PRODUCTION & INVENTORY MANAGEMENT

Published in conjunction with the
American Production & Inventory Control Society

DONALD W. FOGARTY, CFPIM
Southern Illinois University at Edwardsville

JOHN H. BLACKSTONE, JR., CFPIM
University of Georgia

THOMAS R. HOFFMANN, CFPIM
University of Minnesota

COLLEGE DIVISION South-Western Publishing Co.

CINCINNATI

2D EDITION

Publisher: Roger L. Ross
Production Editor: Thomas E. Shaffer
Production House: Sheridan Publications Services
Cover and Interior Designer: Jim DeSollar
Marketing Manager: David L. Shaut

7 D 5

Printed in the United States of America

Library of Congress Cataloging-in-Publication Data

Fogarty. Donald W.
    Production & inventory management / Donald W. Fogarty. John H. Blackstone, Jr., Thomas R. Hoffmann. — 2nd ed.
        p.   cm.
    Rev. ed. of: Production and inventory management. c1983.
    "Published in conjunction with the American Production & Inventory Control Society."
    Includes bibliographical references and index.
    ISBN 0-538-07461-2
    1. Production planning.   2. Inventory control.   I. Blackstone, John H.   II. Hoffmann, Thomas Russell
III. Fogarty, Donald W.   Production and inventory management.
IV. Title.   V. Title: Production and inventory management.
TS176.F64   1991   90-36159
658.5—dc20   CIP

PREFACE

The heightened intensity of global competition has increased the necessity of manufacturing and merchandising organizations to continuously improve production flexibility and product quality, delivery, and cost. Production and inventory management (PIM) professionals must be knowledgeable about the application of Just-in-Time (JIT) concepts and computerized manufacturing control, the use of PCs for many different PIM tasks, the integration of manufacturing planning systems with sales and financial systems, the networking of PCs and the mainframe, the way PIM systems support the overall manufacturing strategy, the continuing development of the theory of constraints, and the use of computer controlled processes, multifunction machining centers, and manufacturing cells.

The goal of *Production and Inventory Management* is to aid in meeting such challenges as the education and certification of many practitioners, the implementation of formal manufacturing planning and control systems in many companies (especially in small manufacturing companies), and the continued education in recent developments of all working in the field. The profession continues to grow in numbers and stature. The American Production and Inventory Control Society (APICS)—in conjunction with whom this text is written—now has more than 65,000 members and more than 30,000 are certified.

Production and Inventory Management is written for two groups of people, those preparing for a career in PIM and professionals interested in reviewing basic concepts and in improving their competence. Although the material in the text is integrated and each chapter inherently deals with the material in more than one area, most of the chapters can be grouped on the basis of the APICS Certification Curriculum module to which they apply most. That grouping is:

Master Planning
- Chapter 2   Long-Range Planning
- Chapter 3   Forecasting
- Chapter 4   Master Scheduling

Inventory Management
- Chapter 5   Inventory Management: An Overview
- Chapter 6   Independent Demand Inventory Management
- Chapter 7   Aggregate Inventory Management
- Chapter 8   Joint Replenishment
- Chapter 9   Distribution and Inventory Control
- Chapter 15   Purchasing Management

Material and Capacity Requirements Planning Management
- Chapter 10   Material Requirements Planning
- Chapter 11   MRP Extensions and Applications
- Chapter 12   Rough Cut Capacity Planning
- Chapter 13   Capacity Requirements Planning

Production Activity Control

Just-in-Time

Although nearly every chapter discusses tactical and technology considerations, those chapters most concerned with these topics are: Chapter 1, Production and Inventory Management (PIM) Environments; Chapter 19, Theory of Constraints; Chapter 20, Production and Inventory Management Systems; and Chapter 21, Managing PIM.

This edition features a more thorough coverage of capacity management, manufacturing resource planning (MRP II), the Just-in-Time approach, the theory of constraints, simulation, and PIM environments. Separate chapters cover rough cut capacity planning and capacity requirements planning. JIT concepts are divided into a chapter concerning general concepts and one concerning quality and preventive maintenance. The theory of constraints chapter includes the most recent developments in this area. The aggregate inventory management chapter contains a new simplified process flow environment example.

Chapter 1 describes five actual organizations, each with an archetypical manufacturing/merchandising environment. These descriptions are used in many different chapters to illustrate the situations to which various concepts, systems, and techniques are applicable.

Many new problems have been added to most chapters. The variety of problem types has been increased and includes some simulation problems.

Acknowledgements We are indebted to many who have supported our work and aided us in deciding how to best treat some basically simple ideas whose applications can be complex. First, our sincere thanks to the APICS Headquarters personnel, especially Hank Sander, Michael Stack, and Charles Mertons, who have been very supportive in preparing both editions of this text. We always will appreciate the vote of confidence that Jim Burlingame, Gary Landis, and Al Perreault, APICS officers, gave us for our first edition. Thanks also to the many academic colleagues and the present officers and members of APICS, including instructors in Chapter education programs and practitioners who offered suggested improvements.

Tom Creahan and Tom Shaffer of South-Western Publishing have been very helpful in preparing and editing the manuscript. Special thanks to our colleagues, Don Aucamp, Bob Barringer, and Jim Cox, who have been very gracious in giving time, serious consideration, and valuable counsel on whether and how to treat various topics.

We owe special thanks to our families and wives, Jean, Lorna, and Melissa, for their patience, understanding, support, and advice.

Donald W. Fogarty, John H. Blackstone, Jr., Thomas R. Hoffman

CONTENTS

1

PRODUCTION AND INVENTORY MANAGEMENT (PIM) ENVIRONMENTS

Production and inventory management (PIM) can be defined as the design, operation, and control of systems for the manufacture and distribution of products. PIM has three levels of applicability in the logistics chain: the retail level, the wholesale (warehouse) level, and the manufacturing level. Manufacturing environments exhibit a great deal of variability from the massive cauldrons full of molten steel found in Pittsburgh to the delicate assembly of computer components, often performed in environments controlled more carefully than surgical rooms. Two factors common to all PIM environments are close contact with people and the need for a consistent, well-defined planning and control system. PIM provides many different, rewarding, career opportunities, in areas such as supervision, materials planning, scheduling, purchasing, inventory control, and management consulting. The career path leads through positions such as material manager, plant manager, vice-president of operations, and beyond.

This book is about both the environments of and the systems for PIM. Both production management and inventory management occur in a variety of environments. Decisions that work well in one context sometimes work poorly in others. For that reason, we will present several specific situations and discuss decision tools appropriate to each. There are three characteristics that determine the efficacy of a management policy, technique, or procedure. These are the product positioning strategy, the general organization of the production process (the process positioning strategy), and the choice of technology. A company must also have a strategy for distributing and providing field support for the product. This chapter begins with the choice of product positioning strategy, production process, and type of technology. These decisions are interdependent. Next, the planning and control functions required for PIM are briefly delineated. The chapter ends with a description of five specific manufacturing and distribution environments.

1

THE PRODUCT POSITIONING STRATEGY

The *product positioning strategy* refers to the type of inventory an organization chooses to maintain. The product positioning strategy may be any one or a combination of the following:

A. Make finished products to stock (maintain and sell from finished product inventory)
B. Assemble finished products to order (maintain an inventory of components, subassemblies, and options)
C. Custom design and make finished products to order (maintain a stock of commonly used material)

The major determinants of the product positioning strategy are the manufacturing lead time, the time a customer is willing to wait for product delivery, and the degree of customization desired by the customer. If the time a customer is willing to wait for delivery is less than either manufacturing lead time or assembly lead time, an organization must maintain an inventory of finished goods for immediate purchase (or lose the business to competitors who have suitable items already available).

If the customer is willing to tolerate some delay in order to have a product custom-assembled (or manufactured), the manufacturer would prefer to operate assemble-to-order or make-to-order. Consider a dress shop with 500 dress styles, 10 dress sizes, and 100 choices of material (varying in color, pattern and composition). Then there can be 500,000 possible dress types. An impossibly large finished goods inventory would be required to stock every one of each type at each retail outlet. However, if the manufacturer is able to deliver any dress within 48 hours and the customer is willing to wait 48 hours to have precisely the desired product, then the inventory required is merely a sufficient stock of each of the 100 choices of material. Some or all of the savings in inventory expense can be passed to the consumer in order to increase the sales volume and profitability of the manufacturer.

Thus, a challenge for any make-to-stock manufacturer is to determine how to lower manufacturing lead time to move to an assemble-to-order or make-to-order strategy. It is not unusual for an organization to have different strategies for different product lines. A company may even have two strategies for one product. For example, automobile companies are primarily make-to-stock but do have some assemble-to-order business.

Make-to-Stock

The positioning strategy of make-to-stock emphasizes immediate delivery of good quality, reasonably priced, off-the-shelf, standard items. In this environment a customer is not willing to tolerate a delay in receiving the product. Management is required to maintain a stock of finished goods. Often the stock of finished goods held is quite large due to the need to provide a variety of sizes, colors, and features.

Assemble-to-Order

Although some products are packaged or finished to order rather than assembled, for convenience, we will refer to this environment as assemble-to-order. The positioning strategy of assemble-to-order is to supply a large variety of high quality, competitively-priced, final products from standard components and subassemblies within a short assembly lead time. The customer and the competition determine what is meant by a short lead time. An automobile may be ordered with or without air conditioning. This requires a different lead time than a hamburger with or without lettuce. In assemble-to-order environments, options, subassemblies, and components are either produced or purchased to stock. By stocking a small supply of components and subassemblies, the manufacturer can quickly assemble any one of an almost limitless number of possible configurations. The customer enjoys the benefit of some customization, yet has a short wait for delivery.

Make- or Engineer-to-Order

The positioning strategy of make-to-order is to provide the technical ability to produce specialty products, such as machine tools. In many situations the final design of the item is part of what is purchased. The final product is usually a combination of standard components and other components custom designed for the customer. Combined material handling and manufacturing processing systems are an example; special trucks for off-the-road work on utility lines and facilities are another. The manufacturer often purchases materials after the order is placed. The customer must therefore be willing to tolerate a long lead time, perhaps years.

PRODUCTION PROCESS DESIGNS (PROCESS POSITIONING STRATEGY)

There are three traditional designs that are useful in classifying production process environments. These designs are called flow shop manufacturing, job shop manufacturing, and fixed site manufacturing. Figure 1-1 depicts a classification of processes and their typical layouts and product positioning strategies.

Flow Shop

The flow shop is sometimes called a product layout because the product always follows the same sequential steps of production. There are four types of flow: (1) continuous flow, (2) dedicated repetitive flow, (3) mixed-model repetitive flow, and (4) intermittent or batch flow.

Figure 1-1
Traditional Classification of Process Design

Process Design	Typical Layout	Typical Product Positioning
Flow Shop	Line	
Continuous	Product Emphasis	Make-to Stock
Dedicated Repetitive		Assemble-to-Order
Intermittent or Batch		
Mixed-Model Repetitive		
Job Shop	Functional	Make-to-Order
	Process Emphasis	
Fixed Site	Fixed Position	Make-to-Order
	Project Emphasis	

Continuous Flow.   Continuous flow usually refers to the production or processing of fluids, wastes, powders, basic metals, and other bulk items. An oil refinery that gradually refines crude oil into various petroleum products or a pipeline for water, oil, or natural gas are examples of continuous flow manufacturing and distribution processes.

Dedicated Repetitive Flow.   Discrete parts such as shafts and connecting rods and discrete assemblies such as microcomputers may be produced by a repetitive flow process. The term *dedicated* implies that the production facility produces only one product, including product variations (such as color) that require no setup delay in the assembly or manufacturing process.

A dedicated line is selected either when the demand for the item justifies the exclusive use of a line or when the manufacturing requirements are sufficiently different from any other item. In the latter case, excess capacity may exist and either the production rate is adjusted to match the demand rate or the line is periodically idle.

Characteristics of Continuous and Dedicated Repetitive Flow Processes.   A flow process is designed specifically for the manufacture of a given product. Figure 1-2 depicts two small representative flow processes. The first flow processes to be designed had linear configurations like that of Figure 1-2A. Recently, U-shaped processes like the one shown in Figure 1-2B have grown in popularity.

The following are the general characteristics of continuous and dedicated repetitive flow processes:

1. Work moves through the process at a fixed rate.
2. The processing and materials handling equipment is individually designed for the production of one product type.

Figure 1-2
A. Typical Flow Line

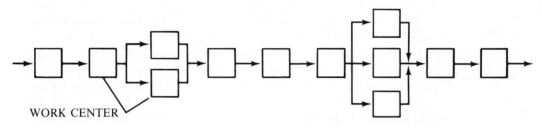

WORK CENTER

B. U-Shaped Line

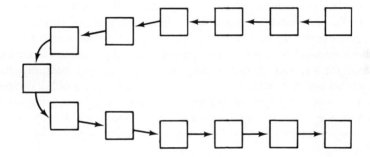

3. The production process generally is arranged to minimize materials handling.
4. Minor changes may be made in the line to incorporate product or process improvements. Most major changes are expensive.
5. The line tends to be run (or to remain idle) for a relatively long time.
6. Inventory planning and control is driven by the rate of flow. The continuous availability of materials and parts is critical.
7. Management usually desires balanced capacity of the different work stations along the line.
8. The rate of flow cannot be significantly changed without substantial modifications to the equipment or the number of personnel.
9. Fixed costs are high and variable costs are relatively low. A dedicated flow facility requires high volume to break even, but with sufficient volume can attain very low per unit costs.

Batch Flow. The batch flow production process is functionally the same as the continuous or the repetitive, except that two or more products are manufactured in the same facility. Because of long setup times in the batch flow shop, manufacturing runs for each product typically last several hours or several days. An example of a continuous batch flow facility is a bottle filling plant that fills bottles with several varieties of liquid. During setup, lines must be cleaned to avoid product contamination from the previous product. Sometimes bottle height changes, requiring adjustment of line or machine height. A batch repetitive flow manufacturer makes discrete parts; changing parts requires a setup. Often the products may differ only in color, but changing colors may require a long setup for painting.

The batch flow process overlaps the line flow and job shop classifications. Batch flow is used when the cost of a line process is justified, even though the item is not produced continuously. Relatively low demand parts, assemblies, and nondiscrete items, such as pharmaceuticals, are often produced using intermittent or batch flow production. Quality control requirements, such as those present in the production of pharmaceuticals, frequently demand batch processing.

In some cases, a given work space may be used for two or more single-model lines when each is not run continuously. These are batch lines consecutively occupying the same space, but they are not mixed-model lines. For example, in the assembly of certain carburetors for which there is a relatively low demand, a line may be operated until the required quantity (production lot) for a specific model is completed. The tools and assembly fixtures for that model are then placed in an adjacent storage area and the different tools and equipment required for the next scheduled model are used to set up the new line. Such lines are being replaced with mixed-model lines as Just-in-Time and zero inventory concepts are adopted by many organizations.

Characteristics of Batch Flow.   The following are characteristics of an intermittent or batch flow production process:

1. Equipment tends to be more general purpose, and thus less efficient, than continuous or dedicated repetitive production.
2. Equipment and personnel must be continually scheduled.
3. The equipment is cleaned and adjusted for the required temperature, pressure, and time prior to running a different item.

Mixed-Model Repetitive Flow.   Mixed-model repetitive flow processes are also used to manufacture two or more models. However, the changeover time between models is minimal (frequently zero), and the different models are intermixed on the same line. Hall (1983) describes such a mixed-model line with the following flow sequence, where A, B, C, and D represent different models: A-B-C-A-B-C-A-B-A-D. Thus, for every D produced, there would be four As, three Bs, and two Cs manufactured.

Characteristics of Mixed-Model Repetitive Flow.   The following characteristics typify a mixed-model repetitive flow line:

1. The equipment is general purpose in order to facilitate manufacture of several models.

2. Workers are multifunction, i.e., capable of performing many different tasks on one line or of moving to different lines in the same plant.
3. Setup times are very short. The ideal setup time is small enough to accommodate run lengths of one unit, switching models after every item.
4. The line produces at the market rate of sales. Workers are added and subtracted and manufacturing tasks are reassigned as needed to support the market rate on all models.

Objectives of Flow Shop Design

Possible objectives of a flow design are as follows:

1. Combine activities requiring one or more of the following: the same special skill, the same tooling or equipment, or the same materials or parts.
2. Meet operation relationship requirements, such as segregating dust-producing activities from activities requiring a clean environment.
3. Limit the number of physically demanding tasks at each work station in a manual line.
4. Provide flexibility to meet changes in output rates. Work stations can be reorganized by changing assignments of activities with minimum difficulty and cost.
5. Minimize the space requirements.

Job Shop

A job shop process is characterized by the organization of similar equipment by function (such as milling, drilling, turning, forging, and assembly). As jobs flow from work center to work center, or department to department, a different type of operation is performed in each center or department. Orders may follow similar or different paths through the plant, suggesting one or several dominant flows. The layout is intended to support a manufacturing environment in which there can be a great diversity of flow among products. Figure 1-3 depicts a job shop process design.

The following are salient characteristics of job shop processes:

1. Multipurpose production and materials handling equipment can be adjusted and modified to handle many different products.
2. Many different products are run in lots or batches through the plant, and many lots are usually being processed at a given time. Low demand per product usually does not justify flow production.
3. The processing of orders requires detailed planning and control due to the variety of flow patterns and the separation of work centers.

Figure 1-3
Order Flow Patterns in a Job Shop

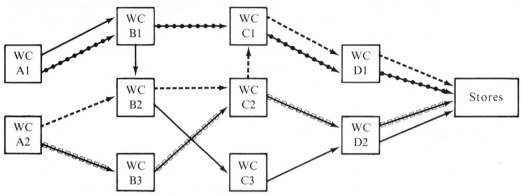

4. Control requires detailed job and shop information, including processing sequence, order priority, time requirements of each job, status of jobs in process, work center capacity, and capacity requirements of critical work centers by time period.
5. Work center loads differ greatly; that is, they have different percent-capacity utilizations. Critical capacity centers (bottlenecks) caused by relative scarcity of manpower or machinery must be determined. A change in product mix may cause the bottleneck to shift from one work center to another.
6. Resource availability, including materials, personnel, and tooling, must be coordinated with order planning.
7. The amount of work-in-process material tends to be high relative to that in a flow process due to the queues and long in-process times.
8. Using traditional scheduling techniques, the total time, from the beginning of the first operation to the end of the last, is relatively long compared to total operation time. An order often spends 95 percent or more of its time in the plant waiting to be moved to the next work center or waiting at a work center for processing.
9. Direct labor personnel are usually more highly trained and skilled than those in a flow process operation.

Job shop operations, like intermittent (batch) flow operations, are characterized by batches. However, unlike intermittent flow processes where batches and batch size are determined by setup time constraints and demand volumes, the batch size of job shop processes often is dictated by the size of a specific order. Thus, large and small batches of very similar, or in some cases identical products, are processed concurrently by the job shop.

Large job shop processes have characteristics that are very similar to repetitive flow or intermittent batch flow operations. High setup costs are prorated over larger lots and specialization of labor and equipment are thus permitted. Alternatively, small job shop operations produce anywhere from ten to several hundred units per setup, and consequently they rely on highly flexible labor and lower-cost, flexible, general purpose equipment. A commercial printer is typical of a small job shop. Jobs are often quoted in terms of setup costs and then additional costs per unit, per hundred, or per thousand of production.

Objectives of Job Shop Design

Job shops permit a highly skilled worker, using general purpose equipment, to manufacture products to exacting specifications from blueprints. A job shop is chosen for:

1. Making prototypes of new products.
2. Making small batches for test marketing or early in the production of a product.
3. Making unique or low-volume products such as machines, tools, and fixtures used to produce other products.
4. Ensuring quality whenever highly skilled labor is required to meet specifications. Examples include the production of mirrors for telescopes and the production of other scientific instruments.
5. Providing the worker with the opportunity to make all of a part or component. Specialization of labor is efficient, but in some cases is not effective due to worker boredom.

Fixed Site (Project)

The key identifying characteristic of fixed site (project) production is that the materials, tools, and personnel are brought to the location where the product is to be fabricated. This type of process is found in shipbuilding, construction, road building, and the final assembly of large, special-purpose trucks, turbines, aircraft, pressure vessels, and any other items that are difficult to move from work center to work center.

Fixed site production is sometimes used in conjunction with other processes. After the product reaches a certain size, it is often more practical to keep it stationary and move the necessary components to its location.

Characteristics of fixed site production include the following:

1. Direct labor personnel frequently are highly trained, very skillful, and independent. They work from blueprints and general instructions rather than detailed process sheets.
2. Order quantities are small and orders frequently have custom design features.
3. Tooling, personnel, materials, and other resources should be available at the proper time to avoid nonproductive capacity.

The Production Process Continuum

Pure production process designs (flow shop, job shop, and fixed site) are rarely found. Most production processes combine two, or sometimes all three, of these designs. For example, building construction usually is regarded as a fixed site project. The construction of suburban housing units, however, often employs job shop and flow shop techniques. Earthmovers dig cellars, create lakes, and build noise-dissipation berms for all houses in the subdivision. Then paved roads, utility lines, concrete forms for basements, and curbs are sequentially added for each of the homes. Because the houses are produced with the same type of flow as an automobile assembly line, such housing construction can be likened to a flow shop process. One difference is that the car is moving on the assembly line, but the house assembly tools and processes are moving sequentially to different fixed sites in the housing development. Thus, housing production combines some elements of a fixed site operation with some elements of a line flow.

Further, consider that some houses are built without cellars, and thus require different concrete forms. This and other design customizations suggest characteristics of a job shop process. Each house must be adjusted for various semi-custom modifications, as in a job shop. To minimize the amount of investment in fixed inventory (in this case, a finished but unsold house), this integrated production process must be closely coordinated with the progress of house sales.

The three pure production processes, when considered in terms of applications, are better represented as a continuum. Examples of a continuous flow might be an oil pipeline, a sugar refinery, or a radio transmission. At the other extreme, a plumbing repair or a bridge construction project are reasonably fixed processes. Between these two relatively pure extremes there are numerous possible adjustments of process design.

One important reason to identify the design of the production process is that each production process type requires specific types of job flow, implying specific layout and scheduling techniques and different management concerns and tasks. In turn, different production processes suggest different product positioning strategies. The interrelationships of product positioning, production process choice, and technology choice have been ably developed by Hayes and Wheelwright (1984) as shown in Figure 1-4. Hill (1989) points out that the relationships are more valid if volume is defined as work content rather than unit volume. Even though airplanes have a low unit volume, they are built in dedicated repetitive flow shops because they have a high volume of work content.

Figure 1-4 identifies a matrix of the product and process relationships. The product continuum is shown at the top with several further descriptors, including volume and degree of standardization. The production process continuum is shown at the left. The dominant competitive-criterian continuum is at the bottom, ranging from flexibility/quality to delivery/cost.

Figure 1-4
Product Positioning—Process Choice Focus

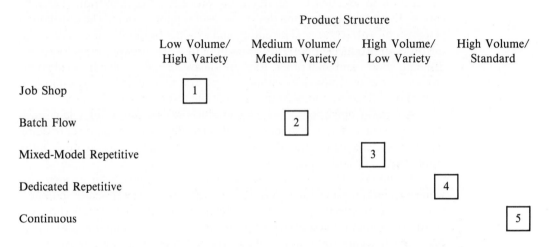

	Product Structure			
	Low Volume/ High Variety	Medium Volume/ Medium Variety	High Volume/ Low Variety	High Volume/ Standard
Job Shop	1			
Batch Flow		2		
Mixed-Model Repetitive			3	
Dedicated Repetitive				4
Continuous				5

Product/Market/Process Characteristics

	Group 1	Group 2	Group 3	Group 4	Group 5
Order Winner	High quality	High quality	High quality	Competitive cost	Low cost
Variety	High flexibility	Some flexibility	Some flexibility	Low flexibility	Standardized
Implication	High cost	High cost	Medium cost	Some automation	Automated
Machinery	General purpose	General purpose	General purpose	Specific purpose	Specific purpose
Product Position	Make-to-order	Assemble-to-order	Assemble-to-order	Make-to-stock	Make-to-stock

Modified from Hayes and Wheelwright *Restoring Our Competitive Edge*, Figure 4-7.

Companies can define their exact position within the framework of the matrix, although they are constrained somewhat by the type of product and the state of product development. For example, auto assembly is generally considered to be a repetitive process, but many luxury and sports automobiles are built in job shops—sometimes even in a semi-fixed position. Examples are Rolls Royce, some Volvo models, and the Studebaker Avanti. (Note that these examples are low volume products with high customization, while the Ford Taurus is a high volume product with little customization.)

The flexibility afforded by programmable logic controllers (microprocessors similar to ones that control a microwave oven) are changing the nature of the volume-process choice relationship. The subject of flexible manufacturing systems and computer controlled production is discussed in Chapter 20.

DISTRIBUTION PROCESS DESIGN

In addition to selecting a manufacturing process, an organization also must choose distribution outlets and design the field support system. The distribution system choice affects several inventory and product support issues. In descending order of product support, distribution outlets are turnkey, specialty shops, discount shops, and mail order. Each of the above may receive finished goods from a central or regional warehouse. Turnkey and mail-order operations also may obtain finished goods from an assemble-to-order manufacturer.

A *turnkey* operation delivers material to the user, sets it up, and ensures it is working properly. The supplier usually provides a service contract providing on-site maintenance for the user. Examples are computers, large duplicating equipment, and large machinery.

A *specialty shop* is a retailer of one type of item, such as men's or women's clothing, sporting goods, jewelry, and so on. The specialty shop provides advice on selection and usage of items. Frequently, a specialty shop will customize an item, making the shop the last stage of the manufacturing process. The specialty shop may provide service under the product warranty.

A *discount shop* is a retailer carrying a very broad line of products. Prices are lower than in specialty shops, but no advice or customization is provided. If the customer experiences problems with a product, the discount store may exchange the product, but usually warranty service must be arranged through the manufacturer, not the retailer.

For items that are small enough to be mailed or shipped by common carrier, *mail order* is an increasingly popular alternative. By centralizing the point of contact with the customer, the mail-order house often is able to provide a more knowledgeable sales clerk than is the discount shop. Exchange policies for reputable mail-order vendors are similar to those of discount houses, but the customer who must exchange a defective item encounters the delay and expense of mailing the product back and awaiting replacement.

TECHNOLOGICAL CHOICES

Manufacturers constantly seek the product or process characteristics that will give them a competitive edge. They need information on changing production process developments, product technology, information management systems, and product distribution methods. The computer is playing an increasing role at all levels of production and distribution process design. In Figure 1-5, the production and distribution process is presented as a system. This system includes product design, supplier selection, product fabrication, assembly, inspection, and distribution. The system must also provide for customer contact and for redesign of the product, the production process, and the distribution process based on continuing input from the customer.

Figure 1-5
Production and Distribution Viewed as a System, with
Computer Integrated Manufacturing Links Indicated

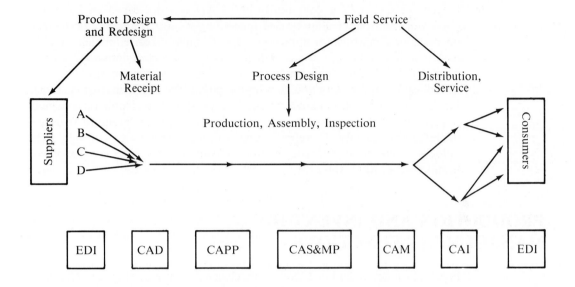

Modified from Deming, W. E., *Out of the Crisis*, Figure 1.

       The computer provides a way to exchange documents with suppliers and customers (electronic data interchange, EDI) and to assist in the design of products (computer aided design, CAD) and of production processes (computer aided process planning, CAPP). The computer can also assist in scheduling and material planning (CAS&MP), in manufacturing (CAM), and in instructing the user in the proper use of the product (CAI). Collectively, these techniques are known as computer integrated manufacturing (CIM).

       The ultimate objective of CIM is to design the product on the computer (CAD) and pass the design electronically to a system that designs the production process (CAPP), including arrangements with suppliers (EDI). The process planning system transfers files electronically to the scheduling and materials planning system, which coordinates material production and purchase (CAS&MP). The process planning system may also transfer specific instructions on how to make the part to robots and to computer or direct numerically controlled machines (CAM). Contact with distributors, like that with vendors, is electronic (EDI). An emerging trend is the inclusion of computer aided instruction (CAI) on the use of the product. This trend is expected to grow exponentially with the introduction of interactive compact disk technology, permitting the mixing of text, images, and sound on a compact disk that can be played on a CD player.

The realization of CIM is not straightforward. Computer aided design, computerized scheduling and material control packages, computer controlled machines and robots, and computer aided instruction all arose independently. Often these technologies exist on machines that do not share a common file format for data or for communication. CAD was developed on dedicated CAD work stations. Computerized scheduling is most frequently performed on plant or departmental minicomputers. Computerized equipment usually has an on-board microprocessor, which may not have been designed for communication with a larger computer. Computer aided instruction was developed for education and is only now developing popularity as a means of customer service. Finally, the company's accounts payable and receivable records may well be on a mainframe computer at a central location far removed from the manufacturing facility. Therefore, a company must decide which of these technologies, if any, is appropriate for the company. Each technology is explored in more detail in Chapter 20.

PRODUCTION AND INVENTORY MANAGEMENT FUNCTIONS

From a production and inventory management viewpoint, all companies must perform certain necessary planning functions. All must forecast demand for their products. All must determine when to increase facility size, how to staff the facilities, when to make or buy items, and how many to make or buy. In the sections that follow, we discuss the planning cycle and introduce the concepts that are used throughout the rest of the text.

Planning

Planning is the first step in management. It consists of selecting measurable objectives and deciding how to achieve them. Planning is a prerequisite for execution and control. Without plans there is no basis for action and no basis for evaluating the results achieved. Planning not only provides the path for action, it also enables management to evaluate the probability of successfully completing the journey.

Execution is the carrying out (performance) of plans. *Control* is comparing actual results with desired results and deciding whether to revise objectives or methods of execution.

Planning, execution, and control are iterative processes that should occur continuously. Initiation of control does not require that plans actually be executed—only that their results be simulated and evaluated. Thus, at times it is difficult to identify an activity as uniquely planning or uniquely control. However, describing planning, execution, and control separately leads to a better understanding of these activities.

Length of the Planning Horizon

Plans can be long range, medium range, or short range depending on the time required to complete the execution. The time spans of these different ranges depend on the operational environment of the organization. The long-range planning horizon should exceed the time required to acquire new facilities and equipment. This may require 10 years or longer for organizations involved in the extraction process where new mines must be developed. It may be as short as 18 months for the machine shop where facilities and equipment are catalog items.

Medium-range planning is the development of the aggregate production rates and aggregate levels of inventory for product groups within the constraints of a given facility. Expansion of capacity within the medium-range planning period is limited to increasing personnel or shifts, scheduling overtime, acquiring more efficient tooling, subcontracting, and perhaps adding some types of equipment that can be obtained on short notice.

Medium-range planning usually covers a period beginning 1 to 2 months in the future and ending 12 to 18 months in the future. Its exact boundaries depend on the time constraints for changing levels of production in a particular situation. The planning horizon for medium-range planning is usually at least as long as the longest product lead time. In this context, we define lead time as the time from recognizing that an order for material must be placed until that material is present in a finished good. If medium-term planning uses a horizon shorter than this, material planning cannot properly be performed.

There is no precise definition for the length of the short-term planning horizon. Although detailed schedules and assignments of men and machines to tasks usually do not occur until well within the short-range period, the development of the production schedule frequently bridges the medium- and short-range planning periods. Planning is a continuous activity, and refinement of medium-range forecasts and plans to the detail required in preparing the first draft of a short-range version of the production schedule may take place gradually over a number of weeks.

Some interactions of PIM activities are shown in Figure 1-6. These activities frequently take place in more than one time frame. For example, resource requirements planning for facilities may be performed years in advance of production, while some equipment purchases can be initiated a few months before needed. In addition, the master production schedule frequently covers both the medium-range and short-range planning periods. A brief overview of these activities is presented here before we examine them in detail in subsequent chapters.

Long-Range Planning

Long-range planning activities include business forecasting, product and sales planning, production planning, resource requirements planning, and financial planning. These activities are interdependent; we must establish that each is feasible and that all are compatible.

Figure 1-6
Schematic of Planning Activities

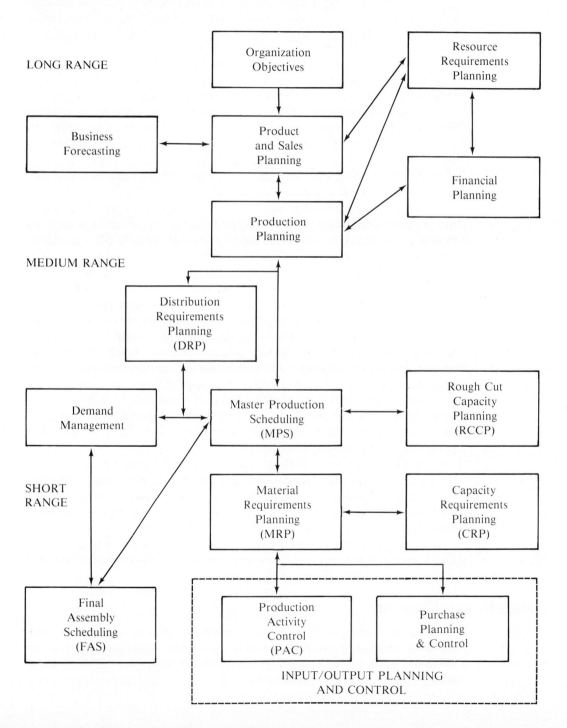

Business Forecasting.   Business forecasting evaluates political, economic, demographic, technological, and competitive factors that will affect the demand for a firm's products. Top management is responsible for this activity. It is not unusual to have a long-range planning task force reporting directly to the chief executive officer and also to employ external forecasting consultants. Business forecasts are aggregated into large product families.

Product and Sales Planning.   Product and sales planning refers to decisions concerning the product lines offered and the markets served (including the target demographic and geographic areas). Product line and sales planning decisions are explicit commitments to an organizational direction. It is usually difficult in the short run to change them. The wisdom of marketing decisions substantially influences organizational growth and prosperity. The business forecast must be disaggregated into product groups appropriate to production planning.

Production Planning.   Production planning uses the forecast from product and sales planning to plan the aggregate rates of production. In production planning, outputs are specified in the broadest terms possible: tons, barrels, yards, dollars, or standard hours of production. The specificity of product line required at this level depends on the equipment required to manufacture it. For example, automotive engine blocks usually are machined on a specially designed high-speed line. A line built for four-cylinder engines ordinarily cannot be used to manufacture six-cylinder engines. Thus, the production plan must separate four- and six-cylinder engine requirements to estimate facility requirements. Production smoothing to compensate for varying seasonal demand rates is planned in this time frame.

Different approaches that might be followed successfully in various situations are discussed in Chapter 2. The production plan establishes customer service level goals, target inventory levels, size of the backlog, production rates, size of the work force, and plans for overtime and subcontracting. The production plan can't be a wish list; it must be within capacity constraints.

The production plan spans the long- and medium-range planning horizons; it serves as a basis for medium-range planning. Some organizations refine the plan gradually until at some point it is more of a master production schedule (see Chapter 4) than a production plan.

Resource Requirements Planning.   Long-range planning is a complex matter. Product, sales, and production planning should interact with resource requirements planning. Decisions concerning products, sales, and output levels should be consistent with planning for facility, equipment, and human resources.

Financial Planning.   Product, sales, and production plans frequently require additional resources that in turn require financing. Normal operations require working capital, and sales generate income. The financial capability of the organization to carry out the long-range plans should be verified. After the availability of the required resources is assured, a commitment can be made to the production plan. Integrated facilities, materials, and financial planning is discussed in Chapter 10.

Medium-Range Planning

Chapters 3, 4, and 10 through 13 examine the problems of medium-range planning and the techniques available to deal with them. An overview of medium-range planning and its constituent activities of distribution requirements planning, demand management, master production scheduling, rough cut capacity planning, material requirements planning, and capacity requirements planning are presented in the following paragraphs.

Distribution Requirements Planning (DRP).   The DRP is the time-phased replenishment needs of branch warehouses summed by period. These requirements are based on the difference between customer demand and the on-hand and in-transit inventory. In a branch warehouse environment the DRP provides a solid link between distribution and manufacturing by providing a record of the quantity and timing of likely orders. DRP is defined in Chapter 9. Interfacing DRP with MRP is discussed in Chapter 10.

Demand Management.   The function of demand management is to determine aggregate demand. This determination reflects forecasts and includes customer orders received, branch warehouse orders, interplant orders, special promotions, safety stock requirements, service parts, and building inventory for later high volume demand periods. Special promotions are used to shift the timing of some demands from peak demand periods to less busy periods in order to avoid adding production capacity. The outputs of demand management are a summation of demand by time period, grouped by product family. Demand management is discussed in Chapter 3.

Master Production Schedule (MPS).   The MPS is a time-phased plan of the items and the quantity of each that the organization intends to build. It is a commitment to meet marketing requirements and to use production capacity. The MPS should be approved by purchasing, production, marketing, and top management.

The MPS covers anything from the present to 1 to 18 months or more in the future. It is used as both a short-range and medium-range planning device. The MPS should be consistent with the production plan. It drives the short-range planning system by providing the input to material requirements planning. Master production scheduling is covered in depth in Chapter 4.

Rough Cut Capacity Planning (RCCP).   Before management approves the production plan or the MPS, it must verify the organization's ability to carry out the plan. Rough cut capacity planning includes the following:

1. Determining that sufficient working capital will be available to meet the cash flow requirements
2. Verifying that production facilities and equipment have adequate capacity
3. Determining that key vendors have the required capacity and obtaining commitment of that capacity

If sufficient capacity is not available and cannot be obtained within the planning horizon, the MPS must be altered to fall within capacity constraints. RCCP techniques are found in Chapter 12.

Material Requirements Planning (MRP).   Time-phased MRP begins with the items listed on the MPS and determines (1) the quantity of all components and materials required to fabricate those items and (2) the date that the components and materials are required.

Time-phased MRP is accomplished by "exploding" the bill of materials and offsetting requirements by the appropriate lead times. This process is described in detail in Chapters 10 and 11.

Capacity Requirements Planning (CRP).   The time-phased requirements obtained from MRP are used in conjunction with other data to determine the capacity required to manufacture the items specified in the MRP. These capacity requirements are compared to available capacity. Corrective action is taken if necessary. Corrective actions include adding overtime, rerouting production, and subcontracting some work.

When available capacity is insufficient despite corrective action, the master scheduler reviews relative priorities and, working with marketing and production, makes the difficult decisions required in revising a schedule.

Revisions in the MPS will require the MRP to be rerun and its output used to verify that capacity requirements are now within constraints. CRP is discussed in Chapter 13.

Short-Range Planning

Short-range planning and control involve both priorities (i.e., determining and meeting due dates) and capacities. Demand management provides the gross requirements' inputs to the MPS, which drives the short-range planning system. The MPS and MRP provide priority planning. The output of the MPS and MRP must be within capacity constraints as determined by CRP. Capacity control is obtained via input/output controls. Priority control is achieved through production activity and purchasing controls.

Final Assembly Schedule (FAS).   The FAS is a statement of the end item configurations that are to be assembled. In an assemble-to-order environment, the FAS frequently is stated in terms of individual customer orders. In an assemble-to-stock environment, it is a commitment to provide a specific quantity of different end product catalogued items.

In some cases the items included on the MPS are the same as those on the FAS. In other cases, the items on the MPS are at a lower level in the bill of materials. This and other aspects of master scheduling are covered in depth in Chapter 4.

Input/Output Planning and Control.   Completion of the MPS, RCCP, MRP, and CRP processes with a schedule of requirements within capacity constraints leads to order release planning. Order release controls the work in process and lead times by controlling the flow of work into the shop. Order release planning principles and techniques are covered in detail in Chapter 14.

Production Activity Control (PAC).   Input/output control, order sequencing, reporting performance, and determining appropriate corrective action are all part of PAC. The function of order sequencing is to determine that the sequence in which tasks are to be performed is consistent with their relative priority. Sequencing decisions are executed by order releases and the dispatch list. The dispatch list, which includes jobs in or soon to arrive in a department and their relative priorities, is the term commonly used to identify the report used to transmit priorities to the production unit.

Reports of actual departmental output, which reveal actual capacity and anticipated late completion of specific jobs, provide the feedback that "closes the loop." This enables management to exercise control by taking the necessary corrective action. Production activity control is covered in Chapter 14.

Purchase Planning and Control.   Planning and controlling the priorities of purchased items are equally important. Some of the approaches may be different from those used for internal production, but the principles are the same. With the growing emphasis on long term relationships with qualified vendors, vendor capacity management is increasingly important. Purchase planning and control are discussed in Chapter 15.

Project Management.   Earlier in this chapter the difference between high-volume, repetitive manufacturing, process manufacturing, and low- to medium-volume batch manufacturing were discussed. Sometimes only one unit is produced. Examples of single unit production include customized software, houses, other large buildings, and large ships. In these situations, the manager's task is complicated by the fact that the job is unique. A set of project management tools have evolved to assist the manager. These tools are discussed in Chapter 16.

Just-in-Time Manufacturing.   The term *Just-in-Time* was introduced in connection with high-volume, repetitive manufacturing. Just-in-Time is an approach to manufacturing that involves eliminating all waste and making the production worker an important part of the decision-making process. Just-in-Time involves not only the production and inventory management function, but many other aspects of a business. Manufacturers that are not high-volume, repetitive manufacturers are finding that the philosophy of continually striving to eliminate waste has much to offer their operations as well. Just-in-Time is discussed in Chapter 17.

Total Quality Control and Preventive Maintenance.   For Just-in-Time manufacturing to function, machines must not break down at critical times, nor can they produce defective parts. Thus, total quality control and preventive maintenance are prerequisites to Just-in-Time system success. Chapter 18 presents an overview of these important topics, each of which could easily form the subject of a large book.

Synchronous Manufacturing.   An alternative approach to attaining world class manufacturing status, introduced by Goldratt (1984), is presented in Chapter 19.

FIVE ENVIRONMENTS

Descriptions of five organizations follow. Although each of these organizations possesses characteristics that make it unique, each has an environment that is very similar to one or some combination of the general types described previously. Recognizing these general characteristics in an organization is the first step in understanding production management.

The companies described range from a family-owned business to a Fortune 500 business and from retail sales to distribution to manufacturing. The five companies are Marvin's, a family-owned building supply retailer; Kickham Boiler and Engineering, Inc., a firm that designs and builds large industrial steam boilers and related products; a division of TRW that produces and distributes replacement parts for automobiles; Wellco Carpet Corp., a carpet manufacturer recently profiled in a study of process industries; and a division of Hewlett-Packard that manufactures computer printers.

Marvin's

Marvin's, headquartered in Birmingham, Alabama, is a family-owned building supply company that operates five stores in northeast Alabama. Marvin's sells primarily to do-it-yourselfers but also supplies contractors. Demand for building products is both seasonal and cyclical. It is seasonal because people undertake home improvement projects in mild weather. It is cyclical, because the economy of Alabama is very sensitive to the state of the manufacturing economy. When the economy is in recession, little building or building improvement occurs.

A customer purchasing a small item, such as a hand tool, brings the item to one of several checkout counters in each store. For larger items, such as lumber or cement mix, the customer drives into a fenced loading area to load his or her vehicle. The customer receives a list of the purchased items to take to the cashier. The cashier enters the stock number and quantity into the cash register, which records this information and displays price information. The cashier gives the customer a printed receipt containing the name of each item and associated price and quantity. Large-item purchasers are given a second receipt to give to a security guard who verifies the purchases as the customer leaves the fenced area.

Every night a small computer in the home office polls each of the cash registers to obtain a list of the day's transactions. The computer then updates inventory records for each store. After updating the inventory records, the computer executes a program designed to order items that have reached their reorder point. Home office personnel review and act on these reorder recommendations the next day. When an item is ordered from a vendor, such as Black & Decker, many items supplied by that vendor are ordered. Ideally, Marvin's would like to have all items provided by a single vendor reach a reorder position at all stores simultaneously. Of course, this ideal never is realized.

The decisions Marvin's must make in managing inventory are when to order, how much to order, and where to stock the inventory among the five store locations. These decisions are typical of inventory decisions in a retail environment.

Kickham Boiler and Engineering, Inc.

Kickham Boiler and Engineering, founded in 1912, is a St. Louis firm whose expertise ranges from minor service calls involving rerolling of boiler tubes to major projects involving the design, fabrication, erection, or repair of the following items: pressure vessels, tanks, smokestacks, ductwork, hoppers, and weldments. A project may include engineering design, manufacturing, or field service.

Manufacturing activities include plate and alloy steel fabrication of various products. Field service activities include erection services and on-site repairs. Kickham builds large structures. Some of the largest include a 230-foot high smokestack, a 35-foot high, 18-foot diameter storage tank, and a 60-ton gate for a river lock.

Kickham's is an example of a custom (project) design and manufacturing environment. Nearly all orders are different and only occasionally is more than one of a kind manufactured. Although components may be fabricated in work centers organized on a functional basis, major subassemblies and the final assembly are completed on site (fixed site production).

In addition to manufacturing, Kickham also performs extensive field service. This work is performed by a different crew than the one that assembled the facility; they use different equipment. Thus, the need to schedule maintenance crews adds to the task of planning and control.

TRW Automotive Replacement Parts Division

TRW Automotive Replacement Parts Division, which we will call simply TRW, makes and distributes parts for the automotive aftermarket, (i.e., the replacement part market). TRW is a wholesale distributor, selling to retail auto parts stores nationwide. TRW maintains 37 branch warehouses (distribution centers) and one central manufacturing/warehouse facility.

The division accounts for $200 million in annual sales. The central facility in Cleveland has more than 30,000 part numbers. Having so many part numbers may seem exceptional, but it really is about average for replacement part operations in any industry. TRW expects the part numbers count to increase sharply in the next few years.

With many different branch warehouses spread throughout the country, it is difficult to have the correct inventory at the proper place. It is not at all uncommon in such an environment to be out of some part, say the carburetor for a 1957 Chevy, in Seattle while having a large supply of the same part in Syracuse. If the part takes a long time to acquire from the plant, TRW may elect to ship the part from Syracuse to Seattle. Unfortunately, this transshipment from one distribution center to another adds no value to the part. TRW would like to avoid such shipments.

To minimize such transshipments, a number of important decisions must be made. First, how many warehouses should there be and where should they be located? Second, which parts should be stocked at branch warehouses and which stocked centrally? Third, what is the appropriate order quantity for parts stocked by branch warehouses? This question requires an accurate forecast of future demand and raises a further question of who should be responsible for the forecast. Many other important questions remain. These and other questions will be discussed at length in the remainder of this book.

Wellco Carpet

Wellco Carpet Corporation manufactures tufted carpets, primarily for commercial and business usage. The carpets are sold through 40 distributors nationwide. The company employs 500 people, including 350 production workers on two 12-hour shifts five days per week. The carpet business is seasonal, with peak demand occurring during the summer, largely because of carpet replacement performed by schools.

The process of manufacturing carpet starts with single strands of yarn. Usually a dyed yarn is used, but sometimes the yarn is natural. An air entangling process creates a multiple strand fiber from several single-strand spools. The entangled yarn then goes through a tufting process at one of 23 tufting machines, capable of producing 400,000 square yards of material per week. After tufting, an average of 20 percent of the fabric is dyed. Two dyeing machines are available. During the peak months, some dye operations are subcontracted. To finish the carpet, a backing is applied and the carpet with backing is baked to cure the latex cement used to apply the backing.

Because of the large number of ways various fabrics can be colored and backed, Wellco produces 5,000 finished carpet styles from only 500 raw materials. Wellco averages a two-month supply of items in inventory (8 weeks × 400,000 yards per week = 3,200,000 square yards of material, or enough to cover more than 600 football fields). Of this inventory, 31 percent is in raw materials, 32 percent is in process, and 37 percent is in finished goods.

When Wellco receives an order, they first try to fill it out of finished goods, then out of unbacked goods (known as griege goods). Orders from contractors always are filled in the exact amount ordered; however, orders from distributors usually are not filled in the exact length requested in order to minimize the creation of short remnants of carpet that are difficult to sell.

Wellco's product positioning strategy is neither purely make-to-stock nor purely assemble-to-order; it does some of both. Mixed environments such as this are quite common. The manufacturing facility is batch flow.

The carpet industry is very competitive, with lead times to the customer of only a few days. The scheduling of tufting, dyeing, and backing operations rarely is done more than one day in advance, so the company can respond quickly to customer orders. Inventory decisions include how much tufted carpet to stockpile prior to the seasonal peak, how much and what dyeing to subcontract, which carpet to back prior to receipt of an order, how long to run one style before changing the tufting, dyeing, or backing operation, and many others.

Wellco has fewer part numbers than TRW and far fewer raw materials. A fabrication and assembly operation, such as TRW, usually has many thousands of raw materials and fewer end items than raw materials. A process industry, such as Wellco, usually makes many end items from a few raw materials using a fixed flow or process (in this case, tufting, dyeing, and backing). As we discuss later in the text, there are many differences between a process industry and a fabrication and assembly shop, but there also are many similarities in the inventory decisions.

Hewlett-Packard, Vancouver Division

Hewlett-Packard is a Fortune 500 company that makes computers and computer peripherals. The Vancouver division makes printers for computers. There are very few models, and each model is made in large volume. High-volume, low-variety operations are ideal for mixed-model repetitive manufacturing and for the Just-in-Time, approach to manufacturing. In Just-in-Time, material for each operation is pulled from a standard container kept near the work station. When the standard container is empty, the worker takes the empty container to the preceding work station and replaces it with a full container. The empty container serves as authorization for the preceding work station to make enough parts to fill the container. If a work station has no empty container to fill, the station does not work ahead. Hewlett-Packard, Vancouver, uses a Just-in-Time system that functions in precisely this manner.

On the final assembly line there is a one unit buffer between stations. Assembly of a new printer is not allowed to proceed at the upstream station unless the buffer between it and the next station is empty. This procedure minimizes the inventory held in manufacturing, but requires a high degree of coordination between stations and also a high degree of quality. The Just-in-Time scheduling system used by Hewlett-Packard is ideally suited for its operation, but is less desirable for a process industry, such as Wellco, or a fabrication and assembly operation, such as TRW. There are, however, certain aspects of the Just-in-Time philosophy (or Japanese management paradigm) that are applicable to the process industry and to low volume assembly operations.

Hewlett-Packard, Vancouver, views suppliers as an extension of the manufacturing process. H-P encourages these suppliers to follow the Just-in-Time philosophy and to achieve a high degree of quality. The division has a formal supplier evaluation process that considers delivery performance, quality, lead time, price, and improvement over time. Part of the Just-in-Time philosophy is to reduce the number of suppliers to a few very good ones.

The Vancouver division managers feel that their system must be responsive to changes in the market. As the system changes, performance measures that are appropriate for evaluating Hewlett-Packard's manufacturing and inventory management change. The relevant criteria for evaluating suppliers change as well.

SUMMARY

Manufacturing enterprises are classified by their product positioning strategy and by their production process. Product positioning strategies are make-to-stock, assemble-to-order, and make-to-order. Production processes are classified as flow shop, job shop, and fixed site. Product positioning strategies and production process design are both influenced by product volume. Products with high volume and standard design tend to be make-to-stock and are usually made in flow shops. Products with low volume and/or high customization tend to be make-to-order and usually are made in job shops or batch flow shops. Most organizations have some variety in both the product positioning and production process dimension. The most common situation is an organization that fabricates components in a job shop area (or separate plant) and assembles finished products in a final assembly area (or plant). The organization makes its most popular products to stock and assembles less popular alternatives to order.

A student of PIM must also understand the technological choices all manufacturers must make. Technology is changing rapidly; microprocessors are becoming a standard part of both products and manufacturing equipment. Computer assistance is available in the design of the product, in the design of the production process, in the production scheduling and material planning process, and in the interchange of data with suppliers and customers. In addition, microprocessors in manufacturing equipment increasingly communicate with a central computer to create a capability for quick programming of many distinct tasks.

The five organizations described in this chapter represent the full spectrum of product positioning strategies and production and distribution process designs. Marvin's is a retail outlet, which on the surface appears to be purely a distribution environment, representing many make-to-stock enterprises. Marvin's is, however, partially a manufacturer—cutting lumber to the specific length desired by a customer is a finish-to-order manufacturing process. Kickham Boiler is make-to-order, employing both a job shop and a fixed site production process. Because specialized engineering skills are required to install their products, Kickham's distribution is turnkey. TRW operates a hybrid job shop, a batch flow line manufacturing facility for automotive replacement parts. Because customers are intolerant of delays in repairing their cars, TRW is forced to operate as a make-to-stock firm with several regional warehouses to support nationwide distribution. Wellco Carpet is a hybrid facility with continuous flow on some looms, batch flow on other looms, and batch flow through their dyeing and finishing operations. Wellco is largely make-to-stock, but does some finish-to-order business. Hewlett Packard, Vancouver, is a mixed-model repetitive flow line, making-to-stock a variety of standard computer printers.

The specific actions common to all manufacturers are forecasting, long-range planning to manage plant and major equipment matters, medium-range planning to manage staffing and materials management matters, short-range planning to schedule production activities, and production control activities to ensure that the plans are met.

To manage production and inventory systems requires a broad range of knowledge. Rapid changes are occurring in the items customers desire to purchase, in the processes used to make those items, and in the procedures used to plan and control their manufacture. Manufacturing management requires constantly learning new techniques. Fortunately, the work is as rewarding as it is challenging, because the manager can see a tangible product created and delivered, and because the job involves a high degree of interaction with people and a high degree of authority and autonomy.

EXERCISES

1. Classify the following products as make-to-stock, assemble-to-order, or make-to-order:

   a. Television set
   b. Eyeglasses
   c. Automobiles
   d. Airplanes
   e. Suits
   f. Portraits
   g. Greeting cards
   h. Chairs

2. Classify the manufacturing process you would expect to find for each of the eight products shown in Exercise 1 (fixed site, job shop, repetitive flow, continuous flow).

3. Discuss the difference between batch repetitive flow lines and mixed-model repetitive flow lines. What implications does the choice between these two process designs have on the consumption of components?

4. Classify the distribution facilities usually found for the eight items listed in Exercise 1 as turnkey, specialty shop, discount store, or mail order.

5. Discuss the relationship between volume and product positioning strategy. Does a house built on speculation fit this pattern?

6. Why would a make-to-stock manufacturer wish to become assemble-to-order? What trends in today's society contribute to the ability and/or necessity to be assemble-to-order?

7. Discuss the relationship between the choice of production process and the mix of skills and equipment needed by the process.

8. Discuss the advantages and disadvantages of controlling the manufacture, distribution, and retailing in a make-to-stock environment. List examples of firms that control the entire process that compete with firms that control only manufacturing.

9. Discuss the advantages and disadvantages of frequent product design changes and new product introductions from a marketing viewpoint and from a manufacturing viewpoint. Does the choice of technology and production process influence the manufacturing viewpoint?

10. Discuss the applicability of computer integrated manufacturing to Kickham Boiler, given the information contained in this chapter.

SELECTED READINGS

Browne, Jimmie, John Harhen, and James Shivnan. *Production Management Systems: A CIM Perspective*. Wokingham, England: Addison-Wesley Publishing Company, 1988.

Cohen, Oded. "The Drum-Buffer-Rope (DBR) Approach to Logistics." In *Computer-Aided Production Management*, edited by A. Rolstadas. New York: Springer-Verlag, 1988.

Craighead, Thomas G. "EDI Impact Grows for Cost Efficient Manufacturing." *PIM Review* (July 1989): 32.

Deming, W. Edwards. *Out of the Crisis*. Cambridge, MA: The MIT Press, 1986.

Dertouzos, Michael L., Richard K. Lester, Robert M. Solow, and The MIT Commission on Industrial Productivity. *Made in America: Regaining the Productive Edge*. Cambridge, MA: The MIT Press, 1989.

Drucker, Peter F. *Management: Tasks, Responsibilities, Practices*. New York: Harper & Row, Publishers, Inc., 1974.

Fox, Edward A. "The Coming Revolution in Interactive Digital Video." *Communications of the ACM* (July 1989): 794.

Goldratt, Eliyahu M., and Jeff Cox. *The Goal: A Process of Ongoing Improvement*. Croton-on-Hudson, NY: North River Press, Inc., 1986.

Hall, Robert W. *Attaining Manufacturing Excellence*, Homewood, IL: Dow Jones-Irwin, 1987.

Hall, Robert W. *Zero Inventories*. Homewood IL: Dow Jones-Irwin, 1983.

Hayes, Robert H., and Steven C. Wheelwright. *Restoring Our Competitive Edge: Competing Through Manufacturing*. New York: John Wiley & Sons, Inc., 1984.

Hayes, Robert H., Steven C. Wheelwright, and Kim B. Clark. *Dynamic Manufacturing: Creating the Learning Organization*. New York: Free Press, 1988.

Hill, Terry. *Manufacturing Strategy: Text and Cases*. Wokingham, England: Addison-Wesley Publishing Company, 1989.

Imai, Masaaki. *Kaizen: The Key to Japan's Competitive Success*. New York: Random House Business Division, 1986.

New, C. Colin. "MRP and GT: A new Strategy for Component Production." *Production and Inventory Management* 18, no. 3 (1977): 50-62.

Pascale, Richard T., and Anthony G. Athos. *The Art of Japanese Management*. New York: Simon & Schuster, Inc., 1981.

Peters, Thomas J. *Thriving on Chaos*. New York: Harper & Row, Publishers, Inc., 1987.

Peters, Thomas J., and Robert H. Waterman, Jr. *In Search of Excellence*. New York: Harper & Row, Publishers, Inc., 1982.

Schonberger, Richard J. *Japanese Manufacturing Techniques: Nine Hidden Lessons in Simplicity*. New York: Free Press, 1982.

Shingo, Shigeo. *Non-Stock Production: The Shingo System for Continous Improvement*. Cambridge, MA: Productivity Press, 1988.

Shingo, Shigeo. "SMED The Heart of JIT Production." In *Competing through Quality & Productivity*. Cambridge, MA: Productivity Press, 1989.

Silver, Edward A., and Rein Peterson. *Decision Systems for Inventory Management and Production Planning*. 2d ed. New York: John Wiley & Sons, Inc., 1985.

Skinner, Wickham. "The Focused Factory." *Harvard Business Review* (May-June 1974): 113-121.

Spencer, Michael S. "Scheduling Components for Group Technology Lines." *Production and Inventory Management* (Fourth Quarter 1980): 43-49.

Swann, Don. "What is CIM, and Why Does it Cost $40 Million." *PIM Review* (July 1989): 34.

Part One

Master
Planning

2

LONG-RANGE PLANNING

Chapter 1 included an overview of long-range planning. This chapter examines long-range planning in more detail. It includes descriptions of strategic planning and tactical planning with examples of selected manufacturing strategic considerations. It describes the manufacturing resource (facilities and equipment) planning that precedes completion of the initial production plan. However, an initial production plan is implicitly required when deciding the number and size of facilities because those decisions affect capacity, and capacity limits the options available to production planning. In addition, a numerical example is used in the description of the relationship of production planning, sales planning, and financial planning.

Although manufacturing strategies and plans may be reviewed annually, major changes in strategies and facilities do not occur that often in most organizations. However, production planning does occur on a regular basis. For example, the production plan is extended (rolled forward) by three months every quarter in some firms. Thus, production planning bridges the long- and medium-range planning horizons. By its very nature, the production plan addresses what is known as the *aggregate planning problem*.

The aggregate planning problem is, strictly speaking, a medium-range planning problem because it normally covers a 12-month period. It is included in this chapter because long-range plans must be based on the decision of how the aggregate planning problem will be solved. In particular, the organization needs to decide whether to follow a chase, level, or combination plan, as described later in this chapter.

STRATEGIC VERSUS TACTICAL PLANNING

Strategic planning is the process of establishing corporate goals and objectives along with the plans to accomplish them. *Tactical planning* is the process of selecting the methods of achieving organizational objectives. There is no clear demarcation between strategic and tactical plans. The strategic-tactical dimension is a continuum with classification sometimes depending on the vantage point. For example, an organizational decision to diversify is strategic, while a resulting decision to enter a specific market may be tactical with respect to the diversification strategy. However, the decision to enter a specific market normally is classified as strategic, although at a lower level than the general diversification decision. Similarly, the president of a multidivision corporation may view the purchase of a bank of numerically controlled machines by a division as tactical, while the plant manufacturing manager may view the same decision as strategic.

Strategic planning begins by defining the organization's mission with answers to the following questions:

What is the nature of the present and future environments?

What are the philosophy and basic values of the organization?

What is the organization's business today and what should it be five or ten years from now?

What is the function of the firm's output; what needs do the company's products and services fill?

Who are the organization's customers?

What are the primary factors that will enable the organization to survive and prosper; i.e., what are its competitive strengths?

What factors hinder its growth and prosperity; i.e., what are its weaknesses?

What changes are required and what are the milestones on the route from the organization's present position to its future position when its long-range strategic goals have been achieved?

Although production inventory management personnel participate in long-range and strategic planning by specifying the capacity requirements for proposed plans, they devote most of their time and effort to tactical decisions in the medium and short range. While recognizing the strategic impact of some decisions, this book examines production inventory management (PIM) activities in the context of the long-, medium-, and short-range time spans as does most literature in this field.

Growth

Questions concerning growth in volume and scope must be addressed. As Peter Drucker has pointed out, all growth is not necessarily good. He notes that some growth is analogous to fat and only adds to the weight that the organization's vital systems must carry. Other growth is analogous to cancer gradually destroying vital functions such as engineering, marketing, and production by dissipating these resources on unrelated tasks, each requiring substantial effort. Desirable growth is that which increases the efficiency of functional activities by adding complementary product lines that make good use of present strengths and reduce fixed costs per unit of output.

Ideally, desirable growth should increase the financial strength of the organization, develop personnel and equipment capabilities, and increase the organization's ability to serve present and future markets. Analysis and decisions concerning growth must be made in terms of the unique strengths and weaknesses of each organization. The competitive strategy decision should extend through the manufacturing facilities, processes, and management systems. (Drucker 1974, 775)

It should be noted that a decision to maintain the status quo and not strive for growth in volume, product or market scope, or financial return is also a strategic plan.

Business Forecasting

Long-range planning begins with a business forecast that reflects the total predicted business environment including political, social, economic, technological, and competitive factors. In some organizations, preparing this forecast is a formal process conducted by an economic planning, a business research, or a marketing department. In other organizations, it is an informal process carried out by top management.

Political developments in foreign countries affect not only sources of supply for raw materials but also productive capacity. The impact of political developments on the availability of petroleum products is clear to even the casual observer. A reduction in Mideast oil exports can place a constraint on the production of many products and also can increase consumer demand for products such as diesel automobiles and insulating materials.

Political developments at home must also be considered. The firm should attempt to anticipate formal action by executive, legislative, and regulatory bodies at the local and national levels. What is the probability of price and wage controls being in effect one to five years from today? What specific actions that would affect the organization are federal agencies likely to take? Are the United States Congress or state legislatures likely to revise tax laws or expand (limit) the powers of their agencies? Customer demand is also affected by social factors, such as population growth, the age bracket, and geographic distribution of population.

Economic conditions are another of the factors that will determine an organization's capital structure two to five years hence. Recessions, depressions, inflationary periods, and business upswings all have different effects on the demand for different products. Long-term debt reduction commitments and profits in the intervening period also influence the ability of a business to obtain the additional capital required for planned expansion.

Probable technological developments within the organization or by competitors also must be assessed. Modularized electronic circuits, compact disks, and video recording devices for the home are three products that not only created their own demand patterns but also affected the demand patterns of many other items. Will the electrically powered automobile reach the same state of development and acceptance? Will high-density television or signals transmitted by optical fiber cable dominate future television systems? These are the type of questions long-range planners in some organizations are asking today.

Few of these issues are easy to confront. Nevertheless, solving too many of these problems incorrectly can lead to disaster. In most cases a sensitivity analysis can be performed and contingency plans can be developed. For example, although the strategic planning task force might base product line demand forecasts on a most likely prediction (say, moderate long-run economic prosperity combined with an inflation rate of approximately 7 percent), the impact of the other possible combinations of inflation and economic growth levels should be examined also. Answers to such *what-if* questions will reveal how sensitive predicted outcomes are to vagaries in the total business environment and resulting demand patterns. Contingency plans can then be developed to the degree suggested by the sensitivity of results to conditions. Some firms use computerized, corporate planning, simulation models to assist in this phase of analysis.

The output of the business forecast is a statement of the aggregate annual demand anticipated by product groups, including a forecast of demand for products that may be added to the product line at a future date. The business forecast also may differentiate between new and established market areas, and it is not unusual for these forecasts to be stated in a statistical fashion. They usually are made for each quarter of years 1 and 2 and for each year thereafter. The production plan, described shortly, is a statement of the extent to which the firm plans to meet this demand.

Top management should assume responsibility for business forecasting. It is not unusual to have a long-range planning task force reporting directly to the chief executive officer and also to employ the services of external consulting firms that specialize in this activity. The organization's objectives and the business forecast are the basis for product and sales planning, the business plan, and the production plan.

Philosophy

An organization's statement of its basic mission often describes its philosophy, perceived customers, and products. Basic values vary widely and cover a wide range. They may concern the products, treatment of customers, market, development of human resources, manufacturing technology, and distribution methods. A company's philosophy also usually reveals what the firm perceives as its competitive strength. For example, Minnesota Mining and Manufacturing emphasizes product innovation in adhesives and tapes, among other items. Its objective is to compete with quality products in these areas and to derive the bulk of its profits from products that are less than five years old. On the other hand Kickham Boiler (see Chapter 1) stresses the design and manufacturing of pressure vessels that must meet the rigid and unique requirements of a specific customer.

Competitive Strength

The competitive strength of a Ferrari automobile is obviously not its price. It succeeds by emphasizing style and quality of performance. The point is that, although all factors contribute to the success or failure of a product, most organizations emphasize excelling in one attribute or combination of attributes while attaining a desired reasonably good performance level for other attributes. Thus, an organization may stress quality, price, product variations and options, quick delivery, service after the sale, or some combination. Consistency in achieving the stated objectives is crucial. The competitive posture sought has a substantial effect on the manufacturing policies and methods. Delivery, product variations and options, price, and quality performance are all affected by process type, facility location, human resource management, production and inventory management, and distribution. Therefore, decisions in these areas should be consistent with and support attainment of the stated objectives.

An analysis of the competitive strengths of an organization often will reveal weaknesses relative either to competitors or to the capabilities required to achieve its objectives. These weaknesses may include an inability to serve certain markets due to inadequate distribution, high prices due to uneconomical production and inventory management or processes, inadequate quality, and inadequate design and performance due to poor engineering or manufacturing capabilities. The analysis should point out where improvements are required. This enables management to develop plans to remedy these conditions. For example, many manufacturing firms are implementing the Just-in-Time (JIT) approach and synchronous manufacturing to improve manufacturing economies through improved quality, reduced lead time, reduced work in process, and greater flexiblity.

LONG-RANGE PLANNING

The strategic plan is the basis for long-range planning that includes product and sales planning, manufacturing planning, and production planning. Its final output is an integrated business plan. These planning activities are part of strategic planning and often occur concurrently with the activities described previously. They verify the feasibility, or lack thereof, of the mission and the strategic objectives.

Product and Sales Planning

Product and sales planning includes macrolevel decisions concerning the product lines the company plans to produce, the markets to be served (including the target population and geographic areas), and the levels of demand anticipated for the various product lines. Product line and market planning decisions are explicit commitments to an organizational direction. It usually is difficult in the short run to change them. Organizational growth and prosperity will be influenced substantially by the wisdom of these decisions. Product and sales planning answers the following questions:

What products does the firm plan to produce?
In what areas and to which customer groups does the company plan to sell its products?
What are the quality and pricing level targets?
What are the expected life cycles of the products and where are they now?
What are the market entry and exit strategies of the firm?

The Product and Sales Planning.   Product and sales planning decisions are interrelated. The defined market affects the product design, including all the attributes of quality described in Chapter 18, the production volume, and the desired unit cost. The product and the sales plan are also the dominant determinants of the resources required for marketing, engineering, manufacturing, and distribution.

Expanding sales activities into a new geographic territory, such as the decision of Coca-Coca Bottling Company to enter China, and the entering of a new product or service field, such as the decision of McDonnell Douglas Corporation to market EDP software systems, are two examples of strategic decisions. Both of these decisions reveal a change in the mission of the organizations and had a substantial impact on the resources required.

The demarcation between business forecasting and product and sales planning is not easily discernible in all cases, and information flows in both directions. Using the inputs received from the business forecast and an analysis of the organization's competitive strengths, product and sales planning determines which markets and products are viable in terms of demand, capabilities, and organizational objectives. Final product line and sales planning decisions are not made until the long-range planning loop is closed by verification of manufacturing and financial feasibility as illustrated in Figure 2-1.

Product Life Cycles and Strategies.   The demand for the vast majority of products goes through the stages of growth, stability, and decay. However, the life spans of different products vary. Many toys have life spans of less than a year, whereas durable goods such as refrigerators have life spans of three or more years. The lengths of the different stages for a particular product line are determined by public acceptance, social and economic conditions, and the rate of development of competing technical and styling innovations. For example, a product in the decay stage of its life may be buoyed by healthy economic conditions and merchandising. However, unless it is redesigned, its demand is likely to decrease at an increasing rate. By the same token, the right new product at the propitious moment in a technological-social sense may experience greater demand than economic conditions alone would warrant. This

Figure 2-1
Production Plans

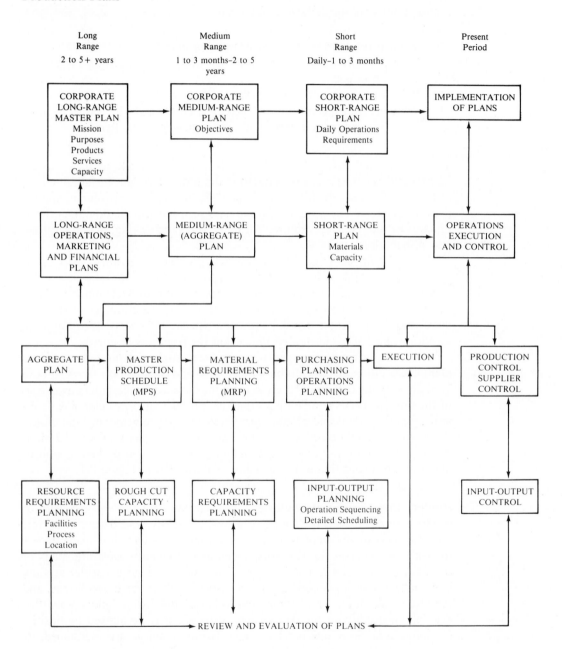

type of analysis leads to recommendations concerning the development of new product lines and the phasing out of some existing products.

Market entry and exit decisions usually have a major effect on manufacturing. Most new products experience a relatively large number of engineering changes as the design develops, and demand tends to be relatively low in the early phases of a developing market. Low demand and frequent variations in design recommend different capacity and processes than the high demand and stable design found in established products. However, successful entry early in the life of a new product usually earns better returns.

The life cycle development is often grouped into four stages, for convenience of discussion, as shown in Figure 2-2. Stage I is product introduction, Stage II is growth, Stage III is maturity, Stage IV is decline. The production facilities appropriate for each stage of production are different. In Stage I the product is usually assembled from purchased parts available from other manufacturers. Parts that are manufactured in-house may be built at special prototyping facilities. Many new products die at this stage for lack of demand.

The products that enter Stage II often are manufactured in a job shop environment or perhaps a batch flow environment. Both environments provide plenty of volume flexibility. Products that become very successful usually are moved to a dedicated flow environment built specifically to manufacture that product for the maturity stage. As the product declines, surplus machines may be removed from the facility, or the facility itself may be converted to a batch flow facility.

Figure 2-2
Product Life Cycle

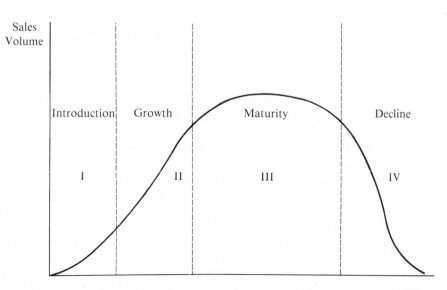

In a Just-in-Time (JIT) system employing a U-shaped line, the facility often is built during the growth stage with sufficient capacity to handle the eventual demand. Because the workers all are multifunctional, changes in demand during Stages II, III, and IV are accommodated by adding or subtracting workers. In the extreme, one worker may walk a part through every stage of manufacture. For non-JIT environments, matching the volume of demand to the proper production environment is a crucial part of competitiveness. For this reason, product managers who stay with the product commonly are employed in addition to the facility managers. For the product manager, it is important to realize that the elements of competition may vary from stage to stage. In Stage I the most important determinant of success is product performance. In Stage II, as the product gains popularity, the most important determinant is price and availability. In Stage III the product often becomes a commodity, competing purely on price. In Stage IV the competition returns to price and availability, as competitors cease production and service parts are important.

Manufacturing Planning

Strategic, long-range, manufacturing planning decisions may be grouped in the following four major areas:

1. Value-added decisions
2. Facility size, location, and degree of focus decisions
3. Manufacturing management philosophy decisions, which include decisions concerning human resource management polices, production and inventory control systems, and management approaches such as Just-in-Time and total quality management
4. Process flow and facility layout decisions, which were described in Chapter 1

As described throughout the text, these decisions should be integrated to maintain consistency and to assure that they are mutually supportive.

Value-Added Decisions.   The term *value-added* refers to the additional utility provided the customer when a product is transformed by the manufacturing process or moved within the distribution system. Few, if any, major clothing manufacturers raise sheep from which to obtain wool for the clothing they manufacture. Some have woolen mills and others do not. The latter purchase material from various textile and woolen mills and manufacture the clothing. Edison Brothers in St. Louis purchases shoes from many different manufacturers and markets them through the hundreds of retail outlets it has throughout North America. Edison Brothers is an example of a company that adds value primarily through distribution and marketing activities. Other companies add value through final preparation, assembly, and packaging. Still others are involved in obtaining raw materials, processing the raw materials, fabricating components, and building the final product. An example of the latter is an oil company that has oil exploration activities, operates oil wells and refineries, and also runs its own distribution systems and retail outlets.

Facility Size, Location, and Focus Decisions.   Facility size is a function of economies and diseconomies of scale, both of which are influenced by the labor- versus capital-intensity of the manufacturing process, the manufacturing focus desired, and the desired number of employees per location. These strategic decisions affect the number of facilities and the task of PIM. (Hayes and Wheelwright 1984; Peters and Watermann 1982)

Manufacturing Management Philosophy Decisions.   The values, norms, and policies that are the underpinning of production procedures and systems should be consistent with the overall organization philosophy. For example, an organization philosophy of "each employee is an associate" will affect hiring, employee development opportunities, layoff policies, and employee participation in decision making. In a similar manner, a policy of "24-hour delivery" should affect production and inventory management practices.

Financial Planning

Product, market, and production plans frequently require additional resources such as facilities and equipment that in turn require financing. Normal operations require working capital, and sales generate income. The financial capability of the organization to carry out the long-range plans should be verified. After the availability of the required resources is assured, a commitment can be made to the production plan.

Integrating Plans

Commitment to a strategic plan does not occur until the long-range planning cycle—including preparation of the business forecast, product and sales planning, production planning, resource planning, and financial planning—has been completed.

Figure 2-1 (page 36) depicts the major long-range level planning activities and their interaction. Although production and inventory management (PIM) personnel play a major role only in production planning and resource planning, an understanding of their role is enhanced by a discussion of all five activities.

Product, sales, and production planning should be conducted interactively with resource planning. The availability of facilities, processes, equipment, and personnel depends on the lead time for acquiring the facilities and equipment, the organization's financial strength, technological difficulty of the tasks, and the availability of the required engineering and other type personnel.

New products may require additional personnel, such as design and process engineers, as well as additional manufacturing capacity. Geographic expansion of the market usually requires additional distribution facilities, and an increased aggregate volume increases manufacturing capacity requirements.

The determination of personnel requirements in areas such as engineering and marketing is the task of the management of those functional areas. Calculation of manufacturing capacity requirements is the point at which PIM usually enters long-range planning. Distribution capacity requirements may be calculated by marketing, PIM, or a joint task force of those two departments. Facilities and equipment required for manufacturing and distribution are affected by value-added, location, plant size, and process decisions.

THE BUSINESS PLAN

The planned aggregate sales income, the planned cost of sales, and all other planned operating expenses for all products and services per period provide a basis for calculating the planned net income of an organization. This enables the organization to calculate the planned return on investment (ROI) or return on assets (ROA) and to estimate what funds will be available for either distribution to stockholders or reinvestment in the organization. In Chapters 10 and 11, we discuss manufacturing resource planning (MRP II). The business plan and resource requirements planning, described later in this chapter, are both part of MRP II.

The business plan, the sales plan, and the production plan must be consistent and mutually supportive. Table 2-1 uses October data developed from the data in Tables 2-3 through 2-7 (pages 45-48) to illustrate the relationships among the production plan, the sales plan, and the business plan. For example, the planned income is based on planned shipments, the sales prices of the products shipped, the projected cost of sales, and other allocated costs. The sales plan projects sales (shipments) of 700 units of Product Group A in October at $45 each, thus generating $31,500 revenue. The total variable and fixed costs allocated to these units is $28,000. Subtracting the total costs from revenue renders a net income of $3,500 for Product Group A in October.

During October the planned income from the sales of Product Groups A, B, and C is $5,300. The natural question is, From where do the income and cost values come? The income of each product group is based on the projected weighted average sales price for the anticipated (forecast) product sales of the items that constitute the group (the product mix). The total revenue is the sum of the revenue from all groups. The variable costs of each group are calculated and then added to the other costs allocated to the group to obtain the group's total costs. Adding the costs of all product groups renders the aggregate costs. The net total income then equals the difference between the total revenue and the total costs. (The costs are a natural derivative of the resource requirements planning system, as described in the following sections; the projected revenue is a natural derivative of the sales plan.)

Table 2-1
Relationship Among Sales, Production, and Financial Plans

Product Group	Production (units) Sept.	Oct.				Financial (dollars)		
A								
	Production	180	720	Cost	$ 40			
				Price	45			
	Shipments		700	Production costs	28,800	Cost of sales	$28,000	
				Revenue	31,500			
	Ending inventory		200	Ending inventory	8,000	Change in inventory	800	Income $3,500
B								
	Production	250	240	Cost	$ 33			
				Price	38			
	Shipments		250	Production costs	7,920	Cost of sales	$8,250	
				Revenue	9,500			
	Ending inventory		240	Ending inventory	7,920	Change in inventory	−330	Income $1,250
C								
	Production	50	160	Cost	$ 35			
				Price	40			
	Shipments		110	Production costs	5,600	Cost of sales	$3,850	
				Revenue	4,400			
	Ending inventory		100	Ending inventory	3,500	Change in inventory	1,750	Income $550
						Total income		$5,300

Aggregate Financial Plan	
Revenue	$45,400
Cost of Sales	40,100
Income	$ 5,300
Ending inventory	$19,420

PRODUCTION PLANNING

The necessary inputs for production planning are:

1. The product and sales plan
2. The management strategy and policy concerning the aggregate planning problem
3. The manufacturing processes for the different product groups
4. The efficiency and capacity of work centers
5. The identification of bottleneck work centers
6. The allocation of manufacturing resources (plants and equipment) to producing specific products

Production planning uses the information from product and sales planning to plan the aggregate rates of production and the inventory levels by time period for groups of products. Output levels are specified in the broadest terms possible: tons, barrels, yards, dollars, and standard hours of production. The specificity of product line and product differentiation required at this level depends on the nature of the product and the equipment required to manufacture it. For example, automotive engine blocks usually are machined on a specially designed high-speed, automated or semi-automated line. A line built for the manufacture of four-cylinder engines ordinarily cannot be used to manufacture six-cylinder engines. Thus, the long-range production plan must separate four- and six-cylinder engine requirements to obtain a valid estimate of facility and equipment requirements. This may be accomplished merely by multiplying the estimated total demand by the anticipated proportion of the various engine sizes.

Smoothing of production to compensate for varying seasonal demand rates is planned in this time frame. The important point is that it is the production plan that establishes customer service level goals, target inventory levels, size of the backlog if any, production rates, size of the work force, levels of hiring and firing, and plans for overtime and subcontracting. The production plan is the basis for determining capacity requirements that must be consistent with capacity availability.

The objective of the production plan is to provide sufficient finished goods by period to meet the sales plan objectives while staying within financial and production capacity constraints. When demand varies from period to period, planning production to exceed demand in one period can provide inventory to fill excessive demand in a following period.

Table 2-2 illustrates a production plan for the three product groups shown in Table 2-1. The number of product groups used to encompass all products should be no greater than that required to determine resource requirements. Individual production plans may be required for divisions or plants within a firm. As the production period approaches, planning becomes more refined and a master production schedule (MPS) is developed. The MPS is a statement of

Table 2-2
Two-Year Production Plan, Product Groups A, B, and C

Period	Month							Quarter					
	Sept.	Oct.	Nov.	Dec.	Jan.	Feb.	Mar.	2	3	4	1	2	3
Weeks/Period[1]	5	4	4	5	4	4	5	13	13	13	13	13	13
Production Days/Period		20	18	22	19	19	25	64	63	60	63	64	63
Group A													
Production rate: units/day[2]		36	36	36	36	36	36	36	40	40	40	40	40
Production		720	648	792	684	684	900	2,304	2,520	2,400	2,520	2,560	2,520
Shipments		700	760	850	500	500	875	2,500	2,500	2,300	2,600	2,700	2,700
Ending inventory	180	200	88	30	214	398	423	227	247	347	267	127	−53
Group B													
Production rate: units/day[3]		12	12	12	12	4	4	4	4/12	12	12/4	4	4/12
Production		240	216	264	228	76	100	256	444	720	404	256	444
Shipments		250	300	350	250	60	60	180	370	900	370	180	370
Ending inventory	250	240	156	70	48	64	104	180	254	74	108	184	258
Group C													
Production rate: units/day[4]		8	8	8	8	20	20	20	22/9	9	9/22	22	22/9
Production		160	144	176	152	380	500	1,280	1,034	540	1,060	1,408	1,034
Shipments		110	115	120	180	400	460	1,340	1,060	500	1,100	1,450	1,000
Ending inventory	50	100	129	185	157	137	177	117	91	131	91	49	83

[1] The weeks per month in each quarter are assigned arbitrarily as *4, 4, 5.* For example, April and May have 4 weeks, June has 5. The plant does not close for vacation.

[2] The production rate is 36 units per day for the first three quarters, 40 units per day thereafter. There is level production throughout the year. The rate change is due to long-term positive demand trend.

[3] The production rate is 12 units per day for September through January and 4 units per day for February through August, due to seasonal sales.

[4] The production rate is 8 units per day for September through January and 20 units per day for February through August. These rates increase to 9 and 22 units per day, respectively, due to long-term positive demand trend.

all anticipated manufacturing of items within product groups by planning period (see Chapter 4). In some firms the production plan is developed in greater detail into what is called a medium-range plan and later is refined into an MPS. In others, the production plan is unfolded directly into the MPS at some point, nine months prior to execution, for example. In other firms the production plan and the MPS may be one and the same. The approach selected by a specific organization depends on the diversity of its product lines, the manufacturing processes, and its data processing capabilities.

The term *aggregate planning* denotes planning for a group in order to obtain a view of the planned total results. An aggregate plan may encompass a product line; the output of a plant, division, or entire organization; or planned sales in a geographic area. Aggregate financial plans are expressed in dollars and are based on the corresponding sales, production, employment, and inventory plans. All of the latter are expressed in both the appropriate units and dollars. In a large organization the grand aggregate is the total of the aggregate plans for all divisions, incorporating the sales of many different products in many different markets. The example developed in this chapter is relatively simple; there are only three product lines (Groups A, B, and C) and only one market. Aggregate plans are developed in the long range and used through the medium and short ranges as an overall control and guide for more detailed plans, such as the MPS. On occasion they may be modified in the medium or short ranges to cope with unforeseen developments, such as a plant fire or flood, an energy crisis, an abrupt shift in demand due to a strike at a competitor, or a sharp price decrease by a competitor.

RESOURCE REQUIREMENTS PLANNING

The resources required by the production plan in any period include labor, materials, facilities, and equipment (usually identified by work center), and the funds required to pay the employees, purchase the materials, and pay other expenses. (This analysis omits resources required for capital improvements, such as building new facilities, purchasing new equipment, or substantially modifying existing facilities and equipment.)

The resource requirements are determined in the following manner:

1. Obtain the planned production for each product group by period.
2. Determine the resource profile for each product group.
3. Determine the materials profile for each product group.
4. Using the planned production, resource profile, and materials profile, calculate the resource and material requirements.

Resource Profile

The product group *resource profile* states the resources required to produce one unit of a product group. It is based on the anticipated product mix of the group and includes the processing time required for all components and subassemblies and for the final assembly. Table 2-3 illustrates how assembly labor is determined for Product Group A, which consists of three different items: 1, 2, and 3. The anticipated percentage of each item in the group is multiplied by the standard assembly time for the item. These results are then summed to obtain the standard assembly time for the average item in Product Group A. For example, Item 1 sales are forecast to be 50 percent of Product Group A total sales and to have a standard assembly time of 0.342 hours. Multiplying 0.50 by 0.342 gives 0.171 hours. Adding 0.171 hours to the values obtained in a similar computation for Items 2 and 3 gives an average assembly time of 0.301 hours for Product Group A, as shown in Table 2-3.

Table 2-3
Assembly Labor for Average Unit, Product Group A

Item	Typical Percentage (1)	Standard Assembly Hours per Unit (2)	Average Assembly Time (1) × (2)
1	0.50	0.342	0.171
2	0.30	0.294	0.088
3	0.20	0.210	0.042
	1.00		0.301

Using the information in Table 2-3 concerning the labor (time) required for assembling a typical unit of Product Group A, and similar information for all of the product groups and resource centers, the resource profiles for Product Groups A, B, and C are developed as shown in Table 2-4.

Table 2-4
Resourse Profiles for Product Groups A, B, and C
Average Standard Hours per Unit

Resource Center	Standard Hours			Week
	A	B	C	
Assembly	0.301	0.285	0.256	1
Electrical subassembly	0.274	0.222	0.241	2
Mechanical subassembly	0.250	0.185	0.241	2
CNC machining	0.112	0.098	0.108	3
Other	0.205	0.182	0.198	3
Total	1.142	0.972	1.044	

Since all of the processes required to produce a complex assembly and its components must be included, and since many of the components must be manufactured a week or so in advance of the assembly activities, the timing of the requirements for various resources must be recognized. This is accomplished using lead-time offset information as shown in Figure 2-3. This lead-time offset

Figure 2-3
Lead-Time Offsets, Product 1

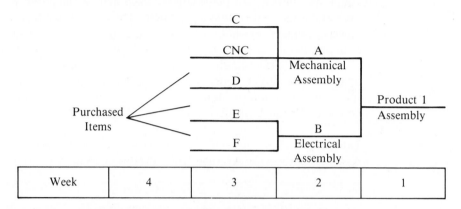

information reveals that the mechanical subassembly is usually completed one week prior to the final assembly and that the processing of components in the CNC machining department takes place two weeks prior to the final assembly. This information is especially important when planning on a weekly basis, but it will not affect less-refined plans made on a monthly basis. As an organization achieves Just-in-Time production (see Chapter 17), most resources will be required in the same week.

Resource Requirements

The standard labor hours required for each product group in a resource center during a period are obtained by multiplying a product group's standard time per unit in the resource center by the quantity of the group to be produced during the period. For example, multiplying the 0.301 hours required for assembling one unit of Product Group A by the 720 units planned in October renders a requirement of 216.72 standard hours for Product Group A during October in the assembly department. Performing similar calculations for Product Groups B and C and adding the requirements for all groups gives 326.08 standard hours required in the assembly department for Product Groups A, B, and C during October. To arrive at the actual hours required, the efficiency of the resource centers must be considered. Efficiency can be measured as follows:

$$\text{Efficiency} = \frac{\text{Standard Hours}}{\text{Actual Hours}}$$

which may be transformed to

$$\text{Actual Hours} = \frac{\text{Standard Hours}}{\text{Efficiency}}$$

In our example, the efficiency of the assembly department is 0.95. Thus, the actual total hours required for Product Groups A, B, and C in the assembly department during October is 343.24 hours. The resource requirements for all periods and all departments are calculated in the same manner. These values are shown in Table 2-5.

Table 2-5
Resource Requirements (Standard and Actual Hours in October)

Product Group	Assembly	Electrical Subassembly	Resource Center Mechanical Subassembly	CNC Machining	Other
A	216.72	197.28	180.00	80.64	147.60
B	68.40	53.28	44.40	23.52	43.68
C	40.96	38.56	38.56	17.28	31.68
Total standard hours	326.08	289.12	262.96	121.44	222.96
Efficiency	0.95	0.95	0.95	0.95	0.95
Actual hours	343.24	304.34	276.80	127.83	234.69

Although a group of chapters is devoted to the issue of control later in the text, it is important to note that control begins in the planning process as the planned resource requirements are compared to the available capacity as shown in Table 2-6. The available capacity in standard hours is based on the actual output that each department (resource center) has achieved in standard hours of output in the recent past. Table 2-6 reveals that sufficient capacity exists in all departments except assembly.

Table 2-6
Comparison of Required and Available Capacity by Resource Center

Resource Center	Capacity Requirements (standard hours) A	B	C	Total	Available (Demonstrated) Capacity	Deficiencies
Assembly	216.72	68.40	40.96	326.08	300	−26.08
Electrical subassembly	197.28	53.28	38.56	289.12	320	
Mechanical subassembly	180.00	44.40	38.56	262.96	280	
CNC machining	80.64	23.52	17.28	121.44	200	

Financial Resources

The financial resources required are the sum of materials, direct labor, and all other costs. The direct labor costs per unit are equal to the cost of labor per hour times the estimated actual labor hours required. The total cost of labor in our example is $20 per hour, which includes wages and fringe benefits such as insurance, holidays, and vacation. For the typical unit of Product A, 1.142 standard hours are required. Using the equation above, the actual hours equal $1.142 \div 0.95 = 1.202$. Thus, the labor cost per unit is $24.04 ($1.202 \times \$20$). This information is recorded in Table 2-7 along with the labor requirements and costs for Product Groups A, B and C.

Table 2-7
Total Cost per Unit

Product Group	Total Standard Hours	Total Actual Hours	Cost of Labor	Cost of Materials	Sales and Administrative Costs	Total Cost
A	1.142	1.202	$24.04	$7.96	$8.00	$40.00
B	0.972	1.023	20.46	5.54	7.00	33.00
C	1.044	1.099	21.98	6.02	7.00	35.00

Materials costs are available from the bill of material, which lists all purchased materials and components as well as their costs (see Chapter 4). The composite cost per unit of a product group is obtained in the same manner as the average labor cost per unit. That is, the typical materials costs of Product Group A equal the weighted average of the materials costs of the three products in the group.

INTEGRATION OF PLANS

Tables 2-2 (page 43) and 2-8 depict an example of an integrated sales, production, and financial plan for the next 24 months. Table 2-2 gives the shipments (sales), production, and inventory investment in units. Table 2-8 lists the same information, as well as the change in inventory and net income in dollars. Both plans are stated in monthly periods for the next 6 months and in quarterly periods for the last 18 months of the two-year plan. It is a common practice to present plans for the more proximate periods in smaller time increments. For example, in the chapters that follow, master planning and rough cut capacity planning will develop weekly plans for the first few months.

Although aggregate planning is a generic term covering many different plans, references to "the aggregate planning problem" are concerned with the specific decision situation described in the remainder of this chapter.

Table 2-8
Two-Year Production Plan (Units and Dollars)

Period	Sept.	Oct.	Nov.	Dec.	Jan.	Feb.	Mar.	Quarter 2	3	4	1	2	3
Group A													
Production		720	648	792	684	684	900	2,304	2,520	2,400	2,520	2,560	2,520
Shipments		700	760	850	500	500	875	2,500	2,500	2,300	2,600	2,700	2,700
Inventory (End)	180	200	88	30	214	398	423	227	247	347	267	127	−53
Cost of Sales		$28,000	$30,400	$34,000	$20,000	$20,000	$35,000	$100,000	$100,000	$92,000	$104,000	$108,000	$108,000
Revenue		$31,500	$34,200	$38,250	$22,500	$22,500	$39,375	$112,500	$112,500	$103,500	$117,000	$121,500	$121,500
Profit		$3,500	$3,800	$4,250	$2,500	$2,500	$4,375	$12,500	$12,500	$13,000	$13,000	$13,500	$13,500
Inventory value	$7,200	$8,000	$3,520	$1,200	$8,560	$15,920	$16,920	$9,080	$9,880	$13,880	$10,680	$5,080	($2,120)
Group B													
Production		240	216	264	228	76	100	256	444	720	404	256	444
Shipments		250	300	350	250	60	60	180	370	900	370	180	370
Inventory (End)	250	240	156	70	48	64	104	180	254	74	108	184	258
Cost of Sales		$8,250	$9,900	$11,550	$8,250	$1,980	$1,980	$5,940	$12,210	$29,700	$12,210	$5,940	$12,210
Revenue		$9,500	$11,400	$13,300	$9,500	$2,280	$2,280	$6,840	$14,060	$34,200	$14,060	$6,840	$14,060
Profit		$1,250	$1,500	$1,750	$1,250	$300	$300	$900	$1,850	$4,500	$1,850	$900	$1,850
Inventory value	$8,250	$7,920	$5,148	$2,310	$1,584	$2,112	$3,432	$5,940	$8,382	$2,442	$3,564	$6,072	$8,514
Group C													
Production		160	144	176	152	380	500	1,280	1,034	540	1,060	1,408	1,034
Shipments		110	115	120	180	400	460	1,340	1,060	500	1,100	1,450	1,000
Inventory (End)	50	100	129	185	157	137	177	117	91	131	91	49	83
Cost of Sales		$3,850	$4,025	$4,200	$6,300	$14,000	$16,100	$46,900	$37,100	$17,500	$38,500	$50,750	$35,000
Revenue		$4,400	$4,600	$4,800	$7,200	$16,000	$18,400	$53,600	$42,400	$20,000	$44,000	$58,000	$40,000
Profit		$550	$575	$600	$900	$2,000	$2,300	$6,700	$5,300	$2,500	$5,500	$7,250	$5,000
Inventory value	$1,750	$3,500	$4,515	$6,475	$5,495	$4,795	$6,195	$4,095	$3,185	$4,585	$3,185	$1,715	$2,905

THE AGGREGATE PLANNING PROBLEM
AND CAPACITY PLANNING

The aggregate planning problem concerns the allocation of resources such as personnel, facilities, equipment, and inventory so that the planned products and services (the output) are available when needed. The aggregate plan usually covers a 12- to 24-month period, and as time passes, may be updated monthly or quarterly. Prior long-range facility decisions limit the capacity available and may limit aggregate planning options. Thus, long-range facility planning must consider the aggregate planning strategy.

Let's examine the cause of the aggregate planning problem and some approaches for meeting the challenge. Not only do snow blowers and lawn mowers have seasonal demand, but furniture, appliances, automobiles, clothing, small tools, and many other items have demand with substantial seasonal variation, year after year. Variation in the demand for consumer goods generates seasonal demand for the raw materials, components, and supplies used in their manufacture. Figure 2-4 shows three typical situations: (1) relatively stable demand—bread and milk, for example; (2) single cycle demand, or one high and one low demand cycle annually—retail sales of many items at Christmas, for example; and (3) dual high and low cycles annually—shaving lotion peaks at Christmas

Figure 2-4
Typical Monthly Aggregate Demand Patterns

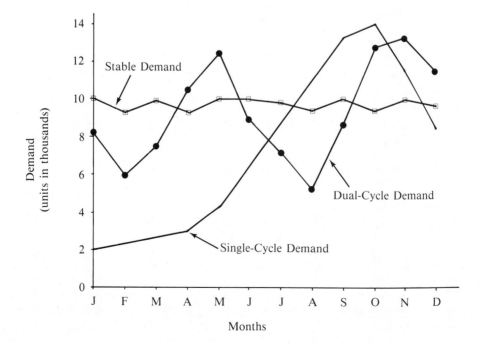

and Father's Day, for example. Other seasonal variations in demand are possible, but examination of these three patterns will provide a basis for studying the concepts and techniques useful for aggregate planning under all situations.

With relatively steady demand, there is no aggregate planning problem. Facilities, capacity, the work force, and materials are planned for production at that steady rate. However, seasonal demand patterns present management with the following three options:

1. Modify or manage demand.
2. Manage supply (output) in the following ways:
   a. Provide ample capacity and flexibility to have the output match demand (the chase strategy).
   b. Produce at a level rate and store some of the output to meet peak demand (the level production strategy).
3. Some combination of 1 and 2.

Managing Demand

Changing the demand pattern can reduce the aggregate planning problem and in some cases uncover other sources of income and profit. Possible methods of modifying demand include the following:

1. **Complementary products.** Developing and marketing new products whose primary demand is in the present off-season can reduce the demand-capacity imbalance. For example, some lawn equipment companies have been successful in manufacturing and marketing snow removal equipment, while swimsuit manufacturers have entered the ski-apparel business. Many service organizations have developed complementary services: combining heating and air conditioning repair; adding weekend courses and evening continuing education programs at educational institutions traditionally offering only weekday programs; and adding a breakfast menu at a fast-food restaurant.
2. **Promotion, advertising, and price incentives.** The right combination of a desired service or product, value for the price, and promotion can increase customer demand in normally slack periods. Major league baseball in the United States has been very successful in using attractions such as glove night and jacket night to increase attendance at games that normally have small- to medium-sized crowds.

   Reduced pricing can shift demand to periods that normally have low demand. Local transit companies offer shoppers reduced bus fares in nonrush hours. Theaters often have reduced prices for matinee and dinner-hour shows, and many restaurants have early bird specials. Other examples include reduced rates for off-season travel and time period differentials in long distance telephone rates. Special financing arrangements may also be used to manage demand. For example, department stores offer November purchasers the option of a late January payment without interest. Similarly, some manufacturers of recreational boats offer retailers the option of later payment without interest for purchases in the preseason months. Thus, the manufacturing company reduces its storage space needs and obtains the sale, while the retailer avoids the financial cost of the inventory and has a better opportunity for early sales to the final customer.

3. **Reservations and backlogs.** Service organizations frequently ask or require that customers reserve capacity by means of an appointment. This could include a reservation for dinner where a specific time is reserved, or a specific space reservation, such as a hotel room or airline seat. This practice enables both the customer and the service provider to plan with greater certainty. In other instances, customers are willing to enter a waiting line for a service. For example, customers often must wait until a restaurant table, service technician, or emergency room physician is available. The service provider agrees to serve the customer as soon as the capacity is available.

   Similar conditions exist in manufacturing, especially in a seller's market. The customer must order well in advance of the actual need date. Thus, the customer places an order for later delivery (similar to an appointment), and the manufacturer produces to a backlog of orders. For example, the Custom Shirt Shop of New Jersey has retail outlets throughout the United States that accept the customer's order with payment. The factory then mails the tailor-made shirts to the customer six to eight weeks later. Using a backlog as a planning approach is feasible only when the customer perceives the quality of the product worthy of the wait—and the cost.

Although modifying demand often makes an important contribution to solving the aggregate planning problem, it rarely solves it completely. Other actions are required to manage the supply so that it meets surges in demand. The primary methods of doing this are described next.

Managing Supply

Two basic strategies represent opposite ends of the spectrum of supply management approaches used in solving the aggregate planning problem. One, the *chase strategy*, is designed to allow for sufficient capacity and flexibility to enable production output to match the demand. Using this approach, the production rate may vary widely, as illustrated in Figure 2-5. The rationale of the chase strategy is to avoid high inventory carrying cost when demand varies substantially by varying employment levels, using overtime, subcontracting, and/or assigning production employees to maintenance or training activities during low demand periods. In some cases, such as agriculture, this is a

Figure 2-5
The Chase Production Strategy

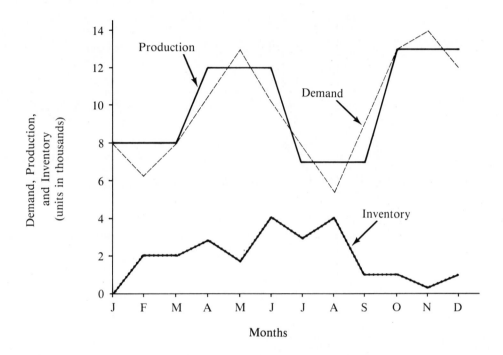

necessity; harvesting must take place when the crop is ready. It also is a necessity for some service organizations. For example, the hospital emergency room must be able to handle trauma cases as they arrive. However, the chase strategy is not necessary or economically practical in many situations. Examples include situations in which employees have a guaranteed annual wage and those in which equipment capacity is well below the maximum demand rate.

At the other end of the spectrum is the *level production strategy*. This strategy is designed to allow for the same production rate throughout the year and to have inventory or backorders absorb variations in demand, as illustrated in Figure 2-6. This makes sense when demand is relatively stable, but following this approach in some situations, such as the manufacture of artificial Christmas trees, will result in excessive inventory carrying costs.

Traditionally, the aggregate planning problem has been viewed as an analysis of the trade-off between production rate change costs and inventory carrying costs. (These and other costs will be examined in the next section of this chapter.) However, more flexible manufacturing and service systems are being developed in many organizations. These systems have the ability to change output rates quickly and inexpensively.

Figure 2-6
The Level Production Strategy

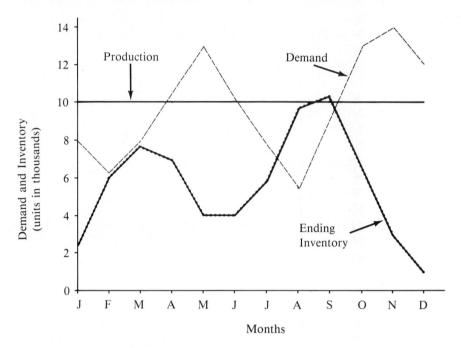

Costs Relevant to the
Aggregate Planning Decision

The costs resulting from the aggregate planning decision fall into two major categories: (1) inventory costs and (2) production rate change costs.

Inventory Costs.   Inventory costs include the following: (1) the costs of carrying inventory and (2) the capital costs of added storage facilities beyond those required for level production. Manufacturing items in one period for sale in later periods during which forecast demand exceeds planned production results in inventory carrying costs. These carrying costs include the costs of storage, capital invested, insurance, taxes for the items held in storage, as well as breakage, deterioration, and obsolescence. In addition, increasing inventory beyond certain levels requires additional storage capacity, which requires additional storage facilities, equipment, and possibly personnel. Furthermore, when working capital requires additional debt, interest rates may be increased due to the altered capital structure of the organization. This, in turn, may increase the carrying cost rate.

Management often views inventory as occupying free space—that is, space not useful for any other purpose. This is misleading. Marion Laboratories, Inc., of Kansas City has reduced its inventory space requirements by more than 75,000 square feet through improved inventory management. Miller Fluid Power of Bensenville, Illinois, has achieved similar savings. Both companies achieved these savings through increased production flexibility and improved production planning, purchasing, and aggregate planning. Both have also converted this space to income-producing activities. Figure 2-7 depicts the general nature of the inventory costs that affect the aggregate planning decision. Note that carrying costs increase at a constant rate from that point at which inventory exists. Discontinuities occur when additional capacity is required (Point B). As inventory shortages (negative inventory investments) increase, backorder and stockout costs rise exponentially.

Production Rate Change Costs. Production rate change costs include the following items:

1. Facilities and equipment (greater capacity)
2. Hiring and releasing employees
3. Overtime and undertime
4. Part-time and temporary personnel
5. Subcontracting
6. Cooperative agreements

Figure 2-7
Aggregate Inventory Costs Versus Inventory Investment

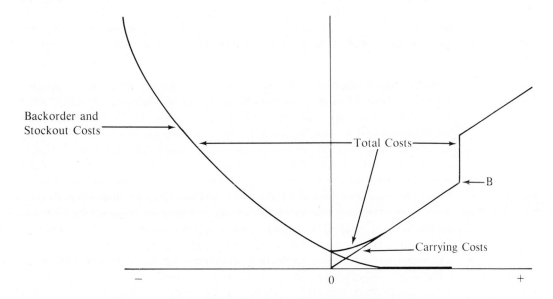

Backorder and
Stockout Costs

Total Costs

B

Carrying Costs

−

0

+

Inventory Investment

Facility and Equipment Costs.   The processing capacity required to match peaks in demand (a chase strategy) is greater than that required to maintain a level production rate. This often means that a larger facility and more equipment are required when initiating or changing to a chase strategy than when following a level production strategy. These decisions and costs are usually part of long-range facility planning. Thus, they provide de facto policy constraints within which aggregate capacity planning decisions must be made. For example, restaurants have a given number of tables, manufacturing plants have equipment with specific processing capabilities and speeds, and elementary schools have a limited number of classrooms and seats. Increasing the facility capacity usually takes longer than one year. The exception is when an existing facility can be purchased and readied for use in a few months. For example, beverage bottling companies occasionally are able to purchase and modify a competitor's plant in a relatively short time.

Hiring and Releasing Employees.   In some cases, increased capacity requires hiring and training new employees, an expensive activity. There are learning curve effects (see Chapter 10), and new employees usually require more instruction than experienced employees. In general, new employees are more susceptible to accidents, more likely to generate scrap, and generally less productive. In a tight market, new employees tend to be marginal and the situation is worsened. Even in a labor market with an abundance of skilled labor, the recruiting, selection, and training costs can be substantial.

Releasing employees increases unemployment insurance and often lowers morale and productivity. Organizations with a policy of seasonal layoffs often have difficulty obtaining the more competent employees. In addition, some labor agreements require the employer to pay furloughed employees a substantial portion of their base pay for periods of up to one year.

Overtime and Undertime.   Increasing labor capacity by scheduling overtime avoids the costs of hiring and training and does not increase the total fringe benefit costs for holidays, vacations, and insurance. However, direct costs usually increase due to both premium wages and decreasing productivity rates. This decrease in productivity is especially true when weekly overtime becomes excessive or lasts for more than a month or so. Undertime exists when there are more personnel on the payroll than required to produce the planned output. The costs of undertime can be reduced by having a flexible work force, flexible work rules governing personnel utilization, and appropriate planning. For example, Sunnen Products Company, a St. Louis manufacturer of honing equipment and hones, has avoided layoffs during slack periods for approximately a half century by (1) using production personnel for plant and equipment maintenance and factory layout changes, (2) running smaller production quantities (more setup time), and (3) providing training programs. Sunnen has operated profitably with a no-layoff policy, good wages and benefits, no strikes, and a productive work force.

Part-Time and Temporary Personnel. Part-time employment is often beneficial for both the employer and the employee. Many individuals in the work force desire less than full-time employment and fill the organization's need for personnel to work only during peak demand periods. Relatively permanent part-time employees can be effective and efficient members of an organization. Some temporary personnel also return on a regular basis, every Christmas or summer for example, and possess much of the experience and knowledge of permanent full-time employees. Since the wages and fringe benefits of part-time employees are frequently less than those of full-time employees, there is a savings in both hours worked and rate of pay. On the other hand, since temporary and part-time employees have a minimal relationship with an organization, it is difficult to imbue them with a full understanding and appreciation of organizational goals and policies concerning critical areas, such as quality and customer service. Inconsistent quality and service from excessive use of poorly trained part-time or temporary personnel can more than counterbalance the cost savings.

Subcontracting. Using other firms on a regular basis to perform manufacturing and professional services, such as engineering, marketing research, and software development, can be an effective method of balancing supply and demand. Subcontractors can be especially valuable when treated as an important link in the production chain. They should be provided with an adequate description of the product requirements (specifications, quantity, and due date) and production process as well as assistance with tooling. As trust and confidence develop, subcontractors often suggest improvements in the product design, manufacturing process, or marketing approach.

Subcontracting is a two-way street. Manufacturing companies producing a product for either an industrial market or the general public often subcontract their excess capacity. For example, the Kidder-Stacy Company of Springfield, Massachusetts, machines parts for other firms when their machine shop capacity is not being utilized fully.

Cooperative Agreements. Working agreements based on the sharing of personnel and equipment to meet surges in demand or the need for expertise or equipment possessed by only one or two members of a group of organizations is common. For example, neighboring fire protection districts, hospitals, and police departments often share in providing paramedic services. Electric utilities often have cooperative agreements through power sharing. In addition, many universities offer off-campus courses and programs at community colleges, and some share faculty.

Aggregate Planning Models and Decision Techniques

Many different approaches are available for solving the aggregate planning problem. The more prominent methods include the following:

1. Trial and error or heuristic methods
2. Linear programming cost minimization (LP)
3. Linear decision rules (LDR)
4. Search decision rules (SDR)
5. Goal programming (GP)
6. Simulation

Trial and error is by far the most commonly used method. Since 1970, methods 2 through 5 have slowly gained greater acceptance. Recently, Goldratt (1989) has argued persuasively that interaction among constraints can be captured accurately only by simulation. This argument is explored in Chapter 23.

Trial and Error.   Nearly all organizations have developed a set of aggregate planning rules based on their experience. These rules of thumb vary from firm to firm but often include information and guidelines such as the following:

1. Identify bottleneck work centers and their capacity.
2. Know the point at which overtime produces diminishing results. For example, working the fifth, six-day week in succession is usually followed by at least 25 percent of the work force being absent at least one day in the following week.
3. Avoid reducing the work force below 75 percent of the normal or there will be a permanent loss of skilled and efficient workers.
4. Avoid changing the work force level more than four times a year or the administrative capability of the organization will be overloaded. The industrial relations department will have insufficient time for handling grievances, negotiating labor contracts, and promoting labor productivity through cost reduction and profit-sharing plans.

The archetypal trial and error method consists of the following steps:

1. Prepare an initial production plan on the basis of forecast demand and established guidelines.
2. Determine if the plan is within capacity constraints. If not, revise it until it is.
3. Cost the plan.
4. Alter the plan to lower costs, perform Steps 2 and 3 on it, and compare the costs of the two plans.
5. Continue this process until a satisfactory plan is developed.

6. Perform sensitivity analysis to evaluate the effect of changes in such parameters as the carrying cost rate, the cost of hiring, and demand.
7. Track the plan. (Compare actual results to the planned results.)

This approach leads to a feasible and satisfactory solution, but not necessarily the optimum one. Frequently, the two extreme plans, a level production rate and a production rate that approximates demand, are developed first. Compromises within these extremes are then developed and evaluated.

Let's consider an example. First, the costs of the two production plans illustrated in Figure 2-5, the chase plan, and Figure 2-6, the level plan, are determined. Then the costs of the two plans are compared. A later section examines the sensitivity of the results to changes in the values of certain parameters.

Assume the following information is available from the product's resource profile and operating policies. Production is planned in increments of 1,000 units.

1. Stockouts are not permitted.
2. The minimum planned level of inventory is 1,100 units.
3. Unit costs equal $50 (labor = $8, materials = $30, and overhead = $12).
4. Overtime unit costs equal $53.50 (labor = $12, materials = $30, and overhead = $11.50).
5. Carrying cost rate equals 0.30 per year per dollar of inventory.
6. Hiring cost equals $600 per worker. (This is a weighted average of hiring and rehiring costs.)
7. Layoff costs equal $200 per worker.
8. Labor cost per hour equals $10.
9. Capacity per worker per month equals 160 hours.

There is a direct ratio of 1:200 between direct laborers and output when production is in the range of 5,000 to 12,000 units per month. That is, one additional worker is required for each additional 200 units produced per month. Overtime must be used to produce more than 12,000 units per month. Since management policy limits overtime to 40 hours per worker per month, the maximum monthly capacity is 15,000 units [12,000 units in regular time + (60 direct laborers × 1.25 units per hour × 40 overtime hours per worker)].

Table 2-9 gives the total cost, $84,125, of the level production plan. The values in the table are calculated as follows:

$$EI_i = BI_i + P_i - D_i \quad \text{and} \quad BI_i = EI_{i-1}$$

where EI_i = ending inventory of Period i
  BI_i = beginning inventory of Period i
  P_i = the production quantity in Period i
  D_i = demand in Period i

Table 2-9
Cost of Aggregate Production Plan I—Level Production

Month	Beginning Inventory (thousands)	Production (thousands)	Demand (thousands)	Ending Inventory (thousands)	Overtime Cost	Production Rate Change Cost	Inventory Carrying Cost
January	1.1	10	9.0	2.1	—	—	$ 2,625
February	2.1	10	6.2	5.9	—	—	7,375
March	5.9	10	8.0	7.9	—	—	9,875
April	7.9	10	11.0	6.9	—	—	8,625
May	6.9	10	13.2	3.7	—	—	4,625
June	3.7	10	10.0	3.7	—	—	4,625
July	3.7	10	8.0	5.7	—	—	7,125
August	5.7	10	6.0	9.7	—	—	12,125
September	9.7	10	9.5	10.2	—	—	12,750
October	10.2	10	13.0	7.2	—	—	9,000
November	7.2	10	14.0	3.2	—	—	4,000
December	3.2	10	12.1	1.1	—	—	1,375
Total		120	120.0	67.3			$84,125

Total cost of level production $84,125

Previous December (Period − 1) production level was 10,000 units.

For example, for Period 1 (January),

$$EI_1 = 1,100 + 10,000 - 9,000$$
$$= 2,100$$

Inventory carrying costs are calculated as follows:

$$IC_i = EI_i \times C \times \frac{k}{12}$$

where
IC_i = inventory carrying cost of Period i
EI_i = ending inventory of Period i
C = unit cost
k = yearly carrying cost rate

For example, for Period 1,

$$IC_1 = 2,100 \times \$50 \times \frac{0.30}{12}$$
$$= \$2,625$$

The total cost of the level production plan is \$84,125 and consists entirely of inventory carrying costs.

The total cost of the chase plan, in which the planned monthly production equals the forecast demand, is \$76,750, as shown in Table 2-10. The models for calculating these costs and some examples follow.

If $WF_i > WF_{i-1}$ then $CL_i = 0$ and $CH_i = \$600(WF_i - WF_{i-1})$

If $WF_i < WF_{i-1}$ then $CH_i = 0$ and $CL_i = \$200(WF_{i-1} - WF_i)$

$$WF_i = \frac{P_i}{200}$$

The maximum value of WF for any period is 60; production from 12,001 to 15,000 units is on overtime.

If $P_i < 12,000$, then $COT_i = 0$

If $P_i > 12,000$, then $COT_i = \$3.50(P_i - 12,000)$

where
WF_i = number of workers in Period i
CL_i = cost of layoffs in Period i
CH_i = cost of hiring in Period i
COT_i = cost of overtime in Period i

Table 2-10
Cost of Aggregate Production Plan II—Chase Strategy

Month	Beginning Inventory (thousands)	Demand and Production (thousands)	Change in Work Force	Overtime Cost $3.50 Each	Hiring Cost $600 Each	Layoff Cost $200 Each	Inventory Carrying Cost
January	1.1	9.0	−5			$1,000	$ 1,375
February	1.1	6.2	−14			2,800	1,375
March	1.1	8.0	+9		$ 5,400		1,375
April	1.1	11.0	+15		9,000		1,375
May	1.1	13.2	+5+OT	$ 4,200	3,000		1,375
June	1.1	10.0	−10			2,000	1,375
July	1.1	8.0	−10			2,000	1,375
August	1.1	6.0	−10			2,000	1,375
September	1.1	9.5	+18−UT		10,800		1,375
October	1.1	13.0	+12+OT	3,500	7,200		1,375
November	1.1	14.0	0+OT	7,000			1,375
December	1.1	12.1	0+OT	350			1,375
Total		120.0		$15,050	$35,400	$9,800	$16,500

Total cost of chase strategy $76,750

Previous December (Period − 1) production level was 10,000 units. OT = overtime and UT = undertime.

For example, for Period 2 ($i = 2$) and Period 3 ($i = 3$),

$$WF_1 = \frac{9,000}{200} = 45, \; WF_2 = \frac{6,200}{200} = 31, \text{ and } WF_3 = \frac{8,000}{200} = 40$$

Because $WF_2 < WF_1$,

$$CH_2 = 0 \text{ and } CL_2 = \$200(45 - 31) = \$2,800$$

Because $WF_3 > WF_2$,

$$CL_3 = 0 \text{ and } CH_3 = \$600(40 - 31) = \$5,400$$

For Period 11, $P_{11} > 12,000$, so

$$COT_{11} = \$3.50(14,000 - 12,000) = \$7,000$$

The other values in Tables 2-9 and 2-10 are calculated in the same manner—with one exception. The planned increase in production from August to September for the chase plan in Table 2-10 is 3,500 units, which requires the addition of 17.5 workers. Since workers are added as full-time employees, 18 are added. This means that one worker will not be fully employed in October (undertime exists). Therefore, in the following period when an additional 12.5 workers are required, we need add only 12. In addition, the ending inventory is never less than 1,100 units in either the chase or level plan. This is because management is planning a reserve (safety) aggregate stock of 1,100 units to cover the contingency of actual demand exceeding forecast demand. The annual cost, $16,500, of carrying these units results from that decision and is not affected by the selection of a chase plan, level plan, or some combination of the two. It is a result of the decision concerning the aggregate level of safety stock in the capacity plan.

Since the estimated cost of the chase plan is $7,375 less than that of the level plan, the next step is to attempt to modify the chase plan and reduce the total cost. Consecutive periods with oscillations in employment levels (April through September, for example) are a logical place in a chase plan to look for a possible cost reduction. One approach for reducing these oscillations is to have only three or four employment levels throughout the year. Table 2-11 gives the cost of a compromise solution that includes only three production levels and less inventory than the level plan. Its total cost is $66,125, $10,625 less than the cost of the chase plan.

Plan III, the compromise plan, is the most economical. However, before adopting it some additional questions should be addressed. For instance, could the five workers scheduled for layoff in January and rehiring in March be assigned temporarily to other duties? Also, what is the expected effect of labor force attrition on the costs of the various plans? The level production plan

Table 2-11
Cost of Aggregate Production Plan III—Compromise Solution

Month	Beginning Inventory (thousands)	Production (thousands)	Demand (thousands)	Ending Inventory (thousands)	Overtime Cost	Production Rate Change Cost	Inventory Carrying Cost
January	1.1	9	9.0	1.1	—	$1,000 (−5 workers)	$ 1,375
February	1.1	9	6.2	3.9	—	—	4,875
March	3.9	10	8.0	5.9	—	$3,000 (+5 workers)	7,375
April	5.9	10	11.0	4.9	—	—	6,125
May	4.9	10	13.2	1.7	—	—	2,125
June	1.7	10	10.0	1.7	—	—	2,125
July	1.7	10	8.0	3.7	—	—	4,625
August	3.7	10	6.0	7.7	—	—	9,625
September	7.7	10	9.5	8.2	—	—	10,250
October	8.2	10	13.0	5.2	—	—	6,500
November	5.2	11	14.0	2.2	—	$3,000 (+5 workers)	2,750
December	2.2	11	12.1	1.1	—	—	1,375
Total		120	120.0	47.3		$7,000	$59,125

Total cost of compromise plan $66,125

Previous December (Period − 1) production level was 10,000 units.

costs $18,000 more than the compromise plan. If new workers are not hired to replace those who retire, those who voluntarily resign, and any who take extended sick or injury leave, what is the expected cost difference? This requires estimates of the probability of these events. (Note that up to this point the cost of replacing workers lost to attrition was treated as the same for all plans).

Mathematical Aggregate Planning Models.   The following sections present an overview of various mathematical aggregate planning models. These models are used by relatively few operations managers on a regular basis because of one or more of the following:

1. Aggregate planning decisions may be dominated by a policy decision, such as a no-layoff policy.
2. A single factor such as a labor contract, available capital, capacity limitations, or product shelf life may dominate the decision.
3. Trial and error methods based on years of experience have developed acceptable decision rules. Electronic spreadsheets make this process quite efficient.
4. Much of the literature on mathematical aggregate planning models is written for management scientists and not operations managers.

Although these mathematical models have shortcomings, they can provide management with improved insight concerning a situation and possible opportunities to improve productivity substantially. Thus, the adoption of these modeling techniques is expected to increase gradually as operations managers gain experience with them and as microcomputer software becomes more available.

Linear Programming.   Linear programming (LP) formulations, ranging from simple to very complex, exist for solving the aggregate planning problem. The LP formulation of the problem generally establishes an objective function and identifies constraints on the decision. In aggregate planning, the objective function usually is to minimize the total costs of carrying inventory, changing production rates, subcontracting, and overtime. Typical constraints include the maximum production capacity, the maximum investment in inventory due to either storage or capital limitations, limits on overtime, and restrictions concerning the furloughing or reassignment of the work force. (An example of a relatively simple formulation is shown in Chapter 22.) Shortcomings of the LP approach to aggregate planning include the assumptions that cost functions are both linear and continuous. Both assumptions often are false. For example, the overtime cost per hour may increase as overtime increases due to a decrease in production efficiency. Larger production quantities may result in a lower unit cost at certain points due to quantity discounts or changes in the manufacturing process—justified by the larger quantity. In addition, cost minimization solutions are not necessarily profit maximization solutions. Nonetheless, LP models can provide a reasonable estimate of costs in some situations and also provide valuable insights and guidance to management (Greene et al. 1959).

The Linear Decision Rule.   Holt, Modigliani, Muth, and Simon raised the level of interest in the aggregate planning problem with their description of the linear decision rule (Holt, Modigliani, and Simon 1955; Holt et al. 1960). The linear decision rule (LDR) represents the costs associated with production rate changes, inventory, and overtime as quadratic functions of the production and work force level. Linear decision rules for determining the optimum work force levels and production rates are derived by differentiating the aggregate quadratic cost function.

Although this approach was a valuable step in the continued development of aggregate planning models, it has not had widespread industrial acceptance due to certain inherent limitations. First, it requires that cost functions be quadratic for differentiating, and this is often not a valid assumption. Second, it places no constraints on the decision variables, which are in practice frequently constrained.

Goal Programming.   There are usually multiple goals when developing the aggregate capacity plan or master production schedule for the medium range. A typical set of such goals might include the following:

1. The schedule must be within productive capacity.
2. Production should be sufficient to meet demand requirements.
3. Production and inventory costs should be minimized.
4. Inventory investment should not exceed a specified limit.
5. Overtime costs should be within a specified limit.
6. Any decrease in employment levels will be handled by attrition.

Since most mathematical programming methods require that all goals be expressed in a single dimension, these goals either are formulated in terms of dollars or converted into constraints. This approach has two shortcomings: (1) the actual constraints may not be as rigid as indicated in an LP formulation and (2) not all goals have the same priority. For example, there may be no objection to exceeding either the overtime cost or inventory investment limits on occasion, if substantial improvements in delivery performance are achieved.

Goal programming overcomes these objections. It allows the different goals to be expressed in their natural form and provides a solution that achieves the goals in priority order. Since some of the goals are in opposition to each other, it may not be possible to achieve all of them. For example, a goal of stable employment may be inconsistent with minimized production costs. Goal programming enables the manager to analyze the deviations from a given goal, which are required to achieve another goal, and to decide how much the organization may deviate from one goal to achieve another.

Lee and Moore (1974) have described the application of goal programming to the development of a schedule for a manufacturer of large electric transformers. The goals and their priorities in that situation were as follows:

1. Operate within the limits of productive capacity.
2. Meet the contracted delivery schedule.
3. Operate at a minimum level of 80 percent of regular-time capacity.
4. Keep inventory to a maximum of three units.
5. Minimize total production and inventory costs.
6. Hold overtime production to a minimum.

The first four goals were achieved. However, overtime production and costs for production and inventory were not kept to a minimum in one month in order to meet the delivery schedule, which is a higher priority goal. Goal programming provides for a straightforward analysis of such trade-offs.

Simulation. The inherent difficulty of developing a realistic analytical model that is easily solved invites the application of simulation techniques to the aggregate planning decision (see Chapter 23). Analytical aggregate planning models rigidly assume specified relationships between decision variables. For example, some require that costs be linear in relation to the production quantity. Others require that the cost-quantity relationship be quadratic. None of these models allow these relationships to change over the planning horizon. In an actual situation, some costs may vary linearly while others vary in a quadratic relationship to production quantities. In addition, labor and material costs may change over a 12- to 18-month period due to the labor contract and changes in the prices of purchased materials. The arrival of new equipment may be scheduled during the planning horizon, which results in increased setup costs and capacity and decreased unit processing costs. Analytical approaches cannot handle these changes without a prohibitive increase in model complexity.

Simulation enables the planner to formulate a model with different types of cost relationships (linear, quadratic, exponential, etc.) and with costs that change at specific points in time or at specific production quantities. Thus, simulation models can approximate reality more closely than their analytical counterparts in most situations. Analytical models such as linear programming, however, guarantee an optimum solution—albeit to an oversimplification of reality—while running a simulation model does not guarantee an optimum solution.

Sensitivity Analysis

The aggregate production plan is based on a set of forecast demands and costs. They are treated as certain, but that is rarely the case. Important questions to answer include: If the actual demand is higher or lower than the forecast, what penalty will the organization pay in each case? Will the plan selected still be the most economical if the actual production rate change costs and inventory carrying costs turn out to be substantially different from the estimates?

In the latter case, the production planner can use the existing forecast demand and revised estimates, both higher and lower, of inventory carrying costs and production rate change costs to determine how sensitive the decision is to changes in these parameters. For example, if the cost of money changes rather quickly and the actual carrying cost per dollar of inventory per year is $0.40 instead of the forecasted $0.30, then the cost of the three plans described previously in Tables 2-9, 2-10, and 2-11 change as shown in Table 2-12.

Table 2-12
Sensitivity Analysis for Carrying Cost Rate Change

| Plan | $0.30 Carrying Cost Rate | | | $0.40 Carrying Cost Rate | | |
	Level	Chase	Compromise	Level	Chase	Compromise
Inventory	$84,125	$16,500	$59,125	$112,167	$22,000	$78,833
Hire/Fire	—	45,200	7,000	—	45,200	7,000
Overtime	—	15,050	—	—	15,050	—
Total	$84,125	$76,750	$66,125	$112,167	$82,250	$85,833

The information in Table 2-12 reveals that the compromise plan now costs nearly $4,000 more than the chase plan, whereas it had cost $10,525 less. Clearly, the economics of the decision are sensitive to a one-third increase in the carrying cost rate. The effect of changes of different degrees and direction, a decrease to $0.25 per dollar of inventory for example, and of changes in other costs can be examined in a similar manner.

Controlling the Aggregate Plan

Once the plan is implemented and execution occurs, management must exercise control. Rarely are actual production and demand quantities equal to the planned quantities. Comparing actual cumulative demand and production with forecast demand and production enables the planner to determine if the situation is under control. Either unexpectedly high demand or actual production that is substantially below the planned level will result in insufficient inventories to fill all orders during subsequent peak demand periods. Unusually low demand or production exceeding the plan can result in excessive inventory. Tabulating and plotting actual and planned results enables the planner to determine if the spread between planned and actual requires remedial action.

Case A in Table 2-13 and Figure 2-8 illustrates a situation in which demand for the initial periods is below the forecast, production is as planned, and inventories are becoming excessive. Management must decide if the lower demand levels will continue or if purchases have been postponed and will increase in the future. Case B depicts a situation in which demand has exceeded the forecast for the first few periods, production is as planned, and inventories

Table 2-13
Inventory Under Planned, Low, and High Demand

Production Period		The Plan		Case A Decreased Demand		Case B Increased Demand	
Period	Production	Cumulative Demand	Ending Inventory	Cumulative Demand	Ending Inventory	Cumulative Demand	Ending Inventory
1	8	9.0	1.1	8.5	1.6	9.1	1.0
2	8	15.2	2.9	14.0	4.1	16.6	1.5
3	8	23.2	2.9	21.5	4.6	24.8	1.3
4	12	34.2	3.9	31.7	6.4	36.8	1.3

Beginning inventory is 2.1.

Figure 2-8
Effect of Demand Variation on Inventory

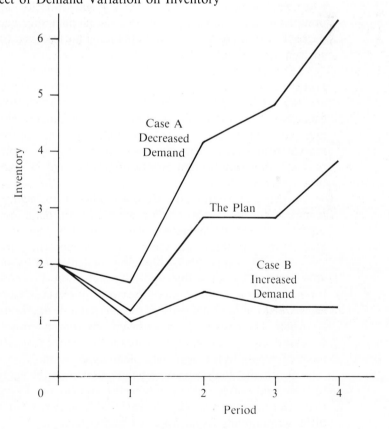

are precariously low. They are insufficient to meet the forecast peak demand in the immediate future. Management must decide if this increased demand will continue or if purchases were made early and demand in the immediate future will be less than forecast.

The point is that the graphs and tables can often alert operations planners and the master scheduler that a significant difference exists between planned and actual demand, production, or inventories. However, the numbers do not in themselves reveal the causes of the difference between actual and planned demand. For example, if increased demand is due primarily to early purchases, no action is required; demand will be less than planned in the near future. If, on the other hand, increased demand is due to a strike at a competitor or the unforeseen development of a new market, the aggregate plan should be increased.

Aggregate planning is a dynamic planning and control device. The aggregate plan is not static; it is reviewed monthly and revised as required.

CONCLUSIONS

Facility planning, resource planning, aggregate capacity planning, and production planning are all elements of long-range planning. Each encompasses the degree of detail appropriate to its planning horizon and to the organization's environment and objectives.

Capacity planning at all levels in the capacity planning hierarchy is connected to measures of product and service outputs. These measures usually are stated in both physical and monetary units. In fact, both the required new capacity resources (facilities, equipment, labor, and information) and required material inputs must be converted to financial terms for the financial planning management system. Capacity planning at all levels should focus on critical resources (bottlenecks) that may be processing centers, engineering, or systems programmers.

Aggregate planning decisions are inherent to facility planning, resource planning, and master production planning. Although most organizations do not use mathematical aggregate planning models, they do recognize the aggregate planning problem and make decisions concerning it.

The aggregate capacity planning challenge can be met by attempting to alter demand, by managing supply through control of production output and inventories, or a combination of the two. The chase and level production strategies are at the opposite ends of the spectrum of aggregate capacity planning strategies. The costs of carrying inventory to meet future demand peaks and the cost of changing output rates are the two major costs affecting the management of supply in the aggregate planning decision.

Sensitivity analysis should be performed on the aggregate capacity plan to evaluate the effects of changes in costs or demand. This analysis can be used to develop contingency plans to deal with the situation when actual parameters differ substantially from projected parameters.

As time unfolds and the plan is implemented, control must take place. This requires that actual inventory, shipments, and costs be compared to the plan and that corrective action be taken as required.

The following are some of the principles found in this chapter:

1. The production plan should be consistent with and support the sales plan, the financial plan, and the business plan.
2. Aggregate plans, including the aggregate production plan, are not static. They should be reviewed at least quarterly to determine that marketing, finance, and production are operating as a team with the same game plan.
3. The more accurate and reliable the resource and production planning, the fewer the difficulties that will occur in master scheduling.
4. Available capacity should be based on the actual (demonstrated) output of the key work centers.
5. Control begins in the planning process by comparing the planned resource requirements to the estimated available requirements.

EXERCISES

Use the following data for Product Group A in Exercises 1 through 5.

Item	Typical Percentage	Standard Assembly Hours per Unit	Production Plan Month	Quantity
1	0.30	0.497	1	1,000
2	0.20	0.291	2	1,200
3	0.10	0.720	3	1,500
4	0.40	0.535	4	1,800

1. Calculate the assembly department resource profile for Product Group A.

2. If the efficiency of the assembly department is 0.90, calculate the actual hours that must be planned for 1,000 units of Product Group A.

3. Calculate the standard hours of capacity required in each of the four months.

4. Due to possible variations in the percentage of demand among the three items in the group, the company decides to overplan for each item in the group by increasing the base percentage of each item by 10 percent; for example, increase 30 percent to 33 percent and 20 percent to 22 percent. Given this decision and zero beginning inventory, calculate the standard hours and the actual hours to produce 1,000 units of Product Group A.

5. Repeat the calculations required in Exercise 4 with the exception that the beginning inventories for Items 1 through 4 are 70, 25, 20, and 60 units, respectively.

Use the following data in Exercises 6 through 18. Electronic spreadsheets are very useful for performing the calculations required by these problems.

Resource Center	Resource Requirements in Standard Hours per Unit				Efficiency Rate	Cost/ Hour	Capacity Available
	Product Group						
	A	B	C	D			
Assembly	7.54	4.34	3.91	5.51	0.90	$12.50	2,000 hr
Subassembly	4.12	2.36	4.78	5.34	1.05	10.75	2,000 hr
Welding	2.53	4.71	3.34	3.92	0.92	11.25	2,000 hr
Machining	5.28	2.68	4.11	3.73	0.95	17.50	2,000 hr
Material Cost per Unit	$ 57.50	$ 43.25	$ 61.10	$ 39.86			
Sales Price	400.00	300.00	350.00	350.00			

Sales Cost per Unit = $10.00

6. Using the above data, calculate the required capacity in standard hours for 100 units in each product group.

7. Calculate the actual hours to be used when scheduling.

8. Calculate the capacity required in each work center and compare it to the capacity available.

9. Calculate the total labor cost, total material cost, and total material and labor cost when planning 100 units of each.

10. Using the above data, calculate the required capacity in standard hours and the actual (clock) hours for the following planned monthly production: Product Group A—150 units, B—80 units, C—120 units, and D—50 units.

11. Using the planned quantities in Exercise 10, calculate the costs required by Exercise 9.

12. Using the planned quantities in Exercise 10 and a 10 percent increase in material costs, a 5 percent increase in labor costs, and a 4 percent increase in efficiency, calculate the total labor and material costs when planning 100 units of each group.

13. What percentage increase in efficiency is required to counterbalance the increased labor and material costs calculated in Exercise 12?

14. Given, in addition to material and labor costs, marketing costs of $10.00 per unit, calculate the total costs of 100 units of each product group.

15. Calculate the percent of value added by the firm for each product group; include sales costs.

16. Calculate the percentage that profit is of manufacturing costs for each product group.

17. Using the preceding data, prepare an integrated production, sales, and financial plan for the next six months (Month 2 through Month 7) for each of the following cases.

a.

					Month		
	1	2	3	4	5	6	7
Projected Shipments	—	50	70	90	110	130	150
Production	—	100	100	100	100	100	100
Inventory	60						

b.

					Month		
	1	2	3	4	5	6	7
Projected Shipments	—	70	70	70	130	130	130
Production	—	100	100	100	100	100	100
Inventory	60						

c.

					Month		
	1	2	3	4	5	6	7
Projected Shipments	—	60	80	100	100	120	140
Production	—	100	100	100	100	100	100
Inventory	60						

18. Using the data in Exercise 17, a carrying cost rate of 0.30 annually, and a flat dollar cost of $1,000 to change the production rate, calculate the costs of each of the plans in Exercise 17.

19. The Preiswert Manufacturing company of New Baden estimates that it will have an inventory of 2,000 units at the beginning of January, which is the company's minimum requirement for ending inventory. It is mid-December, and the current production is 10,000 units per month. Stockouts are not allowed. Projected monthly demand (in thousands) for the coming year is as follows:

	Month											
	Jan	Feb	Mar	Apr	May	Jun	Jul	Aug	Sep	Oct	Nov	Dec
Demand	9	10	11	14	15	17	12	12	14	15	14	13

a. Plot this data and analyze it.
b. If management decides to follow a level production strategy, what level of production should be planned?
c. If each item in inventory at the end of the month costs $1.50, what is the total cost of changing inventory at the end of the year?

20. Use the information in Tables 2-9, 2-10, and 2-11, to calculate the cost of each plan for each of the following conditions. Determine which, if any, of these conditions results in a different, more economical plan.
    a. The carrying cost rate is 0.40 per dollar of inventory rather than 0.30.
    b. The cost of hiring an employee is $500 instead of $600, and the cost of a layoff is $400 per worker instead of $200.
    c. The cost of manufacturing on overtime is $55.00 rather than $53.50.
    d. All of the preceding conditions exist.

21. Concerning Tables 2-9 through 2-11, added information confirms that the company loses an average of three workers each month due to normal attrition. Take this information into consideration and develop a revised plan.

22. Use the data applicable to Tables 2-9 through 2-11, except that the regular labor cost of an item is $20 and overtime cost is $24, to determine what the most economical plan would be.

23. Use the data applicable to Tables 2-9 through 2-11, except that backorders are now permissible at a cost of $15 per unit, and determine what plan to recommend.

24. Referring to the data in Table 2-10, an unexpected surge in demand has occurred due primarily to the addition of a distributor in Canada. Actual demand in August is 7,000 units. The forecast for September and October has been increased by 1,000 units for each month. The forecasts for November through December have been increased by 1,500 units each. There is some concern that at least half of the August increase was due to filling the pipeline and that the forecasts for the fall months are too high. What change, if any, in the existing plan do you recommend and why?

25. Given the following forecast demand and production data

						Month						
	Jan	Feb	Mar	Apr	May	Jun	Jul	Aug	Sep	Oct	Nov	Dec
Demand	40	40	40	32	32	32	48	48	48	60	60	60

Required safety stock	5
Holding cost per unit per month	$300
Hiring cost per worker	$50
Layoff cost per worker	$100
Labor cost per month	$480
Overtime cost per hour	$18
Units of production per worker per period	8
Workdays per month	21
Current work force	5

    a. What is the cost of the chase strategy?
    b. What is the cost of the level production strategy?

    c. If you were the production manager, which cost factor would you pay the most attention to? What suggestions do you have that might reduce that burden?

26. Demand for price-marking machines for the next eight quarters is as follows:

	Quarter							
	1	2	3	4	5	6	7	8
Demand	35,000	40,000	39,000	32,000	39,000	46,000	44,000	45,000

Hiring cost per worker	$400
Layoff cost per worker	$600
Straight-time wages	$3,000
Inventory carrying cost per unit per period	$1
Overtime factor	1.5
Units of production per worker per period	1,000
Current work force	40
Initial inventory	10,000
Minimum safety stock level	10,000

    a. What would be the total cost of production for the chase strategy, not including raw material costs or overhead charges?

    b. What would be the total cost of production for the level production strategy, not including raw material costs or overhead charges?

SELECTED READINGS

Anthony, Robert N. *Planning and Control Systems: A Framework for Analysis.* Cambridge, MA: Harvard University Graduate School of Business Administration, 1965, 26-47.

Bowman, E. H. "Production Scheduling by the Transportation Method of Linear Programming." *Operations Research* (February 1956): 100-103.

Britan, Gabriel R., and Arnoldo C. Hax. "On the Design of Hierarchical Planning Systems." *Decision Sciences*, No. 8 (January 1977).

Drucker, Peter F. *Management: Tasks, Responsibilities, Practices.* New York: Harper & Row, Publishers, Inc., 1974.

Goldratt, Eliyahu M. *The Theory of Constraints Journal* 1, no. 5 (July-August 1989).

Greene, J. H., et al. "Linear Programming in the Packing Industry," *Journal of Industrial Engineering* 10, no. 5 (September/October 1959): 364-372.

Groover, Mikell P. *Automation, Production Systems, and Computer-Aided Manufacturing.* Englewood Cliffs, NJ: Prentice-Hall, Inc., 1987, 119-128.

Hall, Robert W. *Zero Inventories.* Homewood, IL: Dow Jones-Irwin, 1983.

Hax, Arnoldo C., and H. C. Meal. "Hierarchical Integration of Production Planning and Scheduling." *Studies in Management Sciences, Logistics* Vol. 1. Edited by M. A. Geisler. New York: North Holland, 1973.

Hayes, Robert H., and Steven C. Wheelwright. "Link Manufacturing Process and Product Life Cycles." *Harvard Business Review* (January-February 1979).

Hayes, Robert H., and Steven C. Wheelwright. *Restoring Our Competitive Edge: Competing Through Manufacturing*. New York: John Wiley & Sons, Inc., 1984.

Hofer, C. W., and D. Schendel. *Strategy Formulation: Analytical Concepts*. St. Paul, MN: West Publishing Co., 1978.

Holt, Charles C., Franco Modigliani, and Herbert Simon. "A Linear Decision Rule for Production and Employment Scheduling." *Management Science* 2, no. 1 (October 1955): 1-30.

Holt, Charles C., et al. *Planning Production, Inventories, and Work Force*. Englewood Cliffs, NJ: Prentice-Hall, Inc., 1960.

Lee, Sang M., and L. J. Moore. "A Practical Approach to Production Scheduling." *Production and Inventory Management* 15, no. 1, (1974): 79-92.

Lee, W. B., and B. M. Khumawala. "Simulation Testing of Aggregate Production Planning Models in an Implementation Methodology." *Management Science* 20, no. 6 (February 1974): 903-911.

Lee, W. B., and C. P. McLaughlin. "Corporate Simulation Models for Aggregate Materials Management." *Production and Inventory Management* 15, no. 1 (1974): 55-67.

Peters, Thomas J., and Robert H. Waterman, Jr. *In Search of Excellence*. New York: Harper and Row, Publishers, Inc., 1982.

Schwarz, Leroy B., and Robert E. Johnson. "An Appraisal of the Empirical Performance of the Linear Decision Rule for Aggregate Planning." *Management Science* 24, no. 8 (April 1978): 844-849.

Skinner, Wickham. *Manufacturing: the Formidable Competitve Weapon*. New York: John Wiley & Sons, Inc., 1985.

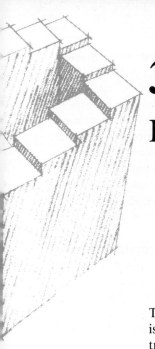

3
FORECASTING

The first step in planning production and inventory management activities is forecasting future demand. The American Production and Inventory Control Society (APICS) considers a forecast to be an objective procedure, using data collected over time. A forecast involves an assumption that current trends will continue into the future. The term *prediction* is used to describe any activity that includes subjective evaluation. This chapter considers both objective and subjective procedures. However, the focus of the chapter is on objective procedures.

The foundation for any production activity is either an actual order or the forecast of future orders. In a make-to-stock environment, production activities are based entirely on forecasts, because orders must be filled from existing stock. In a make-to-order environment, however, production activities are not based solely on actual orders. Consider, for example, the case of Wellco Carpet, discussed in Chapter 1, whose business is substantially make-to-order.

Wellco's ultimate customers are contractors, who must complete the construction or renovation of a building. Often these contractors cannot wait for Wellco to order yarn, to receive it, to entangle the yarn, to weave it, to dye it, and to back it to make finished carpet. Therefore, Wellco must stock partially completed carpet. A large finished goods inventory is held. If an order cannot be filled from finished goods, Wellco checks work in process and fills the order from partially completed carpet, choosing the highest available stage of completion that is consistent with the order. Wellco's purchasing, entangling, and weaving operations are planned based largely on forecasts. The dyeing and backing activities are planned partially on forecasts and partially on actual orders.

A discussion of forecasting usually focuses on quantitative techniques to manipulate data, neglecting how the data are obtained. We should recognize, however, that the maxim "garbage in, garbage out" applies to forecasting as well as to other computerized techniques. Therefore, we first discuss how the data are obtained, verified, and recorded. No forecasting system can afford to neglect these critical activities.

It is also important to understand that whenever there is reason to suspect that the future will not be like the past, a prediction is preferable to a forecast. Electric utilities experienced average annual demand growth of 7 percent to 8 percent for a quarter century following the end of World War II. When the creation of OPEC sent oil prices skyrocketing, the companies continued to forecast based on the past, ignoring predictions that the rate of demand growth must fall in response to rising prices. The oversupply of power plants (particularly nuclear power plants) that resulted is well known. Before making a forecast, consider whether a prediction is more appropriate.

Production planning personnel are not responsible for forecasting for the long-range planning that is needed for planning facility construction and major equipment purchases. Rather, they perform shorter range forecasts used in medium-term production planning and short-range master production scheduling, as shown in Figure 3-1. In this text, we limit our discussion to shorter range forecasts that are used to schedule production and to make short-term capacity plans.

Figure 3-1
The Role of Forecasting in the Production Planning Process

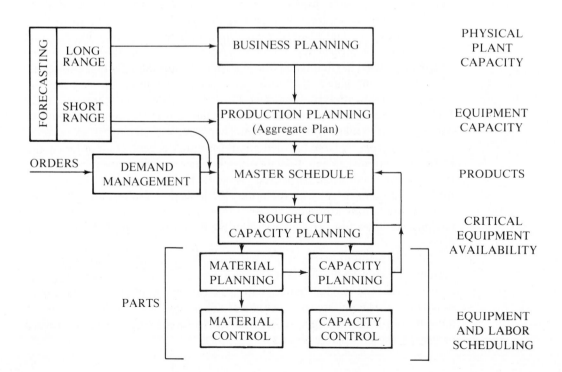

DATA

Forecasting systems *extrapolate* time series data. A time series is a historical record of the past activity. A fundamental assumption for extrapolation is that the future is related to the past in some way. This assumption does not require tomorrow to be just like today; it only requires stable relationships. Even in today's rapidly changing environment, fundamental relationships usually hold, at least in the short term. Some typical time series are shown in Table 3-1. Some characteristics to note are the time intervals (weeks, months, years, etc.), the dimensions (units, dollars, kilograms, etc.), and the degree of data variability.

Time series data are of two types, intrinsic and extrinsic. *Intrinsic* time series data are data concerning past sales of the product to be forecast. *Extrinsic* time series data are data that are external but are related to sales of the product. For example, data describing sales of a related product are extrinsic. Before examining formal techniques to extrapolate time series data, let's first look at some sources of extrinsic data.

Table 3-1
Typical Time Series Data

Weekly Demand for Item 05880-Red Desk Lamp						
Week Number	122	123	124	125	126	127	128
Demand	9	7	8	13	18	22	27

Monthly Shipments of Part 5149-Detergent 127					
Month	March	April	May	June	July	August
Kilograms	10	15	10	25	10	30

Net Sales of XYZ Corporation						
Year	1983	1984	1985	1986	1987	1988	1989
$	437,626	475,998	480,700	641,283	711,193	765,818	802,295

Japanese Imports of Manufactured Goods					
Year	1982	1983	1984	1985	1986	1987
$ (in billions)	6.0	9.2	11.3	9.4	10.9	12.0

Number of Jobs Run per Hour on Computer A					
Time (military)	1000	1100	1200	1300	1400	1500
Quantity	78	85	40	75	105	120

Extrinsic Data Sources

Several sources for extrinsic data exist. One source is demographic data, data related to the characteristics of our customers. Suppose we wish to forecast sales for TRW automotive replacement parts by region. Data clearly of interest are data related to population trends in each region. Beyond total population data, we are interested in the driving age population, the driving age population by specific age group, and the population by income category. Another item of interest is the average time a car is kept. In the early 1980s the length of time people kept their cars began increasing, probably because of the increasing cost of new cars. Presumably, as the average automobile age increases, demand for replacement parts will also increase.

Demographic data are maintained in most large libraries, especially university libraries. Most such libraries employ research librarians whose job is to know where to find these data.

Data can also be collected within a company. Foremost among company data sources are various types of market intelligence, such as survey information, test panel data, and sales force feedback. Frequently, this type of data is considered of questionable value to production control, but the fault is often in its interpretation, not in the quality of the data itself. Market survey data are primarily obtained to aid in product promotion and new product introduction decisions. The specific procedures to conduct a market survey will not be covered in this text. We wish to point out that market survey data, because they are intended primarily for marketing purposes, must be viewed carefully in making production decisions. For example, a survey that establishes an intent to increase purchases may be useful in planning production capacity. Also the sample may shed light on the marketing mix (size, color, configuration) of the demand. These attributes are important in determining manufacturing mix.

Another source of data is sales force feedback. As salespeople contact customers or potential buyers, they accumulate information about what customers say they want and what competitors are offering or plan to offer (or withdraw from) the market. There are several difficulties in using these data for production decisions. Because the data are not obtainable in an orderly and regular manner, their comparability to other information is difficult to establish. Does the reported fact that Customer X intends to buy 15 percent more next month represent demand over that already scheduled? Since it is quite common to use already forecast sales to set sales force goals and hence compensation, the incentive exists to manipulate or withhold data to influence personal pay. The extent of deliberate bias is difficult to determine, and thus sales force feedback is questionable, but not altogether unusable.

Modifying Intrinsic Data

At this point we will examine some sample time series data originating within a company and discuss the need for data modification. Activities that often bias data are sales promotion and new advertising campaigns. While it is obvious that production should be aware of any such activities, it nevertheless happens that such activities are not communicated adequately. Perhaps of greater concern is that the effects of such campaigns or promotions cannot be estimated accurately. Marketing and manufacturing personnel must share responsibility for both the forecast and the manufacturing schedule. Too often marketing estimates that X units will be sold; manufacturing, in the belief that marketing's estimates are optimistic, makes X less 10 percent. When the results are in, each blames the other for excess inventories or shortages. The only way to eliminate this problem is to have a master schedule on which both groups agree.

Two issues that relate to forecasting when special promotions occur are forecasting sales for the period after the promotion and adjusting the data to reflect the promotion. Consider the following sequence of sales data:

Month	1	2	3	4	5
Sales	100	100	100	200	?

Given this sequence, what sales prediction would you make for Month 5? Write your answer before reading further. When this question was asked of a large audience of experienced forecasters at a 1983 APICS conference, a majority responded that they would forecast 0 for Month 5. Their reasoning was that in Month 4 there must have been a promotion, causing customers to overstock. This would, in turn, result in no orders until customers used their existing stocks.

No time series approach would reach this conclusion, logical though it is. Furthermore, a time series analysis package will derive distorted forecasts, given these data. Suppose a nonrecurring promotion did occur in Month 4 and sales for the first six months were:

Month	1	2	3	4	5	6
Sales	100	100	100	200	15	85

Clearly, a more useful set of sales data to give the forecasting system is simply six months of demand of 100 units each. This example demonstrates that modification of sales data is sometimes justified to improve forecast accuracy.

Data modification should be limited to correction of large anomalies having known causes. Furthermore, these causes should not recur on a regular basis. Data should not be modified because it appears to be peculiar and no cause for the irregularity is known. It is a mistake to alter data simply to reduce random variation. One arrives at too small an estimate of forecast error and, worse, too little effort to protect against forecast error.

Data Quality and Accuracy

The validity and appropriateness of our data sources must be ascertained. We must also control for errors and make appropriate modifications for nonrecurring events.

An important source of errors is often found in data recording. These errors may be with regard to numeric quantity (recording 71 instead of 11) or identification (part 6A5Z instead of 6A52) or dimensionality (seven dozen in place of seven gross). The data processing system, whether manual or computerized, should be developed to find such errors, if possible, and to correct them or at least point them out for further investigation as to cause.

Check Digits.   Check digits provide a way to catch most recording errors regarding part numbers. Errors in recording a part number are particularly insidious because they create errors in the data for two parts: the part that should have been entered and the part that was entered erroneously. Most check digits involve an algebraic manipulation of the first $n - 1$ digits of an n digit number to obtain the correct value for the nth digit. The example presented here uses a simpler scheme than is usually used, but serves to illustrate the general principle. Suppose a company has 500 end items that it has numbered 001 to 500. The company desires to add a check digit to the numbering system. A simple procedure is to use

$$X_4 = (X_1 + 2X_2 + 3X_3) \bmod 10$$

That is, the fourth digit is found by adding the first digit plus twice the second digit plus three times the third digit and extracting the unit position digit from the sum. Using this procedure, the check digit for part 134 is $(1 + 2 \times 3 + 3 \times 4) \bmod 10 = (1 + 6 + 12) \bmod 10 = 19 \bmod 10 = 9$. (The mod operator yields the remainder after long division is performed.) The revised part number becomes 1349. A common error in recording data is to transpose two digits. If part number 1349 is incorrectly recorded as 1439, the check digit procedure evaluates the check digit as $(1 + 8 + 9) \bmod 10 = 18 \bmod 10 = 8$. The computer will refuse to accept this part number entry because the final digit must be 8 not 9. Well designed check digit systems will catch more than 99 percent of all errors in recording part numbers.

Demand Filters.   A demand filter is created by recording a range of reasonable data for each part number. If in the past several months demand never has fallen below 100 or exceeded 200, 100 and 200 might be set as limits. The computer would automatically question any entry less than 100 or greater than 200. To avoid too much manual intervention, we must establish appropriate limits as a compromise between chasing down nonexistent errors and allowing erroneous data to enter the system. In choosing a value for a demand filter, one should use a fairly wide band for unimportant items and a narrow band for expensive and high volume items. The reason for a variable band width is that for low dollar volume items it is cheaper to carry safety stock to cover the effects of the error than it is to spend valuable management time correcting the error. For high dollar volume items, the reverse is true.

Orders Versus Shipments. Many forecasting errors have been made through failure to recognize the difference between orders and shipments. For example, orders and shipments differ in timing. Orders precede shipments by manufacturing lead time (make-to-order environments) or at least by order filling time (make-to-stock environments). Quantities shipped may be less than quantities ordered for a variety of reasons. Partial shipments may be made over a period of time to fill one order. Shipments may exceed orders because spare parts or allowances for defects may be included. Whatever the reason, the distinction between orders and shipments must be taken into account when using historical data to forecast.

Price Changes. Another factor to consider is that price changes may cause increased sales dollars but not increased unit sales. Historical variations in unit prices are frequently overlooked, and errors arise because a single conversion factor is used to translate past sales dollars into past unit sales. For example, a price increase from $2.50 to $2.75 last July means that the first six months' sales of $30,000 and the second half sales of $32,000 actually represent a decline in unit sales.

Summary of Data Quality. To summarize, one must examine the source and accuracy of the data on which forecasts will be built. No amount of ordinary photographic development technique can transform a fuzzy negative into a clear, sharp picture. Similarly, no forecasting technique can transform poor data into a good forecast. Figure 3-2 presents an overview of the forecasting process, including data considerations.

FORECAST HORIZON AND SCOPE

The forecast horizon for a product must be at least as long as that product's total lead time. If the forecast horizon is shorter, then the earliest production activities, such as placing purchase orders for long lead time components, are performed with insufficient information. The forecast horizon should be as long as possible, i.e., as long as can be forecast accurately. The frequency of forecast updating depends on the value of the information obtained and on the volatility of product sales. Forecasts should be updated frequently for high dollar volume items, less frequently for low dollar volume items. For high dollar volume items, the additional accuracy obtained by frequent updating is recovered by eliminating expensive safety stock. For items having volatile sales, i.e., sales subject to large changes in volume, frequent forecast updating helps to avoid expensive overproduction and underproduction. The value of the additional information must exceed the cost of obtaining it.

In general, forecasts are made for product groups rather than for individual items. Forecasts can then be divided by historical product mix to obtain individual item forecasts. Forecasts for individual items are rarely needed.

Figure 3-2
The Forecast/Prediction System

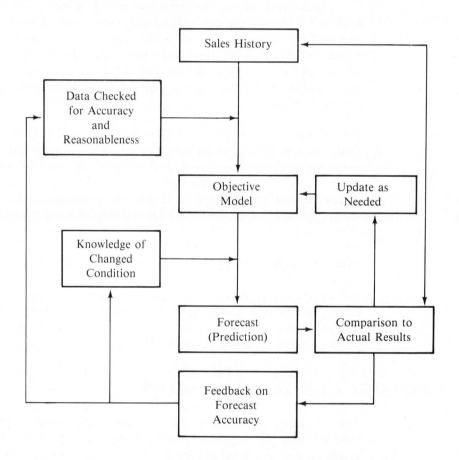

Consider again the case of Wellco Carpet. To plan the weaving operation, one needs a forecast of carpet sales grouped by type of weave. We do not need to know how much of each weave will be dyed each color to plan weaving. Similarly, to plan the dyeing operation our principle concern is the quantity of carpet to be dyed each color, independent of weave type.

Information on both weave style and color can be obtained from the same forecast. Suppose our forecast calls for 100,000 square yards of carpet to be sold per day on the average. Suppose also that 23 percent of past sales was for Weave A and 18 percent was for Weave B. Then our plan for weaving calls for 23,000 square yards of Weave A and 18,000 square yards of Weave B. Using the same aggregate forecast of carpet sales, one can apply historical color mixes to plan the dyeing operation.

BASIC FORECASTING TECHNIQUES

Forecasting techniques (using the term *forecasting* in its broadest sense) can be divided into two categories: qualitative and quantitative. The former, which may involve numbers, uses methodology that is not mathematical. Qualitative techniques rely on judgment, intuition, and subjective evaluation. Among the major techniques within this category are market research (surveys), Delphi (panel consensus), historical analogy, and management estimation (guess). In APICS terminology, all of these techniques represent predictions rather than forecasts (in the narrow sense). The other class of techniques, quantitative, can be divided into intrinsic and extrinsic types.

Intrinsic techniques often are called *time series analysis techniques*. They involve mathematical manipulation of the demand history for an item. These techniques are the most commonly used in forecasting for production and inventory control. The other group of quantitative techniques, extrinsic methods, creates a forecast by attempting to relate demand for an item to data about another item, a group of items, or outside factors (such as general economic conditions).

Qualitative Techniques

We mentioned some aspects of market research in discussing data sources. While these techniques are based on good theory and can yield valuable information for marketing decisions, they are not intended directly to support inventory decisions. Rather, they are intended to support product development and promotion strategies. Data gathered by these methods should be considered in some aggregate inventory or capacity planning decisions, but should not be the sole data source for such decisions.

The Delphi, or panel consensus, method may be useful in technological forecasting, that is, in predicting the general state of the market, economy, or technological advances five or more years from now, based on expert opinion. (The name for this method comes from the ancient Greek oracles of Delphi who forecast future events.) The process of creating a Delphi forecast is a variation of the following: A panel of futurists is asked a question, such as, In the next ten years which consumer products do you envision containing microprocessors as an integral part? Each specialist independently submits a list of such items to the panel coordinator. The combined lists then are sent back to each panel member for evaluation and rating of likelihood of occurrence. Panel members may see something that they hadn't thought of and rate it highly. Also members may have second thoughts about items they themselves previously submitted. After a sufficient number of cycles (generally two or three), the result is a list with high consensus. The Delphi technique is not a suitable technique for short-range forecasting, certainly not for individual products.

When attempting to forecast demand for a new item, one faces a shortage of historical data. A useful technique is to examine the demand history for an analogous product. If the related product is very similar, quantitative techniques may be used. But if the relationship is tenuous, it may be more appropriate to relate the products only qualitatively in order to get an impression of demand patterns or aggregate demand. For example, the seasonal demand pattern for an established product such as tennis balls may be used to estimate the expected demand pattern for tennis gloves. The actual levels and trends for the latter cannot be determined in this manner with any precision, but the seasonal pattern may be expected to be similar.

Finally, we must not overlook management estimation (intuition) as a prediction method. It is widely practiced with regard to new products or unexpected changes in demand for established product lines. Not everyone has estimation talent, however. Some studies have shown that a mathematical technique, consistently followed, will lead to better results than the "expert modification" of those forecasts. Nonetheless, many mathematical techniques need significant quantities of historical data that may not be available. When substantial data are lacking, subjective management judgment may be the better alternative.

Quantitative Techniques

Intrinsic techniques use the time-sequenced history of activity for a particular item as source data to forecast future activity for that item. Such a history is commonly referred to as a time series. Some typical time series patterns are shown in Figure 3-3. The characteristics of such series can be labeled in various ways, and the algebraic representation of such graphs can be accomplished by a variety of methods.

Generally, a time series can be thought of as consisting of four components or underlying factors: (1) cyclical, (2) trend, (3) seasonal, and (4) random (or irregular). The cyclical factor traditionally refers to the business cycle, to long-range trends in the overall economy. The cyclical factor can be very important in forecasting for long-range planning. However, it is of little use in forecasting demand for individual products, which rarely have sufficient data to permit a distinction between the effect of the business cycle and the effect of the product life cycle. For that reason, the time series used for short-term forecasting generally have only trend, seasonal, and random components. The trend component generally is modeled as a line, which is described by an intercept or base level, which we designate L, and a slope, which we designate T. The trend line may be modified by a seasonal phenomenon (S). All data are somewhat muddied by a random, irregular, or otherwise unpredictable variation (R).

Figure 3-3
Typical Time Series Patterns

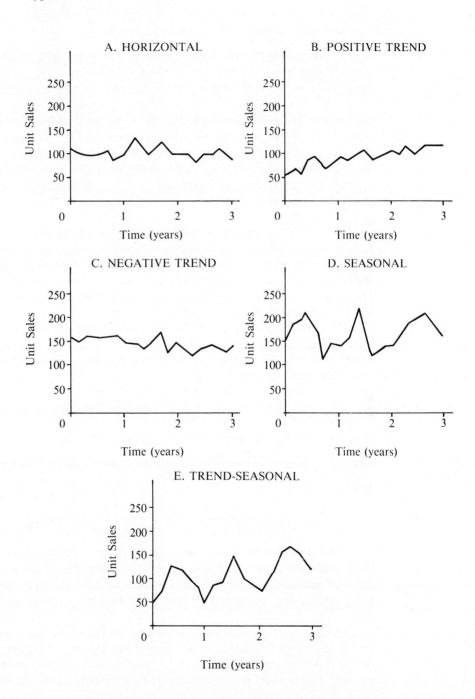

Mathematically this process is based on a combination multiplicative and additive model of the following sort:

$$D = (L + T) \times S + R \qquad (3\text{-}1)$$

where D is demand. In this version T, trend, is expressed in the same units as L, level, and T may be positive or negative. R, random, is expressed in the same units. Its expected value is 0. S, seasonal, is a dimensionless number having an expected value of 1. For example, we may know that the demand for a certain Bruce Springsteen anthology is averaging 10,000 units per month, with a trend of minus 500 per month (the pattern is to sell 500 fewer units each month). However, the month currently being forecast is December; due to seasonal variation, December averages 40 percent higher than the typical month. Average forecast error using this model has been 800 units. In this example the demand forecast is

$$D = (10,000 - 500) \times 1.4 + 0 = 13,300 \text{ units}$$

Because the average forecast error has been 800 units, and because errors twice the average are not uncommon occurrences, we would not be surprised if December's actual sales were anywhere from $13,300 - 1,600 = 11,700$ units to $13,300 + 1,600 = 14,900$ units.

Models of the form shown in Equation 3-1 are the most common, but pure multiplicative models are sometimes used. A pure multiplicative model would express both the trend and random components as percentages, so that the model could be expressed as:

$$D = L \times T \times S \times R \qquad (3\text{-}2)$$

Converting the Springsteen anthology example to this notation, L is still 10,000 units, T is now $\dfrac{10,000 - 500}{10,000} = 0.95$, S is still 1.4, and R becomes 1. The forecast is then

$$D = 10,000 \times 0.95 \times 1.4 \times 1 = 13,300 \text{ units}$$

One approach to time series analysis attempts to determine the underlying components of trend and seasonal factors. The federal government uses this approach in forecasts of economic factors (unemployment, cost of living, and so on). The approach also is used by a few firms in aggregate sales forecasting.

While it may seem straightforward to determine the components of the series, sometimes referred to as *decomposition*, that is not always possible or practical. Obtaining sufficient data for time series decomposition may not be possible, due to short product lifetimes. Four years of consistent data usually are required to make such a forecast (that is, four years of data after the item reaches the maturity stage of its product life cycle). Seasonal factors often are determined for a family of items by assuming groupings based on judgments. Time series decomposition is discussed in detail in the next section.

TIME SERIES ANALYSIS

This section discusses some of the most common techniques for forecasting from intrinsic time series without explicitly looking for seasonal or trend factors. It also examines time series decomposition.

Moving Averages

Perhaps the simplest of all time series forecasting techniques is a moving average. To use this method, we calculate the average of, say, three periods of actual demand and use that to forecast the next period's demand. For example,

$$D_{5,6,7} = \frac{D_5 + D_6 + D_7}{3} = F_8 \tag{3-3}$$

$$D_{6,7,8} = \frac{D_6 + D_7 + D_8}{3} = F_9 \tag{3-4}$$

where D_i = actual demand in Period i
F_i = forecast demand in Period i

Let's use the data in Table 3-2 to solve Equations 3-3 and 3-4. From Table 3-2, Periods 5, 6, and 7 (May, June, and July) have demands of 302, 274, and 162, respectively. Adding these three numbers and dividing by 3 yields 246. If this three-period average is to be used as a forecast, it would have to forecast demand in a future period, such as Period 8. Note that the Average column in Table 3-2 contains the value 246, the average of the previous three periods. When the actual demand of Period 8 (194) is known, Equation 3-4 can be used to produce a forecast for Period 9. The value for Period 5 is dropped, and the values for Periods 6 and 7 are averaged with Period 8 to obtain an average of $\frac{274 + 162 + 194}{3} = 210$.

Because each average moves ahead one period each time, dropping the oldest value and adding the most recent, this procedure is called a *moving average*. The number of periods to use in computing the average may be anything from 2 to 12 or more, with 3 or 4 periods being common. If the time series is essentially like that in Figure 3-3A, in other words, if there is no upward or downward trend, then the moving average is a satisfactory technique. If, however, there is any trend or any seasonal effect, then the moving average will not work very well. Moving averages lag behind any trends as illustrated in Figure 3-4, in which a three-period moving average is applied to the data from Table 3-2.

Table 3-2
A Three-Period Moving Average Projected Forward as a Forecast

Period	Month	Demand	Average
1	January	90	
2	February	106	
3	March	152	
4	April	244	116.0
5	May	302	167.3
6	June	274	232.7
7	July	162	273.3
8	August	194	246.0
9	September	312	210.0
10	October	359	222.7
11	November	215	288.3
12	December	126	295.3
13	January	94	233.3
14	February	125	145.0
15	March	147	115.0
16	April	273	122.0
17	May	349	181.7
18	June	310	256.3
19	July	178	310.7
20	August	182	279.0
21	September	323	223.3
22	October	400	227.7
23	November	252	301.7
24	December	179	325.0
25	January	131	277.0
26	February	142	187.3
27	March	186	150.7
28	April	307	153.0
29	May	398	211.7
30	June	348	297.0
31	July	217	351.0
32	August	228	321.0
33	September	384	264.3
34	October	460	276.3
35	November	273	357.3
36	December	206	372.3
37	January	152	313.0
38	February	141	210.3
39	March	194	166.3
40	April	353	162.3
41	May	449	229.3
42	June	415	332.0
43	July	236	405.7
44	August	253	366.7
45	September	420	301.3
46	October	504	303.0
47	November	343	392.3
48	December	231	422.3

Figure 3-4
Moving Average Lags Behind Actual Data

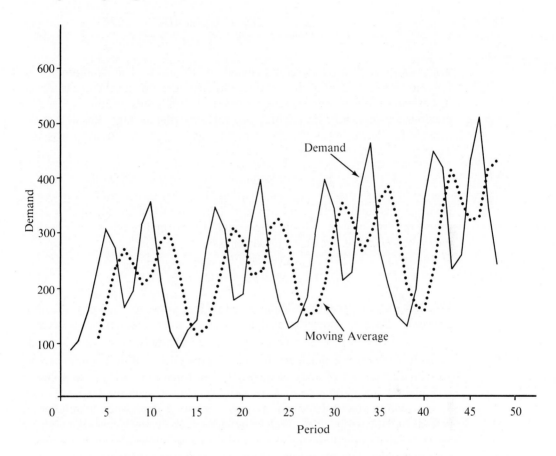

Figure 3-4 shows that during periods in which demand is rising, a moving average produces a forecast that is consistently low. When the forecast is decreasing, a moving average produces a forecast that is consistently high. Furthermore, the turning point in the forecast is consistently later than the turning point in the data. This phenomenon is known as a *lag effect*; i.e., the forecast is consistently later than (lags behind) the original data.

Weighted Moving Averages

More recent data are more indicative of the future than are older data. Often a weighted moving average, one that is computed to give more weight to more recent data, is more reliable than an unweighted average. A weighted moving average is computed by multiplying each period by a weighting factor and dividing the resulting product by the sum of all weighting factors. An example equation is

$$D_{5,6,7} = \frac{2D_5 + 3D_6 + 4D_7}{2 + 3 + 4} \tag{3-5}$$

where $D_{5,6,7}$ is used to forecast demand for Period 8. The denominator of Equation 3-5 is the sum of the weights. The weighted moving average is moved just as in a simple moving average system. Let's apply this formula to the data previously used for the unweighted or simple moving average. Recall that the demand for Period 5 was 302, for Period 6 was 274, and for Period 7 was 162. Then the numerator of Equation 3-5 is

$$(2 \times 302) + (3 \times 274) + (4 \times 162) = 2,074$$

Dividing this total by the sum of the weights (9) yields 230.44, or 230 when rounded to the nearest integer. One could also normalize the weights so that they add to one, as shown in Equation 3-6.

$$D_{5,6,7} = \tfrac{2}{9}D_5 + \tfrac{3}{9}D_6 + \tfrac{4}{9}D_7 \tag{3-6}$$

You may wish to repeat the calculation performed above to verify that the same answer is obtained, subject to a slight rounding error that may occur because $\tfrac{2}{9}$, $\tfrac{3}{9}$, and $\tfrac{4}{9}$ cannot be expressed precisely as decimals. Because the magnitude of the forecast error is much greater than the magnitude of the rounding error, the rounding error is of no consequence. Thus, Equation 3-6 is just as accurate as Equation 3-5, although the two may not yield precisely the same solution.

Usually, weighted moving averages are used only when a number of periods of data are included. Weighting factors can be any values. Weights are the subjective evaluation of the forecaster of the importance of more recent data and older data in making a forecast. If a product is new and is going through the growth stage of the product life cycle, there often is not enough data to estimate the trend and seasonal components of the time series. A simple moving average is undesirable because of its tendency to lag behind a trend. The weighted moving average will alleviate this problem slightly by placing more weight on the latest data. But weighted averages still lag behind the trend and produce a forecast that is consistently low during periods of rising demand.

As a comparison of weighted and unweighted moving averages, examine Table 3-3. Although here the error-squared column indicates that the second weighted moving average had the least error, this does not mean it will for all series of data.

An impediment to the use of weighted moving averages to forecast thousands of items is that N periods of data must be retained (N being the number of demand periods used in the average). And N multiplications, $N - 1$ additions, and one division must be performed for each forecast. This amounts to

Table 3-3
Comparison of Moving Averages

Period	Actual Demand	Three-Period Moving Average Forecast	Three-Period Moving Average Error Squared	Three-Period Weighted Average Weights—2, 3, 4 Forecast	Three-Period Weighted Average Weights—2, 3, 4 Error Squared	Three-Period Weighted Average Weights—1, 5, 9 Forecast	Three-Period Weighted Average Weights—1, 5, 9 Error Squared
January	90						
February	106						
March	152						
April	244	116	16,384	123	14,641	133	12,321
May	302	167	18,225	183	14,161	204	9,604
June	274	233	1,681	249	625	273	1
July	162	273	12,321	277	13,225	281	14,161
August	194	246	2,704	230	1,296	209	225
September	312	210	10,404	201	12,321	189	15,129
October	359	223	18,496	239	14,400	263	9,216
November	215	288	5,329	307	8,464	332	13,689
December	126	295	28,561	285	25,281	269	20,449
January	94	233	19,321	207	12,769	171	5,929
February	125	145	400	132	49	113	144
March	147	115	1,024	115	1,024	115	1,024
April	122	128	136				
Sum of errors			134,850		118,256		101,892

a great deal of data and many calculations. Exponential smoothing, presented next, offers a method that is equivalent to a weighted moving average, but that requires fewer data and calculations.

Exponential Smoothing

Probably the most popular method used to forecast item demand are the various exponential smoothing techniques. Simple or first-order exponential smoothing can be viewed several ways. One viewpoint is that it is a forecasting technique based on the forecasting errors. If the forecast, F, for Period n is F_n and the actual demand for Period n is D_n, then one can forecast the next period as being F_n plus some fraction, α, of the current error $(D_n - F_n)$.

$$F_{n+1} = F_n + \alpha(D_n - F_n) \tag{3-7}$$

or, rearranging the terms of Equation 3-7,

$$F_{n+1} = \alpha D_n + (1 - \alpha)F_n \tag{3-8}$$

One advantage to this method is that the data required are only the last forecast, the last actual demand, and the value of α. Computation is reduced to two multiplications and one addition for each forecast. It should also be noted that this is really a weighted moving average. Large values of α place heavier weight on the most recent actual demand data and lesser weight on historical values. To see why this is true, consider Equation 3-8:

$$F_{n+1} = \alpha D_n + (1 - \alpha)F_n$$

For Period $n - 1$,

$$F_{(n-1)+1} = F_n = \alpha D_{n-1} + (1 - \alpha)F_{n-1} \tag{3-9}$$

and for Period $n - 2$,

$$F_{(n-2)+1} = F_{n-1} = \alpha D_{n-2} + (1 - \alpha)F_{n-2} \tag{3-10}$$

Therefore, combining Equations 3-9 and 3-10

$$F_n = \alpha D_{n-1} + (1 - \alpha)[\alpha D_{n-2} + (1 - \alpha)F_{n-2}] \tag{3-11}$$

or

$$F_n = \alpha D_{n-1} + \alpha(1 - \alpha)D_{n-2} + (1 - \alpha)^2 F_{n-2} \tag{3-12}$$

Similarly, Equation 3-12 can be substituted in Equation 3-8:

$$F_{n+1} = \alpha D_n + (1 - \alpha)[\alpha D_{n-1} + \alpha(1 - \alpha)D_{n-2} + (1 - \alpha)^2 F_{n-2}] \tag{3-13}$$

and by combining terms

$$F_{n+1} = \alpha D_n + \alpha(1 - \alpha)D_{n-1} + \alpha(1 - \alpha)^2 D_{n-2} + (1 - \alpha)^3 F_{n-2} \tag{3-14}$$

Since α must be between zero and one, this amounts to a moving average with decreasing weights of

$$\alpha \qquad \alpha(1 - \alpha) \qquad \alpha(1 - \alpha)^2$$

and so on.

The forms shown in Equation 3-9 through 3-14 are never used, but they are logically equivalent to Equation 3-8. As shown in Table 3-4, the weights decrease rapidly for α close to one and slowly for values of α close to zero. In practice, an equivalent moving average of N periods may be approximated by using a value of α equal to

$$\alpha = \frac{2}{N + 1}$$

Table 3-4
Decreasing Weights for Older Time Periods

Period	1	2	3	4	5
Weights	α	$\alpha(1 - \alpha)$	$\alpha(1 - \alpha)^2$	$\alpha(1 - \alpha)^3$	$\alpha(1 - \alpha)^4$
$\alpha = 0.9$	0.9	0.09	0.009	0.0009	0.00009
$\alpha = 0.6$	0.6	0.24	0.096	0.0384	0.01536
$\alpha = 0.1$	0.1	0.09	0.081	0.0729	0.06561

We now apply simple exponential smoothing to a small sample in order to demonstrate the technique. Later, the technique is used on data from Table 3-2 to provide a basis for comparison with a moving average. The only data required to produce a forecast for Period $n + 1$ are the values of α, F_n, and D_n. Let α be 0.3, F_n be 100 and D_n be 90. Then, using Equation 3-8, we have

$$\begin{aligned} F_{n+1} &= (0.3)(90) + (0.7)(100) \\ &= 27 + 70 \\ &= 97 \end{aligned}$$

Now suppose the demand in Period $n + 1$ is 95. The forecast for Period $n + 2$ is then

$$\begin{aligned} F_{n+2} &= (0.3)(95) + (0.7)(97) \\ &= 28.5 + 67.9 \\ &= 96.4 \\ &= 96 \text{ because forecasts need to be integer units} \end{aligned}$$

Finally, suppose demand in Period $n + 2$ happens to be 96. The forecast for Period $n + 3$ is then

$$\begin{aligned} F_{n+3} &= (0.3)(96) + (0.7)(96) \\ &= (0.3 + 0.7)(96) \\ &= 96 \end{aligned}$$

Table 3-5 presents the results obtained when single exponential smoothing is applied to the data from Table 3-2. Following a procedure similar to that used to develop Table 3-3, both a low and a high value of α are used to demonstrate the result of placing more weight on the most recent observations. This effect may also be seen in Figure 3-5.

The problem with simple exponential smoothing is that, as with any moving average technique, it lags behind changes in the series. This problem is clearly seen in Figure 3-5. Figure 3-5 illustrates that whenever the time series is increasing, the exponential forecast is biased low, and that whenever the time series is decreasing, the exponential forecast is biased high. Also shown

Table 3-5
Comparison of Exponential Forecasts

Period	Actual Demand	Forecast $\alpha = 0.1$		Forecast $\alpha = 0.4$		Forecast $\alpha = 0.7$	
		Forecast	Error Squared	Forecast	Error Squared	Forecast	Error Squared
January	90	90		90		90	
February	106	90	256	90	256	90	256
March	152	92	3,600	96	3,136	101	2,601
April	244	98	21,316	118	15,876	137	11,449
May	302	113	35,721	168	17,956	212	8,100
June	274	132	20,164	222	2,704	275	1
July	162	146	256	243	6,561	274	12,544
August	194	148	2,116	211	289	196	4
September	312	153	25,281	204	11,664	195	13,689
October	359	169	36,100	247	12,544	277	6,724
November	215	188	729	292	5,929	334	14,161
December	126	191	4,225	261	18,225	251	15,625
January	94	185	8,281	207	12,769	164	4,900
February	125	176	2,601	162	1,369	115	100
March	147	171	576	147	0	122	625
		169		147		140	
Sum of errors			161,222		109,278		90,779

in Figure 3-5 is the fact that exponential forecasts always miss the turning point. The magnitude of the bias can be altered by changing α, but the existence of bias cannot be altered.

We have to this point mentioned, but not discussed, two measures of the quality of a forecast, forecast error and forecast bias. In the next two sections, measures of error and bias are defined. Following that, two techniques are illustrated that can produce unbiased forecasts when seasonality is present in the data.

Forecast Error Measurement

In Tables 3-3 and 3-5 we computed the square of the difference between the actual and forecast demand and the sum of those squared errors. Assume the function generating a demand series is of the form

$$D = d + r \tag{3-15}$$

where d is a constant and r is a random component that is normally distributed with a mean of zero. If you subtracted d from every observed D and computed the sum of the differences, it should be zero (or close to it). Thus, the sum of

Figure 3-5
Exponential Smoothing Forecast Lags Behind Actual Data

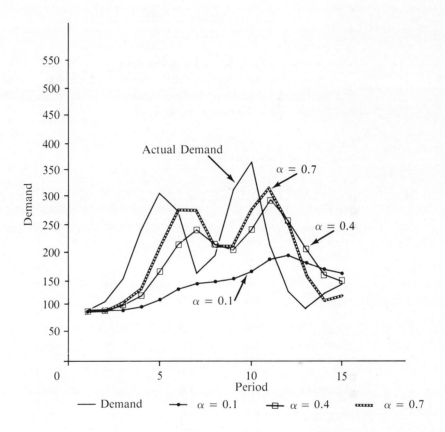

forecast errors (hence, the average of forecast errors) is not a good measure of forecast accuracy. However, the variance estimate

$$s^2 = \sum_{n=1}^{N} \frac{(D_n - d)^2}{N} \tag{3-16}$$

would not equal zero because every term is nonnegative. By squaring each forecast error, we create a series that does not approach zero, but we do not produce an estimate of r. Rather than squaring each term to produce a sequence of nonnegative terms, we could have taken the absolute value of each term (the value without regard for the sign). The average of this sequence is known as the *mean absolute deviation (MAD)*, because it is produced by taking the mean (average) of the absolute values of the deviations of the forecast from the actual data.

$$MAD_i = \frac{\Sigma |e_i|}{n} = \frac{\Sigma |D_i - F_i|}{n} \qquad (3\text{-}17)$$

where i is the ith period and e is the error.

In order to see how these different measures behave, consider the actual and forecast data shown in Table 3-6 (which is taken from Table 3-5, $\alpha = 0.1$) and the corresponding error measures.

Table 3-6
Measures of Forecast Errors

Month	Actual	$\alpha = 0.1$	Deviation	Deviation Squared	Absolute Deviation
January	90	90			
February	106	90			
March	152	92			
April	244	98	146	21,316	146
May	302	113	189	35,721	189
June	274	132	142	20,164	142
July	162	146	16	256	16
August	194	148	46	2,116	46
September	312	153	159	25,281	159
October	359	169	190	36,100	190
November	215	188	27	729	27
December	126	191	−65	4,225	65
January	94	185	−91	8,281	91
February	125	176	−51	2,601	51
March	147	171	−24	576	24
Average errors:			57.0	13,113.8	95.5
Square root				114.5	

Notice in Table 3-6 that although the average of the deviations is not zero, it is much smaller than the *MAD*, and thus is not a good estimate of the random component. The *MAD* is the most common measure of forecast error and usually forms the basis for actions taken to offset forecast error (such as maintaining a safety stock of finished goods). Some people feel that forecasts that are far off have a more negative impact than the positive effect of forecasts that are very close. The *mean squared error (MSE)*, found by averaging the squared deviations, places more weight on the large errors than on the small ones. Note that the mean squared error is not on the same scale as the *MAD* or average error, as the mean squared error deals with squared data. One can correct the scale by taking the square root of the mean squared error. This value is not intended to measure r, only the *MAD* estimates r. The mean squared error may, however, be a better indicator of which of two forecasting techniques produces the more usable results.

The following example, admittedly fabricated, illustrates why the mean squared error may be a better indicator than the *MAD*. Suppose two techniques are used to estimate a time series for 10 periods. The first technique always misses by 100 units, sometimes up, sometimes down. The second technique is perfect nine times and misses by 1,000 units the tenth. Clearly, the *MAD* for both techniques is 100. The *MSE* for the first is 10,000 ($10 \times 100^2 \div 10$). The *MSE* for the second is 100,000 ($1,000^2 \div 10$). The *MAD* indicates we should be indifferent between the techniques. The *MSE* indicates a clear preference for the first approach. A moment's reflection on the actions needed to protect against forecast error in the two situations should be sufficient to convince you that the first method is preferable.

To summarize this section, the *MAD* should be used to estimate r, the average of the random component of the time series. The *MSE* is preferable if one wishes to determine which of a set of forecasting techniques produces the most desirable results.

The Tracking Signal

The tracking signal, *TS*, helps to keep the forecast unbiased. It is usually computed as the ratio of the average error to the *MAD*; that is

$$TS_i = \frac{E(e_i)}{MAD_i} \qquad (3\text{-}18)$$

where $E(e_i)$ is the average, or expected value, of the error through i periods.

TS_i, of course, can be positive or negative. If all is going well, it should stay within reasonable limits and not be biased (that is, constantly negative or constantly positive). As the tracking signal approaches -1 or $+1$, it indicates that the error is constantly negative or constantly positive. When the tracking signal exceeds some threshold, the *trip value*, an action message is printed indicating that forecast bias is suspected. A fundamental change apparently has taken place in the average demand. Two courses of action are possible: (1) searching for a cause (e.g., marketing campaign, data error, etc.) or (2) temporarily revising the coefficient α to a higher value. The first action may or may not cause a revision in the forecast parameters, while the second attempts to allow the system to right itself by placing heavy emphasis on the more recent data. One must remember that a large tracking signal may only be a statistical aberration and that it is possible that nothing is actually wrong or in need of correction.

The choice of tracking signal trip value usually depends on the importance of the item. For important items, the trip value may be 0.3 to 0.4. For unimportant items, the forecaster is likely better off spending little time correcting the forecast. For these items, a trip value of 0.7 or so is used.

One solution to correcting for biased forecasts is to use the absolute value of the tracking signal as the value of α in exponential smoothing. This action chooses the second corrective mechanism. This forecasting procedure is called *adaptive smoothing*, because the value of α adapts, i.e., becomes high when the forecast is poor, to correct, and becomes low when the forecast is good, to ignore random events. Adaptive smoothing is described in detail in the next section.

Table 3-7 illustrates the computation of the tracking signal. Note that for these data the initial one or two values are large. This is because all errors were initially assumed to be zero. Also note that the tracking signal is computed as the ratio of sums rather than of averages. Equation 3-18 indicates averages are used. Since the change to sums merely multiplies both the numerator and the denominator by N, the number of periods used to obtain the average, the tracking signal value is not affected by the choice of sums or averages in its computation.

Table 3-7
Tracking Signal Computations

Actual	Forecast	Error e_i	$\Sigma(e_i)$	$\Sigma\lvert e_i\rvert$	Tracking Signal
150	153	-3	-3	3	-1.00
146	155	-9	-12	12	-1.00
156	147	9	-3	21	-0.14
152	145	7	4	28	0.14
145	155	-10	-6	38	-0.16
146	154	-8	-14	46	-0.30
153	148	5	-9	51	-0.18
157	146	11	2	62	0.03

To close the topic of tracking signals, we note that this section discusses one of several variations of tracking signals. Some signals are defined by the sum of the errors divided by the *MAD*. In this case, the tracking signal ranges from $-N$ to $+N$, where N is the number of observations. We prefer a signal normalized to the range -1 to $+1$ for convenience and to facilitate adaptive exponential smoothing.

Adaptive Exponential Smoothing

When a tracking signal is tripped, i.e., crosses the threshold value, some action must be taken to reevaluate the data. It is likely that a shift in the trend line (intercept or slope) has occurred. The usual corrective action is to discard older data that represents a past trend in order to properly define the current trend. This evaluation process consumes valuable managerial or analyst time. A procedure that takes this corrective action automatically would be useful, especially for low dollar volume items that merit little managerial attention.

A technique that performs automatic correction is exponential smoothing with the value of the smoothing constant, α, taken to be the absolute value of the tracking signal. If the forecast becomes biased, the tracking signal's absolute value increases, thereby increasing α, thereby placing more weight on recent data and less weight on older data. This is precisely the desired correction. On the other hand, if the forecast is unbiased, the tracking signal is close to 0. This yields a smoothing constant close to 0. If a random fluctuation occurs, the low α value causes little weight to be given to the random fluctuation. However, should the random fluctuation become a new trend, then the value of α will increase, causing an automatic correction.

Whenever there are a very large number of parts to be forecast, the use of adaptive smoothing for unimportant items frees managerial time to be spent on improving the forecasting procedure for the important items.

Time Series Decomposition

In this section we demonstrate how to decompose a time series into the trend, seasonal, and random components of which the series is made. We then show how to use the decomposed series to forecast demand. For time series decomposition to function properly, it is best to have at least 48 months of demand history.

Determining Seasonal Indices. The usual approach to time series decomposition has five steps. Step 1 is to calculate a 12-month centered moving average. Because the average is for an entire year, seasonality is eliminated. Step 2 is to estimate seasonal indices using the ratio of actual demand to the 12-month centered moving average. Step 3 is to fit a line to the "deseasonalized" data. The intercept and slope of this line provide the values needed to estimate the trend factor. Step 4 is to extrapolate the line found in Step 3 into the future, providing a "forecast" of what demand would be like were seasonality nonexistent. Step 5 is to multiply each deseasonalized forecast value by its seasonal index to obtain the final forecast.

The details of this procedure are straightforward. In Step 1, the moving average of each 12 months is calculated. This average is placed on the first day of the seventh month, which is the center of the 12-month period. Thus, an average from January 1 to December 31 centers on July 1, an average from February 1 to January 31 centers on August 1, etc. Unfortunately, the 12-month moving averages do not align properly with the monthly data. A monthly demand from July 1 to July 31 centers on July 15, not July 1. To align the original data and the moving averages properly, a 2-month moving average is performed on the 12-month moving average. The average of the 12-month moving averages centered July 1 and August 1 centers midway between July 1 and August 1, on July 15. Thus, the 2-period moving average taken on the 12-month moving average is centered precisely where the monthly values are centered. Table 3-8 illustrates the computation of the 12-month moving averages and the 2-month centered moving averages. The final result of this process is called a 12-month centered moving average. The name indicates that the 12 monthly averages center properly on the monthly data.

The second step in the process of computing seasonal indices is to find the ratio of each period's actual demand to the centered 12-month moving average. If several years of data are available, the average of all July monthly indices is computed and used as the index value for July. All other monthly indices are found in a similar fashion. We call the ratio of any given July (or other month) to the corresponding 12-month centered moving average a *seasonal factor*. The term *seasonal index* is reserved for the final average of seasonal factors. The process of defining seasonal indices works fairly well. The effectiveness of the process is a function of the size of the random component. If the random component is large, the estimate of the seasonal component is not as accurate as when the random component is small.

Table 3-8 shows the computation of the seasonal factors and seasonal indices for the 48-month data set given in Table 3-2. Figure 3-6 shows a graph of the actual data and the centered moving average. The centered moving average plots as a straight line with random variations. Because the effects of seasonality have been removed, the centered moving average data are known as *deseasonalized* data.

Figure 3-6
12-Month Centered Moving Average

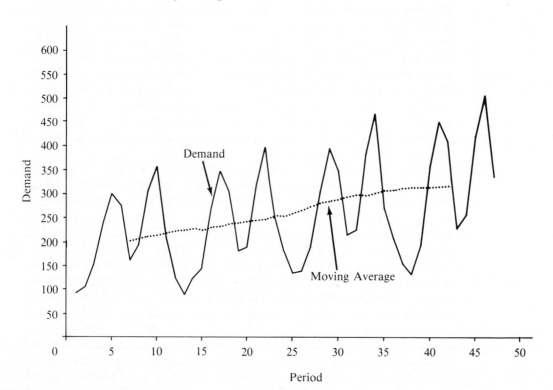

Table 3-8
Seasonal Index Computation

Period	Month	Demand	12-Month Moving Average	12-Month Centered Moving Average	Seasonal Factor	Seasonal Index
1	January	90				
2	February	106				
3	March	152				
4	April	244				
5	May	302				
6	June	274				
7	July	162	211.33	211.50	0.766	
8	August	194	211.67	212.46	0.913	
9	September	312	213.25	213.04	1.465	
10	October	359	212.83	214.04	1.677	
11	November	215	215.25	217.21	0.990	
12	December	126	219.17	220.67	0.571	
13	January	94	222.17	222.83	0.422	0.487
14	February	125	223.50	223.00	0.561	0.532
15	March	147	222.50	222.96	0.659	0.676
16	April	273	223.42	225.13	1.213	1.183
17	May	349	226.83	228.38	1.528	1.495
18	June	310	229.92	232.13	1.335	1.324
19	July	178	234.33	235.88	0.755	0.771
20	August	182	237.42	238.13	0.764	0.835
21	September	323	238.83	240.46	1.343	1.401
22	October	400	242.08	243.50	1.643	1.659
23	November	252	244.92	246.96	1.020	0.993
24	December	179	249.00	250.58	0.714	0.668
25	January	131	252.17	253.79	0.516	
26	February	142	255.42	257.33	0.552	
27	March	186	259.25	261.79	0.710	
28	April	307	264.33	266.83	1.151	
29	May	398	269.33	270.20	1.473	
30	June	348	271.08	272.20	1.278	
31	July	217	273.33	274.20	0.791	
32	August	228	275.08	275.04	0.829	
33	September	384	275.00	275.34	1.395	
34	October	460	275.67	277.59	1.657	
35	November	273	279.50	281.63	0.969	
36	December	206	283.75	286.54	0.719	
37	January	152	289.33	290.13	0.524	
38	February	141	290.92	291.96	0.483	
39	March	194	293.00	294.50	0.659	
40	April	353	296.00	297.84	1.185	
41	May	449	299.67	302.59	1.484	
42	June	415	305.50	305.50	1.358	
43	July	236				
44	August	253				
45	September	420				
46	October	504				
47	November	343				
48	December	231				

The value for the seasonal index is determined by averaging all the relevant observations. For July there are three observations, 0.766, 0.755, and 0.791. The value used in forecasting is the simple average of these three numbers, 0.771. Similarly, the values for May are 1.528, 1.473, and 1.484, which yield a seasonal index for May of 1.495.

It is clear from Figure 3-6 that for peak demand periods the seasonal factor is greater than one and for off-peak periods the seasonal factor is less than one. It can also be seen from Figure 3-6 that the process of creating a 12-month centered moving average results in the moving average having one year less data than the original data. Thus, 48 months of demand produces 36 months of moving average. Since we must have both the demand and the average to estimate a seasonal factor, only 36 estimates are possible, 3 for each of the 12 months.

Step 3 of the decomposition process is to estimate the trend line. We could use the 36 months of data contained in the 12-month centered moving average or the 48 months of data contained in the demand. The usual procedure is to use the actual data, with seasonality removed. To remove seasonality we divide each demand by the corresponding seasonal index. The least squares method can be used to fit a line to the deseasonalized data. Table 3-10 shows the original demand data and the deseasonalized data. The least squares method is used to estimate the y-intercept and slope of a line describing the deseasonalized data. The least squares method is described elsewhere in detail and will not be explained here. A simple way to implement the method is to use Lotus 1-2-3, version 2 or higher, or a comparable product such as Quattro. Lotus 1-2-3 has a command sequence (/ **Data Regression**) that can be used with the period numbers as the independent variable and the deseasonalized data as the dependent variable. The output from this process includes the estimate of the y-intercept and slope, as shown in Table 3-9.

Table 3-9
Regression Output from Lotus 1-2-3

Regression Output:		
Constant		187.1795
Std Err of Y Est		14.18510
R Squared		0.885688
No. of Observations		48
Degrees of Freedom		46
X Coefficient(s)	2.790157	
Std Err of Coef.	0.147794	

The data of interest are the constant (y-intercept of the line) and the X Coefficient (slope). These values were estimated to be 187.1795 and 2.790157, respectively. Thus, the line that best describes our deseasonalized data is $y = 187.1795 + 2.790157x$, where x is the period number. The other data in Table 3-9 will not be used. We now have an estimate for the trend component: For each added month, demand increases on the average by 2.790157 units. Step 2 is now complete. The time series has now been decomposed into underlying factors, the trend factor and the seasonal factor. The trend line is shown in Figure 3-7 and the seasonal indices in Figure 3-8.

Steps 4 and 5 produce the actual forecast. In Step 4, the trend line for deseasonalized data is extrapolated into the future. In Step 5 the extrapolated data are reseasonalized by multiplying each monthly datum by its corresponding seasonal index. The trend line is extended by substituting the future period number for x in the trend equation. For example, deseasonalized demand for Period 49 is estimated by the equation $y = 187.1795 + 2.790157 \times 49$. The results of extrapolating deseasonalized demand to Months 49 through 60 are shown in Table 3-10. In each instance the deseasonalized demand has been rounded to an integer. The final phase is to multiply each period by its seasonal index. Since Month 49 is January, the deseasonalized estimate of 324 is multiplied by 0.487 to obtain the forecast value of 158. February's deseasonalized estimate of 327 is multiplied by February's index of 0.532 to obtain the forecast of 174 for Month 50, and so on. Forecasts are rounded to integer values.

Figure 3-7
Trend Line Fitted to Deseasonalized Data

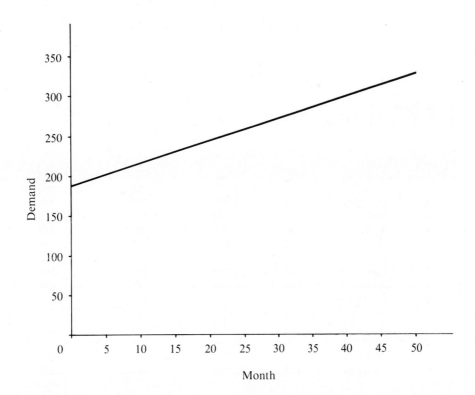

Month

Figure 3-8
Seasonal Indices Repeated Four Times

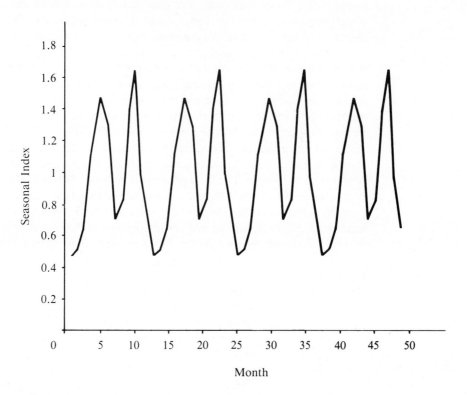

Month

Table 3-10
Trend Line, Final Forecast, Using Time Series Decomposition

Period	Month	Actual	Seasonal Index	Deseasonalized Data	Trend Line	Forecast
1	January	90	0.487	185	190	93
2	February	106	0.532	199	193	103
3	March	152	0.676	225	196	132
4	April	244	1.183	206	198	234
5	May	302	1.495	202	201	300
6	June	274	1.324	207	204	270
7	July	162	0.771	210	207	160
8	August	194	0.835	232	210	175
9	September	312	1.401	223	212	297
10	October	359	1.659	216	215	357
11	November	215	0.993	217	218	216
12	December	126	0.668	189	221	148
13	January	94	0.487	193	223	109
14	February	125	0.532	235	226	120

Table 3-10 (Continued)

Period	Month	Actual	Seasonal Index	Deseasonalized Data	Trend Line	Forecast
15	March	147	0.676	217	229	155
16	April	273	1.183	231	232	274
17	May	349	1.495	233	235	351
18	June	310	1.324	234	237	314
19	July	178	0.771	231	240	185
20	August	182	0.835	218	243	203
21	September	323	1.401	231	246	345
22	October	400	1.659	241	249	413
23	November	252	0.993	254	251	249
24	December	179	0.668	268	254	170
25	January	131	0.487	269	257	125
26	February	142	0.532	267	260	138
27	March	186	0.676	275	262	177
28	April	307	1.183	260	265	313
29	May	398	1.495	266	268	401
30	June	348	1.324	263	271	359
31	July	217	0.771	281	274	211
32	August	228	0.835	273	276	230
33	September	384	1.401	274	279	391
34	October	460	1.659	277	282	468
35	November	273	0.993	275	285	283
36	December	206	0.668	308	288	192
37	January	152	0.487	312	290	141
38	February	141	0.532	265	293	156
39	March	194	0.676	287	296	200
40	April	353	1.183	298	299	354
41	May	449	1.495	300	301	450
42	June	415	1.324	313	304	402
43	July	236	0.771	306	307	237
44	August	253	0.835	303	310	259
45	September	420	1.401	300	313	439
46	October	504	1.659	304	315	523
47	November	343	0.993	345	318	316
48	December	231	0.668	346	321	214
49	January				324	158
50	February				327	174
51	March				329	222
52	April				332	393
53	May				335	501
54	June				338	448
55	July				341	263
56	August				343	286
57	September				346	485
58	October				349	579
59	November				352	350
60	December				354	236

Estimating the Random Component.   If a forecasting procedure is unbiased, the average forecast error should be 0. In most situations, the error should be positive as often as negative. In fact, an unbiased forecast is thought to produce a series of error terms that are random, following the normal (bell shaped) distribution, with mean 0. One way to evaluate the quality of a forecast is to examine a plot of the error terms over time. Table 3-11 shows the calculation of the error terms that would have occurred had the time series decomposition derived above been used to forecast the first 48 months. Figure 3-9 shows a scatter plot of those error terms. If no bias exists in the forecast, there should be no discernable trend in this scatter plot. The center of the plot should be approximately 0. Most of the values should be close to 0, with roughly half above 0 and half below 0, suggesting that the observations fit a bell-shaped distribution. The bell shaped distribution is confirmed by a bar chart of the same data, shown in Figure 3-10. We can therefore conclude that the forecast is unbiased. A plot of the error terms yields much more information than computation of the tracking signal. However, examination of forecast accuracy to this degree can be justified only for very high dollar volume items.

Figure 3-9
Scatter Plot of Error Terms

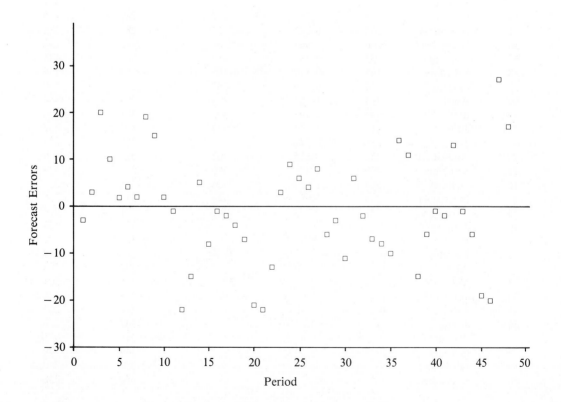

Table 3-11
Computation of Error Terms

Period	Month	Demand	Hypothetical Forecast	Error
1	January	90	93	−3
2	February	106	103	3
3	March	152	132	20
4	April	244	234	10
5	May	302	300	2
6	June	274	270	4
7	July	162	160	2
8	August	194	175	19
9	September	312	297	15
10	October	359	357	2
11	November	215	216	−1
12	December	126	148	−22
13	January	94	109	−15
14	February	125	120	5
15	March	147	155	−8
16	April	273	274	−1
17	May	349	351	−2
18	June	310	314	−4
19	July	178	185	−7
20	August	182	203	−21
21	September	323	345	−22
22	October	400	413	−13
23	November	252	249	3
24	December	179	170	9
25	January	131	125	6
26	February	142	138	4
27	March	186	177	8
28	April	307	313	−6
29	May	398	401	−3
30	June	348	359	−11
31	July	217	211	6
32	August	228	230	−2
33	September	384	391	−7
34	October	460	468	−8
35	November	273	283	−10
36	December	206	192	14
37	January	152	141	11
38	February	141	156	−15
39	March	194	200	−6
40	April	353	354	−1
41	May	449	450	−2
42	June	415	402	13
43	July	236	237	−1
44	August	253	259	−6
45	September	420	439	−19
46	October	504	523	−20
47	November	343	316	27
48	December	231	214	17

Figure 3-10
Distribution of Forecast Errors

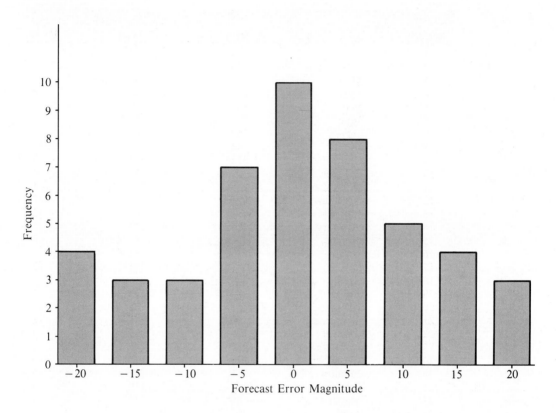

It is instructive to compare the error terms obtained from the time series decomposition approach (Table 3-11) to those obtained by the exponential smoothing approach (Table 3-6). The time series decomposition approach has much smaller errors whenever seasonality is present. The authors' experience indicates that there is seasonality in demand for most products. Even industrial products used year-round have pronounced peaks and valleys caused by companies that attempt to minimize inventory held prior to the annual physical inventory.

The degree of forecast error is the primary determinant of safety stock. The use of time series decomposition to reduce forecast error can reduce safety stock. Time series decomposition requires more computer time than exponential smoothing. As the cost of computing declines, the set of items for which time series decomposition is economically favorable grows.

A barrier to the use of time series decomposition is insufficient data. Where the use of time series decomposition is indicated but insufficient data is available, Winters' three-factor model is an attractive compromise.

Winters' Three-Factor Model

Time series decompostion is usually the preferred method to forecast seasonal, high-dollar volume items. Unfortunately, with product lifetimes typically less than four years, we often lack the data needed to perform time series decomposition properly. Simple exponential smoothing can be used to forecast demand when few data are available, but this technique produces biased forecasts whenever trend or seasonal factors are present in the data. A compromise is to use Winters' three-factor method, which employs separate smoothing factors for the base (deseasonalized) demand, trend, and seasonal index estimators.

A forecast is made with Winters' method in exactly the same fashion as with time series decomposition:

$$F_n = (B_{n-1} + iT_{n-1})S_{n-p} \qquad (3\text{-}19)$$

where B_n = forecast base (deseasonalized) demand in period n (i.e., intercept + n × slope)

T_n = estimate of the slope for period n

S_n = seasonal index for period n

i = number of periods in the future

p = number of periods in a year

It may seem contradictory that this formula can be used with little data in Winters' method since the same formula cannot be used with little data in time series decomposition. The difference is that Winters' method begins with subjective estimates of the base, trend, and seasonal factors and improves these estimates by exponential smoothing as additional data become available. The most critical initial estimate is that of the seasonal indices. The other factors can be derived even if as little as one year of data is available. The estimated seasonal indices can be obtained by using those of a similar product or other product thought to have similar seasonality.

Suppose demand for Acme computers, in thousands, is summarized by quarter as in Table 3-12. Computers are thought to be highly seasonal with peaks at the start of the school year and at Christmas. Based on seasonal factors for other expensive items useful both at home and at school, Acme arrives at seasonal indices of 0.9, 0.7, 1.1, and 1.3 for Quarters 1 to 4, respectively. Demand for the first year can then be divided by these factors to establish four estimates of base demand. The trend can be estimated as follows:

$$T_4 = \frac{B_4 - B_1}{3}$$
$$= \frac{12}{3}$$
$$= 4$$

That is, take the most recent base estimator minus the oldest base estimator and divide by the number of periods that have occurred between observations.

Table 3-12
Initial Base and Trend Estimation

Quarter (n)	Demand	S_n	B_n	T_n
1	112	0.9	124	
2	115	0.7	164	
3	124	1.1	113	
4	177	1.3	136	4

The forecast for Period 5 can be found by substituting into Equation 3-19:

$$F_n = (B_{n-1} + iT_{n-1})S_{n-4}$$
$$F_5 = (136 + 4)(0.9)$$
$$= 126$$

Suppose further that actual demand during Period 5 is 112. The base, trend, and seasonal factors may now be updated using exponential smoothing. We will first derive the general formulas and then apply them to obtain a forecast for Period 6.

Three smoothing constants will be required, which we will designate α, β, and γ. The smoothing constant for the base estimate is α, for the trend is β, and for the seasonal index is γ. In all instances, exponential smoothing is accomplished by

New Estimate = Constant × Actual Data + (1 − Constant) × Old Estimate

This yields:

$$B_n = \alpha B_n + (1 - \alpha)(B_{n-1} + T_{n-1}) \tag{3-20}$$

$$T_n = \beta T_n + (1 - \beta)T_{n-1} \tag{3-21}$$

$$S_n = \gamma S_n + (1 - \gamma)S_{n-p} \tag{3-22}$$

Note that the new seasonal index will be used to forecast one year in the future. The other indices are for one period (month, quarter, week) in the future. The new estimators must be derived in the sequence shown, B_n, T_n, then S_n.

The actual values cited in Equations 3-20 to 3-22 are found as follows:

$$B_n = \frac{X_n}{S_{n-p}} \tag{3-23}$$

$$T_n = B_n - B_{n-1} \tag{3-24}$$

$$S_n = \frac{X_n}{B_n} \tag{3-25}$$

where X_n is the actual demand observed in Period n.

Equation 3-23 says that the deseasonalized demand for Period n is found by dividing actual demand by the existing seasonal index for Period n (which was established in Period $n - p$). Equation 3-24 says that the latest value for trend is found by subtracting the previous base estimator from the current one. Equation 3-25 says that the current seasonal factor is the ratio of actual demand to deseasonalized demand. Substituting Equations 3-23 to 3-25 into Equations 3-20 to 3-22 yields:

$$B_n = \alpha\left(\frac{X_n}{S_{n-p}}\right) + (1 - \alpha)(B_{n-1} + T_{n-1}) \qquad (3\text{-}26)$$

$$T_n = \beta(B_n - B_{n-1}) + (1 - \beta)T_{n-1} \qquad (3\text{-}27)$$

$$S_n = \gamma\left(\frac{X_n}{B_n}\right) + (1 - \gamma)S_{n-p} \qquad (3\text{-}28)$$

Suppose we elect to use 0.2, 0.1, and 0.05 as the values of α, β, and γ, respectively. We can now use Equations 3-26 to 3-28 to determine B_5, T_5, S_5, and F_6.

$$\begin{aligned}
B_n &= 0.2\left(\frac{112}{0.9}\right) + 0.8(136 + 4) \\
&= 24.9 + 112 \\
&= 137
\end{aligned}$$

$$\begin{aligned}
T_5 &= 0.1(137 - 136) + 0.9(4.0) \\
&= 0.1 + 3.6 \\
&= 3.7
\end{aligned}$$

$$\begin{aligned}
S_5 &= 0.05\left(\frac{112}{137}\right) + 0.95(0.9) \\
&= 0.896
\end{aligned}$$

$$\begin{aligned}
F_6 &= (137 + 3.7)(0.7) \\
&= 98
\end{aligned}$$

In creating the forecast for Period 6, the new base and trend estimators are used, but the seasonal index for one year prior to Period 6 (Period 2) is used. The new seasonal index for the first quarter of the year (S_5) will be used to forecast Period 9, the first quarter of the third year.

Table 3-13 shows one possible realization of five years of demand using Winters' method. In this example, the initial estimates of the four seasonal indices seem to be good. Table 3-13 displays the *MAD* and tracking signal obtained during several years of forecasts. There is no discernable bias and the *MAD* is fairly small.

Table 3-13
Application of Winters' Method

Period	Demand	Base	Seasonal Index	Trend	Forecast	Error	Absolute Error
1	112		0.900				
2	115		0.700				
3	124		1.100				
4	177	136.0	1.300	4.0			
5	112	136.9	0.896	3.7	126	14	14
6	101	141.3	0.701	3.8	98	−3	3
7	185	149.7	1.107	4.3	160	−25	25
8	202	154.3	1.300	4.3	200	−2	2
9	129	155.7	0.893	4.0	142	13	13
10	107	158.3	0.700	3.9	112	5	5
11	186	163.4	1.109	4.0	180	−6	6
12	251	172.5	1.308	4.5	218	−33	33
13	177	181.2	0.897	4.9	158	−19	19
14	133	186.9	0.701	5.0	130	−3	3
15	188	187.4	1.104	4.6	213	25	25
16	249	191.7	1.308	4.6	251	2	2
17	182	197.6	0.898	4.7	176	−6	6
18	159	207.2	0.704	5.2	142	−17	17
19	237	212.9	1.104	5.3	234	−3	3
20	266	215.2	1.304	5.0	285	19	19

$\alpha = 0.2$
$\beta = 0.1$
$\gamma = 0.05$
MAD 12.1875
$E(e_i)$ −2.4375
TS −0.2

EXTRINSIC TECHNIQUES

Extrinsic techniques use data in addition to or instead of the time series of the values to be forecast. For example, we can express the number of repair parts needed next year as a function of the number of new machines sold in each of several previous years. Or we can forecast the number of absent employees tomorrow based on the weather forecast for tomorrow. The repair parts example illustrates the use of a leading indicator: machines sold leads (in time) demand for spare parts. The absenteeism example illustrates a less reliable relationship, since to use it to forecast absenteeism we must first have a forecast of the weather. Perhaps a more useful example of the use of a forecast of one time series to forecast a second time series is the U.S. Department of Agriculture forecast of crop yields that is sometimes used to forecast harvesting work force needs.

We need not limit extrinsic forecasts to just one external variable. For example, spare parts demand could be a function of machines sold, dollar cost of the machines, fraction of that cost represented by the part's cost, expected useful life of the machine, etc. In this case, spare parts demand is the dependent variable, and the others are independent variables. A whole body of statistical knowledge is devoted to this concept of multiple regression/correlation. Such techniques can be very useful if: (1) the indicators lead by enough time so that one can take action or the indicators are easily forecasted; (2) the correlation is strong; and (3) data are available. Extrinsic techniques usually are used for aggregate forecasts of demand for product groups rather than for individual item forecasts. However, for large dollar volume items, the use of extrinsic techniques should be considered. The decision criterion is whether the additional accuracy provides sufficient benefit to offset the cost of using the model.

FORECAST ERRORS IN INVENTORY SYSTEMS

The only thing always correct about forecasts is that they are wrong—sometimes by a little, sometimes by a great deal. There is always some error.

It is common in both literature and practice to label all differences between actual and forecast values as errors. But this is like saying that all imperfect performances, be they in games, the classroom, or life, are mistakes. Sometimes inaccurate forecasts (those with serious errors) are because of true error, such as data entry error. Other times inaccuracies are due to the inherent difficulty of the task. We should recognize and eliminate real errors.

Another serious forecasting error is to select the wrong model to match the phenomenon it is to forecast. For example, suppose the true series is actually generated by a function of the following kind:

$$D = d + r$$

in other words, a level demand affected only by random fluctuations. Then use of a higher order model such as $F = a + bt + r$ will cause the forecasting model to amplify each random fluctuation, since it is looking for a trend that really doesn't exist. Any mismatch between the model and the real world can thus be viewed as a true error and should be eliminated. However, this is often difficult because we don't really know the nature of real world phenomena.

What we've chosen to call inaccuracy due to the inherent difficulty of the task refers to inaccuracy caused by the random component of the time series. In the simplest case, where $D = d + r$, the best we can hope to do is to identify correctly the value of d. If we do so, then our forecast will equal d and hence

$$D - d = r$$

and

$$D - F = r = \text{error}$$

Thus, the observed error will reflect the true variability of the underlying process. While we can determine the average variability, the specific deviation on one given forecast is something that cannot be predicted. For example, if we roll one pair of six-sided dice, we know that the average value from many rolls is 7. We know further that the largest value obtainable is 12 (two 6s) and the smallest is 2 (two 1s). By calculating a standard deviation, we can measure average process variability. If we were to forecast a given roll, the forecast that would minimize our forecast error over the long run is 7, the expected value, or average, of the process. For any given roll, the absolute value of forecast error could be anything from 0 to 5. The precise value of forecast error on a particular roll is impossible to predict. Because we have an analogous problem in forecasting demand that is subject to random fluctuation, we have to make plans to protect our customers from imperfect forecasts. By determining the average forecast inaccuracy, or error, we can determine safety stock levels of finished goods needed to almost always have an item in stock. We can also establish safety lead times for scheduling or other contingency plans. The topic of safety stock determination is discussed in Chapter 6; safety lead time is discussed in Chapter 15.

The problem in labeling all differences between forecast and actual demand, whatever their cause, to be errors is that the forecasting system is too often the scapegoat for inadequate actions in other areas. For example, if missed shipping dates are always blamed on poor forecasts, there is no pressure to control other sources of missed shipments. Some problems that may lead to our failure to deliver on time include the variability of suppliers in meeting their delivery dates and specified quantities, poor quality control on a production process, and excessive work-in-process inventories.

SUMMARY

Forecasting techniques are classified as qualitative, involving primarily judgment, and quantitative, involving primarily historical data and mathematical models. Quantitative techniques use both intrinsic data, data pertaining to the item to be forecast, and extrinsic data. All quantitative forecasting methods involve the implicit assumption that the near future will be similar to the recent past. To be reliable, all quantitative forecasting techniques require accurate data. Insuring accurate data requires that the data be monitored carefully to eliminate data input error and to adjust for one-time occurrences, such as special promotions.

The study of a set of data describing demand over time is called time series analysis. Three common techniques of time series analysis are moving averages, exponential smoothing, and time series decomposition. Time series decomposition is the most accurate of the three, but there is often too little data to permit decomposition. Winters' three-factor model, the most complex exponential smoothing application, is a good compromise whenever seasonal variation in demand exists but there is insufficient data to use time series decomposition.

All forecasts are subject to error, even when the model used for the forecast is properly defined. Production and inventory managers require an estimate of the average forecast error to determine appropriate levels of safety stock and other precautionary measures. The most frequently used measure of forecast error is the mean absolute deviation (*MAD*), the average of the absolute values of the forecasts minus the actual demands.

EXERCISES

1. Discuss the use of check digits. Is it possible to use a check digit if the part number contains an alphabetic character?

2. Describe the use of demand filters. Should the demand filter have the same relative width for all part numbers? Why or why not?

3. Name three different extrinsic types of data that will be useful in forecasting demand for audio compact disks.

4. The sales and finance departments of the Orange Computer Company estimate total sales of 1,000 computer systems, each valued at an average cost of $247,000. Assuming their forecast is correct, of what use is it and how must it be interpreted by the manufacturing division?

5. The following table shows the demand for George's Creme Soda. Forecast total demand using (a) a three-period moving average, (b) simple exponential smoothing ($\alpha = 0.2$), and (c) the least squares method to fit a trend line $y = a + bx$, where x is the period number. What problems are encountered in using each method?

| | George's Creme Soda Demand | | |
| | | Sales (in thousands) | |
Month	Liters	750 ml*	2,500 ml*
January	154	176	65
February	126	179	80
March	118	189	73
April	131	177	86
May	160	192	78
June	159	187	94
July	170	194	93
August	162	186	86
September	183	207	99
October	173	197	92
November	187	200	94
December	187	208	107

*milliliter

6. Using the data given in Exercise 5, develop a forecast for (a) liter containers, (b) 750 ml containers, and (c) 2,500 ml containers using (1) a four-month moving average, (2) simple exponential smoothing ($\alpha = 0.3$), and (3) the least squares method to fit a trend line.

7. Considering the forecasts made in Exercises 5 and 6, which is likely to be more accurate, that in Exercise 5 or those in Exercise 6? Is it possible to arrive at the estimate for Exercise 5 by summing those obtained in Exercise 6? Are there advantages to forecasting in this manner? Is it possible to arrive at the estimates in Exercise 6 by prorating the forecast determined in Exericse 5? Are there advantages to this approach?

8. Construct monthly seasonal indices based on the following data using the 12-month centered moving average technique.

Month	1987	1988	1989
January	217	220	246
February	224	226	250
March	233	249	281
April	234	238	264
May	226	227	275
June	244	257	286
July	248	279	299
August	258	284	301
September	244	262	293
October	222	235	263
November	208	220	248
December	218	246	270

9. Using the data given in Exericse 8, prepare a forecast for 1990 using the time series decomposition approach.

10. The following set of data purports to be demand for pencils that are boxed 12 to a carton and have a price of 27 cents each or $3 a carton. Point out which entries are likely to be wrong. Why? How can such errors be caught and corrected?

Week	Quantity	Week	Quantity
27	107	39	255
28	121	40	243
29	181	41	45
30	135	42	219
31	147	43	220
32	165	44	6,468
33	2,016	45	6,501
34	2,232	46	612
35	189	47	189
36	222	48	189
37	232	49	171
38	720	50	171

11. Having corrected the data in Exericse 10, assume you are at Week 32. Forecast demand for Weeks 33 through 43 using (a) a four-week moving average, (b) simple exponential smoothing ($\alpha = 0.1$), and (c) Winters' three-factor model ($\alpha = 0.3, \beta = 0.1, \gamma = 0.0$). Use the data from Weeks 27 to 32 to develop an initial estimate of the trend factor.

12. Use the data from Exercise 11b to develop estimates of the MAD, MSE, and tracking signal. Based on these data, what is your estimate of the random component for this time series?

13. In order to forecast demand for a new product, you may use an existing product for which you have historical data. Identify four such pairs and tell how their demand patterns might be similar.

14. Given the seasonal indices developed for Exercise 8, deseasonalize the data. Why isn't each month's deseasonalized value equal to 100?

15. Use a spreadsheet such as Lotus 1-2-3 to analyze the total demand in Exercise 5, using simple exponential smoothing with three different coefficient values ($\alpha = 0.2, 0.3, 0.9$). Prepare a table showing a values versus degree of smoothing and showing error measures (MAD, MSE, tracking signal). Explain the findings in the table.

16. Use a spreadsheet such as Lotus 1-2-3 to implement Winters' three-factor exponential smoothing model. Apply it to the data in Exercise 8 and use it to forecast 1990.

17. Using the data from Exercise 16 for 1989, estimate the MAD, MSE, and tracking signal. Comment on the appropriateness of the Winters' three-factor model for this data.

18. Using the data from Exercise 8, develop a forecast for 1989 using (a) a six-period moving average and (b) simple exponential smoothing ($\alpha = 0.3$). Estimate the MAD and tracking signal. Comment on the appropriateness of the simple exponential smoothing model for this data.

Exercises 19-24 use the following data set:

Year	Quarter	Demand	Year	Quarter	Demand
1987	I	81	1989	I	112
	II	90		II	129
	III	120		III	158
	IV	177		IV	238
1988	I	97	1990	I	133
	II	113		II	146
	III	145		III	177
	IV	205		IV	262

19. Use simple exponential smoothing to forecast 1990. Start with an estimate of 80 for the first quarter of 1987. Use $\alpha = 0.2$. Calculate the MAD, MSE, and tracking signal for 1990. Comment on the appropriateness of simple exponential smoothing for this data.

20. Use data for 1987 to 1989 to forecast 1990 using the time series decomposition approach.

21. Using the results of Exercise 20, calculate the *MAD, MSE*, and tracking signal for 1990. Based on these results, would you choose time series decomposition to forecast 1991 using this data? Why or why not?

22. Use the data for 1987 to 1989 to initialize the base, trend, and seasonal factors for Winters' three-factor model. Forecast 1990 using $\alpha = 0.3$, $\beta = 0.1$, $\gamma = 0.05$.

23. Use the results of Exercise 22 to determine the *MAD, MSE*, and tracking signal. Comment on the appropriateness of the model for this data.

24. Use the results of Exercises 20 and 22 to discuss the advantages and disadvantages of time series decomposition and Winters' three-factor model as forecasting techniques. Compare single exponential smoothing to both of them.

SELECTED READINGS

Armstrong, J. Scott. *Long-Range Forecasting*. New York: John Wiley & Sons, Inc., 1978.

Box, George E., and G. M. Jenkins. *Time Series Analysis: Forecasting and Control*. Oakland, CA: Holden Day, Inc., 1970.

Brown, Robert G. *Smoothing, Forecastings and Prediction of Discrete Time Series*. Englewood Cliffs, NJ: Prentice-Hall, Inc., 1963.

Newbold, Paul, and Theodore Bos. *Introductory Business Forecasting*. Cincinnati: South-Western Publishing Co., 1990.

Ryan, Thomas A. Jr., Brian L. Joiner, and Barbara F. Ryan, *MINITAB Student Handbook*. North Scituate, MA: Duxbury Press, 1976.

Trigg, D. W., and A. G. Leach, "Exponential Smoothing with an Adaptive Response Rate." *Operational Research Quarterly* 18 (March 1967): 53-59.

Wheelwright, Steven C., and Spryros Makridakis. *Forecasting Methods for Management*. New York: John Wiley & Sons, Inc., 1985.

Willis, Raymond E. *A Guide to Forecasting for Planners and Managers*. Englewood Cliffs, NJ: Prentice-Hall, Inc., 1987.

Winters, P.R. "Forecasting Sales by Exponentially Weighted Moving Average." *Management Science* 6 (April 1960): 324-342.

4

MASTER SCHEDULING

Chapter 2 described production planning and resource requirements planning, which are aggregate plans of production and capacity generally taking one to ten years to complete execution. These plans combine (aggregate) similar products into product groups, combine demand into monthly totals, and often group personnel requirements across departments. The time comes when individual products and services must be scheduled at specific work centers. This is accomplished by *master scheduling*—producing a plan to manufacture specific items or provide specific services within a given time period.

Rough cut capacity planning (RCCP) is the process of determining if the plan is feasible; it determines whether the organization has sufficient capacity to carry out the plan. Although RCCP is more refined than resource requirements planning (RRP), it is called "rough cut" because it is less refined than capacity requirements planning (CRP).

Figure 4-1 illustrates how master scheduling and rough cut capacity planning relate to the corporate and operations planning described in Chapter 2.

This chapter presents a general picture of master scheduling, the master production schedule (MPS) and its relationship to rough cut capacity planning, the projected on hand (POH) inventory, and order promising using the available-to-promise (ATP) quantity. Since these terms and processes are used primarily in manufacturing, we describe them in that context. However, their counterparts exist in many service organizations. A description of the development of the master schedule including the ATP, the POH inventory, and the MPS and its relationship to the RCCP follows. Rough cut capacity planning is described in detail in Chapter 12.

Figure 4-1
Relationship of Master Production Scheduling to Other
Manufacturing Planning and Control Activities

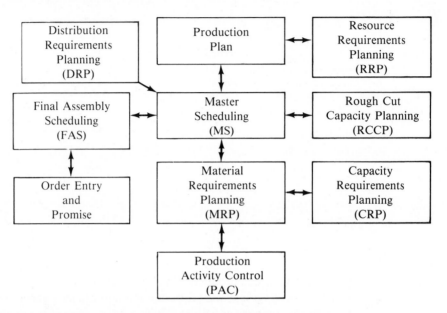

MASTER SCHEDULING AND THE MPS

The master schedule (MS) is a presentation of the demand, including the fore-cast and the backlog (customer orders received), the master production schedule (the supply plan), the projected on hand (POH) inventory, and the available-to-promise (ATP) quantity. The master production schedule (MPS) is the primary output of the master scheduling process. The MPS specifies the end items the organization anticipates manufacturing each period. End items are either final products or the items from which final assemblies (products) are made, as described later in this chapter. Thus, the MPS is the plan for pro-viding the supply to meet the demand. An example of a master schedule only including the MPS and the backlog is shown in Table 4-1. This example is developed further in the chapter.

Table 4-1
Master Schedule, Product 1, Group A

	Week			
	32	33	34	35
Forecast	150	100	50	50
MPS	169	169	22	0
Backlog (Orders booked)	110	80	5	15

The rough cut capacity plan (RCCP) calculates the capacity, often in standard hours, required to achieve the MPS. It is based on the MPS.

INTERFACES

The master schedule (MS) is a key link in the manufacturing planning and control chain. The MS interfaces with marketing, distribution planning, production planning, and capacity planning. It also drives the material requirements planning (MRP) system as shown in Figure 4-1.

Master scheduling calculates the quantity required to meet demand requirements from all sources. Table 4-2 shows a case in which the distribution requirements are the gross requirements for the MS. Material requirements planning, as described in Chapter 10, is used to calculate the quantity required. For example, the 15 units in inventory at the end of Week 3 are subtracted from the gross requirements, 85 units, of Week 4 to determine the net requirements of 70 units for Week 4.

Table 4-2
Warehouse Requirements

		Week							
Warehouse		1	2	3	4	5	6	7	8
Toronto		15	15	15	15	15	15	15	15
Los Angeles		30	30	30	30	30	30	35	35
St. Louis		20	10	20	20	10	20	20	20
Atlanta			20		20		20		20
Dallas		15	—	15	—	15	—	15	—
Total		80	75	80	85	70	85	85	90
Master Schedule									
Gross Requirements		80	75	80	85	70	85	85	90
POH*	250	170	95	15					
Net Requirements					70	70	85	85	90

Beginning inventory = 250

The MS enables marketing to make legitimate delivery commitments to field warehouses and final customers. It enables production to evaluate capacity requirements in a more detailed manner. It also provides the necessary information for production and marketing to agree on a course of action when customer requests cannot be met by normal capacity. Finally, it provides to management the opportunity to ascertain whether the business plan and its strategic objectives will be achieved.

Before describing the activities involved in creating and managing the MS, we examine the different organizational environments in which master scheduling takes place. These environments are determined in large measure by an organization's strategic response to the interests of customers and to the actions of competitors. An understanding of these environments, of the bill of material, and of the planning horizon is essential to the first stage of master planning activities—designing the master schedule.

THE ENVIRONMENT

The competitive strategy of an organization may be any of the following:

A.   Make finished items to stock (sell from finished goods inventory)
B.   Assemble final products to order and make components, 20 subassemblies, and options to stock
C.   Custom design and make-to-order

The competitive nature of the market and the strategy of the organization determine which of the MS alternates it should use. It is not unusual for an organization to have different strategies for different product lines and, thus, use different MS approaches.

Make-to-Stock

The competitive strategy of make-to-stock emphasizes immediate delivery of reasonably priced off-the-shelf standard items. In this environment the MPS is the anticipated build schedule of the items required to maintain the finished goods at the desired level. Quantities on the schedule are based on manufacturing economics and the forecast demand as well as desired safety stock levels. An end item bill of material (BOM) (described later in the chapter) is used in this environment. Items may be produced either on a mass production (continuous or repetitive) line or in batch production. Case I in Figure 4-2 represents this situation. Note that the MPS is the same as the final assembly schedule (FAS) in this case.

Assemble-, Finish-, or Package-to-Order

In this environment, options, subassemblies and components are either produced or purchased to stock. The competitive strategy is to be able to supply a large variety of final product configurations from standard components and subassemblies within a relatively short lead time. For example, an automobile may be ordered with or without air conditioning, an option, and a fast-food restaurant will deliver your hamburger with or without lettuce. This environment requires a forecast of options as well as of total demand. Thus, there is an MPS for the options, accessories, and common components as well as a final assembly schedule (FAS). This is Case II in Figure 4-2.

Figure 4-2
Some Possible Relationships

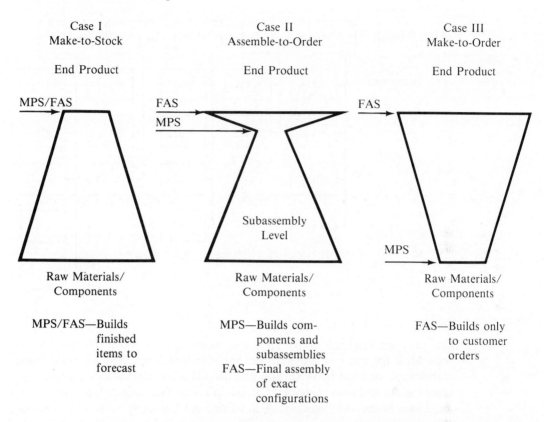

Case I	Case II	Case III
Make-to-Stock	Assemble-to-Order	Make-to-Order

MPS/FAS—Builds finished items to forecast

MPS—Builds components and subassemblies
FAS—Final assembly of exact configurations

FAS—Builds only to customer orders

The advantage of this approach is that many different final products can be produced from relatively few subassemblies and components. This reduces inventory substantially. Figure 4-3 represents such a situation. Each final product contains four major subassemblies and a component. However, each subassembly and the component has different variations (alternates). There are four different variations of SA1, two of SA2, four of SA3, three of SA4, and five of C, which results in $4 \times 2 \times 4 \times 3 \times 5$ or 480 final product configurations. Assembling to order enables the firm to stock $4 + 2 + 4 + 3 + 5$ or 18 different items rather than 480.

Custom Design and Make-to-Order

In many situations the final design of an item is part of what is purchased. The final product is usually a combination of standard items and items custom designed to meet the special needs of the customer. Combined material handling and manufacturing processing systems are an example, special trucks for

Figure 4-3
Final Products with Subassemblies and Components

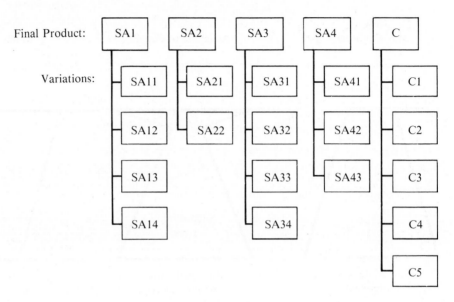

off-the-road work on utility lines and facilities are another. Thus, there is one MPS for the raw material and the standard items that are purchased, fabricated, or built to stock and another MPS for the custom engineering, fabrication, and final assembly. Case III in Figure 4-2 represents this situation. Kickham Boiler and Engineering, described in Chapter 1, exemplifies such an organization.

As we proceed with the discussion of the policies and procedures of master scheduling and its relationship to rough cut capacity planning (RCCP), we will examine further the relationship of these environments to the MPS task.

THE BILL OF MATERIAL

An inclusive definition of a final product includes a list of the items, ingredients, or materials needed to assemble, mix, or produce that end product. This list is called a *bill of material* (BOM). The BOM can take several forms and be used in many ways. It is created as part of the design process and is used by manufacturing engineers to determine which items should be purchased and which items should be manufactured. Production control and inventory planning uses the BOM in conjunction with the master production schedule to determine the items for which purchase requisitions and production orders must be released. Accounting uses it to cost the product.

The BOM is a basic required input for many production planning and control activities, and its accuracy is crucial. In computerized systems the BOM data is contained in *BOM files*, a data base organized by the *BOM processor* that also produces the BOM in the various formats required by the organization.

Single Level Bill of Material

The way in which the BOM files are organized and presented is called the structure of the bill of material. The simplest format is a *single level BOM*, as depicted in Table 4-3. It consists of a list of all components needed to make the end item, including for each component (1) a unique part number, (2) a short verbal description, (3) the quantity needed for each single end item, and (4) the part's unit of measure.

Table 4-3
Single Level Bill of Material for Assembled Lamp

ABC Lamp Company Bill of Material, Part LA01-Lamp			
Part Number	Description	Quantity for Each Assembly	Unit of Measure
B100	Base assembly	1	Each
S100	14″ Black shade	1	Each
A100	Socket assembly	1	Each

Multilevel Tree Structure and Levels

While the single level BOM is sufficient when a product is assembled at one time from a set of purchased parts and raw materials, it does not adequately describe a product that has subassemblies. If we decided to make the base and socket assemblies in Table 4-3, then each of those would have subitems that were purchased or manufactured. To illustrate the product structure, we can draw a "tree" having several levels, as shown in Figure 4-4. Note that by convention the final product is at Level 0, and the level numbers increase as one looks down the tree.

Corresponding to this tree structure is the multilevel BOM shown in Table 4-4. Each part or assembly is given a unique number. To aid in understanding the structure, the numbers for the components of each subassembly are indented under the respective subassembly numbers. When a component is used in more than one subassembly a common parts bill may be produced for use by inventory planning. In this type bill there is only one occurrence of the item along with its total quantity per final assembly.

Figure 4-4
Multilevel Tree Structure

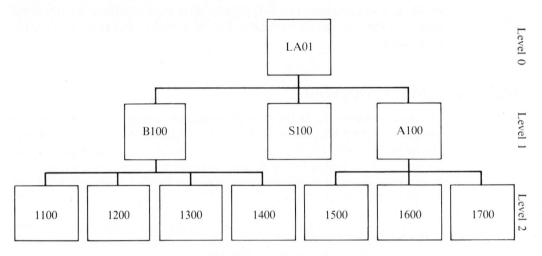

Table 4-4
Indented Bill of Material

ABC Lamp Company			
Bill of Material, Part LA01			
Part Number	Description	Quantity for Each Assembly	Unit of Measure
B100	Base assembly	1	Each
1100	Finished shaft	1	Each
1200	7″-Diameter steel plate	1	Each
1300	Hub	1	Each
1400	1/4-20 Screws	4	Each
S100	14″ Black shade	1	Each
A100	Socket assembly	1	Each
1500	Steel holder	1	Each
1600	One-way socket	1	Each
1700	Wiring assembly	1	Each

If the wiring assembly were itself a subassembly, then its components would be listed. On the indented BOM, the component part numbers would be further indented, as shown in Table 4-5. As you see, the multilevel product structure is really made up of building blocks of single level product trees; that is, a BOM can be drawn up for each subassembly and only these single level bills need be retained. This is important when producing many different end items that have common subassemblies. We do not need to change every end item BOM when an engineering change takes place in a single common subassembly.

Table 4-5
A Level Three Bill of Material

ABC Lamp Company Bill of Material, Part LA01			
Part Number	Description	Quantity for Each Assembly	Unit of Measure
B100	Base assembly	1	Each
1100	Finished shaft	1	Each
2100	3/8″ Steel tubing	26	Inches
1200	7″-Diameter steel plate	1	Each
1300	Hub	1	Each
1400	1/4-20 Screws	4	Each
S100	14″ Black shade	1	Each
A100	Socket assembly	1	Each
1500	Steel holder	1	Each
1600	One-way socket	1	Each
1700	Wiring assembly	1	Each
2200	16-Gauge lamp cord	12	Feet
2300	Standard plug terminal	1	Each

To illustrate this and several other real-life complexities, let's assume that we manufacture lamps with three different shades, two alternate base plates, and two types of sockets. Our original lamp was designated LA01. Working with the different components, we now can have 12 different final products. To clarify this, we can produce a common parts bill in a matrix format, as shown in Table 4-6. An examination of the matrix shows that some parts are common to all models. To ease the planning task, we could group together the wiring assembly and the finished shaft with a new part number, say 4000, on the bill of material. Although these components are produced independently of one another, they can be grouped as common parts on the BOM for administrative purposes. This part number is never stocked and so it is called a *phantom* part. Its only purpose is to reduce the number of items on the BOM. We can go further with the concept of restructuring our BOMs and, for some products, create new numbers to represent new subassemblies (for example, subassemblies of plate, hub, and screws) in order to shorten lead times.

Another type of BOM is often useful in planning and handling engineering charges. It is referred to as a *planning bill*, a *pseudo bill*, a *phantom bill*, a *super bill*, or a *family bill*. From the matrix form of the summary bill (Table 4-6), a simplified product structure diagram (Figure 4-5) can be created for the family of lamps that consisted of pseudo subassemblies—base assemblies, shades, and socket assemblies. For each of these, in place of the quantity for each unit assembled, the percentage split for each type of component is stated. Now, as we plan for a total of 10,000 lamps for each month, this planning bill can be used to derive the number of each type of component to build. Furthermore, if we decide to change to, say, a 16-inch green shade, only this single BOM, this modular bill, needs to be altered.

Table 4-6
Planning Bill of Material in Matrix Format, Part LA01 (Quantity for Each Assembly)

Part Number	Description	Unit of Measure	Model											
			01	02	03	04	05	06	07	08	09	10	11	12
1100	Finished shaft	Each	1	1	1	1	1	1	1	1	1	1	1	1
2100	3/8″ Steel tubing	Inches	26	26	26	26	26	26	26	26	26	26	26	26
1200	7″-Diameter steel plate	Each	1		1	1	1	1	1	1	1	1	1	1
1201	8″-Diameter steel plate	Each		1										
1300	Hub	Each	1	1	1	1	1	1	1	1	1	1	1	1
1400	1/4-20 Screws	Each	4	4	4	4	4	4	4	4	4	4	4	4
S100	14″ Black shade	Each	1	1			1	1		1				
S101	15″ White shade	Each			1				1		1	1		
S102	15″ Cream shade	Each				1							1	1
1500	Steel holder	Each	1	1	1	1	1	1	1	1	1	1	1	1
1600	One-way socket	Each	1	1	1	1		1	1	1		1	1	
1601	Three-way socket	Each					1				1			1
1700	Wiring assembly	Each	1	1	1	1	1	1	1	1	1	1	1	1
2200	16-Gauge lamp cord	Feet	12	12	12	12	12	12	12	12	12	12	12	12
2300	Standard plug terminal	Each	1	1	1	1	1	1	1	1	1	1	1	1
B100	Base assembly—7″	Each	1		1	1	1	1	1	1	1	1	1	1
B101	Base assembly—8″	Each		1										
A100	Socket assembly— one-way	Each	1	1	1	1		1	1	1		1	1	
A101	Socket assembly— three-way	Each					1				1			1

Figure 4-5
Simplified Product Structure Diagram

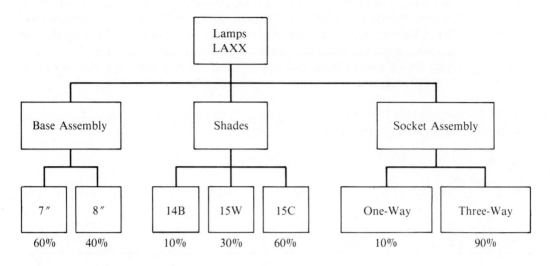

Option Overplanning

If the exact percentage split is uncertain, the percentage of each option can be increased to cover the uncertainty. This results in the total being more than 100 percent, as illustrated in Figure 4-6. The amount added can be calculated in the same manner as safety stock (see Chapter 5). Using this procedure to cover possible high side demand for each option is called *option overplanning*.

Figure 4-6
Option Overplanning

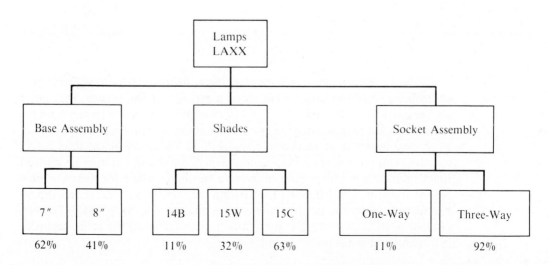

THE PLANNING HORIZON

A principle of planning is that a plan must cover a period at least equal to the time required to accomplish it. This means that the MS planning horizon must be at least as long as the lead time required to fabricate the MS items. This includes production and procurement time as well as engineering time in a custom design environment. Delivery-to-customer response times (lead times) in the different production environments are illustrated in Figure 4-7.

Figure 4-7
Delivery-to-Customer Response Times

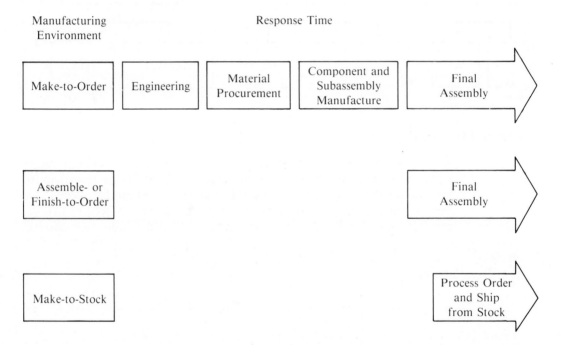

Many organizations divide the planning horizon into periods with different controls on schedule changes. The closer a period is to the present, the tighter are the controls on schedule changes. For example, *time fences* (boundaries between different periods) may be established at the fourth week and the eighth week (two months), as shown in Table 4-7. The location of the time fences and the nature of the approval required depend on the situation. Varying lead times, market conditions, and processing flexibility make for different time fences, sometimes at different plants within the same firm. Time fences should be tailored to specific product groups as lead time may vary widely between groups. In all cases, the MS is the vehicle for coordinating the achievement of marketing and manufacturing goals.

Table 4-7
MS Planning Horizons

Period	Time Horizon	Conditions	Approval Required
A	0 to 4 weeks	Emergency	Top management
B	4 to 8 weeks	Dramatic shift in requirements	Marketing-manufacturing negotiation
C	Beyond 8 weeks	Normal	Master scheduler

In Period C (a time horizon beyond two months in Table 4-7) the MPS is consistent with the production plan. A good production plan will make preparation of the MS straightforward in this time frame.

In Period B (a time horizon of four to eight weeks in Table 4-7) things become a bit sticky when operating at full capacity. A zero sum game exists; that is, any additions to the schedule must be counterbalanced by comparable deletions or increases in capacity. Changes in demand patterns, unusual orders, or equipment failures may warrant changes in the MPS. These changes are usually negotiated between marketing and manufacturing with the master scheduler determining their feasibility before the final decision. The product mix may change but not the production rate.

In Period A (a time horizon of zero to four weeks in Table 4-7) only an act of God or top management can change the MPS.

As the time for order execution and manufacturing approaches, labor and material are committed. A change in the schedule can be disruptive and costly, and the costs must be compared with the benefits of the change. Following time-fence-control guidelines, which reflect realistic lead time constraints and competititve factors, will result in an MPS that promotes manufacturing stability and productivity while providing reasonable flexibility in meeting marketing demands. However, the competitive environment may force decisions to restructure the BOM, to develop a modular BOM, to produce to stock at a higher level in the BOM, or to move time fences.

DESIGNING, CREATING, AND MANAGING THE MASTER SCHEDULE

Master scheduling activities take place in three stages: (1) designing the MS, (2) creating the MS, and (3) controlling the MS.

A. Designing the MS includes the following steps:
   1. Select the items; that is, select the levels in the BOM structure to be represented by the items scheduled (both components and final assemblies may be included).
   2. Organize the MS by product groups.

3. Determine the planning horizon, the time fences, and the related operational guides.
4. Select the method for calculating and presenting the available-to-promise (ATP) information.

B.   Creating the MS includes the following steps:
1. Obtain the necessary informational inputs, including the forecast, the backlog (customer commitments), and the inventory on hand.
2. Prepare the initial draft of the master production schedule (MPS).
3. Develop the rough cut capacity requirements plan (RCCP).
4. If required, increase capacity or revise the initial draft of the MPS to obtain a feasible schedule.

C.   Controlling the MS includes the following activities:
1. Track actual production and compare it to planned production to determine if the planned MPS quantities and delivery promises are being met.
2. Calculate the available-to-promise to determine if an incoming order can be promised in a specific period.
3. Calculate the projected on hand to determine if planned production is sufficient to fill expected future orders.
4. Use the results of the preceeding activities to determine if the MPS or capacity should be revised.

Up to this point, this chapter has emphasized MS design factors and practices. Now we are ready to discuss preparing the initial draft of the master schedule—creating the MS. However, as you will note, creating and controlling activities are interwoven. Remember, the MPS lists by period the planned quantity of each MPS item to be built. The MS includes the demand, the available-to-promise, the projected on hand, and the MPS quantity by period.

Creating the Master Schedule

Let's consider creating the MS in a make-to-stock environment with no safety stock. Table 4-8 provides the type of information available for a product group. It reveals that Product 3 has sufficient inventory to cover the requirements of Weeks 32, 33, and 34 but not Week 35. Product 2 has sufficient inventory to cover the requirements for Weeks 32 and 33 but not Week 34. Product 1 must be produced in Week 32. At this point there is no production scheduled yet, so the POH merely equals the POH of the preceeding period minus the forecast requirements. An MPS quantity should be planned in the first week that an item has a negative POH. Thus, Product 1 must be scheduled in Week 32, Product 2 in Week 34, and Product 3 in Week 35. In some situations an organization may decide that an MPS quantity should be scheduled whenever the POH reaches some safety level, 25 units for example. In the latter case, production is planned in the first period that the POH is less than the safety stock level.

Based on a weighted average capacity of 180 units per week, the first plan calls for manufacturing Product 1 in Weeks 32 and 33, manufacturing Product 2 in Week 34 and the first part of Week 35, and manufacturing Product 3 in the last part of Week 35, as shown in Table 4-9. Calculation of the POH quantities demonstrates that the plan will cover forecast requirements.

The POH for the first week equals the beginning inventory plus the MPS quantity minus the forecast, and, for all remaining weeks, it equals the POH of the preceeding period plus the MPS quantity minus the forecast requirements of the current period. Thus, the POH of Product 1 in Week 32 equals $10 + 180 - 150 = 40$ units; and in Week 33 it equals $40 + 180 - 100 = 120$. The other POH quantities are calculated in the same manner. The next question is, "Is there sufficient capacity to produce the MPS quantities?"

Table 4-8
Calculating the POH Inventory for Product Group A

		Week		
		32	33	34	35
Product 1					
Forecast		150	100	50	50
MPS					
POH	10	− 140	− 240	− 290	− 340
Product 2					
Forecast		20	40	60	90
MPS					
POH	70	50	10	− 50	− 140
Product 3					
Forecast		30	30	35	45
MPS					
POH	100	70	40	5	− 40

Table 4-9
The Master Schedule for Product Group A

		Week			
		32	33	34	35	Total
Product 1						
Forecast		150	100	50	50	350
MPS		180	180			360
POH	10	40	120	70	20	
Product 2						
Forecast		20	40	60	90	210
MPS				180	36	216
POH	70	50	10	130	76	
Product 3						
Forecast		30	30	35	45	140
MPS					144	144
POH	100	70	40	5	104	

Rough Cut Capacity Planning (RCCP).   RCCP calculates the critical work center capacity requirements for all items on the MPS. It provides an early warning of insufficient capacity and the need for capacity actions. Capacity in some work centers—the paint shop, for example—may be well beyond that ever required, while capacity in other work centers—welding and heat treating, for example—may be relatively low and a frequent bottleneck. Planning should focus attention on the potential bottleneck work centers. *Capacity actions* is the term used to describe rectifying a situation in which the available capacity is less than the required capacity.

Figure 4-8 shows the relationship of the various stages of capacity planning—resource capacity planning (RCP), rough cut capacity planning (RCCP), and capacity requirements planning (CRP)—to the specific production processes of a product group. (RCP was described in Chapter 2, RCCP is described in Chapter 12, and CRP is described in Chapter 13.) Table 4-10 highlights the salient characteristics of these different stages of capacity planning.

Figure 4-8
Stages of Capacity Planning

| Type of Planning | Items on Plan | Tree Diagram |

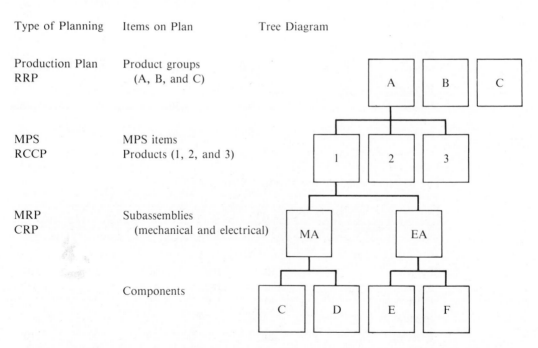

The primary differences between RCP and RCCP planning are that the latter plans in smaller time increments, usually weekly rather than monthly, and considers the production lead time of the various components and subassemblies required to produce the products on the MPS.

Table 4-10
Capacity Planning Stages

Stages	Input	Outputs
Resource requirements planning (RRP)	Production plan (product groups) Resource profile (bill of labor, capacity bill)	Resource requirements by month
Rough cut capacity planning (RCCP)	Resource capacity available MPS Product load profile with lead-time offset	Rough cut capacity requirements by week
Capacity requirements planning (CRP)	Material requirements plan (MRP) Capacity available Inventory status	Capacity requirement plans by week or day

Revising the MPS. This section reveals once again that control takes place in the planning process. An initial MPS is developed for Products 1, 2, and 3 of Product Group A from the production plan for Product Group A as shown in Table 4-11. The capacity required by this initial MPS is shown in Table 4-12. Calculation of these requirements is described in Chapter 13.

Table 4-11
Production Plan and MPS, Group A, October

Group	October
A	720
B	240
C	160

	Group A, Master Production Schedule, October Week					
Product	32	33	34	35	Total	Percent
1	180	180			360	50
2			180	36	216	30
3				144	144	20
Total	180	180	180	180	720	100

Table 4-12
Capacity Report, Assembly Work Center
Demonstrated Capacity: 58 Standard Hours

	Week			
Capacity	32	33	34	35
Required	61.56	61.56	52.96	47.73
Shortfall	3.56	3.56	−5.08	−10.27

The comparison of capacity requirements to available capacity reveals if the present MPS is feasible. Table 4-12 shows a shortfall 3.56 hours of assembly capacity in both Weeks 32 and 33 and surplus capacity in Weeks 34 and 35. This presents the master scheduler with the following options:

1. Increase capacity in Weeks 32 and 33.
2. Reduce production quantities in Weeks 32 and 33 and increase production quantities in Weeks 34 and 35.
3. Some combination of Options 1 and 2.

In this case the choice is Option 2, as shown in Table 4-13, which also reveals that sufficient capacity is available with the revised MPS. The revised MPS quantities were obtained by scheduling the maximum possible quantity of Product 1 in Weeks 32 and 33 and completing those requirements in Week 34. The remaining requirements for Products 2 and 3 were roughly balanced between Weeks 34 and 35, producing Product 2 first. The resulting POH values are shown in Table 4-14, which reveals that sufficient units will be available to cover forecast demand for Product 1. Similar calculations will reveal that the forecast demands for Products 2 and 3 are also covered. Later, as orders arrive, it may be necessary to revise the MPS again if actual orders are substantially different from the forecast on which the production plan and the MPS are based.

Many organizations have computerized the calculation of rough cut capacity requirements while others have standard forms and procedures that facilitate manual computations. In any event the rough cut capacity required to implement the MPS must be compared to available capacity to determine if any capacity actions are required. Table 4-13 reveals that the MPS is within the capacity constraints of the assembly department. It is also necessary to

Table 4-13
Revised MPS and Capacity Requirements

Master Production Schedule				
	Week			
Product	32	33	34	35
1	169	169	22	0
2			160	56
3				144

Assembly Department, Group A Capacity Requirements				
	Week			
Product	32	33	34	35
1	57.80	57.80	7.52	
2			47.04	16.46
3				37.15
Total	57.80	57.80	54.56	53.61

Table 4-14
Revised Master Schedule with POH

		Week			
		32	33	34	35
Product 1					
Forecast		150	100	50	50
MPS		169	169	22	0
POH	10	29	98	70	20

verify that the plan does not require more than the available capacity in the departments used in the manufacture of subassemblies and components.

At first glance this may seem to be a rather complicated procedure. However, once it is understood and the appropriate software obtained or developed, it readily provides information extremely valuable for planning. Once this initial revised feasible MPS is developed, creating the master schedule is completed.

Controlling the Master Schedule

The MS serves as a control in three distinct ways. Actual production is compared to the MPS to determine if the plan is being met. The available-to-promise is calculated to determine if an incoming order can be promised for delivery in a specific period. The projected on hand is calculated to determine if the supply is sufficient to fill expected future orders.

The Available-to-Promise (ATP).   Promising delivery to customers should be based on what is or will be available (not committed). *Available-to-promise* (ATP) is defined by the *APICS Dictionary* (1987) as "The uncommitted portion of a company's inventory or planned production. This figure is normally calculated from the master production schedule and is maintained as a tool for customer order promising." However, when one is informed that there are "25 units available-to-promise in Week 7 and 20 units available-to-promise in Week 8," the meanings are not clear until the method of calculation is known. The three basic methods of computing the ATP are the discrete, the cumulative without lookahead, and the cumulative with lookahead. Descriptions of these methods follow.

Calculating the Discrete ATP.   The discrete available-to-promise (ATP:D) is computed as follows:

1. For the first period, the available-to-promise is the sum of the beginning inventory plus the MPS for the first period (in this case zero) minus customer commitments for the first period and all periods following the first period up to, but not including, the next period for which an MPS quantity has been planned.

2. For all periods after the first, there are two possibilities:
   a. If a master production quantity has been scheduled for the period, the available-to-promise is the quantity scheduled minus all customer commitments for the period and for all following periods up to, but not including, the next period for which a master production quantity has been scheduled.
   b. If no master production quantity has been scheduled for the period, the available-to-promise is zero, even if deliveries in the period have been promised. The promised shipments often are shown as backlog (customer commitments) in the period with the most recent production (MPS).

As an example, suppose after the MPS has been constructed, total actual orders received (total customer commitments) for Product 1 are as follows: 110 units for delivery by the end of Week 32, 80 units for delivery by the end of Week 33, 5 units for delivery by the end of Week 34, and 15 units for delivery by the end of Week 35. The discrete ATP of Product 1 in Week 32 equals $10 + 169 - 110 = 69$ units. The discrete ATP in Week 34 equals $22 - 20$ (there is no MPS in Week 35) = 2 units. The discrete ATPs for all products are shown in Table 4-15.

Table 4-15
Master Schedule
Showing a Discrete Display of the Available-to-Promise (ATP:D)

		Week		
	32	33	34	35
Product 1				
Beginning on hand inventory = 10 units				
MPS		169	169	22	0
B*		110	80	5	15
ATP:D	10	69	89	2	0
Product 2				
Beginning inventory = 70 units				
MPS		0	0	160	56
B*		35	20	45	24
ATP:D	15**	0**	0**	115	32
Product 3				
Beginning inventory = 100 units				
MPS		0	0	0	144
B*		13	15	10	104
ATP:D	62**	0	0	0	40

*Backlog, commitments to customers; some organizations record customer commitments only in an MPS period and show actual delivery date promises on the shipping schedule. Thus, a B of at least 55 would have been shown as existing prior to Week 32 for Product 2.
**This value would be associated with the previous MPS period.

If in addition to the 110 units of Product 1 that had already been promised for delivery in Week 32, an order for 15 more units was received for delivery in Week 32, the ATP would be 54 in Week 32 and all the other ATPs would remain the same.

Note that in computing the ATP:D it is not necessary to have the forecast and the projected on hand inventory in the master schedule. That is because at this time the master scheduler is not creating a master schedule, but is, instead, managing an existing schedule. The master scheduler is promising delivery to customers of units that will be available either from units already on hand when construction of the master schedule began or from units scheduled to be built in accordance with the master production schedule. Therefore, the forecast and POH are not included in the tables that follow.

Calculating the Cumulative ATP. The cumulative method can be used without or with the "lookahead" calculation. We describe both methods. Table 4-16 is an example of the cumulative calculation of the ATP without lookahead (ATP:WOL) for Products 1, 2, and 3.

The cumulative ATP without lookahead equals the ATP in the preceeding period plus the MPS, minus the backlog (customer commitments) in the period being considerd. Thus, in Week 32 the ATP:WOL for Product 1 is $10 + 169 - 110 = 69$. In Week 33 it equals $69 + 169 - 80 = 158$. The salient difference between this method and the discrete method is that the ATP in any period

Table 4-16
Master Schedule
Example of the Cumulative ATP without Lookahead (ATP:WOL)

		Week			
	31	32	33	34	35
Product 1					
Beginning on hand inventory = 10 units					
MPS		169	169	22	0
B*		110	80	5	15
ATP:WOL	10	69	158	175	160
Product 2					
Beginning inventory = 70 units					
MPS		0	0	160	56
B*		35	20	45	24
ATP:WOL	70	35	15	130	162
Product 3					
Beginning inventory = 100 units					
MPS		0	0	0	144
B*		13	15	10	104
ATP:WOL	100	87	72	62	102

*Backlog, commitments to customers

is likely to *include units also included in the ATP of other periods.* For example, the 158 unit ATP of Week 33 includes the 69 units in the ATP of Week 32, which are also included in the ATP of all other weeks. Furthermore, when there is no lookahead procedure, the ATP for a week may include units committed to fill requirements for a later week. For example, 15 of the units in the ATP of Week 34 are committed to customer orders promised in Week 35. Although some planners may function well with such a system because they understand the data and are able to extract accurate information from it, the data is misleading. The lookahead approach resolves this problem. Table 4-17 is an example of the cumulative with lookahead calculation of the ATP (ATP:WL).

Table 4-17
Master Schedule
Example of the Cumulative ATP with Lookahead (ATP:WL)

	Week				
	31	32	33	34	35
Product 1					
Beginning on hand inventory = 10 units					
MPS		169	169	22	0
B*		110	80	5	15
ATP:WL	10	69	158	160	160
Product 2					
Beginning inventory = 70 units					
MPS		0	0	160	56
B*		35	20	45	24
ATP:WL	15**	15**	15**	130	162
Product 3					
Beginning inventory = 100 units					
MPS		0	0	0	144
B*		13	15	10**	104
ATP:WL	62**	62**	62**	62	102

*Backlog, commitments to customers
**This value is associated with the previous MPS period.

The difference between this method and the cumulative ATP without lookahead is that units produced in one period and committed for use in a future period are omitted from the ATP in all periods preceeding that in which they are promised. The ATP of Table 4-17 gives a very clear picture: there are 62 units of Product 3 that can be promised for any of the Weeks 32 through 34, and a total of 102 units, including the 62 available earlier, that can be promised for delivery in Week 35. The ATP:WL of a period equals the ATP:WL of the preceeding period plus the MPS of the period minus the backlog of the period minus the sum of the differences between the backlogs and master production schedules of all future periods until, but not including, the period from which point production exceeds the backlogs. This is shown by the following model. Although this description and the following model seem cumbersome, the actual calculations usually are not. This is because proper management of the MS, including the MPS and promises to customers, usually will prevent the backlog from exceeding the MPS for an extended time. Fogarty and Barringer (1984) have described a simple algorithm and computer program for calculating the cumulative ATP with lookahead.

ATP:WL Model: $\quad ATP_i = ATP_{i-1} + MPS_i - B_i - \Sigma(B_j - MPS_j)$
$\quad\quad\quad\quad\quad\quad\quad$ until $\Sigma MPS_j > \Sigma B_j$, where $j > i$

Consuming the Forecast. This chapter previously described how to calculate the POH without changing the forecast or the MPS. Under the *consuming-the-forecast* concept, the master schedule presents the forecast as only the quantity yet to be ordered by customers, as opposed to the initial forecast. Thus, each time an order is received, the forecast quantity on the MS may be changed. Two different situations exist when using this approach.

In the first case, the existing total sales forecast still is seen as an accurate forecast of the total eventual units to be sold for delivery in the period. The revised forecast equals the original forecast minus the orders received (the backlog) for the period; the forecast is "consumed" by the orders received. This situation is illustrated in Weeks 32, 33, and 34 of Table 4-18. The orders received have been subtracted from the forecast. For example, the forecast for Week 32 now equals 150 (the initial forecast) − 110 = 40. The forecast now represents the remaining orders expected, and the POH equals the POH of the preceeding week plus the MPS minus the sum of the forecast and the backlog (B). For example, the POH of Week 34 equals 98 + 22 − (45 + 5) = 70. (The resulting value of the POH is the same as when not consuming the forecast but is calculated differently.)

Table 4-18
Revised Master Schedule with POH

		Week			
	31	32	33	34	35
Product 1					
Forecast*		150	100	50	50
Forecast		40	20	45	45
MPS		169	169	22	0
B		110	80	5	15
POH	10	29	98	70	10
ATP:WL	10	69	158	160	160

Initial forecast prior to receipt of orders

The second situation differs in that the existing total forecast no longer is viewed as accurate. For example, suppose an unexpected order is received from a new customer and there is no reason to believe that the regular customers will not order as forecast. This situation is illustrated in Week 35 of Table 4-18. Ten of the units ordered for delivery in Week 35 come from a new customer; the planner decides that there will still be additional orders for 45 units. Thus, only 5 units of the 15 ordered are subtracted from the forecast. This also requires that another 10 units be subtracted from the POH in Week 35 as the original forecast for Week 35 has effectively been increased by 10 units. For example, the POH of Week 35 now equals $70 + 0 - (45 + 15) = 10$. Thus, the POH for Week 35 is different from that shown in Table 4-14. Consuming the forecast is an effective method of recognizing either potential stockouts or excessive inventory and the need to revise the MPS. The likelihood of excessive inventory would be spotted when present sales suggest that eventual total orders will be less than the existing forecast.

THE FINAL ASSEMBLY SCHEDULE

The final assembly schedule (FAS) is a statement of those final products that are to be assembled from MPS items in specific time periods. In some organizations—those producing power tools, for example—MPS items and final products are identical, and one document serves as both the MPS and the FAS. In many other situations, especially when there are many more final products than there are items at the next BOM level, the two are separate and distinct.

In some cases final products differ only by the labeling or packaging of the same MPS item. In others painting or finishes may constitute the difference. In still others a vast difference may exist in the transformation of items into a variety of final products. In each of these cases an FAS that is distinct from but consistent with the MPS must be prepared. In the manufacture of automatic washers, for example, the motor, transmissions, control units, consoles, tubs, sets of assembly hardware, and various optional accessories would be MPS items, and the different models available to the customer would be final assemblies. Thus, the manufacture of motors can be authorized long before each motor is committed to the assembly of a particular model. Since the FAS is constrained by the availability of those items scheduled on the MPS plus those in inventory, the MPS and the FAS must be coordinated. This is true for both purchased and manufactured components.

Table 4-19 is an example showing the relationship between the FAS for an assembly, A, made-to-order, and an MPS for two optional subassemblies, SA1 and SA2, which are made-to-stock with option overplanning. The assembly may be ordered with either an SA1 or an SA2 subassembly. Sales records reveal that each has an equal probability of being selected; each has received a maximum of 60 percent of the orders in any week. Thus, with an FAS for a maximum of ten A's in Week 2, no beginning inventory for any item, and a lead time of one week for subassemblies, the MPS calls for six each of SA1 and SA2 in Week 1. Three possible demand combinations exist: five each of SA1 and SA2, four of SA1 and six of SA2, and six of SA1 and four of SA2. Two subassemblies will not be used immediately; they will be carried in stock to the next week.

Week 1 passes: Actual orders are for ten A's, four with SA1 and six with SA2. Two SA1's are in inventory at the end of the week. This results in an MPS calling for producing four SA1's and six SA2's in Week 2 to assemble a maximum of ten A's in Week 3. The FAS and the MPS are coordinated.

Table 4-19
Coordinated FAS and MPS

Final Assembly Schedule Week			Master Production Schedule Week		
Item	1	2	3	Item	1	2	3
A		10	10	SA1	6	4	
				SA2	6	6	

In an assemble-to-order environment, the FAS frequently is stated in terms of individual customer orders and must be consistent with the shipping schedule. In a make-to-stock environment, the FAS is a commitment to produce specific quantities of catalog final products. The shipping schedule depends on available inventory and available capacity. Capacity is required for assembly and for any items that may be controlled by the FAS and not the MPS. Examples are painting, packaging, crating, and preparing shipping documents.

In any event, authorization of the final assembly schedule should be held to the last possible moment. This provides the greatest flexibility in meeting actual demand and improves customer service. Since assembly lead time and MPS item availability constrain the FAS, any planning and design that reduce this lead time and increase flexibility aid in achieving customer service objectives.

Preparation, measuring of actual output, and control of the FAS should rest with the master scheduler. This enables one individual to control all demands on resources and coordinate MPS items and the FAS, order entry items, and order-promising activities.

The Master Scheduler

Most organizations should have a master scheduler. This individual is the link between marketing, distribution, engineering, manufacturing, and planning. The tasks of the master scheduler include the following:

1. Provide delivery promise dates for incoming orders; match actual requirements with the master schedule as they materialize.
2. Evaluate the impact of top-down inputs, such as a request for the introduction of a new product in much less than the normal delivery time.

3. Evaluate the impact of bottom-up inputs, such as anticipated delay reports from the shop or purchasing indicating that particular components will not be available as scheduled or that planned production rates are not being attained.
4. Revise the master schedule when necessary because of lack of material or lack of capacity.
5. Call basic conflicts of demand and capacity to the attention of other members of management, especially marketing and manufacturing, who need to participate in resolving the problems.

Whether or not a firm has someone formally designated as the master scheduler, the tasks are essential. Combining them under the jurisdiction of one individual improves the likelihood that they will be coordinated and managed properly. Most importantly, it provides a focal point for the required coordination of marketing, manufacturing, distribution, and planning as well as a place to look for answers when things are not going as planned.

MPS Information Systems and Analysis

The complexity of most manufacturing environments requires a computerized production planning and control system with human interfaces at appropriate decision points. As noted previously, the master scheduler requires such an interface. The requirement for computer assisted planning is due to a combination of the number of items on the MPS, the large number of subassemblies and components, and the magnitude of recording and processing inventory transactions, material requirements, and capacity requirements. Today, there are literally hundreds of commercial software systems available. Some are for use with mainframe computers, others for use with minicomputers, and a growing number for use with personal computers.

The installation and availability of such a computer system often allows the organization to perform what-if analyses to answer questions such as: (1) What will be the effect of a shift in product mix on capacity requirements? (2) What will be the effect of a 10 percent increase in demand on capacity requirements? Answers to these questions, available from a computerized simulation run, will enable management to prepare plans for such contingencies.

SUMMARY AND COMMENTS

Although the preparation and maintenance of all the elements of the master schedule may be complex in some situations, the principles and concepts are not. All have been developed in practice and are well documented in the literature and have been discussed in this chapter.

The MPS is a vital link in the operations planning and control system due to its links (interfaces) with many other activities and systems in manufacturing, marketing, and engineering (product and process design). The items on the MPS, in particular their level in the BOM, should be consistent with the organization's competitive strategy. The efficacy of the master scheduling process and the MPS requires an accurate and reliable capacity planning system.

The master scheduler plays a key role in the master scheduling function. This individual plays a key role in marketing and manufacturing working to the same plan.

Available-to-promise information is very useful for responding to customer requests for delivery. POH data is very helpful in indicating when the MPS is inadequate or will result in excessive inventory.

If actual production is consistently below the planned MPS, it suggests that actual capacity is less than the "capacity available" used in creating the MPS. And if actual orders completed in each period consistently differ substantially from those in the MPS, it suggests that the priority plan established by the MPS is not being followed throughout the system or that the MPS is not being controlled (revised) as unplanned changes in material, equipment, or personnel occur.

EXERCISES

1. a. Construct a tree structure bill of material (BOM) from the following indented BOM.
    b. Which of the items are purchased?

Item	Description	Quantity	Lead Time (weeks)
A	Assembly	1	1
B	Component	2	3
C	Subassembly	1	1
D	Component	1	2
E	Component	3	4
F	Subassembly	2	1
G	Component	1	2
H	Component	4	3

2. Use the information in Exercise 1 to calculate the minimum planning horizon for the MPS if all items are either purchased or made to order.

3. Use the information in Exercise 1 to calculate the minimum planning horizon for the MPS if all purchased items (B, D, E, G, and H) are in stock and A, C, and F are made to order.

4. Using the information in Exercise 1 and the additional requirement of two weeks of engineering time to adapt the unit to each customer's requirements, calculate the minimum planning horizon.

5. Develop an indented bill of material for the assembly represented by the following product structure tree.

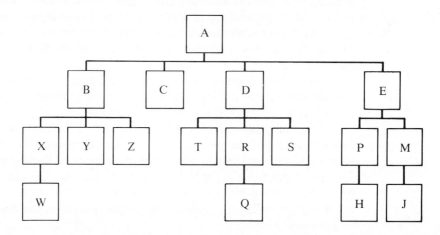

6. a. Using the information in Exercise 5, determine the level of each item.
   b. Using the information in Exercise 1, determine the level of each item.

7. Use the following data to calculate the standard hours required in the assembly department to manufacture the MPS quantities in a four-week period as indicated below. The requirement is that all must be shipped by the end of the four weeks. The department has a capacity of 40 standard hours per week. Revise the schedule as required.

| | Assembly | | MPS | | | |
| | Standard Time | Quantity | Week | | | |
Product	per Unit	Required	1	2	3	4
A	1.10 hours	80	40	40		
B	0.90 hours	40			40	
C	0.80 hours	40				40

8. A product group (three similar assemblies: A, B, and C) is manufactured to stock on a batch flow process assembly line. Each is usually manufactured in batch quantities of 20 units or more. The cost of changing from the manufacture of any one assembly to any other is the same. The gross requirements, line capacity, safety stock, and present inventory of each assembly is given below.

Assembly	Inventory On Hand	Weekly Forecast	Weekly Capacity	Safety Stock
A	45	15	50	10
B	20	5	50	5
C	35	25	50	15

a. Which assembly should be manufactured first?
b. Develop an MPS without safety stock, that is, assume safety stock is zero for all assemblies.
c. Develop an MPS considering the safety stock requirements.

9. Develop graphs representing the cumulative production output, cumulative demand, and projected on hand inventory for the following situation.

						Week						
	1	2	3	4	5	6	7	8	9	10	11	12
Forecast	5	5	5	5	10	10	10	15	15	15	15	10
Production	10	10	10	10	10	10	10	10	10	10	10	10

Beginning inventory = 5

10. The Midwestern Equipment Company supplies hoists to a wide variety of customers. They offer any combination of the five following major subassemblies to their customers. The subassemblies and the number of choices available for each are given below.

Subassembly	Number of Choices
Motors	8
Drums	10
Gear boxes	6
Pendants*	5
Hooks	4

*Cable with device for attaching hook on its free end

a. If the company decides to store final assemblies, calculate the number of different assemblies (unique part numbers) it will have in finished goods inventory.
b. If the company decides to store major subassemblies and make final assemblies to order, calculate the number of different subassemblies (unique part numbers) it will have in inventory.
c. The pendants and hooks can be added in less than 10 minutes during final packaging. Of the 480 different possible configurations (combinations) of motors, drums, and gear boxes, five account for 50 percent of sales; each accounts for approximately 10 percent. What does this suggest regarding stocking policies?
d. If the five combinations in Part c are manufactured without the pendants and hooks, how would the BOM be modified?

11. The company described in Exercise 10 has experienced the following demand proportions for the six gear box models. In the past these proportions have been accurate within 20 percent. For example, a 10 percent estimate has never been less than 8 percent or more than 12 percent.

Model	Percentage	On Hand
A	20	8
B	10	3
C	25	6
D	5	0
E	30	7
F	10	2

Given the above stock on hand and a forecast of maximum sales next month of 200 hoists, calculate the number of each model of the gear boxes that should be on the MPS to meet this demand without any stock-outs. Assume ample time remains this month and in the beginning of next month to produce the gear boxes required.

12. A Taiwan manufacturing company manufactures wheelbarrows which it ships unassembled. The customers assemble them after the purchase. In each packaged final product, they provide the items listed below in a plastic bag (a kit) for each of their three most popular models.

		Quantity per Model	
Item	Midget	Garden	Construction
Plastic bag B22	1	1	1
Nut 1/4	8	10	10
Bolt 1/4 - 2	6	4	4
Bolt 1/4 - 3	2	4	2
Bolt 1/4 - 5		2	4
Washer 1/4	8	10	10
Screw 6 - 3	2		
Instructions IM	1		
Instructions IG		1	
Instructions IC			1

a. Assign a part number to the kit required for each model and develop an indented BOM for each kit.

b. The company plans to ship 1,000 wheelbarrows next month: 200 Midgets, 500 Gardens, and 300 Construction models. Calculate the number of each of the above components required to complete this schedule.

13. Two products, A1 and A2, are processed in four departments as described below. Given: a lead time of one week for each operation and the manufacturing data that follows.

			Week		
Product	1	2	3	4	5
A1				15	20
A2				20	30

	Operation Standard Times (Hours) per Unit			
Product	Machining	Welding	Subassembly	Assembly
A1	3.0	1.0	2.0	2.0
A2	2.0	1.5	3.0	1.0

Capacity Available (Standard Hours per week) per Department			
Machining	Welding	Subassembly	Assembly
150.0	60.0	120.0	65.0

a. Calculate the weekly capacity requirements for each product.
b. If any overtime is required in any week, calculate how much in each department.
c. Now forget overtime, and adjust the MPS so that capacity requirements do not exceed that available and the delivery schedule is met.

14. Calculate the net requirements and the projected on hand inventory by period for the master schedule, given the following forecast, a beginning inventory of 150 units, and scheduled receipts of 80 units in Week 3. Finally, calculate the MPS if the product is produced in lots of 80 units. Use a lead time of 0 and schedule items in the first week they are required.

	Month							
	1	2	3	4	5	6	7	8
Forecast	80	50	60	40	30	70	60	40
Scheduled Receipts			80					

Beginning Inventory = 150

15. Use the data in the following table to:
a. Calculate the ATP using the discrete (period-by-period) method. The beginning inventory is 5.
b. Revise the solution to Part a to include a new order for 10 units that has just arrived. Shipment has been promised in Week 8.

	Week										
	1	2	3	4	5	6	7	8	9	10	11
Forecast	15	15	15	15	15	15	15	15	15	15	15
Backlog	20		35			20			10		
MPS	30		45			45			45		

16. Using the data from Exercise 15, calculate the POH without consuming the forecast.

17. Using the data from Exercise 15, calculate the POH using the consuming the forecast method and the assumption that orders are following their normal pattern (the original total forecast is still valid).

18. Using the data from Exercise 15, calculate the POH using the consuming the forecast method and the assumption that 15 of the units ordered in Week 6 are from a new customer. All other orders are following a normal pattern (the original total forecast must be increased).

19. Using the data from Exercise 15 and the receipt of an additional order for 40 units in Week 6, calculate both the revised ATP—cumulative with lookahead—and the revised POH.

20. Use the requirements for the four warehouses given below to construct the gross requirements for the organization's master schedule. (The gross requirements equal the sum of all the warehouse requirements.)

Product A: Warehouse Requirements Week								
Warehouse	1	2	3	4	5	6	7	8
Toronto	20		20		20		20	
Los Angeles	15	15	15	15	15	15	15	15
Atlanta		25			25			25
Dallas	10	—	20	—	—	20	—	10
Total	45	40	55	15	60	35	35	50

21. A company produces one product and output is measured in gallons. The MPS for each of the last four weeks has called for production of 2,000 gallons. Ample raw materials have been available. Actual production output has averaged 1,820 gallons. What does this suggest? What actions do you recommend?

22. The MPS of a company has called for the production of 15 A's and 30 B's during each of the last four weeks. Actual production has varied widely with production of A's being sequentially 12, 22, 25, 3 and B's being 41, 15, 18, and 43 during the four-week period. What does this suggest?

SELECTED READINGS

Everdell, Romeyn. *Master Scheduling: APICS Training Aid*. Falls Church, VA: American Production and Inventory Control Society, 1987.

Fogarty, Donald W., and Robert L. Barringer. "The Available-to-Promise (ATP) Quantity." *APICS International Conference Proceedings* (1984): 153-156.

Ling, Richard C. "Demand Management: Let's Put More Emphasis on this Term and Process." *APICS International Conference Proceedings* (1983): 11-12.

Malko, Richard W. "Master Scheduling: A Key to Results." *APICS International Conference Proceedings* (1980): 408-412.

Malko, Richard W. "Product Groups: A Prerequisite For Production Planning." *APICS International Conference Proceedings* (1986): 322-323.

Proud, John F. "Consuming the Master Schedule with Customer Orders." *APICS International Conference Proceedings* (1983): 21-25.

Sari, F. John. "The Planning Bill of Material—All It's Cracked Up To Be?" *APICS Conference Proceedings* (1982): 324-327.

Schwendinger, James R. "Master Production Scheduling Available to Promise." *APICS Conference Proceedings* (1978): 316-330.

Wallace, Thomas, ed. *APICS Dictionary*. 6th ed. Falls Church, VA: American Production and Inventory Control Society, 1987.

Ware, Norman, and Donald W. Fogarty. "The Same or Different?" Working paper concerning MS, MPS, ATP, and POH accepted for publication, *Production and Inventory Management*.

Part
Two

Inventory
Management

5

INVENTORY MANAGEMENT: AN OVERVIEW

Inventory includes all those goods and materials that are used in the production and distribution processes. Raw materials, component parts, subassemblies, and finished products are all part of inventory, as are the various supplies required in the production and distribution process.

Inventory ties up capital, uses storage space, requires handling, deteriorates, sometimes becomes obsolete, incurs taxes, requires insurance, can be stolen, and sometimes is lost. Furthermore, inventory frequently compensates for sloppy and inefficient management, including poor forecasting, haphazard scheduling, and inadequate attention to setup and ordering processes. In other words, inventory may hide inadequacies and allow management to ignore them (see Chapter 17). In such cases inventory increases costs and productivity without enhancing net income. It is "liability" regardless of where it is carried on the organization's balance sheet. In addition, if an organization has the wrong items in inventory, the situation is worsened.

However, the benefits of a properly managed inventory outweigh the costs of maintaining it. The absence of the appropriate inventory will halt a production process. Lack of component parts will shut down an assembly line with partially completed assemblies collecting dust. An expensive piece of earth-moving equipment may be idled by lack of an inexpensive replacement part. A patient may die due to the unavailability of plasma. The learning process will be hampered by the nonarrival of texts. And in many cases, good customers may become irate and take their business elsewhere if the desired product is not immediately available. The availability of the right items at the right time and in the right place supports the organizational objectives of customer service, productivity, profit, and return on investment. This is true in manufacturing, wholesale, retail, health care, and educational organizations. Inventory can be an asset in the full sense of the word. Measures of performance and productivity may differ among organizations, but all need adequate inventory management.

INVENTORY DECISIONS

Inventory management objectives, policies, and decisions should be consistent with overall organizational objectives and should be consistent with marketing, financial, and manufacturing objectives as shown in Figure 5-1.

Figure 5-1
Relationship of Functional Goals

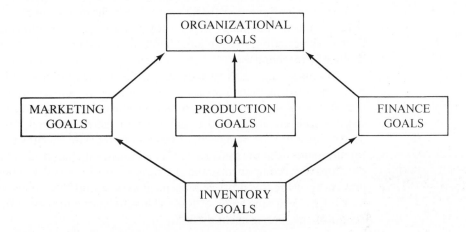

Inventory decisions are intertwined with capacity planning decisions throughout the long-, medium-, and short-range planning time frames, as well as in the execution and control phases of operations management. Facility size and related aggregate planning decisions determine the inventory necessary to meet seasonal high demand (see Chapter 2). The type of process—line, job shop, fixed site, and so on—affects work in process inventory. Decisions concerning distribution methods and the number of warehouses affect finished goods inventory. (See Chapter 9.) Purchasing and production decisions to combine items for joint replenishment affect inventory as described in Chapter 8.

Inventory management of individual items encompasses the principles, concepts, and techniques for deciding what to order, how much to order, when it is needed, when to order for purchase or production, and how and where to store it. Decisions at each of these levels should be consistent with decisions at the other levels (integrated) and should support organizational objectives by (1) defining and attaining desired levels of customer service and (2) achieving inventory investment objectives.

Inventory Management Systems

In an operational setting, inventory management is accomplished through the use of a set of procedures, frequently called an *inventory management system* (see Figure 5-2). An inventory management system embodies a set of decision rules and guides for various inventory situations. It utilizes information processing capabilities to determine the nature of different situations as they arise on the planning horizon. Using the information describing the decision variables, the system will make automatic decisions on the basis of explicit models of some situations. In other less structured situations, the system will provide the relevant information to a decision maker for human action.

Prerequisites to Inventory Decisions

Where should one begin in the management of inventories? In calculating economic order quantities (EOQ's)? Or in purchasing a computer and a material requirements planning (MRP) software package? Or in hiring a consultant? Each of these actions may do more harm than good unless an adequate analysis is made beforehand.

Inventory managers must determine the boundaries, magnitude, and composition of the aggregate inventory before they can expect to make decisions that are rational in terms of the organization's objectives and the nature of a specific decision situation. The point is that there is no inventory model, set of decision rules, or management system appropriate for all situations—even for all situations in the same firm. Characteristics such as demand pattern, lead time, delivery requirements, and the various cost factors determine the appropriateness of the inventory management system and the model on which it is based. Let's examine some of these characteristics and their influence on the design of the management system.

First, we will examine the functional classifications of inventories since they have a major impact on the selection of management systems and techniques. Next, we will discuss inventory management performance measures, and then follow with an examination of measures of value and how value affects the approach to managing inventory. Descriptions of various costs and the measuring of inventory decision related costs conclude the chapter.

FUNCTIONAL CLASSIFICATIONS

The primary function of inventory is a buffering, decoupling one. Inventory serves as a shock absorber between customer demand and the manufacturer's production capability, between finished assembly requirements and component availability, between the input materials required for an operation and the output of the preceding operation, and between the manufacturing process and the supplier of raw materials. It decouples—separates—demand from immediate dependence on the source of supply. Functional classifications of inventory

Figure 5-2
Inventory Management System Development Flowchart

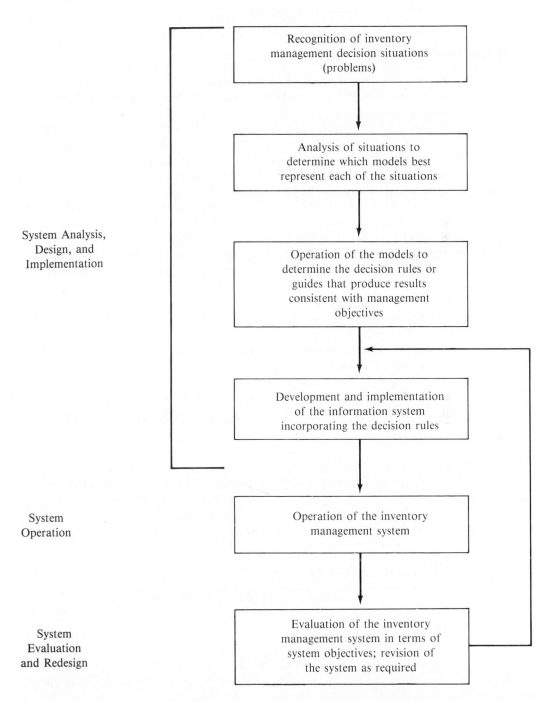

typically include anticipation inventory, lot size inventory, fluctuation inventory, transportation inventory, and service parts. Inventory serves as a special type of buffer in each of these cases.

Anticipation Inventories

Vacation shutdowns, peak sales periods, sales promotions, and possible strikes are all situations that can lead to an organization producing or purchasing additional finished goods, components, materials, or supplies. This anticipation inventory allows an organization to cope with either the anticipated surge in demand or the supply drought. Anticipation inventories, discussed at length in Chapter 2, differ from hedge inventories. George Plossl (1973, 98) has defined hedge inventories as those purchased or built to take advantage of present costs or to avoid anticipated substantial price increases.

Decisions concerning acquisition of hedge inventory are excellent examples of investment decisions with a risk element. Additional carrying cost is incurred by purchasing the inventory early. This cost must be less than the expected savings to justify acquiring anticipation inventory. For example, a hospital in the Northwest had the opportunity to double its order quantity and purchase an additional three months' supply, 1,000 units, of surgical kits at the present unit price of $6.50 with an anticipated price increase to $6.75 in three months. The purchasing agent estimated the probability of a price increase to be 90 percent. The agent knew that space and capital were available. Policy was to purchase not more than six months' supply. Should the agent make the purchase? Let's see.

$$\text{Total Expected Savings} \times \text{Order Cost Savings} + \text{Expected Savings in Material Costs}$$

where

$$\begin{aligned}
\text{Expected Material Savings} &= \text{Number of Units} \times \text{Savings per Unit} \\
&\quad \times \text{Probability of Cost Increase} \\
&= 1,000 \times 0.25 \times 0.9 \\
&= \$225
\end{aligned}$$

and

$$\text{Order Cost Savings} = 1 \text{ Order at } \$30$$

Thus,

$$\text{Total Expected Savings} = \$255$$

Using a carrying cost rate of 25 percent a year (we will discuss carrying costs more later) renders the following costs:

Total Costs = Inventory Investment × Time Period × Carrying Rate

where

$$Investment = 1,000 \times \$6.50$$
$$Time = 0.25 \text{ years (3 months)}$$
$$Rate = 25\% \text{ a year}$$

Thus,

$$Total Costs = 1,000 \times \$6.50 \times 0.25 \times 0.25$$
$$= \$406.25$$

Given these facts, the early purchase does not pay.

The production manager, although always concerned about costs and monetary savings, should be concerned primarily about storing critical commodities and resources. Manufacturing organizations frequently have inadequate machine capacity of a specific type to meet an above average demand rate. In building anticipation inventory during a less than average demand period, the manager should make those items that require scarce machine and work force capacities. Ideally, anticipation inventory should consist of items that have a high labor content and a low material content.

Before leaving anticipation stocks, we should recognize that in those cases involving possible shortages, the cost of not buying can be extremely large when a shortage can shut down a production line, threaten the life of a patient, or damage customer relations.

Lot Size Inventories (Cycle Stock)

It is very inefficient in many cases to produce or purchase goods at the same rate at which they are consumed. Efficient production rates sometimes are much greater than consumption rates. For example, the process for producing die castings for carburetor housings generates output at a much greater rate than the sales of automobiles using a specific carburetor housing. To use a slow method of production that matches the demand rate—for example, machining the housing in sections from raw materials and then assembling it—is much more expensive than casting the housings on an intermittent basis and holding some in stock to be used gradually.

The folly of a hospital purchasing gauze on a daily basis is apparent immediately. The costs of writing the purchase order, delivering the gauze, and processing the invoice can very well be greater than the cost of the gauze. In many cases of this type, purchasing a large quantity of material to be used over a period of time is the economical approach.

The economics of manufacturing and purchasing lead to the intermittent purchasing or production of goods and materials in a quantity (lot size) sufficient to meet relatively stable demand during an extended period. Decisions concerning determination of the lot size and timing of the order will be discussed later, as will the crucial issues of selecting the method of determining the lot size and timing the release of orders.

The ideal solution is to be able to economically produce or purchase a quantity of one, the minimum requirement. Being able to produce the exact quantity required eliminates the cost of carrying residual units. This solution requires that fixed costs (ordering and setup costs) be reduced to the point at which small lot sizes are economically feasible. Analysing and improving both the administrative processing of orders and setup is crucial to achieving lot size inventory reduction and production and distribution flexibility. Oil supertankers and ocean-going automobile transports are the result of economical shipping quantities. The manufacture of die castings and plastic injection mouldings usually still requires subtantial lot sizes to justify the fixed cost. Reducing lot sizes is a challenge to manufacturing and distribution.

Fluctuation Inventories

There are both demand fluctuations and supply fluctuations. The sales of canned or frozen beans, sweaters, refrigerators, lawn mowers, fountain pens, fertilizer, shoes, and so on vary from day to day and from week to week. It is, therefore, not realistic in most cases to expect the demand for these products to be perfectly predictable. At best we know a range within which the demand will fluctuate. When it is economical, inventories are provided to meet the high side fluctuations of finished goods demand just as they are provided to absorb the variations in the requirements for raw materials, components, manufacturing supplies, and office supplies. When vendor lead time or in-process time is greater than average, inventory is required to maintain a steady flow of work through the shop.

Such fluctuation inventories are called *safety stock*, *buffer stock*, or *reserve stock*. They enable an organization to service its customers when the demand for that service is above average or when delivery of replenishment stocks takes longer than usual. Fluctuation inventory will be examined further when we look at order points and at controlling lead time.

Transportation Inventories

Stages in the production process are not always physically adjacent. In fact, components frequently are manufactured in one part of the state, country, or world and shipped to another location for assembly. Similarly, finished products often are shipped sizable distances to warehouses, distributors, or customers. Ample inventory, flowing from one stage to the next, must be kept in the pipeline if the production and distribution process is not to be interrupted. Items in movement from one stage to the next are called *transportation inventories*. They include all items being shipped from finished goods warehouses to the customer as well as those items that an organization is shipping from one of its plants to another.

There is a natural tendency to overlook or not fully recognize the transportation inventory cost (TRIC). Such inventory ties up capital and is subject to spoilage, deterioration, damage, insurance, taxes, pilferage, and handling costs. Transportation inventories do exist and do cost money, and this cost can be measured.

TRIC equals the product of the transportation carrying cost rate, the dollar volume shipping rate, and the transit time.

$$TRIC = k \times R \times C \times t$$

where k = transportation carrying cost rate based on cost of capital, insurance, pilferage, and so on (does not include cost of shipment)

  R = requirements (demand) per period

  C = unit cost

  t = transit time

In most cases the actual transportation inventory cost can be determined with sufficient accuracy for decision-making purposes. For example, if a manufacturer of automobile frames ships a daily average of a thousand frames, the frames take a day and a half on the average to reach the assembly plant, the frames have a value of $30 each, and 0.15 is a good estimate of the transportation carrying cost rate, then

$$TRIC = (0.15/year) \times (1,000 \text{ units/day}) \times (\$30 \times 1.5 \text{ days})$$
$$= \$6,750 \text{ per year}$$

Reduction of transportation time from a day and a half to one day would result in an annual savings of $2,250.

Service Parts

Items carried in inventory as replacement parts for operating equipment or other needs are service parts. Service parts deserve a separate functional classification for at least three reasons. First, they often have very low and extremely erratic demand. For example, a sleeve used in pnuematic lines in a Southern Illinois Coal mine has an average demand (usage rate) of four per year, but three have been known to fail within a week. Second, the cost of a stockout is often extremely high. For example, a processing line or a piece of earthoving equipment may be idle without the right replacement part. And third, as a result of the first two reasons, the customer is usually not only willing but happy to pay a price much greater than the cost of producing the item. In

brief, the savings achieved by avoiding a stockout justify carrying a service part
in inventory for a prolonged period. The spare tire is a good example. It is not
uncommon to go for years without needing one. But the consequences of not
having one, if required, justify the carrying costs.

Service parts inventories may be held by:

A.   A user of the equipment in which the service parts are components
B.   The manufacturer of the equipment in which the service parts are com-
     ponents
C.   The manufacturer of the service parts
D.   An organization whose business is to supply organizations with replace-
     ment parts and, in some cases, to also provide repair services

Louisville Gas and Electric is a good example of the first case. They carry more
than a thousand items used as replacements in either their power production
facilities or in their distribution system. The cost of not generating or distributing power can be substantial for any utility. (In some cases the utility is
contractually bound to cover the losses of the customer.) In each of the other
cases reliable and timely provision of service parts can be profitable due both
to the return on the sale of the replacement part and to the increased sales of
the major equipment when replacement parts are known to be readily available.
Caterpillar of Peoria, Illinois, has long been known for its ability to achieve
its commitment to provide replacement parts anywhere in the world within
forty-eight hours.

Summary

The primary function of inventory management is to have items available to
maintain the flow of goods through the production process to the customer
while minimizing the investment required to achieve this service. Achievement
of this goal supports the overall organization goals of productivity, profit, and
return on investment. Methods of achieving these goals are discussed throughout the text. Inventories can be functionally classified as anticipation, lot size,
fluctuation, and transportation inventories and service parts. The importance
of these types of inventories in a particular organization depends on the firm.
The concepts and decision techniques usually employed in managing lot size
and fluctuation inventories are later discussed in detail.

As suggested earlier, management has traditionally perceived inventory
as an asset, something that can be converted to cash and that also fulfills essential functions, such as those of fluctuation (safety) stock and lot size (cycle)
stock. The new perception, the Just-in-Time approach, views inventory as a
liability, a waste that hides poor practices and does not add value. Traditionally, the cost of inventory has been perceived as including the costs of the
capital invested, storage, handling, deterioration, and so on as described later

in this chapter. Only recently has full recognition been given to the fact that inventory is frequently used to compensate for inefficient setups, poor scheduling, and excessive scrap. It is no exaggeration to state that inventory can be a cover-up for sloppy management. Its true total cost may be double or triple that calculated using the traditional method. The challenge to operations management is to minimize setup times, improve quality, and increase the flexibility of manufacturing in order to reduce the need for inventory.

PERFORMANCE MEASURES

The two primary criteria for evaluating inventory management performance are: (1) the levels of customer service achieved and (2) the inventory investment required to achieve those levels. Establishing target levels and measuring performance against those targets are practices followed by many companies (Edwards 1975).

This section examines different measures of customer service and inventory investment emphasizing their application to individual item management.

Customer Service (Service Level)

Operationally, *customer service* is the term used to describe the availability of items when needed by the customer. The customer may be a consumer of a finished product, a distributor, a plant in the organization, or a department in which the next operation is performed. Seldom, if ever, can an organization plan or act so that all items always are available in the proper quantity when desired. Some of the obvious causes of the unavailability of items when desired are an unusually large number of orders, machine failure, and late delivery by suppliers. However, an organization should aim for a high level of customer service and measure performance against this goal. Richard Artes (1977) stated it well, "A good finished goods inventory system will compare actual performance to planned performance and provide a feedback loop to correct significant deviations."

But measuring delivery performance relative to delivery dates is only part of the story. In some situations, backordering and late deliveries are possible. How good a job the organization does in filling backorders should also be determined.

Measures of Customer Service.   There is a plethora of ways for measuring customer service. Each has its strengths and weaknesses and appropriate applications. These measures can be divided into percentage measures and absolute value measures. Both types are suitable for comparison with a standard, perhaps performance in a previous similar period.

The percentage type measures include:

1. Orders shipped on schedule
2. Line items shipped on schedule
3. Total units shipped on schedule
4. Dollar volume shipped on schedule
5. Profit volume shipped on schedule
6. Operating item days not out of stock
7. Ordering periods without a stockout

The absolute value type measures include:

8. Order days out of stock
9. Line item days out of stock
10. Total item days out of stock
11. Dollar volume days out of stock
12. Idle time due to material and component shortages

Percentage Type Measures.   Let's now consider four of the percentage type measures. Others are described in detail by Fogarty and Hoffmann (1980).

1. Percentage of orders shipped on schedule. For an order to be counted as shipped on schedule, all items included in the order must be shipped on schedule. This is a good measure of service to the external customer, if all orders are of approximately equal value. But if 99 percent of the orders constitutes only 50 percent of the volume and profit while the 1 percent shipped months late constitutes the other 50 percent, a 99 percent customer service level achievement is misleading.
2. Percentage of line items shipped on schedule. This measure overcomes a deficiency of the previous measure in that it recognizes that different orders may be for different numbers of items. However, it does not recognize the possible dollar differential in line items and the lateness of the order. In addition, the complexity and cost of the measure are increased by having to record the number of items on each order.
3. Percentage of total units shipped on schedule. This measure recognizes the differences in quantities in orders and line items. But, again, dollar volume and the lateness in delivery variations could distort the picture. For example, if a company sells automotive brake sets and also sells rivets, the percentage of total units shipped on schedule is not very helpful. The measurement is more costly and complex than the previous measures.
4. Percentage of ordering periods not out of stock. If an item is ordered monthly and there is one stockout during the year, the customer service level according to this measure is 91.67 percent (11 ÷ 12). This method lends itself to the determination of order points (an order is

placed when stock on hand reaches the order point) that provide specific levels of customer service. It provides a good starting point in many situations for establishing customer service objectives. Then refined measures can be implemented on selected items.

Absolute Value Type Measures. Since the percentage measures related to absolute value measures 8 through 11 (order days, line item days, total item days, and dollar volume days out of stock) were discussed previously, these measures will not be discussed individually. Each possesses shortcomings similar to its counterpart. The combination of a percentage measure and its absolute value counterpart removes the inherent disadvantage of either measure used individually.

Results obtained using absolute value type measures can be evaluated only if a basis for comparison exists. As mentioned previously, comparison can be made to a standard—for example, 10 order days out of stock per year—or to results obtained in previous periods.

Idle time due to material and component shortages is a very useful measure of purchasing control and production activity control, including queue management and input/output control (see Chapters 13 and 14). The measure for a period can be compared to the performance in a period of similar plant activity. It is not uncommon for this measure to be taken monthly. Any manufacturing facility operating against standard production times usually maintains a record of productive and nonproductive hours with the latter's causes noted. Admittedly in some situations the causes of idle times are multiple and in others it is difficult to judge, but, with a little practice, the dominant cause can be determined in most cases. Thus, the data required to measure idle time due to material and component shortages are frequently available.

Comparison of Measures. To see how a single situation can give rise to different values, consider the following data. During a one-year time span, a firm supplied 152,700 units of a particular product. Of the 1,227 orders received, 46 could not be filled from stock. This represented a total of 5,560 units not shipped from stock. Over the 52-week period, the company was out of stock 9 times. What was its service level on this one part?

On the basis of the percentage of items shipped on schedule [(152,700 − 5,560) ÷ 152,700], the service level was 96.36 percent. On the basis of the percentage of orders shipped complete on schedule [(1,227 − 46) ÷ 1,227], it was 96.25 percent. But on the basis of the percentage of the periods in which no stockout occurred [1 − (9 ÷ 52)], it was only 82.70 percent. This comparison reveals why the latter measure is viewed as conservative.

None of the methods described is "right" or "wrong." Individual circumstances will determine which is most appropriate.

All customer service measures are surrogates for how the customer rates the organization's service. Peters (1987) recommends that all managers and many workers visit customers to acquire this information firsthand.

Backorder Delivery Performance.   In the design and manufacture of equipment, zero defects seldom if ever occur. Even when a piece of equipment malfunctions only rarely, the customer is concerned with how long it takes to repair. Many inventory management situations are analogous to this. When backorders (late deliveries) are possible, inventory management must be concerned not only with customer service relative to the original goal but also with the organization's ability to rectify the situation. As Henry Jordan (1976) has noted, "In addition to measuring delivery performance, the system should provide a means of analyzing delinquent orders." In brief, how fast are the backorders filled? It is one thing if all backorders are shipped the following day, but quite another if it takes weeks or months.

Here again there are many different ways of measuring performance. Goals should be established and performance measured against those goals. Some of the measures are:

1. The percentage of backorders shipped within different time periods. For example, one manufacturer of small tools has a goal of shipping 80 percent of all backorders within five working days and 100 percent within ten working days.
2. The average time and the standard deviation of the time it takes to ship a backorder.
3. An aging of backorders similar to an aging of accounts receivable may take place with limits established as goals on the various brackets.

To measure delivery performance against scheduled shipping dates without measuring the delivery performance on backorders is to possess only half a picture.

Selecting the Measure of Customer Service.   The foregoing undoubtedly did not exhaust all the possible measures of customer service, but it does indicate the myriad of possibilities. How does management determine which, if any, of the above are cost beneficial and worthy of implementation? Perhaps the most important questions to be asked concerning the selection of a measure of service are the following:

1. Are the data available?
2. Can the results being measured be affected by the manager's decisions?
3. Do the results being measured have an impact on productivity, profit, and return on investment?

Obviously, if the data are not available, the measure is not feasible. Estimated costs of obtaining the data must be compared to the benefits of the measure. For example, measuring and recording the profitability of items completed on schedule versus those that are late may cost more than the increase in profit that can be achieved with the added information.

A manager's decisions may not always affect results. For example, shortages of scarce purchased items (items available only from a single source) are situations in which the manager may be able to do little to achieve on-time delivery. An accumulation of circumstances similar to the foregoing can lead to measure results not indicative of the manager's performance.

If the measure is not related to productivity, profit, and return on investment, it has little value. An indication of something wrong and where to go to correct it does have value, because it does relate to performance.

The fundamental measurement problem is aggregation. A single measure used across all items and orders is bound to be deceptive. Thus, it is necessary to group items and orders by their important characteristics. What different types of inventories are being managed? What are the competitive pressures? Are all stockouts of equal importance? Are some customers more important than others?

In summary, customer service measures are in most cases a surrogate measure of the customer's satisfaction with the organization's delivery performance. How unhappy a customer is with a specific late depends on how pressing the customer's need is at that time. One measure that is not a surrogate is idle time due to material and component shortages. It, in fact, does measure how well a particular type of inventory fulfills its function. Obtaining this measure is not especially difficult when both the items needed for production and the production facility are controlled by the same organization.

Finally, different measures of customer service are appropriate for different sets of circumstances. These circumstances include the nature of the inventory, the availability of data, the use of the measures by management, the relation of the measures to organizational objectives, and the cost of the measures.

Customer Service Objectives.   After an organization selects customer service measures for its different types of inventory, performance objectives must be established. For example, should the organization aim for a 90 percent or a 95 percent level of customer service for finished goods? How much idle time in the plant due to material and component shortages is acceptable? Again, these are not easy questions to answer. But there are rational approaches that can be followed to establish reasonable objectives.

To begin, different performance objectives are usually appropriate for different types of items. The controlling factors in establishing the customer service objective for an item are the cost of carrying the item and the cost of a stockout. Inexpensive, easily stored items whose absence results in relatively high costs should have high customer service performance objectives. For example, it doesn't seem unreasonable that a 100 percent customer service level objective be established for all hardware items, such as washers, nuts, bolts, screws, pins, and so on, used in assembly operations. Theoretically, it is true that a 100 percent customer service level is impossible over an infinite time span or for an infinite number of parts, but the typical organization measures performance on a finite number of parts over a period seldom longer than a year. Elton Throndsen (1971), of General Electric, recommends that customer service level objectives be established on the basis of the delivery service needed to serve the market and obtain the desired return on investment given the inventory investment required to achieve the specific level of service.

In a dependent demand environment with a time-phased requirements planning system, a 100 percent service level is necessary for component parts if assemblies are to be fabricated. Planned service levels of less than 100 percent at the component level will diminish the assembly service level in a cumulative fashion due to joint probability (Orlicky 1975, 24). For this situation, the (joint) probability is computed as follows: The probability of all the assembly being completed on schedule is equal to the product of the probabilities of each of the components being available multiplied by the probability that assembly will be completed within the standard lead time given that the parts are available. For example, suppose an assembly consists of three parts, each with a 0.95 service level. If the probability of fabricating the assembly within the standard lead time is 0.98, the service level of the assembly being completed on schedule equals $0.95 \times 0.95 \times 0.95 \times 0.98$, or 0.84. Eighty-four percent may not seem terrible (not too good either), but change the 0.95 service levels to 0.90 and the 0.98 to 0.95 and the service level of the assembly is 0.69—certainly not a praiseworthy performance.

Some practical approaches can help in establishing customer service objectives. For finished goods sold from stock, determine the customer service level achieved during the past year. Was it satisfactory? What were the level and intensity of customer complaints? How much business was lost due to shortages or backorders? Estimates, if not exact figures, can be obtained from marketing, the customer service department, or the order entry department. If the data are not available, provisions should be made to collect the information. After such information has been obtained, the acceptability of present performance can be evaluated in terms of competitors' performance, customers' expectations, and the cost of improving the customer service level.

In the same fashion, information concerning machine center downtime and assembly line downtime due to material and component shortages is usually available. If not, it should be. Although it may be necessary to slip the scheduled fabrication of an assembly, it is not unreasonable to have an objective of never shutting down an assembly line for lack of components. In brief, once the assembly fabrication is begun, a 100 percent customer service for items required in the assembly is not unusual.

Customer Service and Inventory Investment.   In a large organization with inventories of many types, the aggregate customer service level achieved has an exponential relationship to aggregate investment in inventory. That is, for each additional percentage increase in customer service, a greater increase in investment is required than was required to achieve the previous percentage point increase in customer service, as shown in Figure 5-3. Note that Figure 5-3 assumes that all other factors remain the same. Such is not always the case. For example, if the inventory management system is improved, it is not unusual to increase the level of customer service while simultaneously decreasing investment in inventory. This possibility is illustrated by the family of curves shown in Figure 5-4.

Figure 5-3
Customer Service Versus Inventory Investment

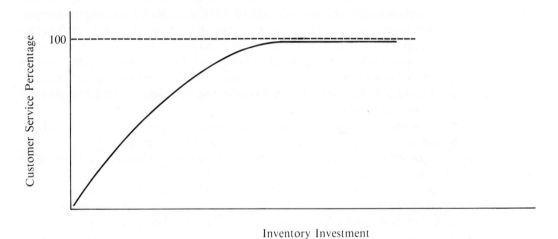

Figure 5-4
Customer Service Versus Inventory Investment
with Different Management Systems

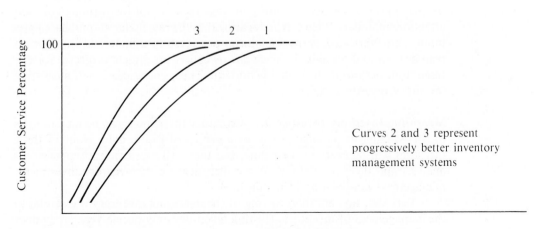

Curves 2 and 3 represent progressively better inventory management systems

In addition, it is possible to increase the inventory investment and decrease customer service even when the investment has been made in those items needed most. This happens whenever a system is overburdened physically or administratively. Continual increases in work in process eventually will reach the point where all or some of the following conditions result: lots are lost; movement of material through the shop is inefficient; foremen combine lots for setup cost savings and so create more costly scheduling problems; the information system is not capable of handling the volume. In a similar fashion, exceeding storage capacity may result in some of the following: weather damage due to outside storage; misplacement of lots due to inability to use the normal storage locations; item damage due to aisle storage. In brief, overloading the system physically and administratively may reduce customer service and create chaos. The success of Just-in-Time inventory systems verifies what can be accomplished with good management, reduced work in process, and top management commitment: reduced inventory investment, reduced manufacturing lead time, and improved customer service.

In summary, there are many measures of customer service, each with its strengths, weaknesses, and appropriate applications. Management should establish customer service objectives consistent with market demands and inventory investment objectives. Different performance measures and different objectives frequently will be appropriate for different types of items. Dependent demand items virtually require a 100 percent service level because of the multiplicative effect of joint probabilities. And, finally, to measure delivery performance based only on meeting scheduled shipping dates without establishing the cause of the problem and measuring the delivery performance on backorders is to do only half the job.

Inventory Investment

Oliver Wight (1974, 184-188) made an excellent point when he wrote that "Most people in production and inventory management do not focus enough of their attention on dollars." He was advocating that the raw material, purchase parts input, and fabricated output quantities projected in a materials requirement plan be used to determine the aggregate inventory investment projected for different time periods in the planning horizon. Thus, our discussion of measuring inventory investment begins.

Measuring Inventory Investment.   Inventory investment can be measured as of a past date, as of today, or as of a projected future date. None of these measures will be exact to the penny, but they will be sufficiently precise for analysis and decision making. Without a measure of inventory investment, management is operating in the dark.

Periodic, say monthly, costing of the aggregate inventory is essential to the management of inventory. Costing inventory only once a year rarely does the job. Annual physical counts of inventories commonly are taken at atypical times, and it is not entirely unknown for organizations to manipulate inventories at that time to obtain desired balance sheet results or to avoid property taxes. Even if that is not the case, an annual evaluation of inventory investment completely misses fluctuations in investment that occur during the year. Periodic, say monthly, accounting evaluations combined with a cycle counting program enable an organization to spot short-term seasonal fluctuations, to discern long-term trends early, and to avoid the end-of-year inventory surprises that perennially haunt some organizations. Having obtained a measure of inventory investment, how can we use it?

Absolute Measures of Investment. Determination of the total dollars invested in raw materials, work in process, and finished goods constitutes an absolute measurement of inventory investment. The value obtained can then be used for comparisons and to obtain relative measures of investment. First, actual levels can be compared to budgeted target levels, and variances can be analyzed (Edwards 1975). Are variances (differences between actual and budgeted) due to an increase (decrease) in volume, scrap rate, labor costs, or lead time? The results of such analyses are the basis for corrective action. Projected inventory investments by period are necessary for cash flow analysis and to determine whether inventory investment will be within the financial capability of the organization. If it will not, management has the option of revising the production plan to bring projected inventory investment within financial constraints. The above decision is one more opportunity for applying the ABC principle (described in this chapter) of concentrating on the high dollar volume items to achieve the necessary changes.

Relative Measures of Investment. Once the inventory investment has been measured, the inventory turnover rate (*ITR*) can be determined:

$$ITR = \frac{\text{Cost of Sales}}{\text{Inventory Investment}}$$

To avoid obtaining a misleading value, we must not mix apples and oranges. The ratio of actual cost of sales to actual investment or, as an alternative, the ratio of standard cost of sales to inventory investment at standard cost, will produce a legitimate and meaningful measure. If total sales, rather than cost of goods sold, are divided by the inventory investment, the measure is distorted by the changing profit percentages contained in the total sales. Use of standard cost data will provide for a more uniform measure that is not contaminated by cost variances and that is more suitable for period to period comparisons. However, in some cases—when estimating the *ITR* of another firm—only sales data is available.

Krupp (1981) argues that the cost of sales value used in calculating this ratio should be based on a historical smoothed cost of sales (for a period of three months or so) divided by the present value of inventory.

$$DITR = \frac{\text{Sum of Last Three Months Cost of Sales} \times 4}{\text{Instantaneous Inventory}}$$

where $DITR$ = dynamic inventory turnover ratio.

Close (1970) recommends a projected inventory turnover rate ($PITR$) calculated in the following manner:

$$PITR = \frac{\text{Annualized Forecast Cost of Sales}}{\text{Inventory Investment Today}}$$

Although their approaches differ, both models have the same objective: providing a meaningful measure of inventory investment in a dynamic environment. One method does this by using forecast cost of sales and the other does it by changing the target turnover rate to reflect planned production and sales.

When using past rather than future sales (as in the $DITR$ model), the inventory turnover rate target will change in response to shifts in the demand forecast (Krupp 1981). Turnover targets usually will be lower when high demand is anticipated and vice-versa. This model provides data that more clearly indicates the situation when seasonal demand or substantial trends in demand exist. For example, if a firm is entering its slow season after having just completed its fast sales period, the cost of goods sold annualized for the past three quarters is relatively high while the present inventory investment is relatively low. Using historical volume to calculate the ratio will generate a very low ITR when the inventory was in fact at an appropriate level to meet forecast demand.

What about using an instantaneous inventory value, such as the value of inventory on, say, the 25th of the month? Are there any pitfalls? There usually are. An usually large shipment or receipt of goods on the 24th is an event that will distort the ratio. Professional alertness and integrity will assist in avoiding this problem. If an event of unusual magnitude takes place shortly before inventory investment is measured, then any report including the ITR also should include a statement describing the event and its impact. In accounting, this is called the principle of full disclosure.

How are the $PITR$ calculations made? First, the forecast sales must be obtained for a period long enough to provide some stability and at the same time reflect shipments for which the present inventory will be used. Then this forecast must be annualized by multiplying it by the appropriate factor. This factor can be obtained by dividing the number of months in a year, 12, by the length of the forecast period in months. The annualized cost of sales is then divided by the present inventory. For example, suppose forecast cost of goods sold for the next three months is $30 million, and the cost of present inventory is $28 million.

$$\text{Annualized Cost of Goods Sold} = \frac{\$30 \text{ million} \times 12}{3} = \$120 \text{ million}$$

$$PITR = \frac{\$120 \text{ million}}{\$28 \text{ million}} = 4.29 \text{ per year}$$

Sensitivity Analysis.   Sensitivity analysis, especially on the pessimistic side, is appropriate here. What if in the preceding example our forecast is high and the standard cost of actual sales turns out to be only $108 million in the next three months? Then: *PITR* with 10 percent decrease in sales = $108 million ÷ $28 million = 3.86. Such an analysis enables us to predict both a pessimistic *PITR* and an expected *PITR*. Inventories exist primarily for future requirements. If the errors in projecting future inventories are relatively small and the *ITR* experienced is continually lower than the *PITR*, changes in the cost of goods sold are the likely problem area and not the inventory management system.

The above figures can be used very easily to determine such common measures as weeks of sales on hand. For example,

$$\frac{\text{Weeks of Sales}}{\text{on Hand } (WS)} = \frac{\text{Present Inventory } (I)}{\text{Projected Average Weekly Cost of Sales } (AWCS)}$$

and

$$QWCS = \frac{\text{Annualized Cost of Sales}}{\text{Weeks per Year}}$$

Thus,

$$AWCS = \frac{\$120,000,000}{52} = \$2,310,000 \text{ per week}$$

and

$$WS = \frac{\$28,000,000}{\$2,310,000} = 12.12 \text{ weeks}$$

Check:

$$PITR = \frac{\text{Weeks per Year}}{\text{Weeks of Sales on Hand}} = \frac{52}{12.12} = 4.29$$

Obsolete Inventory.   A company with a large dollar amount of obsolete inventory carried at cost will have an *ITR* that understates inventory management performance. Furthermore, if an unusually large amount of such inventory is purged with the appropriate accounting entries, the increase in the *ITR* will reflect not a stroke of genius in the inventory management department but more likely an increase in the value of scrap or a belated resolution of an obsolescent inventory problem.

The Inventory Turn Ratio Objective.   There is no magic *ITR* goal for all organizations and all periods of activity. In fact, different ratio performance objectives may be appropriate for different inventories within the same firm. Establishment of the *ITR* objectives should be a joint venture of inventory management, marketing, and financial management. It should reflect cash flow requirements, customer service objectives, and the individual characteristics of the business. As Plossl and Wight (1967, 332) have pointed out, "Two companies in the same business may have extremely different rates of turnover, depending upon the degree of manufactured versus purchased material contained in the end product, whether the business is make-to-stock or make-to-order or both, consignment stocking policies, distance from suppliers, the number of warehouses maintained, and many other considerations that vary substantially affect the companies' ability to turn inventory." In brief, the *ITR* objective should be based on customer service objectives, process cycle time, purchased and fabricated parts ratios, and stocking policies.

Like many management tools, the *ITR* has been abused and misapplied (Campbell 1975). As a result, its credibility has suffered. It is, nonetheless, still a useful technique. It is easy to understand and explain, can be measured and monitored, and reacts with minimum lag in reflecting change.

ABC ANALYSIS

If not the first, certainly one of the first steps in gaining a handle on an inventory situation should be the performance of an ABC analysis.

Vilfredo Pareto, a nineteenth century Renaissance man, was the first to document the Management Principle of Materiality, which is the basis of ABC analysis. Pareto, educated as an engineer and renowned as an economist, sociologist, and political scientist, noted that many situations are dominated by a relatively few vital elements in the situation. Thus, he surmised that controlling the relatively vital few will go a long way toward controlling the situation.[1]

Applying the ABC principle to inventory management involves:

1. Classifying inventory items on the basis of relative importance
2. Establishing different management controls for different classifications with the degree of control being commensurate with the ranked importance of each classification

---

1. Ford Dickie (1951), of General Electric, has illustrated how this principle could be applied to inventory management.

The letters A, B, C represent different classifications of descending importance, but there is nothing sacred about having three classes. Criteria for classification should reflect the difficulty of controlling an item and the impact of the item on costs and profitability.

ABC analysis usually is illustrated using the annual dollar volume criteria as in Table 5-1, but that is only one of many criteria that may affect the value of an item. Factors that affect the importance of an item and that may be criteria for classifying items in an ABC analysis include the following:

1. Annual dollar volume of the transactions for an item
2. Unit cost
3. Scarcity of material used in producing an item
4. Availability of resources, manpower, and facilities to produce an item
5. Lead time
6. Storage requirements for an item
7. Pilferage risks, shelf life, and other critical attributes
8. Cost of a stockout
9. Engineering design volatility

Whether lead time, storage requirements, possibility of pilferage, shelf life, or scarcity of resources such as raw materials, work force personnel or facilities for production should be considered in the classification of a group of items can be determined only by examining the situation. For example, Paul Conroy (1977) discusses the use of average weekly usage at Data General to establish breakpoints for an ABC classification.

Table 5-1
Example of ABC Analysis

Item	Unit Cost	Annual Usage	Annual Dollar Usage	Total Annual Percentage Usage
1	0.05	50,000	$2,500	34.3
2	0.11	2,000	220	3.0
3	0.16	400	64	0.9
4	0.08	700	56	0.8
5	0.07	4,800	336	4.6
6	0.15	1,300	195	2.7
7	0.20	17,000	3,400	46.7
8	0.04	300	12	0.2
9	0.09	5,000	450	6.2
10	0.12	400	48	0.7
		81,900	$7,281	100.1

Criteria Other than Dollar Volume

Table 5-2 illustrates how criteria can be applied in a programmed manner with the classification of an item being determined by the yes answer that results in the highest classification.

Table 5-2
Typical Decision Table for ABC Classification

Question	Class Based on a Yes Answer*
1. Is annual usage more than $50,000?**	A
2. Is annual usage between $10,000 and $50,000?	• B
3. Is annual usage less than $10,000?	C
4. Is the unit cost more than $500?	A
5. Is the unit cost between $100 and $500?	B
6. Does the physical nature of the item cause special storage problems?	B
7. Is the lead time longer than 6 months?	A
8. Is the lead time between 3 and 6 months?	B
9. Is shelf life less than 3 months?	A
10. Is shelf life greater than 3 months but less than 6 months?	B

*Final classification of an item is based on the highest classification received.
**The exact values used in annual usage, unit cost, lead time, and other criteria depend on the situation.

The Procedure

With one more caveat, that annual dollar volume alone should not be used to classify an item, the following procedure and simplified examples (Tables 5-1, 5-3, and 5-4) for classifying items on the basis of dollar volume are presented.

1. Determine the annual usage for each item in inventory (Table 5-1).
2. Multiply the annual usage of each item by the cost of the item to obtain the total annual dollar usage of each item (Table 5-1).
3. Add the total annual dollar usages of all items to determine the aggregate annual dollar inventory expenditures (Table 5-1).
4. Divide the total annual dollar usage of each item by the aggregate annual expenditure for all items to obtain the percentage of total usage for each item (Table 5-1).
5. List the items in rank order on the basis of the percentage of aggregate usage (Table 5-3).
6. Examine annual usage distribution and group items on basis of percentage of annual usage (Table 5-4).

Tables 5-3 and 5-4 typify real world situations in that the classifications of some items are clearly discernible while others are debatable. Items 7 and 1 are clearly A items while the classification of Items 2 and 6 could be either B or C. A graph illustrating A, B, and C items is shown in Figure 5-5.

Table 5-3
ABC Analysis—Rank by Percentage of Usage

Item	Annual Dollar Usage	Percentage of Total	Cumulative Percentage	Item Classification
7	$3,400	46.7	46.7	A
1	2,500	34.3	81.0	A
9	450	6.2	87.2	B
5	336	4.6	91.8	B
2	220	3.0	94.8	B
6	195	2.7	97.5	B
3	64	0.9	98.4	C
4	56	0.8	99.2	C
10	48	0.6	99.8	C
8	12	0.2	100.0	C

Table 5-4
ABC Analysis—Rank by Classification

Item Classification	Items	Percentage	Percentage Value
A	7, 1	20	81.0
B	9, 5, 2, 6	40	17.5
C	3, 4, 10, 8	40	2.5

Examples of different controls that might be used for different classifications are:

A Items
1. Frequent evaluation of forecasts and forecasting method
2. Frequent, perhaps monthly, cycle counting with tight tolerances on accuracy
3. Daily updating of records
4. Frequent review of demand requirements, order quantities, and safety stock; usually resulting in relatively small order quantities
5. Close follow-up and expediting to reduce lead time

B Items
Similar to controls for A items with most control activities taking place less frequently

C Items
1. Basic rule is to *have them*
2. Simple records or no records; perhaps use a periodic review of physical inventory
3. Large order quantities and safety stock
4. Store in area readily available to production workers or order fillers
5. Count items infrequently (annually or semiannually) with scale accuracy (weighing rather than counting) acceptable

Figure 5-5
Distribution of Inventory by Value

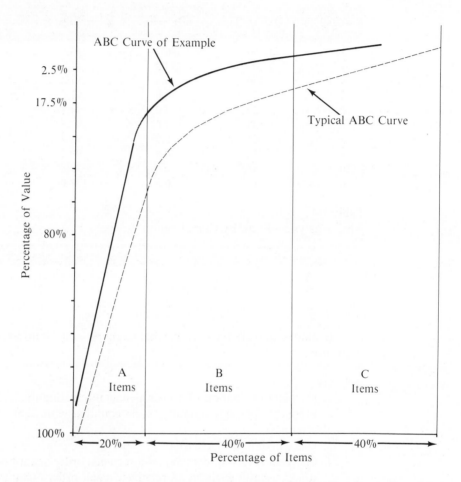

Widespread application of electronic data processing to inventory management has had an impact on some applications of ABC analysis. Accurate and
timely records now can be maintained economically on all items except very
low cost ones, such as standard rivets, washers, and other pan stock items. For
record-keeping purposes, only A and C items may exist. But record-keeping
procedures are only one aspect of inventory management. Other planning and
control procedures, such as evaluation of forecasts and cycle counting frequencies, still may be influenced by the result of an ABC analysis.

   Application of ABC analysis principles does not require the use of only
three classifications or even that the classifications be designated A, B, and C.
In an interesting presentation, Kenneth L. Campbell (1975) recommends the
adoption of a descriptive classification system with five different categories

each related to the functional use of the items rather than classification based only on annual dollar volume of transactions.

Before leaving ABC analysis there are at least two or three other points that should be made. Distinct ABC analyses should be performed for different product groupings. Purchased items, manufactured items, assemblies, sub-assemblies, independent demand items, and dependent demand items should be analyzed separately in most situations. The analysis should not ignore trends in demand or future plans. Most items experience a product life cycle. Some are on the upswing, experiencing an increasing demand; others may have leveled off and be declining. Historical usage patterns can be misleading if followed blindly. In addition, marketing may be planning to drop a product or engineering may be planning to redesign a component. Such information must be obtained by inventory management and used in establishing planning and control procedures.

In addition to inventory management, the principles of ABC analysis can be applied to many production and inventory control decisions. Gary Zimmerman (1975), of McCormick & Company, Inc., discusses the use of the ABC principle in establishing "trigger limits" for tracking signals in forecasting, in evaluating orders in relationship to capacity planning on the basis of the amount of critical capacity (worker or machine hours) required by the order, in scheduling by noting those primary operations that provide the bulk of the load on secondary operations, and in determining the frequency of cycle counting. Rolf Norbom (1973) reports on the use of ABC principles by the Philco-Ford Corporation in controlling purchase part deliveries, inventory levels, and investment at a medium-sized assembly plant.

INVENTORY COSTS

Costs are the crux of inventory management decisions at all levels. What about profits? Lost profits (profits foregone) can be and, in fact, are viewed as a cost in some inventory management decisions. As mentioned previously, when an organization selects a customer service objective less than 100 percent, it does so on the premise that the lost profits that are incurred by lack of inventory on certain occasions are less than the costs of carrying sufficient stock to cover all demand situations. Although different costs may occur in different situations in somewhat different ways and magnitudes, there is a common cost structure applicable to most inventory management decisions.

Before exploring the elements of that common structure, a brief discussion of the following aspects of costs and costing should be helpful.

Relevant, Opportunity, and Sunk Costs

Full cost accounting procedures record all manufacturing costs and assign these costs to an organization's output. In brief, all costs incurred in the production process end up in cost of goods sold (expense) or in various inventories (assets).

As a general rule, the inventory planner should include only relevant costs in the decision-making process. *Relevant costs* are costs that are incurred because of a decision. The ordering costs, setup costs, and direct labor and material costs related to a lot size decision are examples of relevant costs. Costs that will be incurred regardless of a decision are not relevant costs. For example, the cost of heating the plant seldom is affected by lot size or order release decisions.

Opportunity costs are returns on capital that would have been obtained from an alternate foregone investment. They represent the gains surrendered because one possible venture is neglected due to the use of limited resources for another. Such costs usually are not recorded in financial accounting records, but must be considered by the decision maker. For example, if an organization has large cash reserves, the financial accounting system normally will not record the cost of funds invested in inventory even though the organization could earn income on those funds if invested in treasury bills or another income producing vehicle. The decision maker should recognize opportunity costs. In many cases the average expected return from feasible alternative investment is used as an estimate of opportunity costs.

Sunk costs are expenditures that already have been incurred and that will not be affected by a decision. These costs include capital expenditures for equipment and land and training costs for new personnel. Expenditures for raw materials or purchased parts already received usually cannot be considered as sunk costs. The assumption is that, if the materials or parts are not used unless used now to complete a particular order, they will be used in the near future for another order. An exception occurs when consideration is being given either to using materials with a fast expiring shelf life or to using scrap. Costs of personnel for whom no alternate tasks are available in a period also may be viewed as sunk costs. For example, the cost of under-utilized setup personnel may be considered as a sunk cost if no other productive tasks are available and laying the personnel off is not practical. This is a valid, although sometimes hazardous, assessment of setup personnel, production workers, or office staff. The hazard is that this approach may be adopted to justify an emotionally desired decision when in fact resourceful management would have discovered other and more profitable opportunities to employ these resources. Sunk costs should not be included in the decision maker's calculations.

Incremental Costs, Cost Breakpoints, and Marginal Costs

The change in total costs resulting from a sizable change in output is an *incremental cost*. For example, if output increases from 250 to 500 tons and causes an increase in total costs from $25,000 to $40,000, the incremental cost of this change is $15,000.

Equally important to the decision maker are the *cost breakpoints*, points on the total cost curve where discontinuity exists. Let's add the following information to the example:

1. As given, 250 tons will cost $25,000.
2. An increase from 250 to 350 tons will cost $25 a ton.
3. Any increase beyond 350 tons will require a capital investment of $11,000.
4. Additional output from 350 tons to 700 tons will cost $10 a ton.

This cost function is shown in Figure 5-6. The critical point is the discontinuity of the cost function at 350 tons. Considerations of cost breaks such as this will arise often in our examination of inventory costs.

Figure 5-6
Incremental Costs and Cost Breakpoints

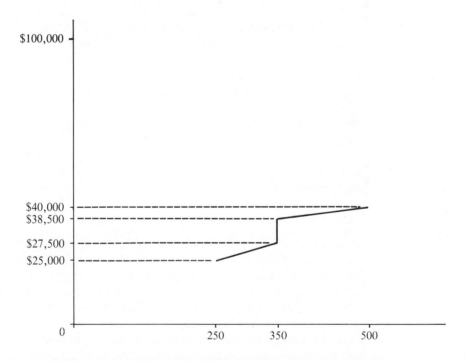

Marginal costs are those incurred to produce one additional unit. In the previous example the marginal cost of the 251st ton was $25; the marginal cost of the 351st ton was $11,010; and the marginal cost of the 352d ton was $10. Marginal cost is a particular type of incremental cost; the two differ by degree. For example, the additional (marginal) cost incurred in building one more supertanker is rather large to be called marginal.

Direct, Indirect, and Overhead Costs

Direct costs are those that can be traced directly to the fact that an order, task, or lot of parts has been produced. Material and labor costs fall into this category; they are clearly direct out-of-pocket costs in most cases. In fact, most accounting systems call these Direct Material and Direct Labor costs. Relevant and out-of-pocket costs are used synonymously in this text. Even depreciation cost changes may be relevant because of their effect on taxes.

Indirect costs are those not directly traceable to a specific item. Frequently, they are synonymous with manufacturing overhead. Cutting oils, lubricants, material handling, perishable tools such as drill bits and cutters, plant supervision, and other manufacturing support and services usually are recorded as indirect costs and are allocated to products on some common proportional basis such as a multiple of the direct labor hours or material costs of each item. Some of these costs—drill bits, for example—may be out-of-pocket costs, but, for the most part, these costs are not affected by an individual lot size decision. An aggregate level decision to increase or decrease the production output rate usually will affect these costs; thus, they should be included in an aggregate level type decision.

Overhead costs are those expenditures for heating, lighting, buildings, equipment, top management, sales, and general services such as plant security and the personnel department. They are affected by individual item level decisions only if that item constitutes a major portion of the production and the decision has aggregate level impact. This situation sometimes exists in the refining, mining, and chemical process industries but rarely in job shop situations. Thus, in the former case these may be out-of-pocket costs, but in the latter they are not. Their inclusion in the decision-making process depends on the nature and peculiarities of the organization and the particular situation being considered.

Fixed and Variable Costs

Fixed costs, by definition, do not vary with output level. Total variable costs change as a function of the output quantity. In short-range nonaggregate decisions, production inventory managers are not concerned with fixed costs; their decisions are based primarily on variable out-of-pocket costs. This can lead to the pitfall of neglecting factors that contribute to fixed costs. The magnitude and time horizon of a decision determine what is fixed cost and what is variable cost. A decision to increase the lot size of one item by 20 percent rarely requires purchasing additional equipment, hiring personnel, or building additional storage space. In other words, these costs are fixed. But the decision to increase the output rate from 100 to 200 gallons an hour may require additional manufacturing and distribution capacity and, hence, these costs are variable. As described here, they are an incremental type of variable cost. Again, what are fixed costs and what are variable costs depends on the nature of the decision.

Actual Costs and Standard Cost

Expenditures recorded as having been incurred as the result of a decision are *actual costs*. Such costs are available only after products have been made or after a project is completed.

Standard cost is a preestablished criterion or norm, based on efficient operating procedures, of what an item should cost to produce or purchase. Material, labor, and overhead costs usually are included.

In practice, actual costs seldom are equal to the standard cost. In some cases they oscillate about the standard cost. In other situations—for example, where incentive plans exist—they may be consistently below standard cost. While in another situation—for example, a measured day rate nonincentive plant—they may be consistently above standard cost. In those situations where actual costs exhibit a bias with respect to standard cost, that bias should be recognized by the decision maker's calculations. If actual costs vary about the standard cost with no consistent bias, the standard cost may be used in the calculations.

Intangible Costs

Some costs are very difficult to quantify and some cannot be valued in ordinary economic terms. The cost of a dissatisfied customer due to the unavailability of stock depends on numerous, difficult-to-measure variables such as the degree of the customer's unhappiness and the impact it will have on his or her future purchases. The value of having the proper blood type for a transfusion or of having life-saving medication when required does not lend itself to economic analysis. In such situations it is common to establish system objectives such as always having certain quantities of various blood types and medicines available.

INVENTORY DECISION COSTS

There are four types of costs relevant to inventory management decisions: (1) preparation costs, (2) carrying costs, (3) stockout costs, and (4) capacity related costs.

Preparation Costs

Preparation costs include the costs of all activities required in issuing a purchase or production order. They include the cost of writing the order, preparing specifications, recording the order, order follow-up, processing of invoices or plant reports, and preparation of payment. Production orders, sometimes called shop orders or manufacturing orders, are orders for internal fabrication of items as opposed to purchases. They usually require a setup, including the mounting of fixtures, adjustment of machine settings, checking the first items produced, and tearing down the setup at the end of the operation. The labor and machine costs of these activities are part of the preparation costs. Preparation costs sometimes are called ordering costs or setup costs. Since the connotations of these terms are limited, preparation cost is used in this text to indicate the broad nature of these costs. See Appendix 5A for a discussion of the practical aspects of calculating preparation costs.

Setup Costs.   Preparation costs for production orders—the internal fabrication or assembly of items as opposed to purchasing the items—also include the costs of machine setup. This involves activities such as obtaining tools, mounting fixtures, receiving instructions concerning the job, adjusting machine settings, checking the first items produced, tearing down the setup, and often cleaning the equipment when the job is complete.

Labor costs and machine costs are the components of setup costs. Labor costs can be determined in a straightforward manner by multiplying standard setup times by the applicable efficiency factor and the hourly cost of labor. If standard times are not available, good estimates usually can be obtained from shop supervision. Consider the following labor setup calculation example.

Setup labor costs = $15 per hour

Standard time for setup on a particular operation = 1.8 hours

Rated efficiency of setup workers on this task = 0.80

$$\text{Estimated Setup Cost} = \frac{\text{Cost} \times \text{Average Actual Time}}{\text{Hours}}$$

$$\text{Average Actual Time} = \frac{\text{Standard}}{\text{Efficiency}} = \frac{1.8}{0.8} = 2.25 \text{ hours}$$

$$\begin{aligned} \text{Estimated Setup Labor Cost} &= \$15.00 \times 2.25 \\ &= 33.75 \end{aligned}$$

When setup personnel do not operate equipment, have substantially less than a full workload, and will be retained on the payroll in any event, setup labor is a sunk cost. It can be treated as free in a lot sizing decision.

The determination of machine costs is not quite that straightforward. To begin, machine costs should not include depreciation costs or any other absorption of sunk costs. The lost profits and foregone contribution to overhead when equipment is being set up rather than operating and producing output are the machine costs. These are opportunity costs and, although usually not readily available in the accounting records, they must be considered by the planner. Such costs exist only if setup activities are consuming time that otherwise would be used for production. This occurs only when equipment is being used at or near capacity. A resulting rule of thumb is that during slack periods, other things being equal, orders with relatively large setup times should be run. This increases equipment utilization during the slack period and places fewer material dollars in inventory for a given labor investment and machine utilization. It usually will result in a higher proportion of operating (productive) time and in a lower proportion of setup (nonproductive) time in periods of high demand. Thus, production run sizes will decrease in slack periods and increase in high demand periods.

The opportunity costs of setup (profit and contribution to overhead lost by not producing output) exist only when a plant or machine center is operating at or near capacity. If a machine center is used to produce many products, these lost profits depend on which product is not being manufactured because all items are not equally profitable. The equipment to manufacture a particular product may include some machine centers that are rarely utilized fully, some that are loaded to capacity on occasion, and some bottleneck type work centers that usually are utilized fully. These factors make estimating setup machine costs difficult in job shop operations. In such cases, it makes sense to use average profit and overhead contributions, but only for those work centers that are usually or frequently operating at full capacity. Continuous flow operations such as those found in paper making, some textile plants, paint factories, and food processing present a less complex picture.

In general, it seems that setup machine costs are not investigated as often as they might be when analyzing production and inventory decisions. In many cases these costs may be negligible and not worthy of inclusion. However, this decision should be a conscious one and not one made by default.

Consider the following example where a part is processed through five departments: A, B, C, D, and E. The following conditions exist.

Department*	Setup Time (hours)	Percentage of Work Center Utilization
A	0.6	60
B	1.2	100
C	0.0	100
D	0.5	95
E	0.4	85

Average profit and overhead contribution = $20.50 per hour.

The process of determining the machine opportunity costs of setup involves:

1. Establishing a utilization cutoff point and determining those departments in which such costs are not incurred
2. Adding the setup time for those departments that are utilized above the utilization cutoff point
3. Multiplying total setup hours by overhead and profit contribution per hour
4. Determining if cost is sufficient to include in total preparation costs

Now, apply these steps to the foregoing data:

1. Setup time is not required in Department C. Utilization is only 60 percent in Department A. Setup machine costs are not incurred in either of these departments. Setup time is incurred in Departments B and D, and they are fully utilized for all practical purposes. What about Department E? Is 85 percent utilization sufficiently high to believe that additional setup hours will affect productive output? Perhaps not; but, for the purpose of this example, a cutoff point of 80 percent for full utilization exists. This is a policy decision that must be based on the number of hours reserved for flexibility to handle rush orders, unplanned scrap, and so on.

2 & 3. Add the opportunity cost setup hours and multiply them by the contribution rate.

Department B	1.2
Department D	0.5
Department E	0.4
Total	2.1 hours

$$\begin{aligned}\text{Machine Costs} &= \text{Total Setup Hours} \times \text{Contribution Rate/Hour} \\ &= 2.1 \times \$12.50 \\ &= \$26.25 \end{aligned}$$

4. In this instance, $26 is a cost worthy of including in most lot size decision calculations.

How are overhead and profit contribution costs per hour determined? Accounting can help here if production management does not have such costs available. Sometimes a general model or formula has been established by management for estimating these costs. For example, every dollar of labor expended requires $1.50 of manufacturing overhead and should generate 40 cents profit.

Neglecting fixed costs and the factors that contribute to them is a dangerous trap that often leads to fixed costs dominating the decision and limiting production flexibility. Accepting a high fixed cost environment as unavoidable leads to large lot sizes, high inventory investment, long manufacturing lead times, and difficulties in competing on cost and delivery.

Carrying Costs

Carrying costs are those costs incurred by the very fact that an item is in stock. Included are the cost of the capital invested; the costs of deterioration, obsolescence, pilferage, insurance, and taxes; and the storage costs due to handling, security, space, and record-keeping requirements. Each of these is a very real cost although its relative importance may vary from item to item. For example, in the manufacturing of men's clothing, the probability of obsolescence may be negligible for classic single-breasted blazer jackets but rather high for fashion items with abrupt changes in demand.

Costs of pilferage, spoilage, obsolescence, and damage vary from industry to industry and even from product to product. Some costs are incurred to prevent pilferage or spoilage. Experience can be used to estimate these costs as a proportion of the value of inventory. Accounting should be able to provide the cost of insurance. It may be a flat rate based on estimated value of inventory. This easily translates into a percentage of dollar value. Taxes vary by geo-political boundaries.

The cost of space again raises the challenge of separating sunk and opportunity costs. An organization with a half full warehouse incurs few if any additional warehouse storage costs if inventory is increased. The cost of the building and utilities plus security will exist whether or not inventory is doubled. This is true regarding warehouse space, but seldom, if ever, true concerning work in process. Even with excellent shop floor control, space in the plant is usually at a premium. In addition, half empty warehouses have a habit of filling up overnight. The product line in some organizations may make it possible to charge for storage at a constant rate based on the value of an item. Such is not always the case. Large bulky items may cost much more to store per dollar of value than their small size high dollar value counterparts. In the latter situation it is appropriate to use different rates per dollar volume for different size items.

Handling costs are similar to space costs in that many are sunk costs and others are related to the bulkiness and weight of the item rather than its cost.

The cost of capital can be based on the higher of either the actual cost of capital or the opportunity costs. If a firm is paying two points over the prime rate, the cost of capital is straightforward although it may vary from time to time as the prime rate changes. If a firm continually earns an ROI of at least 15 percent before taxes, the opportunity costs of capital invested in inventory are at least 15 percent. This assumes that opportunities for further investment exist as in the following:

Costs of capital are 15 percent	0.150
Insurance costs are 0.5 percent of value	0.005
Taxes are 2.5 percent of value	0.025
Pilferage, spoilage, and damage	0.010
Obsolescence	0.010
Storage space and handling	0.040*
Carrying cost rate	0.240

See determination that follows.

Even in the best of situations, these calculations result in an estimated cost. As many have pointed out, the actual carrying cost rate used is a management policy variable whose selection is determined by the financial condition of the firm among other factors (Plossl and Wight 1967, 56; Brown 1977, 210). Carrying costs are obtained by multiplying the carrying rate by the cost of the items being stored whether they are purchased or produced internally.

Storage Costs.   Storage and handling costs were determined from the following information. Out-of-pocket costs for storage space and handling include the following annual costs:

Utilities	$ 25,000
Material handling personnel	110,000
Equipment maintenance	12,000
Building maintenance	13,000
Security personnel	20,000
	$180,000

The average dollar value of inventory in stores is $4,500,000. Dividing $180,000 by $4,500,000 renders an annual rate of 0.04. These calculations are based on the assumption that all items in storage require essentially the same storage space and services per unit of value. If this is not the case, the ratio of the requirements of the different classes of items must be determined and the costs proportioned accordingly.

Item Costs.   The cost of purchased items usually is readily available. The cost of internally produced items traditionally consists of labor, material, and overhead costs. The cost of labor per item can be determined in the usual manner by multiplying the standard hours by the average efficiency level achieved in producing that product and by the labor charge per hour. The cost of material can be obtained from accounting or purchasing.

Occasionally the argument will be presented that, in those cases where material is used for many products and producing a lot of a specific finished product will not require the purchase of an additional lot of material, material costs are sunk costs and need not be included when determining the lot size of the finished item. Unless the material is scrap, or approaching obsolescence or spoilage, this reasoning is fallacious. Eventually an order for a finished item will require ordering additional materials. Consistency then demands that the order that triggers a new order for raw materials be assigned the cost of all the new raw materials. Although the availability of materials must be considered in the release of orders, it makes little economic sense to subject the lot size decision to such vagaries. If the use of materials is lumpy and dependent on demand for finished goods, it would make more sense to use MRP rather than the economic order quantity (EOQ) approach. (See Chapter 10.)

Stockout Costs

A stockout occurs whenever insufficient stock exists to fulfill a replenishment order. The sources of stockout costs are easy to describe but very difficult to calculate. If stock is not available, two possible conditions—backorder or no backorder—may exist.

In a backorder situation, the customer is willing to wait to receive the item. The customer may be the purchaser of the finished product or, in fact, an internal user such as the final assembly department. In a no backorder situation, the customer doesn't wait; the order is lost.

In the case of a backorder, there are at least the costs resulting from the paperwork of keeping track of the backorder. There is also the possibility of the loss of future sales due to the customer's inconvenience in waiting. Emergency shipment costs also are possible.

When the sale is lost in the no backorder situation, there is the loss of the possible profit plus the loss of the contribution to overhead costs. Here, too, there is the possibility of additional losses due to future orders being placed with competitors. Repeated inability to deliver in a competitive manner can generate a poor delivery reputation, loss of goodwill, and loss of sales.

Stockout costs are virtually impossible to calculate in a straightforward, explicit manner. Part of the cost is lost customer goodwill, an intangible. How lost goodwill transforms into future buying habits of a customer is uncertain. How much adverse publicity results from a stockout? How does that publicity affect future sales and profits? What impact does lack of parts have on the assembly department's morale and efficiency? No one doubts the results of stockouts, but direct quantification of these results has not been achieved to any great extent. Instead, the approach followed most frequently is for management to establish a desired level of customer service. Since the marginal cost of each level of service can be determined, this approach implicitly assigns a cost to a stockout. For example, suppose the following:

1. A part is ordered 20 times per year.
2. A stockout is defined as any period in which inventory is insufficient to cover demand.
3. Present level of service is 90 percent and management desires to raise the service level to 95 percent. Two stockouts per year were permitted, now only one will be.
4. An additional $440 in stock must be added to safety stock—and therefore to average inventory—to achieve this goal.
5. The annual carrying rate for inventory is 0.25.

Then, implicitly, management is stating that the total cost of a stockout is greater than $0.25 \times \$440$, or $110.

This example is also an approach to measuring the cost of achieving various levels of customer service.

Capacity Related Costs

Costs of expanding or contracting capacity are incurred as a result of aggregate planning decisions of either the middle- or long-range type. Short-term decisions to run a work center or an entire facility overtime for a brief period are predominately scheduling problems, although they may result from a poor inventory position relative to demand.

When capacity is increased, costs are increased by some or all of the following:

1. Hiring and training direct laborers
2. Hiring and training supervisors
3. Adding service personnel in receiving, the warehouse, and so on
4. Learning curve experiences
5. Purchasing equipment

A substantial decrease in capacity results in costs due to

1. Layoffs (terminal pay and unemployment compensation)
2. Fixed overhead spread across a smaller volume
3. Temporary inefficiency due to change in production rate and reassignment of personnel
4. Low morale

Consideration of the costs of changing output rates were examined in greater detail in Chapter 2.

CONCLUDING COMMENTS

Whether inventory is an asset used to accomplish the objectives of an organization or a liability depends on its management; both conditions may exist in the same firm at the same time. The primary function of inventory is to decouple customer demand and production capacity. Functionally, inventory can be divided into anticipation, lot size, transportation, and fluctuation inventories and service parts. Each serves as a buffer between demand and production in a particular type of situation. However, in some instances inventory may be used to compensate for ineffective management.

Inventory management performance is measured in terms of customer service and inventory investment. There are many measures of customer service, and backorder service is an important component of any measure. Measuring customer service by multiple methods is a good idea in any situation. The availability of data, the effect of decisions on the measured results, and the relationship of the measured results to profit and productivity influence the selection of customer service measures.

Inventory investment is measured in both an absolute and a relative manner. An absolute value—$1 million, for example—serves as an upper limit constraint on inventory while an inventory turn ratio measures inventory investment in relation to the cost of goods sold. Both types of measures should be employed in most situations.

ABC analysis, based on Pareto's Principle of the Vital Few, divides items into ranked categories on the basis of monetary value, scarcity, and other factors influencing the desired degree of control. Different control procedures are established for the different classes.

Inventory costs are easier to describe than they are to calculate. Preparation costs, carrying costs, stockout costs, and capacity related costs affect inventory management decisions. Capacity related costs are associated with medium-range aggregate type decisions more than with individual item decisions. Cost calculations should include opportunity costs as well as direct costs, while sunk costs should be excluded.

Determination of inventory classifications, performance measures, and costing procedures should precede aggregate, intermediate, and individual item inventory management decisions.

EXERCISES

1. Describe a circumstance in which inventory is truly an asset, describe another in which inventory is a liability, and describe a third in which it clearly results from ineffective management.

2. Give an example of each of the following functional types of inventory: anticipation, fluctation, transportation, and lot size.

3. Compare two organizations, one with a line flow process and manufacturing-to-stock and the other with a job shop process and manufacturing-to-order. How would you expect their inventories to differ?

4. The Klingenbaum Mortuary has four funeral homes in a large metropolitan area. The most popular casket it sells has an average demand of 30 units per month. They purchase these caskets in truckload quantities of 60 units every two months for shipment to their warehouse. They use a carrying cost rate of 0.30 per year and an ordering cost of $30. For practical purposes, they have unlimited storage space. The present cost is $1,200 per unit. They believe that there is an 80 percent chance that the unit price will be increased to $1,350 each in two months. They are about to place an order. What should the quantity be?

5. A division ships a truckload of 1,000 transmissions to its assembly plant twice each week. One shipment leaves the plant around noon on Monday and arrives around noon on Thursday; the other leaves around noon on Thursday and arrives at the assembly plant about noon on Monday. What is the annual cost of transmission transportation inventory if the annual carrying cost rate is 0.20?

6. Using the data in Exercise 5, calculate the savings in transportation inventory if the transportation time is reduced to one day.

7. A local manufacturer uses 100 gallons of zinc chromate primer a month at a steady rate throughout the year. The present EOQ is 80 gallons. The supplier has a practice of increasing prices each June 1. On May 1 the company estimates that there is a 95 percent probability that the price of the primer will be increased from $10 to at least $11 per gallon. What quantity should be ordered when the order point is reached on the 15th of May? Ordering costs are $15 an order and the company policy is to use a carrying cost rate of 0.25 per year.

8. A multinational corporation ships components via rail and ship to its European assembly plant at a cost of $1 a unit. Total transit time is one-half month; unit cost is $40; the carrying cost rate is 0.24. They have the opportunity to ship by air at a cost of $1.80 a part. Air shipment will consume three calendar days. How should they ship?

9. Aggregate planning was discussed in Chapter 2. With which type of inventory is it primarily concerned? Describe the costs considered in the aggregate planning decision.

10. The owner of a relatively small retail establishment in East St. Louis has approximately $300,000 of small and medium size motors in inventory. They are sold primarily to industrial and commercial establishments as replacements. The demand for most varies between zero and five per year, and demand for most items is very erratic. A student study group expresses concern over the relatively low inventory turn ratio—about 1.5—achieved by the firm. The owner responds with a smile that, "That inventory is my gold mine". Is the owner demented, or can you suggest a probable basis for the comment?

11. What are the factors that should be considered in selecting the measure of customer service?

12. Give four examples, two from manufacturing and two from service organizations, of situations in which a 100 percent service level is a reasonable customer expectation. Remember that other departments and warehouses also are customers.

13. The B & J Home Supply Company carries lighting fixtures that it sells to small contractors and do-it-yourself homeowners. Last year it sold 1,240 of the most popular fixture. Sales of another 50 items were lost when stockouts caused contractors to find other suppliers. On another

occasion a contractor waited three days for a shipment of an order for 12 fixtures. What level of customer service did B & J achieve?

14. The Von Bester Qualitat Manufacturing Company of Germantown, Illinois, manufactures electonic assemblies. The plant manager tells you that all ten components of a major assembly have availability probabilities (customer service) performance histories of 0.99 each and that the final assembly has a 0.96 probability of 95 percent of being completed on schedule if all the components are available. Calculate the probability that an order for the final assembly will be completed on schedule.

15. A manufacturer of roller bearings supplies distributors and manufacturers from its warehouse. The following table describes the sales of the five bearings that constitute its most popular items. Items not shipped were backordered. How many measures of customer service are possible using these data? What measure of customer service did the manufacturer achieve in each?

Demand	Cost per Unit	Profit per Unit	Shipped from Stock
8,000	0.90	0.10	7,500
6,000	1.25	0.15	5,800
4,000	1.00	0.12	4,200
4,500	0.80	0.10	3,900
3,000	0.60	0.12	2,850
25,000			

16. Product A is assembled by the North Central Fabricating Company from four components, B, C, D, and E. Purchasing and component part machining departments have achieved their objective of a 98 percent service level relative to supplying the final assembly department. When the assembly department has all the components on time, it has completed the assembly on time 99 percent of the time. What level of service do you think the company achieves in shipping assemblies to customers? Do you recommend any changes in its objectives?

17. The South Plains Manufacturing Company produces sporting goods apparel for which demand is seasonal, as indicated in the data below. Company forecasts are relatively accurate. The company president wants to know the inventory turnover ratio at the end of Period 3. What will you report?

Months	Forecast	Demand	Inventory
1	6.4	6.3	8.2
2	6.5	6.4	9.4
3	6.6	6.7	10.0
4	9.2		
5	10.4		
6	11.4		

18. The president of the South Plains Manufacturing Company is unhappy with your answer to Exercise 17. The president wants to know how many weeks of sales are in inventory. What are you going to report?

19. Some contend that ABC analysis is no longer appropriate because computers can maintain tight control on all items. Comment.

20. An electronics component manufacturer produces high precision assemblies for the aeronautics and space industry, controls for kitchen appliances, and some items for industrial equipment. Classify the following sample of the company's purchased parts according to ABC principles and the following data.

Product	Unit Cost	Annual Volume	Other Factors
575	$ 93.00	3,200	
607	31.00	2,500	
625	212.00	320	Single source
811	130.00	475	
947	618.00	300	
024	720.00	300	
413	0.25	25,000	
483	0.60	6,800	Engineering change anticipated in next two months
495	1.25	15,000	
211	6.30	3,000	Lead time six months

21. Give an example of a sunk cost that could be erroneously considered relevant to the decision concerning the replacement of the present inventory management system.

22. How do preparation costs affect the amount of gasoline purchased by a motorist? A friend of yours tells you that the cost of ordering (preparation) are virtually zero. How do you respond?

23. Carrying costs and preparation costs are difficult to measure precisely. So what is accomplished by applying them in the decision-making process?

24. The inventory manager of a chain of department stores is reviewing the carrying cost rates used for small tools, paper products, and small appliances. The controller has reported the cost of capital as 16 percent. The company is borrowing at a point and one-half over the prime rate, which is 14 percent. The inventory manager collects the following information:

| | Costs as a Percentage of Item Value | | |
	Small Tools	Paper Products	Small Appliances
Insurance	0.5	0.5	0.5
Taxes	1.0	1.0	1.0
Pilferage and damage	2.0	0.2	2.4
Obsolescence	1.0	0.3	0.6
Storage space and handling	5.4	11.0	5.5

What is the carrying cost rate for each of the product groups? Why do you think the storage space and handling costs of the paper products are substantially higher than the other two groups?

25. A pottery manufacturer makes coffee mugs for an international hotel chain. Orders are received throughout the year from new hotels and for replacements from established hotels. The mugs use the same raw materials as other items manufactured by this firm. The mugs account for approximately 20 percent of the annual use of these materials. The inventory control department has obtained the following data concerning the cost of this item.

Work Center	Setup Time (hours)	Process Time	Department Utilization	Operators
A	2.4	0.0055	100%	1
B	0.6	0.0500	65%	1
C	0.0	0.0167	80%	1

Labor costs are $12.50 an hour, and the hourly contribution of equipment to overhead costs and profit is $25. Raw material costs 2 cents per unit and the yield rate equals 90 percent (the scrap rate is 10 percent). If the typical lot size is 2,000 units, what item cost should be used in the lot size calculation?

SELECTED READINGS

Artes, Richard P. "Making Some Cents out of Service Level." *Production and Inventory Management* 18, no. 4 (1977): 59.

Brown, Robert G. *Materials Management Systems*. New York: John Wiley & Sons, Inc., 1977.

Campbell, Kenneth L. "Inventory Turns and ABC-Analysis-Outmoded Textbook Concepts?" *American Production and Inventory Control Conference Proceedings* (1975): 420.

Close, Arthur C. "Projected Inventory Velocity Measurement." *Production and Inventory Management* 11 no. 3 (1970): 66.

Conroy, Paul G. "Data General ABC Inventory Managment." *Production and Inventory Management* 18, no. 4 (1977): 63.

Dickie, H. Ford. "ABC Inventory Analysis Shoots for Dollars." *Factory Management and Maintenance* (July 1951): 92.

Edwards, J. Nicholas, "Target Level Inventories." *American Production and Inventory Control Conference Proceedings* (1975): 309.

Fogarty, Donald W., and Thomas R. Hoffmann. "Customer Service." *Production and Inventory Management* (First Quarter 1980).

Greene, James H. *Production and Inventory Control Handbook*, 2d ed. New York: McGraw-Hill Book Co., 1987.

Jordan, Henry. "Relating Customer Service to Inventory Control." *American Management Association's Advanced Management Journal* 39, no. 4 (October 1974).

Jordan, Henry. "How to Plan and Control Inventories." *APICS Conference Proceedings* (October 1976): 305.

Krupp, James A. "Inventory Turn Ratio, as a Management Control Tool." *Inventories and Production* 1, no. 4 (September/October 1981): 18-21.

Norbom, Rolf. "The Simple ABC's (A Loose Piece Float System)." *Production and Inventory Management* 14, no. 1 (1973): 16.

Orlicky, Joseph. *Material Requirements Planning.* New York: McGraw-Hill Book Co., 1975.

Peters, Thomas J. *Thriving On Chaos.* New York: Harper & Row, Publishers, Inc., 1987.

Plossl, George W. "How Much Inventory is Enough?" *Production and Inventory Management* (Second Quarter 1971).

Plossl, George W. *Manufacturing Control: The Last Frontier for Profits.* Reston, VA: Reston Publishing Company, Inc., 1973.

Plossl, George W., and Oliver W. Wight. *Production and Inventory Control.* Englewood Cliffs, NJ: Prentice-Hall, Inc., 1967.

Throndsen, Elton C. "Performance Measurement Criteria for Inventory Management." *American Production and Inventory Control Society Conference Proceedings* (Third Quarter 1971): 256.

Wight, Oliver W. *Production and Inventory Management in the Computer Age.* Boston, MA: Cahner Books, 1974.

Zimmerman, Gary. "The ABC's of Vilfredo Pareto." *Production Inventory Management* 16, no. 3 (1975): 1-9.

APPENDIX 5A
MEASURING PREPARATION COSTS

One good way of examining different costing approaches is to look at an example. Let's estimate the cost of issuing a purchase order under the following conditions.

1. During the last three years the purchasing department placed an average of approximately 10,000 purchase orders annually. The total number of personnel and the number per wage classification were constant during that period.

2. Cost of purchasing agents (*CPA*) is the direct and indirect costs of five purchasing agents. This cost is projected as $140,000 next year.

3. Cost of purchasing management, stenographers, and clerical personnel (*CPMS*) is the total direct and indirect costs of these persons. It is

forecast as $80,000 next year. This includes $38,000 for a purchasing manager and $42,000 for three stenographers and two clerks.

4. Cost of services (*CSER*) is the cost of copying, communications, and miscellaneous supplies. It is forecast as $30,000 next year.

5. Building and equipment amortization charges, building and equipment maintenance, and utilities are grouped under general and administrative overhead. The corporation is considered as an ongoing concern; these costs are viewed as sunk costs, not affecting the purchase lot size decision.

6. Industrial engineering has studied the purchasing department using work sampling and some standard time data for clerical functions. They have found the following: The average purchase order requires 0.1 standard hours of the purchasing manager's time, 1.0 standard hours of the purchasing agent's time, 0.5 standard hours of stenographic and clerical time, and $2 of copying and communication cost. Paper costs are 25 cents per order. The average monthly direct and indirect compensation of stenographic personnel is $875. Estimates are based on next year's costs.

What does it cost to place a purchase order? "Your guess is as good as mine," is the reaction of many. We can do better than that—much better, in fact. Three alternative approaches to the problem follow. Each approach is demonstrated and its strengths and weaknesses discussed.

The Aggregate Approach

This approach consists of dividing the total costs of the activity (purchasing in this case) by the total number of purchase orders to obtain the average cost of an order. Using the data from the foregoing example:

$$
\begin{aligned}
\text{Total Costs} &= CPA + CPMS + CSER \\
&= \$140,000 + \$80,000 + \$30,000 \\
&= \$250,000
\end{aligned}
$$

$$
\begin{aligned}
\text{Cost per Order} &= \frac{\text{Total Costs}}{\text{Total Orders}} \\
&= \frac{\$250,000}{10,000} \\
&= \$25 \text{ per Order}
\end{aligned}
$$

The Standard Cost Approach

Adding the standard costs of personnel time, materials, and services required for each order is another approach. For the sake of simplicity we will assume that all efficiency factors are 1.00 (for personnel performances and usage of materials and services).

Standard Cost
of Purchasing $= \dfrac{\$38,000 \text{ per Year} \times 0.1 \text{ Hour per Order}}{50 \text{ Weeks per Year} \times 40 \text{ Hours per Week}}$
Manager's Time
$= \$1.90 \text{ per Order}$

Standard Cost
of Purchasing $= \dfrac{\$140,000 \text{ per Year} \times 1.0 \text{ Hour per Order}}{50 \text{ Weeks per Year} \times 40 \text{ Hours per Week} \times 5 \text{ Agents}}$
Agent's Time
$= \$14 \text{ per Order}$

Standard Clerical
and Stenographic $= \dfrac{\$42,000 \text{ per Year} \times 0.5 \text{ Hour per Order}}{50 \text{ Weeks per Year} \times 40 \text{ Hours per Week} \times 5 \text{ Persons}}$
Costs
$= \$2.10 \text{ per Order}$

Paper Costs = $0.25 per Order

Copy and Communication Costs = $2.00 per Order

Total costs: $ 1.90 Purchasing Manager's Time
              14.00 Purchasing Agent's Time
               2.10 Stenographic and Clerical Time
               2.00 Copy and Communication Costs
               0.25 Paper Costs
             $20.25 per Order

(Estimated costs equal standard costs since the efficiency factor is 1.00 for all costs.)

The Marginal Out-of-Pocket Cost Approach

If placing an additional order does not require an additional purchasing agent, additional stenographic and clerical personnel, additional management, additional accounting or receiving personnel, or additional office equipment, then the added costs of placing the order consist of the paper consumed plus telephone and telegraphic expenses resulting directly from this order. In summary, the cost of the purchase order would be the out-of-pocket costs of paper and communication costs cited earlier in this analysis. The out-of-pocket marginal costs of the purchase order being considered are:

Paper Costs   = $0.25
Copy and Communication Costs =   2.00
                                  $2.25

Thus, we can use $25, $20.25, or $2.25 as the cost of a purchase order. This should enable us to justify whatever action we want to take (the essence of agile management). Will it really though? Not if we analyze the underlying assumptions and premises of each of these approaches.

Assumptions and Premises of the Aggregate, Standard, and Marginal Cost Approaches

The aggregate approach assumes that (1) all the purchasing department does is place orders with vendors and follow up on the orders and (2) the rated capacity of the purchasing department is represented by the average production of the last few years. The second assumption is frequently invalid and the first should be if it is not. In addition to issuing purchase orders, an effective purchasing department will be searching for new and additional sources, participating in value analysis activities, participating in material board review of damaged items, developing the purchasing management systems, reviewing developments in decision techniques, and so on.

Assuming that the average purchasing activity of the previous two or three years is an accurate measure of the purchasing department's capacity is precarious. If those years were unusually busy ones in a period of high business activity, then nine-hour days and Saturday morning work in purchasing may have been common. Thus, the 10,000 orders were above a reasonable upper limit of the activity the department can maintain without additional personnel, chaos, or disgruntled employees. If the preceding years were a slack period, the 10,000 orders annually may be substantially below what the department can handle.

A major weakness of the standard cost approach to determining the cost of a purchase order is that it assumes, at least in the form presented, that all purchase orders are equally demanding. Such is not the case. Many orders are routine, present little or no problem in vendor selection, and have few if any quality and delivery problems associated with them. Different orders require substantially different commitments of purchasing time. Vendor selection, price and contract negotiations, vendor performance in the fulfillment of the product quality, and delivery promises vary widely for different orders. For example, the introduction of new products or new product lines may involve establishing purchasing relations with new suppliers. If the standard cost approach is used, it makes sense in many organizations to establish rates for at least four types of purchase orders, A, B, C, and D.

A: Orders for which considerable difficulty in vendor selection, contract negotiation, purchase order approval, supplier quality, delivery performance, or production setup is expected

B: Orders for which moderate difficulties are anticipated or have been experienced

C: Routine, straightforward orders

D: Joint orders

Some purchasing agents will tell you they don't have any of the C type situations and few of the B types. That may be true if they are the elite of the department and assigned the difficult tasks. However, in most organizations

Pareto's principle will hold: a relatively small number of items, 10 to 20 percent, will generate most of the problems. Under such circumstances different standards can be established for the types of purchase orders with different levels of administrative difficulty. How to establish such standards is more appropriately within the realm of a text on clerical and administrative work measurement. Such standards can be established with the cooperation of the purchasing department. The standards may not represent reality precisely to the third decimal place, but they are precise enough for decision making. In addition, they are more accurate than a single average for all purchase orders. A similar approach can be followed in measuring the clerical and administrative costs of production orders.

As noted in the previous discussion of marginal costs, this approach is of questionable validity except in unusual circumstances. It is valid if the department is operating far below capacity and dismissal of personnel is not desirable for long-term economic reasons or for other reasons. If applied to its logical extreme, it means that lot sizes would be relatively small and a much larger number of orders would be placed. It also means that the organization would eventually reach a point at which an additional order would require the addition of a purchasing agent and, to maintain consistency, that order would cost thousands of dollars. Such an approach is unrealistic.

What is a valid approach? The standard cost approach, modified to include actual costs of personnel time, processing, and forms while excluding sunk costs such as building and equipment overhead, is adopted frequently. The aggregate approach, modified to include only those costs related to the number of orders processed, should produce similar results. The proportion of personnel time devoted to activities such as vendor selection and value analysis should be excluded from the order preparation costs because, in most cases, they are not related to the number of orders. If these two approaches result in substantially different results, it suggests that the calculations should be reviewed.

6

INDEPENDENT DEMAND INVENTORY MANAGEMENT

Individual items include assemblies, subassemblies, fabricated components, purchased components, and purchased materials. They are found in finished goods, spare parts, work in process, and raw materials. Prior to analyzing individual items, decisions have been made at the aggregate and intermediate levels concerning such things as constraints on inventory, grouping of items, customer service objectives, and the development and implementation of inventory management information systems.

Individual item management activities begin with selecting the appropriate inventory management system (decision rules for how much to order and when to release the order) for the different individual items. Table 6-1 lists the names of the basic methods for managing individual items.

Table 6-1
Names of Basic Ordering and Lot Size Rules (Grouped by Type of Rule)

Demand	When to Order Rules	Quantity to Order Rules
Independent	Order Point	Fixed Order Quantity
		Economic Order Quantity
	Periodic	Variable Order Quantity
	Time-Phased Order Point	Fixed or Discrete Order Quantity
Dependent	Time Phasing	Discrete Order Quantity
	(Material Requirements Planning)	

Many different combinations of lot size and order point rules are possible. Different combinations are appropriate under different conditions. In this chapter we will examine the data required for inventory management decisions, the situational characteristics determining the appropriateness of different management systems, and the nature of basic inventory management decision rules and the systems that they constitute.

DATA REQUIREMENTS

Certain data concerning each item are required for inventory management decisions. In less complex situations (low volume transactions and few levels in the bill of material), this data may be processed manually and stored on cards. However, the complexity of most situations and the availability of relatively inexpensive computer hardware and software have led to increased computerization of inventory management support systems. The data usually are organized in the following manner:

1. The inventory record file, also called the part master file or the item master file
2. The bill of material (BOM) file
3. The master production schedule (MPS)

The BOM file and the MPS were discussed in Chapter 4. The inventory record file contains a record, identified by part number, for each item. Each record usually contains inventory status and cost data required for cost estimating and production activity control in addition to the following data required for inventory management:

1. Part number—the unique part number assigned to the item
2. Part description—the name of the item
3. On-hand quantity—the number of units of this item in stock
4. Allocated quantity—the number of units of this item that has been assigned to previously planned future orders
5. Available quantity—the difference between the on-hand quantity and the allocated quantity
6. Lot size quantity—the normal number of units of this item produced at one time (the order quantity), a quantity that will vary in many situations
7. Lead time—the normal time required to manufacture (or purchase) this item in a typical lot quantity range
8. Item cost—the standard cost of the item
9. Preparation costs—the sum of administrative, clerical, and shop costs incurred in issuing and monitoring the order (Machine setup time is included in these costs for manufactured orders.)
10. Carrying cost—the annual cost of carrying one unit of this item in inventory
11. Group code—An indication as to whether this item is to be purchased or produced as one of a group of items in a joint lot size decision process
12. Where used (next assembly)—the identification of the assembly or assemblies in which this item is used
13. Safety stock—a number of units usually held in inventory to protect against fluctuations in demand and/or supply
14. Average demand—the average quantity required per period

FACTORS IN INVENTORY DECISIONS

The nature of a situation determines the appropriateness of an inventory management system. Although it is not feasible to examine all the possible combinations of factors, each of which can define a unique situation and set of considerations, it is possible to describe those that are most important in selecting an inventory management system and why they are important. Those factors are: (1) demand pattern, (2) source—common suppliers or production process, and (3) customer requirements.

The Demand Pattern

The nature of the demand pattern has an effect greater than any other possible factor on the appropriateness of the when-to-order decision rules and, thus, on the design of the inventory management system. A relatively gradual and steady usage pattern is characteristic of independent demand (see Figure 6-1). On the other hand, a pattern of abrupt and dramatic changes in usage is characteristic of dependent demand (see Figure 6-2)

Independent Demand. Distribution inventories (i.e., items held as finished goods for sale) and service parts purchased by many different customers usually experience a relatively stable demand, as illustrated in Figure 6-1. This demand, which may be affected by trends and seasonal patterns, does not depend on demand for other items; it is independent demand.

Figure 6-1
Relation of Demand and Stock Dissipation Patterns Over Time
(Independent Demand)

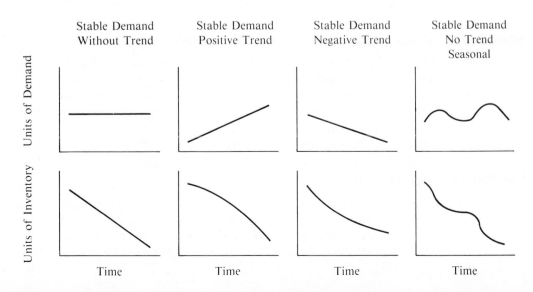

Dependent Demand.   Subassemblies, component parts, and raw materials have a demand that is primarily dependent on the demand for the final products in which they are used. If the final products are fabricated intermittently in lots (batches), the demand for these items is relatively abrupt and dramatic as illustrated in Figure 6-2. They are dependent demand items. Material requirements planning should be used for these items.

Figure 6-2
Relation of Demand and Stock Dissipation Patterns Over Time
(Dependent Demand)

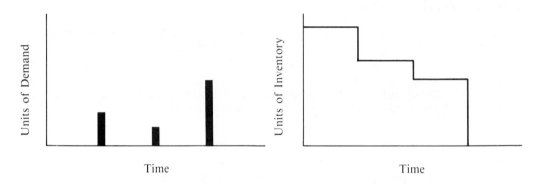

Of course, there are exceptions. Finished goods purchased in relatively large quantities only a few times a year by one or two customers will likely exhibit an abrupt and irregular demand pattern similar to dependent demand. On the other hand, raw materials, common hardware items, and components used in many different final products may experience a relatively stable demand similar to that usually associated with independent demand items. The demand pattern for each item must be evaluated on its own merits.

Source: Common Supplier or Production Process

Parts purchased from a single supplier frequently are grouped together to facilitate joint purchase orders, joint product quantity discounts, transportation, and communications with suppliers. Items produced in the same department or on similar machines also should be analyzed for common setups. Items purchased from a common supplier or produced on common facilities are candidates for joint periodic review inventory management. (See Chapter 8.)

Customer Requirements

When a group of items is ordered by a single customer, the production or purchase of these items may be grouped to enable concurrent delivery. This practice enables joint shipping and invoicing. None of the items may have value to the customer unless all are delivered, and, in practice, some purchase orders predicate payment upon receipt of all items. This situation may exist when all the items are required in an assembly produced by the customer.

Other Factors

Demand and design stability, shelf life, and lead time also affect inventory decisions. Items susceptible to the whims of fashion or engineering changes may be ordered in quantities smaller than otherwise would be the case. Limited shelf life also imposes limits on the quantity ordered. Dependent demand parts and materials with long lead times relative to final assembly delivery requirements may require an order point system to achieve customer service objectives.

JIT concepts, discussed in Chapter 17, and purchasing arrangements, discussed in Chapter 15, should be examined before deciding on order quantities and order release decisions.

INVENTORY MANAGEMENT MODELS AND DECISION RULES

A company may manufacture or purchase an item in three different ways: (1) after receiving an order for the item (production to order), (2) in anticipation of customer orders (production to stock), or (3) as modular components that are produced to stock and then final assembled after receiving an order.

In the first instance, production to order, the firm may produce the quantity ordered by customers, or it may produce that quantity plus additional units in anticipation of further orders.

The principles and techniques of material requirements planning (MRP), discussed in Chapter 10, are used in determining the order release dates and lot sizes of items produced only to order. In the case of production to stock or production of modular components, the decision rules governing lot size and order release timing are a function primarily of an item's demand characteristics. A fixed order quantity—an order point type system or a periodic review type system—usually is appropriate for managing independent demand items. Dependent demand items usually are managed best by an MRP type system.

Production of customer order requirements plus anticipated requirements on receipt of an order frequently involves a combination of MRP and order point management systems. In fact, most real world systems are hybrid; they combine features of the different systems to cope with real world complexities. This introduction to lot size and order release decision rules views inventory management situations as relatively simple and neat. The principles and techniques developed under these conditions will aid in handling the more complex situations discussed later.

The two objectives of an inventory management system are to provide a level of customer service and to minimize the costs of providing that service. The order release mechanism is used by the inventory planner as the major determinant of the level of customer service, while order quantity size is the primary determinant of inventory costs. This is important because the inventory planner selects the inventory management model that best achieves the system objectives.

First, we examine the fixed order quantity model because it clearly illustrates the cost structure of lot size decisions. Presentation of the statistical order point model follows as the concepts involved are relevant to any demand situation. Treatment of periodic review systems, visual review systems, and the time-phased order point follow. Material requirements planning is covered in Chapter 10.

Fixed Order Quantity and the Economic Order Quantity

The fixed order quantity lot size decision rule specifies a number of units to be ordered each time an order is placed for a particular item. This quantity may be arbitrary, such as a two-week supply or 100 units, but is frequently the economic order quantity (EOQ). The EOQ is the most economical under a given set of conditions. The fixed order quantity lot size determination method can be combined with each of the different methods for determining the order release. Later we will examine the conditions appropriate for the different combinations of methods.

The assumptions of the basic economic order quantity are:

1. Lead time is constant and known, and demand occurs at a relatively constant and known rate; thus, there are no stockouts.
2. Preparation costs and total carrying costs are constant and known.
3. Replenishment is instantaneous; items arrive at an infinite rate at a given time.

Situations in which all the relevant factors—demand, lead time, and costs—are known with complete certainty are rare. But assuming deterministic conditions is legitimate when analyzing some inventory factors (demand, lead time, and costs) for at least three reasons. First, situations do exist in which the facts are known with near certainty, for example, the newsprint to publish a Sunday paper or the requirement for staple food items such as milk and bread. Second, the effect of the decision frequently is relatively insensitive to small changes in decision factors. And third, understanding the fixed order quantity model can aid in the modeling of more complex situations.

Two graphs are essential in analyzing inventory management situations. One displays the quantity in inventory over time, and the other illustrates the relationship of cost to lot size (see Figure 6-5). In the case of the fixed order quantity, the quantity versus time relationship takes the sawtooth shape in Figure 6-3.

The straight vertical lines in Figure 6-3 represent the arrival of items in inventory just as the stock level reaches zero. The number of units in stock

Figure 6-3
Units in Inventory Versus Time
(Fixed Order Quantity Model with Demand and Lead Time Certain)

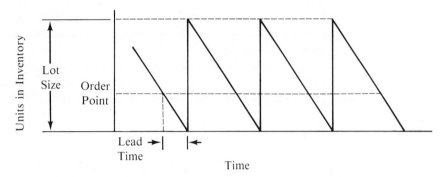

then increases instantaneously by *Q*, the amount ordered and received. This graphic representation of the arrival of an order instantaneously is a very accurate depiction of the arrival of a lot of purchased parts. It is also an accurate representation of the arrival of parts produced within the organization when the time between the manufacture of the first item and the last is relatively brief.

Withdrawals of items from inventory under constant demand conditions actually take place in an incremental step fashion, which is approximated by the straight line slope shown in Figure 6-4.

Figure 6-4
Constant Withdrawals from Inventory Over Time

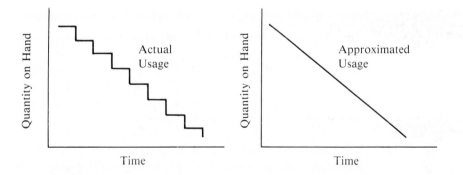

Costs incurred in a lot size decision include carrying costs, preparation costs, stockout costs, and the cost of the item itself. The cost of the item, the purchase price or the cost of material and labor and overhead in the case of an item produced internally, can change in those situations where purchase or production of larger quantities will achieve economies of scale. For the purpose of this analysis, the cost of an item is treated as a constant, and stockouts do not occur. Therefore, the total costs incurred during a period as a result of the lot size decision when using the basic economic order quantity decision rule are formulated as follows:

Total costs equal preparation costs plus carrying costs.
Preparation costs equal cost per preparation times the number of preparations in the period.
Carrying costs equal the average quantity in inventory times the cost of carrying one unit for the period or the average quantity in inventory times unit cost times the cost rate of carrying one unit for the period.

Therefore,

$$TC = \frac{SR}{Q} + \frac{QK}{2} \quad \text{or} \quad TC = \frac{SR}{Q} + \frac{QkC}{2}$$

where TC = total costs per period, usually a year
        S = cost per preparation in dollars
        R = period requirements in units
        Q = lot size in units
        K = cost of holding one unit in inventory for the period
        C = cost of one unit
        k = cost rate of carrying one unit in inventory for the period
        $K = kC$

From Figure 6-3 it can be determined that average inventory equals one-half the lot size. Inventory decreases at a constant rate from a maximum lot size to a minimum of zero. Thus, the average inventory equals $\frac{Q + 0}{2}$ or $\frac{Q}{2}$.

The period used for these calculations is usually one year. However, it may be appropriate to use a different length period; for example, the planning period of some items may be only six months. You should note that the requirements, demand, and the carrying cost per unit will be proportionately less for the shorter period. Either a calculus or a graphic approach can be used to find the lot size that results in minimum costs.

The Graphic Solution.   Graphing carrying costs, preparation costs, and total inventory costs in relation to lot size reveals a critical relation between carrying costs and preparation costs at that point, lot size, where total costs are a minimum. Let's look at an example.

A ball bearing distributor has an item that has an annual demand of 60,000 units at a relatively constant rate throughout the year. Preparation costs are $45 each time an order is placed; the carrying cost rate is $0.30 per dollar of inventory per year; and the units cost $2 each. To graph the relationship of lot size and total costs, it is necessary to calculate the total costs for different lot sizes, as shown in Table 6-2 and graphed in Figure 6-5.

Table 6-2
Tabulation of Inventory Costs for Different Lot Sizes
$S = \$45$, $R = 60,000$, $k = 0.30$, $C = \$2$

Lot Size (Q)	Preparation Costs $\left(\dfrac{SR}{Q}\right)$	Carrying Costs $\left(\dfrac{QkC}{2}\right)$	Total Cost
10	$270,000	$ 3	$270,003
100	27,000	30	27,030
500	5,400	150	5,550
1,000	2,700	300	3,000
1,500	1,800	450	2,250
2,000	1,350	600	1,950
2,500	1,080	750	1,830
3,000	900	900	1,800
3,500	771	1,050	1,821
4,000	675	1,200	1,875
6,000	450	1,800	2,250
10,000	270	3,000	3,270
15,000	180	4,500	4,680
30,000	90	9,000	9,090
60,000	45	18,000	18,045

Figure 6-5
Fixed Order Quantity
(Cost Versus Lot Size: An Example)

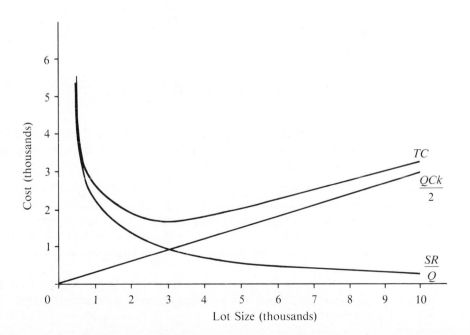

Note that the preparation costs, $\dfrac{SR}{Q}$, shown in Table 6-2 or Figure 6-5, decrease at a *geometrically* decreasing rate and that the carrying costs, $\dfrac{QCk}{2}$, increase at an *arithmetically* increasing rate. Additionally, the total cost values and the graph reveal two interesting facts: (1) total period costs are lowest at that point where preparation costs equal carrying costs (lot size equals 3,000) and (2) the total costs are approximately the same for a wide range of lot sizes centered on the minimum cost lot size. In fact, preparation costs are approximately equal to carrying costs for the minimum total cost lot size in most continuous demand situations. You may want to tabulate and graph other examples to verify this. The width of the span of lot sizes in which there is little change in total costs is called the *inelastic portion* of the total cost curve and depends on the values of the parameters (carrying costs, preparation costs, and annual demand). We will return to this topic later when discussing the sensitivity of the model. The first observation enables us to establish the general procedure: set preparation costs equal to carrying costs and solve for the EOQ.

Since the EOQ is that quantity where preparation costs equal carrying costs:

$$\frac{QkC}{2} = \frac{SR}{Q}$$

Thus, solving for Q gives:

$$Q^2 = \frac{2SR}{kC}$$

and, therefore,

$$Q^* \text{ (optimum value)} = \left(\frac{2SR}{kC}\right)^{1/2}$$

The EOQ can be determined using the above model. Graphing the cost functions versus lot size will also provide valuable insight concerning the increase in total cost as the lot size is increased or decreased in a particular case.

The Calculus Optimization Approach.   The calculus approach is presented to illustrate a technique useful for deriving a decision rule in many inventory situations. One need not possess a knowledge of calculus to use the resulting decision rule.

Using the basic calculus optimization technique, the first derivative of the total cost expression with respect to Q is set equal to zero. The value of

Q that satisfies that equation is an optimum. Taking the first derivative of TC, TC', with respect to Q,

$$TC = \frac{SR}{Q} + \frac{KQ}{2}$$

$$TC' = \frac{-SR}{Q^2} + \frac{K}{2} = 0$$

and, so,

$$\frac{K}{2} = \frac{SR}{Q^2}$$

Multiplying both sides of the equation by Q^2 and $\frac{2}{K}$ gives:

$$Q^2 = \frac{2SR}{K}$$

$$Q^* = \left(\frac{2SR}{K}\right)^{1/2}$$

This is the same decision rule we obtained using the graphic approach, except that kC has been replaced by K.

To determine if this point is a maximum or minimum we must next take the second derivative of TC, TC'', and determine if it is positive or negative at Q^*. This is formulated as follows:

$$TC'' = \frac{2SR}{Q^3}$$

Since R, S, and Q are always positive, the test of a minimum solution is met; TC'' will be positive for Q^*. Therefore, the solution obtained by solving the second derivative is a minimum. That is, it gives the value of Q that will result in the minimum total period costs.

Total Period Costs and Sensitivity.   Both approaches result in the same lot size, 3,000 units. The total annual costs resulting from using a lot size of 3,000 are determined in the following manner:

$$TC(Q^*) = \frac{SR}{Q^*} + \frac{CkQ^*}{2}$$

$$TC(3,000) = \frac{\$45 \times 60,000}{3,000} + \frac{\$2 \times 0.3 \times 3,000}{2}$$

$$= \$900 + \$900$$

$$= \$1,800$$

Increasing the lot size, Q, by 10 percent results in a little less than a one-half percent increase in total costs given the parameters of this situation, as shown in the following calculations.

$$TC(3,300) = \frac{\$45 \times 60,000}{3,300} + \frac{\$2 \times 0.3 \times 3,300}{2}$$
$$= \$818.18 + \$990$$
$$= \$1,808.18$$

Decreasing the lot size, Q, by 10 percent results in slightly more than a one-half percent increase in the total annual inventory costs, as shown by the following calculations.

$$TC(2,700) = \frac{\$45 \times 60,000}{2,700} + \frac{\$2 \times 0.3 \times 2,700}{2}$$
$$= \$1,000 + \$810$$
$$= \$1,810$$

Total costs resulting from the lot size decision do not seem to be overly sensitive to changes in the lot size if the foregoing example is any indication. Let's look at the general case.

The relationship of the total cost, TC, of a nonoptimum lot size to the total cost, TC^*, of the optimum lot size can be determined as follows.

$$TC^* = \frac{SR}{Q^*} + \frac{Q^*K}{2}$$

and

$$TC = \frac{SR}{Q} + \frac{QK}{2}$$

Therefore,

$$\frac{TC}{TC^*} = \frac{\dfrac{SR}{Q} + \dfrac{QK}{2}}{\dfrac{SR}{Q^*} + \dfrac{Q^*K}{2}}$$

Substituting $Q^* = \left(\dfrac{2SR}{K}\right)^{1/2}$ and then manipulating algebraically to remove S, R, and K gives:

$$\frac{TC}{TC^*} = \frac{1}{2}\left(\frac{Q^*}{Q} + \frac{Q}{Q^*}\right)$$

Thus, the effects of a specific percentage change in Q can be calculated. For example, let $Q = 1.10Q^*$ (a 10 percent increase). Then,

$$\frac{TC}{TC^*} = \frac{1}{2}\left(\frac{Q^*}{1.10Q^*} + \frac{1.10Q^*}{Q^*}\right)$$
$$= \frac{0.909 + 1.10}{2}$$
$$= 1.0045$$

These results correspond to those obtained when analyzing the sensitivity of total costs to changes in the lot size of the previous examples. Thus, in general, the percentage difference in inventory costs is relatively small in comparison with the difference in lot sizes around the EOQ. This inelasticity of the total cost curve in the vicinity of the EOQ gives the inventory planner some flexibility.

Variations of the EOQ Model.   There are literally dozens of ways the basic EOQ model can be modified to fit different situations. Because of their broad applicability, the dollar lot size model and the noninstantaneous receipt model are examined.

The dollar lot size model provides the optimum lot size value in monetary units rather than physical units. This approach is especially useful when developing and applying a model to determine the minimum cost lot size of a group of items. Letting:

$$Q_\$ = \text{lot size in dollars,}$$
$$A = \text{period requirements in dollars, and}$$
$$TC = \frac{kQ_\$}{2} + \frac{SA}{Q_\$}$$

Following the calculus approach to determine the value of $Q_\$$ that results in the minimum total period costs, TC^*, yields the following.

$$Q_\$^* = \left(\frac{2AS}{k}\right)^{1/2}$$

And, using data from the previous example, where $C = \$2$, $R = 60{,}000$, $k = 0.3$, and $S = \$45$:

$$A = CR = \$2 \times 60{,}000 = \$120{,}000$$
$$Q_\$^* = \left(\frac{2 \times \$120{,}000 \times \$45}{0.3}\right)^{1/2} = \$6{,}000$$
$$Q^* = \frac{Q_\$^*}{C} = \frac{\$6{,}000}{\$2} = 3{,}000$$

Note that this is the same answer as obtained earlier.

Noninstantaneous Receipt. When items are produced internally, they frequently enter inventory gradually on a day-to-day basis during a substantial portion of the consumption period rather than at once as when a purchased lot arrives. Thus, the investment of dollars in inventory takes place day by day during the production run, as illustrated in Figure 6-6, and units continue to be withdrawn from stock as the newly produced items arrive. Thus, in this case of noninstantaneous receipt, known lead time, and no safety stock, the inventory level is never as large as the lot size.

Figure 6-6
Inventory Versus Time, Fixed Order Quantity
(Noninstantaneous Receipt)

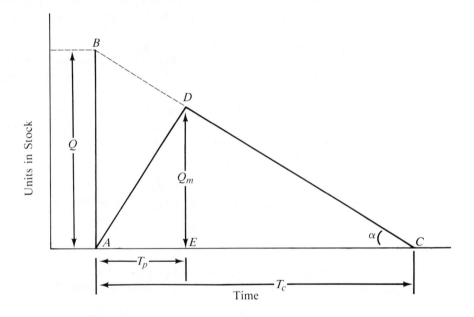

Inventory is both produced and consumed during the period of production, T_p. The rate, P, at which an item is produced is equal to the production lot size, Q, divided by T_p. The demand rate, D, is equal to Q divided by the consumption period, T_c. When T_c equals a year, D equals R (the annual requirements). These are, then, formulated as follows:

$$P = \frac{Q}{T_p} \quad \text{and} \quad D = \frac{Q}{T_c}$$

Therefore,

$$T_p = \frac{Q}{P} \quad \text{and} \quad T_c = \frac{Q}{D}$$

Both P and D are expressed in units per the same time period—often units per day. In this case, as in the instantaneous receipt case, the TC resulting from the lot size decision is equal to the preparation costs plus the carrying costs. Preparation costs again equal the cost per preparation times the number of preparations in the period as described previously. Carrying costs again equal average inventory quantity (or value) times the cost (or cost rate) of carrying one unit for the period. The difficulty is that average inventory is not one-half the lot size, $\frac{Q}{2}$, in this case. An examination of Figure 6-6 reveals that average inventory is equal to $\frac{Q_m}{2}$, but the value of Q_m is not immediately apparent. A little basic geometry will allow us to determine it from the known parameters. Two similar triangles, each having a common angle alpha (α), can be seen in Figure 6-6. Triangle ABC has sides of Q and T_c while triangle EDC has corresponding sides of Q_m and $T_c - T_p$. From the rules of geometry,

$$\frac{Q}{T_c} = \frac{Q_m}{T_c - T_p}$$

since both ratios describe the angle α. Thus,

$$Q_m = \frac{Q(T_c - T_p)}{T_c}$$

Previously described relationships between Q, T_c, T_p, P, and D, showed that

$$T_p = \frac{Q}{P} \quad \text{and} \quad T_c = \frac{Q}{D}$$

Substituting $\frac{Q}{P}$ for T_p and $\frac{Q}{D}$ for T_c gives

$$Q_m = \frac{Q\left(\dfrac{Q}{D} - \dfrac{Q}{P}\right)}{\dfrac{Q}{D}}$$

Multiplying the numerator and denominator on the right side of the equation by $\frac{D}{Q}$ gives

$$Q_m = Q\left(\frac{D}{D} - \frac{D}{P}\right) = Q\left(1 - \frac{D}{P}\right)$$

Therefore, the average inventory in the noninstantaneous case, $\frac{Q_m}{2}$, is equal to one-half the lot size multiplied by one minus the ratio of the consumption rate to the production rate. Intuitively this makes sense; one would expect the average inventory to decrease in proportion to the ratio of the consumption and production rates due to the fact that units are being withdrawn from stock as they are produced and enter stock.

This example illustrates a useful approach for determining average inventory under many different circumstances that do not correspond exactly to the basic model. Thus, substituting

$$\tfrac{1}{2}Q\left(1 - \frac{D}{P}\right)$$

for $\dfrac{Q}{2}$ in the basic decision rules gives the following.

$$TC = \frac{SR}{Q} + \tfrac{1}{2}kCQ\left(1 - \frac{D}{P}\right)$$

$$Q^* = \left[\frac{2RS}{kC\left(1 - \dfrac{D}{P}\right)}\right]^{1/2}$$

Noninstantaneous Receipt Example. Let's return to the previous example of the ball bearings. We assume the same facts except that the situation has changed to one of a manufacturer producing these items for finished goods, and the production capacity is 960 units per eight-hour shift. Thus, we have the following.

$$R = 60,000 \text{ units per year}$$
$$S = \$45 \text{ per order}$$
$$k = \$0.30 \text{ per \$ per year}$$
$$C = \$2 \text{ each}$$
$$P = 960 \text{ units per eight-hour shift}$$
$$D = 60,000 \text{ units per year}$$

If we casually insert the given demand and production rates directly into the formula we have developed for this situation, we will have a mixture of apples and oranges—fruit salad. Consequently, we must first convert either P or D to the same base as the other. They should not be stated in units for different time periods. In this case let's convert P to the same base as D, an annual one.

Since the plant works one shift a day, five days a week, and 50 weeks a year, the annual production rate is calculated as

$$P = 960 \times 5 \times 50$$
$$= 240,000 \text{ units/year}$$

The minimum cost order quantity is

$$Q^* = \left[\frac{2RS}{kC\left(1 - \dfrac{D}{P}\right)} \right]^{1/2}$$

$$= \left[\frac{2 \times 60,000 \times 45}{2 \times 0.3\left(1 - \dfrac{60,000}{240,000}\right)} \right]^{1/2}$$

$$= 12,000,000^{1/2}$$

$$= 3,464.1$$

The exactness of this answer raises practical considerations. First, a fractional ball bearing is not a meaningful quantity; second, it probably makes sense to round the lot size to 3,500 or 3,400 units. The increased unit costs should be relatively small and the record keeping much easier. Using a lot size of 3,464 or 3,465 is attributing greater precision to the estimated parameter values than is justified in most cases.

In summary, the fixed order quantity model is useful for determining the lot size under relatively stable, independent demand. Total costs are relatively insensitive to the actual lot size differing slightly from the optimum lot size. Minor modifications to the basic model are required to provide decision rules for more complex situations.

Order Release Decisions

As mentioned previously, deciding when to release an order for purchase or production and deciding the quantity to order are the two objectives of individual item management. There are four basic methods of deciding when to order independent inventory items: (1) statistical order point, (2) periodic review, (3) hybrid methods, and (4) time-phased order point.

Traditionally, the EOQ, fixed order quantity, lot-sizing approach has been combined most frequently with the statistical order point method of deciding when to order. Thus, we will examine the statistical order point first. The periodic review method of ordering and the variable order quantity are interwoven inextricably; an examination of this method and common hybrids follows. The use of the time-phased order point in conjunction with the EOQ in independent demand situations, also is presented.

The Statistical Order Point

The statistical order point system places an order for a lot whenever the quantity on hand is reduced to a predetermined level, known as the order point, *OP*, as illustrated in Figure 6-7. This type system can be used effectively for independent demand items with relatively stable demand.

Figure 6-7
Typical Quantity in Stock Versus Time
(Order Point System, LT = Lead Time)

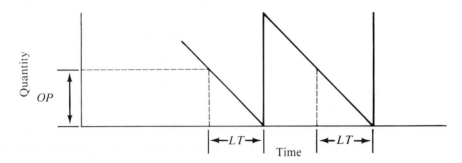

If the demand rate and the replenishment lead time, LT, are constant, it is not difficult to determine exactly how low the stock level of an item can drop before an order must be placed to avoid a stockout. For example, if an automobile parts distribution warehouse experiences a constant demand for 250 ball joint sets every two weeks—month in and month out—and it always takes exactly two weeks to obtain a replenishment order from the factory, the order point should be set at 250 sets, exactly two weeks of stock. However, this is not the common case. More typically the demand would vary, for example, from approximately 200 to 300 sets, and the lead time might vary between $1\frac{1}{2}$ weeks and $2\frac{1}{2}$ weeks. An order point without safety stock will result in stockouts in 50 percent of the ordering periods if demand and lead time varied randomly. In this more realistic case, the order point is established to cover average usage during average lead time plus some of the expected high side variations in demand or in lead time. Stock held to cover these variations is called safety stock, SS, buffer, or reserve stock. The amount of variation covered depends on the level of customer service desired. The relationships between order point, lead time, and safety stock are shown in Figure 6-8.

The purpose of carrying a safety stock is to allow routine handling of the normal fluctuations that can be expected in any real situation. Safety stock is not intended to prevent all stockouts or to eliminate completely the need for expediting, that is, emergency follow-up on delayed orders or requests for quick delivery in unusual situations. Safety stock is present to allow management by exception, where the exceptions are truly unusual delays or surges in demand. Analysis of demand and lead time data should suggest a usage during lead time that is exceeded only rarely. If it is exceeded, management considers it an exception to deal with as a special case.

Safety stock can be determined using techniques based on statistical measures of forecast error that may be due to random variations in demand or techniques based on the ratio of maximum covered demand to normal demand during lead time. We will examine both.

Figure 6-8
Relationship Between Inventory Level, Order
Point, Safety Stock, and Lead Time

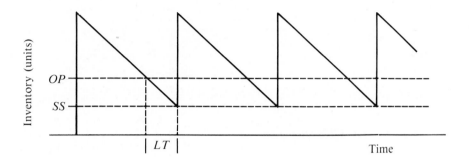

This section determines the safety stock required to cover a proportion of unbiased forecast errors due to variations in demand. Thus, the order point is equal to average demand during normal lead time, LT, plus the safety stock, SS. This is represented by the model

$$OP = D \times LT + SS$$

where D = the average demand rate. The required safety stock is a function of the random variation in demand per forecast period, the desired customer service level, and the ratio of the lead time, LT, to the forecast period, FP. Variation in demand may be measured by two different techniques: standard deviation, s, or mean absolute deviation, MAD, which were defined in Chapter 3.

The service level is defined as the percentage of order cycles in which inventory is sufficient to cover demands, or $1 - r$, where r is the stockout probability. A safety factor may be defined for any desired customer service level; it is used with the measure of variation to compute safety stock. Assuming that forecast errors are normally distributed as shown in Figure 6-9, the safety factor to be used with the standard deviation, s, of demand during lead time is the Z value, z, from the table of areas under the normal curve in Appendix A. Since 50 percent of the time (the left-hand side of the curve) demand is less than the forecast and is covered without any safety stock, adding enough safety stock to cover 42 percent of the time when demand is above forecast during lead time (the right side of the curve) gives a 92 percent service level. The safety factor corresponding to a 92 percent customer service level is 1.41. The Z value of 1.41 corresponds to an area of 0.4207, or approximately 0.42 of the right half of the curve. Safety factors required to provide other levels of customer service can be determined in the same fashion. The safety stock is calculated as

$$SS = s \times z$$

Figure 6-9
Typical Distribution of Demand During Lead Time

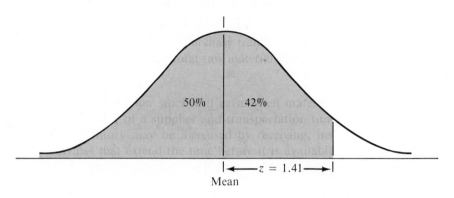

$$\text{\textemdash}z = 1.41\text{\textemdash}$$
Mean

An alternate method of computing the safety factor is with the *MAD*. If the distribution of deviations, $F_i - D_i$, is normal, the value of *MAD* calculated for a distribution approximates 0.8 times the standard deviation of this distribution. Thus, a *MAD* safety factor, *SF*, can be derived from a list of Z values by merely multiplying the corresponding Z value by 1.25. Safety stock can be calculated as

$$SS = MAD \times SF$$

The statistical order point (*OP*) can be calculated as the normal demand during lead time plus safety stock, (*SS*).

$$OP = D \times LT + SS$$

To use the preceding model, the lead time must equal the forecast period. We can see how this would work with an example. A demand of 250 ball joint sets ($D = 10$ per day; $LT = 10$ days) was forecast for each of 10 two-week periods during the preceding 20 weeks. (For ease of calculation this problem uses data from only 10 periods. In a real world example analysis of more data is desirable.) Lead time equals the forecast period, two weeks. Table 6-3 lists the demand that then occurred in each period.

Inspection of this data reveals that the sum of the absolute deviations for the 10 periods is 150 units. Dividing 150 by 10 (the number of forecasting periods covered in the data) yields a *MAD* of 15. If management desires a customer service level of 95 percent, the safety factor is 2.06 (see Table 6-4). The safety stock, and the order point are calculated as

$$SS = 15 \times 2.06 = 30.9 \quad \text{and} \quad OP = 250 + 30.9 = 280.9$$

or 281. Safety stock calculations must be rounded *up* to prevent the service level falling below the objective.

Table 6-3
Determination of Deviation in Demand; MAD and Standard Variation
Forecast = 250 units/period

Period	Demand (D)	Deviation (Forecast Error) (F − D)	(F − D)²
1	262	12	144
2	276	26	676
3	240	− 10	100
4	252	2	4
5	236	− 14	196
6	282	32	1,024
7	240	− 10	100
8	237	− 13	169
9	222	− 28	784
10	253	3	9

For purposes of comparison, let's determine what OP would result from using the standard deviation as a measure of variation. From the 10 periods observed as a sample, the estimated standard deviation is 18.87 and the value of z for a service level of 95 percent (corresponding to 45 percent of the area under the right half of the normal curve) is 1.65 (Table 6-4). Therefore,

$$OP = 250 + 1.65 \times 18.87$$
$$= 250 + 31.14$$
$$= 281.14 \text{ or } 282$$

The results of these two methods differ only because the sample distribution is not a perfect normal distribution. The observed measure of variation is based on sample data and is always, therefore, an estimator of the true standard deviation.

Table 6-4
Common Safety Factors
(Multiples of MAD and the Normalized Standard Deviation Corresponding to Given Customer Service Levels and Stock Out Probabilities)

MAD SF Values	Z Values	Service Level	Stockout Probability
1.60	1.28	0.90	0.10
2.06	1.65	0.95	0.05
2.56	2.05	0.98	0.02
2.91	2.33	0.99	0.01
3.75	3.0	0.9986	0.0014
5.0	4.0	0.9999	0.0001

Maximum/Normal Demand Ratio Approach.   For most statistical distributions the maximum demand rate can be infinite. However, analysis of actual past data should suggest some usage rate that is exceeded only rarely, and when it is exceeded management treats it as an exception.

In many situations both demand rate and lead time vary. Protection against stockout to a maximum tolerable rate of combined demand rate and lead time variations can be obtained using a relatively simple analysis. Figure 6-10 illustrates what happens when demand rises from a normal rate (D_n) to a maximum rate (D_m) just after an order has been placed and lead time increases to a maximum (T_m) length. In that case,

$$SS = LT_m D_m - LT_n D_n$$

and

$$OP = LT_n D_n + SS$$

Thus,

$$OP = LT_m D_m$$

For example, if normal lead time (T_n) is five days with an average demand of 4 units per day while the maximum lead time has been nine days with the maximum demand over any nine-day period being 50 units, an order point of 50 units would likely provide coverage for virtually all situations.

Figure 6-10
Safety Stock Required To Meet Maximum Demand
During Maximum Lead Time

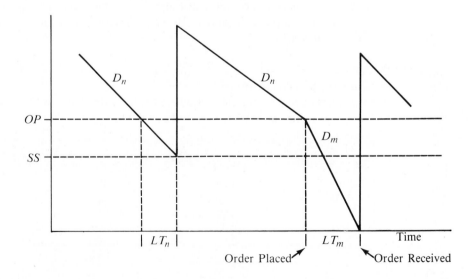

The above discussions of safety stock apply to a fixed order quantity system. Safety stock in a periodic review system must be provided not only for demand during the lead time but also for demand over the time between reviews as well. This will be examined in the section covering the periodic review system later in this chapter.

Other Considerations. A number of additional questions arise. What measure of customer service is being used in these calculations? What if the forecast period and lead time are not equal? In fact, do not the demand rate and the length of the lead time both vary simultaneously? What if the distribution of demand is not normal? In the following sections, we will examine these issues.

When using the standard deviation or *MAD* in calculating safety stock, customer service is defined as the percentage of replenishment periods during which the stock available will be equal to or greater than the demand. Little work has been done in defining order points using other measures of customer service.

Unequal Lead Time and Forecast Period. When variation in demand is measured over a period smaller than the lead time, the model for safety stock must be modified to the following:[1]

$$SS = s \times z \times \sqrt{\frac{LT}{FP}}$$

where FP = the forecast period. Let lead time be four weeks (two periods) in the previous example with all other factors remaining the same. Then,

$$OP = 250 \times 2 + 1.65 \times 18.87 \times \sqrt{\frac{4}{2}}$$

$$= 500 + 44.03 = 544$$

In this case, do not overlook the fact that the calculation of normal usage during lead time must reflect the fact that lead time includes multiple forecast periods, in this case two periods. Whenever practical, the forecast period is set equal to the lead time. This is done by the practice of recording demand during lead time and developing a forecast for that length of time.

Simultaneous Variations in Lead Time and Demand. Safety stock is held to cover both the variations in the demand rate and the variations in lead time, as is illustrated in Figure 6-11. Operationally, there are a number of ways of handling these concurrent variations. Perhaps the simplest is merely to record the actual joint variations and treat the result as a single distribution. For

---

1. This modification is based on the sum of the standard deviations equaling the square root of the sum of the variances.)

Figure 6-11
Lead Time and Demand Distributions

A. Distribution for Varying Demand and Constant Lead Time

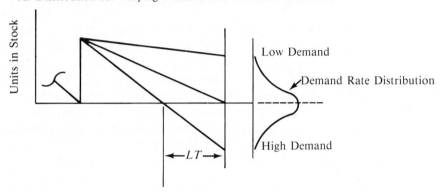

B. Distribution for Constant Demand and Varying Lead Time

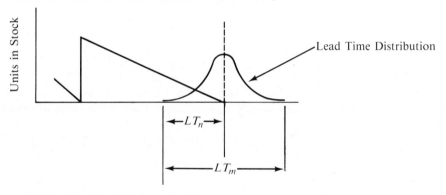

C. Joint Distribution for Varying Lead Time and Varying Demand

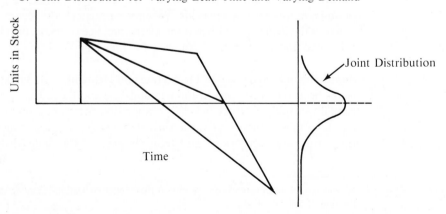

example, if Table 6-3 contains data for 10 periods during which both lead time and demand vary, we have an average demand of 250 units per lead time and a standard deviation of 18.87.

Greene (1974) presents an excellent discussion of the factors that influence the demand, withdrawal distribution and the lead time, replenishment distribution. He also points out—and we should remember—that basing order point calculations on withdrawal and replenishment distributions of historical data assumes that the future will correspond to the past. Changing economic conditions, the actions of competitors, new products, and unusual events such as strikes, wars, and threats of war may make that assumption tenuous. Additionally, Chapter 3 reminds us that demand forecasts must consider seasonal and trend factors as well as promotions. Order point calculations also should recognize these factors.

Implementation of an Order Point System. A statistical order point system requires a mechanism that alerts management when the order point has been reached. There are two basic methods of accomplishing this: (1) a perpetual inventory system and (2) a two-bin inventory system.

Perpetual Inventory System. A record is kept of each transaction, receipt or withdrawal from inventory, and the new on-hand balance is recorded. Computerized systems of this type usually are programmed to output an exception message when the stock balance is at or below the order point. Manual systems require the inventory planner to compare the stock balance to the order point after each transaction.

Two-Bin System. The inventory is physically separated into the order point quantity and the remaining units. The latter are consumed first and an order is placed on their consumption. Material may be placed in different bins or physically separated within the same bin. The order point quantity may be placed in a special container or designated by a line on the storage bin or drum. When the container is opened or stock reaches the designated line an order is placed. This type system depends on stockroom personnel recognizing that an order point has been reached. The two-bin system is best suited for independent demand and for low value items with short lead times. Office supplies and common hardware items are likely candidates.

Periodic Review

The characteristics of many inventory items do not make them amenable to the continuous review inherent in a statistical order point system. Some items, especially dependent demand items, are managed best by a material requirements planning type system, while some others are managed more appropriately by a periodic review type system.

The adoption of a periodic review system, or one of its derivatives, is suggested by one or more of the following conditions:

1. Independent demand is the usual situation.
2. It is difficult to record withdrawals from stock and continuous review is expensive. Although optical scanning and modern computer systems have reduced this problem—even in some grocery stores—it still exists in many situations.
3. Groups of items are purchased from a common supplier and the total preparation costs per item are greatly reduced by combining the items into one order. Small tools; manufacturing supplies; common commercial parts such as nuts, bolts, washers; and office supplies are examples.
4. Items that have a limited shelf life (perishables) are ideal candidates for fixed period review management. Dairy items and fruits and vegetables are the classic examples. Many chemicals, pharmaceuticals, solvents, etc., used directly or indirectly in the manufacturing process, also may be managed most effectively by a periodic review type system.
5. There is an economic advantage in generating full carload shipments or fully utilizing available production capacity. This type situation will be examined when discussing joint replenishment.

The System.   A periodic review system in its basic form involves determining the amount of an item in stock at a specified, fixed, time interval and placing an order for a quantity that, when added to the quantity on hand, will equal a predetermined maximum level. Since the time period between reviews of the quantity on hand is fixed, this approach sometimes is called the *fixed review period system*.

The *maximum inventory level*, *M*, is the sum of the anticipated demand during lead time, the anticipated demand during the replenishment period, and the safety stock. It is sometimes called the *target level inventory*. The inventory on hand will never reach this level unless demand (withdrawals from stock) ceases during the lead time.

This system is described by the following model.

$$M = D(R + LT) + SS$$

where M = maximum inventory level
LT = lead time duration
D = demand rate
R = review period duration
SS = safety stock

And, with I = inventory and Q = order quantity, the order quantity is equal to the maximum level minus the quantity on hand (inventory):

$$Q = M - I \quad \text{or} \quad Q = D(R + LT) + SS - I$$

There may be some items on order in those cases where the lead time is greater than the review period ($LT > R$). These cases are very rare.

Figure 6-12 illustrates the relationship of the inventory versus time for a periodic review system. It clearly reveals that $t_1 = t_2 = t_3$, and that Q_1, Q_2, Q_3, and Q_4 are not necessarily equal. Thus, the review period is fixed, and the order quantity may vary. In the traditional fixed order quantity, order point system the order quantity is fixed, and the period between orders may vary.

Figure 6-12
Units in Stock Versus Time
(Periodic Review System)

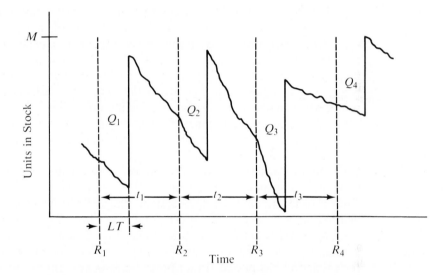

Let's examine a periodic review example. A company uses a zinc based primer that is obtained along with other paints, solvents, etc., from a local supplier. Normal usage is 3 gallons per day, the review period is every two weeks (ten working days), lead time is three days, and safety stock is 4 gallons. Inventory is reviewed at the appropriate time, and there are 15 gallons in stock. Thus, the maximum inventory level and the order quantity can be calculated as follows.

$$M = D(LT + R) + SS$$
$$= 3(3 + 10) + 4$$
$$= 43$$

$$Q = M - I$$
$$= 43 - 15$$
$$= 28$$

An order should be placed for 28 gallons.

What if the inventory on hand had been 6 gallons instead of 15? This is insufficient to cover normal usage during the three-day lead time. In all likelihood, the company will be able to obtain some on short notice by special order. However, if this is not possible, the question of the permissibility of backorders must be addressed. In this example, a stockout in primer paint can result in a schedule delay and in some items being painted late (after the paint arrives). The order quantity then will be calculated in the normal fashion as follows:

$$Q = M - I$$
$$= 43 - 6$$
$$= 37 \text{ gallons}$$

Let's look at a slightly different situation. When a stockout occurs, the company uses a substitute primer. In this case the minimum inventory on hand will be 9 gallons for practical purposes since the requirements during the lead time are covered by a substitute. Then, $Q = 43 - 9 = 34$ gallons.

A similar situation frequently exists when the periodic ordering system is used in managing finished goods. If the customer usually goes to a second source when an item is not available, the minimum value of I in the calculation is the demand during lead time. Hardware stores, grocery stores, drug stores, and manufacturing supply houses frequently operate under such conditions.

Safety Stock Considerations.   The purpose of safety stock is to cover high side variations in demand from the placement of an order to the arrival of a subsequent order. In an order point system, unusually heavy demand will trigger another order as soon as the order point is reached. This may occur immediately after the receipt of the first order. In a strictly periodic system (one without an order point mechanism), another order will not be placed until the review period has passed. In an order point system safety stock must cover only variations in demand during lead time, but in a strictly periodic system the safety stock must cover variations in demand during the combined review and lead time period. As illustrated in Figure 6-13, the quantity ordered at R_1 must recognize possible variations in demand from R_1 to D_2 (date of delivery of order No. 2). Thus, safety stock is calculated by multiplying the safety factor times the standard deviation of demand during the sum of the lead time plus the review period. The value of the safety factor depends, of course, on the customer service level desired. For example, the safety factor for a customer service level of 95 percent is 1.65 (see Table 6-4) when using the standard deviation as the measure of variation. Service level is defined here as the percentage of periods during which all customer orders are filled (a stockout does not occur). Without any safety stock, the service level will be 50 percent since demand is less than or equal to the average demand 50 percent of the time.

Returning to our earlier example of the zinc based primer, let the standard deviation of demand during the combined lead time and review period be 2.42 units and the desired service level be 95 percent. Then, safety stock will equal $2.42 \times 1.65 = 3.993$, or 4 units.

Figure 6-13
Safety Stock
(Periodic Review System)
Order size determined at R_1 and R_2
Deliveries occur at D_1 and D_2

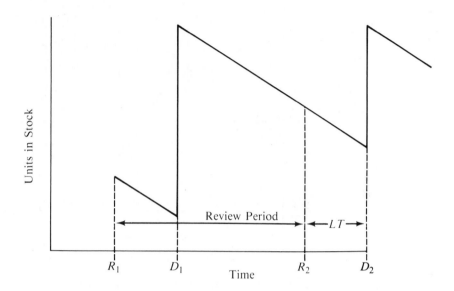

Hybrid Systems

There are many different ways of combining the features of the periodic ordering system and the order point system. The two most common will be described.

The first (the order point-periodic review combination system) combines the order point feature with the periodic review. In brief, if the inventory level drops below a specified level prior to the review date, an order is placed; if not, the order quantity is determined at the end of the period in the basic periodic review manner (see Figure 6-14). This system is appropriate when relatively large variations in demand are common and the cost of safety stock required to cover these variations during the combined lead time and review period is excessive (greater than the cost of a combination system). A combination periodic review-order point system requires safety stock to cover variations in demand during the lead time only. To function, this system must have a mechanism for indicating when the order point is reached. If perpetual records are not available, then a form of the two-bin system, described earlier, must be installed. A combination order point-periodic review type system frequently is used to manage families of independent items.

If an item frequently reaches the order point before the review period has expired, examination of the value of D, demand rate, and M, the maximum inventory level, is in order.

Figure 6-14
Units in Stock Versus Time
(Periodic Review-Order Point Combination)

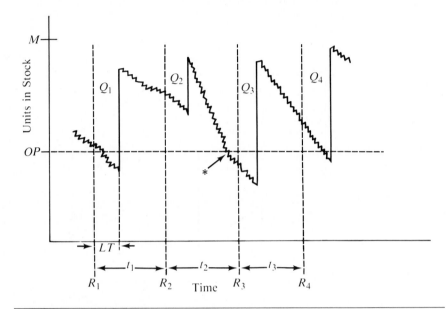

*Order is placed before scheduled review as stock drops below order point.

The second hybrid inventory management system is the optional (s, S) replenishment system. This method is also known as the s, S model, where S represents the maximum inventory level, which we have called M, and s represents the order point, which we have designated as OP. In this periodic review-order point combination system, an order is placed only if the quantity on hand is below a specific level (see Figure 6-15). This method enables an organization to avoid placing orders for relatively small quantities. This approach is useful when periods of dormant demand are possible, shelf life is important, and aging is undesirable. Although staleness, dust, rust, oxidation, and other attributes of age may not prevent an item from being sold if it is needed, they do not enhance customer satisfaction. The optional replenishment system diminishes the probability of these deficiencies, but it does increase the probability of a stockout.

Establishing the order point in this type system is extremely complex if one desires to have the mathematical assurance that the order point guarantees that the sum of the carrying costs, ordering costs, and expected stockout costs are being minimized. This assurance is always tempered by a few assumptions including one concerning the demand distribution.

The main point is that this type system is used successfully by numerous organizations. We have observed on many occasions a storeroom or supply

Figure 6-15
Units in Stock Versus Time
(Optional Replenishment System)

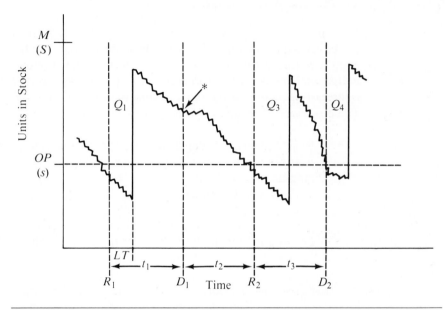

*Order is not placed. Stock level is above the order point.

clerk who reviews commercial items on a periodic basis (such as on the fifth and twentieth of every month) and orders only if an item has reached the order point. In some cases, the order point may be relatively high since the carrying costs are relatively low compared with the cost of ordering. (Ordering costs include the costs of writing the order, receiving it, moving it to stores, and processing the payment.)

In other cases, such as fresh food markets, seasonal goods, bookstores, restaurants, and pharmacies, the order point may be set relatively low since the cost of a stockout is balanced against the cost of obsolete, unusable, inventory.

Visual Review Systems

Both periodic review and order point systems can be implemented using a physical review of the stock on hand rather than a perpetual inventory record system. For example, in many retail outlets the customer is the stock picker and real time records of the quantity on hand do not exist. Thus, periodic physical count of the stock to determine the order quantity is common.

The two-bin system of inventory storage is a common method of operating a visual review order point system. It is appropriate for the management of independent demand, low value items with short lead times, such as office supplies and common hardware items.

Time-Phased Order Point System

Many items have large seasonal variations in demand. Statistical order points can be revised to correspond to these demand changes. The time-phased order point uses forecast demand by period. Thus, it explicitly recognizes changes in forecast demand. The information prerequisites for this type system include a forecast of requirements, the lead time of the item, and the order quantity. The procedure to compute a time-phased order point is as follows.

1. Requirements, scheduled receipts, and the on-hand quantity are projected by week for the short-range planning period, usually two to six months.
2. The week is determined in which the on-hand quantity, excluding safety stock, falls below zero. This is the outage period.
3. An order release is planned for the outage period minus the lead time. For example, if the lead time is two weeks and the projected outage occurs in Week 8, an order release should be planned for Week 6.

Let's see how this works with an example. The following is known about a service part that is not used in currently produced assemblies.

Lead time = 3 weeks
Weekly demand forecast = 20 units
Safety stock = 30 units
Order quantity = 100 units
An order of 100 units is scheduled for receipt in Week 2
On-hand quantity = 40 units

The projected gross requirements, scheduled receipts, and on-hand quantity by week are given in Table 6-5.

Table 6-5
Material Requirements Projections

						Week				
		1	2	3	4	5	6	7	8	9	10
Gross Requirements		20	20	20	20	20	20	20	20	20	20
Scheduled Receipts			100								
Projected On Hand	40	20	100	80	60	40	20	0	(20)	(40)	(60)
Planned Order Releases											

◄———————————►
Lead-time Offset

The projected on hand (POH) for Week t is equal to the POH of Week $t - 1$ plus the scheduled receipts in Week t minus gross requirements in Week t. For example, the POH of Week 2 is $20 + 100 - 20 = 100$. The on-hand quantity is projected to fall below the safety stock level of 30 in Week 6. An order release must be planned for Week 3 to have a scheduled receipt in Week 6. The planned release of an order in Week 3 and its planned receipt in Week 6 are incorporated in the planning document in Table 6-6. We also have determined that an order receipt will be required in Week 11 and have included its planned release and planned receipt.

Table 6-6
Material Requirements with Time-Phased Order Points

			Week									
		1	2	3	4	5	6	7	8	9	10	11
Gross Requirements		20	20	20	20	20	20	20	20	20	20	20
Scheduled Receipts			100									
Projected On Hand	40	20	100	80	60	40	120	100	80	60	40	120
Planned Order Releases				100					100			
Planned Receipts							100					100

Lead-time Offset   Lead-time Offset

The time-phased order point system reveals when orders for an item likely will be placed during the entire planning horizon. It can be used to furnish both suppliers and manufacturing with advance notice of likely future orders, as described in Chapter 10. Other basic systems do not have this capability.

Other Considerations

Even the most complex inventory management models only approximate reality. The cost, demand, and lead time values used in calculating lot sizes and order release timing are estimates. The inventory planner should not use the results of lot size and order release calculations without considering practical factors such as rounding, material usage, tool life, package or container size, yield, etc.

Rounding. Lot size and safety stock calculations frequently result in fractional values that are obviously not feasible in the case of discrete parts. For example, one cannot sell 97.2 transmissions. Rounding a number such as 97.2 or 98.0 up to 100 makes sense in most cases. Total carrying and setup costs would change little and numbers ending in one or more zeros facilitate human memory and recognition.

Material Usage. Frequently, it makes sense to increase a lot size to use all of the material available in a coil, rod, sheet, or container rather than returning a small leftover amount to stores. The added material and processing costs may be less than the costs of handling and storing small amounts.

Tool Life.   The required periodic replacement or maintenance of a tool or process, such as a dye, cutting blade, filter, or treatment solution, may consume as much production capacity (machine downtime) as the machine setup. Increasing production lot sizes so that the end of the production run and the maintenance requirement occur currently will decrease downtime. Since such tools, solutions, and filters must be replaced or cleaned when a different item is run, coordinating required maintenance and setup activities may be equivalent to eliminating a setup.

Care should be taken not to reduce the lot sizes of dependent demand items required for an assembly. The savings in machine downtime and maintenance costs will be small compared to the costs resulting from the missing parts.

Package or Container Size.   Items are often purchased or stored in standard size containers or packages. Increasing lot sizes to fill containers may be justified by reduced transportation, storage, and handling costs per unit.

Yield.   The scrap or yield rate of a process should be considered when calculating lot sizes. In a material requirements system using lot-for-lot order quantities, scrap and yield factors require that the actual order quantity be greater than the net requirements. This quantity can be calculated in the following manner for lot sizes in a given range.

$$Q = \frac{\text{Net Requirements } (NR)}{1.0 - \text{Maximum Likely Scrap Percentage } (MLS)}$$

Or

$$Q = \frac{\text{Net Requirements}}{\text{Yield Rate } (y)}$$

where $y = 1 - MLS$. For example, if the net requirement is 500 and the maximum likely scrap percentage is 10 percent,

$$Q = \frac{500}{1.0 - 0.10}$$
$$= 556$$

Minimums and Maximums.   Floors and ceilings may be established by policy to eliminate overloading of production and order handling capacity by a large number of small orders and to prevent production of quantities greater than required in a reasonable planning horizon. These limits may be stated in absolute terms, such as no fewer than 10 units and no more than 100 units, or in demand related terms, such as no less than a two-week supply and no more than a six-month supply. Rarely does it make sense to produce more than a year supply.

Implementation of Multiple Factors. It is common for more than one practical consideration to affect the order quantity decision. When ordering dependent demand items, top priority is to order at least the net requirements. Maximum and minimum limits usually rank next, followed by yield calculations, tool life, and material usage. However, the planner should evaluate each situation on its own merits as the costs related to the various factors can differ widely from case to case.

Just-in-Time

Implementation of world class manufacturing practices such as total quality management, development of human resources, uniform flow, reduced setup times and costs, flexible equipment and employees capable of handling different assignments, and more frequent deliveries from suppliers has led to Just-in-Time inventory management by many organizations in some situations. In these instances the economic order quantity is reduced substantially, reaching a single unit in the ideal case (see Chapter 17).

SUMMARY

Individual item management concerns when to order (the order release) and how many to order (the lot size). The dependent demand-independent demand dichotomy is the major determinant of the appropriateness of the different models for a given item. The lot sizing decision rules are based on models that minimize the sum of carrying and preparation costs. Order point decision rules are predicated on a customer service level objective. A timely and accurate information processing system is required to implement these decision rules.

EXERCISES

1. A purchased item in the finished goods warehouse has an annual demand of 14,400 units with no seasonality or trend. Unit costs are 40 cents, holding costs are estimated to be 25 percent of average inventory value, and ordering costs are estimated as $20.
   a. What should the economic ordering quantity be?
   b. How often should an order be placed?
   c. What are the total annual inventory costs?
   d. If the same company decides to produce these items at a cost of 30 cents each with a total preparation cost of $45 per order and its annual capacity is 21,600 units, what is the economic order quantity?

2. The Near East Electronics Sales Company sells 16,000 Model 19A meters every year. There is no seasonality or trend in the demand pattern. They pay $2 for the meters and sell them for $3, $3.50, or $4 depending on the quantity the customer purchases. The company uses a carrying cost rate of 0.30 and estimates preparation costs as $40. What is the economic purchase lot size?

3. Near East (see Exercise 2) discovers that they can assemble Model 19A meters for a total labor, material, and overhead cost of $1. Total preparation costs will be $45; annual production capacity is 16,000 units. What is the economical production lot size?

4. A pottery company experiences a rather steady independent demand of 25,000 units annually for an ashtray. They have the capacity to produce 50,000 units annually. Carrying costs are estimated to be 10 cents per unit per year, and the total preparation costs are $25.
   a. What is the economic production lot size?
   b. What will total inventory costs be if the company mistakenly estimates total preparation costs to be $36?

5. West End Auto Supply purchases gasket g906 in lots of 500 boxes, which is a three-month supply. The cost per box is $10, and the ordering cost is $25. The carrying cost is estimated as 25 percent of average inventory per year.
   a. What is the economic order quantity?
   b. What is the total annual cost of the present inventory policy?
   c. How much would be saved annually by employing the EOQ?

6. A manufacturer of power take-offs forecasts a steady demand of 1,000 units next year for its most popular model. The company can produce 10 units per day, and there are 250 working days available. It costs $900 to set up the production line, and the unit production cost is estimated at $2,750. The holding cost per year is $750. Demand is independent.
   a. What is the economic production quantity?
   b. How many runs should be made during the year?

7. A radar detector manufacturer forecasts a steady demand of 25,000 units of Model 997 Fuzzbuster in the coming year. The company produces 250 units per day, and there are 250 working days each year. It costs $900 to set up the production line, and the cost of each unit is $275. The carrying cost per unit per year is $75.
   a. Calculate the economical production quantity.
   b. How many lots will be produced during the year?
   c. How would applying JIT concepts and techniques alter this situation?

8. The firm manufacturing radar detectors in Exercise 7 has a customer service level objective of 99 percent and desires two weeks notice before setting up a production line. If the variance in average demand during lead time is 15 units, what should their order point be? Assume that units can be shipped the day they are produced.

9. The firm described in Exercises 7 and 8 decides to use a time-phased order point (TPOP) system.
   a. Develop a chart for the next 10 weeks in this situation with a beginning inventory of 1,600 units under constant demand.
   b. Develop a chart with a demand of 400 units in the first week and increasing by 20 units for each of the next 9 weeks.

10. A distributor estimates that 4,000 Model G198Z motors will be sold during the coming year. Demand consists of many relatively small orders spread rather evenly throughout the year. The cost of the motors to the firm is estimated to be $15 per motor. Taxes ($T$) and insurance ($I$) for motors in storage are a total of 20 cents per motor per year, based on one-fourth of the maximum inventory. Costs of deterioration, pilferage, handling, heat, light, etc. (P) come to 30 cents per motor per year, based on maximum inventory. The cost of ordering, receiving, and inspecting the motors before acceptance is $50 per lot. Lead time is two weeks and the plant closes for two weeks for vacation each year. The cost of capital is 20 percent per year.
    a. Develop the TC model assuming constant deterministic demand and no stockouts.
    b. Derive the EOQ model and determine the EOQ.
    c. What are the total inventory costs for the year?

11. Given the following data for an item with independent demand:

    > Annual demand = 26,000 units
    > Economic order quantity = 500 units
    > Lead time = one week
    > Mean absolute deviation = 200 units per order interval
    > Management has set the tolerable number of stockouts per year at one.

    Determine:
    a. The number of exposures per year
    b. The service rate percentage
    c. The reserve, safety stock
    d. The order point

12. A local distributor sells an average of 100 CB radios, Model 784DJ, each week. The standard deviation of weekly sales is 20 units. Lead time to obtain replacement stock from the manufacturer is one week.
    a. What should the reorder point be if a customer service level of 50 percent is desired?
    b. What should it be if a 98 percent customer sevice level is desired?
    c. What percentage of time would the distributor be out of stock if the order point is 120 units?

13. An Atlanta equipment supply distributor stocks pumps, valves, and similar items used in the chemical, pharmaceutical, and similar wet processing industries. The average weekly demand for Pump 19X7 is 20 units with a standard deviation of 5 units. Pumps are ordered from the main warehouse in Chicago every 25 working days, and the company is interested in achieving a 95 percent service level on these pumps. If lead time is one week, what should the order point be (based on the traditional statistical approach)? What should the order point be if the lead time is two weeks?

14. The parts department of a large automobile dealership uses a combination periodic review-order point system to manage the inventory of a fuel pump, Model 75A, used on many different models of the automobiles it has sold. The following conditions exist:

   (1) A review is made late every second Wednesday, and an order for many different parts is placed with the regional warehouse. Parts arrive late Monday.
   (2) Four Model 75A pumps are used on the average each day, either for repairs in the shop or for purchases by individuals doing their own work. The parts department is open five days a week. The standard deviation of demand during the Monday to Wednesday lead time is 2.
   (3) Special orders can be placed for individual items with delivery in two days.
   (4) The firm's customer service objective is to approach 100 percent.

   a. What should the order quantity be if the stock on hand is 20 units on a given Wednesday?
   b. What should the order point be for special orders?

15. The local grocery supermarket uses a fixed interval inventory management system to determine the number of frozen chickens it orders each week. (The policy is to have a stockout only once every 20 weeks.) The store places an order every Wednesday morning for delivery at 6 a.m. on Monday. It sells 20 chickens on the average each day of the week except Sunday when the store is closed. The mean absolute deviation of daily sales is 3 chickens. The poultry department manager determines that there are 85 frozen chickens in the store on a Wednesday immediately before opening at 8 a.m.
   a. How many chickens should he order?
   b. What if there are 65 frozen chickens and backorders are not allowed?

16. The Ace Publishing Company is printing a textbook for a course in production control. It estimates the demand to be 5,000 books per year. The production cost of each book is $13, inventory carrying costs are computed using $k = 0.25$, each order requires a fixed setup cost of $500, and up to 15,000 books may be printed and bound a year. No shortages

are allowed; if the publisher is out of stock, another printing will be run immediately. Suppose, however, that the publisher is in error, and the actual demand for the book is 7,500 copies a year. To what extent has this lack of perfect information affected the optimal inventory policy? How much would the publisher be willing to pay to have a perfect estimate of demand?

17. The Mendell Chemical Company is experiencing expensive stockouts with an inexpensive compound it uses in relatively small quantities. The compound is essential to many of its manufacturing processes, and the president has asked you to suggest an ordering policy to eliminate stockouts. You check and discover that records of past usage do not exist. The general manager tells you that they use an average of 100 pounds weekly and at most 135 pounds each week. The only supplier is some 500 miles away. The normal lead time is one week; but on one occasion in the last two years it took two weeks for delivery. What order point would you recommend?

18. Four basic methods of managing the inventory of individual items are:

    (1) EOQ combined with the statistical order point
    (2) Periodic review system
    (3) Material requirements planning
    (4) Combined periodic review and order point

    For each of the following situations, indicate which of the above methods of managing inventory would likely be most appropriate:
    a. Replacement brake shoes, part no. 727A5, carried at a regional auto parts warehouse and sold to automative repair garages and service stations
    b. Cottage cheese sold in various ways to employees at an organization's cafeteria
    c. A solenoid, part no. 2719, used in the final assembly of a piece of farm equipment assembled in small lots four or five times a year
    d. Whole blood stored in a hospital primarily for emergency purposes

SELECTED READINGS

Arrow, K. J., S. Karlin, and H. Scarf. *Studies in the Mathematical Theory of Inventory and Production*. Stanford, CA: Stanford University Press, 1958.

Brown, Robert, G. *Advanced Service Parts Inventory Control*. Norwich, VT: Materials Management Systems, Inc., 1982.

Buchan, Joseph, and Ernest Koenigsberg. *Scientific Inventory Management.* Englewood Cliffs, NJ: Prentice-Hall, Inc., 1963.

Greene, James H. *Production and Inventory Control Handbook.* 2d ed. New York: McGraw-Hill Book Co., 1986.

Greene, James H. *Production and Inventory Control Systems and Decisions.* 2d ed. Homewood, IL: Richard D. Irwin, Inc., 1974.

Orlicky, Joseph. *Material Requirements Planning.* New York: McGraw-Hill Book Co., 1975.

Plossl, George W. *Production and Inventory Control: Principles and Techniques.* 2d ed. Englewood Cliffs, NJ: Prentice-Hall, Inc., 1985.

Silver, Edward A., and Rein Peterson. *Decision Systems for Inventory Management and Production Planning.* 2d ed. New York: John Wiley & Sons, Inc., 1985.

Silver, Edward A., and Rein Peterson. *Inventory Management Reprints.* Falls Church, VA: American Production and Inventory Control Society, 1989.

7
AGGREGATE INVENTORY MANAGEMENT

Aggregate inventory encompasses the raw materials, purchased parts, work in process, and finished goods in different stages of the production-distribution process. These components of aggregate inventory fulfill the anticipation, fluctuation, cycle stock, and transportation inventory functions at various stages in the production-distribution process, as illustrated in Figure 7-1.

Inventory is an asset on the balance sheet. (However, in some situations it may be considered a liability. See Chapters 5, 17, and 19). Table 7-1 is a list of typical measures for evaluating the management of inventory assets. The primary objective usually is to attain a minimum level of performance relative to each goal; the secondary objective is to raise performance relative to each measure in keeping with its priority. Priorities should be consistent with the organizational strategies and policies.

Table 7-1
Typical Measures of Inventory Management

1. Customer service
2. Inventory investment
3. Inventory turnover ratio

Performance relative to goals is affected by many decisions including:

1. The distribution plan
2. The production (aggregate) plan
3. The master production schedule
4. Purchasing commitments
5. Family (group) lot-sizing decisions
6. Item lot-sizing decisions
7. Safety stock levels
8. Quantity discount and hedge purchases
9. Transportation modes and decisions

Figure 7-1
The Locus and Flow of Inventory Through a Production and Distribution Process

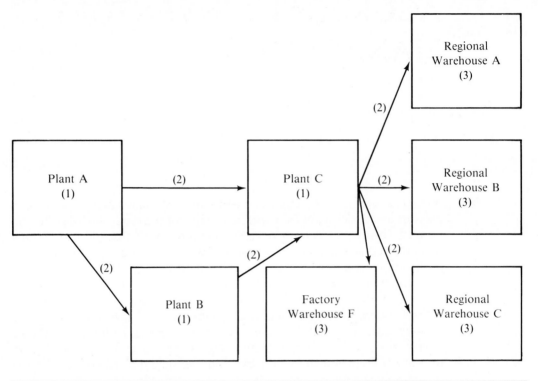

(1) Plants A, B, and C have raw materials, purchased parts, and work-in-process inventory. It may be cycle stock, demand and supply fluctuation (safety) stock, or anticipation stock.
(2) Transportation inventory exists between the plants and between Plant C and the regional warehouses.
(3) The warehouses have finished goods inventory including service parts. This inventory is cycle stock, fluctuation stock, and anticipation stock.

Aggregate inventory management concentrates on the trade-offs between the costs of inventory and the benefits it provides in other situations. This chapter examines the conflicting objectives of aggregate inventory management; the pitfalls of superficial analyses; projecting the value of aggregate inventory in a high volume, make-to-stock environment, and in a job shop, make-to-order environment; dealing with constraints on aggregate inventory; and the trade-offs that often are made in managing different types of inventory.

AGGREGATE INVENTORY INVESTMENT

Inventory balance sheet totals can be misleading if not viewed in terms of the needs the inventory is fulfilling at a given time. The gross totals illustrated graphically in Figure 7-2, which may represent inventory investment in past periods or planned future investment, do not provide sufficient information concerning the uses, i.e., benefits, of the inventory. For example, when the projected total inventory balance appears to be excessive (Point *A*), inventory may in fact be inadequate to meet requirements; and the opposite may be true at Point *B*.

Figure 7-2
Graphic Representation of Aggregate Inventory
Without Analysis of Need[1]

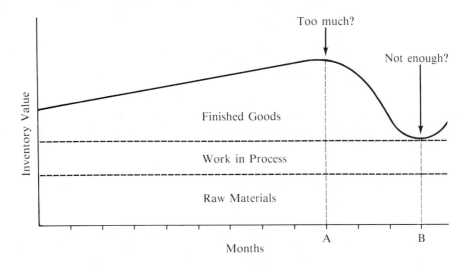

Comparing each inventory requirement to projected availability is necessary to judge whether inventory is excessive, just right, or inadequate. Figure 7-3 graphically illustrates the division of aggregate inventory by state and functional class. This information not only is necessary for comparing projected investment to projected needs but also provides controls for evaluating actual investments later. In addition, if inventory must be decreased due to capital or storage constraints, this information is very helpful in selecting inventories for reduction.

Figures 7-1 and 7-3 indicate the determinants of aggregate inventory investment. Inventory fulfills anticipation (leveling), transportation (pipeline), cycle (lot size), and fluctuation (buffer) objectives; it exists as raw materials, purchased parts, work in process, and finished goods.

The production plan has a major impact on aggregate inventory investment in any environment. In the typical high volume, make-to-stock environment, the production rate usually dominates all other factors in determining

1. Adopted from George Brandenburg's presentation "Master Planning" at the AIDS National Conference, Las Vegas, 1980.

Figure 7-3
Inventory Investment Versus Time (By State)

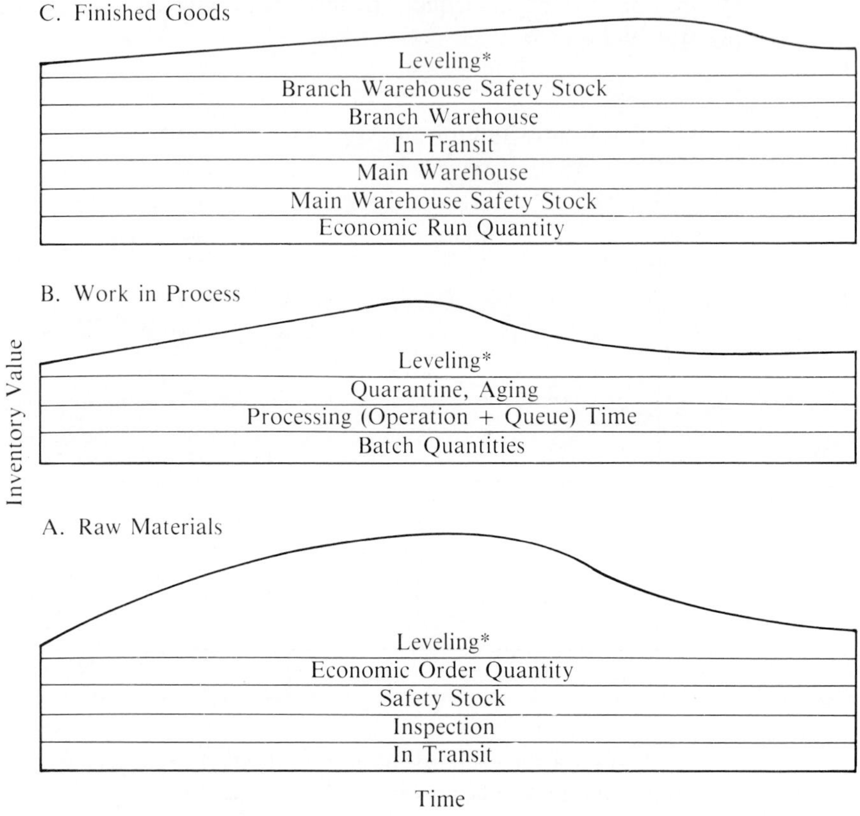

C. Finished Goods

| Leveling* |
| Branch Warehouse Safety Stock |
| Branch Warehouse |
| In Transit |
| Main Warehouse |
| Main Warehouse Safety Stock |
| Economic Run Quantity |

B. Work in Process

| Leveling* |
| Quarantine, Aging |
| Processing (Operation + Queue) Time |
| Batch Quantities |

A. Raw Materials

| Leveling* |
| Economic Order Quantity |
| Safety Stock |
| Inspection |
| In Transit |

Time

Leveling may take place in each of the functional classifications.

the aggregate inventory investment. In the typical job shop environment, the nature of specific orders is the dominating factor. We will use examples to demonstrate how projected aggregate inventory investment can be calculated in each of these situations.

MAKE-TO-STOCK ENVIRONMENT

Inventory in a continuous (or repetitive) process, make-to-stock environment is somewhat analogous to fluid in a pipeline. Just as the amount of fluid in the system depends on the length of the pipeline, the diameter of the pipe, and the number and volume of sumps or reservoirs in the system, the total inventory in a manufacturing-distribution system depends on the time required to pass through the system, the processes through which the material must pass, and reservoirs of material held at various points in the system (queues, anticipation, and safety stock).

Inventory in a continuous process system usually includes raw material (RM), work in process (WIP), and finished goods (FG). The finished goods may be stored only at the factory or it also may exist throughout a distribution system. RM, WIP, and FG may each include anticipation, fluctuation, cycle, and transportation inventory.

Data Requirements

Calculating projected inventory under these conditions requires the following information:

A. **The forecast and the master production schedule.** The quantities of end items scheduled for production each period are a major determinant of raw material, work in process, and finished goods inventory. Projected production output and demand are required to calculate finished goods inventory.

B. **Manufacturing and distribution lead times.** Raw material and work in process inventory depend on purchasing policies and manufacturing lead time; and distribution inventory is affected by transportation and warehousing policies.

C. **Bill of Material (BOM).** The BOM lists the ingredients and the quantities required. These data are necessary for calculating inventory investment.

D. **A description of the manufacturing process.** A full description of the manufacturing process will include interplant transportation time requirements, intraplant material handling time, process time requirements, and yield. It also will reveal whether or not the process is batch flow and whether or not it involves cycle stock. Although many continuous (and repetitive) manufacturing activities do not require cycle stock, batch flow processes may. Cycle stock may exist in a batch continuous process when two or more operations are involved, when a delay exists between the two operations, and when the run time of the first operation is relatively long. Even when continuous or repetitive processing dominates, some components or ingredients may be produced in batches.

E. **The value added at milestones in each item's production process.** If a process takes a relatively short time, this information is not necessary. When, however, the process is relatively long with, say, interplant transfers between two or more continuous processess, this information is required to calculate the value of work in process.

F. **A quantitative measure of safety stock.** Safety stock may exist in raw materials, work in process, or finished goods to cover variations in supplier deliveries, process yields, and demand.

G. **Interplant and warehouse transportation time and shipping practices.** Transportation stock is a function of these characteristics.

The following examples are simplistic in that they do not include all of the variations possible in the real world. They do illustrate how the value of inventory may be projected (estimated) under most types of situations. They include samples of raw material, work in process, and finished goods projections.

Finished Goods Inventory—No Remote Warehouses

The first example is based on the production (aggregate) plan for the next six months, a unit cost of $5, and all sales from the factory (no distribution system), as shown in Table 7-2.

Table 7-2
Production Plan (in Thousands of Units)

				Month			
	0	1	2	3	4	5	6
Production	—	7	7	8	8	9	9
Demand	—	7	4	9	9	10	9
Ending Inventory	1	1	4	3	2	1	1

The ending finished goods inventory in any month equals the ending inventory of the previous month plus the production for the month minus the demand for the month. Thus,

$$EI_i = EI_{i-1} + P_i - D_i$$

where i = the period (month)
        EI = ending inventory
         P = production output
         D = demand (shipments)

The value of finished goods is calculated by

$$FG_i = C \times EI_i$$

where FG = finished goods investment
          C = unit cost

If, for example, each finished unit costs $5, the value of finished goods at the end of Month 3 is calculated as follows.

$$FG_3 = \$5 \times 3,000 = \$15,000$$

The value of finished goods at the end of each month is listed in Table 7-3.

Table 7-3
Projected Finished Goods Inventory Investment (in Thousands of Dollars)

	Month					
	1	2	3	4	5	6
Ending Inventory	1	4	3	2	1	1
Inventory Investment	$5	$20	$15	$10	$5	$5

With the point of sale being the company's shipping dock, this example does not include any transportation inventory in finished goods nor any warehouse cycle stock, a condition that will be changed shortly.

The finished goods inventory at the factory consists of anticipation stock and safety stock. Since the lowest amount of finished goods inventory planned in any month is 1,000 units, these units are inherently safety stock; they have no planned use except to cover high-side variations in demand. The remaining inventory is anticipation stock; it exists to cover demand in those future months in which forecast demand exceeds planned production. Thus, in this example, the finished goods inventory can be divided into safety stock and anticipation inventory as illustrated Table 7-4.

Table 7-4
Projected Finished Goods Inventory
Safety Stock and Anticipation Inventory (in Thousands of Units)

	Month					
	1	2	3	4	5	6
Safety Stock	1	1	1	1	1	1
Anticipation Inventory	0	3	2	1	0	0
Total	1	4	3	2	1	1

Dividing finished goods inventory into components, such as anticipation and safety stocks, enables management to treat each separately. Management, for example, can remove $2,500 from finished goods investment by cutting the safety stock in half. This could be done by increasing the production rate to 8,000 units in the middle of Month 3 rather than at the beginning. The average inventory during any month in a continuous or repetitive flow environment with a constant rate of production throughout the month equals one-half the sum of the beginning inventory and the ending inventory. Thus, the average finished goods inventory during the third month equals 3,500 units $\left(\dfrac{4,000 + 3,000}{2}\right)$.

Finished Goods Inventory with Distribution

Let's increase the complexity of the situation by adding two warehouses, one on each coast, as shown in Figure 7-4.

Figure 7-4
Flow of Finished Goods

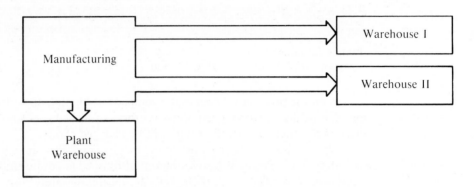

The following information describes the situation.

A. Thirty percent of production is shipped to each of the coastal warehouses
    and 40 percent is kept at the centrally located plant warehouse.
B. Loading, transportation, and unloading takes approximately one week
    for each of the warehouses.
C. Each of the three warehouses has 400 units of safety stock. This is an
    increase in safety stock from the previous example.
D. The time for delivery from a warehouse to a customer is insignificant.
E. Forty percent of each day's production goes directly to the factory ware-
    house. Thus, both receipts and withdrawals (demand) at the factory
    warehouse occur at a relatively continuous rate during any given period.
    Deliveries to each of the other two warehouses occur once a week and
    demand occurs continuously. The warehouses, as a result, have cycle
    stock. These conditions are illustrated in Figure 7-5.

Finished Goods Transportation Inventory.   A total of 60 percent of each
week's production is always in transit to the two warehouses, and there are
$4\frac{1}{3}$ weeks in each month (the exact number in each month could be used). The
value of finished goods transportation inventory during any month is calculated
as follows (1 week = 0.23 months).

$$FG(T)_i = 0.60 \times 0.23 \times C \times P_i$$

where i = the period (month)
        $FG(T)$ = value of finished goods transportation inventory
             C = unit cost
             P = production output

In Month 3, for example, $FG(T)_3 = 0.60 \times 0.23 \times \$5 \times 8,000$ or $5,520.
The finished goods transportation inventory during each month is calculated
in the same manner and listed in Table 7-5.

Table 7-5
Finished Goods Transportation Inventory (in Dollars)

	Month					
	1	2	3	4	5	6
$FG(T)$	$4,830	$4,830	$5,520	$5,520	$6,210	$6,210

Figure 7-5
Inventory at Warehouses Including Cycle, Anticipation, and Safety Stock

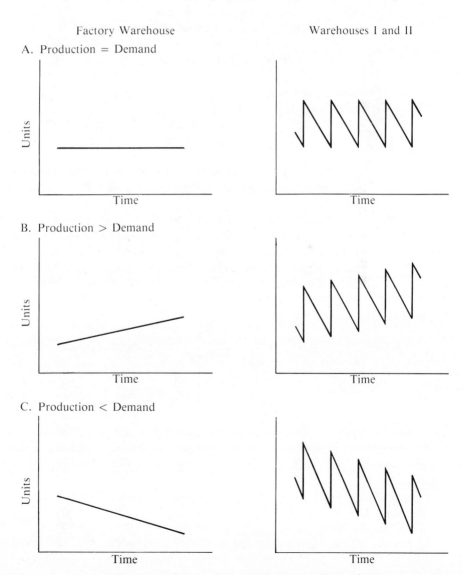

Finished Goods Cycle Stock (in the Distribution System). Cycle stock results from the weekly shipments to the warehouses as illustrated in Figure 7-5. The cycle stock value in each of the two coastal warehouses decreases to zero immediately preceeding the arrival of a shipment and then peaks at the arrival.

The average value of cycle stock equals the sum of cycle stock at the two warehouses, and the cycle stock at each warehouse equals one-half of the shipping quantity. Thus,

$$FG(C)_i = 2 \times 0.50 \times 0.23 \times 0.30 \times C \times P_i$$
$$= 0.23 \times 0.30 \times C \times P_i$$

where i = the period (month)
     $FG(C)$ = value of finished goods cycle stock
         C = unit cost
         P = production output

Thus, in our example,

$$FG(C)_4 = 0.23 \times 0.30 \times \$5 \times 8,000$$
$$= \$2,760$$

The total finished goods cycle stock at the two warehouses during the other periods is calculated in the same manner. These values are included in Table 7-6.

A comparison of the aggregate finished goods inventory in the two situations, Case B with two regional warehouses (Table 7-6) and Case A with none (Table 7-3), reveals that the additional inventory in Case B is due to the addition of transportation stock, cycle stock at the two coastal warehouses, and the increased safety stock.

Table 7-6
Finished Goods Inventory

				Month			
	0	1	2	3	4	5	6
Transportation	—	$ 4,830	$ 4,830	$ 5,520	$ 5,520	$ 6,210	$ 6,210
Cycle	—	2,415	2,415	2,760	2,760	3,105	3,105
Safety Stock							
Plant Warehouse	$2,000	2,000	2,000	2,000	2,000	2,000	2,000
Warehouse I	2,000	2,000	2,000	2,000	2,000	2,000	2,000
Warehouse II	2,000	2,000	2,000	2,000	2,000	2,000	2,000
Anticipation							
Plant Warehouse	—	—	6,000	4,000	2,000	—	—
Warehouse I	—	—	4,500	3,000	1,500	—	—
Warehouse II	—	—	4,500	3,000	1,500		
		$13,245	$28,245	$24,280	$19,280	$15,315	$15,315

Anticipation Stock. As shown in Table 7-4, anticipation stock is 3,000 units in Month 2, 2,000 units in Month 3, and 1,000 units in Month 4. Thus, total investment in anticipation inventory is $15,000, $10,000, and $5,000 in Months 2, 3, and 4, respectively. Anticipation stock is divided among the three warehouses using the same 40 percent, 30 percent, 30 percent split used for other shipments. Thus, for Month 2 in Table 7-6, the plant warehouse anticipation stock is $6,000, and each of the coastal warehouses have $4,500 in anticipation stock. The anticipation stock for Months 3 and 4 is calculated in a similar manner.

Work In Process

The value of work in process (WIP) depends on the planned production output and the manufacturing lead time. The simplest approach to calculating projected WIP is to estimate it as a percentage of planned production. The following model is applicable in this continuous process example.

$$WIP_i = p \times C \times P_{i+1}$$

where

i = the period (month)
p = appropriate percentage
WIP = value of WIP at the end of the period
C = unit cost
P = units shipped

The percentage used in the calculation can be determined by a comparison of past actual WIP and planned production quantities. Suppose in our example that measurements of WIP have revealed that the value of WIP approximates 25 percent of the value of the next month's planned shipments. Using that value to calculate the value of WIP at the end of Period 3 results in

$$WIP_3 = 0.25 \times \$5 \times 8,000 = \$10,000$$

The values at the end of the other periods are calculated in the same manner and listed in Table 7-7.

Table 7-7
WIP Value (End of Month)

	1	2	Month 3	4	5	6*
WIP	$8,750	$10,000	$10,000	$11,250	$11,250	$11,250

*P_7 = 9,000

The above model is merely an example; other models must be developed for other situations. When there is more than one product being produced at the same time, perhaps on different lines, the WIP of each must be calculated.

Raw Material

The ideal practice is to have purchased materials or components arriving daily or more often, at a rate equal to their use in manufacturing. The supplier's production methods and transportation economics frequently make this impractical; in such cases economical purchase-transportation lot sizes are purchased.

Before calculating the total raw material (*RM*) inventory investment, it should be noted that:

A.   *RM* transportation stock will exist when material is purchased at the loading dock of a supplier and transportation time is substantial.
B.   *RM* inventory may be increased by receiving, inspection, and testing activities that extend the time before it is available for manufacturing.
C.   *RM* may be purchased as "anticipation" inventory against known price increases or supplier shutdown.

When any one of the above conditions exist, calculation of the projected value of *RM* must include these factors. Our example includes only cycle stock and safety stock in raw material.

Lot-Size (Cycle Stock) Inventory.   The value of lot-size raw material inventories can be projected in the same manner as finished goods cycle stock. Manufacturing lead time, of course, affects the relationship. In the example, suppose data from earlier production has revealed that the value of raw material cycle stock equals, on the average, 25 percent of the value of the raw material required for the next month's production. This does not include safety stock. Purchased items account for 30 percent of the total cost of the final product. Thus, the model for the value of raw material cycle stock is

$$RM(C)_i = C \times p \times P_{i+1} \times COSP$$

where i = the period (month)
    $RM(C)$ = value of *RM* cycle stock at the end of the period
        C = unit cost
        p = percentage, expressed as a decimal, of *RM* requirements in stock, on the average
        P = production output
    $COSP$ = value of *RM* as a decimal percentage of the total unit cost of sales

In the example, the value of $RM(C)$ at the end of Month 4 is

$$RM(C)_4 = \$5 \times 0.25 \times 9{,}000 \times 0.30 = \$3{,}375$$

The values of $RM(C)$ at the end of each month are calculated in the same manner—assuming the production output in Month 7 is also 9,000 units—and listed in Table 7-8.

Table 7-8
$RM(C)$ Value (End of Month)

	Month					
	1	2	3	4	5	6
$RM(C)$	$2,625	$3,000	$3,000	$3,375	$3,375	$3,375

Safety Stock.   Since lower production quantities can sometimes result in smaller lot sizes but the same order interval, safety stock may remain relatively constant in order to achieve the same customer service level (measuring customer service in terms of the percentage of exposure without stockouts). Thus, the relationship of raw material safety stock investment to production output may be constant when production output varies monthly by only 20 percent or less. In the example, analysis has revealed that raw material safety stock, $RM(S)$, averages about $625 over the present production range. Other relationships may exist in other situations.

The total RM investment in the example is given in Table 7-9.

Table 7-9
Raw Material Inventory by Month

	Month					
	1	2	3	4	5	6
$RM(C)$	$2,625	$3,000	$3,000	$3,375	$3,375	$3,375
$RM(S)$	625	625	625	625	625	625
RM	$3,250	$3,625	$3,625	$4,000	$4,000	$4,000

Aggregate Inventory Investment

The aggregate inventory value is obtained by adding the values of finished goods, work in process, and raw material. The aggregate inventory for our example, shown in Table 7-10, includes the finished goods inventory with distribution stock.

Table 7-10
Aggregate Inventory Investment

	Month					
	1	2	3	4	5	6
FG	$13,245	$28,245	$24,280	$19,280	$15,315	$15,315
WIP	8,750	10,000	10,000	11,250	11,250	11,250
RM	3,250	3,625	3,625	4,000	4,000	4,000
	$25,245	$41,870	$37,905	$34,530	$30,565	$30,565

The foregoing models are examples. The relationships of raw material, work in process, and finished goods inventory to planned production must be determined for each organization and appropriate models developed.

Also, these relationships are dynamic. For example, changes in manufacturing processes and lead time may change work in process even though planned output is not changed.

JOB SHOP ENVIRONMENT

In a continuous process or mass production environment, the projected inventory investment depends primarily on the rate of flow and the products being produced. Projecting inventory investment in a job shop environment requires an order-by-order and operation-by-operation or operation group-by-group analysis. The detailed procedures and calculations appropriate in a situation depend on the characteristics of that situation. However, the approach is the same.

Required prerequisite information includes purchasing and manufacturing lead times, a master production schedule (MPS), bills of material, and the value added at milestones in the production process of each item.

The following discussion explains and illustrates an approach for calculating projected WIP increases and decreases by period in the planning horizon.

Calculating changes in the WIP inventory consists of:

1. Calculating the time-phased increase in inventory for each item on the MPS
2. Adding by period these increases for all items on the MPS
3. Adding to these totals the funds allocated for anticipation type purchases
4. Decreasing period totals by an estimate of the purchases that have been made previously in anticipation (Step 3)

We will use Assembly 675000 to illustrate this approach. The MPS calls for 100 of these assemblies to be shipped in Week 30. Fabricating a 675000 assembly requires two subassemblies (level one in the BOM), a purchased part, and paint. One of these subassemblies, Part 675200, is fabricated from three production parts; the other first level subassembly, Part 675100, is the assembly of two second level subassemblies, Parts 675110 and 675120. Table 7-11 is a bill of material listing all items required in the manufacture of 675000 and describing the foregoing relationships. It also lists the lead times of all items based on the manufacture of a lot of 100 assemblies; in addition, it lists the value added per 100 units for each item.

Figure 7-6 is a process chart indicating when material must be available and when fabrication operations must be completed if the one hundred 675000 assemblies are to be completed in Week 30. The chart is based on normal manufacturing lead times. For example, Figure 7-6 reveals that the raw material,

Table 7-11

Illustration of a Bill of Material, Item Lead Times, and Item Value Added for an MPS Item

Part No.*	Quantity**	Value Added	Item Lead Time (weeks)	Cumulative Lead Time (weeks)	Start*** (week)
675000	1	$ 4.60	2	2	28
675100	1	2.50	1	3	27
675110	1	4.80	2	5	25
675111	1	5.40	3	8	22
M2787	2 lb	0.30	2	10	20
675112	1	14.40	8	13	17
M3523	3 lb	0.30	2	15	15
675113	2	8.10	4	9	21
M8619	3.5 lb	1.10	1	10	20
675120	1	8.40	3	6	24
675121	1	7.20	4	10	20
P7472	1	0.25	3	13	17
675122	1	3.60	2	8	22
M2786	6.5 lb	1.20	1	9	21
P1314	2	0.84	2	8	22
675200	1	7.20	3	5	25
675210	1	3.60	2	7	23
P4423	2	5.25	2	9	21
675220	1	1.80	1	6	24
M3391	4 ft	0.40	1	7	23
675230	1	8.10	4	9	21
M1851	2 lb	0.25	2	11	19
P2783	1	6.70	4	6	24
M1467	5 gal	13.00	1	3	27

*An M prefix indicates raw material and a P prefix indicates a purchased part.
**Raw material quantity requirements usually are specified in pounds, gallons, linear feet, or other bulk measure.
***See Figure 7-6.

M3523, must be available by Week 17, and the purchased part, P7472, must be available by Week 20.

Table 7-12 tabulates the increases in WIP as purchased items arrive, parts are manufactured, and assemblies are completed. For example, plans are for M3523 to be available in Week 17, for 675121 to be completed by Week 24, and for 675100 to be assembled by Week 28. The value added by completing these and similar activities for 100 items is recorded. The increases in WIP due to partial completion of an item's manufacture are not recorded in order to keep the example simple. For example, although labor is added to WIP during Weeks 25 and 26, no increase in WIP is recorded since no activities are completed. However, estimates of partial completion could be made and WIP increased accordingly.

Figure 7-6
Inventory Investment Value Added
(Time-Phased with the MPS)

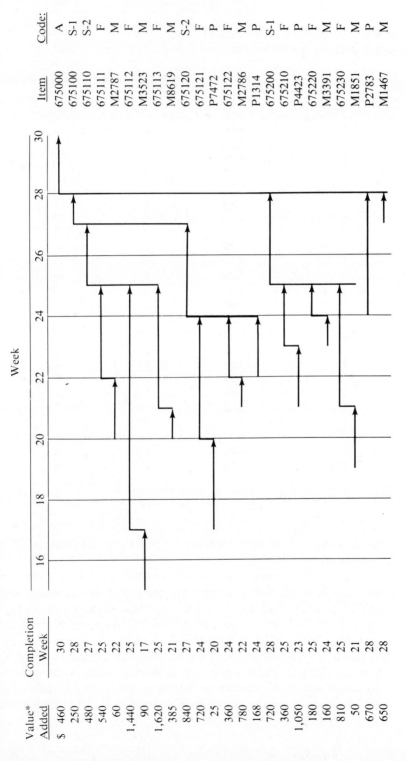

Week

Value* Added	Completion Week	Item	Code:
$ 460	30	675000	A
250	28	675100	S-1
480	27	675110	S-2
540	25	675111	F
60	22	M2787	M
1,440	25	675112	F
90	17	M3523	M
1,620	25	675113	F
385	21	M8619	M
840	27	675120	S-2
720	24	675121	F
25	20	P7472	P
360	24	675122	F
780	22	M2786	M
168	24	P1314	P
720	28	675200	S-1
360	25	675210	F
1,050	23	P4423	P
180	25	675220	F
160	24	M3391	M
810	25	675230	F
50	21	M1851	M
670	28	P2783	P
650	28	M1467	M

*Based on values in Table 7-11.

Table 7-12
Cumulative Increases in Work-in-Process Value per Week by
Completion of Manufacturing and Purchasing Activities

						Raw Materials			
						Week			
Item	17	20	21	22	23	24	27	28	30
M3523	$90								
M8619			$385						
M1851			50						
M2787				$ 60					
M2786				780					
M3391						$ 160			
M1467								$ 650	
Cumulative Value	$90	$90	$525	$1,365	$1,365	$1,525	$1,525	$2,175	$2,175

						Purchased Parts			
						Week			
Item	17	20	21	22	23	24	27	28	30
P7472		$25							
P4423					$1,050				
P1314						$ 168			
P2783								$ 670	
Cumulative Value	0	$25	$25	$25	$1,075	$1,243	$1,243	$1,913	$1,913

						Fabricated Parts			
						Week			
Item	17	20	21	22	23	24	27	28	30
675121						$ 720			
675122						360			
675111							$ 540		
675112							1,440		
675113							1,620		
675210							360		
675220							180		
675230							810		
Cumulative Value	0	0	0	0	0	$1,080	$6,030	$6,030	$6,030

						Assemblies			
						Week			
Item	17	20	21	22	23	24	27	28	30
675110							$ 480		
675120							840		
675100								$ 250	
675200								720	
675000									$ 460
Cumulative Value	0	0	0	0	0	0	$1,320	$2,290	$2,750

	Total								
	Week								
17	20	21	22	23	24	27	28	30
$90	$115	$550	$1,390	$2,440	$3,848	$10,118	$12,408	$12,868

Table 7-13 adds the investment for all items on the MPS. To keep the example relatively simple we have added only two other MPS items, Assemblies 445000 and 925000. Table 7-13 also adds investment in raw material, purchased parts, fabricated parts, subassemblies, and assemblies. For example, the totals are $610 for Week 16, $54,959 for Week 28, and $51,786 for Week 30. The $8,434 for Item 445000 is removed from the total in Week 30 since Item 445000 was shipped in Week 29. This is a laborious task when performed manually for a large number of MPS items. However, once the investment pattern of each MPS item is established and software developed, a computer can perform the summations by period with relative ease.

Table 7-13
Aggregate Inventory Investment from MPS, Multiple Items

| | MPS Item | | | |
| | 675000 | 445000 | 925000 | |
Week	Quantity = 100	Quantity = 50	Quantity = 200	Total
16	$ —	$ —	$ 610	$ 610
18	90	210	3,520	3,820
20	115	720	6,405	7,240
22	1,390	3,120	12,167	16,677
24	3,448	4,210	22,815	30,473
26	3,448	7,826	28,374	39,648
28	12,408	8,434	34,117	54,959
30	12,868	—*	38,918	51,786

*Assembly 445000 has been shipped to a customer.

MANAGEMENT UNDER CONSTRAINTS

The shortage of financial resources frequently leads management to limit the capital available for inventory. When the projected inventory investment exceeds the limit, reductions in one or more of the functional types of stock can bring the investment within the acceptable boundary. Since initial aggregate inventory plans usually are based on minimum cost strategies, reducing inventory investment often will increase total costs. Comparing the increased costs resulting from the reduced investment to the benefits gained will enable management to evaluate the constraint.

However, the pressure to lower inventory can often lead an organization to adopt the JIT approach and obtain reduced inventories through reduced setup time, more frequent deliveries of purchased parts, uniform flow, transfer lot sizes substantially smaller than production lot sizes, manufacturing cells, and improved quality. Successful implementation of JIT can lead to both reduced inventory and reduced operating costs, as described in Chapter 17.

Anticipation Inventory

Building inventory prior to vacation shutdowns or peak sales periods is a common practice in industry. An analysis comparing the costs of carrying anticipation inventory to the costs of changing production levels was included in Chapter 2.

Cycle (Lot-Size) Inventories

Finished goods with independent demand may be produced in economic lot sizes to minimize the sum of carrying and setup costs. Purchased parts and raw material used in production at a relatively constant rate also may be purchased in economic order quantities (EOQ). Cycle stock inventory investment changes in direct proportion to purchase and production lot sizes, as illustrated in Figure 7-7. Thus, reducing lot sizes reduces inventory investment. However, the smaller lot sizes result in more orders per year and increased preparation (setup and ordering) costs. Figure 7-8 illustrates this relationship.

Figure 7-7
Lot Size and Average Inventory
(Finished Goods and Purchased Items with Independent Demand)

A. Lot Size $= M$; Average Inventory $= \dfrac{M}{2}$

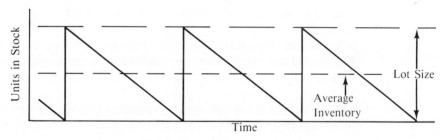

B. Lot Size $= \dfrac{M}{2}$; Average Inventory $= \dfrac{M}{4}$

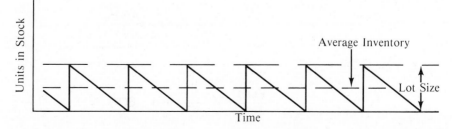

Figure 7-8
Cycle Stock Investment Versus Ordering Costs

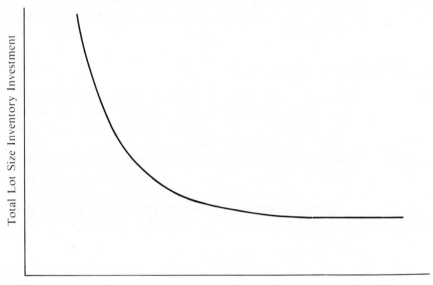

Total Preparation Costs

Two common approaches to controlling cycle stock investment by modifying lot sizes are: (1) treating the carrying cost rate (k) as a policy variable and (2) using the LIMIT procedure. We will examine both.

The Carrying Cost Rate as a Policy Variable.   Robert G. Brown (1967, 30) has pointed out that lot size adjustments can be made by treating the carrying cost rate (k) as a management policy variable. Increasing k will decrease the lot size in proportion to the square root of the ratio of the old to the new value of k, as proved in the following: Designate the new values of k and the EOQ as k' and EOQ', respectively, and recall that

$$EOQ = \sqrt{\frac{2SR}{kC}}$$

Then

$$EOQ' = \sqrt{\frac{2SR}{k'C}}$$

Thus,

$$\frac{EOQ'}{EOQ} = \frac{\sqrt{k}}{\sqrt{k'}} \quad \text{and} \quad EOQ' = EOQ\sqrt{\frac{k}{k'}}$$

As an example, let the old EOQ be 20 units and the carrying cost rate be increased by 50 percent, then

$$EOQ' = 20\sqrt{\frac{k}{1.5k}}$$
$$= 20\sqrt{0.667}$$
$$= 16.32, \text{ or } 17 \text{ units}$$

To reduce the average lot size stock investment by a percentage (p), one can calculate the ratio of the new carrying cost rate (k') to the old carrying cost rate (k) using the following model.

$$\frac{k'}{k} = \frac{1}{(1 - p)^2}$$

For example, if a 25 percent reduction in the average cycle stock investment is desired and the present carrying cost rate is 0.20, then

$$\frac{k'}{0.20} = \frac{1}{(1 - 0.25)^2}$$
$$k' = 0.2(1.78)$$
$$k' = 0.36$$

Thus, a management decision to reduce lot size inventory investment by 25 percent in this case is an implicit statement that k is 0.36 rather than 0.20.

LIMIT.   Harty, Plossl, and Wight (1963, 21) introduced the lot-size inventory management interpolation technique (LIMIT) to calculate minimum total cost lot sizes when the production of EOQ lot sizes will exceed production capacity constraints. Hoffmann (1964) extended the LIMIT approach to cover situations where the normal EOQ's exceeded investment constraints. The procedure, which also can be used to cope with storage constraints, does require that the carrying cost rate be the same for all items.

The Procedure.   This technique determines the relation of the aggregate EOQ requirements to the limited resource available and revises all the lot sizes by the same proportion to bring the aggregate EOQ resource requirements within the limit. When capital or storage space is insufficient, the EOQ's must be reduced; when production capacity is insufficient, the EOQ's must be increased. In the latter case, production capacity requirements are lowered as a result of the decreased setup requirements. When production capacity and either capital or storage space available are exceeded by the EOQ requirements, the manager must decide on the trade-off between added production capacity costs and added investment or storage costs. The procedure is described next and an example follows.

1. Group items on the basis of common carrying cost rates, common resource requirements, or common space requirements.
2. Determine the multiplier (M). The exact nature of the calculation depends on the constrained resource. The values described here relate to the group being analyzed and the applicable constraint.
   a. Capital constraint

   $$M = \frac{\text{Limit on the Cycle Stock Investment}}{\text{Aggregate EOQ Investment Required}}$$

   b. Production capacity constraint

   $$M = \frac{\text{Aggregate EOQ Setup Hours Required}}{\text{Limit on Setup Hours}}$$

   c. Space constraint

   $$M = \frac{\text{Maximum Space Available for Cycle Stock}}{\text{Aggregate EOQ Space Requirements}}$$

3. Multiply the EOQ of each item in the group by M to obtain the LIMIT order quantity (LOQ) for each item.
4. Calculate the aggregate capital (production or space capacity) required by the LOQ's, and determine if the new requirements are within the limit.
5. Calculate the aggregate preparation (ordering and setup) and carrying costs of the LOQ's.
6. Decide if the benefits of operating within the constraint are greater than the added costs.

An Example.   Table 7-14 contains data concerning four independent demand items that have the same carrying cost rate, 0.30. The economic production lot size of these four final products is calculated using the basic model described in Chapter 6. For example, the EOQ for Item A is calculated as follows:

$$\text{EOQ} = \sqrt{\frac{2RS}{kC\left(1 - \dfrac{D}{P}\right)}}$$

where $R = 1{,}000$ units $k = 0.30$
        $C = \$10$ $P = 50$ units per day
        $S = \$36$ $D = \dfrac{1{,}000}{250} = 4$ units per day

$$\text{EOQ}(A) = \sqrt{\frac{2(1{,}000)(36)}{(0.30)(10)\left(1 - \frac{4}{50}\right)}} = 161.51$$

$$\text{EOQ}(A) = 162$$

The average lot size investment $(\bar{I}_{\$_i})$ for an item equals the product of the average quantity in inventory and the cost of an item. Thus,

$$\bar{I}_{\$_i} = \frac{Q\left(1 - \dfrac{D}{P}\right)C}{2}$$

and

$$\bar{I}_{\$_A} = \frac{162(1 - \frac{4}{50})10}{2} = \$745.20$$

The annual carrying cost and annual preparation costs were calculated as described in Chapter 6. The aggregate average cycle stock investment for the four items (A, B, C, and D) is $6,028.17 as recorded in Table 7-14. The limit for average cycle stock investment in this group of items is $5,000. (Similar limits have been established for other groups to bring the aggregate investment for all cycle stock within a given constraint.) Therefore,

$$M = \frac{\$5,000}{\$6,028.17} = 0.8294$$

The new order quantity, the LOQ, for each item equals 0.8294 times the EOQ. Thus,

$$LOQ(A) = 0.8294 \times 162 = 134.36$$
$$LOQ(A) = 134$$

The LOQ's for Items B, C, and D are obtained in the same manner, and average investment required by the LOQ is calculated in the usual manner.

$$\bar{I}_{\$} = \frac{LOQ\left(1 - \dfrac{D}{P}\right)C}{2}$$

Thus,

$$\bar{I}_{\$}(A) = \frac{134(1 - \frac{4}{50})10}{2} = \$616.40$$

Table 7-14 includes the results of these calculations for all items.

The LOQ lot sizes require an aggregate average investment of approximately $5,000, annual carrying costs of $1,499.21, and preparation costs of $2,180.30. Thus the trade-off is a $373 ($2,180 − $1,807) increase in preparation costs for a decrease of approximately $1,030 ($6,028 − $4,997) in inventory

Table 7-14
Average Cycle Stock Investment*
Annual Carrying Costs and Preparation Costs

k = 0.30

Annual Requirements (R)	Item	Unit Cost (C)	Preparation (Setup and Ordering) Costs (S)	Daily Production Rate (P)	With the EOQ				
					EOQ	Average Inventory Investment	Annual Carrying Costs	Annual Preparation Costs	$1 - \frac{D}{P}$
1,000	A	$10.00	$36	50	162	$ 745.20	$ 223.56	$ 222.22	0.92
40,000	B	2.50	28	800	1,932	1,932.00	579.60	579.68	0.80
15,000	C	4.00	48	500	1,168	2,055.68	616.70	616.42	0.88
8,000	D	6.00	25	200	514	1,295.29	388.58	389.11	0.84
					Total	$6,028.17	$1,808.44	$1,807.43	

With the LOQ

Item	LOQ	Annual Inventory Investment	Annual Carrying Costs	Annual Preparation Costs
A	134	$ 616.40	$ 184.92	$ 268.65
B	1,602	1,602.00	480.60	699.12
C	969	1,705.44	511.63	743.03
D	426	1,073.52	322.06	469.48
Total		$4,997.36	$1,499.21	$2,180.28

Constraint: Maximum
Average Investment = $5,000($I_K$)

$$\text{Multiplier}(M) = \frac{I_K}{I}$$
$$= \frac{\$5,000}{\$6,028.17}$$
$$= 0.8294$$

$$\text{LOQ} = M(\text{EOQ})$$

*250 operating days per year

investment and a savings of $309 ($1,808 − $1,499) in carrying costs. However, the actual increase in aggregate setup costs when the LOQ lot sizes are implemented depends on the utilization of equipment and personnel prior to the change as described in Chapter 5.

If the affected workers and machines are operating on *undertime* (scheduled production is less than that normally obtained from available equipment and personnel), the added setups may be accomplished by otherwise idle personnel and machines, and the increased preparation costs will be substantially less than the straightforward calculations indicate. Conversely, if the affected workers and machines already are operating at capacity or on overtime, the increase in setup hours will exacerbate the capacity problem, and the costs of the added setups will be much greater than the standard calculations indicate. The inventory planner always should evaluate how well a model fits a given situation. The foregoing situations are good examples of cases in which the cost model should be altered.

Insufficient Capacity. Additional capacity may be gained by reducing the number of manufacturing orders per year for each item and, thus, reducing the total number of setups. Some of the time previously devoted to setting up machines then can be used to produce output. When the preparation cost (S) is directly proportional to setup time and the cost per hour of setup time is the same for all items in a group, the LIMIT approach will provide LOQ's that provide the added production capacity and that minimize the sum of carrying and setup costs under the constraint.

For example, if the EOQ's of a group of items require 2,000 hours of setup time in a work center and an additional 400 hours of production capacity are required in that work center, the LIMIT on setup hours is 1,600. Thus,

$$M = \frac{2,000}{1,600} = 1.25$$

and

$$\text{LOQ's} = 1.25 \times \text{EOQ's}$$

Buffer Stock

Customer service is related directly to safety stock investment, as illustrated in Figure 7-9. An increase in safety stock increases customer service, all things being equal. Thus, management must evaluate the inventory investment-customer service trade-off when establishing safety stock policy and decision rules.

Figure 7-9
Safety Stock Investment Versus Customer Service

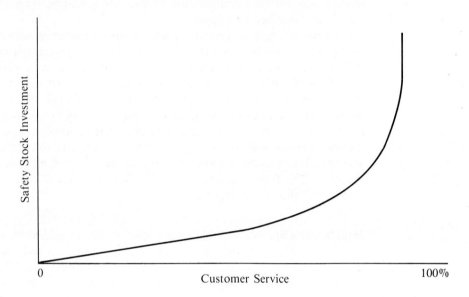

Factors such as the following must be considered when evaluating safety stock policy:

1. Each additional investment in safety stock gains a diminishing increase in customer service.
2. The exchange curve describing the trade-off between safety stock investment and customer service depends on the customer service objectives and the decision rule used to achieve these objectives (Brown 1977, 191).
3. Customer service, safety stock, and lot size interact. Small lot sizes result in more orders per year and increased exposure to stockouts. This relationship supports the application of the ABC principle to safety stock management. Control should be concentrated on those items with a relatively large number of exposures, long lead times, and high stockout costs. Safety stock for slow moving, inexpensive items will be relatively high (a high safety factor), but require minimum investment.
4. Anticipation inventory can fill the safety stock function during periods when production exceeds demand.
5. The required customer service level for dependent demand items is 100 percent. The stockout of a component for a subassembly can result in stockouts at each of the remaining BOM levels in the manufacturing process. Safety stock is frequently replaced by safety time when ordering dependent demand items. This enables new orders to be released on an expedited basis in the event of scrap.

CONCLUDING REMARKS

Managing aggregate inventory is a complex and crucial challenge. It is intertwined with purchasing, transportation, and production scheduling. It usually involves decisions on trade-offs among customer service, inventory investment, and the number of production and purchase orders in an environment with investment and production capacity constraints.

The JIT approach to managing manufacturing challenges many traditional approaches as well as reminding the inventory manager that factors such as setup times and costs, manufacturing scheduling practices, and supplier delivery practices should be analysed for possible changes that can lead to reduced inventory and improved operating efficiencies (see Chapter 17).

EXERCISES

1. What elements of inventory are included in aggregate planning as described in Chapter 2?

2. A fellow student contends that the major Japanese automobile manufacturers have no inventory. Can you name the one type of inventory in which they have an obvious large investment?

3. Explain why a company whose lowest value of planned finished goods inventory during the next 18 months never falls below $150,000 is said to have $150,000 of safety stock.

Use the following aggregate planning information in Exercises 4 through 13:

The standard weighted average unit cost of finished goods is $40. The forecast demand and the planned aggregate production in thousands of units for the next 12 months is:

	Month												
	−1	1	2	3	4	5	6	7	8	9	10	11	12
Production		8	8	8	12	12	12	7	7	7	13	13	13
Demand		9	6	8	11	13.5	10	8	6	9.5	13	14	12
Ending Inventory*	2												

Includes anticipation and buffer stock only.

4. Calculate the projected aggregate finished goods buffer stock in units and in dollars.

5. Calculate the projected aggregate buffer finished goods inventory at the end of each month in units and in dollars.

6. Calculate the value of the aggregate finished goods anticipation inventory at the end of each month in units and in dollars.

7. What is the value of the average aggregate finished goods anticipation stock each month in units and in dollars?

8. Shipment to five warehouses takes place when production allocated to a given warehouse is complete. Thus, the shipment to Warehouse B is made at the end of Tuesday's production. Transportation time, including loading and unloading, to Warehouses A and B is two days each, to Warehouse C is five days, and to Warehouses D and E is eight days each. The following table lists the allocation of daily production to the five warehouses.

Day	M	T	W	Th	F
Production %	20	20	20	20	20
Warehouse			Shipments		
A	15				
B	5	20			
C			20		
D				20	10
E					10

Calculate for each month the maximum and the average number of units and the dollar value in transport to each warehouse. What is the average aggregate value of transportation inventory each month?

9. What is the finished goods cycle stock in units and in dollars at each warehouse during each month?

10. What is the total average finished goods each month? at the end of each month?

11. Components are manufactured at Plant A and shipped to Plant B for assembly. The weighted (by value) average cycle time of work in process is two weeks at Plant A and one week at Plant B. Transportation time between the two plants is two days; shipments are made daily. The weighted average cost of WIP when it leaves Plant A is 55 percent of the cost of goods sold. One day's buffer stock of incoming material is planned at Plant B.
   a. Calculate the projected WIP cycle stock at Plant A and at Plant B each month.
   b. Calculate the projected WIP safety stock at Plant B at the end of each month.
   c. Calculate the projected average WIP transportation stock each month.
   d. Calculate the projected total value of WIP at the end of each month.

12. The weighted average of *RM* cycle stock is 0.4 of a month's supply. The *RM* required at Plants A and B—primarily at A—equals 35 percent of the cost of goods sold. Incoming orders take an average (weighted by value) of 2 working days per month to clear inspection. (Use 20 working days per month.) On average, the company-owned raw material in transit equals 1 percent of the month's purchases. Manufacturing lead time causes the *RM* expenditures for a given month to equal 40 percent of the *RM* required for the present month and 60 percent of the *RM* required for the following month's output. *RM* safety stock is approximately 1.5 days stock.

   a. Calculate the average *RM* cycle stock value during each month.
   b. Calculate the average *RM* safety stock value during each month.
   c. Calculate the average *RM* in-transit stock value during each month.
   d. Calculate the total average *RM* stock value during each month.

13. Calculate the average inventory investment for each month.

14. Explain how a company might have transportation inventory in its raw material.

15. A company has approximately one million dollars of inventory in transit to customers during 10 of every 20 working days but never on the last day of the month when inventory is measured. Discuss the ramifications of measuring inventory in this manner.

16. Eighty of Assembly 9800 are scheduled for completion in Week 20. Calculate the increase in WIP per week on the basis of the lead times and value-added amounts shown in the following table. An indented manufacturing BOM for Assembly 9800 is listed.

Part No.*	Quantity	Value Added (each)	Item Lead Time**
9800	1	$10.00	2
P635	2 gal	9.00	0.5
9810	2	8.60	1
9811	1	15.00	2
M348	4	1.50	1
P2715	1	6.00	3
9820	1	21.00	1.5
9821	3	8.40	1
9822	1	4.20	1
P376	2 ft	0.75	1

*P prefix on number indicates purchased component. M prefix on number indicates material.
**In weeks.

17. Given the data in Table 7-14 and a maximum allowable average inventory investment of $5,500, calculate the LOQ's for Items A, B, C, and D. Calculate the affect on annual carrying costs and annual preparation costs.

18. Given the data in Table 7-14, calculate the new value of k that will result in average inventory investments of $5,500 and $5,000.

19. Change the values of k for Items A, B, C, and D in Table 7-14 to 0.20 and leave all other data the same.
    a. Calculate the LOQ's.
    b. Calculate the difference in the inventory related costs of the LOQ's and the EOQ's.
    c. Repeat Parts a and b for an inventory investment constraint of $4,500.

20. Change the values of k for Items A, B, C, and D in Table 7-14 to 0.25 and leave all other data the same.
    a. Calculate the LOQ's.
    b. Calculate the difference in the inventory related costs of the LOQ's and the EOQ's.
    c. Repeat Parts a and b for an inventory investment constraint of $4,500.

21. Some contend that the LIMIT approach and similar methods are no longer relevant given the proven merit of the JIT approach. Describe the value of JIT concepts when inventory investment is constrained and also the continuing value of the LIMIT and similar approaches in such situations.

22. Use the data in Table 7-14 plus the following information. The EOQ of the four items requires 200 hours of setup time in Work Center 28 during the next six months. Management has decided to gain 40 hours of additional capacity in Work Center 28 by changing the lot sizes of Items A, B, C, and D. Calculate the new lot sizes.

SELECTED READINGS

Brown, Robert G. *Decision Rules for Inventory Management*. New York: Holt, Rinehart & Winston, 1967.

Brown, Robert G. *Materials Management Systems*. New York: John Wiley & Sons, Inc., 1977.

Edwards, J. Nicholas. "Target Level Inventories." *American Production and Inventory Control Conference Proceedings* (1975): 309.

Harty, James D., George W. Plossl, and Oliver W. Wight. *Management of Lot Size Inventories*. Falls Church, VA: American Production and Inventory Control Society, 1963.

Hoffmann, Thomas R. "LIMIT Extended." *APICS Quarterly Bulletin* (January 1964): 65-70.

Plossl, George W. *Production and Inventory Control: Principles and Techniques*. 2d ed. Englewood Cliffs, NJ: Prentice-Hall, Inc., 1985.

8

JOINT REPLENISHMENT

To this point we have focused on managing individual items or stockkeeping units (SKUs). Many firms order several items simultaneously, rather than individually. In Chapter 3 we considered forecasting for a family of products. In this chapter, we consider the simultaneous purchase of several items, known as *joint replenishment*. An order for several items is known as a *joint order*.

Marvin's uses joint replenishment almost exclusively. Suppose that Marvin's Auburn store needs to reorder $\frac{3}{8}''$ reversible drills from Black & Decker. They will at the same time order whatever other Black & Decker tools are in short supply. The precise details of deciding which items to include in an order are discussed in this chapter. The principle concept behind these calculations is that the marginal cost of adding one line item to an existing order is much less than the marginal cost of later ordering the item individually. There also may be savings on shipping costs, as it is generally cheaper to ship one large lot than to ship several small ones. Finally, vendors often give discounts based on the total value of an order, giving a further incentive to large purchases.

It is also possible to obtain economies in manufacturing setup costs. Since some items are manufactured using the same equipment and tooling, one major setup frequently serves the entire group with only minor changes required for each item.

Joint replenishment requires decisions concerning:

1. The aggregate value of the order
2. The order quantity of each item
3. The order intervals for individual items within a group
4. The timing of order releases

These decisions are used in the management of:

1. Purchased items
2. Production parts manufactured on (a) equipment dedicated to one group and (b) equipment used in the production of two or more groups

This chapter first examines joint replenishment decisions when there is constant demand and each item is ordered every cycle. A discussion of different order intervals for items within a group precedes an explanation of using equal-run-out order quantities to cope with variations in demand. Models are provided to suggest appropriate order quantities for jointly considered items. The second part of the chapter covers the establishment of order release points for joint orders and the evaluation of quantity discounts.

JOINT PURCHASE ORDER QUANTITY

The economic order quantity (EOQ) model for groups is derived in the same manner as the EOQ for individual items. The assumptions of the basic (deterministic demand, instantaneous replenishment) EOQ model apply; namely

1. The demand rate for each item is constant and known with certainty. Lead time is also known with certainty. Thus, there are no stockouts and no stockout costs.
2. Replenishment or lead time is common to all items. All ordered items arrive at one point in time each cycle.
3. The carrying cost rate, individual item costs, and preparation costs are known. There are no discontinuities in the cost of units (such as quantity discounts), setup costs, and the carrying cost rate.

Figure 8-1 graphically depicts inventory over time in this situation. Under these conditions, the total cost of an aggregate lot size decision is equal to the sum of preparation costs and carrying costs during the period.

The formal derivation of the joint order quantity is shown in Appendix 8A. Recall that in Chapter 7 we derived an optimal order quantity equal to the square root of the quantity two times the annual unit demand times the setup cost divided by the holding cost in dollars per year. We should not be surprised to find a similar formula for joint orders, and in fact, the formula is the square root of the quantity two times the annual dollar volume of all items times the sum of all order costs divided by the carrying cost as a proportion of item cost. This is stated formally in Equation 8-1.

$$Q_\$^* = \sqrt{\frac{2(S + \Sigma s_i)A}{k}} \tag{8-1}$$

where S = cost of placing an order
s_i = marginal cost of adding Item i to the order
A = annual dollar volume of all items
k = carrying cost rate (proportion)
$Q_\$^*$ = optimal lot size in dollars

Figure 8-1
Stock on Hand Versus Time (Aggregate Purchased Lots)
LT = Lead Time, OP = Order Point, $Q_{\$_i}^*$ = Economic Order Quantity (in dollars) for Item i, and $Q_\$^*$ = Optimal Aggregate Lot Size in Dollars

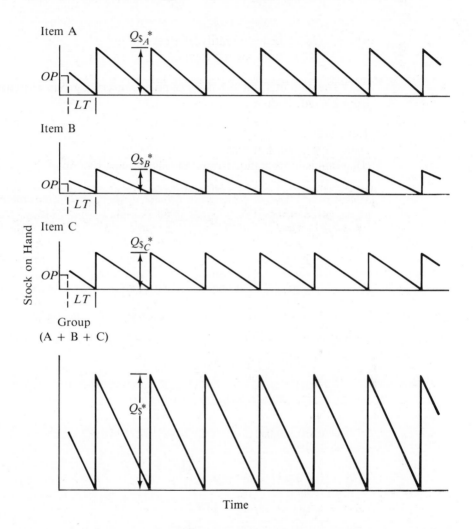

The individual order quantity in dollars is found by prorating the total order by annual dollar volume, as shown in Equation 8-2.

$$Q_{\$_i}^* = \left(\frac{a_i}{A}\right)Q_\$^* \tag{8-2}$$

where a_i = annual dollar volume of Item i
$Q_{\$_i}^*$ = order quantity of Item i in dollars

The individual order quantity in units equals the dollar value of the item order divided by the cost of the item. Thus, we have the following equation

$$Q_\$^* = \frac{Q_{\$_i}^*}{C_i} \qquad (8\text{-}3)$$

where $Q_\$^* =$ order quantity of Item i in units
$\quad\quad\ C_i =$ unit cost of Item i

The data in Table 8-1, for example, concern a group of items purchased from a single source.

Table 8-1
Data, Aggregate Lot Size
(Deterministic Demand, Instantaneous Receipt Example)

Item	Annual Demand	Unit Cost	Annual Dollar Requirements (a_i)	Item Preparation Costs (s_i)	$\dfrac{a_i}{A}$
1	1,000	$ 5.00	$ 5,000	$ 5	0.0567
2	2,500	6.00	15,000	10	0.1701
3	800	3.50	2,800	15	0.0317
4	3,200	12.00	38,400	10	0.4354
5	1,800	15.00	27,000	10	0.3061
			$88,200	$50	1.0000

$k = 0.30$ and $S = \$70$

$$Q_\$^* = \sqrt{\frac{(2)(70 + 50)(\$88,200)}{0.30}}$$

$$= \sqrt{\frac{(2)(120)(\$88,200)}{0.30}} = \sqrt{\frac{\$21,168,000}{0.30}}$$

$$= \sqrt{\$70,560,000}$$
$$= \$8,400$$

$$Q_{\$_i}^* = \left(\frac{a_i}{A}\right) Q_\$^* \quad \text{and} \quad Q_i^* = \frac{Q_{\$_i}^*}{C_i}$$

$Q_{\$_1}^* = 0.0567 \times \$8,400 = \$476.28$
$Q_{\$_2}^* = 0.1701 \times \$8,400 = \$1,428.84$
$Q_{\$_3}^* = 0.0317 \times \$8,400 = \$266.28$
$Q_{\$_4}^* = 0.4354 \times \$8,400 = \$3,657.36$
$Q_{\$_5}^* = 0.3061 \div \$8,400 = \$2,571.24$
$Q_1^* = \$476.28 \div \$5.00 = 95.26$
$Q_2^* = \$1,428.84 \div \$6.00 = 238.14$
$Q_3^* = \$266.28 \div \$3.50 = 76.08$
$Q_4^* = \$3,657.36 \div \$12.00 = 304.78$
$Q_5^* = \$2,571.24 \div \$15.00 = 171.42$

Practical aspects must be considered when implementing these results. First, order quantity must be an integer. Second, order quantity is usually rounded to a multiple of 5 or 10. And third, container and package size can affect the order quantity. Thus, the order quantities for Items 1 through 5 might be 100, 240, 80, 300 and 175, respectively. Calculation of the optimum aggregate production quantity is described in Appendix C.

Purchasing an optimum aggregate order of items under deterministic conditions results in the order being placed at a constant interval throughout the year. This enables us to approach the same problem in terms of the optimum order interval.

Optimum Order Interval

The number of orders per year (N) equals the aggregate annual demand for the family of items divided by the aggregate lot size. (Thus, $N = A \div Q_\$^*$.) In the previous example, annual dollar usage is \$88,200. The optimal order size is \$8,400 per order. The ratio \$88,200/\$8,400 indicates that just over ten orders will be placed each year, which equals an order every five weeks.

The interval between orders (T) can be expressed as a proportion of the period—a year in most cases—by dividing the period length in years by the number of orders. Thus,

$$T^* = \frac{1}{N} = \frac{1}{\dfrac{A}{Q_\$^*}} = \frac{Q_\$^*}{A}$$

Practical considerations must be recognized when using this approach to establish the interval between reviews in a periodic review type system. In the preceding example the optimum interval (T^*) is 0.095 years, approximately five weeks. This is a feasible solution. However, the optimum interval could have been 0.025 years, which is equivalent to approximately 6.25 working days. In such a case an interval of one week usually would be the practical solution.

Varying Item Cycles

Frequently, it is not economical to order each item every cycle. Aggregate preparation costs equal aggregate carrying costs for the minimum cost aggregate lot size. Although individual item carrying costs and preparation costs approach equality at the minimum cost aggregate lot size, they usually are not equal. Items with relatively large annual dollar demand have a greater influence on the aggregate lot size, especially when minor preparation costs are equal. Items that have a relatively low ratio of annual dollar demand to minor preparation cost (a_i/s_i) are likely candidates for ordering less frequently. Any marked lack of balance suggests that multiple cycles be investigated. Using the example data in Table 8-1, we calculate the ratios of preparation costs to carrying costs per cycle for each item, as shown in Table 8-2.

Table 8-2
Data, Aggregate Lot Size, Multiple Intervals

(1)	(2)	(3)	(4)	(5)	(6)	(7)	(8)
Item	Carrying Cost	Minor Preparation Costs (s_i)	$\dfrac{(3)}{(2)}$	$\dfrac{a_i}{A}$	$S\left(\dfrac{a_i}{A}\right)$	(3) + (6)*	$\dfrac{(7)}{(2)}$
1	$ 6.80	$ 5	0.74	0.0567	$ 3.97	$ 8.97	1.32
2	20.00	10	0.50	0.1701	11.91	21.91	1.10
3	3.81	15	3.95	0.0137	2.22	17.22	4.52
4	52.00	10	0.19	0.4354	30.47	40.47	0.78
5	36.83	10	0.27	0.3061	21.43	31.43	0.85
	$119.44				$70.00	$120.00	1.00

*Allocated total preparation costs

Using the carrying cost results obtained when assuming that all items are ordered each cycle gives the ratio of minor preparation costs to carrying costs listed in Column 4 and the ratio of allocated total preparation costs to carrying costs listed in Column 8. The following calculations for Item 1 illustrate how the carrying costs per period are obtained.

Carrying cost per period equals lot size times period length times annual carrying rate divided by two.

$$K = \frac{Q_{\$_1} Tk}{2}$$
$$= \frac{\$476.28 \times 0.0952 \times 0.3}{2}$$
$$= \$6.80$$

Carrying costs and setup costs approach a balance for all items except Item 3. The data in both Columns 4 and 8 reveal that setup costs far exceed carrying costs for Item 3; the ratios are 3.95 and 4.52. Thus, an investigation of the use of multiple intervals is in order. R. G. Brown (1967, 48-52) and E. A. Silver (1975) have recommended different methods of determining the interval multiples (n_i) for each item. We will examine both methods.

Brown's Approach.   Let's look first at Robert Brown's technique, which has a number of steps to obtain a solution:

1. Compute an initial estimate of the order interval (T) assuming that all items are ordered each cycle using the model developed earlier; i.e., $T = [2(S + \Sigma s_i) \div (kA)]^{1/2}$.

2. Determine n_i's using the model:

$$n_i = \frac{1}{T}\left(\frac{2s_i}{ka_i}\right)^{1/2}$$

Since n_i is rarely an integer, use Table 8-3 to round the n_i's. If all n_i's equal 1, the solution was obtained in Step 1; if not proceed to Step 3.

Table 8-3
Rounding Rules; Multiple Intervals

Range of Calculated Multiple n^*	Use an n of
0 to 1.414	1
1.414 to 2.449	2
2.449 to 3.464	3
3.464 to 4.472	4
4.472 to 5.477	5
5.477 to 6.480	6
6.480 to 7.483	7

For calculated values of n greater than 6, use the integer part of (n + 0.52). For example, if calculated n = 8.9, then n + 0.52 = 9.42, and an n of 9 should be used.

3. Determine a new value of T using the following model that incorporates the possibility of different order intervals.

$$T = \left[\frac{2\left(S + \sum\frac{s_i}{n_i}\right)}{k\sum n_i a_i}\right]^{1/2}$$

4. Return to Step 2 and calculate the new n_i's. If none of the interval multiples, n_i's, change, Step 3 has provided the solution. If one or more of the n_i's has changed, repeat Step 3 with the revised n_i's and continue the process until none of the n_i's change. This process converges rapidly, frequently on the first iteration. Let's see next how this would work out using the example data in Table 8-1, $T = \frac{1}{10.47}$.

$$n_1 = 10.47\left(\frac{2 \times 5}{0.3 \times 5,000}\right)^{1/2}$$

$$n_1 = 0.85 \rightarrow 1 \text{ (referring to Table 8-3)}$$

Calculating n_2 through n_5 in the same manner gives:

$$n_2 = 0.698 \rightarrow 1 \qquad n_4 = 0.43 \rightarrow 1$$
$$n_3 = 1.97 \rightarrow 2 \qquad n_5 = 0.52 \rightarrow 1$$

Calculating the new T produces the following:

$$T = \left[\frac{2\left(S + \sum \frac{s_i}{n_i}\right)}{k\sum n_i a_i}\right]^{1/2}$$

$$= \left[\frac{2\left(70 + \frac{5}{1} + \frac{10}{1} + \frac{15}{2} + \frac{10}{1} + \frac{10}{1}\right)}{0.3(5,000 + 15,000 + 2 \times 2,800 + 38,400 + 27,000)}\right]^{1/2}$$

$$= \left(\frac{2(112.5)}{0.3(91,000)}\right)^{1/2} = 0.091$$

Calculating the new n_1 gives:

$$n_1 = \frac{1}{T}\left(\frac{2s_1}{ka_1}\right)^{1/2} = \frac{1}{0.091}\left(\frac{2 \times 5}{0.3 \times 5,000}\right)^{1/2}$$
$$= 10.99 \times 0.082 = 0.9 \rightarrow 1$$

Calculating n_2 through n_5 in the same manner gives the following:

$$n_2 = 0.72 \rightarrow 1 \qquad n_4 = 0.44 \rightarrow 1$$
$$n_3 = 2.07 \rightarrow 2 \qquad n_5 = 0.55 \rightarrow 1$$

Since none of the n_i's have changed, we have a solution:

$$T = 0.091; \ n_1, n_2, n_4, \text{ and } n_5 = 1; \text{ and } n_3 = 2$$

Silver's Approach. As opposed to R. G. Brown, Edward Silver employs the following procedure to determine interval multiples for individual items:

1. Determine the item that has the smallest ratio of minor setup costs to annual dollar demand (s_i/a_i), and set its cycle interval equal to one.
2. Determine the interval multiple (n_i) for each item by rounding the value obtained from the following model to the nearest integer greater than zero. Use the following formula for n_i.

$$n_i = \left(\frac{s_i}{a_i} \times \frac{a_j}{S + s_j}\right)^{1/2}$$

where j = that item with the lowest s_i/a_i ratio.

The results from applying this approach to the data in Table 8-1 are shown in Table 8-4. These are the same results obtained with Brown's approach. This is not always the case. Silver's method is not iterative and, thus, slightly less tedious to determine manually. Neither approach guarantees the optimum. See Silver's (1975) article for further discussion.

Table 8-4
Results of Silver's Method

Item	$\dfrac{s_i}{a_i}$	$\dfrac{s_i}{a_i} = \dfrac{a_j}{S + s_j}$	n_i
1	0.00100	0.480	0.69 → 1
2	0.00067	0.319	0.57 → 1
3	0.00536	2.571	1.60 → 2
4	0.00026*	0.124	0.35 → 1
5	0.00037	0.178	0.42 → 1

*Item 4 has the lowest $s_i \div a_i$ ratio; thus, $a_j \div (S + s_j) = 480 \, [38,400 \div (70 + 10)]$.

UNCERTAINTY: ORDER QUANTITIES AND ORDER RELEASE

In a deterministic situation, all items in a purchased group reach their order points simultaneously as illustrated in Figure 8-1. Thus, an order for the optimum item lot sizes (which constitute the optimum aggregate lot size) is placed when the items reach their order point.

However, independent item demand rates rarely are deterministic. They vary daily, and sporadic surges in demand occur for particular items. Although dependent demand item requirements are calculable, they can change abruptly due to late orders, scrap, order cancellations, etc. Provisions for handling the reality of uncertainty must be incorporated in lot size and order release models and decisions. We will examine the impact of varying demand on lot sizes first.

Equal Runout Order Quantity

Figure 8-2 illustrates the case of one item in a purchased group reaching its order point prior to the other items. The objective in this case is to bring the item stocks back into balance, to attain an equal time supply, days of stock, for each item. It is accomplished by ordering each item's EOQ adjusted by the difference between its expected order point and its available stock when the order is placed. The resulting modified lot size frequently is called the equal runout quantity. The following model accomplishes this adjustment.

$$Q_{\$_i} = \left(\frac{a_i}{A}\right)(Q_\$^* + \Sigma I_{\$_i}) - I_{\$_i} \quad \text{or} \quad Q_{\$_i} = \left(\frac{d_i}{D}\right)(Q_\$^* + \Sigma I_{\$_i}) - I_{\$_i}$$

where $Q_{\$_i}^*$, A, and a_i are as defined earlier
$I_{\$_i}$ = dollar inventory of Item i when order is triggered
d_i = daily usage, demand, rate of Item i
$D = d_i$

Figure 8-2
Stock on Hand Versus Time (Varying Demand)
LT = Lead Time, OP = Order Point, t = Item B reaches its order point prior
to Items A and C, R = Remnant Stock, Q_i = Order Quantity, BO = Backorders permitted. Quantities are in dollars.

Item A

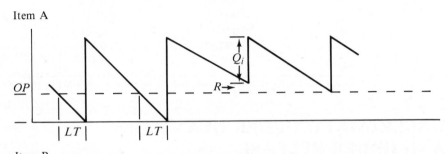

Item B

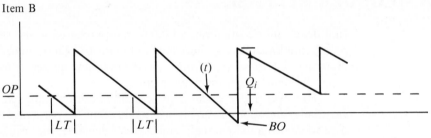

Item C

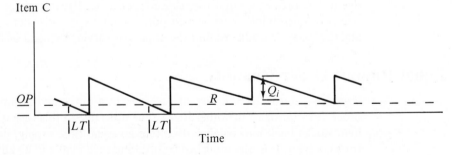

Since $D = \dfrac{A}{250}$ (working days per year), and

$$d_i = \frac{a_i}{250}$$

then,

$$\frac{d_i}{D} = \frac{a_i}{A}$$

Let's return to the example described in Table 8-1 and add additional data (see Table 8-5) describing a situation in which one item reaches its order point prior to the rest of the group.

Table 8-5
Data, Purchased Group
Varying Demand Example

Item	Daily Usage (d_i)	EOQ	Order Point*	Quantity on Hand $(I_{\$_i})$
1	$ 20.00	$ 476.28	$ 200	$ 240.00
2	60.00	1,428.84	600	660.00
3	11.20	266.28	112	168.00
4	153.60	3,657.36	1,536	1,536.00
5	108.00	2,571.24	1,080	1,108.80
	$352.80	$8,400.00	$3,528	$3,712.80

Two weeks, ten working days, is the lead time.

The data in Table 8-5 reveal that Item 4 is the first to reach its order point. The order quantities are calculated as follows.

$$Q_{\$_1} = \left(\frac{\$20}{\$352.80}\right)(\$8,400 + \$3,712.80) - \$240 = \$446.66$$

$$Q_1 = \frac{\$446.66}{\$5} = 89.33$$

The days of stock provided by the inventory on hand plus the order quantity is calculated as follows:

$$t_i = \frac{I_{\$_i} + Q_{\$_i}}{d_i}$$

where t_i = time period in days covered by the sum of the order quantity plus the inventory on hand of Item i. Thus,

$$t_i = \frac{\$240 + \$446.66}{\$20} = 34.33 \text{ days}$$

Calculating these values for the other items gives the results in Table 8-6. Table 8-6 reveals that the aggregate order quantity is still $8,400 as in the basic case, but item order quantities have been adjusted to provide the same time supply for all items.

Table 8-6
Equal Runout Time, Balanced, Lot Sizes

(1)	(2)	(3)	(4)	(5)	Days Supply
	Order		Inventory		(5)
Item	Quantity	Daily Usage	on Hand	(2) + (4)	(3)
1	$ 446.66	$ 20.00	$ 240	$ 686.66	34.33
2	1,400.00	60.00	660	2,060.66	34.33
3	216.53	11.20	168	384.53	34.33
4	3,737.91	153.60	1,536	5,273.91	34.33
5	2,598.92	108.00	1,108	3,707.92	34.33
	$8,400.02	$352.80	$3,712	$12,113.02	34.33

Remnant Stocks and Added Costs

Varying rates of demand and placement of a joint order when only one item reaches its order point result in increased costs and *remnant stock* (inventory in excess of an order point when an order is placed), as illustrated in Figure 8-2.

Since an order is placed prior to the expiration of the normal order interval (T) more orders are placed each year. The stock on hand when the replenishment order arrives equals the remnant stock if expected lead time demand occurs. The increase in cost per year can only be estimated since both the value of the remnant stock and the decrease in the interval length vary. Estimated increased annual carrying costs equal the estimated average remnant stock times the carrying cost rate. The estimated increased preparation costs equal the cost of a preparation times the estimated increased number of preparations per year. The estimated average remnant stock equals the estimated average inventory on hand when an order is placed minus aggregate demand during lead time, the aggregate order point. The calculation of these estimated costs can be illustrated by using the data in Table 8-6 as the average case in the example given next.

Records of the past two years reveal that:

1. The quantity on hand data in Table 8-5 represent the average position of inventory on hand when an order is placed.
2. Approximately one additional order is placed each year.

Estimated average remnant stock = $3,712 − $3,528 = $184.

Increased carrying costs = 0.3 × $184 = $55.20.

Increased ordering costs = 1 × $120 = $120.

Total increase in costs = $55.20 + $120 = $175.20.

The estimated percentage increase in costs

$$= \frac{\text{Estimated Total Annual Increase in Costs}}{\text{Minimum Total Annual Costs} \times 100}$$

$$= \frac{\$175.20}{\left(\dfrac{0.3 \times \$8,400}{2} + \$120 \times 10.5\right) \times 100}$$

$$= \frac{\$175.20}{\$2,520 \times 100}$$

$$= 6.9 \text{ percent}$$

This calculation provides a rough estimate of the added costs of the increased customer service protection provided by ordering equal runout quantities as soon as one item reaches its order point rather than waiting until the aggregate order point is reached. A method for minimizing the costs of remnants is presented in Appendix 8B.

ORDER RELEASE

A time-phased order point system, a traditional (statistical) order point system, or a periodic review system can be used to trigger the release of joint orders. An MRP system with time-phased order release is the best system for managing dependent demand items. A periodic review system or a continuous review system incorporating either time-phased ordering logic or a traditional order point approach is appropriate for making order release decisions concerning independent demand items. Situational characteristics influencing the selection of individual item inventory management systems were examined in Chapter 7; the same criteria apply to the release of joint orders. General explicit decision rules have not been developed for releasing joint orders to attain an optimum balance between inventory cost and customer service objectives, but feasible approaches do exist for making rational joint order release decisions in specific situations. An examination of these approaches follows a discussion of the role of safety stock in joint ordering decisions.

Safety Stock and Joint Orders

Safety stock is used to achieve customer service objectives in the management of individual items with probabilistic demand or supply. Joint ordering, in general, reduces safety stock requirements as an order typically is placed before all items, except one, reach their individual order points. Providing safety stocks for all items in a group can result in excessive carrying costs. Each time an order is received, both remnant stock and safety stock likely will exist for all items, except the item that triggered the order. Conversely, the costs of stockouts can be expensive. This dilemma can be resolved by applying the

ABC principle, i.e., control the vital few. Application of the ABC principle in this case requires that safety stock be provided only for those items that meet criteria such as the following:

1. A stockout is expensive.
2. Carrying costs are relatively low.
3. Surges in demand have a relatively high probability.

Because carrying costs for C items are low and because stocking out of a single C item usually causes an order to be placed when A items are plentiful (stockouts are expensive), safety stock should be carried for all C items. By similar logic, most B items should have safety stock.

Continuous Review (Order Point) System

In a basic continuous review (s, Q) system, a fixed order quantity (Q) is ordered whenever the stock on hand reaches the order point (s). In a variation of this system the quantity ordered equals the difference between an order-up-to-level (S) and the stock on hand (s). This is known as the order point, order-up-to-level (s, S) system. If the stock on hand of an item managed by an s, S system is less than the order point, the quantity ordered is greater than it would be under an s, Q system.

The S, c, s System

Silver (1974) has suggested that an S, c, s system be used for managing coordinated items in a continuous review, coordinated replenishment system. An S, c, s system incorporates an order-up-to-level (S), a can-order level (c), and a must-order level (s) for each item. A joint order is placed whenever the inventory of any item descends to s. Orders are placed for each item whose stock is at or below its c or s to raise its inventory level to S. The rationale is that when a joint order is triggered by one item reaching its order point, individual decisions to order (or not to order) the other items can reduce total inventory-related costs. An item should be included in the joint order only if its inventory is below a predetermined level.

The S, c, s system reduces ordering costs by eliminating the minor ordering costs associated with items not ordered, and it reduces inventory carrying costs by reducing remnant stocks. However, total inventory costs may increase if the average interval between joint orders decreases substantially due to items that were not ordered triggering a new order in less than the normal interval.

Implementation of an S, c, s system requires extensive prior study. For example, an item that has not reached its can-order level may be experiencing a postponed demand. In such a case demand in the immediate future would be greater than normal and an S, c, s system would be very inappropriate. An

S,c,s system is appropriate when minor setup costs are substantial, carrying costs are high, and recent demand is a good predictor of the short-term future demand.

Periodic Review Systems

In a basic periodic review system, each item is ordered in a quantity that, when added to the stock on hand, will equal the safety stock plus the demand during the lead time and the demand during the replenishment period (see Chapter 7). Using a periodic review system to manage joint replenishment has inherent problems. A periodic review system requires a larger safety stock than a continuous review system, given the same variations in demand (forecast error), because safety stock must cover variations in demand during the replenishment period as well as during the lead time. Accumulation of safety stock across a large number of items ordered jointly can be substantial. IBM's Wholesale IMPACT System includes a service point method of determining whether a joint order should be placed or postponed for a period.[1] The decision is based on a comparison of the expected shortage (if no order is placed) with the allowed average shortage.

Time-Phased Order Point (TPOP) System

Managing a group of items by a TPOP system can provide a straightforward estimate of the benefits and costs of omitting any item from a joint order. A prerequisite of a TPOP system is known requirements, i.e., a forecast of demand for each item. In deciding whether to include any item in the joint order, one of three situations can exist, as described below and illustrated in Table 8-7.

1. Requirement greater than the quantity in stock does not occur until after the next joint order will be triggered. Thus, a shortened order interval is not anticipated.
2. Requirement greater than the quantity in stock does occur before the normal order interval, but after an order is triggered by a requirement for another item in the group.
3. Requirement greater than the quantity in stock does occur before the normal order interval and before an order is triggered by a requirement for any other item in the group.

The savings that are gained by omitting an item when ordering a group are (1) s_i—the minor ordering costs associated with the item and (2) $Q_i K t$—the cost of carrying the item order quantity until the next order is placed. Omitting

---

1. See IBM, *Wholesale IMPACT—Advanced Principles and Implementation Reference Manual E20-0174-1* (White Plains, NY, 1971) for the development and further discussion.

an item results in added costs only if the next joint order is placed sooner as a result (the order interval is reduced). This situation is analyzed by determining the least cost option available. Analysis of the data in Table 8-7 illustrates this approach.

Table 8-7
Time-Phased Order Point System
Normal Interval Between Orders, $T = 5$ Weeks
(Group Consists of Items A, B and C)

Ordering Costs	Item Costs	Minimum Lot Sizes
$S = \$80$	A = $ 70	A—50 units
$S_A = 30$	B = 100	B—50 units
$S_B = 20$	C = 60	C—50 units
$S_C = 20$	$k = 0.3$	

| | | | Planned Order Releases | | | | | | |
| | | | | | | Period | | | |
	Items	Past Due	1	2	3	4	5	6	7
Case 1	A	0	65	0	0	0	0	0	0
	B	0	50	0	0	0	0	50	0
	C	0	0	0	0	0	0	0	60
Case 2	A	0	65	0	0	0	0	50	0
	B	0	50	0	50	0	0	0	0
	C	0	0	0	0	60	0	0	0
Case 3	A	0	65	0	0	0	0	50	0
	B	0	50	0	0	0	0	50	0
	C	0	0	0	0	50	0	0	0

Returning to the three situations just mentioned, the following analyses can be made.

Case 1—An order for the item that may be omitted is not planned until after the normal order interval has passed. Case 1 in Table 8-7 illustrates this situation. An order is not planned for Item C for seven weeks; the normal order interval is five weeks. Omitting Item C from the joint order in Period 1 will result in no additional costs, only savings. This typifies this situation; Item C should be omitted from the order.

Case 2—An order for the item that may be omitted is not planned until after an order is triggered for another item in the group. This analysis is similar to Case 1. There are no added costs; omit Item C from the first order. This situation is illustrated in Case 2 of Table 8-7. One should also question the wisdom of ordering 65 units of A in Case 2. An order quantity large enough to cover demand for two weeks is an alternative that might be preferable.

Case 3—An order for the item is planned before the normal order interval and before requirements trigger an order for another item. Table 8-7's Case 3 illustrates this situation. The three available options for this situation and their relevant costs are as follows.

1. Order Items A, B, and C in Period 1 as a group and Items A and B in Period 6.

    Setup Costs

    Period 1—$150.00
    Period 6— 130.00
              $280.00

    Carrying Costs
    $50 \times \$60 \times 0.3 \times 3 \div 50 = \$\ 54.00$
    Total = $334.00

2. Order Items A and B in Period 1 and in Period 6, and order Item C in Period 4.

    Setup Costs

    Period 1—$130.00
    Period 4— 100.00
    Period 6— 130.00
              $360.00

    Carrying Costs   None
    Total = $360.00

3. Order Items A and B in Period 1 and order Items A, B, and C in Period 4.

    Setup Costs

    Period 1—$130.00
    Period 4— 150.00
              $280.00

    Carrying Costs
    $50 \times \$70 \times 0.3 \times 2 \div 50 = \$\ 42.00$
    $50 \times \$100 \times 0.3 \times 2 \div 50 =\ \ \ 60.00$
                                      $102.00
    Total = $382.00

Option 1 is the minimum cost decision in the illustration contained in Table 8-7. However, not only are the cost differences small but other factors such as capacity must be considered before a final decision is made. These other factors are discussed in the remainder of this chapter and in Chapters 13 and 14.

Order Release, Joint Production Lots

Demand patterns, production capacity, and production sequence requirements affect decision rules governing order release for joint production lots. A given decision can involve any combination of the demand, production sequence, and capacity factor variations listed in Table 8-8.

Table 8-8
Factors Affecting Joint Production Lot
Order Release Decision Rules

I. Demand	II. Capacity	III. Production Sequence
a. Dependent	a. Dedicated	a. Optional
b. Independent	b. Nondedicated	b. Prescribed

Demand.   Order releases for dependent demand items are predicated on the material requirements plan (MRP) flowing from the master production schedule (MPS). The MRP seldom calls for the individual item lot quantities suggested by the economic lot size model. Decisions to increase production lot quantities above the MRP quantities depend on available capacity and a comparison of the expected increased carrying costs with expected savings in setup costs as previously described. See Chapter 10 for a further discussion of MRP (discrete requirements) lot sizes.

Order releases for production of independent demand items should be planned on the basis of order releases established in the manner suggested for joint purchased orders. Final release also depends on production sequence and capacity requirements.

Capacity.   Some multi-item production groups are manufactured by *dedicated facilities*, equipment used exclusively for the production of one group. Other groups are manufactured on equipment used in the manufacture of many different items and groups. In the latter case, the nature of demand, process sequence, and available capacity determine the release of orders. Order release and scheduling problems under these conditions are examined in Chapters 13 and 14.

Dedicated Equipment.   Decisions concerning groups manufactured on dedicated equipment include the following:

1. Determining the minimum group lot size and the minimum interval between lots to provide the capacity required
2. Establishing order release points for individual items
3. Determining when production of all items should be interrupted

Minimum Group Lot Size.   Effective capacity, frequently expressed in standard hours, is a function of the standard hours available, production efficiency, and equipment utilization. It usually is obtained by multiplying the actual hours available by a factor that reflects production efficiency and utilization experience. The total time required for setup and processing must not be greater than effective capacity if requirements are to be produced within available capacity. The relationship of the maximum number of cycles per year and the effective available annual capacity is:

$$N(T_s + \Sigma t_{si}) + \Sigma(D_i \div p_i) \leq C$$

$$N \leq \frac{C - \Sigma(D_i \div p_i)}{T_s + \Sigma t_{si}}$$

and, since $T = \dfrac{1}{N}$, then

$$T \geq \frac{T_s + \Sigma t_{si}}{C - \Sigma(D_i \div p_i)}$$

where N = maximum number of cycles per period
T_s = major setup time
t_{si} = minor setup time for Item i
D_i = period demand for Item i
p_i = hourly production rate for Item i
C = period effective capacity in hours
T = interval between cycles

If more than N cycles are run per year, there will be insufficient time for the required setups and production runs. Calculation of the upper limit on the number of cycles per year, for example, is illustrated using the data in Table 8-9.

Table 8-9
Data, Capacity Requirements, Equipment Dedicated
to a Multi-Item Production Group (T_s = 9 hours)

Item	Time per Minor Setup (hours) (t_{si})	Annual Demand (D_i)	Hourly Production Rate (p_i)	$D_i \div p_i$	Annual Production Rate* (P_i)	$D_i \div P_i$
1	0.2	10,000	20	500	36,000	0.28
2	0.3	9,000	20	450	36,000	0.25
3	0.2	12,000	48	250	86,400	0.14
4	0.3	6,000	12	500	21,600	0.28

Based on 1,800 hours of effective capacity

Effective annual capacity equals the hours available each year multiplied by the decimal fraction reflecting operating efficiency and utilization. In this case there are 50 weeks, five days per week, one eight-hour shift per day and an effective capacity multiplier of 0.9. This is formulated in the following:

$$C = 50 \times 5 \times 8 \times 0.9 = 1,888 \text{ hours per year}$$

$$N \le \frac{1,800 - (500 + 450 + 250 + 500)}{9 + 1}$$

$$N \le 10$$

$$T \ge 0.1 \text{ years or 5 weeks}$$

Quantity Discounts

Some suppliers offer price discounts based on the total dollar value of an order. The number of different items on the order is not restricted. For example, a 3 percent discount may be given on all orders of more than $10,000. When the $Q_\$^*$ is less than the order value required to obtain the discount, the order quantity should be increased to the discount quantity if the net benefits are positive. Increasing the aggregate lot size to earn a quantity discount will produce the following three results: (1) decrease the costs of the material, (2) increase the annual carrying costs due to the increase in average inventory, and (3) decrease the annual preparation costs due to the fewer number of orders per year.

A decision in a given situation can be made by comparing the savings to the added costs. As an example, let's use the data in Table 8-1 and grant a 2 percent discount on all orders equal to or greater than $15,000. Consequences would be as follows.

$$Q_\$^* = \$8,400$$
$$k = 0.3$$
$$S = \$120$$
$$A = \Sigma a_i = \$88,200$$
$$d = \text{discount} = 2 \text{ percent if } Q_\$^* \ge \$15,000$$

A good rule is to increase the order quantity to the discount quantity if the net savings are positive, if neither constraints nor practical considerations override the decision, and if the rate of return on the increased investment is satisfactory. We can calculate this in the following manner:

$$\text{Net Savings} = \text{Purchase Price Discount} + \text{Preparation Cost}$$
$$\text{Savings} - \text{Increased Carrying Cost}$$

$$\text{Purchase Price Discount} = \text{Annual Requirements} \times \text{Discount Percentage}$$
$$= \$88,200 \times 0.02$$
$$= \$1,764$$

Preparation Cost Savings = Cost per Preparation × Decrease in Number of Preparations per Year

$$= \$120\left(\frac{\$88,200}{\$8,400} - \frac{\$88,200}{\$15,000}\right)$$

$$= \$554.40$$

Increased Carrying Cost = Carrying Cost Rate × Increased Average Inventory

$$= \frac{0.3(\$15,000 - \$8,400)}{2}$$

$$= \$990$$

Net Savings = \$1,764 + \$554.40 - \$990

$$= \$1,328.40$$

If financial and storage constraints are not violated, an aggregate lot size of \$15,000 should be purchased. Next, the individual item order quantities are calculated in the usual manner:

$$Q_{\$_i}^* = \left(\frac{a_i}{A}\right)Q_{\$}^* \quad \text{and} \quad Q_i^* = \frac{Q_{\$_i}^*}{C_i}$$

Therefore,

$$Q_{\$_1}^* = 0.0567 \times \$15,000 = \$850.50$$
$$Q_{\$_2}^* = 0.1701 \times \$15,000 = \$2,551.50$$
$$Q_{\$_3}^* = 0.0317 \times \$15,000 = \$475.50$$
$$Q_{\$_4}^* = 0.4354 \times \$15,000 = \$6,531.00$$
$$Q_{\$_5}^* = 0.3061 \times \$15,000 = \$4,591.50$$
$$Q_1^* = \$850.50 \div \$5.00 = 170.1$$
$$Q_2^* = \$2,551.50 \div \$6.00 = 425.25$$
$$Q_3^* = \$475.50 \div \$3.50 = 135.86$$
$$Q_4^* = \$6,531.00 \div \$12.00 = 544.25$$
$$Q_5^* = \$4,591.50 \div \$15.00 = 306.10$$

Practical considerations such as container size and round numbers influence the actual order quantity. Order quantities for Items 1 through 5 in a specific situation might be 170, 425, 135, 550, and 300, respectively.

Capital and storage constraints, shelf life, possible engineering changes, and the return on other possible investments must be considered prior to a final decision.

SUMMARY

Items obtained from the same supplier may be purchased as a group with reduced total inventory costs due to the savings in ordering costs being greater than any increases in carrying costs for individual items. Coordinating the production of items that share a major setup can achieve similar savings. The optimum (minimum total cost) group lot size can be calculated for purchased items and production parts with known and steady independent demand. Derivation of the optimum lot size model is similar to derivation of the individual item optimum lot size model. Purchase or production of those items with relatively low demand may take place less than every cycle in some cases. Ordering up to the equal runout quantity is one approach for dealing with uncertainties in demand.

Order releases for purchased parts may be based on either a time-phased order point system, a periodic review system, or a statistical order point system. The nature of order releases for joint production lots depends on the type of demand, the group production sequence requirements, and capacity considerations. Explicit decision rules for calculating safety stocks to achieve specified customer service levels have not been developed yet. When producing a group on dedicated equipment, conditions can arise that warrant producing larger than the optimum lot size of an item in order to maintain a balanced inventory.

Decisions concerning purchasing larger than the straightforward EOQ to obtain quantity discounts are made on the basis of minimum total costs and the rate of return on the increased investment.

Economies are available through astute management of joint orders. However, establishing order release decision rules in situations with relatively large item demand variations can require lengthy analysis of data regarding a specific situation.

EXERCISES

1. A medium size manufacturer of specialized (low volume) construction equipment purchases four sizes of hydraulic hoses. The demand for each is relatively steady throughout the year. Hosing is purchased in a continuous segment and cut to size in the plant where the couplings are added. The company usually buys all four types on one purchase order to save the costs of four separate purchase orders. Given the following information:

    Plant operates 250 days a year. Annual carrying cost rate of 0.30 has been established by management. The major cost of this type purchase order is estimated as $75.

Usage and Cost Data			
Item	Annual Usage	Cost per Foot	Additional Ordering Cost
Hose H25	2,000 ft	$0.30	$4
Hose H29	10,000 ft	0.50	4
Hose H48	6,000 ft	0.20	8
Hose H73	2,000 ft	0.60	4

a. Determine the aggregate order quantity and the order quantity of each type (in dollars and units).
b. If the company presently orders hoses once a month, what would you estimate the total annual savings to be if the new aggregate order quantity was used?
c. Describe the nature of the savings found in Part b.

2. The Demart Locker and Cabinet Company purchases five types of hardware from the same firm. These items are used in many products at a rather steady rate throughout the year. The inventory manager has decided to combine the purchase of these items in a joint order. The following information is available.

Item	No.	Annual Requirements (units)	Unit Cost	Minor Order Costs
Hook	H95	12,000	$0.75	$5
Handle	H122	8,000	3.00	5
Handle	H197	6,000	2.25	5
Lock	L79	15,000	3.00	8
Hinge	H478	35,000	1.10	5

Annual carrying cost rate = 0.25
Major cost of a purchase order = $40

a. What is the joint economic order quantity?
b. What is the quantity of each item in that order?

3. The lathe department of a company that fabricates material handling equipment produces four pins. Each pin is used at a relatively steady rate throughout the year. The pins are pan stock items and are required in many standard products as well as in special design material handling systems. Manufacturing runs the pins as a joint lot to gain the benefits of a single major setup for all four items. Given the following information make the ensuing determinations:

The company operates 250 days a year.
An annual carrying cost rate of 0.30 is used.
The major costs of ordering and setup are $80.

Item	Annual Usage	Unit Cost	Daily Production Rate (units)	Minor Setup Costs
P121	$6,000	$3	48	$3
P127	5,000	5	32	3
P132	3,600	9	24	5
P143	2,400	6	40	4

   a. What should the aggregate lot size be?
   b. What should the economic quantity of each be?

4. An order is being placed for the hydraulic hoses described in Exercise 1. How many feet of each item should be ordered if the inventory on hand for each item is as follows?

Item	Present Inventory
Hose H25	$ 12.00
Hose H29	200.00
Hose H48	120.00
Hose H73	38.40

5. A decision has been made to run the pins described in Exercise 3. How many of each pin should be run if the inventory on hand is as follows?

Item	Present Inventory
P121	30
P127	300
P132	180
P143	54

6. Using Brown's method to determine whether each item should be ordered each interval:
   a. Use the data in Exercise 1 and determine T^*.
   b. Repeat this process with the data in Exercise 2.

7. Determine whether each item should be ordered each interval applying Silver's approach to the data in Exercise 3.

The following data applies to Exercises 8 through 10.

Bob's Hardware buys the following products from a leading drill manufacturer:

Item	Quantity Sold per Month	Purchase Price
3/8″ Reversible Drill	100	$19.95
Mixed Drill Bit Sets	200	1.50
Individual Drill Bit A	100	0.25
Individual Drill Bit B	200	0.29
Individual Drill Bit C	300	0.22

Bob estimates that the cost of placing an order is $100. The cost of adding an additional item to an existing order is $10. Bob uses a 35 percent carrying cost rate for items held in inventory.

8. Using the economic order quantity approach, determine the optimal order quantity for each item, treating each as though it is the only item to be ordered. Using the methods shown in this chapter, determine the optimal order frequency if drill bits are ordered whenever drills are ordered. Estimate the savings achieved by using a joint order strategy.

9. The drill manufacturer offers a 10 percent discount for orders exceeding $15,000. Should Bob take advantage of this discount?

10. Assume that today is January 2. Bob presently has 75 drills in stock, 175 drill bit sets, and 200 each of drill bits A, B, and C. Assume further that demand for drills and drill bits is seasonal, with the following seasonal indices:

Month	Index
January	0.50
February	0.60
March	0.80
April	1.10
May	1.20
June	0.90
July	0.80
August	0.80
September	1.20
October	1.10
November	1.30
December	1.70

Set up a time-phased order point template for each of the five items using an electronic spreadsheet. Assume that all five will be ordered whenever an order is placed. Start with an order placed in each of the twelve months. Determine by trial and error whether this policy can be improved. Is there a more systematic way to make this determination?

SELECTED READINGS

Brown, Robert G. *Decision Rules for Inventory Management*. New York: Holt, Rinehart & Winston, 1967.

Brown, Robert G. *Management Decisions for Production Operations*. Hinsdale, IL: The Dryden Press, 1971.

Brown, Robert G. *Materials Management Systems*. New York: John Wiley & Sons, Inc., 1977.

Fogarty, Donald W. "Material Flow in Manufacturing Cell and Material Requirements Planning Environment: Problems and a Solution." *Material Flow* 4 (1987): 139-146

Fogarty, Donald W., and Robert L. Barringer. "Joint Order Releases Under Dependent Demand." *Production and Inventory Management* (First Quarter 1987): 55-61.

IBM. *Wholesale IMPACT-Advanced Principles and Implementation Reference Manual E20-0174-1*. White Plains, NY, 1971.

Johnson, Lynwood, and Douglas C. Montgomery. *Operations Research in Production Planning, Scheduling and Inventory Control*. New York: John Wiley & Sons, Inc., 1974.

Magee, John R., and David M. Boodman. *Production Planning and Inventory Control*. 2d ed. New York: McGraw-Hill Book Co., 1967.

Plossl, George W. *Production and Inventory Control: Principles and Techniques*. 2d ed. Englewood Cliffs, NJ: Prentice-Hall, Inc., 1985.

Silver, Edward A. "A Control System for Coordinated Inventory Replenishment." *International Journal of Production Research* 12, no. 6 (1974): 647-671.

Silver, Edward A. "Modifying the Economic Order Quantity (EOQ) to Handle Coordinated Replenishment of Two or More Items." *Production and Inventory Management* 16, no. 3 (1975): 26-38.

Silver, Edward A., and Peter Kelle. "More on Joint Order Releases Under Dependent Demand." *Production and Inventory Management* (First Quarter 1988).

Silver, Edward A., and Rein Peterson. *Decision Systems for Inventory Management and Production Planning*. 2d ed. New York: John Wiley & Sons, Inc., 1985.

APPENDIX 8A
CALCULATING PREPARATION COSTS
AND CARRYING COSTS FOR JOINT
ORDER QUANTITY

Total preparation costs equal the number of preparations in the period times the cost of preparation. The latter equals the major cost of processing an order plus the sum of the costs associated with the addition of each item to the order. The number of orders per period equals the aggregate of all item requirements divided by the aggregate lot size. Both aggregate values must be calculated in monetary units for dimensional consistency as shown in the following.

$$\text{Total Preparation Costs} = \frac{(S + \Sigma s_i)A}{\Sigma Q_{\$_i}}$$

where S = preparation costs independent of the number of items (sometimes called major setup costs or header costs)

s_i = incremental preparation costs incurred by the inclusion of a specific item. (These are the clerical, receiving, and expediting costs associated with Item i; sometimes called minor setup costs.)

a_i = period requirement for Item i in dollars

$A = \Sigma a_i$ = aggregate requirement for the period in dollars

$Q_\$ = \Sigma Q_{\$_i}$ = aggregate lot size in dollars

$Q_\$^*$ = optimal aggregate lot size in dollars

Total carrying costs are equal to the carrying cost rate per year (k) times the average inventory value, which in the case of instantaneous receipt and deterministic demand is equal to one-half the aggregate lot size.

$$\text{Total Carrying Costs} = \frac{k}{2}(\Sigma Q_{\$_i})$$

Therefore,

$$\text{Total Costs } (TC) = \frac{(S + \Sigma s_i)A}{\Sigma Q_{\$_i}} + \frac{k}{2}(\Sigma Q_{\$_i})$$

Solving for the minimum cost lot size by setting the first derivative of TC with respect to $Q_\$$ equal to zero and solving for $Q_\$^*$ yields the following.

$$TC'(Q_\$) = \frac{-(S + \Sigma s_i)A}{(\Sigma Q_\$^*)^2} + \frac{k}{2} = 0$$

$$(\Sigma Q_\$^*)^2 = \frac{2(S + \Sigma s_i)A}{k}$$

$$Q_\$^* = \Sigma Q_{\$_i}^* = \left[\frac{2(S + \Sigma s_i)A}{k}\right]^{1/2}$$

Applying the second derivative test produces the following.

$$TC''(Q^*) = \frac{2(S + \Sigma s_i)A}{(Q_\$^*)^{-3}}$$

Since S, Σs_i, A, and $Q_\$^*$ are positive under all conditions, $TC''(Q^*)$ is positive. Thus, TC is a minimum at $Q_\$^*$.

The minimum cost lot size of each item is determined by multiplying the minimum cost aggregate lot size by the ratio of the item's period requirements to aggregate period requirements. Thus,

$$Q_{\$_i}^* = \left(\frac{a_i}{A}\right) Q_{\$}^*$$

APPENDIX 8B
MINIMIZING THE COST OF REMNANTS

As is noted in Chapter 8, when several items are ordered simultaneously from one vendor, it is sometimes helpful to design the system so that one should run out of A items while B and C items are still relatively plentiful. This tactic is intended to minimize the total value of the inventory by lowering the average value of remnants existing when the replenishment order arrives. Carrying additional stock of B and C items permits the order to almost always be triggered by an A item, which also means that the inventory of the A items gets quite low. Since A items typically account for 80 percent of the total volume and a large portion of the total inventory, increasing the remnants of B and C items to lower the stock of A items can be a beneficial trade-off.

In the example shown in Tables 8B-1 to 8B-4, there are 10 items ordered from one vendor, consisting of 1 A item, 3 B items, and 6 C items. All items have an average demand of 100 units per week. All items are subject to fluctuations in demand. Specifically, weekly demand is uniformly distributed on the range (0, 200). The A item, Item 1, costs $80. The B items, Items 2, 3, and 4, cost $5, $5, and $4, respectively. The C items, Items 5 through 10, each cost $1. The percentage of total sales by category is 80 percent A, 14 percent B, and 6 percent C, while the distribution of part numbers by category is 10 percent A, 30 percent B, and 60 percent C. Thus, the example is quite ordinary from an ABC classification viewpoint.

Three different ordering policies are used. All three are hybrid (s, S) policies with weekly review of the inventory position, a reorder point (s) for all items set to 190 units, and an order-up-to point (S) that differs by category of item. The order-up-to point is of the form y^x. For all three order policies, x is 0 for the A items, 1 for the B items, and 2 for the C items. For Table 8B-1, y is 1, for Table 8B-2, y is 1.1, for Table 8B-3, y is 1.2. The result of this formula is that for Table 8B-1 the order-up-to point is 1,000 units for all 10 items. For Table 8B-2, the order-up-to point is 1,000 for A items, 1,100 for B items, and 1,210 for C items. For Table 8B-3, the order-up-to point is 1,000 for A items, 1,200 for B items, and 1,440 for C items. The formula was used so that a two-way data table could be created in Lotus 1-2-3 to evaluate the results of a simulation of the three policies.

Table 8B-1
A Portion of the Monte Carlo Spreadsheet, Equal Order-Up-To Points

Item	Unit Price	Volume	Dollar Volume	Begin	Week	1	2	3	4	5	6	7	8	9	10	11	12	13
1	80	100	8000	1000	Demand	20	106	43	11	33	158	113	72	67	42	27	132	136
					Balance	980	874	831	820	787	629	887	815	748	706	679	547	411
					Value	78400	69920	66480	65600	62960	50320	70960	65200	59840	56480	54320	43760	32880
2	5	100	500	1000	Demand	167	40	68	179	197	76	132	88	66	35	192	41	5
					Balance	833	793	725	546	349	273	868	780	714	679	487	446	440
					Value	4165	3965	3625	2730	1745	1365	4340	3900	3570	3395	2435	2230	2200
3	5	100	500	1000	Demand	123	20	187	127	189	119	71	59	28	113	166	72	154
					Balance	877	857	670	543	354	235	929	870	842	729	563	491	337
					Value	4385	4285	3350	2715	1770	1175	4645	4350	4210	3645	2815	2455	1685
4	4	100	400	1000	Demand	197	164	28	21	148	100	118	81	53	89	89	124	30
					Balance	803	639	611	590	442	342	882	801	748	659	570	446	416
					Value	3212	2556	2444	2360	1768	1368	3528	3204	2992	2636	2280	1784	1664
5	1	100	100	1000	Demand	51	183	133	189	165	96	88	157	77	138	179	74	23
					Balance	949	766	633	444	279	183	912	755	678	540	361	287	264
					Value	949	766	633	444	279	183	912	755	678	540	361	287	264
6	1	100	100	1000	Demand	138	94	198	183	30	51	111	91	132	144	83	191	148
					Balance	862	768	570	387	357	306	889	798	666	522	439	248	100
					Value	862	768	570	387	357	306	889	798	666	522	439	248	100
7	1	100	100	1000	Demand	3	63	141	75	181	117	61	96	145	12	183	167	49
					Balance	997	934	793	718	537	420	939	843	698	686	503	336	287
					Value	997	934	793	718	537	420	939	843	698	686	503	336	287
8	1	100	100	1000	Demand	132	141	96	65	126	53	32	189	75	126	53	120	123
					Balance	868	727	631	566	440	387	968	779	704	578	525	405	282
					Value	868	727	631	566	440	387	968	779	704	578	525	405	282
9	1	100	100	1000	Demand	91	28	44	139	17	179	131	13	1	108	109	58	32
					Balance	909	881	837	698	681	502	869	856	855	747	638	580	548
					Value	909	881	837	698	681	502	869	856	855	747	638	580	548
10	1	100	100	1000	Demand	145	136	149	133	33	55	176	123	53	125	169	145	119
					Balance	855	719	570	437	404	349	824	701	648	523	354	209	90
					Value	855	719	570	437	404	349	824	701	648	523	354	209	90
					Order:	0	0	0	0	0	1	0	0	0	0	0	0	1

Table 8B-2
A Portion of the Monte Carlo Spreadsheet, B Items 1.1 times A Items

Item	Price	Unit Volume	Dollar Volume	Begin	Week	1	2	3	4	5	6	7	8	9	10	11	12	13
1	80	100	8000	1000	Demand	168	49	200	156	196	64	61	45	73	88	138	163	157
					Balance	832	783	583	427	231	167	939	894	821	733	595	432	275
					Value	66560	62640	46640	34160	18480	13360	75120	71520	65680	58640	47600	34560	22000
2	5	100	500	1100	Demand	159	174	147	101	75	6	20	71	4	1	171	77	43
					Balance	941	767	620	519	444	438	1080	1009	1005	1004	833	756	713
					Value	4705	3835	3100	2595	2220	2190	5400	5045	5025	5020	4165	3780	3565
3	5	100	500	1100	Demand	188	193	43	105	153	190	99	86	121	104	96	188	140
					Balance	912	719	676	571	418	228	1001	915	794	690	594	406	266
					Value	4560	3595	3380	2855	2090	1140	5005	4575	3970	3450	2970	2030	1330
4	4	100	400	1100	Demand	177	48	13	121	64	174	157	151	19	93	158	35	157
					Balance	923	875	862	741	677	503	943	792	773	680	522	487	330
					Value	3692	3500	3448	2964	2708	2012	3772	3168	3092	2720	2088	1948	1320
5	1	100	100	1210	Demand	45	70	39	74	120	1	168	16	172	117	180	37	6
					Balance	1165	1095	1056	982	862	861	1042	1026	854	737	557	520	514
					Value	1165	1095	1056	982	862	861	1042	1026	854	737	557	520	514
6	1	100	100	1210	Demand	159	54	15	84	116	54	158	64	184	48	51	47	50
					Balance	1051	997	982	898	782	728	1052	988	804	756	705	658	608
					Value	1051	997	982	898	782	728	1052	988	804	756	705	658	608
7	1	100	100	1210	Demand	169	190	59	147	5	54	120	115	88	189	180	127	108
					Balance	1041	851	792	645	640	586	1090	975	887	698	518	391	283
					Value	1041	851	792	645	640	586	1090	975	887	698	518	391	283
8	1	100	100	1210	Demand	86	162	78	92	100	101	153	91	35	150	64	30	105
					Balance	1124	962	884	792	692	591	1057	966	931	781	717	687	582
					Value	1124	962	884	792	692	591	1057	966	931	781	717	687	582
9	1	100	100	1210	Demand	18	82	178	173	1	128	139	46	21	68	35	2	186
					Balance	1192	1110	932	759	758	630	1071	1025	1004	936	901	899	713
					Value	1192	1110	932	759	758	630	1071	1025	1004	936	901	899	713
10	1	100	100	1210	Demand	96	133	154	181	80	13	195	155	28	63	118	17	81
					Balance	1114	981	827	646	566	553	1015	860	832	769	651	634	553
					Value	1114	981	827	646	566	553	1015	860	832	769	651	634	553
					Order:	0	0	0	0	0	1	0	0	0	0	0	0	0

Table 8B-3
A Portion of the Monte Carlo Spreadsheet, B Items 1.2 times A Items

Item	Price	Unit Volume	Dollar Volume	Begin	Week	1	2	3	4	5	6	7	8	9	10	11	12	13
1	80	100	8000	1000	Demand	52	26	123	31	92	180	62	76	4	42	163	180	115
					Balance	948	922	799	768	676	496	434	924	920	878	715	535	420
					Value	75840	73760	63920	61440	54080	39680	34720	773920	73600	70240	57200	42800	33600
2	5	100	500	1200	Demand	157	141	132	125	94	130	110	28	17	159	78	155	184
					Balance	1043	902	770	645	551	421	311	1172	1155	996	918	763	579
					Value	5215	4510	3850	3225	2755	2105	1555	5860	5775	4980	4590	3815	2895
3	5	100	500	1200	Demand	121	80	154	95	189	108	133	61	172	48	46	75	57
					Balance	1079	999	845	750	561	453	320	1139	967	919	873	798	741
					Value	5395	4995	4225	3750	2805	2265	1600	5695	4835	4595	4365	3990	3705
4	4	100	400	1200	Demand	189	193	62	165	132	93	194	72	76	51	167	77	196
					Balance	1011	818	756	591	459	366	172	1128	1052	1001	834	757	561
					Value	4044	3272	3024	2364	1836	1464	688	4512	4208	4004	3336	3028	2244
5	1	100	100	1440	Demand	64	94	47	172	163	20	2	27	174	94	73	70	46
					Balance	1376	1282	1235	1063	900	880	878	1413	1239	1145	1072	1002	956
					Value	1376	1282	1235	1063	900	880	878	1413	1239	1145	1072	1002	956
6	1	100	100	1440	Demand	39	49	123	63	190	65	170	151	32	60	44	50	6
					Balance	1401	1352	1229	1166	976	911	741	1289	1257	1197	1153	1103	1097
					Value	1401	1352	1229	1166	976	911	741	1289	1257	1197	1153	1103	1097
7	1	100	100	1440	Demand	103	184	67	38	56	190	167	193	191	191	152	180	48
					Balance	1337	1153	1086	1048	992	802	635	1247	1056	865	713	533	485
					Value	1337	1153	1086	1048	992	802	635	1247	1056	865	713	533	485
8	1	100	100	1440	Demand	70	65	200	165	188	20	178	122	8	151	112	196	177
					Balance	1370	1305	1105	940	752	732	554	1318	1310	1159	1047	851	674
					Value	1370	1305	1105	940	752	732	554	1318	1310	1159	1047	851	674
9	1	100	100	1440	Demand	46	150	23	135	68	113	102	188	11	126	6	166	103
					Balance	1394	1244	1221	1086	1018	905	803	1252	1241	1115	1109	943	840
					Value	1394	1244	1221	1086	1018	905	803	1252	1241	1115	1109	943	840
10	1	100	100	1440	Demand	28	122	119	74	85	120	100	175	50	144	89	63	78
					Balance	1412	1290	1171	1097	1012	892	792	1265	1215	1071	982	919	841
					Value	1412	1290	1171	1097	1012	892	792	1265	1215	1071	982	919	841
					Order	0	0	0	0	0	0	1	0	0	0	0	0	0

Table 8B-4
Total Inventory Cost by Value of y

Trial	1	1.05	1.1	1.15	1.2
1	25862	26151	25313	24658	26100
2	26687	25796	25345	25254	24290
3	27733	26452	24591	24000	25776
4	25608	25003	25308	25448	26391
5	26247	24839	24602	24472	25253
6	26183	24939	24105	24326	24156
7	26595	25573	24817	25940	25228
8	26294	27037	23787	25573	25486
9	27403	25861	25070	24967	25896
Average	26512	25739	24771	24960	25397

The simulation proceeds as follows: (1) Each of the 10 parts is initialized with an inventory equal to the order-up-to point, i.e., all 10 parts begin at the "full" level. (2) For each of the 10 parts a random demand for the week is drawn. In Lotus 1-2-3, this is accomplished by placing the formula **@ROUND(@RAND*200,0)** in the proper cell. The Lotus formula says "Draw a random number between 0 and 1, multiply it by 200, and round to the nearer integer." (3) Subtract demand from the previous balance to obtain the current balance. (4) After the current balance has been obtained for all 10 parts, determine whether any of the 10 has a current balance less than 190 units. If so, place an order to arrive the next week. (5) Go to the next week and repeat the process beginning at Step 1.

Partial results of the three simulations are shown in Tables 8B-1 to 8B-3. Since demand averages 100 units per week and the order-up-to point is about 1,000, one might expect an order about every 10 weeks. This expectation is true only for Table 8B-3. Why?

As Table 8B-4 shows, for this example, cost is minimized when the order for B items is 1.1 times the size for A items. This example illustrates how Lotus 1-2-3 can be used to determine safety stock.

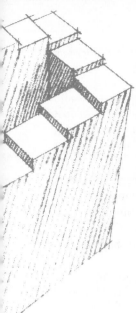

9

DISTRIBUTION AND INVENTORY CONTROL

This chapter discusses the management of distribution inventory and the integration of administrative and physical control systems with the inventory planning system.

Time and place have value. The objective of distribution inventory management is to have inventory in the right place at the right time at reasonable cost. In brief, the objective is to achieve a desired level of customer service at or below a specified cost.

Distribution decisions affect:

1. Facilities
2. Transportation
3. Inventory investment
4. Stockout frequency
5. Manufacturing
6. Communication and data processing

Distribution strategies and policies should be part of an integrated organization strategy encompassing all functional areas. Decisions made by marketing, engineering, finance, and manufacturing are linked. Decisions in one area also affect results in other areas.

The major distribution related questions include the following:

1. Should the company build to stock or build to order?
2. What part of the distribution function should the company perform, and what part should it subcontract?
3. What, if any, manufacturing or packaging should be performed at distribution facilities?
4. Where should distribution centers be located?
5. Should the company own and operate the transportation system?
6. Exactly what modes of transportation should be used?
7. How should distribution inventory be managed?

This chapter concentrates on the management of distribution inventory and addresses the other questions only briefly.

Although most products made completely to order are shipped directly from the factory to the purchaser, many require that assistance be provided to the purchaser during installation and initial operations. Thus, distribution takes the form of field service technical assistance in bringing the equipment to an operating condition.

When the volume of sales is low in a particular area, it frequently costs less to purchase distribution services than to purchase and maintain wholly owned facilities. Warehouses can be leased. Other firms with complementary product lines and existing distribution facilities may provide distribution services for a fee. The primary purpose of some organizations is to provide distribution services.

Distribution centers often can perform some fabrication jobs more economically than the factory. For example, manufacturers of special truck bodies and related equipment, such as derricks, aerial devices, and diggers, frequently ship the equipment and the truck body to a distributor for final assembly. The mounting of equipment and the installation of hydraulic, pneumatic, and electrical lines frequently can be performed less expensively by a distributor or fabricator. In addition, shipping costs usually are less as the truck chassis is shipped directly from the truck manufacturer to the distributor rather than through the truck body manufacturer. When final assembly, finishing, and packaging operations are performed at distribution centers, bulk shipments from the plant to the distribution point are less expensive than shipping assembled products. The distance from the plant to the distribution point is usually substantially greater than the distance from the distribution center to the customer, so considerable savings can result. A distribution center may purchase packaging materials locally and achieve additional transportation savings.

Selecting the lowest cost location for each of several warehouses in a distribution network is a complex problem. More than one plant may supply each warehouse, and shipments may be made between warehouses. It usually is best, however, to hold inventory at the central facility until the proper allocation to warehouses is clear. This avoids expensive movements between warehouses. Mathematical programming and simulation are useful for analyzing these problems. Arthur M. Geoffrion (1974, 1976) developed a trade-off curve of the sum of warehousing and transportation costs against the average level of response time to customer orders. Grouping the plant locations and customer demand by geographic area and product type, he used a computer model of this relationship to calculate the lowest cost network of warehouse locations.

DISTRIBUTION INVENTORY MANAGEMENT SYSTEMS

Distribution managers frequently encounter the classic transportation network problem described in Chapter 22, i.e., how to allocate resources from multiple sources to fill requirements at multiple locations. For example, consider the allocation of output from three plants to four distribution centers as illustrated in Figure 9-1.

The objective is to minimize the total transportation costs (TC) while providing the warehouses with their requirements (D_j) from available sources (S_i). The general model for this problem follows.[1]

$$\Sigma X_{ij} \leq S_i \qquad (1 \leq i \leq m)$$
$$\Sigma X_{ij} = D_j \qquad (1 \leq j \leq n)$$
$$X_{ij} \geq 0$$
$$\text{Minimum } TC = \Sigma\Sigma C_{ij} X_{ij}$$

where X_{ij} = quantity shipped from Plant i to Warehouse j
       m = number of plants
       n = number of warehouses
       C_{ij} = cost of shipping one unit from Plant i to Warehouse j

Figure 9-1
Allocation of Production to Warehouses
Multiple Plants (S_i) and Multiple Warehouses (D_j)

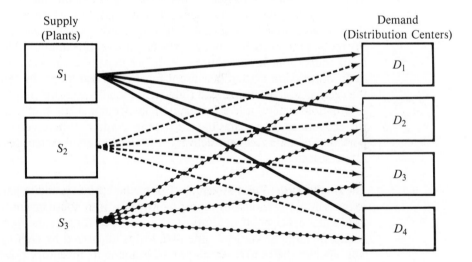

Distribution inventory management systems can be classified as pull or push systems. In a *pull* system, the warehouse determines its requirements and orders from the factory; it "pulls" inventory into the warehouse. In a *push* system, the forecast requirements for all warehouses are summed by period, and scheduled production and available inventory is allocated to the warehouses. The inventory is "pushed" into the warehouses. Actual systems frequently combine features of both push and pull systems.

---

1. Chapter 22 describes its solution.

Pull Systems

The archetype pull system orders without regard for the needs of other warehouses, the inventory available at the central warehouse, or the production schedule. The warehouse controls the ordering system. Traditional pull systems include the order point system, the periodic review system, the double order point system, and the sales replacement system.[2] The base stock system is primarily a pull system but may exhibit some push system characteristics.

The Order Point System.   In the order point system, the branch warehouse orders from the main warehouse whenever the quantity in stock at the branch reaches its order point. The order point is based on the normal demand during the average time required to obtain the order from the central warehouse (replenishment lead time) plus the safety stock. There is little interaction between the branch warehouse and the central warehouse (which receives the orders without any warning). This system can result in very erratic demand on the central warehouse. It requires a relatively large safety stock at the central warehouse in addition to the safety stocks at the branch warehouses.

The Periodic Review System.   With this system (sometimes called the fixed order interval system or the cycle review system), branch warehouse inventory status is determined at a regular interval, and the warehouse orders the quantity required to bring inventory to the target level (maximum). All other things being equal, branch warehouse safety stock must be greater in this system than in an order point system because it must cover variations in demand during the cycle as well as during lead time. Traditionally, this method has been used in situations where orders for many items from a single source are combined for economies of purchasing and transportation. Where economical transportation permits frequent delivery, the fixed interval system results in small safety stocks.

The Double Order Point System.   This method provides additional information to the central warehouse by reporting when the warehouse inventory equals the traditional order point quantity (OP_1 in Figure 9-2) plus the normal demand during manufacturing lead time (MLT), as illustrated by OP_2 in Figure 9-2. This enables the central warehouse to examine its inventory position relative to anticipated warehouse orders and take appropriate action. Theoretically, the central warehouse need not carry safety stock since it is forewarned of pending orders and adds inventory required to meet those orders. (Porter 1979)

The Sales Replacement System.   In this system each warehouse periodically (perhaps quarterly) establishes a stocking level for each item based on local

---

2. Chapter 6 contains a description of the principles and basic techniques of the order point, periodic review, and combination order point-periodic review systems.

Figure 9-2
Double Order Point System

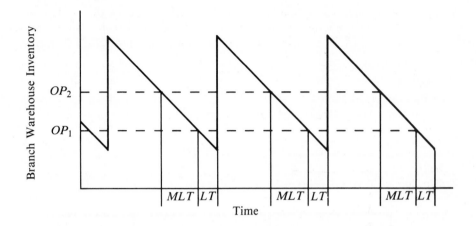

demand. Sales at each warehouse are reported to the central warehouse at periods shorter than the normal order interval. Shipments replacing the quantities sold are sent to each warehouse at the end of the replenishment periods. Periods usually are established to obtain economical shipments such as full truckloads. Increased warehouse reporting of sales to the central warehouse decreases the effect of erratic demand on the central warehouse. It enables manufacturing and purchasing to improve the coordination of planned orders and warehouse sales. (Plossl and Wight 1967, 403-420)

Advantages and Disadvantages of Pull Systems.   The advantages of a pull system are that it can operate autonomously and has low data processing and communication expenses. However, pull systems that usually employ large order quantities have inherent disadvantages. In a strictly pull system, orders are placed on the central warehouse without any knowledge or consideration of the needs of other warehouses. The ordering warehouse usually is unaware of shipping plans that may include the combination of shipments to two or more warehouses or the use of a different size truck or railroad car. Orders also are submitted without regard to available inventory, production schedules, or irregular occurrences, such as the addition of a new private label customer. As these deficiencies in pull systems have been recognized, communication between regional warehouses and the central supply has increased, and greater control of shipping quantities has been placed at the central supply. Thus, many actual systems with the basic characteristics of a pull system have taken on some characteristics of push systems. The base stock system is such a pull system.

The Base Stock System.   In this system each retail outlet (if company owned) and each warehouse periodically (perhaps quarterly) establishes a stocking level for each item. Sales are reported on a weekly or, preferably, a daily basis to all inventory-holding facilities rather than only when ordering. (See Figure 9-3.) Thus, the regional warehouse, the central warehouse, and the factory are aware of demand trends. This system usually is not subject to shock waves of un-expected demand. The primary advantage of this system is that it enables manufacturing, the central warehouse, and regional warehouses to plan and react on the basis of actual customer demand rather than on the basis of the

Figure 9-3
The Base Stock System
Flow of Sales Data, Orders, and Inventory

Demand Data
Inventory Flow
Order Flow

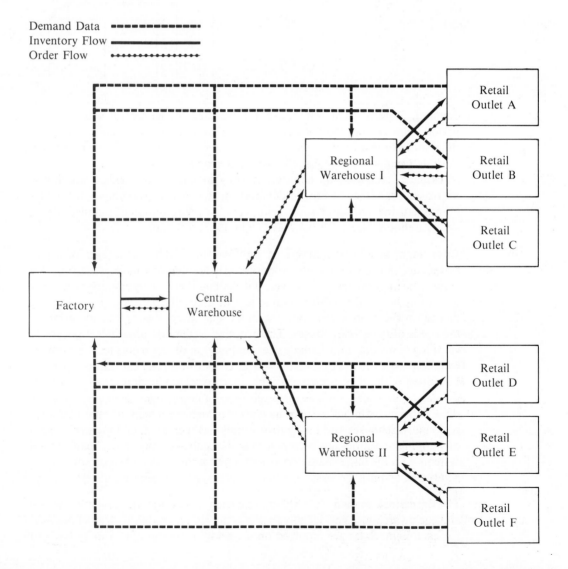

replenishment orders filled at secondary stock points, such as regional warehouses. The system reduces the unpredictability of demand on the warehouses and the factory. The total demand for an item across the entire system is usually more stable than demand measured by individual stocking points in the system.

The base stock level at each stocking location equals the normal demand during replenishment lead time and the interval between sales reports plus the safety stock. The supplying operation rather than the stocking location initiates replenishment orders on the basis of customer demand and available stock. This system eliminates many of the inherent deficiencies of the classic pull systems by incorporating features now identified with push systems. (Magee and Boodman 1967, 223)

Push Systems

Push systems consider total projected requirements (all warehouse and direct sales requirements), inventory available at the regional warehouses and the central warehouse, inventory in transit, and scheduled receipts from the source (plant or supplier) and determine the quantity available for each warehouse and direct factory sales. This allocation is controlled centrally on the basis of such criteria as equal days coverage, shipping schedules, and competitive factors. The central warehouse decides what to send, i.e., push, to the regional warehouses.

Distribution Requirements Planning (DRP).   DRP ties production and distribution planning together by determining aggregate time-phased net requirements at the same point in the material flow as the master production schedule (MPS). (See Figure 9-4.) When the items on the MPS are not the final product and require finishing, packaging, or fabrication into a final assembly, these final operations can be viewed as the first stage in distribution. James Heskett (1977) points out that automobile assembly plants are distribution centers equipped to receive orders, fabricate individually designed final assembly configurations from standard components, and deliver them in a reasonable time.

Figure 9-4 illustrates the application of DRP to a situation with three warehouses and sales direct from a central warehouse. Here the lead time, economic shipping quantity, forecast demand, projected orders, and projected on-hand balance each week for each warehouse are given. The projected warehouse orders and the direct sales constitute the demand on the central supply source (warehouse). Thus, Warehouse A's planned order of 500 in Week 1 combines with Warehouse B's planned order of 200 and with direct sales of 50 to yield the gross requirement of 750 at central supply. Subtracting these requirements from the on-hand balance (950 units) at the central warehouse results in a projected on hand of 200 units at the end of Week 1. The time-phased netting logic used in time-phased order point is continued. The projected on-hand in Week 4 would be negative unless an order were received, so a planned receipt is scheduled in Week 4. When the three-week lead time is applied, the order is planned for release in Week 1.

Figure 9-4
Distribution Requirements Planning (DRP)

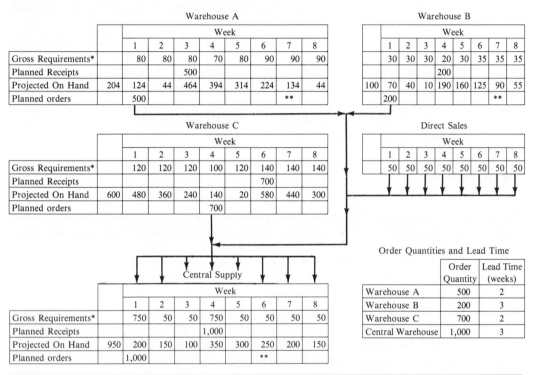

*Forecast
**As Weeks 9 and 10 are added, planned orders will be created in Week 7 for Warehouses A and B, and in Week 9 for Warehouse C. This, in turn, creates a planned order in Week 6 by the central warehouse.

This process is followed for all of the end items simultaneously. Therefore, consolidated shipments on a regular basis are possible. Central supply's planned orders are passed on to the manufacturing facility where they are absorbed into the master production schedule. Thus, distribution requirements are linked directly to the MPS.

Advantages of DRP Systems.   In a traditional order point system, an apparently excellent inventory position at the central warehouse can evaporate overnight if two or more warehouses reach their order point at the same time. (Martin 1980) To illustrate this, let's calculate the order point for each warehouse and change the on-hand quantities at Warehouses B, C, and Central as shown in Table 9-1.

The stock in the central warehouse is above its order point and all appears well, but Warehouses A and C have just dropped below their order points. They then place orders for 500 and 700 units, respectively, (another 50 units is required this week for direct sales). A total of 1,250 units are required, but only 1,150 are available. The central warehouse can make partial shipments

Table 9-1
Order Point Example

	Warehouse			
	A	B	C	Central
On Hand	204	150	350	1,150
Forecast per Week	80	30	120	280**
Order Point*	240	120	360	1,120
Order Quantity	500	200	700	1,800
Lead Time (weeks)	2	3	2	3

*Equals demand during lead time plus 1 week's safety stock.
**Includes 50 units sold each week direct from central warehouse.

to Warehouses A and C while holding stock for direct sales. (The central warehouse has not been informed of the forthcoming order from Warehouse B next week.) Next week, Warehouse B will be put on backorder. Unless the central warehouse can expedite the production of its order and/or the shipment to Warehouse B, B will have a stockout.

DRP avoids such problems by projecting branch warehouse requirements by period and generating planned orders on the central warehouse. The joint occurrence of two branch warehouse orders will be predicted and a factory order placed by the central warehouse to meet these requirements. DRP is especially beneficial when shipping cost factors make it advisable to ship in large quantities at relatively infrequent intervals.

Both the double order point system and the base stock system will provide early warnings to the central warehouse of future orders and reduce these difficulties somewhat. Nonetheless, they can result in orders not necessarily aligned with true needs and in relatively large safety stocks in regional warehouses. DRP is based on future time-phased requirements rather than on past sales and maintains most safety stock at the central warehouse.

In a strict pull system, branch warehouse orders are based on demand in one geographic area only. Filling such orders on a first-come-first-served basis leads to suboptimization, achieving one goal at the expense of other equally important goals. The branch warehouse lacks information concerning the needs of other warehouses, possible special shipping arrangements, central inventory, and manufacturing requirements. Also, in a pull system, branch warehouse managers usually are evaluated on the performance of their warehouse only. This frequently encourages decisions that hinder the accomplishment of organizational goals.

DRP provides the information needed for distribution and manufacturing management to effectively allocate inventory and productive capacity, to increase customer service, and to reduce inventory investment.

Allocation and Push Systems. The latest ship date is a common criterion for assigning priorities to warehouse shipments. The latest ship date is the day projected stock at a given warehouse will reach zero, minus the normal replenishment lead time of that warehouse. For example, if the stock of Item 927 at Warehouse H is projected to reach zero on Day 85 and the replenishment lead time is 8 days, the latest ship date is Day 77.

Up to this point, we have addressed only the distribution of individual items. However, it is common to combine many items in one shipment (a joint shipment). In a joint shipment the major fixed cost of shipping is spread across many items with only a minor fixed shipping cost for each additional item. This is analogous to major and minor setups in production and to combined purchase orders. The economies result from full carloads and reduced paperwork per item.[3] The quantity of an item sent to a given warehouse may be limited by truck or train car capacities and the requirements for other items. In such cases, a good practice is to ship equal runout quantities of each item.

We also have assumed that the central warehouse has sufficient stock of an item to meet the requirements of all branch warehouses. When this is not the case, a reasonable approach is to send an equal runout quantity to each warehouse. These quantities, sometimes called fair shares, will provide each warehouse with coverage for the same number of days of projected sales.

For example, suppose the central warehouse has 140 units of Product A when the latest ship date for that product arrives in the Minneapolis branch warehouse. Additional receipts are not expected at the central warehouse for at least a week. The inventory and the requirements of the four warehouses are as follows:

Warehouse	On Hand	Requirements/Week					Daily Usage
Minneapolis	10	25	25	25	25	25	5
Atlanta	20	30	30	30	30	30	6
Denver	18	20	20	20	20	20	4
Pittsburgh	10	15	15	15	15	15	3
Total	58	90	90	90	90	90	18

The system has a total of 198 units: 140 units at the central warehouse plus 58 units at the four regional warehouses. Since 18 units are used each day, there is an 11-day supply in the system. The objective is to ship each warehouse the quantity required to bring its stock to an 11-day supply. Thus,

$$TS = \frac{\Sigma I_i}{\Sigma d_i}$$

$$R_i = TS \times d_i$$

$$Q_i = R_i - I_i$$

---

3. Calculation of economical joint order quantities was treated in Chapter 8.

where TS = time supply in days
        I_i = inventory on hand in Warehouse i
        d_i = daily demand for Warehouse i
        Q_i = shipping quantity for Warehouse i
        R_i = requirements for Warehouse i during runout period

In the example, $TS = 198 \div 18 = 11$, and for the Minneapolis warehouse, $Q = 5 \times 11 - 10 = 45$. The quantities for the other warehouses are calculated in the same manner and are as follows:

Warehouse	Quantity Allocated
Atlanta	46
Denver	26
Pittsburgh	23
Total	95

Thus, the 140 units have been allocated to provide coverage for an equal time period in all warehouses. The central warehouse ships 45 units to the Minneapolis warehouse. If carriers are leaving shortly for the other warehouses, their respective fair shares may be sent to the other warehouses. The space available on a carrier is assigned on the basis of the relative priority of the items vying for shipment. This is similar to the technique Porter (1979) calls the Force-Balance method and to the allocation procedure described in American Software's *Inventory Management Systems* (Newberry 1978). Thomas Newberry and Carl Bhame (1981) have pointed out the need to tie distribution to demand forecasting using forced consensus on a bottom up, top down basis. A push allocation system works especially well when there are regular shipments to branch warehouses, say, every week or two, or when shipping costs do not require the shipment of relatively large quantities. Push allocation can combine the projection of branch warehouse and central supply requirements by period. Research and analyses of distribution systems have increased in the last few years and DRP and push allocation systems have resulted. We can look forward to further developments and refinements.

INVENTORY ACCOUNTING AND PHYSICAL CONTROL

Successful inventory management requires adequate administrative, physical, and financial controls. These controls are achieved by inventory records and record-keeping practices, auditing practices, inventory evaluation methods, and storekeeping and security.

Inventory status may be recorded on a perpetual or a periodic basis. Perpetual recording consists of recording each inventory transaction as or immediately after it occurs. Thus, a perpetual inventory record is an up-to-the-instant (real time) record of transactions and a statement of the current (1) quantity on order (and not received), (2) quantity in inventory, (3) quantity allocated (but still in inventory), and (4) quantity available for allocation. A perpetual recording system is required by the statistical order point inventory management and MRP systems.

In a strictly periodic inventory recording system, the inventory is counted or measured at a fixed interval, e.g., every two weeks, and the record of stock on hand is then updated. The quantity ordered, if any, is based on the quantity in stock and the expected usage.

Marvin's data processing system updates inventory records daily; other systems use shorter intervals, say, every four hours. This updating is effectively a perpetual system if multiple transactions on any item during one day are unlikely. If the occasionally required remedial action is inexpensive, the use of frequent updates is more cost effective than a truly perpetual system.

Distributed computer systems with data entry from widely separated locations (hundreds or thousands of miles) are becoming relatively inexpensive. Communication and software, however, are not inexpensive. These cost conditions lead to maintaining real time inventory data on micro or mini computers at distribution centers and reporting periodically, for example, daily. This has increased the feasibility of perpetual inventory recording and DRP.

The Inventory Record

An inventory record (see Figure 9-5) contains permanent information and variable information. Each transaction changes the variable information; the permanent information changes only occasionally. Permanent information includes data such as the following:

1. Part number
2. Part name
3. Description
4. Storage location
5. Order point (if applicable)
6. Lead time
7. Safety stock
8. Suppliers and their ratings
9. Cost
10. Yield
11. Group (if any) to which the item belongs
12. Assemblies in which the item is used (if any)
13. Shelf life
14. Batch control requirements
15. Substitutes (if any)
16. Item classification

Figure 9-5
Inventory Record Example

Part No. __B281__	Order Quantity __400__	Suppliers
Name __Bearing__	Order Point* _____	_____
Location __B-3__	Lead Time __1 week__	_____
Class __B__	Yield __1.00__	_____
Group __12__	Shelf Life __N/A__	_____
Substitutes __None__	BCR** __N/A__	_____
Used on _____	Cost __$3.75__	_____
Description __Bearing__	Safety Stock __50__	_____

	Ordered		Received		Issued		Balance	Allocated		Available
Date	Order No.	Quantity	Order No.	Quantity	Order No.	Quantity		Order No.	Quantity	Quantity
1/6							470			470
1/8								M-62	300	170
1/10								M-78	100	70
1/10	P891	400								470
1/15					M84	300	170	M-62	−300	
1/17			P891	400				570			

Based on time-phased requirements.
**Batch control requirements.*

This information is not truly permanent. It may change as the result of engineering changes, manufacturing process changes, or inventory management analysis.

Variable information usually includes the following:

1. Quantities ordered, the dates ordered and dates due, and the production or purchase order number
2. Quantities received, the dates, and the production or purchase order number
3. Balance on hand
4. Quantities issued, the date, and the production or shipping order number
5. Quantities allocated, the date, and the production or shipping order number
6. Quantities previously allocated that have been issued
7. Available balance
8. Batch identification

The variable information required depends on the situation. For example, batch identification is not required in all circumstances. Shelf life, customer demands, trade practices, or statutes require it for some products, especially in the food and pharmaceutical industries.

Sound inventory management requires accurate inventory records. Inaccurate records lead to the following:

1. Excess inventory of some items due to premature orders
2. Stockouts, assembly and component fabrication department downtime
3. Increased overtime, extra setups, and increased expediting
4. Inaccurate monthly or quarterly profit and loss statements resulting in unexpected profits or losses when the annual physical inventory count occurs
5. Overplanning to guarantee enough, leading to excess inventories and high obsolescence

Six ingredients essential to obtain accurate inventory records are:

1. An appropriate attitude on the part of management
2. Clearly designating specific persons as responsible for maintaining the accuracy of each recording activity
3. Providing tools to minimize errors
4. Providing instructions and training
5. Establishing accuracy goals and then measuring performance
6. Auditing records and determining and correcting the underlying cause of each error

Management must lead by demanding accurate records. Bank tellers, bookkeepers, nurses' aides, and university admissions clerks all respond positively to an expectation of accurate records. Manufacturing, inventory, and purchasing personnel respond in the same manner when their supervisors demand accuracy. If an individual's performance evaluation depends on accuracy, the accuracy of records increases substantially.

Counting and identification of items occurs in several places in the organization. Individuals performing these activities should be informed explicitly that their tasks require accuracy. For example, receiving clerks must count and identify incoming material accurately. The same holds for shipping clerks and outgoing items. Storekeepers must identify, count, and record material received and issued. In addition, they must record material locations accurately. If scrap occurs, the quantity of acceptable production and of scrap should be recorded by the operator.

Accurate records are difficult to maintain without adequate support. Containers holding a designated quantity, counting scales (the number of items is given by the weight), hand counters, and orderly storage facilitate accurate counts and records. Data describing issues, receipts, shipments, completions of operations, scrap, and allocation must be processed by the production and inventory management (PIM) information system in a timely manner.

Adequate training of personnel is relatively inexpensive; inadequate training may be very expensive. Documentation of proper recording procedures with clear examples of the typical transactions can aid both the experienced and the new employee. Formal training is an excellent foundation for an understanding and appreciation of appropriate and accurate recording of transactions.

Auditing Inventory Records. Physically counting the quantity of each item in inventory is necessary to verify the accuracy of inventory records. The two basic methods are (1) a periodic, usually annual, count of all items and (2) a cyclic, usually daily, counting of certain items, where specific criteria determine the items to be counted during a given day.

An annual physical inventory does not support day-to-day inventory record accuracy. Its primary purpose is to validate the aggregate inventory values used for financial accounting statements. Production usually is discontinued while the annual count is taken by a combination of line and staff personnel on temporary assignment. This relatively large group is not familiar with the appearance of most items, their location, and the engineering changes that obsolete some items. Production downtime is expensive; pressure to quickly complete the count may cause accuracy to suffer.

Cycle counting involves the following:

1. Selecting and training a limited number of personnel to be (preferably) full-time counters
2. Establishing criteria for selecting items to count
3. Selecting items for counting each day
4. Counting those items, comparing counts to the inventory record, and determining the causes of any errors
5. Taking the action required to prevent recurrence of the error, or at least to reduce the likelihood of recurrence
6. Measuring the quality of records and changes in quality over time

Initiating a Cycle-Counting Program. Beginning the program by repetitively counting a small representative sample of items can spotlight problem areas very rapidly. Henry Jordan (1980) has pointed out that the sample should include some purchased items, some manufactured items, some difficult-to-count items, and some items whose unit of measure changes as they are processed. When all problems have been resolved and the physical count and inventory records agree over a period with numerous transactions, extend the cycle-counting program to all parts.

Selecting Items to Count. The frequency with which an item is counted should be related directly to the likelihood and importance of an error with the item. Inexpensive, low usage items that can be obtained quickly are low risk items.

They are C items in the typical ABC classification system that can be used to determine the frequency of counts. Selection of an item for counting frequently is based on activity criteria such as counting when:

1. An order is placed
2. An order is received
3. The inventory record balance is zero or negative
4. The last item is issued from stores
5. A specified number of transactions has been recorded

Each of these criteria usually results in an unbalanced work load for the counters. In such cases A items usually are counted first, B items next, and then C items. Counters may have other storekeeping tasks assigned on days when the work load is low.

The block system, which counts items in the same storage area each day, may be used. It results in a balanced work load and is a more efficient process in terms of counts per hour. If, for the most part, different storage areas are used for A, B, and C items, the frequency of area counts can vary by classification.

All items should be counted at least once a year. Location audits also should take place to guarantee that all items physically in storage are counted.

Since operations continue during cycle counting, cutoff procedures must exist so that ongoing transactions do not alter the inventory record before a comparison is made. In an on-line system this problem is minimized since the count can be checked with the record immediately. Cycle counting may be performed at the end of the day or transactions may be suspended in the items to be counted during a given day. The practicality of any approach depends on the situation.

Accuracy Goals and Performance Measurement.   Whenever the count and the record differ, the record must be adjusted. When that difference is beyond the specified tolerance, an analysis should be made to determine the cause, and the accounting department should be notified of the difference. Table 9-2 gives tolerances recommended by the APICS cycle-counting training aid (Jordan 1980).

Table 9-2
APICS Recommended Tolerances

Inventory Class	Percentage of Quantity
A	±0.2
B	±1
C	±5

Preparing a monthly cycle count cumulative variance report, as illustrated in Table 9-3, enables management to track the progress of inventory accuracy. The variance report indicates the difference of the inventory count from the inventory record in dollars and as a percentage of the inventory record value.

Table 9-3
Cycle Count Cumulative Variance Report
(Month: March)

Inventory Class	Previous Month Variance (dollars)	Previous Month Value (percentage)	Current Month Variance (dollars)	Current Month Value (percentage)	Year-to-Date Variance (dollars)	Year-to-Date Value* (percentage)
A	−6,122	0.750	−5,137	0.623	−19,022	2.330
B	485	0.059	−402	0.049	671	0.082
C	−95	0.012	87	0.010	−33	0.004

Based on present inventory value.

Inventory Evaluation Methods

There are four principal methods of costing inventory: FIFO (first in, first out); LIFO (last in, first out); the moving average cost; and the order (specific) cost. The value of inventory sold is included as an expense in calculating profit. The value of items in stock at the end of the period is included as an asset on the balance sheet. Thus, the inventory valuing procedure will affect the book value of inventory investment, profit, taxes, and cash flow (via taxes).

FIFO.   This method assumes that items are issued from stock in the same sequence that they are received. Oldest items leave first. The cost of sales is based on the cost of the oldest items in inventory and the asset value of the items remaining in stock is based on the cost of the newest items. During an inflationary period this procedure results in a lower cost of goods sold, increased earnings before taxes, increased taxes, and decreased cash flow when compared with other methods. The opposite results during a deflationary period. Table 9-4 is a simple example of the application of FIFO with an increasing item cost.

On January 1, there are 400 units in stock, each valued at $3.00. On January 10, 300 of these are sold, leaving a balance of 100 valued at $3.00 each. On January 25, 300 units costing $3.30 each arrive. There are then 100 units valued at $3.00 each and 300 units valued at $3.30 each for a total inventory value of $1,290.

LIFO.   This method assumes that the most recent arrivals in inventory are issued first. The newest items leave first. The cost of goods sold reflects the cost of the most recent arrivals in inventory and the asset value of the items remaining in inventory is based on the cost of the oldest items in inventory. During an inflationary period (newer items cost more than older items) this method results in a higher cost of goods sold, decreased earnings before taxes, decreased taxes, and increased cash flow when compared with other methods. The opposite results during a deflationary period. Table 9-5 is a simple example of LIFO with an increasing item cost.

Table 9-4
FIFO Costing of Inventory

Date	Receipts Units	Unit Cost	Total Cost	Issues Units	Unit Cost	Total Cost	Balance* Units	Unit Cost	Total Cost
January 1							400	$3.00	$1,200
January 10				300	$3.00	$ 900	100	3.00	300
January 25	300	$3.30	$ 990				100	3.00	
							300	3.30	1,290
February 3				100	3.00	300	300	3.30	990
February 18				200	3.30	660	100	3.30	330
March 1	400	3.35	1,340				100	3.30	
							400	3.35	1,670
March 10				100	3.30				
				200	3.35	1,000	200	3.35	670
March 25	400	3.40	1,360				200	3.35	
							400	3.40	2,030
						$2,860			

*Quarter cost of goods sold = $2,860; asset value = $2,030.

Table 9-5
LIFO Costing of Inventory

Date	Receipts Units	Unit Cost	Total Cost	Issues Units	Unit Cost	Total Cost	Balance* Units	Unit Cost	Total Cost
January 1							400	$3.00	$1,200
January 10				300	$3.00	$ 900	100	3.00	300
January 25	300	$3.30	$ 990				100	3.00	
							300	3.30	1,290
February 3				100	3.30	330	100	3.00	
							200	3.30	960
February 18				200	3.30	660	100	3.00	300
March 1	400	3.35	1,340				100	3.00	
							400	3.35	1,640
March 10				300	3.35	1,005	100	3.00	
							100	3.35	635
March 25	400	3.40	1,360				100	3.00	
							100	3.35	
						$2,895	400	3.40	1,995

*Quarter cost of goods sold = $2,895; asset value = $1,995.

Table 9-5 is identical to Table 9-4 until the February 3 transaction. Using LIFO, the 100 units issued are valued at $3.30 each; using FIFO (Table 9-4), they are valued at $3.00 each.

Weighted Moving Average.   This method calculates the value of items in inventory on the basis of their weighted average cost. The cost of items consumed by production equals the current weighted average unit cost of inventory. When an order is received, a new weighted average value is computed. The new average is found by adding the value of the order to the value of the on-hand inventory and then dividing that value by the sum of the units on hand plus those just received. For example, in Table 9-6 an order worth $990 arrives. Adding the $990 to the $300 on-hand inventory yields $1,290. Dividing $1,290 by 400 units on hand gives a unit value of $3.225. This method smooths the effect of inflation and deflation on the valuation of inventory and the cost of goods sold. Table 9-6 is a simple example of this method with increasing item costs. Since Tables 9-4, 9-5, and 9-6 use the same data for the beginning balance, receipts, issues, and item costs, they provide a comparison of the results of LIFO, FIFO, and the weighted moving average.

Table 9-6
Weighted Average Costing of Inventory

Date	Receipts Units	Receipts Unit Cost	Receipts Total Cost	Issues Units	Issues Unit Cost	Issues Total Cost	Balance* Units	Balance* Unit Cost	Balance* Total Cost
January 1							400	$3.00	$1,200.00
January 10				300	$3.00	$ 900	100	3.00	300.00
January 25	300	$3.30	$ 990				400	3.225	1,290.00
February 3				100	3.225	322.50	300	3.225	967.50
February 18				200	3.225	645	100	3.225	322.50
March 1	400	3.35	1,340				500	3.325	1,662.50
March 10				300	3.325	997.50	200	3.325	665.00
March 25	400	3.40	1,360				600	3.375	2,025.00
						$2,865.00			

Quarter cost of goods sold = $2,865; asset value = $2,025.

Order (Specific) Cost.   This method ties the cost of goods sold directly to the cost of the actual items used in production (or sold directly). The value assigned to items remaining in inventory also equals the actual costs of those items. This method is applicable to large expensive items with relatively low demand and costs that may vary widely. It requires an information-processing system capable of tracing the flow of each purchase and each production lot through the entire production and distribution system.

Selecting a Costing Procedure. The accounting or finance department usually selects the inventory costing procedure. The product process structure of an organization, the organization's objectives, and legal requirements influence the selection. The results of the different systems are very similar when costs are stable. United States companies must obtain approval from the Internal Revenue Service to use LIFO.

Storekeeping and Security

Administrative control (records accuracy) and physical control are interdependent. Misplaced items, unrecorded issues, and pilferage can annul records accuracy. The principles of storekeeping and security (physical control) apply to all situations. The appropriate method to implement these principles depends on the situation.

Storerooms should be locked and all material issues and movement should be authorized and recorded. Receipts must also be recorded. Although physically enclosing all items is not always possible—for example, bulk commodities such as coal and sand may have to be stored outdoors—all issues and receipts should be recorded. Other items may move directly from the receiving dock to the production line or from the final production work center to the shipping dock. In both cases, clearly defined control points must exist with the information system recording changes in inventory status when movement occurs. This situation is prevalent in continuous and repetitive production where containers of material may move from the receiving dock to the production line at regular intervals, e.g., every hour.

Fixed locations, random locations, and zoned random locations may be used to determine the point of storage. The fixed location method permanently assigns a specific space to each item. This method minimizes problems in finding items. It is appropriate when item inventory levels are relatively stable, when receipt and withdrawal frequencies are stable, and when space is not a problem. Using this method when item inventory levels vary widely can lead to inefficient space utilization.

Storing items in part number sequence is possible in a fixed location system. This facilitates location but can be inefficient if handling and storage requirements vary widely for items in the same number range. Frequency of use and handling difficulty also is a sound basis for assigning locations. Convenient access should be provided for high volume items whose bulk or weight causes handling difficulties. The nature of certain items requires that they be segregated as a group and stored in temperature, humidity, or dust controlled facilities.

The random location approach assigns items to an available space. Different lots of the same item may be stored in different locations. Item location may become variable rather than permanent information on the inventory record. The locations of an item should be updated at each receipt and withdrawal. The method can use space efficiently when item inventory levels vary widely. However, it requires that storekeepers and material handlers frequently consult the inventory records before obtaining items or placing them in stores. Lax recording practices will lead to an inability to find items in a reasonable time. Some companies having large inventories now use an automated storage and retrieval system (ASRS) in which a computer directs an automatically guided vehicle to the appropriate bin location. An ASRS uses random locators.

Zoned location combines some of the benefits of both the fixed and the random location systems. Items are located in a space available basis within a designated zone. Grouping similar items in the same zone reduces the location problems that may result from the random location approach. Grouping may be based on storage requirements, nature of the item (for example, storing all hydraulic components in the same area), or on the basis of product line usage.

No single technique will necessarily meet all the needs of any one company. Many organizations, consequently, use a combination of these methods.

EXERCISES

Use the following information for Exercises 1 through 13.

Central Warehouse: On Hand = 1,600; Safety Stock = 250								
	Week							
	1	2	3	4	5	6	7	8
Warehouse A								
Forecast Demand	0	60	60	60	60	60	60	60	60
On Hand	300								
Warehouse B								
Forecast Demand	0	150	150	150	150	200	200	200	200
On Hand	600								
Warehouse C								
Forecast Demand	20	40	60	80	20	100	40	40	60
Planned Receipts	0	200							
On Hand	0								

Replenishment lead times are two weeks for Warehouse A and one week for both Warehouses B and C. The economic shipping quantity is 250 units to Warehouse A, 500 units to Warehouse B, and 200 units to Warehouse C. Finished goods units cost $18. The cost of placing an order is $125. The holding cost rate used by the enterprise is 30 percent. Manufacturing lead time is three weeks. Based on the history of the past several months, average weekly demand at warehouses A, B, and C is 80, 180, and 70 units, respectively.

1. If all the warehouses use a basic order point system with safety stocks of 60, 100, and 50 units at Warehouses A, B, and C, respectively, what is the order point of each warehouse? If actual demand is the same as forecast demand, in which periods will each warehouse place its next order?

2. Given the information in Exercise 1, calculate the economic order quantity for each warehouse. Use the average weekly demand to estimate annual demand. Then calculate the projected inventory each week in each warehouse and calculate the average inventory cost for each warehouse (the sum of ordering cost and carrying cost).

3. The central warehouse has 1,100 units at the beginning of Week 1; the safety stock is 250 units; the production order quantity is 2,000 units; the average weekly demand is 230 units; and the manufacturing lead time is three weeks. Calculate the order point for the stock at the central warehouse, the periods in which orders are released and received, and the quantity on hand at the end of each week.

4. Calculate the total inventory for each week in units and in dollars when the four warehouses are using the order point system.

5. If the *MLT* is three weeks, calculate the second order point for each warehouse. What are the implications of the results of the calculations in this case using the double order point system?

6. Assume a sales replenishment system is used to manage the stock in Warehouses A, B, and C. The replenishment period is four weeks for each of the warehouses. Warehouse A's stock is replenished in Weeks 1, 3, and 7; Warehouse B's stock is replenished in Weeks 2 and 6; and Warehouse C's stock is replenished in Weeks 1 and 5. Given the safety stocks for these warehouses in Exercise 1 for an order point system,
   a. Estimate the approximate safety stock for each warehouse in order to achieve the same level of service with the sales replenishment system.
   b. Calculate the stocking level for each warehouse.
   c. Assume that actual demand equals forecast demand. Calculate the order quantity each review period for each warehouse and the on-hand balance at the end of each week at each warehouse. (Refer to the treatment of periodic review systems in Chapter 6.)
   d. Using an *OP* of 1,000 units and an order quantity of 2,000 units, calculate the inventory on hand each week at the central warehouse.
   e. Calculate the total inventory in the distribution system (the four warehouses) for each week in units and in dollars.

7. Using a DRP system, determine the planned orders for each warehouse and the projected inventory on hand at each warehouse each week. There is no safety stock at Warehouses A, B, and C. Calculate the order release timing, order receipt periods, and inventory on hand at the central warehouse each week. (Use a production order quantity of 2,000 and a safety stock of 250 at the central warehouse.)

8. Calculate the total inventory in the distribution system for each week in units and dollars when using a DRP system.

9. Compare the costs of carrying inventory in the order point, the sales replenishment, and the DRP systems for the eight-week period. Use a k of 0.30. Calculate the estimated differences in cost between the three methods for a year.

10. Using a DRP system, determine the planned orders for each warehouse and the projected on hand inventory at each warehouse each week. Use the period order quantity method to determine the size of each order. There is no safety stock at Warehouses A, B, and C. Calculate the order release timing, order receipt periods, and inventory on hand at the central warehouse each week. (Use a production order quantity of 2,000 and a safety stock of 250 at the central warehouse.)

11. Using a DRP system, determine the planned orders for each warehouse and the projected on hand inventory at each warehouse each week. Use the least total cost method to determine the size of each order. There is no safety stock at Warehouses A, B, and C. Calculate the order release timing, order receipt periods, and inventory on hand at the central warehouse each week. (Use a production order quantity of 2,000 and a safety stock of 250 at the central warehouse.)

12. Compare the results of Exercises 7, 10, and 11 and comment on the desirability of each lot sizing technique for use in a distribution requirements planning system.

13. Demand at each of the three warehouses really represents a forecast. Assume that the forecasts are unbiased, that is, forecast error has a mean of 0. Assume further that the forecast error is normally distributed with a coefficient of variation of 0.2, that is, the standard deviation of the forecast distribution is 20 percent of the forecast. Determine the safety stock level needed in each warehouse.

14. Using an electronic spreadsheet, perform a simulation of the system derived in Exercises 10 and 13. Use the distribution requirements plan developed in Exercise 10 as a starting point. First, add the safety stock you calculated in Exercise 13 to the beginning on-hand amount for each part. Then insert two rows at the top of the time-phased plan for each part. Label the first row "Actual Demand" and the second row "Actual on Hand." In the first row generate a random demand equal to **.75*Forecast(n)** + (**@RAND** + **@RAND**)***.5*Forecast(n)**, where **Forecast(n)** is the forecast for period n and **@RAND** is the spreadsheet's built-in random number generator. (Technical note: For Lotus 1-2-3, **@RAND** is the actual function. The function name may be different for other spreadsheets. The distribution created by the approach used in this exercise is not a normal distribution, but rather a symmetric triangular distribution that is a rough approximation of a normal distribution.) Repeat this process for every period for each of the three warehouses. Calculate the

"Actual on Hand" for each warehouse. Next, subtract the "Actual Demand" and add in any planned receipts. Repeat this process for each period. Carry the planned order release information down to the next level and repeat. Comment on the adequacy of the safety stock you acquired. Did the schedule change in any way? What are the implications of a schedule change to the manufacturing process?

15. A distribution manager wishes to change his system from a pull system with three autonomous warehouses, one central warehouse, and a manufacturing facility, to a distribution requirements planning environment. Discuss the advantages and disadvantages of making this change. Recommend a solution intermediate to the current system and the proposed system.

16. Assume the central warehouse in Exercise 7 finds that a recording error has caused it to incorrectly estimate the quantity on hand, which really is 400, rather than the 1,600 shown by the computer. Assume further that the normal manufacturing and distribution lead times cannot be shortened. Use the equal runout approach to establish a corrected DRP.

Use the following information for Exercises 17 through 21.

A small company buys original molds and dies for popular antique cars and makes replacement parts from these original fixtures. The company supplies parts nationwide from one manufacturing facility through two central warehouses and four regional warehouses. The customers order directly from the four regional warehouses, which in turn order from the two central warehouses, which order from the manufacturing facility. Central Warehouse 1 (CW1) serves Regional Warehouses 1 and 2 (R1 and R2) exclusively. Central Warehouse 2 (CW2) serves Regional Warehouses 3 and 4 (R3 and R4) exclusively. There is a two-week manufacturing lead time. Delivery lead time from the manufacturing facility to each of the two central warehouses is one week. Delivery lead time from the central warehouse to either of its regional warehouses is one week. The manufacturing facility maintains no finished goods inventory; when a batch is finished it is shipped to one or both central warehouses.

There are three parts supplied by the company, Parts 101, 102, and 103. Information about these parts is as follows:

Part	Cost	On Hand CW1	On Hand CW2
101	$8	500	600
102	$6	200	300
103	$5	600	900

The cost for any of the six warehouses to place an order is $100. The cost to add to an existing order is $10. The enterprise uses a 40 percent carrying cost rate for items held in inventory. The cost to set up the manufacturing facility to build a batch of any part is $500. Manufacturing capacity is not limited. The manufacturing facility has two batches presently in progress, both due at the end of the first week: one batch of Part 101, size 800, and one batch of Part 102, size 800.

Demand forecasts for the next 12 weeks are as follows (the "forecast" for Period 0 is the quantity presently on hand):

Part	0	1	2	3	4	5	6	7	8	9	10	11	12
							Period						
Regional Warehouse 1													
101	150	120	110	95	90	130	160	180	160	120	80	60	50
102	70	50	80	100	120	100	80	60	60	80	130	140	70
103	230	200	180	160	140	120	100	120	140	160	180	200	220
Regional Warehouse 2													
101	250	240	205	180	230	270	300	340	310	270	180	160	130
102	100	100	110	110	110	110	90	90	90	90	100	110	90
103	340	300	290	280	270	260	250	260	270	280	290	300	310
Regional Warehouse 3													
101	190	160	150	130	120	180	200	190	190	150	110	80	70
102	80	70	100	130	150	150	110	90	100	130	180	180	100
103	260	250	240	220	210	200	190	190	200	200	220	240	250
Regional Warehouse 4													
101	350	300	300	300	250	350	350	350	350	300	250	250	200
102	250	150	200	250	300	300	200	200	200	250	350	350	200
103	530	500	500	450	400	400	400	400	400	400	400	500	500

17. Using a DRP system, determine the planned orders for Warehouses R1, R2, and CW1. Use the period order quantity method to determine the size of each order. There is no safety stock at any warehouse.

18. Using a DRP system, determine the planned orders for Warehouses R1, R2, and CW1. Use the economic order quantity method to determine the size of each order. There is no safety stock at any warehouse.

19. Using a DRP system, determine the planned orders for each of the six warehouses and for the manufacturing facility. Use the period order quantity method to determine the size of each order. There is no safety stock at any warehouse.

20. Using a DRP system, determine the planned orders for each of the six warehouses and for the manufacturing facility. Use the economic order quantity method to determine the size of each order. There is no safety stock at any warehouse.

21. Demand at each of the four regional warehouses really represents a forecast. Assume that the forecasts are unbiased, that is, forecast error has a mean of 0. Assume further that the forecast error is normally distributed

with a coefficent of variation of 0.2, that is, the standard deviation of the forecast distribution is 20 percent of the forecast. determine the safety stock level needed in each warehouse.

22. Using an electronic spreadsheet, perform a simulation of the system derived in Exercises 19 and 21. Use the distribution requirements plan developed in Exercise 19 as a starting point. Add the safety stock you calculated in Exercise 21 to the beginning on-hand amount for each part. Construct the spreadsheet as described in Exercise 14. Comment on the adequacy of the safety stock you acquired. Did the schedule change in any way? What are the implications of a schedule change to the manufacturing process?

23. Design an inventory record for a dependent demand item used in 10 to 15 different assemblies. The beginning balance and quantity available are both 650. Record the events on the following dates:

6/18	250 units allocated to order M93
6/21	300 units allocated to order M107
7/8	500 units ordered (M207)
7/8	450 units allocated to order M123
7/16	300 units issued (M107)

24. Prepare a cumulative cycle count variance report based on the following information. (Use these two months for year-to-date calculations.)

Inventory Class	Previous Record Value	Month Actual Value	Current Record Value	Month Actual Value
A	$782,490	$775,200	$791,600	$781,800
B	15,208	15,321	15,675	15,790
C	4,920	4,915	5,176	5,320

25. Based on the receipts and issues during the last two months (see table that follows), determine the cost of goods sold for the two months and the asset value of the inventory at the end of the two months using (a) FIFO, (b) LIFO, and (c) the weighted moving average.

	Receipts		Issues	Balance	
Date	Units	Unit Cost	Units	Units	Unit Cost
March 1				200	$4.00
March 10	300	$4.20			
March 15	200	4.25	100		
March 30			200		
April 5	300	4.40			
April 10			300		
April 25					

SELECTED READINGS

Brown, Robert G. *Materials Management Systems*. New York: John Wiley & Sons, Inc., 1977.

Ford, Quentin. "Distribution Requirements Plannings and MRP." *APICS 24th Annual International Conference Proceedings* (1981): 275-278.

Geoffrion, Arthur M. "Better Distribution Planning with Computer Models." *Harvard Business Review* (July-August 1976): 92.

Geoffrion, Arthur M. "Multicommodity Distribution System Design by Benders Decomposition." *Management Science* (January 1974): 822.

Herron, David P. "Managing Physical Distribution for Profit." *Harvard Business Review* (May-June 1979): 121-132.

Heskett, James L. "Logistics-Essential to Strategy." *Harvard Business Review* (November-December 1977): 85-96.

Jordan, Henry. *APICS Training Aid: Cycle Counting for Records Accuracy*. Falls Church VA: American Production and Inventory Control Society, 1980.

Magee, John R., and David M. Boodman. *Production Planning and Inventory Control* 2d ed. New York: McGraw-Hill Book Co., 1967.

Martin, Andre J. "Distribution Resource Planning (DRP 11)." *APICS 23d Annual International Conference Proceedings* (1980): 161-165.

Martin, Andre J. *Distribution Resource Planning, Distribution Management's Most Powerful Tool*. Essex Junction, VT: Oliver Wight Limited Publications, Inc., 1983.

Newberry, Thomas L., ed. *Inventory Management Systems*. Atlanta, GA: American Software, (October 1978): 8-1 and 8-2.

Newberry, Thomas L., and Carl D. Bhame. "How Management Should Use and Interact with Sales Forecasts." *Inventories and Production Management* 1, no. 3 (July-August 1981): 4-11.

Plossl, George W., and Oliver W. Wight. *Production and Inventory Control*. Englewood Cliffs, NJ: Prentice-Hall, Inc., 1967.

Porter, Robert W. "Centralized Inventory Management in the Multilevel Distribution Network." *APICS 22d Annual International Conference Proceedings* (1979): 81-82.

Root, Cary M., Andre J. Martin, and Paul N. Lomas. "The ABC's of DRP." *APICS 22d Annual International Conference Proceedings* (1979): 83 and 84.

Stenger Alan J., and Joseph L. Cavinato. "Adapting MRP to the Outbound Side-Distribution Requirements Planning." *Production and Inventory Management* 20, no. 4 (1979): 1-13.

Part Three

Material Requirements Planning

10

MATERIAL REQUIREMENTS PLANNING

The acronym, MRP, is used in three different but related contexts. Each of these contexts marks a stage in the development of MRP concepts. These different but related contexts are:

1. MRP I—material requirements planning
2. Closed-loop MRP
3. MRP II—manufacturing resource planning

Figure 10-1 is an overview of MRP I, closed-loop MRP, and MRP II and their relationships. MRP I is part of closed-loop MRP which is part of MRP II.

MRP I was the initial development in MRP. It is sometimes called little MRP or just MRP. It calculates the exact quantity, need date, and planned order release date for each of the subassemblies, components, and materials required to manufacture the products listed on the master production schedule. Prior to MRP I the vast majority of manufacturing organizations controlled subassemblies and components using traditional order point methods. This chapter describes MRP I in detail and its advantages over the traditional order point approach for managing dependent demand items.

Closed-loop MRP was a natural evolutionary step in the development of a more formal and explicit manufacturing control system. It includes capacity requirements planning and feedback describing the progress of orders being manufactured. On the front end it links the master production schedule to the production planning process. It uses the material requirements plan to develop a capacity requirements plan. It then compares the planned capacity utilization resulting from the MPS and the MRP to the available capacity to determine if the plan is attainable. Once an attainable plan is developed, shop floor control and purchasing control are exercised to close the planning and

Figure 10-1
Overview of MRP II, Including Closed-Loop MRP and MRP I

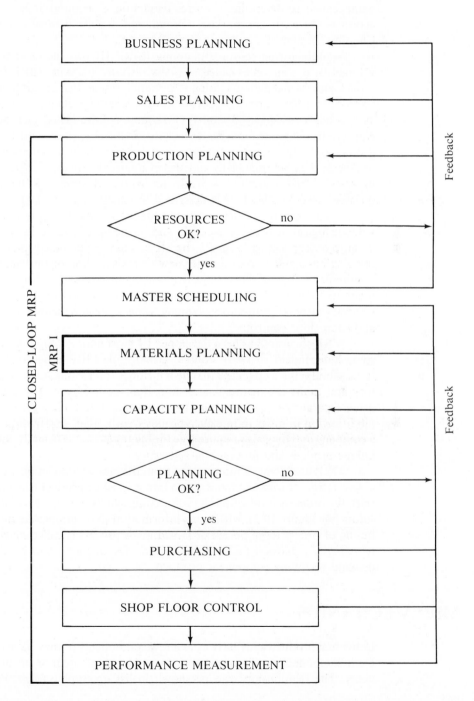

control system. That is, actual production and supplier performances are measured and compared to the plan. (The loop is closed.) This feedback enables management to determine if corrective action is required and, if it is, what action is the most appropriate. (Production activity control is described in Chapters 14 and 15.)

Manufacturing resource planning (MRP II) was the most recently developed. It is sometimes called *business resource planning* (BRP™). It is an explicit and formal manufacturing information system that integrates marketing, finance, and operations. It coordinates the sales and manufacturing plans to assure their consistency. It converts resource requirements, such as facilities, equipment, personnel, and material, into financial requirements and converts production outputs into monetary terms. It evaluates the organization's ability to execute the plan financially and also evaluates the financial merit of the plan in terms of such measures as profit, return on investment (ROI), and return on assets (ROA). (MRP II is described in Chapters 2 and 11.)

Today, nearly all MRP software systems are closed-loop systems that provide the logical tie between the MPS and the detailed inventories and purchase or shop orders needed to satisfy the MPS. They are designed to do this on an ongoing basis and to create either new or revised shop or purchase orders as requirements change. Their objectives are (1) to determine what to order, how much to order, when to order, and when to schedule delivery, and (2) to keep priorities current for inventory planning, capacity requirements planning (CRP), and shop floor control.

MRP software has been developed by most major computer vendors and some independent software houses. Usually the MRP program is part of a total manufacturing package that also includes forecasting, order entry, inventory and BOM file maintenance, shop floor control, etc. The programs are often separately priced and vary in their capabilities. They generally require modification in order to interface properly with other information systems in a company and may also require fine tuning to operate efficiently with a firm's unique product and process characteristics.

MRP uses demand information from the master production schedule with a description of what components go into a finished product (the bill of material), the order or production times for components, and the current inventory status (see Figure 10-2). MRP uses information to determine the quantity and timing of orders to be placed or issued. This process is called *product* or *bill of material explosion* because the demand for one end item breaks up into demand for many component products.

MRP MECHANICS

Individual products may have only a few components or may have thousands. Each component itself may be composed of a single item or of many sets of items. The relationships can be shown in list or graphic form. Figure 10-3

Figure 10-2
Inputs and Outputs of Material Requirements Planning

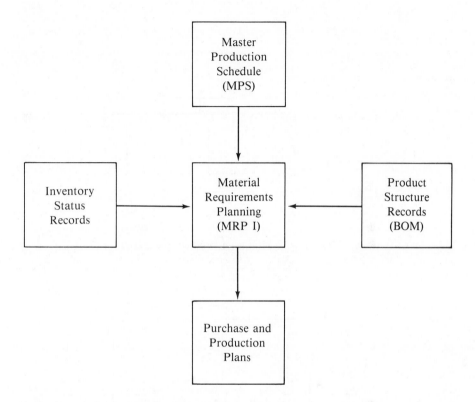

illustrates product structure diagrams and what are referred to as *product structure levels*. The end product or end item is set at Level 0 and its immediate components and subassemblies are at Level 1. Each level is similarly divided into successively lower (but by convention, numerically higher) levels down to fundamental components, that is, purchased parts and raw materials.

The multilevel structure shown has both horizontal and vertical demand dependency relationships. These relationships and netting and lead-time off-setting are the basic processes of MRP I.

Vertical and Horizontal Dependencies

The product explosion process illustrates vertical and horizontal dependent demand. For example, let's consider the simplified product structure for a lamp, as shown in Figure 10-4. Vertical dependent demand is exemplified by the requirement for wiring assemblies to manufacture socket assemblies. Similarly, the requirement for terminals is dependent on the schedule for wiring assemblies because terminals are a component of wiring assemblies. This type

Figure 10-3
Simple and Multilevel Product Structures

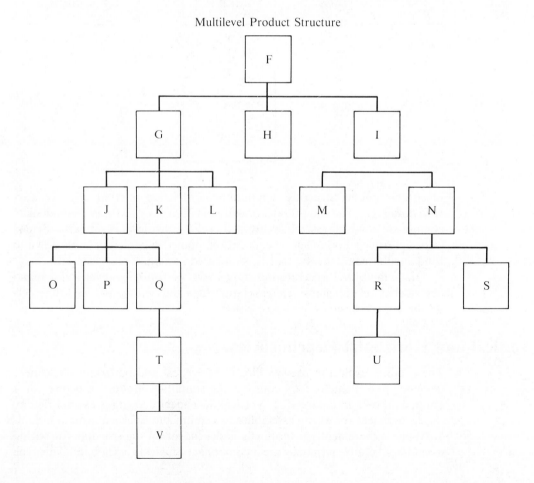

Simple Product Structure

Multilevel Product Structure

of dependency may involve one or more subcomponents and occurs between different levels of the BOM. The holder, the socket, and the wiring assembly are horizontally dependent; that is, they are at the same level in the BOM and all are required in the socket assembly. Having two of the three is of little value; all three are required. In contrast, the demand for the lamp itself is independent. Another example of independent demand is the demand for the wiring assembly as a service (repair) part. Thus, the MPS might contain forecast demand for wiring assembly service parts in addition to calculated requirements to build new lamps.

Gross to Net (Netting)

In order to understand the basic problem that MRP I addresses and how its logic works, consider Figure 10-4. To simplify the example, consider only the

Figure 10-4
Simplified Product Structure for a Lamp

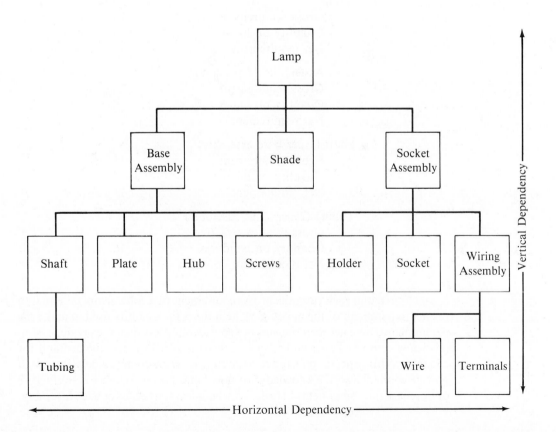

left branch of this diagram—lamp, base assembly, shaft, tubing. Assume we receive an order for 25 lamps. We have the following items on hand:

Lamps	3
Base assemblies	7
Shafts	4
Tubing	16 feet

(In this instance each shaft requires 2 feet of tubing.) How many of each of these items should we order? A simple response would be 22 lamps (25 − 3), 18 base assemblies (25 − 7), 21 shafts (25 − 4), and 34 feet of tubing (25 × 2 − 16). However, this is incorrect, because each unit in a level contains all of the components that are below it. Each lamp already contains one base assembly; each base assembly already contains one shaft; and each shaft already contains 2 feet of tubing. Thus, the gross requirement for 25 lamps must be analyzed sequentially at each level to get the correct net requirement for each item. The gross to net logic is as follows:

Lamp
Gross requirement	25
Quantity on hand	− 3
Net requirement	22

Base Assemblies (1 per lamp)
Gross requirement	22
Quantity on hand	− 7
Net requirement	15

Shaft (1 per base assembly)
Gross requirement	15
Quantity on hand	− 4
Net requirement	11

Tubing (2 per shaft assembly)
Gross requirement (feet)	22
Quantity on hand	− 16
Net requirement	6

Note that in each case, the gross requirement of a subassembly is equal to the net requirement of the next higher item times the quantity used to make the parent item. These net requirements are considerably less than the previous, simplistically computed ones and represent the true needs to meet the demand for 25 lamps. This process, referred to as *netting* or *gross to net* calculation, must now be combined with a knowledge of how long it takes to either manufacture or purchase the components in order to schedule a start date for each assembly.

Lead-Time Offsetting

The time intervals necessary to either manufacture or purchase the components are referred to as the lead times. In our example, the lead times are as follows:

Lamps	2 weeks
Base assemblies	1 week
Shafts	2 weeks
Tubing	3 weeks

These lead times are used to compute *lead-time offsets* for each component. If the order is to be shipped in Week 27, then the offsets are as shown in the schematic representation in Figure 10-5. Notice how the beginning date for one level is the completion or arrival date for the next. Thus, an order for 6 feet of tubing must be placed in Week 19 in order for the lamps to be shipped in Week 27.

Figure 10-5
Lead-Time Offsets

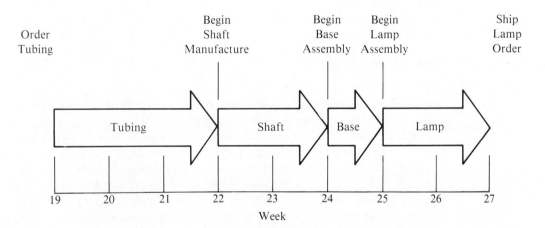

The essence of the MRP logic can be expressed in three relationships: (1) horizontal and vertical dependencies, (2) gross to net, and (3) lead-time offset. Specifically, horizontal and vertical dependencies establish end item, subassembly, component, and purchased material gross number relationships, gross to net considers the effect of current inventories, and the lead-time offset backs off production or order lead time. The logic for a simple product like this lamp is quite straightforward. However, when dealing with thousands of items and varying product structures, the situation in practice is much more complicated.

The MRP Chart

A table or chart similar to Table 10-1 is often used to illustrate the management of a dependent demand item. The gross requirements come from the net requirements of the next level (upper) in the BOM and ultimately from the MPS; the beginning inventory in Period 1 comes from the inventory records; and the projected on hand inventory in each period is calculated. A net requirement exists whenever projected on hand is less than safety stock. If a fixed order quantity is used, a planned receipt is created in that amount whenever a net requirement exists. The planned order release value and location on the chart indicates the quantity to be ordered and the period in which it is planned to give either production or purchasing the authority to execute the order.

Table 10-1
MRP Chart
Lead Time: 3; Lot Size: 25; Safety Stock: 0; Quantity on Hand: 30

		Period					
		1	2	3	4	5	6
Gross Requirements		10	15	15	10	15	10
Scheduled Receipts				25			
Projected On Hand	30	20	5	15	5	15	5
Net Requirements						10	
Planned Order Receipts						25	
Planned Order Releases			25				

Scheduled Receipts and Planned Order Receipts.   Note that scheduled receipts, by definition, come from orders already released either to manufacturing (production, manufacturing, or shop orders) or to suppliers (purchase orders). When an order is released it becomes an *open order* and has scheduled receipts. Lower level requirements due to planned receipts of production orders (released earlier) were added earlier to the gross requirements of lower level items. Purchase orders have no lower level requirements for the purchaser. However, planned order releases result in planned order receipts and cause requirements at lower levels. Planned order receipts differ from scheduled receipts in that they have not been released. Since net requirements exist in Period 5 and the lead time is 3 periods, a planned order release is required in Period 2.

Remember that this is a plan, however, and plans can change. If gross requirements in Period 3 should fall to 5, then the plan would change to that shown in Table 10-2.

It is important to note that planned order releases are easier to change than released orders (open orders). Changes or cancellation of open purchase orders can result in cancellation charges. Open production orders frequently

Table 10-2
MRP Chart
Lead Time: 3; Lot Size: 25; Safety Stock: 0; Quantity on Hand: 30

		Period					
		1	2	3	4	5	6
Gross Requirements		10	15	5	10	15	10
Scheduled Receipts				25			
Projected On Hand	30	20	5	25	15	0	15
Net Requirements							10
Planned Order Receipts							25
Planned Order Releases				25			

are in process, with lower level purchase and production orders also having been issued; and change is disruptive and costly. Changes in released orders also reduce manufacturing's confidence in the system's output and their adherence to it.

Time Periods (Buckets).   Time periods also are called *time buckets* in MRP jargon. The time buckets in the previous example are weeks. The immediate (current) period in the planning horizon, Period 1 in the example, is the *action period* (the *action time bucket*). Planned order releases usually are not released until this period. This practice provides the planner with maximum flexibility and diminishes disruptions in the plant and at suppliers' facilities.

Bucketless MRP systems use a time period of one day. (Thus, they are not truly bucketless). Scheduled receipts, planned order releases, and planned order receipts are specified for a certain date. The smaller the time bucket, the more time buckets there are in the planning horizon, and the greater precision possible in planning and control of lead times. The costs of smaller time buckets include larger computer storage requirements and increased computer processing and outputs. Many companies have successfully implemented bucketless systems.

If lead-time precision permits it, a bucketless system can specify requirements, releases, and receipts in terms of a specific shift, a four-hour period, or an hour. As the execution of manufacturing planning and control continues to improve, this will be achieved in some firms. It is consistent with the objectives of the Just-in-Time approach (see Chapter 17).

Time Conventions.   Interpreting production and inventory management records requires an understanding of the timing conventions used. Inventory quantities, for example, frequently are listed explicitly as either beginning inventory or ending inventory. When a production quantity is stated for a given period, the understanding usually is that the quantity will be produced by the end of the period. MRP charts also require the use of such conventions for consistent use. The charts in this chapter use the following conventions:

Gross requirements	Needed by end of period
Projected on hand	Ending Inventory
Net requirements	Needed by end of period
Scheduled receipts	Needed by end of period
Planned order receipts	Needed by end of period
Planned order releases	Needed by end of period

Thus, if the lamp of Figures 10-4 and 10-5 has net requirements in Week 27 and lead time is two weeks, a planned order release for lamps must exist in Week 25. Note that if the order is released at the beginning of Week 25, manufacturing has a one week safety lead time, because—by convention—the lamps are not required until the end of the Week 27.

Low Level Coding.   Some items are required at more than one level in the BOM. For example, in Figure 10-6, Item B has a low level code of 2. Net requirements for such an item are obtained by adding gross requirements for that item through the lowest level that the code is found in the BOM structure. BOM software assigns a level code to each item corresponding to the lowest level at which it is required. This is known as *low level coding*.

A bill of material explosion proceeds level by level. First, all Level 0 parts are time phased and their net requirements added to the gross requirements of

Figure 10-6
Low Level Coding

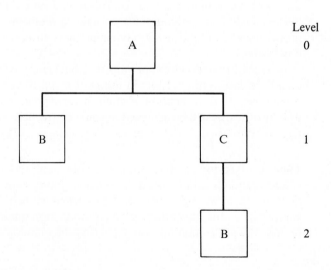

their components. Then, time-phased and gross requirements are carried down to their components, and so on. By waiting until the lowest level of usage for an item is reached, the processor avoids duplication of effort.

Lot Sizing

The preceding example used a fixed lot size of 25, but the lot-size decision should not be made lightly. It can substantially affect inventory levels, setup and ordering costs, capacity requirements and availability, and delivery. Factors affecting the lot-size decision include the number of levels in the BOM, the cost of a setup or purchase order, the cost of carrying an item in inventory, the use of joint orders and manufacturing cells, and the low level code of a given item. The effects of many of these factors are described in the following paragraphs; others are described throughout the text. Consider the situation shown in Table 10-3. A lot size of 25 might be proper given capacity and other factors. However, the seeming lack of correlation between quantities needed and quantities ordered raises questions concerning the appropriateness of this schedule. There are several methods of selecting lot size that may achieve better results.

Table 10-3
MRP Chart
Lead Time: 2; Lot Size: 25

						Period				
	0	1	2	3	4	5	6	7	8	9
Gross Requirements		12	15	9	17	8	10	16	7	11
Scheduled Receipts		25	25							
Projected On Hand	0	13	23	14	22	14	4	13	6	20
Planned Order Receipts					25			25		25
Planned Order Releases			25			25	25			

Ordering and Carrying Costs.   One, but not the only, criterion for evaluating lot sizes for dependent demand items is the sum of the preparation (setup) and carrying costs resulting from a particular method. If the preceeding lot-sizing algorithm (order 25 units each time a requirement exists) were followed over the nine-period planning horizon, it would require five setups and the carrying of inventory as indicated in the projected on hand row. If setup costs are $5.75 each and inventory carrying costs are $0.05 per unit (part) per period, total setup costs would be 5 × $5.75 or $28.75, and total carrying costs would be 13 + 23 + . . . + 20 or 129 part periods at $0.05 or 129 × $0.05 = $6.45. The total costs over the nine-period horizon would be $28.75 + $6.45 = $35.20. These costs will be compared to the total setup and carrying costs of other methods before discussing other factors.

Lot-for-Lot (L4L). Assuming that orders can be for any quantity, then ordering the exact quantity that is actually needed (referred to as the *lot-for-lot* or *L4L* ordering rule) results in no on-hand inventory. In practice this doesn't always occur for several reasons: orders arrive late or early, orders are canceled, quantities made or delivered are under or over those ordered, or the economics or technology dictate constant lot sizes or multiples thereof.

If we take our previous example and are planning lot-for-lot order releases, the situation would be described by Table 10-4.

Table 10-4
MRP Chart
Lead Time: 2; Lot Size: L4L

		0	1	2	3	4	5	6	7	8	9
							Period				
Gross Requirements			12	15	9	17	8	10	16	7	11
Scheduled Receipts			12	15							
Projected On Hand		0	0	0	0	0	0	0	0	0	0
Planned Order Receipts					9	17	8	10	16	7	11
Planned Order Releases			9	17	8	10	16	7	11		

To cost the lot-for-lot method, there are nine setups at $5.75 each and no inventory is held. The total cost by this method is $51.75. In this particular example, the total costs are notably higher for the lot-for-lot method. However, there are situations where a production planner would have no choice but to select the lot-for-lot method. For example, the L4L method would have to be used for perishable food items or for items for which the market fluctuates widely. When excess capacity exists and labor costs are fixed, the marginal costs of additional setups may be zero. In addition, this method is consistent with the Just-in-Time philosophy of eliminating all unrequired inventory.

Least Unit Cost (LUC). A second method of determining the lot size is the least unit cost. This method produces the demands of the present period, then, on a trial basis, evaluates future periods. The algorithm chooses the least unit cost (setup + inventory carrying cost per period) over successive periods by adding the total carrying costs to the setup costs and finding the period for which the per unit cost is the smallest. The LUC lot sizing of our example data is shown in Table 10-5, and the computations are as shown in Table 10-6. The data in Table 10-6 includes the cost of the scheduled receipts quantity, which was based on this method.

The LUC method would order the first period, then sequentially evaluate future periods for the least unit cost. The holding cost of $0.05/period and setup cost of $5.75 are used, giving the computations shown in Table 10-6.

Table 10-5
MRP Chart
Lead Time: 2; Lot Size: LUC

		Period								
	0	1	2	3	4	5	6	7	8	9
Gross Requirements		12	15	9	17	8	10	16	7	11
Scheduled Receipts		53								
Projected On Hand	0	41	26	17	0	44	34	18	11	0
Planned Order Receipts						52				
Planned Order Releases				52						

Table 10-6
Lot-Sizing Computations of the LUC Method

Period	Number Ordered	Setup Cost	Carrying Cost	Total Cost	Cost/ Unit
1	12	$5.75	0	$ 5.75	$0.479
1-2	27	5.75	15 × 0.05 = $0.75	6.50	0.240
1-3	36	5.75	15 × 0.05 + 9 × 0.10 = $1.65	7.40	0.205
1-4	53	5.75	15 × 0.05 + 9 × 0.10 + 17 × 0.15 = $4.20	9.95	0.188
1-5	61	5.75	15 × 0.05 + 9 × 0.10 + 17 × 0.15 + 8 × 0.20 = $5.80	11.55	0.189

For Period 1, the number ordered is 12, the setup cost is $5.75, and carrying costs are 0. Thus, the total cost of $5.75 is divided by the number of units to obtain the cost per unit of $0.479. The per unit cost for Periods 1 and 2 is then evaluated as follows: Demands are 12 + 15 = 27, and setup costs are $5.75. Carrying costs are $0.05 for each of the 15 items demanded in Period 2, or $0.75. Thus, the total cost is $6.50, and the cost per unit is $0.240. Similar computations indicate that the cost per unit decreases when the demands through Period 4 are ordered in one lot. But these per unit costs increase when the demand for the fifth period is added to the initial order. Thus, the method would order the 53 items through Period 4 and plan a subsequent order to cover Periods 5 through 9. Similar computations would result in a planned order release of 52 in Period 3, with a planned receipt in Period 5.

The total cost of the LUC method to manage demand for the nine-week horizon would be two setups at $5.75, or $11.50 for setup costs, and a total of 191 part-periods (41 + 26 + . . . + 11 + 0) at $0.05, or $9.55 total carrying cost. The total cost of the LUC method then would be $9.55 + $11.50 = $21.05. However, more than nine periods are required to evaluate any method.

Least Total Cost (LTC). This approach selects lot sizes (order quantities) and times their release so as to obtain the least total cost (the minimum sum of ordering and carrying costs) over the planning horizon. It does this by combining requirements until carrying costs approximate ordering costs. Based on the logic that the total cost curve is discrete (can be evaluated on a period-by-period basis) for dependent demand decisions, the minimum total cost still usually occurs at the point closest to a balance of carrying and ordering costs. This approach is executed as follows:

1. Begin with the first period in which an order is required.
2. Add the requirements of future periods, one at a time, ordering up to and including that period at which the cumulative carrying costs come closest to the ordering cost. (Another method of exercising the LTC logic is to add requirements in all future periods until, but not including, the period in which cumulative carrying costs exceed the order cost.)
3. Begin the next order with the first period not covered by the previous order and continue in the same manner.

Using the same data as the L4L and LUC examples, the ordering cost is $5.75, and the carrying costs are $0.05 per period per unit. The requirements and scheduled receipts are given in Table 10-7. (The scheduled receipts order quantity was determined using the LTC method as described shortly.) Table 10-8 shows the calculations for this example.

Table 10-7
MRP Chart
Lead Time: 2; Lot Size: LTC

						Period				
	0	1	2	3	4	5	6	7	8	9
Gross Requirements		12	15	9	17	8	10	16	7	11
Scheduled Receipts		61								
Projected On Hand	0	49	34	25	8	0	34	18	11	0
Planned Order Receipts							44			
Planned Order Releases					44					

Table 10-8
Calculations for LTC Solution

Period	Units	Periods Carried	Period Carrying Costs	Cumulative Carrying Costs
2	15	1	$15 \times 0.05 \times 1 = \$0.75$	$0.75
3	9	2	$9 \times 0.05 \times 2 = 0.90$	1.65
4	17	3	$17 \times 0.05 \times 3 = 2.55$	4.20
5	8	4	$8 \times 0.05 \times 4 = 1.60$	5.80

The first order is for at least the 12 units required in Period 1. The first decision is whether or not to add the 15 units required in Period 2 to the order arriving in Period 1. If the carrying cost of adding these units is less than the cost of ordering again, they are added. Since total carrying costs are 15 × $0.05 × 1 or $0.75, the 15 units for Period 2 are included in the order arriving in Period 1. Considering Period 3 requirements next gives a total carrying cost of $1.65. Therefore, these units also are added to the first order. The results of continuing these calculations are given in Table 10-8. The 10 units required in Period 6 are not included in the first order because their addition generates a carrying cost much greater than the ordering cost. The planned order receipt for 44 units in Period 6 is calculated in the same manner. In fact, up to 13 parts for Period 7 could be added to the order without requiring another setup.

The total cost of the using the LTC approach for the 11 weeks in the example problem is $20.45, or about 2 percent less than the LUC approach. Which of the many different approaches will work best in a given situation can be evaluated by simulation, as described in Chapter 23. Capacity considerations also are included in the final decision, as described in Chapter 12.

Part Period Balancing. Part period balancing is a variation of the LTC approach. It converts the ordering cost to its equivalence in part periods, the economic part period (EPP), by dividing the ordering cost by the cost of carrying one unit for one period. The EPP is calculated as follows:

$$EPP = \frac{S}{K}$$

where EPP = the economic part period
S = the cost of ordering
K = the cost of carrying one unit for one period

Using the data from the previous LTC example, the EPP equals $5.75 divided by $0.05 or 115 part periods. Using part period balancing, requirements are added period by period until the generated part periods approximate the EPP. This approach is shown in Table 10-9.

Table 10-9
Application of Part Period Balancing

Period	Requirements	Periods Carried	Part Periods	Cumulative Part Periods
2	15	1	15	15
3	9	2	18	33
4	17	3	51	84
5	8	4	32	116
6	10	5	50	166

Since 116 is the closest value to 115, the requirements for Periods 2 through 5 should be included in the order due in Period 1. The advantage of this approach is that it is usually easier to compute part periods than carrying costs.

Another technique, which in theory produces optimal orders, is the Wagner-Whitin dynamic programming algorithm (Wagner and Whitin 1958). Given a finite time horizon and known demands, it optimally balances costs. In the example problem the Wagner-Whitin method selects the same sizing as the LTC method. A major problem with this method is its complexity and its sensitivity to change. While our planning horizon must be long enough to cover the total lead times for all our items, the dynamics of the real world cause the specific quantities and times to change. Hence, the optimal solution changes. Small changes at high levels of the BOM can cause "nervous" changes and instability in dependent demand plans. This is undesirable and is one factor that argues for fixed lot sizes. For example, if the demand changes slightly in our first example and the lot size were 30, there would be no change in planned orders.

The difficulty with fixed lot-sizing techniques is that they only look at one level in a multilevel system. The setting of lot sizes for Level 1 of the product structure has impact all the way down through the explosion of that structure. Trying to take into account the carrying and setup costs for all levels simultaneously to establish optimal lot sizes is an area just now being investigated.

The Period Order Quantity (POQ).   This method uses the standard EOQ, calculating a fixed number of period requirements to include in each order. Thus, the POQ avoids *remnants*—that is, quantities carried in inventory until the next requirement—whereas using the EOQ for discrete demand frequently results in remnants. In cases with low demand per period, relatively high setup costs, and relatively few levels in the BOM, it results in lower total inventory costs than the L4L method because it combines the requirements for more than one period in a single order. The procedure is as follows:

1. Calculate the EOQ in the standard manner.
2. Use the EOQ to calculate N, the number of orders per year, by dividing the annual requirements (R) by the EOQ.
3. Calculate the POQ by dividing the number of requirements planning time periods per year by N. Round the result to obtain the POQ.
4. Begin with the first period that has requirements and place an order to cover them plus those in the periods that follow until the number of periods specified by the POQ are covered.

This can be illustrated with an example of a purchased item. If $R = 1,440$ units annually, $S = \$60$ per order, $k = 0.3$ per year, $C = \$90$ per unit, with 50 planning weeks per year, then following the procedure we have:

1. $\text{EOQ} = \sqrt{\dfrac{2RS}{kC}} = \sqrt{\dfrac{2 \times 1,440 \times \$60}{0.3 \times \$90}} = 80$

$$2. \ N = \frac{R}{\text{EOQ}} = \frac{1,440}{80} = 18$$

$$3. \ \text{POQ} = \frac{\text{Planning Periods per Year}}{18} = \frac{50}{18} = 2.8 \text{ or } 3$$

An equivalent alternate method is to calculate the ratio of the EOQ to the annual requirements $\left(\dfrac{\text{EOQ}}{R} = \dfrac{80}{1,440} \text{ or } 0.056\right)$ and multiply this ratio by the number of periods per year ($0.056 \times 50 = 2.8$).

Applying this result to a given set of requirements when the lead time is two weeks results in the planned order releases shown in Table 10-9.

Table 10-9
MRP Chart
On Hand: 0; Lot Size: POQ = 3 Periods; Lead Time: 2 Weeks

						Week						
	1	2	3	4	5	6	7	8	9	10	11	12
Net Requirements	*	*	20	34	8	50	0	51	0	9	38	13
Planned Order Receipts			62			101				60		
Planned Order Releases	62			101				60				

Covered by a previous order.

This approach does not minimize ordering and carrying costs, but it frequently is less costly than ordering each period or arbitrarily selecting a fixed order period.

Other Considerations. In practice, it may be possible to have complicated lot-sizing rules, although fixed sizes or minimum lot sizes are the most common alternatives to L4L ordering. Even the fixed size rule should be subject to review and periodic recomputation as costs, normal demand levels, or technology change. In addition, human judgment by the production planners should review schedules and use firm planned orders (described shortly) when appropriate.

Safety Stock and Safety Time

As long as parts procurement and manufacturing lead time are constant and the MPS is frozen (fixed) for a sufficient period of time to allow for parts procurement or production, no safety stock is required. However, competitive pressures frequently prevent the MPS from being fixed for a period as long as the total lead time. Figure 10-7 illustrates a situation in which the MPS must be frozen for at least 16 weeks if there is to be no variability in any requirements.

Figure 10-7
Activity Lead Times

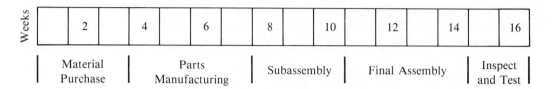

If customers expect delivery in six weeks, then subassemblies must be planned to a forecast. Parts and materials requirements are based on the schedule of subassemblies. And if demand cannot be forecast with certainty—which usually is the case—safety stocks are required at the subassembly level to assure that a desired percentage of the demand for final assembled products will be filled within the six-week lead time.

Given a fixed schedule for an assembly (either a final assembly or a sub-assembly as described previously) both the delivery of purchased material and the manufacturing of parts involve uncertainties. For example, if parts are scrapped late in the manufacturing process, a new lot cannot be produced within normal lead time. Vendors often do not ship the quantity promised. Also, vendors have manufacturing and procurement problems; late delivery and short quantities result. If an item experiences either vendor delivery or manufacturing problems in a regular fashion, safety stock is appropriate. Safety stock requirements are determined as described in Chapter 6.

To illustrate how safety or buffer stocks impact system behavior, consider our previous example with a fixed lot size of 15. With a safety stock of 10 units, the plan is illustrated in Table 10-10. Net requirements equal the safety stock minus the POH prior to the receipts.

Table 10-10
MRP Chart
Lead Time: 2; Lot Size: 15; Safety Stock: 10

		Period								
	0	1	2	3	4	5	6	7	8	9
Gross Requirements		12	15	9	17	8	10	16	7	11
Scheduled Receipts		15	15							
Projected On Hand	10	13	13	19	17	24	14	13	21	10
Net Requirements				6	8	1		12	4	
Planned Order Receipts			15	15	15		15	15		
Planned Order Releases		15	15	15		15	15			

Planned order releases are calculated just as before, except that the trigger point is when the inventory falls below 10 rather than below 0. The direct impact of such safety stock is to raise the average inventory level. This negative aspect is offset by the system's ability to handle unexpected demand increases or time advancements. For example, if an additional demand for 10 units were suddenly to occur in Period 3, it could be accommodated. If the demand of Period 5 were to move up to Period 4, it could be met. And if a future demand increase occurred—that is, if the demand in Period 4 were to suddenly become 25—no change in the order release for Period 2 would be required. A shortage would have occurred if no buffer stock were present.

An alternative to safety stocks is safety lead times. By overstating the lead time in the plan, the actual deliveries may arrive early and can then be used to satisfy changed demand. A simulation study by Whybark and Williams (1976) showed that if the uncertainties are in the demand quantities then safety stock quantity is desirable. However, if the uncertainty is in the timing of demand, safety lead times are preferred. Since demand for component items is certain, in the sense that it is dependent demand, in theory there should be no need for safety stock except for independent demand items and end products in the MPS. In practice, however, uncertainty in supply, either purchasing or manufacturing induced, may warrant some type of safety or uncertainty preparedness.

It is important that the MRP system output (report, charts, etc.) clearly distinguish between safety stock requirements and upper level requirements. Safety stock requirements should be visible. In the previous example, if the on-hand quantity falls to 5 units in Period 1 (the action period), an order with insufficient lead times would be triggered. Expediting, broken setups, overtime, and considerable expense could result if the order is released. Replenishing safety stock usually is not a legitimate cause for special orders so the material planner will override the system. The planner can override the MRP system by using a firm planned order.

Firm Planned Orders (FPO)

One of the difficulties in establishing lot sizes is that the traditional economic order quantity (EOQ) formula looks only at the costs associated with one level in the product structure. However, most product manufacture is multilevel, and a lot-size decision results in requirements for items at all lower levels. For example, the act of producing a gear box assembly necessitates the production of all components at levels below it—that is, gears, castings, shafts, bolts, etc. Until recently, the impact of the assembly EOQ on these components has usually not been considered.

Consider the example shown in Table 10-11, in which the rotor is a component of the motor assembly. The need for motor assemblies in Period 4 triggers a planned receipt for a lot size of 35. This in turn generates a planned order release in Period 2 and, hence, a gross requirement for the rotor in the same period. MRP logic causes a past due condition for the planned order release for the rotor. However, the 25 on hand could cover the true need caused by the gross requirements for motor assemblies (5 + 10 + 10), but the

Table 10-11
MRP Chart
Motor Assembly and Rotor

Motor Assembly
Lead Time: 2; Lot Size: 35

				Period			
	1	2	3	4	5	6	7
Gross Requirements				5	10	10	10
Scheduled Receipts							
Projected On Hand	0	0	0	0	30	20	10	0
Net Requirements				5			
Planned Order Receipts				35			
Planned Order Releases		35					

Rotor
Lead Time: 2; Lot Size: 10

				Period			
	1	2	3	4	5	6	7
Gross Requirements		35					
Scheduled Receipts							
Projected On Hand	25	25	0				
Net Requirements		10					
Planned Order Receipts			10				
Planned Order Releases	10						

lot sizing forces a past due situation. Manual intervention by a production scheduler may be required to either expedite the past due order, change the lot size for the motor assemblies, or introduce a firm planned order.

A *firm planned order* (FPO) is an order entered by the planner that supersedes the computer's MRP logic—that is, the planner does not allow the normal MRP gross to net and lead-time offset logic to take place, but rather the planner freezes a particular order. In this example, an FPO for 25 could be entered for the motor assembly and then all lower-level gross requirements would be determined by its value, as shown in Table 10-12. The FPO technique can also be used if the planner believes the lead time can be compressed. In this case the planner might decide that the motor assembly can be made in one week instead of two. Therefore, he or she enters as an FPO a planned order receipt of 35 in Week 5 instead of Week 4. This allows the MRP logic to proceed normally in scheduling the rotor. The computer program will probably issue a warning message (action notice) because it notes the discrepancy between the time the FPO will arrive and when it is logically needed, but the planner just uses this message to prompt expediting.

Table 10-11
MRP Chart
Motor Assembly and Rotor

Motor Assembly
Lead Time: 2; Lot Size: 35

				Period			
	1	2	3	4	5	6	7
Gross Requirements				5	10	10	10
Scheduled Receipts							
Projected On Hand	0	0	0	0	20	10	0	25
Net Requirements*				5			10
Planned Order Receipts				25			35
Planned Order Releases		25F			35		

Rotor
Lead Time: 2; Lot Size: 10

				Period			
	1	2	3	4	5	6	7
Gross Requirements		25			35		
Scheduled Receipts							
Projected On Hand	25	0	0	0	0		
Net Requirements*					35		
Planned Order Receipts					35		
Planned Order Releases			35				

Prior to order receipt

Pegging

Engineering frequently designs families of end products that have a common component. MRP must pool the demands for these items. Consider, for example, the two product structures and their time-phased demands shown in Figures 10-8 and 10-9, respectively.

Some interesting complexities are introduced. If for some reason the production lot of 25 units of A is reduced to 20 units (damage and scrap, low level delays, etc.), what impact should this have on X and Y? The first question is: Has the system kept track of which items gave rise to A's gross requirement of 25 in Period 4? In order to have such a record, valuable computer space must be used to note these parent demands. Furthermore, if this is a multi-level product structure, and it usually is, will the system also keep track of succeeding generations (parents, grandparents, etc.) or derive such information from a knowledge of each parent and/or offspring? These are important system

Figure 10-8
Product Structures

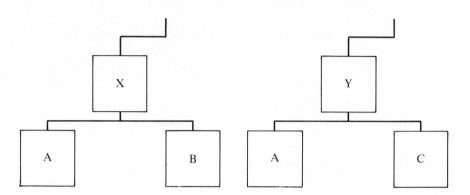

Figure 10-9
Time-Phased Demands

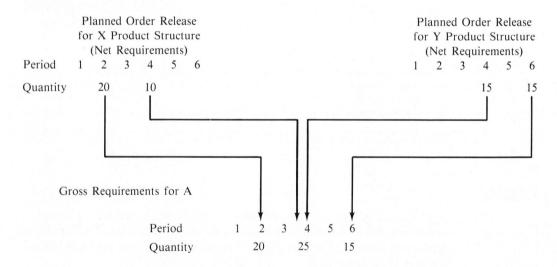

design considerations. This process of keeping track of parents and offspring is termed *pegging*.

More complexity is added by having the same component at different levels or in different branches within the same product. An example is matching decorative hardware on the tables and chairs that constitute a dining room suite of furniture. This is handled by low level coding, discussed earlier.

The final complexity is caused by the sheer number of parts in a typical firm—possibly upwards of 1,000 end items and 20,000 components. The result is no small data processing task. Hence, the rise in the use of MRP parallels decreasing cost and increasing speed of computers. In fact, without computers it would probably be necessary to assume that all demand is independent demand and hence MRP cannot be used. Also, in some instances, although the product structure relationship of the demand for a given item may be dependent, the effect of the many different requirements can be an aggregate demand of a relatively steady rate—in short, an independent demand profile—and a time-phased order point may be used.

BASIC OPERATIONAL CONSIDERATIONS

Implementing and operating an MRP system is a major challenge for many companies. Success requires accurate data, timely data processing, a realistic master production schedule, methods of controlling as well as planning priority, and a balanced approach to processing changes (the handling of unplanned events). Master production scheduling was described in Chapter 4, and priority controls are described in Chapters 14 through 16. Discussions of managing data and the MRP system follow.

Data Accuracy and Dependencies

At the base of all MRP computations are correct BOM and inventory status records. If they are inaccurate, the MRP system will plan the wrong items and the wrong quantities—garbage in, garbage out. Thus, if an engineering change has been communicated to the shop floor but not to the BOM file, the MRP system will order the wrong item. The item withdrawn from inventory—if it is available—will not be same as the item allocated. In addition, if inventory records indicate that parts are available when they are not, the required orders will not be planned. The salient problems resulting from inaccurate records are the lack of required items, disrupted production, and late deliveries. Whether an organization uses MRP, an order point system, or just estimates, it should have an accurate data base. But many do not.

System Processing

The realities of the manufacturing world are that events do not always occur as planned and that the passage of time brings the completion of some orders and the arrival of new ones. These events give rise to two questions concerning the processing of data affecting the MRP system: should the data be entered and, if so, when?

Managing Change.   A critical aspect of any scheduling system is its ability to deal with unplanned events, such as shortages, scrap, machine breakdowns, work stoppages by suppliers, absenteeism, and engineering changes. When any of these occur, it is necessary to note their impact and to take the appropriate action. If any such event is going to cause production delays, we should revise our priorities and produce items that are needed rather than those that are not.

As an example, let's return to the lamp assembly. If wiring assemblies are going to be delayed because of a shortage of terminals, there is no need to retain the original schedule to produce or order base assemblies. Wiring assemblies and base assemblies are horizontally dependent. We may as well work on another order, because otherwise we will have an inventory of base assemblies gathering dust while waiting for the socket assemblies. From this example it can be seen that a key feature of MRP is its ability to de-expedite work when necessary and, hence, to maintain correct priorities so that production can be accomplished on what is really needed.

As information comes in regarding changes, the schedule can be revised immediately. However, this is not always necessary or desirable. First, remember that MRP provides plans; it does not just issue orders. It is likely that only the plans need be changed, not the orders already issued to the shop floor. Second, the time frame of MRP is usually weeks, although bucketless systems are becoming more common. Changes that cause delays of less than a week are not recognized by the system. Third, it is preferable to have stability in the system since excessive changes will diminish production efficiency. This is a stage at which MRP interfaces with the MPS (discussed in Chapter 4) and the shop floor control system (discussed in Chapter 14). The planner must decide which changes are feasible and desirable on the basis of customer requirements, material and tooling availability, and the status of work in the shop.

Net Change Versus Schedule Regeneration.   Somewhat associated with change (but equally the result of time passing and, hence, production orders being completed and new orders received) is the necessity to revise the MRP. This can be done in two ways. One is to start with the current plan and to change it incrementally based on new information: delays, orders, shipments, etc. This is termed the *net change approach*.

While the net change approach may seem simple, in practice it has usually been found easier to start from the same basic information—the MPS, BOM, and inventory status data—and to regenerate the entire schedule. This second way is often called *regen* or *regeneration*.

A number of factors influence whether a firm chooses a net change or a regenerative system. One of these is computer processing time. To effectively perform a net change, the program must have pegging and, depending on the computer environment, about 10 parts per minute might be handled. Thus, 2,400 parts could be done in 4 hours. For a pegged, regenerative system perhaps two or three times as many parts could be handled per unit time, but many more parts must be handled each time the program is run. For a 20,000-part situation, it may take 11 hours to do a complete replanning run. A regenerative system may not contain pegging, in which case processing time is speeded up by a possible factor of three or four. Because product structures, software implementations, and the dynamics of change vary so greatly from company to company, it is impossible to state categorically whether net change or regenerative MRP will require less computer time. Inherently, a net change system is very responsive to changes, particularly if it is an on-line system where changes can be input as soon as they occur rather than grouping them for periodic processing. This makes the plan very current, but also causes it to be "nervous," or extremely volatile in response to changes. The use of time fences to limit the planning horizon within which changes can be made is a very effective way to reduce nervousness. Regenerative systems are less responsive but more stable, and hence fewer variations from the plan are noticed. Thus, closer control may be possible with a net change system, but computer costs and stability may argue for a regenerative system. A possible compromise is to net change weekly and to regenerate monthly.

MRP VERSUS ORDER POINT

Although many firms have implemented MRP systems, many have not. Thus, it is important to review the costs and benefits of changing from the traditional order point method to an MRP system for managing manufacturing inventories. First, an MRP system requires an accurate BOM, accurate and timely processing of inventory transactions, and a realistic MPS. If these conditions do not exist, they require education, training, time, and money to achieve. (See Chapter 20.) However, the improved use of resources resulting in improved delivery performance and competitive position usually make them a worthwhile investment.

Figure 10-10 illustrates a typical relationship between the independent demand and inventory for Assembly A, an item on the MPS, and the dependent demand and inventory for Component B when managed by an MRP system and when managed by an order point system. The shaded area represents the additional time the same inventory is carried when using an order point system. In the order point system example, the component lot size equals the the assembly requirements (an L4L). This is rarely the case in order point systems. As a result, usually either an additional ordering or setup is required or additional units beyond the safety stock are carried until the next order. Thus, Figure 10-10 understates the typical difference in the inventory in order point and MRP systems. Order point systems typically have substantially more inventory—often of the wrong items. Furthermore, when capacity is being used to manufacture items not needed, insufficient capacity may be available to produce required items.

In addition to not considering vertical dependencies, order point systems do not consider horizontal dependencies. For example, if Components B and C are required for Assembly A but Component B will arrive three weeks late from a supplier, an order point system does not consider this factor in deciding when to manufacture Component C. MRP does. Again, the order point system results in unnecessary inventory.

An MRP system looks into the future and calculates when items are needed; it is proactive. An order point system calls for action when inventory reaches the order point; it is reactive. MRP facilitates formal and explicit

Figure 10-10
MRP Versus Order Point

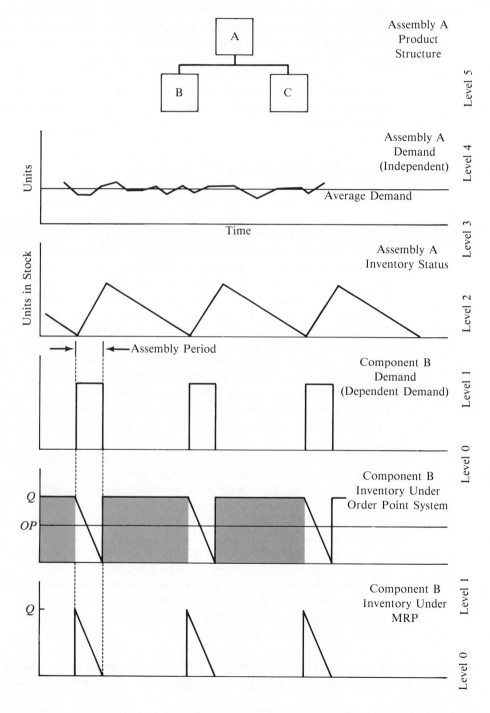

planning. Order point systems for dependent demand items make life more exciting by increasing the number of surprises and decreasing the time operations management has to cope with capacity management challenges.

Any company, regardless of whether it uses MRP or an order point system, should have an accurate data base. Whereas MRP systems can collapse if bills of material are incomplete or inaccurate or if inventory records are inaccurate, physical review order point systems will call for orders when inventory reaches the order point even if the records are inaccurate. The point is that an MRP system requires accurate bills of material and accurate and timely recording of inventory transactions to be effective. Thus, some firms who have not attained these prerequisites, continue to use an order point system until the organization attains an accurate data base. However, effective and efficient management of dependent demand items requires accurate inventory status and BOM files and an MRP system. Manufacturing organizations without this capability operate at a competitive disadvantage.

CLOSED-LOOP MANUFACTURING CONTROL

The MRP I system in Figure 10-2 is an open-loop system; there is no feedback. The manufacturing control system in Figure 10-11 is a closed-loop system. The capacity requirements planning (CRP), supplier performance control (SPC), and production activity control (PAC) systems provide feedback. The CRP system determines if critical work centers gave sufficient capacity during each period in the planning horizon. The PAC and SPC systems provide information concerning the status of orders in the plant and the performance of suppliers. This information enables planners to decide what, if any, action is required to bring production outputs in line with production plans. This action may include: (1) changes in the MPS and everything dependent on it, (2) overtime and/or additional suppliers, (3) expediting, (4) firm planned orders, and (5) some combination of the foregoing. These systems are described in detail in following chapters.

CONCLUSIONS

A closed-loop MRP system has four major advantages over the traditional order point system in the management of dependent demand items. These advantages are: the correspondence of MRP orders to actual demand requirements; the recognition by MRP of vertical and horizontal dependencies among items; the proactive planning and forward visibility of MRP; and the ability of closed-loop MRP to integrate materials and capacity planning and control consistency while maintaining the progress of orders and capacity in the production facility. Implementing a timely information processing system, a valid MPS, and the ability to manage change and priorities.

Figure 10-11
Closed-Loop Manufacturing Control

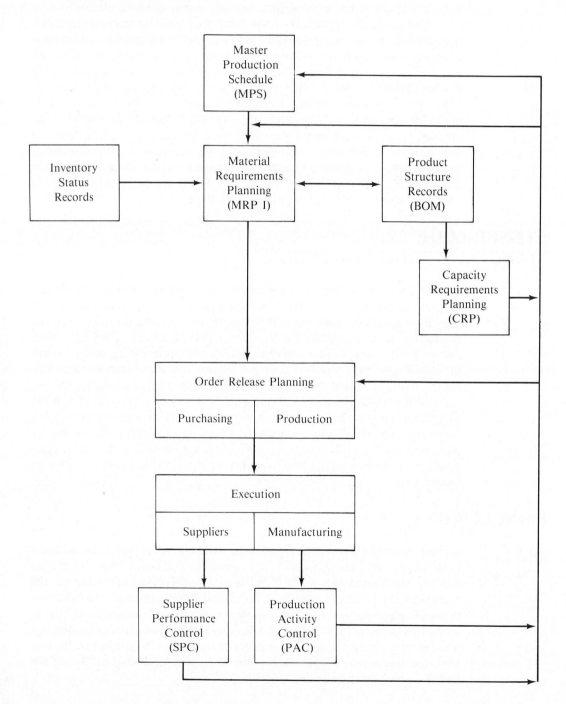

EXERCISES

1. Refer to the multilevel structure in Figure 10-3. If the gross requirement for Product F is 75 units, what are the net requirements for Parts F, G, J, O, P, Q, T, and V given the following on-hand quantities?

Part/Assembly	On Hand	Part/Assembly	On Hand
F	26	P	39
G	15	Q	7
J	12	T	6
O	14	V	4

2. Using the on-hand quantities in Exercise 1 and the BOM in Figure 10-3 except that the BOM requires two Q's for each J subassembly, calculate the net requirements for Parts F, G, J, O, P, Q, T, and V.

3. Referring to Exercise 1, calculate the net quantities to be ordered for Parts F, G, J, O, P, Q, T, and V if the lot sizes are 40—or multiples thereof—for all parts/assemblies.

4. Refer to Figure 10-3. If 120 units of Product F are to be shipped in Week 25, when must Part V be ordered given the following lead times?

Part/Assembly	Lead Time (weeks)	Part/Assembly	Lead Time (weeks)
F	3	P	5
G	2	Q	2
J	1	T	1
O	4V	6	

5. For the following situation, determine the planned order releases.

Lead Time: 3; Lot Size: 25; Beginning Inventory: 20

		Period									
		1	2	3	4	5	6	7	8	9	10
Gross Requirements		15	10	20	0	15	30	0	15	0	20
Scheduled Receipts		25									
Projected On Hand	20										
Net Requirements											
Planned Order Receipts											
Planned Order Releases											

6. If in Exercise 5 the lot-for-lot (L4L) order size rule is employed, what are the planned order releases?

7. If in Exercise 5, a POQ lot size of three periods is to be used, what are the lot sizes and in which periods are the planned order releases?

8. If the ordering cost is $10.00 per order, and the carrying cost is $1.00 per part per period, calculate the total cost associated with:
   a. The solutions for Exercise 5
   b. The solutions for Exercise 6
   c. The solutions for Exercise 7

9. If the ordering cost is $50.00 per order, and the carrying cost is $0.50 per part per period, calculate the total cost associated with:
   a. The solutions for Exercise 5
   b. The solutions for Exercise 6
   c. The solutions for Exercise 7

10. For the following situation determine the planned order releases using the least total cost (LTC) procedure. Ordering cost is $10.00. The carrying cost is 15 cents per unit per period.

Lead Time: 2; Beginning Inventory: 15; Scheduled Receipts: 0													
							Period						
	−1	1	2	3	4	5	6	7	8	9	10	11	12
Gross Requirements		8	6	5	11	4	10	4	7	10	8	6	6
Projected On Hand	15												
Planned Order Receipts													
Planned Order Releases													

11. Given the information in Exercise 10, calculate the total cost for ordering and carrying inventory if the lot size were fixed at 40 units. Do not include costs of carrying inventory that exists because of a previous decision.

12. Refer to the information in Exercise 10 to determine the planned order releases using the least total cost (LTC) procedure. Ordering cost remains at $10.00/order, however, the holding cost is 25 cents per unit per period.

13. Using the information in Exercise 10, determine the planned order releases using the least unit cost (LUC) procedure. Ordering cost remains at $10.00/order, however, the holding cost is 25 cents per unit per period.

14. Given the information in Exercises 10 and 12, calculate the economic part period (EPP) for each situation.

15. a. Solve Exercise 10 using the EPP.
    b. Solve Exercise 12 using the EPP.

16. Calculate the total costs of the least total cost lot-sizing example in Table 10-7.

17. Differentiate the concepts of safety stock and safety time. Give an example of the appropriate use of safety stock and the appropriate use of safety time.

18. Use the BOM in Exercise 1 and the lead times in Exercise 4. Sales vary week-to-week but continue throughout the year. However, substantial sales are being lost to competitors who deliver within one month. What might the company do to regain these sales?

19. The Ajax company has adopted MRP wholeheartedly. They have become aware of the pitfalls of various lot-sizing methods and use lot-for-lot exclusively. They have been working hard at reducing setup times and have made some progress. The present situation is described by the following table. They often have requirements for items in two successive weeks. What suggestions would you make to the planner?

Number of Items	Approximate Setup Cost	Carrying Cost/Week
25	$100 or More	$0.50
250	$40 to $50	0.40
725	Less than $20	0.30

20. a. A company has a forecast demand of 25 units per week for an item used only as a service part. The item has a lead time of three weeks. At present there are 120 of the items in stock. Develop an MRP type chart for the next 12 weeks using the time-phased order point (TPOP) method with a safety stock of 20 and an order quantity of 100. (See Chapter 6.)

  b. Prepare the same chart with no safety stock but with a safety lead time of one week.

SELECTED READINGS

Cate, Dexter, and Gary A. Landis. "How to successfully Integrate a Totally Closed-Loop System: A Case Study." In *31st Annual International Conference Proceedings*, 4-7. Falls Church, VA: American Production and Inventory Control Society, 1988.

DeMatheis, J. J. "An Economic Lot-Sizing Technique: The Part Period Algorithms." *IBM Systems Journal* 7, no. 1 (1968): 50-51.

Material Requirements Planning Reprints. Falls Church, VA: American Production and Inventory Control Society, 1986.

Orlicky, Joseph. *Material Requirements Planning.* New York: McGraw-Hill Book Co., 1975.

Schultz, Terry. *BRP: The Journey to Excellence*. Milwaukee, WI: The Forum, 1982.

Tincher, Michael, and David W. Buker. "Parrel Paths: A New Sucessful Path to Class A Mrp II." In *31st Annual International Conference Proccedings*, 1-3. Falls Church, VA: American Production and Inventory Control Society, 1988.

Wagner, Harvey M., and Thomson M. Whitin. "Dynamic Version of the Economic Lot Size Model." *Management Science* 5 (October 1958): 89-96.

Whybark, Clay D., and J. G. Williams. "Material Requirements Planning under Uncertainty." *Decision Sciences* 7, no. 1 (October 1976): 595-606.

Wight, Oliver W. *MRP II: Unlocking American Productivity Potential*. Boston, MA: CBI Publishing, 1982.

11
MRP EXTENSIONS
AND APPLICATIONS

This chapter covers some extensions to the basic MRP concepts presented in Chapter 10. It also presents specific applications of MRP.

In Chapter 10, MRP was presented as a technique for using the master production schedule for end items to determine the dependent demand for subassemblies, fabricated components, and purchased material. Two critical assumptions of this technique are that the MPS is developed at the end-item level and that a bill of material (BOM) exists for that end item. Recall from Chapter 4 that there are three basic BOM structures, the normal, the hourglass, and the inverted, as shown in Figure 11-1. The presentation of MRP concepts in Chapter 10, which assumes that the MPS is developed at the

Figure 11-1
Basic Bill of Material Types

Finished Goods

Subassemblies

Fabrication

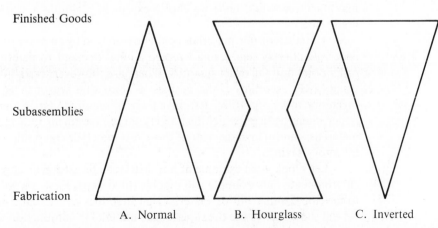

A. Normal   B. Hourglass   C. Inverted

end-item level, is most appropriate when the BOM shape is normal. This chapter discusses the design of an MRP system when the BOM has an hourglass or an inverted shape.

The discussion in Chapter 10 also assumes that a BOM existed at the time the order was received, that is, that the item was a standard product. However, in an engineer-to-order plant (see Chapter 1), the product is designed after the order is received. Clearly, a BOM cannot be created until the product is designed.

Chapter 11 is divided into three sections. In the first section we discuss how MRP can be used in an engineer-to-order environment, that is, in an environment in which the BOM does not exist when the order is received. In the second and third sections we discuss the use of MRP when the BOM shapes are inverted and hourglass, respectively. In the fourth section we discuss MRP II.

MRP IN AN ENGINEER-TO-ORDER ENVIRONMENT

Most engineer-to-order shops have a limited variety of product offerings, within which they have the capability of providing an effectively infinite variety of possible configurations. For example, Kickham Boiler builds boilers, smokestacks, and related products. Within their area of specialization, Kickham can build almost anything.

Often the raw material used for engineer-to-order firms has a very long lead time. The long raw material lead time often makes it difficult to respond to the customer in a timely fashion. As a result, an inventory must be held of certain long lead-time items that are common to many orders. For example, the lead time for many types of sheet steel may be six months. Suppose a manufacturer like Kickham makes custom designed boilers. Suppose further that the nature of competition is such that the manufacturer must promise to deliver within three months if the boiler uses a standard grade of steel. The manufacturer would have no choice except to maintain a stock of standard grade steel.

The stock of raw materials could be managed by an order point/economic order quantity system, using average annual demand to determine both the order point and the order quantity. There are, however, certain advantages to using MRP, especially if the business is somewhat seasonal. By tracking the inventory more carefully, less inventory is required. For a company like a boiler manufacturer, which has a very large investment in a few critical raw materials, careful management of those raw materials can result in a substantial inventory savings.

Let's look at an example of how MRP can be used in an engineer-to-order environment. This example will involve three steps. First, we will discuss how to develop a super bill of material that describes a "typical" product. Then we will show how to use the super bill of material in conjunction with the MRP system to control material purchases. Finally, we will show how to incorporate both actual orders and forecasts of "typical" product sales in order to manage the inventory.

Developing a Super Bill of Material

We will use a simplified example, limited to one family of end items and a single raw material, in order to better convey the concept of how one bill of material can represent a family of items. This hypothetical example is inspired by the use of Kickham Boiler elsewhere in the text. The hypothetical boiler company custom designs all boilers. It makes boilers in a variety of sizes. The management has observed that for planning purposes, the boilers can be split into three families: small boilers, medium boilers, and large boilers. Small boilers average about 10 tons, 100 percent of small boilers use standard steel, and about 20 small boilers are sold each year. Medium boilers average about 20 tons, 60 percent of medium boilers use standard steel and 40 percent use specialty steel, and about 10 medium boilers are sold each year. Large boilers average about 50 tons, 20 percent of all large boilers use standard steel and 80 percent use specialty steel, and about 5 large boilers are sold each year.

For boilers using standard grade steel, the hypothetical company promises delivery in three months. This consists of one month to design the boiler and have the design approved by the purchaser plus two months to manufacturer the boiler. For boilers using specialty steel, the company promises delivery in eight months. This consists of six months to order the specialty steel, during which time the design is completed and approved, plus two months to manufacture the boiler.

In developing bills of material, the company could use a separate bill of material for each boiler size category, as shown in Figure 11-2. Figure 11-2A shows a bill of material for a small boiler, 10 tons of standard steel. This bill of material is also a super bill, designated bill S-1, because 10 tons of standard steel is an average value. The actual order may be for a boiler weighing 6 tons or one weighing 14 tons. Figure 11-2B shows super bill S-2 for a medium boiler, for which 60 percent have standard steel (Part 101, 20 tons each) and 40 percent have specialty steel (Part 201, 20 tons each). Figure 11-2C shows super bill S-3 for a large boiler, for which 20 percent have standard steel and 40 percent have specialty steel. Figure 11-2D shows super bill S-0, a "typical" boiler, that consists of $\frac{20}{35}$S-1, $\frac{10}{35}$S-2 and $\frac{5}{35}$S-3. All boiler sales can be lumped into S-0 for forecasting purposes. The MRP system would then treat S-1, S-2, and S-3 as dependent demand items and would use their bills of material to determine the requirements for Parts 101 and 201, standard and specialty steel. Specialty steel is forecast so the manufacturer can reserve capacity at the steel facility.

Super bill S-0 can be simplified, as shown in Figure 11-3, by a weighted average of the amount of standard and specialty steel in S-1, S-2, and S-3. The average amount of standard steel in a boiler has been 10.6 tons. The average amount of specialty steel in a boiler has been 6.9 tons. We could also get this data by adding all the standard steel and all the specialty steel used in the past X years and dividing the totals by the total number of boilers built.

Figure 11-2
Hypothetical Super Bills of Material

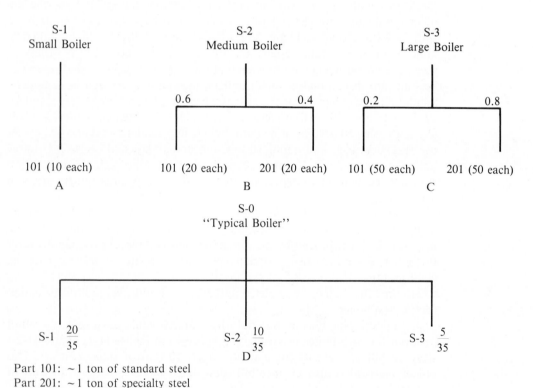

Part 101: ~1 ton of standard steel
Part 201: ~1 ton of specialty steel

Figure 11-3
Simplified Hypothetical Super Bill

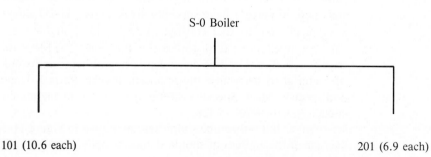

Consuming the Forecast with Actual Orders

Table 11-1 shows a level master production schedule with boiler production set at three boilers per month. This schedule is consistent with observed sales of 35 units in the previous year. We will now show how this information can be combined with orders for actual boilers. To simplify the discussion, assume that the manufacturer sells only five types of boiler, a standard boiler in sizes small, medium and large (10, 20, and 50 tons, respectively) and a specialty boiler in sizes medium and large (20 and 50 tons). Further, assume only one category specialty steel is used. We designate these five boilers by SB1, MB1, LB1, MB2, and LB2, respectively. Note that when the boiler type is determined, its precise steel content is also determined. Specifically, there are bills of material for SB1, MB1, and LB1 showing 10, 20, and 50 tons of standard steel, respectively, and bills of material for MB2 and LB2 showing 20 and 50 tons of specialty steel, respectively.

Table 11-1
Level Master Schedule Exploded to Determine Raw Material Usage

Product	Month											
	1	2	3	4	5	6	7	8	9	10	11	12
S-0	3	3	3	3	3	3	3	3	3	3	3	3
101	31.8	31.8	31.8	31.8	31.8	31.8	31.8	31.8	31.8	31.8	31.8	31.8
201	20.7	20.7	20.7	20.7	20.7	20.7	20.7	20.7	20.7	20.7	20.7	20.7

As an order for an actual boiler is received, the master scheduler enters an order for one of the five boiler types into the MPS and eliminates one of the orders for S-0 in the same period. The MRP system then updates the amount of material required. The full MPS for one year into the future is shown in Table 11-2. Since boiler production capacity is limited to three boilers per month, the MPS may not show more than three boilers due in any one month. The S-0 row, therefore, represents an available-to-promise row for capacity. During the coming month (Month 1) the manufacturer can accept one order for a boiler using standard steel. That order would be promised during Month 4. If more than one order is received this month, the second boiler must be promised in four months, rather than three (Month 5).

From Table 11-2, observe that the amount of material required in a given month is quite variable, despite the level production schedule. Because MRP gives the manufacturer forward visibility of this variability, MRP permits much closer management of the available inventory than does the order point/economic order quantity approach. Most industries have seasonal demand and, as a consequence, seasonal variations in production. This example did not illustrate seasonal demand, but it is reasonable to assume that the presence of seasonal demand increases the month-to-month variability in raw material consumption, further increasing the need for an MRP system.

Table 11-2
Hypothetical Master Schedule for "Typical" and Actual Boilers
Exploded to Determine Raw Material Usage

Product	Month											
	1	2	3	4	5	6	7	8	9	10	11	12
S-0	0	0	0	1	1	1	3	2	3	3	3	3
SB1	2	2	2	1	1	1	0	0	0	0	0	0
MB1	1	0	0	0	1	0	0	0	0	0	0	0
MB2	0	0	1	1	0	0	0	1	0	0	0	0
LB1	0	1	0	0	0	0	0	0	0	0	0	0
LB2	0	0	0	0	0	1	0	0	0	0	0	0
101	40	70	20	20.6	40.6	20.6	31.8	21.2	31.8	31.8	31.8	31.8
201	0	0	20	26.9	6.9	56.9	20.7	33.8	20.7	20.7	20.7	20.7

In the next section, we discuss the use of MRP with a standard product having an inverted bill of material.

MRP IN PROCESS INDUSTRIES—A CASE WITH SEASONAL DEMAND

Most continuous process manufacturers have many end items produced from a few raw materials. For example, a manufacturer of fiberglass insulation has one primary raw material, glass marbles, and a variety of insulation products as end items. A refinery has oil as an input and kerosene and various grades of gasoline as outputs. A textile plant has natural and manufactured fibers as inputs and a variety of types, weights, and colors of cloth as outputs. Most process industry plants have more than one stage of production, such as weaving, dyeing, and finishing in a textile mill. In most cases, the number of options increases as the product moves from stage to stage. As a result, most process industries have an inverted bill of material, as shown in Figure 11-1, with master scheduling performed at the first operation. In a one-stage process industry plant, the master schedule for the first operation is also the master schedule for the whole plant. Another way of saying this is that the master schedule is also the final assembly schedule. MRP, therefore, plans only material purchase. In this case, it is possible to use a super bill approach exactly as described in the previous section.

The more complicated, multiple stage, process industry plant may require separate scheduling of each stage, with inventory held between stages. We present a case that has three stages of production in order to discuss the development of the schedule at each level. To provide a realistic example, we present a case in which demand is seasonal and capacity is limited at each stage, requiring that anticipation inventory be held at several stages.

A carpet manufacturer having a bill of material shape similar to Figure 11-1C is discussed in Finch (1986) and Finch and Cox (1987). This manufacturer has three basic stages of production: weaving, dyeing, and backing. If there are X weave styles, Y colors, and Z types of backing, then there are XYZ possible end items, XY dyed unbacked subassemblies, and only X undyed weaves (known as greige goods). The company described in Finch and Cox chose to master schedule the weaving operation and use MRP to drive purchasing, even though only a few raw materials need to be ordered. Dyeing and backing are scheduled manually.

The example that follows is based loosely on Finch and Cox. The number of options available at each stage is reduced to create a simple example. The example is entirely hypothetical and the practices described respresent a hybrid of approaches used by two different firms.

Master Production Scheduling

Gala Carpet produces 30 carpet styles consisting of 3 weaves (Office 1, Home 1, Home 2; abbreviated O1, H1, H2), 5 colors (gray, brown, blue, off-white, red; abbreviated GR, BR, BL, OW, RE), and two backings (B1 and B2). Product flow is as shown below.

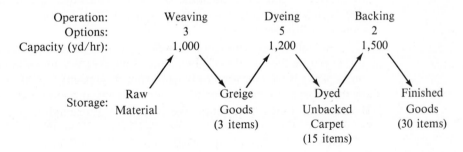

Operation:	Weaving	Dyeing	Backing
Options:	3	5	2
Capacity (yd/hr):	1,000	1,200	1,500

| Storage: | Raw Material | Greige Goods (3 items) | Dyed Unbacked Carpet (15 items) | Finished Goods (30 items) |

Any one of the 30 end products can be designated by a six-digit stock number describing weave, color, and backing. For example H2REB1 is a carpet containing Home 2 weave, dyed red, and using backing 1. Intermediate products are identified with two-digit and four-digit designations. Thus, O1 refers to woven, undyed fabric, and O1GR refers to O1 fabric, dyed gray, as yet unbacked.

Total annual demand is 8,000,000 yards, with a seasonal peak during the summer when many schools replace their carpet. Forecast demand by month is shown in Table 11-3. The plant operates three shifts, 365 days a year. The weaving capacity is 1,000 yards per hour, dyeing capacity is 1,200 yards per hour, backing capacity is 1,500 yards per hour. For simplicity, we will assume this capacity consists of one loom, one dyeing area, and one backing machine. We will also assume that dyed carpet leaves the dyeing area dry and ready to back.

Table 11-3
Total Carpet Demand, Gala Carpet

Month	Demand
1	466,400
2	533,600
3	600,000
4	666,400
5	733,600
6	866,400
7	933,600
8	933,600
9	800,000
10	600,000
11	466,400
12	400,000
Total	8,000,000

To protect against forecast error, Gala management desires to hold 400,000 yards in safety stock. Management desires to hold this inventory as greige goods (i.e., prior to dyeing) to maximize flexibility. Thus, dyeing and backing deliberately are designed to have excess capacity. The significance of this excess capacity will be clear later.

As Table 11-4 demonstrates, weaving is short a total of 643,200 yards of carpet during the months of May, June, July, August, and September. Weaving capacity is found by multiplying the hourly capacity (1,000 yards per hour) by the hours available in a month. Hours available in a month are total monthly hours minus time lost to setup. We chose for this example 12 one-hour setups at weaving. For January, there are 744 hours in the month (31×24) less 12 hours spent in setup equals 732 hours available. Thus, weave capacity for January is 732,000 yards. Weave capacity for February is 660,000 yards: $(24 \times 28 - 12) \times 1,000$ [(24 hours/day $\times$ 28 days $-$ 12 hours for setup) $\times$ 1,000 yards/hour]. And so on.

It is necessary to build anticipation inventory in advance of the seasonal peak to offset the shortfall. Since the capacity shortfall totals 643,200 yards, precisely this amount of anticipation inventory must be built by the end of April. To limit holding cost, this inventory will be built as late as possible. Thus, all of April's surplus is committed first. April's surplus is found by subtracting demand from capacity. Table 11-5 shows the computation of surplus capacity for the months of January through April.

The total anticipation inventory that can be built prior to April is 565,600 yards. Since the shortfall for May to September is 643,200 yards, Gala is 77,600 yards short. Fortunately, sufficient safety stock (400,000 yards) exists to cover this shortfall, otherwise the master schedule would be infeasible. Further, safety stock is reduced by 77,600 yards due to our inability to build enough

Table 11-4
Total Carpet Demand, Available Weaving Capacity,
Weaving Capacity Shortfall, Gala Carpet

Month	Demand	Capacity*	Shortfall
1	466,400	732,000	0
2	533,600	660,000	0
3	600,000	732,000	0
4	666,400	708,000	0
5	733,600	732,000	1,600
6	866,400	720,000	146,400
7	933,600	732,000	201,600
8	933,600	732,000	201,600
9	800,000	708,000	92,000
10	600,000	732,000	0
11	466,400	708,000	0
12	400,000	732,000	0
Total	8,000,000	8,628,000	643,200

Capacity data is based on 12 setups per month.

Table 11-5
Total Carpet Demand, Available Capacity, Capacity
Shortfall, Capacity Surplus, Gala Carpet

Month	Demand	Capacity*	Shortfall	Surplus
1	466,400	732,000	0	265,600
2	533,600	660,000	0	126,400
3	600,000	732,000	0	132,000
4	666,400	708,000	0	41,600
5	733,600	732,000	1,600	
6	866,400	720,000	146,400	
7	933,600	732,000	201,600	
8	933,600	732,000	201,600	
9	800,000	708,000	92,000	
10	600,000	732,000	0	
11	466,400	708,000	0	
12	400,000	732,000	0	
Total	8,000,000	8,628,000	643,200	565,600

Capacity data is based on 12 setups per month.

anticipation inventory. Table 11-6 shows the MPS for weaving for 1990 and
the inventory available at the end of each month. Figure 11-4 illustrates the
buildup and consumption of anticipation inventory.

We can see from Table 11-6 that safety stock at the end of August, the
month with highest demand, is 414,000, approximately the desired level of

Table 11-6
Total Carpet Demand, Available Capacity, Capacity Shortfall,
Capacity Surplus, and Ending Inventory, Gala Carpet, 1990

Month	Demand	Production*	Shortfall	Surplus	Inventory
					400,000
1	466,400	732,000	0	265,600	665,600
2	533,600	660,000	0	126,400	792,000
3	600,000	732,000	0	132,000	924,000
4	666,400	708,000	0	41,600	965,600
5	733,600	732,000	1,600		964,000
6	866,400	720,000	146,400		817,600
7	933,600	732,000	201,600		616,000
8	933,600	732,000	201,600		414,400
9	800,000	708,000	92,000		322,400
10	600,000	677,600	0	77,600	400,000
11	466,400	466,400	0		400,000
12	400,000	400,000	0		400,000
Total	8,000,000	8,000,000	643,200	643,200	

Capacity data is based on 12 setups per month.

Figure 11-4
Building and Consuming Anticipation Inventory

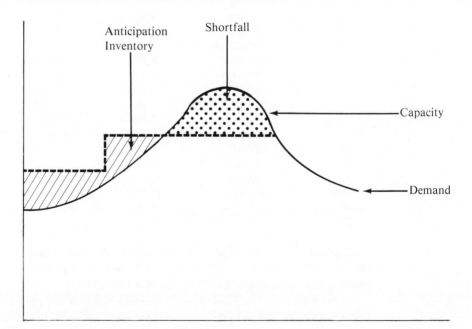

400,000 yards. By the end of September, it dips to 322,400, which is too low. If demand runs 5 percent above the forecast level, ending inventory could reach 0. The lack of safety stock in September may be offset somewhat by surplus capacity in October—some customers might be persuaded to take partial shipments in September. At any rate, if more safety stock is needed in the future it cannot be built prior to October. Safety stock is restored to 400,000 in October. Based on the 1990 forecast, Gala management are considering a proposal to increase the MPS in October to December in order to end 1990 with some anticipation inventory for May to September, 1991.

Allocating the MPS to Specific Products. The MPS for Gala Carpet is expressed in terms of the entire family of weaves. The MPS may be expressed in specific weaves by prorating by historical product mix. As previously mentioned, current product is 60 percent O1, 30 percent H1, and 10 percent H2. Ideally, the 400,000 yards of greige goods held at the end of December should follow the same proportions, 240,000 yards of O1, 120,000 yards of H1, and 40,000 yards of H2. If the product mix shifts, the weave schedule may be modified so the actual MPS may reflect slightly different percentages. Since lead times for raw materials are only a few days, the MPS can readily be adjusted without upsetting material availability.

MPS Horizon Length. Since total lead time is measured in a few days to weeks, one may wonder why the MPS is stated 12 months into the future. The answer is that when the product has seasonal demand and when capacity is inadequate to meet peak demand, the MPS planning horizon needs to be one full year to permit proper planning of anticipation stock.

Run Length. There are several ways run length can be determined. Given that a one-hour setup has a small direct cost and that holding cost of a week's output (165,000 yards of undyed carpet) is substantial, it seems 12 setups per month—running each of the three weaves once a week—is too few setups. If more setups were made the batch sizes would be smaller. According to traditional theory, holding costs would be reduced.

In this instance, however, most of the inventory held is anticipation inventory, due to the fact that weaving cannot meet demand during the peak season. If Gala were to set up weaving more frequently, weaving would lose capacity. The loss of capacity would reduce the quantity available in September. As it is, September's projected ending inventory is below safety stock. October's weaving would have to be increased to offset this loss of capacity. More anticipation inventory would be needed. The anticipation inventory would not be sold until the following September. Thus, in reality, smaller batch sizes in this case lead to more inventory holding costs.

The current process used by Gala is not ideal. Since the safety stock of greige goods represents at least a two-week supply, Gala could gain capacity by going to 6 setups per month, rather than 12. The 54 setups saved from January to September represent 54,000 yards of output. It is also useful to minimize time spent on a single setup at a bottleneck, since setup time represents lost system capacity. Shingo (1985), inventor of the Single Minute Exchange of Dies technique, has a number of useful tips for minimizing setup time. Some setup reduction techniques are discussed in Chapter 17.

Control of Purchasing.   Purchasing of manufactured fiber is fairly routine. Purchasing of cotton, wool, and other natural fibers is somewhat more complicated, because these fibers are subject to limited growing seasons, highly variable year-to-year prices, uneven quality, and other sources of variability not present in manufactured products. In order not to lose the focus of our discussion, we choose to ignore these subtleties. It is possible to develop a bill of material relating the number of pounds (or fractional pounds) of each fiber required to produce a yard of cloth. There is one bill of material for each weave type. Since the specific weave to be used is known only a few days in advance, it is possible to use a super bill representing a "typical" yard of cloth to plan material purchase well into the future. The technique for producing a super bill for a "typical" yard of cloth is identical to the procedure used to produce a super bill for a "typical" boiler.

Subassembly Scheduling

In the Gala example, dyeing represents a subassembly operation, since all dyed carpet must go through a backing operation (final assembly) before it can be sold. There is only a single dyeing area, and it requires extensive cleaning whenever colors are changed. For this reason, Gala prefers to run one color of dye for all weave styles prior to changing colors. Therefore, dyeing must have an inventory of undyed carpet staged between the weaving and dyeing operations. Monthly capacity in the dyeing area is shown in Table 11-7. Because of the large supply of greige goods stocked year round, the dyeing area can be scheduled independently of weaving. To generalize from this example, whenever the MPS is done below the end item level, higher levels usually are planned independently to provide prompt response to the market. To enable this prompt response, the MPS must provide for continuous availability of the components it plans.

   In this example, the dyeing area also is a bottleneck because it has insufficient capacity during June, July, and August, totaling a 231,600 yard shortage. As shown in Table 11-7, anticipation inventory is built during April and May to meet peak demand. When Gala management reviewed the initial subassembly schedule, they perceived a need to move some safety stock from greige goods to dyed goods. If the forecast should be 5 percent low, lack of dyeing capacity could severely limit sales. The downside risk is that one may misguess product mix; there are 15 dyed, unbacked goods and only 3 greige goods. Gala attempts to avoid this danger by building safety stock only in the two or three most popular color-weave combinations.

Table 11-7
Demand, Initial Subassembly Schedule, Initial
Anticipation Inventory, Gala Carpet, 1990

Month	Demand	Capacity Available	Capacity Scheduled	Anticipation Inventory
1	466,400	843,600	466,400	
2	533,600	757,200	533,600	
3	600,000	843,600	600,000	
4	666,400	814,800	788,000	121,600
5	733,600	843,600	843,600	231,600
6	866,400	814,800	814,800	180,000
7	933,600	843,600	843,600	90,000
8	933,600	843,600	843,600	
9	800,000	814,800	800,000	
10	600,000	843,600	600,000	
11	466,400	814,800	466,400	
12	400,000	843,600	400,000	

Again to generalize from this example, whenever anticipation inventory is built, management must not only decide how much anticipation inventory to hold but also what specific part numbers to hold. Most companies choose to build stocks of fast moving items in order to minimize the time the material must be held and to minimize the risk of not selling all the inventory built in anticipation of peak demand.

As shown in Table 11-8, O1GR prepresents 36 percent of total demand, H1GR represents 18 percent, and O1BR represents 12 percent. Gala decided to add 200,000 yards to the January to March dyeing schedule in order to hold some safety stock through the peak months as dyed goods rather than as greige goods. The inventory of dyed goods safety stock is divided among the three most popular products.

Table 11-8
Product Mix, Dyed, Unbacked Goods, Gala Carpet

	Gray	Brown	Blue	Off-White	Red
Office 1	0.36	0.12	0.06	0.03	0.03
Home 1	0.18	0.06	0.03	0.015	0.015
Home 2	0.06	0.02	0.01	0.005	0.005

Table 11-9 shows the revised subassembly schedule, revised dyed goods inventory, and revised greige goods inventory.

Determining Product Mix at the Dyeing Operation. In general, the quantity of any product to be produced during a given month can be obtained by multiplying demand for that month (such as in Table 11-9) by the historical demand

Table 11-9
Demand, Initial Subassembly Schedule, Initial
Anticipation Inventory, Gala Carpet, 1990

Month	Demand	Subassembly Schedule	Dyed Goods Inventory	Greige Goods Inventory
1	466,400	566,400	100,000	565,600
2	533,600	633,600	200,000	592,000
3	600,000	700,000	300,000	624,000
4	666,400	788,000	421,600	544,000
5	733,600	843,600	531,600	432,400
6	866,400	814,800	480,000	337,600
7	933,600	843,600	390,000	226,000
8	933,600	843,600	300,000	214,400
9	800,000	700,000	200,000	122,400
10	600,000	600,000	200,000	200,000
11	466,400	466,400	200,000	200,000
12	400,000	400,000	200,000	200,000

proportion (Table 11-8). Thus, the amount of 01-Red to run during January is 466,400 yards $\times$ 0.03 = 13,992 yards, or 14,000 yards since carpet is cut into 100 yard rolls. However, when inventory is being increased or decreased, the quantity to produce of items affected by this change must be computed differently. For 01-Gray for January, Gala produces 167,900 yards to meet demand. Gala must also add 100,000 yards to total dyed goods inventory. This inventory is to be apportioned among O1GR, H1GR, and O1BR. There are many ways to divide these 100,000 yards. Gala elected to prorate by historical demand proportion among the three. Since O1GR historically accounts for 36 percent of sales, H1GR 18 percent, and 01BR 12 percent, O1GR gets $\frac{36}{36 + 18 + 12}$ = 54.5 percent of the 100,000 yards or 54,500 yards. Adding the 54,500 yards of safety stock to the 167,900 yards anticipated demand yields a total of 222,400 yards of O1GR to be produced in January. A similar process is used on all other dyed, unbacked goods.

Determining the Dyeing Sequence.   The dyeing operation experiences one problem not experienced by weaving—sequence-dependent setup times. The old color must be removed before the new color can be run. The thoroughness of cleaning is a function of how colors react. For example, changing from red to off-white requires a much more thorough cleaning than changing from off-white to red. Table 11-10 gives the time to setup for one color given the present color.

Sequence-Dependent Setups.   Sequence-dependent setups are quite common in process industries and also in discrete parts manufacturing operations, such as painting. Therefore, a discussion of sequence-dependent setup times is appropriate. Whenever sequence-dependent setup times exist, a common approach

Table 11-10
Sequence-Dependent Setup Time, Dyeing

		To				
		Gray	Brown	Blue	Off-White	Red
	Gray	0	2	2	4	3
	Brown	1	0	2	2	2
From	Blue	1	3	0	4	3
	Off-White	1	1	1	0	1
	Red	2	3	3	4	0

Setup Time, Hours

to scheduling is to follow a fixed sequence that minimizes the sum of all setup times. In this example, dyeing would go from one color, through all other colors, and back to the original. This type of problem is known as a *traveling salesman* problem because it was first studied in the context of a salesman who regularly must leave home, travel to several locations, and return home. Solution techniques for the traveling salesman problem are beyond the scope of this text but may be found in any management science text and many production and operations management texts, including Fogarty, Hoffmann, and Stonebraker (1989).

The sequence Gala Carpet uses is GR → BR → OW → RE → BL → GR, with setup times of 2, 2, 1, 3, and 1 hours for a total of 9 hours per set of colors. Each month, Gala goes through the sequence 4 times for a total of 36 hours per month to switch between colors.

Major-Minor Setups.   Once the dyeing area is set up to dye carpet a color, all three weaves will be dyed that color. Changing between O1 weave and H1 weave requires 10 minutes. Changing from H1 to H2 requires 5 minutes. Changes from H2 back to O1 are always done while the dyeing area is being cleaned for a new color and, thus, do not increase setup time. Thus, each of the five colors requires 15 minutes for changing weaves, for a total of 75 minutes. Multiplying 75 minutes per set of colors times 4 sets per month yields 300 minutes or 5 hours. Adding this to the 36 hours previously established for cleaning means that Gala requires an average of 41 hours per month for setup.

The preceeding paragraph illustrates a common manufacturing occurrence known as *major-minor setup*. This refers to a situation in which once a major setup is performed for any member of a family, other members of that family can be run with only minor setups between them. Whenever this situation occurs, it is generaly useful to run an entire family in sequence before switching to the next family. The master scheduler should be aware of all such relationships when setting the master schedule.

Because there is only one loom, which makes quite long runs of one weave style, all three weaves must be stocked as greige goods at all times so that dyeing may operate independently from weaving. The need for greige goods inventory to keep dyeing in operation dictates that at least 100,000 yards of the safety stock be held as greige goods rather than dyed, unbacked carpet.

Setups at Nonbottleneck Operations.   During the period of May to August, dyeing is a bottleneck. A *bottleneck* is any operation that must run 24 hours a day, 7 days a week, to maintain sales. Because any nonproductive time at weaving will result in lost sales (or, at best, sales deferred to September if the customer is willing to wait beyond the peak season), Gala must be very diligent about scheduling the dyeing area. No high priority jobs are permitted to cause a deviation from schedule. During most of this period, Gala holds a large inventory of dyed, unbacked goods, so rush orders usually can be handled by applying a backing to the appropriate dyed carpet.

During the off-peak season, however, dyeing is not a bottleneck. If a large order comes in that cannot be handled from finished goods inventory or through backing already dyed carpet, Gala does not hesitate to break the sequence in the dyeing area. Because slight color differences are inevitable between different dye runs, Gala always fills any order from a single dye run. It is possible, therefore, that an order may arrive for which Gala has enough of the appropriate item, but not enough of one dye run.

It is instructive at this point to consider the real cost of breaking the dyeing sequence. Suppose Gala is running off-white, which would ordinarily be followed by red. A rush order for 5,000 yards of blue carpet is received that cannot be filled from finished goods or dyed goods. Gala could reverse red and blue for this sequence, running OW → BL → RE → GR instead of the usual OW → RE → BL → GR. The three setups are 1, 3, and 2 hours rather than 1, 3, and 1 hour. Thus, one hour is lost to setup. If the lost hour occurs during a month in which Gala has some idle time anyway, what does the setup cost Gala? What would losing the order cost?

Since the cleaning is performed by dyeing personnel, who are employed full time, the setup really costs Gala little. What would the dyeing crew be doing during this time otherwise? In a really well organized shop, they would be performing routine maintenance, cross-training for other tasks, or meeting to consider ways to improve operations in their area. In most cases, however, the workers are likely to be idle. Because dyeing is slightly faster than weaving, the dyeing operation must be idle at times while waiting for weaving. Gala management is far-sighted to use a portion of this time for additional setups in order to be more responsive to market conditions. They must, of course, take care not to turn a nonbottleneck into a bottleneck by breaking too many setups.

Final Assembly Scheduling and Finished Goods Inventory

Gala's finished goods inventory policy varies by ABC classification. For A items, one week's forecast demand is held as safety stock. A items are produced every week. For B items, whenever stock on hand falls below 3,000 yards,

5,000 yards are ordered. For C items, whenever stock on hand falls below 1,000 yards, 3,000 yards are ordered. This policy reflects the following considerations:

1. The distribution of order size is as shown in Table 11-11 and is independent of the specific item ordered.
2. Customers expect immediate delivery on the most popular items. For less popular items they expect delivery within three days for large orders and immediate delivery for small orders.
3. All orders for a given color must be shipped from one dye lot. Therefore, when an item is backed, at least 3,000 yards are backed so that many orders for B and C items can be shipped from existing stock.
4. The backing operation is never a bottleneck. Idle periods are scheduled every week, ideally every day, so that orders that cannot be filled from stock can quickly be backed and shipped.
5. Every order is filled at the highest possible level, i.e., from finished goods if possible; by backing if sufficient dyed, unbacked goods exist; by dyeing and backing as a last resort. During most of the year contingency idle time is master scheduled at the dyeing operation. During the peak period, when dyed, unbacked carpet inventory is on the order of 500,000 yards, a minimum of 5,000 yards is held in each of the 15 dye/weave combinations. This means a large order for a B or C item can be met by using contingency idle time at the backing operation.

Table 11-11
Distribution of Sales by Length of Carpet Purchased

Quantity x	Probability $p(x)$	$x \times p(x)$	$\Sigma p(x)$
100	0.05	5	0.05
300	0.10	30	0.15
500	0.20	100	0.35
1,000	0.30	300	0.65
2,000	0.20	400	0.85
3,000	0.10	300	0.95
5,000	0.05	250	1.00
Total	1.00	1,385	

Table 11-12 shows Gala's finished goods inventory as of January 1, 1990. Gala is about to begin processing gray carpet through the dyeing and backing areas. In order to minimize the need for dyed, unbacked carpet, the backing operation generally follows the same sequence as the dyeing operation.

Among the A items, current inventory typically varies from approximately a one-week supply (the safety stock level) for items next on the schedule for backing to approximately a two-week supply for items that just have been

Table 11-12
Finished Goods Inventory, Gala Carpet, January 1, 1990

	% Sales	Inventory	Forecast
A Items			
01GRB1	25.2	25,000	26,600
O1GRB2	10.8	12,000	11,400
H1GRB1	12.6	16,000	13,300
H1GRB2	5.4	8,000	5,700
H2GRB1	4.2	7,000	4,400
O1BRB1	8.4	10,000	8,900
O1BRB2	3.6	7,000	3,800
H1BRB1	4.2	8,800	4,400
O1BLB1	4.2	8,800	4,400
B Items			
H2GRB2	1.8	6,000	
H1BRB2	1.8	4,000	
H1BRB1	1.4	2,000	
O1BLB2	1.8	5,000	
H1BLB1	2.1	2,000	
O1OWB1	2.1	6,000	
O1REB1	2.1	3,000	
C Items			
H2BRB2	0.6	2,500	
H1BLB2	0.9	800	
H2BLB1	0.7	1,500	
H2BLB2	0.3	2,800	
O1OWB2	0.9	700	
H1OWB1	1.05	1,400	
H1OWB2	0.45	2,000	
H2OWB1	0.35	3,300	
H2OWB2	0.15	2,800	
O1REB2	0.9	1,200	
H1REB1	1.05	900	
H1REB2	0.45	2,100	
H2REB1	0.35	1,500	
H2REB2	0.15	800	

backed. Gala rotates A items through the backing operation in the sequence shown in Table 11-12. Note that O1GRB1, the item to be run next, is down to approximately its safety stock level. The item just completed at backing, O1BLB1, has precisely two weeks of forecast demand.

Among the B items, three have reached their reorder point (3,000 yards) and have been scheduled for production this week: H1BRB1, H1BLB1, and O1REB1. Among the C items, four are below their reorder points and will be produced this week: H1BLB2, O1OWB2, H1REB1, and H2REB2.

In order to understand the final assembly schedule, we must first examine the subassembly schedule for the week, shown in Figure 11-5. In Figure 11-5 the week is divided into 7 days, or 168 hours. Gray is about to be run. Because the dyeing operation has less than 168 hours of work, four contingency idle periods, denoted C1, C2, C3, and C4, are scheduled. If a large order arrives that cannot be filled at higher levels, these contingency idle periods will be used. Otherwise, the dyeing area will be idle and the operators will be engaged in training or other activities. The dyeing sequence shown in Figure 11-5 deviates from the usual sequence to avoid losing an order.

Figure 11-5
Subassembly Sequence with Contingency Periods

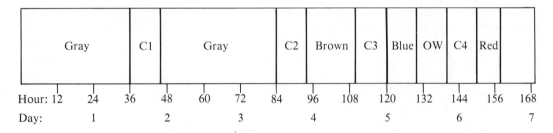

In developing a schedule for backing, the scheduler works with the time dyeing completes a color requirement rather than its start time. Because backing is faster than dyeing (1,500 yards/hour compared to 1,200 yards/hour), if backing started a color when the material was first available from the dyeing operation, the backing operation would frequently have short delays waiting for the next roll of material. Thus, there is an interval of 20 hours, more or less, before the backing operation needs to begin work on gray. We noted from Table 11-12 that three B items and four C items need to be produced. The scheduler begins with some of these, then shifts to gray A items when the dyeing operation completes dyeing gray. The scheduler reserves daily contingency idle periods for the backing operation.

Because B and C items are not backed every week, dyed goods inventory accumulates. This inventory permits rapid response to large orders for slower moving inventory. Gala's dyed carpet inventory as of January 1, 1990, is shown in Table 11-13. The final assembly scheduler must verify that sufficient dyed, unbacked carpet is in stock before scheduling B or C items. The final assembly (backing) schedule is shown in Table 11-14. You may wish to verify that sufficient inventory exists (or will exist) to meet this schedule. (In performing this verification, you will observe that the dyeing area and backing area will need to coordinate the proper weave type sequence in dyeing.)

Thus, Gala Carpet is a hybrid of assemble-to-stock, make components and subassemblies to stock and assemble-to-order and make components to stock and subassemble- and assemble-to-order.

Table 11-13
Dyed Goods Inventory, Gala Carpet, January 1, 1990

Item	Inventory
O1GR	10,000
H1GR	8,000
H2GR	4,000
O1BR	6,000
H1BR	8,000
H2BR	9,000
O1BL	11,000
H1BL	9,000
H2BL	3,500
O1OW	6,000
H1OW	5,000
H2OW	4,500
O1RE	9,000
H1RE	5,000
H2RE	7,500

Table 11-14
Final Assembly Schedule, Gala Carpet, January 6-10, 1990

Item	Quantity	Finish Time (Cumulative)
H2BRB1	5,000	4
H1BLB1	5,000	8
O1REB1	5,000	12
Contingency		22
O1GRB1	27,000	40
O1GRB2	12,000	48
Contingency		58
H1BLB2	3,000	61
O1OWB2	3,000	63
O1REB1	3,000	65
H2REB1	3,000	67
Contingency		77
H1GRB1	16,000	88
H1GRB2	6,000	92
H2GRB1	4,400	95
Contingency		105
O1BRB1	9,000	111
O1BRB2	4,000	114
H1BRB1	4,400	117
Contingency		132
O1BLB1	4,400	135
Contingency		168

MRP IN ASSEMBLE-TO-ORDER ENVIRONMENTS

A firm operates in an assemble-to-order mode whenever the time a customer is willing to wait for delivery is greater than the time required to assemble the product from components but is less than the time required to fabricate the components and assemble the product. A firm operates in a make-to-order mode whenever the customer is willing to wait the entire manufacturing lead time for the product. Most assemble-to-order firms have an hourglass bill of material. (See Figure 11-1C.) An hourglass bill of material is a complex assembly, made from a few major subassemblies that in turn are made from a number of components. The hourglass bill of material usually arises from the number of different ways one can combine modules to produce an end item. There are virtually an infinite number of ways to configure a car from a small number of possible chassis, body style, body color, engine, transmission, and interior option configurations. A customer usually is willing to wait a small amount of time provided he or she can specify precisely the combinations to be used in creating the end item. Because almost any item can be assembled in a short time, assembly lead time is short for almost all products. However, manufacturing lead time is usually quite long. It is therefore not surprising to find that most companies having hourglass-shaped bills of material operate assemble-to-order, and vice-versa.

There are exceptions to the correlation between hourglass-shaped bills and assemble-to-order. Sometimes a firm may purchase all components and simply assemble the end item, yielding an inverted bill of material. An example of such a product is a personal computer that is assembled from off-the-shelf components. There are a number of firms offering such PCs at prices substantially less than the name brands.

Let's examine a hypothetical firm, Athens Computers, that sells to small dealers. Athens Computers buys most component items, but it does build the computer case and some other subassemblies. As the example should make clear, Athens Computers has the typical hourglass shape and operates in an assemble-to-order fashion. The dealers to whom Athens Computers sells usually are willing to wait no more than four weeks for delivery, but will occasionally place small orders up to eight weeks in advance. Athens offers three basic computers, based on the Intel 8088, 80286, and 80386 chips. Athens purchases motherboards from a Taiwanese firm that makes motherboards of identical size so any board will fit a standard case. Each motherboard has 8 expansion slots, all accepting 16-bit boards. Athens chose this configuration to minimize the number of optional boards that must be carried in stock. Standard parts for any computer are the case, a 5.25″ high density drive, 1Mb of 120 nanosecond memory chips to be inserted on the motherboard, a controller board, a monitor board (capable of handling monochrome, EGA, or VGA monitors), a fan, and a cabling kit.

Optional features are as follows:

> Monitor (monochrome, EGA, VGA)
> Keyboard (standard, enhanced)
> Second floppy disk drive (3.5″) or none
> Hard disk (20Mb, 30Mb, 40Mb, 70Mb) or none
> Motherboard (8088, 80286, 80386)

All customers must specify which monitor, keyboard, and motherboard combination(s) are desired. As noted, the hard disk and second floppy disk options may be omitted. This results in 180 possible configurations of PC, since the options may be selected in any configuration. Orders from dealers must be for a minimum of 5 units and sometimes are as large as 50 units. A dealer will occasionally order as many as 10 identically configured machines.

Athens Computers cannot afford to operate as a make-to-stock vendor. To do so would require stocking perhaps 2,000 assembled computers, each having an average cost of approximately $1,000, for a total of $2,000,000 finished goods inventory. In addition to any finished goods inventory, Athens Computers must carry a sufficient inventory of components to keep the assembly line busy. By operating on an assemble-to-order basis, Athens is able to operate with only a small inventory of purchased components and little finished goods inventory.

Like many assemble-to-order operations, Athens can quickly add capacity simply by hiring more assemblers. Training of assembly workers is minimal. Athens' problem is maintaining a sufficient quantity of components for assembly. Suppose, for example, Athens receives an order for 50 PCs: 25 are for 8088 motherboards, monochrome monitors, standard keyboards; 15 are for 80286 motherboards, EGA monitors, enhanced keyboards, 30Mb hard disks; 10 are for 80386 motherboards (5 VGA and 5 EGA monitors), enhanced keyboards, 3.5″ floppy drives, 70Mb hard drives. Athens finds they have only 5 70Mb hard disks in stock and that acquiring the additional 5 hard disks will require a wait of 20 to 30 days because the supplier is backordered. In this situation, the customer will likely decide to acquire all 10 80386 machines from another source in order to keep identical machines (dealers often act as agents for small businesses; all 10 machines may be destined for one of the dealer's customers). There is even some likelihood that Athens will lose the order for all 50 machines due to the lack of 5 hard disks.

Bill of Material Development

In order to avoid situations such as the one just described, assemble-to-order operations often overplan components. This overplanning can be done by using a planning bill as discussed in Chapter 4, except that the proportions for all components add to a number greater than 1. For example, suppose that Athens' historical product mix for motherboards has been 50 percent 8088, 30 percent 80286, and 20 percent 80386. The proportions for these three boards shown on the planning bill might be 0.55, 0.33, and 0.22, respectively. Note that the three proportions add to 1.1.

Suppose Athens plans to order components for 100 PCs. They would order 55 8088 motherboards, 33 80286 motherboards, and 22 80386 motherboards, a total of 110 in all. Suppose the actual orders turned out to be 46 8088 machines, 32 80286 machines and 22 80386 machines. Athens would be left with 10 motherboards (9 8088s and 1 80286) that can be netted out in placing a replacement order. Had they been using a standard planning bill, Athens would have ordered only 30 80286s and 20 80386s. As a result, they would have lost orders for at least 4 machines, and possibly other orders tied to those machines. Overplanning provides a safety stock of components. The planning bill used by Athens Computer is shown in Figure 11-6.

Master Production Scheduling

If the purpose of overplanning is to provide safety stock, why not merely specify safety stock at the component level? MRP will permit this although it is not recommended practice. The reason overplanning is preferred is that as actual orders consume the master production schedule, orders for actual part numbers replace forecasts for the planning bill. As this occurs, an order for 1 specific motherboard replaces the planning bill's demand for 1.1 motherboards. In a typical situation there are orders for specific machines consuming most of the master schedule for several weeks, with booked orders diminishing as one moves farther into the planning horizon. As a consequence, the number of planning bills remaining on the master schedule increases with time, and the amount of overplanning also increases with time. Thus, there is very little overplanning in the near term, when orders are well known, and substantial overplanning in the longer term, where forecast accuracy begins to deteriorate. Let's consider a specific instance involving Athens Computers.

The daily demand for Athens Computers varies between 80 and 100 units, uniformly distributed. In the past, the product mix has been 50 percent 8088 machines, 30 percent 80286 machines, and 20 percent 80386 machines. A breakdown of orders for the coming four weeks is shown in Table 11-15. (To create this hypothetical example, demand was generated using random numbers. The number of units ordered, X, was generated, ranging from 80 to 100. Next, X random draws were made, each having a 50 percent probability of producing demand for one 8088, 30 percent probability of producing demand for one 80286, and 20 percent probability of producing demand for one 80386.)

Athens requests a four-week lead time, usually accepts reasonable orders with shorter lead time, and sometimes gets requests for as many as eight

Figure 11-6
Super, or Planning, Bill of Material, Athens Computers

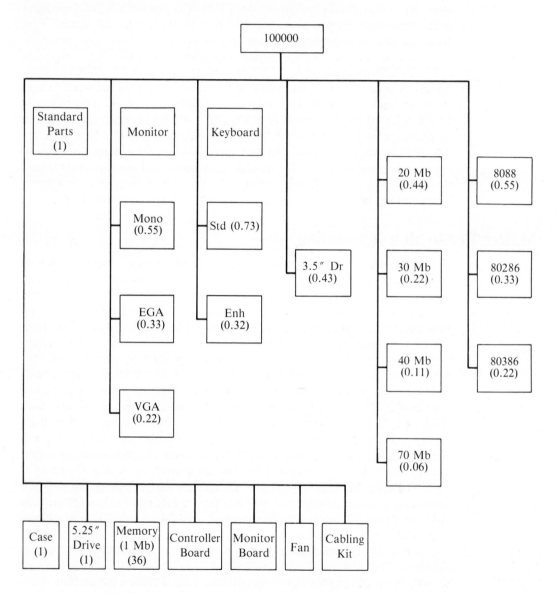

weeks into the future. Since total demand averages 450 units per week, Athens forecasts demand for 450 Part 100000s each week. Part 100000 is a planning bill whose bill of material (the planning bill) is shown in Figure 11-6. Athens also maintains phantom bills 100001, 100002, and 100003, that represent firm

Table 11-5
Demand and Assembly Schedule, Athens Computers,
by Type of Motherboard, by Week

| | Board Type | | |
	8088	80286	80386
Week 1			
Monday	44	29	11
Tuesday	53	27	19
Wednesday	37	25	25
Thursday	45	21	21
Friday	42	25	20
Total	221	127	96
Week 2			
Monday	52	28	18
Tuesday	44	34	22
Wednesday	41	22	21
Thursday	49	28	18
Friday	46	20	17
Total	232	132	96
Week 3			
Monday	53	18	14
Tuesday	44	29	18
Wednesday	42	29	18
Thursday	47	30	18
Friday	40	23	17
Total	226	129	85
Week 4			
Monday	50	26	15
Tuesday	44	22	17
Wednesday	40	33	14
Thursday	48	22	19
Friday	48	25	16
Total	230	128	81

orders for machines requiring the 8088, 80286, and 80386 motherboards, respectively. A phantom bill for part 100001 is simply:

100001 Phantom 8088
MB 8088 (1 each)

For the coming weeks, gross requirements for the four parts are as follows:

Part	Period 1	2	3	4	5	6	7	8	9
100000	6	0	10	11	213	300	403	437	450
100001	221	232	226	230	105	75	10	0	0
100002	127	132	129	128	78	43	22	5	0
100003	96	96	85	81	54	32	15	8	0

Recall that the gross requirement for Part 100000 is initialized to 450 each week, as per the forecast. When an order is accepted, a gross requirement is created for one of the three phantoms tied to a specific motherboard. At the same time, gross requirement for Part 100000 is reduced by 1 (except that the gross requirement for 100000 cannot be negative).

Material Requirements Planning

The full MRP report for the planning bill, the three phantoms, and the three motherboards is shown in Table 11-16. Note that as the period number increases, gross requirement for each of the three motherboards also generally increases, reflecting the added uncertainty caused by having to forecast farther into the future. Also note that Athens is able to meet demand over the entire horizon, provided that the scheduled receipts arrive as promised.

One row, labeled "Revised On Hand," has been added to the time-phased plan for each part. This row permits you to see the on-hand quantity before and after the planned receipt.

For a complex assembly having many components, the probability of being out of stock of any individual component must be kept very small. For example, if there are 50 individual components and the probability of having in stock any single component is 0.98 and is independent of the status of all other components, then the probability of having all 50 components in stock is 0.98 raised to the 50th power or approximately 0.364. Component overplanning provides an effective and relatively inexpensive way to ensure that any single component is available virtually 100 percent of the time.

The example given in this section is rich in detail and requires careful thought and study. The MRP report itself is a home-grown MRP system that Athens has implemented using an electronic spreadsheet. Such systems are quite feasible for small companies. The Revised On Hand row usually does not appear on MRP reports; it is necessary to avoid a circular logic error when MRP is performed using a spreadsheet. See Peek and Blackstone (1987) for further details of performing MRP netting on a spreadsheet.

Table 11-16
Material Requirements Planning, Fixed Period Ordering, Athens Computers

Item 100000
Periods to Order: 1; Lead Time: 0; Safety Stock: 0

					Period					
	0	1	2	3	4	5	6	7	8	9
Gross Requirements		6	0	10	11	213	300	403	437	450
Scheduled Receipts										
Projected On Hand	0	−6	0	−10	−11	−213	−300	−403	−437	−450
Net Requirements		6	0	10	11	213	300	403	437	450
Planned Receipts		6	0	10	11	213	300	403	437	450
Revised On Hand	0	0	0	0	0	0	0	0	0	0
Planned Releases		6	0	10	11	213	300	403	437	450

Item 100001
Periods to Order: 1; Lead Time: 0; Safety Stock: 0

					Period					
	0	1	2	3	4	5	6	7	8	9
Gross Requirements		221	232	226	230	105	75	10	0	0
Scheduled Receipts										
Projected On Hand	250	29	−203	−226	−230	−105	−75	−10	0	0
Net Requirements		0	203	226	230	105	75	10	0	0
Planned Receipts		0	203	226	230	105	75	10	0	0
Revised On Hand	250	29	0	0	0	0	0	0	0	0
Planned Releases		0	203	226	230	105	75	10	0	0

Item 100002
Periods to Order: 1; Lead Time: 0; Safety Stock: 0

					Period					
	0	1	2	3	4	5	6	7	8	9
Gross Requirements		127	132	129	128	78	43	22	5	0
Scheduled Receipts										
Projected On Hand	130	3	−129	−129	−128	−78	−43	−22	−5	0
Net Requirements		0	129	129	128	78	43	22	5	0
Planned Receipts		0	129	129	128	78	43	22	5	0
Revised On Hand	130	3	0	0	0	0	0	0	0	0
Planned Releases		0	129	129	128	78	43	22	5	0

Item 100003
Periods to Order: 1; Lead Time: 0; Safety Stock: 0

					Period					
	0	1	2	3	4	5	6	7	8	9
Gross Requirements		96	96	85	81	54	32	15	8	0
Scheduled Receipts										
Projected On Hand	100	4	−92	−85	−81	−54	−32	−15	−8	0
Net Requirements		0	92	85	81	54	32	15	8	0
Planned Receipts		0	92	85	81	54	32	15	8	0
Revised On Hand	100	4	0	0	0	0	0	0	0	0
Planned Releases		0	92	85	81	54	32	15	8	0

Table 11-16 (Continued)
Material Requirements Planning, Fixed Period Ordering, Athens Computers

Item MB 8088
Periods to Order: 4; Lead Time: 4; Safety Stock: 30

					Period					
	0	1	2	3	4	5	6	7	8	9
Gross Requirements		3	203	232	236	222	240	232	240	248
Scheduled Receipts			907							
Projected On Hand	50	47	751	519	283	61	−179	518	278	30
Net Requirements		0	0	0	0	0	209	0	0	0
Planned Receipts		0	0	0	0	0	929	0	0	0
Revised On Hand	50	47	751	519	283	61	750	518	278	30
Planned Releases	0	0	929	0	0	0	0	0	0	0

Item MB 80286
Periods to Order: 4; Lead Time: 4; Safety Stock: 20

					Period					
	0	1	2	3	4	5	6	7	8	9
Gross Requirements		2	129	132	132	148	142	155	149	149
Scheduled Receipts			553							
Projected On Hand	30	28	452	320	188	40	−102	318	169	20
Net Requirements		0	0	0	0	0	122	0	0	0
Planned Receipts		0	0	0	0	0	575	0	0	0
Revised On Hand	30	28	452	320	188	40	473	318	169	20
Planned Releases	0	0	575	0	0	0	0	0	0	0

Item MB 80386
Periods to Order: 4; Lead Time: 4; Safety Stock: 15

					Period					
	0	1	2	3	4	5	6	7	8	9
Gross Requirements		1	92	87	83	101	98	104	104	99
Scheduled Receipts			386							
Projected On Hand	20	19	313	226	143	42	−56	218	114	15
Net Requirements		0	0	0	0	0	71	0	0	0
Planned Receipts		0	0	0	0	0	378	0	0	0
Revised On Hand	20	19	313	226	143	42	322	218	114	15
Planned Releases	0	0	378	0	0	0	0	0	0	0

Final Assembly Scheduling

In Table 11-16, the gross requirement for 3 MB 8088s in Week 1 is derived from the planned release of 6 Part 100000s in Week 1. Recall that there are 0.55 MB 8088s per planning bill. If 6 additional (rush) orders are not accepted this week, the Week 1 requirement for Part 100000s will disappear and the available MB 8088s will be increased by 3. The gross requirement for 203 MB 8088s in Period 2 comes from 203 units actually ordered that require the 8088 motherboard. The 232 units of gross requirement for MB 8088 in Period 3 come from 226 actual orders and 10 planning bills (0.55×10, rounded up) that have not yet been consumed by actual orders. And so on.

Perhaps you're wondering why MB 8088 shows a safety stock of 30 units when overplanning is done. The answer is that overplanning protects only against variation in product mix. It is also possible for the forecast simply to be low. The safety stock is provided to guard against having too low a forecast and, hence, too few components in general. Of course, if the forecast is accurate, the safety stock provides additional buffer against product mix variation.

Note that MB 80286 and MB 80386 have patterns similar to that of MB 8088. In each case, the minimum projected on hand is somewhat more than the safety stock (except for the final period). The difference between the minimum on hand reached in each cycle and the desired safety stock represents the additional safety buffer created by overplanning. Of course, this overplanning adds to the carrying cost. The cost of providing the protection against product mix variation must be weighed against the cost of backordering or loss of sales caused by not having the stock.

MANUFACTURING RESOURCE PLANNING

Manufacturing resource planning is a concept that extends MRP to include financial functions. In brief, the evolution of MRP is as follows. First, MRP (material requirements planning) was used only to perform materials netting and lead-time offsetting. MRP thus indicated the quantity and timing of production orders and purchase orders. This first system is often called a "launch and forget" system, since there was initially no mechanism for updating MRP information on orders already released. Because the environment in which MRP often is used is very dynamic, i.e., because order quantity and due date changes are not infrequent, there exists a need to update order due date and order status after the order has been launched. Adding this feedback capability to MRP resulted in closed-loop MRP. Today, most systems are closed-loop systems, and the words "closed-loop" no longer need appear. When we hear MRP, we assume closed-loop MRP.

Next came the concept of adding financial functions, called *manufacturing resource planning* or MRP II. Material requirements planning is often called MRP I, little MRP, or mrp. The concept behind MRP II is that MRP should be able to provide virtually all the information financial management needs. MRP provides the timing of purchase orders and their due dates, from which we can easily predict when and how much we will pay various vendors. MRP, fed into the capacity planning system, provides information about staffing levels, overtime, and so on, needed to meet the schedule. From this information it should be possible to determine future payroll obligations. Finally, MRP provides information about the quantity and timing of materials delivered to customers. From this, we should be able to predict receivables with great accuracy.

The reality of manufacturing resource planning is that financial managers, as a general rule, have not accepted MRP II information as being sufficiently accurate. They have rejected the information with good justification—delivery performance under MRP II simply has not been good enough for complete reliability. Also, capacity information tends to be poor because of outdated standard times and, thus, the payroll predictions are not all that accurate. Financial managers demand greater accuracy than MRP II has been able to deliver, because they insist on managing cash very carefully. They desire to keep any excess cash in instruments such as short term Treasury Bills or Certificates of Deposit and, therefore, require accurate information concerning the quantity and timing of cash requirements.

To illustrate how MRP II can be used for predicting cash flows, consider the MRP data given in the Athens Computer example. Let's simplify this example by assuming that only one standard configuration is sold for each motherboard type and that all components except the motherboard are purchased for a cost of $500, regardless of the type of computer, with a two-day lead time. Motherboards sell for $250 for an 8088 board, $750 for an 80286 board, and $1,250 for an 80386 board. Completed computers sell for $1,000 for an 8088 machine, $2,000 for an 80286 machine, and $3,000 for an 80386 machine. Athens employs 20 assemblers, each of whom averages 2 hours to assemble a computer. Athens pays the assemblers $12 per hour plus time and a half for any overtime beyond 40 hours per week. Employees are paid weekly. White collar employees and other overhead average $80,000 per week with little variation. Let's look at the MRP schedule and predict cash flows.

Table 11-17 is constructed as follows: The forecast for computer sales is 450 total units per week. The forecast and other sales data referenced in this discussion are found in Table 11-15. As orders are received, the forecast is decremented. The forecast for Model 8088 units includes actual orders incorporating the Model 8088 motherboard plus 50 percent of any unconsumed forecast. The forecast for Model 80826 units includes actual orders plus 30 percent of unconsumed forecast. The forecast for Model 80386 units is actual orders plus 20 percent of unconsumed forecast.

Projected income in Table 11-17 is found by multiplying the sales forecast times the unit price. There are 224 units of Model 8088 forecast in Week 1, which is multiplied times $1,000; there are 129 units of Model 80286, which is multiplied by $2,000; and there are 97 units forecast of Model 80386, which is multiplied by $3,000. The sum of these products yields the projected income of $773,000 in Week 1.

Projected expense in Table 11-17 breaks down as follows. Assembly cost is $9,600 per week (20 workers × 40 hours × $12 per worker hour) for the first 400 units plus $36 for each unit assembled over 400 in a week. The $36 unit cost is found by multiplying the two-hour assembly time by the $12 hourly cost times 1.5 for overtime. The $80,000 weekly overhead is fixed. This includes assembly worker benefits, all nondirect labor, management salaries, building expense, etc. Motherboards are paid COD at the cost of $250 for an 8088,

Table 11-17
Income and Expense Predictions, Athens Computers

	Period								
	1	2	3	4	5	6	7	8	9
Sales Forecasts									
8088	224	232	231	236	212	225	212	219	225
80286	129	132	132	131	142	133	143	136	135
80386	97	96	87	83	97	92	96	95	90
Projected Income	$773,000	$784,000	$756,000	$747,000	$787,000	$767,000	$786,000	$776,000	$765,000
Projected Expense									
Assembly Cost	$ 10,500	$ 10,680	$ 10,500	$ 10,500	$ 10,518	$ 10,500	$ 10,518	$ 10,500	$ 10,500
Overhead	80,000	80,000	80,000	80,000	80,000	80,000	80,000	80,000	80,000
Motherboards	0	1,124,000	0	0	0	1,136,000	0	0	0
Other Material	225,000	230,000	225,000	225,000	225,500	225,000	225,500	225,000	225,000
Total Expense	$315,500	$1,444,680	$315,500	$315,500	$316,018	$1,451,500	$316,018	$315,500	$315,500
Cash Flow	$457,500	$ −660,680	$440,500	$431,500	$470,982	$ −684,500	$469,982	$460,500	$449,500
Cumulative Cash	$457,500	$ −203,180	$237,320	$668,820	$1,139,802	$455,302	$925,284	$1,385,784	$1,835,284

$750 for an 80286, and $1,250 for an 80386. The quantity and timing of deliveries for motherboards is taken from Table 11-16. Other material is costed at $500 per unit during the week the unit is assembled (there is a two-day lead time for these items, purchased locally).

Cash flow for any week is Projected Income minus Total Expense. Cumulative Profit is the cumulative sum of the Cash Flow row. Note that for the nine-week horizon, projected profit is approximately $1.8 million. Also note, however, that every fourth week, when motherboards are delivered, there is a negative cash flow of approximately $660,000 for the week. The fact that some weeks have large positive cash flows and some weeks large negative cash flows explains the financial manager's concern that the quantity and timing of material receipts and finished goods deliveries be very accurate.

Many businesses exhibit what is known as the "end of the month" syndrome, i.e., a large percentage of monthly shipments are made at the end of the month. The end of the month syndrome is caused by the fact that managers are evaluated by how well they meet shipments on a monthly basis and by how well they meet machine utilization and efficiency targets on a total basis. Assume Weeks 4 and 9 represent the end of the month for Athens Computers. Then actual shipments, allowing for the end of the month syndrome might appear as shown in Table 11-18.

A comparison of the Cash Flow row in Table 11-17 with the Cash Flow row in Table 11-18 reveals that the actual Cash Flow shortfall in Weeks 2 and 6 is $932,600 and $893,600, respectively, more than $250,000 higher than projected. It is fairly obvious, then, that financial managers will not believe financial forecasts coming from the MRP system as long as the end of the month syndrome continues. On the other hand, the end of the month syndrome will not end as long as financial managers judge plant managers based on overall machine utilization and on monthly delivery performance. In other words, financial managers are not likely to start using MRP II data on a wide scale.

It is unfortunate that financial managers will continue to ignore MRP, because commitment from the financial and general managers is necessary for MRP implementation to fully succeed. Yet financial and general managers are unlikely to be as committed to MRP success as they should be unless they see a definite benefit to themselves from MRP implementation. Thus, we have a Catch-22 situation: Financial managers won't use the MRP data because of the end of the month syndrome, but the only practical way to end the end of the month syndrome is to get the financial managers to use the MRP data.

Because the financial aspects of MRP II have not occurred as expected, a number of people have begun using the term MRP II or manufacturing resource planning as though it simply meant closed-loop MRP. Most current references to MRP II are not consistent with the original definition of the term and make no mention of financial applications. While this situation is regrettable, it is not likely to change soon.

Table 11-18
Actual Income and Expense, Athens Computers

	Period								
	1	2	3	4	5	6	7	8	9
Actual Deliveries									
8088	150	140	190	443	105	140	180	232	436
80286	102	94	124	204	87	120	134	124	224
80386	67	64	89	143	54	59	67	88	202
Actual Income	$555,000	$520,000	$705,000	$1,280,000	$441,000	$557,000	$649,000	$744,000	$1,490,000
Actual Expense									
Assembly Cost	$ 9,600	$ 9,600	$ 9,654	$ 16,620	$ 9,600	$ 0	$ 9,600	$ 10,392	$ 17,916
Overhead	80,000	80,000	80,000	80,000	80,000	80,000	80,000	80,000	80,000
Motherboards	0	1,124,000	0	0	0	1,136,000	0	0	0
Other Material	225,000	230,000	225,000	225,000	225,500	225,000	225,500	225,000	225,000
Total Expense	$314,600	$1,443,600	$314,654	$321,620	$315,100	$1,450,600	$315,100	$315,392	$322,916
Cash Flow	$240,400	$−923,600	$390,346	$958,380	$125,900	$−893,600	$333,900	$428,608	$1,167,084
Cumulative Cash	$240,400	$−683,200	$−292,854	$665,526	$791,426	$−102,174	$231,726	$660,334	$1,827,418

EXERCISES

1. The management of Gala Carpet proposes to reduce labor cost by reducing the capacity of the dyeing and backing operations to that of weaving. This capacity reduction is to be achieved by working fewer hours in dyeing and backing than in weaving. Discuss the impact of this change to (1) anticipation inventory, (2) finished goods inventory, (3) work-in-process inventory, (4) raw material inventory, and (5) future sales. Do you agree with this proposal? Why or why not?

2. As a follow-up to Exercise 1, consider the following data regarding Gala Carpet:

   Annual sales: 8,000,000 yards
   Price per yard: $5.00, regardless of style or color
   Annual overhead (management and staff salaries and benefits, rent, utilities, insurance, etc): $15,000,000
   Annual direct labor cost: $2,500,000. A crew of five works each station (weaving, dyeing, backing), and there are four shifts, each working 42 hours/week, 52 weeks/year. All workers receive the same pay, about $14 per hour plus about $5.08 per hour in benefits.
   Raw material cost: $1 per yard of finished cloth
   Annual equipment depreciation: $2,500,000
   Annual marketing and distribution cost: $5,000,000
   Holding cost rate, inventory: 35 percent per year

   a. How much annual profit does Gala project for 1990, given the inventory levels projected in Tables 11-9, 11-12, and 11-13? Assume Table 11-12 is representative of finished goods inventory year round.
   b. How much profit would Gala project if they switched to the policy described in Exercise 1? State your assumptions regarding inventory, sales levels, and any other impact the policy would have on cost or income. In making this assessment, assume actual output from each process is normally distributed having a 30 percent deviation from the mean, measured on an hourly basis.

3. (Advanced) Simulate Exercises 2a and 2b and compare the actual results to your answers in Exercises 2a and 2b. What conclusions do you draw from these results?

4. Develop a detailed subassembly and final assembly schedule for Gala for July, 1990. Assume beginning inventory as of July 1, 1990, is as shown in Tables 11-9, 11-12, and 11-13.

5. Discuss the differences in operation between Gala Carpet and Athens Computers. What implications do these differences have on the way inventory is managed and the way production is scheduled at the two firms?

6. Athens' sole supplier of hard disks faces a labor contract expiration date in three months. Negotiations are not going well. The union has a strike fund that is anticipated to keep workers at 75 percent of normal pay for 45 days. Assume you're in charge of purchasing. What action should you take?

7. A carpet firm in Brazil faces peak demand during December, January, and February, summer months in the southern hemisphere. They propose to furnish 1,000,000 yards each of greige goods and backing material and to pay Gala $1.50 per yard to dye and back the carpet. The Brazilian firm will pay all transportation expense. Material is to be delivered at 250,000 yards per month during November to February. Should Gala accept the offer?

8. At Athens Computers, how can the cost of protecting against product mix shifts be lowered?

9. At Athens Computers, how can the cost of protecting against product mix shifts be avoided? Is that likely to be achieved in this instance?

10. Discuss ways to improve the performance of MRP systems as predictors of financial performance.

SELECTED READINGS

Bolander, Steven F., Richard C. Heard, Samuel M. Sward, and Sam G. Taylor. *Manufacturing Planning and Control in Process Industries*. Falls Church, VA: American Production and Inventory Control Society, 1981.

Davis, Edward W., ed. *Case Studies in Materials Requirement Planning*. Falls Church, VA: American Production and Inventory Control Society, 1986.

Finch, B. J. "Production Planning and Control in the Process Industries." Ph.D. diss., University of Georgia, 1986.

Finch, Byron J., and James F. Cox. *Planning and Control System Design: Principles and Cases for Process Manufacturers*. Falls Church, VA: American Production and Inventory Control Society, 1987.

Fogarty, Donald W., Thomas R. Hoffman, and Peter W. Stonebraker. *Production and Operations Management*. Cincinnati: South-Western Publishing Co., 1989.

Mather, Hal. *Bills of Material*. Homewood, IL: Dow Jones-Irwin, 1987.

Peek, L. E., and John H. Blackstone, Jr. "Developing a Time-phased Order-point Template Using a Spreadsheet." *Production and Inventory Management Journal* 28, no. 4 (1987): 6-10.

Shingo, Shigeo. *A Revolution in Manufacturing: The SMED System*. Cambridge, MA: Productivity Press, 1985.

Wight, Oliver W. *The Executive's Guide to Successful MRP II*. Essex Junction, VT: Oliver Wight Publications, Ltd., 1982.

Part
Four

Capacity
Management

12

ROUGH CUT
CAPACITY PLANNING

Capacity planning and control techniques were introduced briefly in Chapter 4. Material requirements planning (MRP) uses a master production schedule (MPS) of end items to determine the quantity and timing of component part production. MRP is capacity insensitive; it implicitly assumes that sufficient capacity is available to produce components at the time they're needed.

A problem commonly encountered in operating MRP systems is the existence of an overstated MPS. An overstated master production schedule is one that orders more production to be released than the shop can complete. An overstated MPS causes raw materials and WIP inventories to increase because more materials are purchased and released to the shop than are completed and shipped. It also causes a buildup of queues on the shop floor. Since jobs have to wait to be processed, actual lead times increase, causing ship dates to be missed. As lead times increase, forecast accuracy over the lead time diminishes because forecasts are more accurate for shorter periods than for longer ones. Thus, overstated master production schedules lead to missed due dates and other problems. Validating the MPS with respect to capacity is an extremely important step in MRP. This validation exercise has been termed rough cut capacity planning (RCCP).

There is no general agreement on the level of detail that should be incorporated in the MPS validation. An APICS monograph (Berry, Vollman, and Whybark 1979) presents case histories of several companies, including details on the capacity planning process. Some companies used very crude techniques, other used detailed, time-phased, methods. In this chapter, we examine the process of RCCP. First, we examine the role of RCCP in the overall production planning and control system. Then we look at three RCCP techniques and discuss the selection of a technique. Third, we examine the various decisions that are based on RCCP. Finally, we look at two alternative approaches to capacity management, line balancing under the Just-in-Time philosophy, and the drum-buffer-rope technique of the theory of constraints philosophy.

THE ROLE OF RCCP IN THE PRODUCTION PLANNING AND CONTROL SYSTEM

Figure 12-1 shows an overview of the entire production planning and control (PPC) process under MRP. Capacity management techniques usually are separated into four categories: resource requirements planning (RRP), rough cut capacity planning (RCCP), capacity requirements planning (CRP), and input/output control. These represent the four time horizons considered. In an MRP system the typical sequence is to create a master schedule, use rough cut capacity planning to verify that the MPS is feasible, perform the MRP explosion, and send planned order release data to capacity requirements planning. The sequence of our discussion will be (1) rough cut capacity planning (Chapter 12), (2) capacity requirements planning (Chapter 13), and (3) input/output control (Chapter 13).

Plossl and Welch (1979) describe the role RCCP plays in the overall PPC system:

> Production and inventory planning is the process of dealing with flexibility to meet the desires of the customer, the need for stability in manufacturing and the resultant inventory levels to compensate for the mismatch. The process involves performing three functions effectively:
>
> Developing an achievable Master Production Schedule.
> Planning and controlling priorities.
> Planning and controlling capacities.
>
> Priority Planning is the process of specifying batch quantities and their start and finish dates for all items where procurement and manufacture are involved.
>
> Priority Control is making the right things at the right time. It is completely dependent on maintaining a balance between master schedule [MPS] requirements and output rates. If the plant and its vendors do not produce enough in total, they will not be able to hold schedule for the right items.
>
> Capacity planning is the task of determining how much output is needed from plant facilities and from suppliers. If less-than-adequate capacity is available, the problem is unmanageable.
>
> Capacity control is the comparison between planned levels and actual outputs achieved and the identification of significant variances above or below plan. Corrective action must be initiated promptly if control is to be maintained, that usually means adjusting capacity, preferable in most cases to the alternative of changing the master schedule. . . .

In an MRP system, the functions of capacity planning and control are separated from the functions of priority planning and control. As Figure 12-1 illustrates, the capacity planning functions consist of resource requirements planning, rough cut capacity planning, and capacity requirements planning. Capacity control is usually performed by input/output control. Priority planning is the task of the MRP system. Priority control is determined on the shop floor by the use of a dispatching technique to sequence specific tasks on specific machines.

Figure 12-1
An Overview of Capacity Management

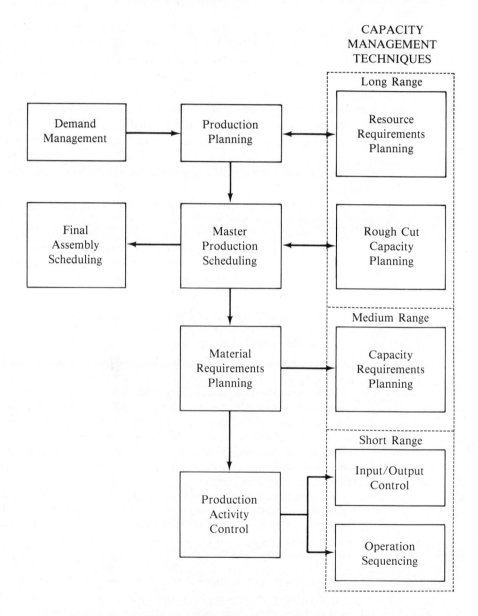

A common criticism of MRP is that it does not manage capacity well. This is a somewhat ironic criticism because few firms fully use the capacity management techniques described here. Two reasons that the techniques are not utilized are: (1) data requirements are quite high and (2) the process is designed to be iterative and, therefore, is time-consuming. A third reason is that many companies do not have a stable MPS. If the MPS is unstable, capacity planning is a futile exercise.

Capacity management should be used by all firms running MRP. Not to perform capacity management is to invite extremely wasteful manufacturing and inventory management. Companies that have unstable master schedules should recognize that the instability is a symptom of inadequate safety stock at the MPS level. The inadequate safety stock may itself be a symptom of the lack of an appropriate forecasting system or failure to measure forecast error. Once a system is in place that does an adequate job of forecasting demand, measuring forecast error, and providing adequate safety stock, the capacity management process can begin.

The capacity management process should begin by insisting on a stable master schedule. Last minute schedule changes are very expensive. Few companies that permit frequent schedule changes make any attempt to measure the cost of these changes to the company's profitability. If they did measure cost, the premium charged for making such changes would likely be much higher. The topic of the cost of MPS instability is discussed in Chapter 13.

The next section develops a simple example that is used to perform rough cut capacity planning. After the master schedule is developed, a discussion of MPS validation is presented.

Developing the Master Production Schedule

In Chapter 4 the development of an MPS is discussed. An example is presented that discusses the assembly of a lamp. A representation of the super bill of material for lamps, originally presented as Figure 4-5, is reproduced here as Figure 12-2. For this chapter, we create a hypothetical lamp manufacturer that we will call Al's Lamps. Al's Lamps has developed an MPS, as shown in Table 12-1.

Figure 12-2
Super Bill of Material, Lamp LAXX

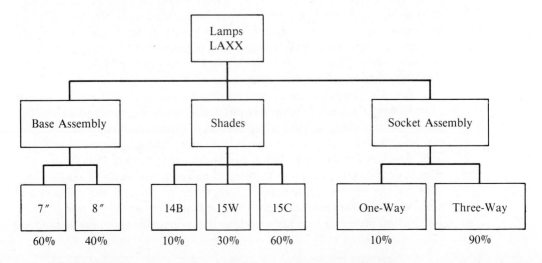

Table 12-1
Master Production Schedule Development at Al's Lamps for 1991

Month	Forecast (thousands)	Regular Production	Overtime Production	Total Production	Inventory Available
					15
January	22	15	0	15	8
February	8	15	0	15	15
March	10	15	0	15	20
April	10	15	0	15	25
May	20	15	0	15	20
June	14	15	0	15	21
July	8	15	0	15	28
August	8	15	1	16	36
September	12	15	4	19	43
October	15	15	4	19	47
November	30	15	4	19	36
December	40	15	4	19	15
	197	180		197	

Al's runs only one shift, 40 hours per week, with a maximum of 10 hours per week overtime permitted. Given present employment levels, monthly production averages approximately 15,000 units without overtime and 19,000 units with maximum overtime. As Table 12-1 reflects, demand for lamps is quite seasonal, with a major peak during the winter holiday season and a minor peak at income tax return time. Al's wishes to have stable employment in order to produce superior quality, so they choose to operate a level production strategy, with overtime as needed.

When a level production strategy is used, finished goods inventory must be built in advance of the seasonal peak (recall this type of inventory is known as anticipation inventory). The minimum level of inventory planned is the safety stock level, which provides protection against forecast error. Because Al's has little excess capacity to permit recovery from poor forecasts, they carry a fairly substantial safety stock, 8,000 units. The maximum level of inventory planned is the amount needed at the end of October to meet the holiday peak season. For 1991, that maximum is 47,000 units.

Because Al's produces a single product family and because Al's strategy of stable employment limits the options available for aggregate planning, the process of preparing the MPS is quite simple. Current inventory is known. The desired year end inventory is known (15,000 units, enough to provide anticipation inventory for January, 1992). Minimum production is 15,000 units per month, or 180,000 units per year. Minimum production yields 17,000 too few units for the year; total demand is forecast to be 197,000 units. Because a maximum of 4,000 units per month can be built using overtime, and because anticipation inventory should be built as late as possible to minimize holding costs, the 17,000 units to be built on overtime are allocated to December, November, October, September, and August, in that sequence. (The observant reader might note that inventory for the year could be lowered by planning to end with 11,000 units rather than 15,000 and planning to use overtime in January, 1992. Al's prefers to use overtime in January only if the forecast for a given holiday season was pessimistic.)

Validating the Master Production Schedule

Al's wishes to validate the master production schedule at five key resources: lamp assembly, oven, base forming, plastic molding, and socket assembly. Lamp assembly assembles the base, the socket, and the shade to complete the lamp. The oven bakes the ceramic clay created at the base forming department. Plastic molding creates the plastic lamp shade. Socket assembly assembles all socket components except the power cord. The RCCP technique is used to verify that adequate capacity exists at each of the five stations. The technique consists of comparing a machine load report of capacity required to planned available capacity at each work center. An example of a machine load report for plastic molding is shown in Figure 12-3. As Figure 12-3 clearly shows, plastic molding has adequate capacity. There are 400 standard hours available without overtime (500 with overtime) during each month of the year. Capacity required varies from 320 standard hours to 380 standard hours. Thus, plastic molding should be able to meet the production schedule all year without overtime.

Figure 12-3
Machine Load Report for Plastic Molding

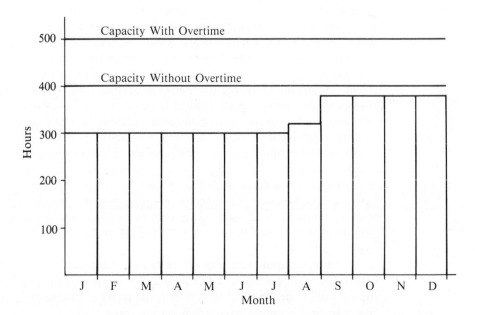

The next section presents three techniques for developing the machine load report to determine capacity required. The following section discusses the determination of capacity available and decisions to be taken if available capacity is inadequate. Both discussions assume a stable MPS. The three techniques are known as capacity planning using overall factors, the bill of labor approach, and the resource profile approach. The section ends with a discussion of selection of an appropriate technique.

RCCP TECHNIQUES

The three techniques discussed in this section are similar in purpose but have substantially different data requirements and computational complexity. All three techniques are designed to convert the master production schedule from units of end items to be produced into the amount of time required on certain key resources. Because the amount of time available on existing key resources can be determined well in advance, the use of RCCP permits planning for expansion of these resources in a timely fashion. In some instances, the RCCP process may reveal that key resources are presently inadequate and that expanding the resources requires more time and/or more money than the company is willing to invest. In these instances, the MPS must be revised.

The three techniques are capacity planning using overall factors, the bill of labor approach, and the resource profile approach. Capacity planning using overall factors requires the least detailed data and the least computational effort. Not surprisingly, it is also the approach that is most affected by any changes that occur in product volume or the level of effort required to build a product.

The bill of labor approach uses detailed data on the time standards for each product at the key resources. A *time standard* is the time it should take an average worker working at a normal pace to produce one unit of an item. The time standard for any part has built into it an allowance for rest to overcome fatigue, an allowance for unavoidable delay, etc. When a time standard first is set, it usually is quite reliable. Because production processes continually are improved, time standards become less reliable; a time standard that is two or three years old is probably somewhat pessimistic. For this reason, many companies are reluctant to use time standards in performing capacity management. Many companies, especially those with incentive systems, do a good job of updating time standards. However, poor standards are not an absolute barrier to capacity planning; the capacity planning process contains an adjustment factor known as "efficiency" that may be used to correct for outdated time standards (although efficiency is not intended to reduce the need to keep standards up to date).

The final, and most detailed, technique is known as the resource profile approach. Like the bill of labor approach, the resource profile approach requires time standard data. In addition, the resource profile approach requires the lead time required to perform certain tasks.

Capacity planning using overall factors can be performed using a calculator. The bill of labor approach and the resource profile approach both can be performed using an electronic spreadsheet on a first generation microcomputer such as the original IBM PC. Computational complexity is therefore not currently a barrier to capacity management, although prior to the introduction of the electronic spreadsheet about 1980, computational complexity was a barrier to capacity management for many companies.

Capacity Planning Using Overall Factors (CPOF)

CPOF requires three data inputs: the MPS, the time the total plant requires to produce one "typical" part, and the historical proportion of total plant time required by each of the key resources. If more than one product family exists, one "typical" part time is required for each family. CPOF multiplies the "typical" time by the MPS quantity to obtain total time required in the entire plant to meet the MPS. This time is then prorated among the key resources by multiplying total plant time by the historical proportion of time used at a given work center. Table 12-2 shows the RCCP for Al's Lamps produced using CPOF.

Al's Lamps has only one product family, lamps. A typical lamp requires 0.22 standard hours of labor/machine time, as shown in Table 12-3. Multiplying each monthly MPS quantity shown in Table 12-1 by 0.22 yields the Total Capacity Requirements row of Table 12-2. The remaining rows of Table 12-2 are found by multiplying the total capacity requirement for the month times the historical proportion for the work center. For example, the value 1,501.5 standard hours for lamp assembly for January is found by multiplying the historical proportion, 0.455, by January's total capacity requirement, 3,300 hours. This computation can easily be performed for all work centers for all months using an electronic spreadsheet; in the pre-microcomuter era, the technique often was performed using a simple four-function calculator.

Bill of Labor Approach

A good definition of the bill of labor (also known as bill of resources or bill of capacity) is given in Conlon (1977):

> The bill of labor is a listing by item number of the amount of labor required by a major labor category to produce that item or group of part numbers. It is not intended to be a routing, but merely a means of estimating the capacity requirements for a particular item. The bill of labor (BOL) may be compiled for every distinct item or for groups of similar items, and extended by the scheduled quantities to determine capacity requirements.

In order to illustrate the concept of the bill of labor approach, we will use data from Al's lamps, introduced in the previous section. The bill of labor for lamp LAXX, a "typical" lamp is shown in Table 12-3. (The time standard data is taken from engineering files. For this hypothetical example, we elected to use the same data used for the CPOF approach.)

Table 12-2
RCCP for Al's Lamps Using the CPOF Approach

Work Center	Historical Proportion	Jan	Feb	Mar	Apr	May	Jun	Jul	Aug	Sep	Oct	Nov	Dec	Total Hours
Lamp Assembly	0.455	1,501.5	1,501.5	1,501.5	1,501.5	1,501.5	1,501.5	1,501.5	1,601.6	1,901.9	1,901.9	1,901.9	1,901.9	19,719.7
Oven	0.045	148.5	148.5	148.5	148.5	148.5	148.5	148.5	158.4	188.1	188.1	188.1	188.1	1,950.3
Base Forming	0.227	749.1	749.1	749.1	749.1	749.1	749.1	749.1	799.04	948.86	948.86	948.86	948.86	9,838.18
Plastic Molding	0.091	300.3	300.3	300.3	300.3	300.3	300.3	300.3	320.32	380.38	380.38	380.38	380.38	3,943.94
Socket Assembly	0.182	600.6	600.6	600.6	600.6	600.6	600.6	600.6	640.64	760.76	760.76	760.76	760.76	7,887.88
Total Capacity Requirements		3,300	3,300	3,300	3,300	3,300	3,300	3,300	3,520	4,180	4,180	4,180	4,180	

Table 12-3
Bill of Labor for Lamp LAXX

	Lamp LAXX
Lamp Assembly	0.10 hr
Oven	0.01 hr
Base Forming	0.05 hr
Plastic Molding	0.02 hr
Socket Assembly	0.04 hr
	0.22 hr

To determine capacity required, the time per piece shown in the bill of labor must be multiplied by the number of lamps to be assembled each month. The assembly requirements are taken from the master production schedule, Table 12-1. To determine the total time required by a department in a given month, the time per lamp in the department is multiplied by the number of lamps to be built during the month. For example, it requires 0.1 hours to build one lamp at lamp assembly. January's MPS quantity is 15,000 lamps. Therefore, 1,500 standard hours are required at lamp assembly during January. All other entries in Table 12-4, the RCCP using BOL, are calculated in a similar fashion. Perhaps you have noticed that these repetitive computations are an ideal electronic spreadsheet application.

Although RCCP using the BOL approach can be performed with an electronic spreadsheet, virtually all of the necessary data is probably on a corporate mainframe. For this reason, many companies prefer to use a commercial capacity management software package. Most commercial software packages have the ability to display the rough cut capacity planning as graphic output, in a form such as Figure 12-3. This graphical representation simplifies identification of occasions in which capacity required exceeds capacity available.

If Al's Lamps produced more than one product, the time required for each product in each department would have to be determined. The sum of all product times for one department gives that department's capacity required. In matrix notation, Table 12-4 is a five row by twelve column (5×12) matrix. Note that the master schedule, Table 12-1, is a one row by twelve column (1×12) matrix and the bill of labor is a five row by one column matrix (5×1). Students familiar with matrix multiplication will have recognized the process used to obtain the rough cut requirements using the bill of labor approach as a matrix multiplication. (The MPS must be transposed to enable multiplication.) In general, assume there are n master scheduled items. Let the bill of labor amount for Product k in Work Center i be denoted a_{ik}. Let the master schedule amount for Product k in Period j be denoted b_{kj}. Then the formula for the capacity required in Work Center k for Period j is given by the following equation.

$$\text{Capacity Required} = \sum_{k=1}^{n} a_{ik} b_{kj} \text{ for all } i, j \qquad (12\text{-}1)$$

Figure 12-4 provides a generalized example of Equation 12-1 for a two product, two month, two work center case. Figure 12-5 provides a specific example. As Figure 12-5 shows, the RCCP value for the first work center for the first month is found by multiplying the time at Work Center 1 for Product 1 by the demand for Product 1, multiplying the time at Work Center 1 for Product 2 by the demand for Product 2, and adding the two results. Further examples of RCCP involving multiple products, and multiple periods can be found in Blackstone (1989).

Table 12-4
RCCP for Al's Lamps Using the BOL Approach

Work Center	Jan	Feb	Mar	Apr	May	Jun	Jul	Aug	Sep	Oct	Nov	Dec	Total Hours
								Month					
Lamp Assembly	1,500	1,500	1,500	1,500	1,500	1,500	1,500	1,600	1,900	1,900	1,900	1,900	19,700
Oven	150	150	150	150	150	150	150	160	190	190	190	190	1,970
Base Forming	750	750	750	750	750	750	750	800	950	950	950	950	9,850
Plastic Molding	300	300	300	300	300	300	300	320	380	380	380	380	3,940
Socket Assembly	600	600	600	600	600	600	600	640	760	760	760	760	7,880
Total Capacity Requirements	3,300	3,300	3,300	3,300	3,300	3,300	3,300	3,520	4,180	4,180	4,180	4,180	

Figure 12-4
Bill of Labor Approach
Two Products, Two Months, Two Work Centers

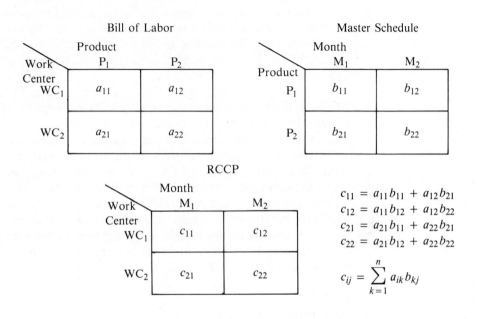

$$c_{11} = a_{11}b_{11} + a_{12}b_{21}$$
$$c_{12} = a_{11}b_{12} + a_{12}b_{22}$$
$$c_{21} = a_{21}b_{11} + a_{22}b_{21}$$
$$c_{22} = a_{21}b_{12} + a_{22}b_{22}$$

$$c_{ij} = \sum_{k=1}^{n} a_{ik}b_{kj}$$

Figure 12-5
Bill of Labor Example, Two by Two

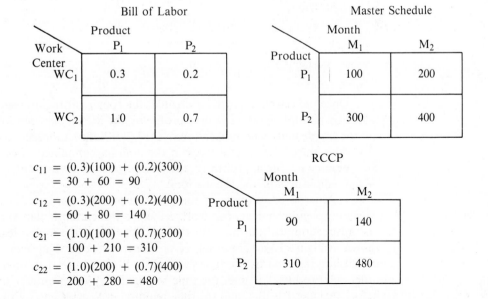

$c_{11} = (0.3)(100) + (0.2)(300)$
$= 30 + 60 = 90$

$c_{12} = (0.3)(200) + (0.2)(400)$
$= 60 + 80 = 140$

$c_{21} = (1.0)(100) + (0.7)(300)$
$= 100 + 210 = 310$

$c_{22} = (1.0)(200) + (0.7)(400)$
$= 200 + 280 = 480$

Resource Profile Approach

Neither the bill of labor approach nor the CPOF approach considers lead-time offsets. Both approaches assume that all components are built in the same time period as the end item. The resource profile technique time phases the labor requirements. Each bill of labor must be time phased for the resource profile approach to be used. The resource profile technique is the most detailed rough cut approach, but is not as detailed as capacity requirements planning (see Chapter 13).

A resource profile for Lamp LAXX is shown in Table 12-5. This table is identical to the bill of labor except that the time at each department is now associated with a specific time period, reflecting the lead time of the part. Al's lamps have a three-month lead time. In the first month, the bases are formed. In the second month, the bases are processed through the oven, socket assemblies are created by the socket assembly department, and shades are created at plastic molding. In the third month, the lamps are assembled from constituent components and subassemblies. These lead times are unrealistically long; the numbers were created to produce a useful example. To create a resource profile, the lead time must be converted to periods prior to the period in which the order is promised. Since the last operation always occurs immediately prior to delivery, it is shown as occurring 0 periods prior to delivery.

Table 12-5
Resource Profile for Lamp LAXX

		Months Before Due Date	
Department	2	1	0
Lamp Assembly	0	0	0.1
Oven	0	0.01	0
Base Forming	0.05	0	0
Plastic Molding	0	0.02	0
Socket Assembly	0	0.04	0

Once the resource profile is created, the rough cut requirements are obtained by multiplying the resource profile by the MPS. This multiplication is not the simple matrix multiplication of the bill of labor approach. Rather, the procedure must keep careful track of the hours accumulated in each period. The resource profile approach is always implemented on a computer because of the tediousness of the calculations.

A generalized example of the resource profile approach for a case involving two end products, two work centers, a three-month planning horizon, and a three-month lead time (for the product having the longer lead time) is shown in Figure 12-6. The resource profile for Product 1 at Work Center 1 is split into three parts, the time required in Work Center 1 in the month the order for Product 1 is due, the time required in Work Center 1 one month before Product 1 is due, and the time required in Work Center 1 two months

Figure 12-6
Resource Profile Approach, Two Products, Two Work
Centers, Three-Month Horizon, Three-Month Lead Time

Time to Due Date	Resource Profile				Master Schedule Month		
Product	2	1	0	Product	M_1	M_2	M_3
P_1	a_{112}	a_{111}	a_{110}	P_1	b_{11}	b_{12}	b_{13}
P_2	a_{212}	a_{211}	a_{210}	P_2	b_{21}	b_{22}	b_{23}

Work Center 1

	2	1	0
P_1	a_{122}	a_{121}	a_{120}
P_2	a_{222}	a_{221}	a_{220}

Work Center 2

$$c_{11} = a_{110}b_{11} + a_{111}b_{12} + a_{112}b_{13} + a_{210}b_{21} + a_{211}b_{22} + a_{212}b_{23}$$
$$c_{12} = a_{110}b_{12} + a_{111}b_{13} \qquad\quad + a_{210}b_{22} + a_{211}b_{23}$$
$$c_{13} = a_{110}b_{13} \qquad\qquad\qquad\quad + a_{210}b_{23}$$
$$c_{21} = a_{120}b_{11} + a_{121}b_{12} + a_{122}b_{13} + a_{220}b_{21} + a_{221}b_{22} + a_{222}b_{23}$$
$$c_{22} = a_{120}b_{12} + a_{121}b_{13} \qquad\quad + a_{220}b_{22} + a_{221}b_{23}$$
$$c_{23} = a_{120}b_{13} \qquad\qquad\qquad\quad + a_{220}b_{23}$$

RCCP

Work Center	Month		
	M_1	M_2	M_3
WC_1	c_{11}	c_{12}	c_{13}
WC_2	c_{21}	c_{22}	c_{23}

before Product 1 is due. Any or all of these times may be 0 for any given product and time until due date at any given work center. To find the time Work Center 1 works on Product 1 during Month 1, we multiply Month 1's demand by the time required at Work Center 1 during the month the product is due, we multiply Month 2's demand by the time required at Work Center 1 one month before the product is due, and we multiply Month 3's demand by the time required at Work Center 1 two months before the product is due. This process is then repeated for Product 2. We then add all six products (i.e., results of the multiplication process) to obtain the final value for the time required at Work Center 1 during Month 1. The equation for this process is represented as the equation for term c_{11} in Figure 12-6.

If a product has a lead time of n periods, there will be an end-of-horizon effect (underestimating the capacity required) during the last $n - 1$ periods of the planning horizon. In the example shown in Figure 12-6, there is a three-month lead time, thus, the end-of-horizon effect occurs during the final two periods, Months 2 and 3. The equation for c_{12} has only four terms, two fewer than the equation for c_{11}. Because the end-of-horizon effect is unavoidable, the planning horizon for the resource profile approach must be quite long. To provide the same unbiased visibility as the bill of labor approach, the planning horizon must equal the bill of labor approach's planning horizon plus the lead time minus one period. For advanced students, implementing the algorithm illustrated in Figure 12-6 using a microcomputer is a reasonable exercise.

The results of RCCP using the resource profile approach for Al's Lamps are shown in Table 12-6. This example is a special case of the resource profile approach, because the product requires effort during only one period for all work centers. For lamp assembly, the results are identical to the BOL results, which has a time offset of 0. For the three operations having a one-month lead-time offset (oven, plastic molding, socket assembly), BOL results are shifted one month to the left. For base forming, results are shifted two months to the left. The left shift of some department times, reflecting the lead-time offset, results in an end-of-horizon effect during November and December, as predicted. Time requirements for November and December are 0 for some departments, reflecting the fact that the end-item orders that require production in these departments will not be due until the following January or February. Since the planning horizon ends at December, no requirement can be shown at present. Users of the resource profile approach must be careful that the planning horizon is sufficiently long so that the first few periods do not exhibit an end-of-horizon effect. The first few periods of a planning horizon are the ones that must be accurate to provide MPS verification.

Choosing an RCCP Technique

Obviously, the resource profile approach requires more computational effort than the bill of labor approach. Is there a return for the additional effort of creating the resource profiles and performing the extra computations? There may be a return, but only if lead times are quite long and the shop uses a lot-for-lot policy in establishing lot sizes.

It is not uncommon to find products whose manufactured lead time runs several months. Most large, complex items such as airplanes, machine tools, and so on have very lengthy lead times. For parts having lengthy lead times, the resource profile approach might be useful because the bill of labor approach assumption that the components and the end item are built during the same

Table 12-6
RCCP for Al's Lamps Using the Resource Profile Approach

| Work Center | Month | | | | | | | | | | | | Total Hours |
	Jan	Feb	Mar	Apr	May	Jun	Jul	Aug	Sep	Oct	Nov	Dec	
Lamp Assembly	1,500	1,500	1,500	1,500	1,500	1,500	1,500	1,600	1,900	1,900	1,900	1,900	19,700
Oven	150	150	150	150	150	150	160	190	190	190	190	0	1,820
Base Forming	750	750	750	750	750	800	950	950	950	950	0	0	8,350
Plastic Molding	300	300	300	300	300	300	320	380	380	380	380	0	3,640
Socket Assembly	600	600	600	600	600	600	640	760	760	760	760	0	7,280
Total Capacity Requirements	3,300	3,300	3,300	3,300	3,300	3,350	3,570	3,880	4,180	4,180	3,230	1,900	

month must be wrong. The resource profile approach avoids this assumption by including the time dimension. However, be aware that although the resource profile will have different information than the bill of labor approach regardless of how lot sizing is done, it is likely to have more accurate information only if lot sizing is lot-for-lot.

To illustrate the effect lot sizing has on the accuracy of the resource profile approach, let's consider the following example. Suppose a product, that for purposes of this discussion we will call a whatsit, has two operations, A and B, performed in Work Centers 1 and 2. Suppose further that the bill of labor and resource profile for the whatsit are as shown in Table 12-7 and that the master production schedule for the coming four weeks is as shown in Table 12-8.

Table 12-7
Bill of Labor and Resource Profile for a Whatsit

Bill of Labor			Resource Profile		
				Week Until Due	
Work Center	Time		Work Center	1	0
1	20		1	20	0
2	30		2	0	30

Table 12-8
Master Production Schedule for a Whatsit

	Week			
	1	2	3	4
Whatsits	100	200	250	100

Then the rough cut capacity plans produced by the bill of labor and resource profile approaches would be as shown in Tables 12-9 and 12-10, respectively. Note the difference in requirements for Work Center 1 in Tables 12-9 and 12-10. Table 12-10 has offset the requirement by a one-week lead time, resulting in a capacity requirement of 0 for Period 4, because no requirement for Period 5 is visible. Periods 1, 2, and 3 represent requirements placed on the work center one week earlier by the resource profile than by the bill of labor approach. Finally, note that 2,000 fewer hours are estimated using the resource profile approach since the resource profile approach assumes the components for the 100 whatsits due in Week 1 have been built.

When demand peaks occur, such as in Period 3 of the MPS, it is important to reflect the timing of the impact of the peak on various work centers. The resource profile does this, provided that the quantity of Operation A in Period $t - 1$ always coincides with the master schedule amount of whatsits in Period t. Suppose, however, that the lot size for Operation A is 700, so that incomplete whatsits are stocked after Operation A. Then both the bill of labor

Table 12-9
Capacity Requirements Using the Bill of Labor

Work Center	Period				Total
	1	2	3	4	
1	2,000	4,000	5,000	2,000	13,000
2	3,000	6,000	7,500	3,000	19,500

Capacity Required in Time Units

Table 12-10
Capacity Requirements Using Resource Profiles

Work Center	Period				Total
	1	2	3	4	
1	4,000	5,000	2,000	0	11,000
2	3,000	6,000	7,500	3,000	19,500

Capacity Required in Time Units

and the resource profile approach are wrong. At some point during the four periods, Work Center 1 will produce 700 incomplete whatsits requiring 14,000 time units. The timing of this demand will depend on the number of incomplete whatsits currently in stock.

Since both the bill of labor and the resource profile results are incorrect when any lot sizing rule other than lot-for-lot is used, the bill of labor approach with time buckets as large as practical is recommended (i.e., monthly or quarterly buckets). For those companies having lot-for-lot lot sizing throughout all operations, the resource profile approach using small (e.g., weekly) buckets will provide quite a bit of additional information.

For an environment in which large batches lead to large week-to-week shifts in product mix, the following analysis is correct: The CPOF approach utilizes less data than the bill of labor approach, but is insensitive to shifts in product mix. (The historical proportions of total hours used by CPOF reflect average product mix. They are insensitive to changes in product mix that occur because of seasonality and/or batching of components.) This statement explains both why CPOF has been used and why it should not be used now that microcomputers are commonplace. In the era before microcomputers (that for business purposes began about 1981) and even before inexpensive hand held calculators (that, perhaps surprisingly, began about 1976), the process of performing all of the multiplications required by the bill of labor approach was quite cumbersome. The CPOF approach was much simpler, requiring only that each proportion be multiplied by each total labor quantity, i.e., one multiplication per cell rather than several. For many situations, CPOF was perhaps the only practical solution.

From the viewpoint of the traditional MRP user, the bill of labor approach is superior to capacity planning using overall factors, because it better predicts the actual change in hours required from week to week. From the viewpoint of the Just-in-Time philosophy discussed in Chapter 17, there should not be such large product mix variations from week to week. If the lot size of each product were very small, then it would be possible to make each product every week. Since it is likely that the product is in fact consumed every week, then there is an advantage to matching the rate of production to the rate of sale or consumption so that inventory need not be stored. A secondary advantage of the "level load" philosophy of Just-in-Time is that capacity management is simplified.

The bill of labor approach captures the changing product mix since each end product has its own bill of labor. For that reason, the bill of labor approach is strongly recommended over the CPOF approach. Given modern electronic spreadsheets, the bill of labor approach is just as simple to perform as CPOF. Thus, CPOF, while a useful technique only a few years ago, is clearly outdated and soon will be discussed only for historical interest.

RCCP DECISIONS

In this section we discuss how to determine the amount of capacity that is available, how to compare capacity available to capacity required, and the options that exist for adjusting capacity available and/or capacity required.

Determining Capacity Available

The plastic molding department of Al's Lamps, presented in the previous section, has three plastic molding machines. Since Al's works one eight-hour shift each day and there are 21 working days in an average month, it might seem that the capacity available to the plastic molding department is 504 hours per month (3 machines times 8 hours/day/machine times 21 days/month). However, two additional factors must be considered. First, the plastic molding machines may not be available all the time. The machines may break down, the worker may be absent, and the mold needed or the material needed may not immediately be available. Second, there must be an adjustment between the time standard average and the actual average production rate of the department. The first adjustment factor is known as utilization. *Utilization* is a number between 0 and 1 that is equal to 1 minus the proportion of time typically lost due to machine, worker, tool, or material unavailability. The second adjustment factor is known as efficiency. *Efficiency* is formally defined to be the average of standard hours of production per clock hour actually worked. If a time standard is exactly right, efficiency is 1. If the time actually required to perform the work is less than the standard, efficiency is more than 1. If the time actually required to perform the work is more than the standard, efficiency is less than 1. As mentioned previously, time standards tend to be slightly pessimistic due to continual improvement in production methods.

Capacity available is found by multiplying time available times utilization times efficiency:

Capacity Available = Time Available × Utilization × Efficiency

Assume that for the plastic molding department of Al's Lamps, utilization is 0.756 and efficiency is 1.05. The time available in a month having 168 working hours (21 eight-hour days) is 504 (3 machines times 168 hours/month/machine). Thus,

Capacity Available = 504 × 0.756 × 1.05 = 400 hours

rounded to the nearest hour.

Comparing Capacity Required to Capacity Available

Most standard software packages can determine both the capacity required and the capacity available and can display them in both tabular and graphical format. The report containing capacity available and required is known as the *machine load report*. The graphical format for the machine load report was shown in Figure 12-3. Graphical formats usually are preferred because one can determine at a glance whether capacity is adequate. Tabular formats are more precise, however, and when capacity is inadequate one needs to know the exact shortage to be covered.

When capacity is inadequate, four basic options are available to increase capacity: overtime, subcontracting, alternate routing, or adding personnel. If no combination of the four options can provide sufficient capacity, the MPS will have to be reduced. Options to adjust capacity required or available are discussed next.

Overtime

Overtime is probably the most popular solution to inadequate capacity because few advance arrangements must be made. Usually workers appreciate having the money provided by some overtime; however, beyond some point, the workers would rather have the time off than the extra money. For this reason, many companies have a policy that limits the amount of overtime during specific periods. Also, almost all departments have to meet a budget for the year, which imposes a constraint on annual overtime.

Subcontracting

A second way to obtain additional capacity is through subcontracting. Arrangements for subcontracting must begin well in advance to permit time to find a vendor capable of performing quality work. Subcontracting usually is more expensive than building an item in house on regular time (otherwise, we would buy the part and not make it). However, subcontracting may be cheaper than building the part in house on overtime. Disadvantages of subcontracting are that lead time usually increases, transportation cost may increase, and it is more difficult to guarantee a quality product.

Alternate Routing

If only a few work centers have excess work, the remaining work centers will tend to have too little work during a given period. It is, therefore, possible to consider a temporary change in the routing of specific parts so that work usually performed in Work Center A temporarily is performed in Work Center B. There are two possible reasons that Work Center B is not presently used— quality and time. If Work Center B cannot achieve the needed quality, alternate routing should not be considered. If Work Center B presently is not used because of time, alternate routing should be considered. Using Work Center B during time in which it otherwise would be idle is preferable to having Work Center A on overtime. Using Work Center B on overtime is an alternative to subcontracting. However, having Work Center B on overtime probably is not an alternative to having Work Center A on overtime. Why?

Adding Personnel

Adding personnel will add capacity provided equipment is not the constraint. There are three ways to add personnel: add a shift, add new hires to an existing shift, or move existing personnel from an underused work center. The time to consider adding a shift is when the master schedule first is formulated, when the demand chase versus level production versus mixed strategy choice is made. Adding new hires to an existing shift is likely to be an option only when the budget for the next fiscal year is being approved. Thus, the only short-term way to obtain additional personnel is to shift people from an underused work center to one that is overloaded. In union shops, union rules may prohibit or limit this option. Enterprises that have restrictions on moving workers between work stations are at a competitive disadvantage to companies that have no such restrictions. The Japanese strongly encourage a worker to cross train and master several different tasks. For this reason, many companies have insisted that union rules on multifunction workers be relaxed; most unions have been willing to trade flexibility for job security or other considerations. Clearly it is not in the union's interest for the enterprise not to be competitive.

Revising the Master Production Schedule

Most companies consider a revision to the MPS to be a solution of last resort in the event of insufficient capacity, to be implemented only when all other options are exhausted. MPS revision actually should be the first thing a company considers. A number of things can cause an order to be expedited. An order is rarely de-expedited. There may be several orders on the existing master schedule that no longer are needed as early as the current due date shows them to be needed. It is not uncommon to find a machine load report that shows too much work in the first two or three periods, but ample capacity beyond that. This problem may be corrected or substantially alleviated merely by putting the true need date on all orders.

If de-expediting, overtime, subcontracting, alternate routing, and shifting personnel collectively cannot provide sufficient capacity, MPS revision does in fact become the technique of last resort. It is important to understand that when an unavoidable capacity overload exists, it must be corrected. If insufficient capacity exists, it is impossible to complete all orders on time. Our choice is to have management decide whose order will be late based on the impact on the whole enterprise or to have a worker on the floor make the choice based on the convenience of one department. The worker must perform his or her tasks in some sequence. It is a mistake to let a more-or-less arbitrary sequencing decision determine that jobs are late. Even if the sequencing decision is ordinarily made by a rule such as earliest-due-date-first, when capacity overloads exist we may prefer to have jobs completed out of strict due date sequence.

Management must take responsibility to see that rough cut capacity planning is performed. If an unavoidable overload exists, management must take the responsibility to revise the job due dates in order to provide a feasible master production schedule. This is the meaning of master schedule validation.

DRUM-BUFFER-ROPE

The rough cut capacity planning process just described is needed because the MRP technique assumes that needed capacity always is available. The medium-range planning systems used by Just-in-Time (JIT) and the theory of constraints (TOC) are somewhat simpler because both involve explicit recognition of capacity limitations.

The JIT approach maintains excess capacity in order to achieve very short lead times and to hold very little inventory. JIT also produces every item every day, changing the quantity per day about once a month to reflect the market rate of sales, so the matter of predicting the quantity and timing of needs for components is trivial. Medium-range planning under JIT consists merely of multiplying the daily rate of sales for the end item by the quantity of components per end item.

The theory of constraints says the constraint must pace the entire system. The constraint may be the market or it may be an internal resource (work center). If the market is the constraint, the theory of constraints schedule essentially would be identical to the Just-in-Time schedule. If an internal constraint exists, the TOC approach, called *drum-buffer-rope*, is to have the master scheduler sequence all jobs through the constraint resource. Since the lead time from the constraint to shipping is known, due dates can then be set for end items with the assurance that they are capacity-feasible. The resulting MPS can be fed to the MRP system, which will set operation due dates for all work centers except the constraint. (Since the process is deterministic, MRP should arrive at precisely the same due dates at the constraint that the master scheduler originally established.)

The name drum-buffer-rope is derived from the following metaphors: the schedule at the constraint is the drum, setting the pace for all work centers; the deterministic lead-time offset from the constraint to order release is the rope, pulling work into the shop at the pace the constraint is completing work; the linkage between the constraint and order release ensures that an essentially constant buffer is maintained at the constraint. If problems never occurred, the buffer would be constant. But since problems such as absenteeism do occur, the buffer at the constraint must be large enough to absorb these fluctuations and avoid idle time at the constraint. Because this technique is used only if demand exceeds capacity, any idle time at the constraint results in lost revenue.

Although drum-buffer-rope is not as yet common practice, a number of writers have recognized that the iterative process of MPS creation (RCCP to validate the MPS → MPS revision → RCCP repeated → perhaps another MPS revision → RCCP a third time → etc.) simply is not an ideal way to perform the scheduling task. Because it is likely that when an overload exists one station is more overloaded than all others, and because a schedule for that one station easily can be created, drum-buffer-rope is a single pass technique that any company can use. Wahlers (1990) reports that Valmont Industries presently is using drum-buffer-rope with a great deal of success. See Chapter 19 for a further discussion of the theory of constraints.

SUMMARY

In this chapter, three approaches to rough cut capacity planning have been examined. The least detailed, the capacity planning using overall factors (CPOF) approach, is quickly computed but is insensitive to shifts in product mix. A second approach, bill of labor, involves multiplying two matrices, the bill of labor and the master production schedule. This approach picks up shifts in product mix, but does not consider lead-time offsets. The third approach, resource profile, takes lead-time offsets into account. Both the bill of labor approach and the resource profile approach implicitly assume a lot-for-lot policy for setting lot sizes. If some other technique, such as economic order quantity or the Silver-Meal algorithm, is used, then either approach is a very rough estimate. For that reason, the bill of labor approach is recommended because it is easily implemented on a microcomputer and is just as accurate as the more cumbersome resource profile approach. In any event, rough cut capacity plans should be used only to determine if sufficient capacity exists over broad time frames such as a month or a quarter.

Drum-buffer-rope is an emerging procedure that eliminates the need for iteration found in all three RCCP approaches. It is presently used by a small but growing number of corporations.

EXERCISES

1. Discuss the differences between the bill of labor approach and CPOF. Suppose the product mix is stable and standard time data by operation is unreliable. Which approach would you use and how would you implement it?

2. Discuss the differences between the bill of labor approach and the resource profile approach. Which approach requires the most data? Which approach would be preferable for a company running an MRP system utilizing the period order quantity lot-sizing technique? State your assumptions regarding period length.

3. For a given plant, the bill of labor at critical work centers is as follows:

| Work Center | Bill of Labor (hours per part) | |
	Part A	Part B
WC 149	2.8	2.7
WC 103	3.2	3.9
WC 56	6.1	8.1

The master production schedule, by quarter, for the next year is:

	Q1	Q2	Q3	Q4
Part A	2,500	2,000	2,000	2,900
Part B	2,200	2,200	2,200	2,400

Using the bill of labor approach, determine the number of hours required in Work Centers 149, 103, and 56 for each quarter. Assume that the times just obtained are completely accurate and that only these three work centers exist in the plant. Determine the factors that would be used by CPOF to prorate total plant time.

4. Using the data from Exercise 3, assume that for Part A the work at WC 149 must be done one quarter prior to the other two operations and that for Part B the work at WC 103 must be done one quarter before the other two operations. Create the appropriate resource profile and the rough cut capacity plan that would result. Discuss the end-of-horizon effect.

5. A plant consists of four departments, A, B, C, D, whose historical proportions of total plant direct labor have been 0.35, 0.32, 0.18, and 0.15, respectively. The plant makes three major product families, F1, F2, and F3, requiring total labor of 20, 32, and 39 hours, respectively. The MPS for the coming year is as follows. Compute required capacity using the CPOF approach.

	Q1	Q2	Q3	Q4
F1	2,000	2,500	2,500	3,000
F2	4,000	4,000	4,500	5,000
F3	3,000	3,500	3,000	4,000

6. A master schedule for table assembly for 1991 is as follows:

Month	Production
January	1,300
February	1,200
March	1,300
April	1,300
May	1,500
June	1,500
July	1,500
August	1,500
September	1,800
October	1,800
November	1,800
December	1,800

To assemble the table, four legs must be lathed, the tabletop must be planed, and four holes must be drilled to accommodate the legs. The total time required in each of these three work centers to complete the components for one table are:

Work Center	Time
Lathe	0.44 hours
Plane	0.24 hours
Drill	0.10 hours

There are five lathes, two planes, and one drill, each available for two shifts per day, five days per week, eight working hours per day. Overtime is available for a maximum of 12 hours per week or 50 hours per month. Historical utilization of all three work centers is 95 percent. The rated efficiency of the lathe, plane, and drill work centers is 105 percent, 112 percent, and 102 percent, respectively. Prepare a machine load report for each work center for the year and indicate whether adequate capacity exists to meet the master production schedule.

SELECTED READINGS

Berry, William L., Thomas E. Vollman, and D. Clay Whybark. *Master Production Scheduling: Principles and Practice.* Falls Church, VA: American Production and Inventory Control Society, 1979.

Berry, William L., Thomas G. Schmitt, and Thomas E. Vollmann. "Capacity Planning Techniques for Manufacturing Control Systems: Information Requirements and Operational Features." *Journal of Operations Management* 3, no. 1 (September 1982): 13-26.

Blackstone, John H., Jr. *Capacity Management*. Cincinnati: South-Western Publishing, Co., 1989.

Conlon, J. R. "Is Your Master Schedule Feasible?" *APICS Master Production Scheduling Reprints*. Falls Church, VA: American Production and Inventory Control Society, 1977.

Orlicky, Joseph. *Material Requirements Planning*. New York: McGraw-Hill Book Co., 1975.

Plossl, George W., and Everett Welch. *The Role of Top Management in the Control of Inventory*. Reston, VA: Reston Publishing Co., 1979.

Wahlers, James. "A Study of Performance Measures of Synchronous Manufacturing in Intermittent Operations." Unpublished Ph.D. diss., The University of Georgia, 1990.

13
CAPACITY REQUIREMENTS PLANNING

The *APICS Dictionary* (1987) defines capacity requirements planning as "the function of establishing, measuring, and adjusting limits or levels of capacity . . . the process of determining how much labor and machine resources are required to accomplish the tasks of production. Open shop orders, and planned orders in the MRP system, are input to CRP, which 'translates' these orders into hours of work by work center by time period (see closed-loop MRP)."

Often associated with capacity requirements planning is a closed-loop MRP system that not only incorporates planning and execution functions, but also provides for feedback from the execution functions so that planning can be kept valid at all times. A closed-loop MRP system is diagrammed in Figure 13-1. The discussion that follows assumes the existence of a closed-loop MRP system.

Capacity requirements planning (CRP) is a detailed comparison of the capacity required by the material requirements plan (MRP) and by orders currently in progress versus available capacity. CRP verifies that there is sufficient capacity to process all orders due to be released within the planning horizon. This verification generally constitutes a final acceptance of the master production schedule (MPS). If the MPS is accepted, CRP determines the load that is expected at each work center during each time period.

CRP LOGIC

Conceptually, CRP is simple. The MPS is exploded via the MRP system. Planned order releases are taken from the MRP system and used to perform a deterministic simulation that uses lead-time offsets to determine the time each order passes through each work station. The deterministic simulation continues by including jobs already released to the shop floor. From this simulation, a machine load report is produced. The machine load report for each work station is compared to capacity available at that station.

The mechanics of CRP become tedious even for small shops. In order to demonstrate the mechanics of CRP, a very simplified example using only

Figure 13-1
Closed-Loop MRP

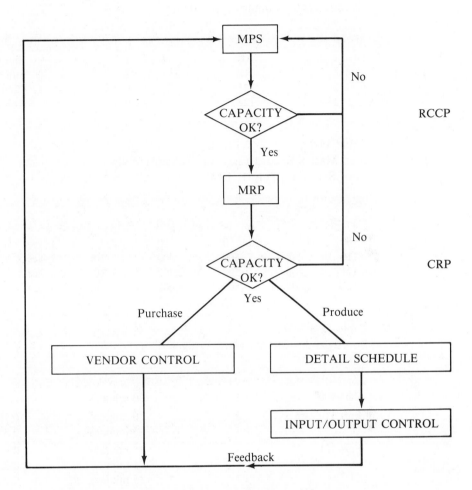

four parts and three work stations has been created. This example demonstrates the mechanics of CRP and illustrates how CRP results can have important differences from rough cut capacity planning.

Example of CRP Mechanics

Standard Widgets makes one widget from a pair of identical subassemblies, which in turn are made from two sets of components. The bill of material for a standard widget is shown in Table 13-1. The item master record for each of the four parts is shown in Table 13-2. The routing for each of the four parts is shown in Table 13-3. The work center master files are shown in Table 13-4. The master production schedule for Standard Widgets is shown in Table 13-5.

Table 13-1
Bill of Material for Standard Widget
Effective Date January 1, 1990

Level	Part	Qty/Parent	Description
0	100	1	Finished Widget
1	110	2	Subassembly
2	121	6	Component A
2	122	10	Component B

Table 13-2
Item Master Record Files for Standard Widget
as of Saturday, July 1, 1990

Item	Order Quantity	On Hand	On Order	Due Date	Lead Time	Allocated
100	LFL	0	250	7/3	1 week	0
110	400	500	400	7/10	2 weeks	0
121	2,400	1,500	2,400	7/10	3 weeks	0
122	6,000	2,500	6,000	7/10	4 weeks	0

Table 13-3
Routing Files for Standard Widget

	Work Center	Setup Time/Lot	Run Time/Piece
Part 100	1	30 minutes	2.5 minutes
Part 110	2	10 minutes	0.75 minutes
	1	15 minutes	0.5 minutes
Part 121	3	15 minutes	0.3 minutes
	1	25 minutes	0.25 minutes
	2	15 minutes	0.25 minutes
Part 122	2	25 minutes	0.75 minutes
	3	30 minutes	0.15 minutes
	1	75 minutes	0.5 minutes
	3	30 minutes	0.75 minutes

Table 13-4
Work Center Master Files, Standard Widget

Work Center	Available	Utilization	Efficiency	Planned Queue
1	2,400 minutes	100%	100%	4 days
2	2,400 minutes	100%	100%	4 days
3	2,400 minutes	100%	100%	4 days

Table 13-5
Master Production Schedule for Part 100

	Week											
	1	2	3	4	5	6	7	8	9	10	11	12
Quantity	250	200	250	150	200	300	150	250	200	200	250	200

Standard Widgets begins its planning process by performing rough cut capacity planning for all three work centers. The results of these rough cut calculations are shown in Table 13-6. The calculations used to derive Table 13-6 are given in Appendix 13A. The rough cut capacity plan is also shown in Figure 13-2. Note that although the required capacity exceeds the capacity available in some periods, the average requirement for each work station for the seven periods is less than the 2,400 minutes available.

Table 13-6
Rough Cut Capacity Requirements, Standard Widget
as of July 1, 1990

	Week							
Work Center	1	2	3	4	5	6	7	Average
1	2,604	2,083	2,604	1,562	2,083	3,125	1,562	2,232
2	2,657	2,125	2,657	1,594	2,125	3,188	1,594	2,277
3	2,734	2,187	2,734	1,640	2,187	3,281	1,640	2,343

Figure 13-2
Rough Cut Capacity Requirements, Standard Widgets

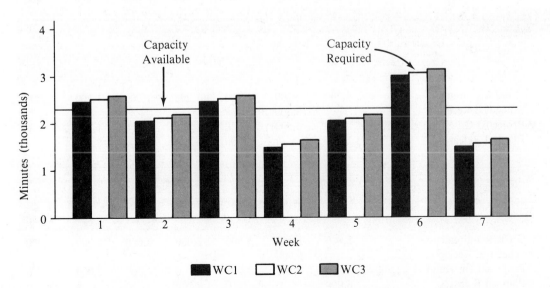

Based on these rough cut results, Marsha Abrams, production planner for Standard Widget, decides that the production plan is reasonable and causes the material requirements planning system to be run. Marsha notes that slight overloads exist in some weeks but feels that these will be offset by underloads in other weeks. The MRP system uses the data given in Tables 13-1 through 13-5 to produce the MRP report shown in Table 13-7. The actual material requirements plan contains 12 periods, but only 7 periods are shown in Table 13-7.

Table 13-7
Material Requirements Plan for Standard Widgets

Item 100
Fixed Period Ordering; Periods to Order: 1; Lead Time: 1

				Period			
	0	1	2	3	4	5	6	7
Gross Requirements		250	200	250	150	200	300	150
Scheduled Receipts		250						
Projected On Hand	0	0	0	0	0	0	0	0
Planned Releases		200	250	150	200	300	150	250

Item 110
Fixed Quantity Ordering; Quantity to Order: 400; Lead Time: 2

				Period			
	0	1	2	3	4	5	6	7
Gross Requirements		400	500	300	400	600	300	500
Scheduled Receipts			400					
Projected On Hand	500	100	0	100	100	0	100	0
Planned Releases		400	400	500	400	400	400	400

Item 121
Fixed Quantity Ordering; Quantity to Order: 2,400; Lead Time: 3

				Period			
	0	1	2	3	4	5	6	7
Gross Requirements		1,200	1,200	1,500	1,200	1,200	1,200	1,200
Scheduled Receipts			2,400					
Projected On Hand	1,500	300	1,500	0	1,200	0	1,200	0
Planned Releases		2,400	0	2,400	0	2,400	2,400	0

Item 122
Fixed Quantity Ordering; Quantity to Order: 6,000; Lead Time: 4

				Period			
	0	1	2	3	4	5	6	7
Gross Requirements		2,000	2,000	2,500	2,000	2,000	2,000	2,000
Scheduled Receipts			6,000					
Projected On Hand	2,500	500	4,500	2,000	0	4,000	2,000	0
Planned Releases		6,000	0	0	6,000	0	0	0

The set of planned order releases from MRP is needed to complete CRP. These planned releases have been extracted from Table 13-7 and summarized to create Table 13-8.

Table 13-8
Planned Order Releases, Standard Widget, as of July 1, 1990

Part	Week						
	1	2	3	4	5	6	7
100	200	250	150	200	300	150	250
110	400	400	500	400	400	400	400
121	2,400	0	2,400	0	2,400	2,400	0
122	6,000	0	0	6,000	0	0	0

The effect of batch production is evident in Table 13-8. Note that Parts 121 and 122 have an irregular production schedule, with nothing produced in some weeks and large batches released in other weeks. This "lumpiness" is not considered in the process of rough cut capacity planning. Note that the MPS (Table 13-5) does not exhibit the lumpiness found in Parts 121 and 122. Because of this lumpiness, the actual work load that Standard Widget is placing on the shop may be much more irregular than that predicted by RCCP in Table 13-6. This difference occurs for any of the three RCCP techniques. The reason CRP is needed even when RCCP has been properly completed is to determine whether batching orders for components has created an uneven flow of work.

CRP Computation

Computation of the capacity requirements plan requires a separate calculation of setup time and run time requirements. This section first discusses setup time computation for planned order releases, then run time calculation for planned order releases, then the inclusion of orders already on the shop floor, and finally a presentation of the CRP machine load report. The discussion presented here is a generic discussion of CRP computation principles. It is not intended to represent the algorithm actually used by any commercial CRP system. There may be algorithms that are more efficient than the one presented here. This discussion is intended to present an approach that is theoretically sound and easily understood.

The setup time matrix is shown in Table 13-9. This table is created directly from the planned order releases of the MRP system. Each operation has a lead time of one week. Thus, if a job due to be released in Week 3 has three operations, setup for Operation 1 is shown in Week 4, setup for Operation 2 is shown in Week 5, and setup for Operation 3 is shown in Week 6. In each case the setup is shown for the appropriate work station.

For a specific example, let's consider Part 122. From Table 13-8 an order for 6,000 Part 122s is to be released in Week 1. From the routing file (Table 13-3), we find that Part 122 is routed to Work Center 2, then to 3, then to 1,

Table 13-9
Setup Time Matrices for Standard Widgets

	Part	Week 1	2	3	4	5	6	7
WC1	100	30	30	30	30	30	30	30
	110	0	15	15	15	15	15	15
	121	0	25	0	25	0	25	25
	122	0	0	75	0	0	75	0
	Total	30	70	120	70	45	145	70
WC2	100	0	0	0	0	0	0	0
	110	10	10	10	10	10	10	10
	121	0	0	15	0	15	0	15
	122	25	0	0	25	0	0	0
	Total	35	10	25	35	25	10	25
WC3	100	0	0	0	0	0	0	0
	110	0	0	0	0	0	0	0
	121	15	0	15	0	15	15	0
	122	0	30	0	30	30	0	30
	Total	15	30	15	30	45	15	30

and finally back to 3. Each operation has a one-week planned lead time. In the setup matrix for WC2, we find a setup in Week 1. In the setup matrix for WC3, we find setups in Weeks 2 and 4. In the setup matrix for WC1, we find a setup in Week 3. The setup times at each station agree with the data given in Table 13-3, the routing file. Each planned release in Table 13-8 yields a similar set of setup requirements in Table 13-9.

The run time matrix, Table 13-10, is computed in a similar fashion except that the times contained there are found by multiplying the lot size times the run time per piece shown in Table 13-3.

The Total row from each setup time and run time matrix can now be extracted and setup time added to run time at each work center to produce capacity required by the planned order releases from the MRP system (see Table 13-11).

We must now account for orders released to the shop. Four orders have been released to the shop according to Table 13-2: (1) an order for Part 100, quantity 250, due Week 1; (2) an order for Part 110, quantity 400, due Week 2; (3) an order for Part 121, quantity 2,400, due Week 2; and (4) an order for Part 122, quantity 4,000, due Week 2. These four orders are all on schedule, i.e., the number of operations remaining to be completed is equal to the number of weeks until due. The information on the location of the jobs in the shop has been taken from a shop floor control report that is not shown in any figure in this chapter. Such information is available in a closed-loop MRP system. Part 100 has one operation to be completed, the other three orders have two operations (the final two) to be completed. From this information and information contained in the routing file, Table 13-12 is created.

Table 13-10
Run Time Matrices for Standard Widget

	Part	Week 1	2	3	4	5	6	7
WC1	100	500	625	375	500	750	375	625
	110	0	200	200	250	200	200	200
	121	0	600	0	600	0	600	600
	122	0	0	3,000	0	0	3,000	0
	Total	500	1,425	3,575	1,350	950	4,175	1,425
WC2	100	0	0	0	0	0	0	0
	110	300	300	375	300	300	300	300
	121	0	0	600	0	600	0	600
	122	4,500	0	0	4,500	0	0	0
	Total	4,800	300	975	4,800	900	300	900
WC3	100	0	0	0	0	0	0	0
	110	0	0	0	0	0	0	0
	121	600	0	600	0	600	600	0
	122	0	900	0	2,100	900	0	2,100
	Total	600	900	600	2,100	1,500	600	2,100

Table 13-11
Capacity Requirements of Planned Releases

	Week 1	2	3	4	5	6	7
WC1	530	1,495	3,695	1,420	995	4,320	1,495
WC2	4,835	310	1,000	4,835	925	310	925
WC3	615	930	615	2,130	1,545	615	2,130

Table 13-12
Capacity Required by Released Orders

Part	WC	Week	Setup Time	Run Time Calculation	Run Time	Total Time
100	1	1	30	250×2.5	625	655
110	2	1	10	400×0.75	300	310
110	1	2	15	400×0.5	200	215
121	1	1	25	$2,400 \times 0.25$	600	625
121	2	2	15	$2,400 \times 0.25$	600	615
122	1	1	75	$6,000 \times 0.5$	3,000	3,075
122	3	2	30	$6,000 \times 0.75$	4,500	4,530

Table 13-12 illustrates an alternate algorithm for producing capacity requirements. First, total operation time is determined by the following equation.

Operation Time = Setup Time/Lot + Quantity × Run Time/Piece

Then, the operation time is placed in the appropriate weekly time bucket.

The data from Table 13-12 may now be collected by work center by week to produce Table 13-13.

Table 13-13
Released Order Capacity Requirements Summary

Work Center	Week 1	2
1	4,355	215
2	310	615
3	0	4,530

The capacity required by the planned order releases is now added to the capacity required by orders already released to the shop to produce the capacity requirements plan in Table 13-14. The CRP is shown graphically in Figure 13-3.

Table 13-14
Capacity Requirements Plan for Standard Widget
as of July 1, 1990

	Week 1	2	3	4	5	6	7
WC1	4,885	1,710	3,695	1,420	995	4,320	1,495
WC2	5,145	925	1,000	4,835	925	310	925
WC3	615	5,460	615	2,130	1,545	615	2,130

Cumulative Capacity Versus Average Capacity

CRP examines cumulative capacity while RCCP is generally interpreted using average capacity. That is, for each week CRP compares capacity required from the beginning of the planning horizon through the end of the week to capacity available for the same period. If for any week in the planning horizon cumulative capacity is insufficient, then a capacity shortfall exists that must be corrected. RCCP compares average capacity required over the entire planning horizon to average capacity available over the entire horizon. Why does this difference exist? Very simply, RCCP does not contain sufficient information regarding the timing of order releases for component items for cumulative capacity required to be portrayed accurately. If RCCP shows sufficient average

Figure 13-3
Capacity Requirements Plan for Standard Widgets

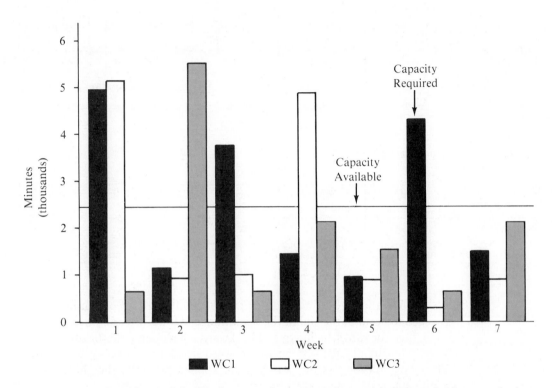

capacity and the load pattern is not grossly overloaded on the front end, then sufficient capacity is presumed. CRP on the other hand is based on a deterministic simulation of the shop using exact order release data from the MRP system. If cumulative capacity is inadequate for any period, then some jobs will be tardy.

FORWARD AND BACKWARD SCHEDULING

Two terms frequently associated with capacity requirements planning are forward and backward scheduling. In *forward scheduling,* activities start at the planned release date and move forward in time. Forward scheduling was used in the Standard Widgets example, although the term was not mentioned. In *backward scheduling*, activities start at the planned receipt date (due date) and move backward in time.

Assume that one lot of 500 Part 121s are due in Week 3. Then backward scheduling of Part 121 would appear as shown in Figure 13-4.

Given that Part 121 has a three week lead time, a job due at the end of Week 3 would be released at the beginning of Week 1. Forward scheduling from the release date would result in Figure 13-5.

Figure 13-4
Backward Scheduling, Part 121

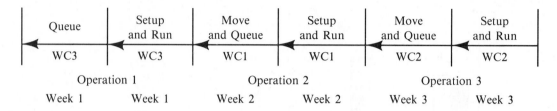

Figure 13-5
Forward Scheduling, Part 121

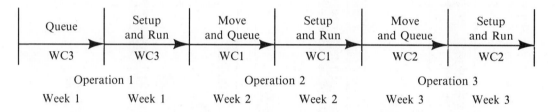

If operation lead times add to the job lead time and operation time is assumed to occur at the end of the operation lead time (after all interoperation time), then forward scheduling and backward scheduling yield the same result. Some commercial CRP systems use forward scheduling, others use backward scheduling. As long as the concepts are applied properly, the choice is not significant.

Note that in both cases the setup and run time is shown at the end of the operation lead time. This procedure is consistent with COPICS, IBM's Communications Oriented Production Information and Control System (1972), which seems to be the standard to which most CRP systems have been designed. This procedure gives the latest date at which a job must start in order to meet its due date. COPICS also recommends the establishment of an earliest start date permissable because of various restrictions (such as material availability). COPICS states further that "It is not known on which day the operation will actually be performed, but it is probable that it will be between these two dates. The actual date will depend on a number of factors, such as completion of the previous operation, tool availability, priority, capacity availability, amount of idle time, etc." (IBM 1972, 37) Thus, as with rough cut capacity planning, CRP develops an estimate of when and how much capacity will be needed.

Let's look again at the definition of CRP: "The term capacity requirements planning in this context is the process of determining how much labor and machine resources are required to accomplish the tasks of production. Open shop orders, and planned orders in the MRP system, are input to CRP, which 'translates' these orders into hours of work by work center by time period." (*APICS Dictionary* 1987) In order to complete the capacity requirements plan, one must perform either backward scheduling from the due date or forward scheduling from the release date for every released order in the shop and for every planned release in the MRP system.

In summation, the primary mission of CRP is to determine that there is adequate cumulative capacity to perform to schedule, taking into account earliest possible start dates where it is necessary to perform some work early, and overtime and alternative routings where overloads exist. If adequate capacity cannot be established, the master production schedule must be modified.

ESTIMATION OF QUEUE TIME FOR CRP

Of all elements of scheduling, as it relates to CRP, estimation of queue time is the most difficult to do properly. A *queue* is a group of elements, each waiting its turn for processing. In many operations, queue time makes up the largest single element of lead time (in some cases 90 percent of lead time). Queue time is also highly variable, as it is a function of how much work is already at a work center, how urgently the job in question is needed, and how badly the other jobs at the work center are needed. But if CRP is to work, lead time, hence queue time, must be predictable. As R. L. Lankford (1978) so aptly put it, "lead time must be planned and controlled, meaning that queues must be planned and controlled. . . . The mission of production control is one of managing queues to the sizes prescribed by a rational plan of shop operation. Queues become an element of operations to be managed—like efficiency, utilization, and material flow—not a condition determined by events and passively accepted as a fact of life by supervision. . . . The proper queue allowance is the one decided upon as appropriate by production management for the average job under normal operating conditions. Queues must then be maintained at or near planned levels as a routine part of production control, otherwise the execution of the manufacturing plan will bear little resemblance to the expectations of MRP and CRP. . . . Input/Output control seeks to control lead times by controlling queues, and to do so by metering input of load into the system based on measurement of output. Even when Input/Output control cannot be used in a formal way, the controlled release of manufacturing jobs to the shop floor can be helpful in maintaining planned queues and avoiding excessive lead time through the manufacturing processes."

If a shop is arranged in assembly line or group technology fashion, so that a gateway operation controls load at a number of work stations, queue control is very achievable. But with a job shop configuration, queue control may be very difficult. Queue control is especially difficult in shops that, like Standard Widgets, have extremely lumpy planned order release schedules. Reducing lot sizes, ideally moving to lot-for-lot ordering, helps to produce a more even flow of work to the shop and, hence, more manageable queues.

Queue control in general, and input-output control in particular, are discussed in Chapter 14.

SUMMARY

In this chapter, a method for creating and evaluating the capacity requirements plan is presented. Note that CRP uses more information than RCCP but still produces only an estimate of the timing and quantity of capacity needed. CRP is a deterministic technique. To the extent that jobs wait in queue longer than expected, machines break down, jobs are completed in a sequence other than planned, and so on, reality deviates from CRP.

Because queue control is such an important aspect of managing capacity within an MRP system, recognizing the random nature of queue lengths is extremely important.

EXERCISES

1. Discuss why CRP is necessary given that rough cut capacity planning has been properly performed.

2. Suppose that CRP reveals a capacity shortfall. Discuss the steps that could be taken to correct this shortfall without modifying the material requirements plan. Why not simply ignore the shortfall and let the shop floor deal with the problem?

3. Take the information given in Table 13-1 of this chapter and modify the bill of material quantities as follows: (1) change the quantity of Part 110 required by Part 100 to 4 per unit and (2) change the quantity of Parts 121 and 122 required by Part 110 to 3 and 5, respectively. Retaining all other data given, develop a CRP report for the first seven weeks of the planning horizon spanned by the master production schedule.

4. Discuss the relationship between queue time and lead time. Discuss the relationship between input/output control and customer service (meeting due dates).

5. Work Center 46 employs two workers on one 40-hour shift. Historical utilization and efficiency figures for Work Center 46 are 93 percent and 112 percent, respectively. Work Center 46 has a planned queue of 15 hours. At present, the actual queue is 35 hours. In the coming five weeks the standard hours of work scheduled to arrive at Work Center 46 are 70, 86, 72, 74, and 84, respectively.
   a. Each worker may work up to 10 hours overtime per week. Schedule Work Center 46 in order to reduce the actual queue by 4 hours each week so that at the end of five weeks the actual queue is 15 hours.
   b. Schedule Work Center 46 so that the actual queue is returned to 15 hours as quickly as possible, i.e., using the full overtime allowable as long as is necessary to return the queue to 15 hours.

   c. Assume an alternate station has been identified that will accept 4 standard hours of work from Work Center 46 each week. Schedule Work Center 46 using no overtime in such a way as to reduce the backlog to 15 hours by the end of the fifth week.

6. Using the data from Exercise 5, assume that Work Center 46 currently has no work. Schedule the next five weeks so that at the end of the period 15 standard hours of backlog exist and so that no overtime is worked during the period. Discuss why such a deliberate buildup of work is desirable.

Exercises 7 to 9 refer to the following data:

	Bill of Material	
Level	Part	Quantity/Parent
0	A	1
1	B1	2
1	B2	4

		Item Master Record				
Item	Order Quantity	On Hand	On Order	Lead Time	Allocated	Safety Stock
A	LFL	228	0	2	0	25
B1	400	354	0	2	0	0
B2	800	430	0	3	0	0

	Routing File			
	Operation	Work Center	Setup/Lot	Run Time/Piece
Part A	10	3	45 minutes	4 minutes
	20	1	80 minutes	2 minutes
Part B1	10	2	35 minutes	1 minute
	20	3	20 minutes	2 minutes
Part B2	10	1	70 minutes	4 minutes
	20	3	40 minutes	3 minutes
	30	2	60 minutes	5 minutes

	Work Center Master File			
Work Center	Available	Utilization	Efficiency	Planned Queue
1	4,800 minutes	80%	110%	2 days
2	4,800 minutes	75%	105%	2 days
3	4,800 minutes	95%	110%	4 days

	Master Schedule for Part A			
		Week		
	1	2	3	4	5
Quantity	120	85	95	115	90

7. Develop a rough cut capacity plan for Weeks 1 to 5 using the data shown above. Is the schedule feasible?

8. Develop a material requirements plan using the data shown above. Assume any orders due to be released prior to Week 1 will be released in Week 1. Develop the capacity requirements plan. Is the MRP feasible?

9. Based on the results obtained in Exercise 8, what recommendation, if any, would you make regarding lot-size policies?

SELECTED READINGS

Blackstone, John H., Jr. *Capacity Management*. Cincinnati: South-Western Publishing Co., 1989.

Carter, Phillip L., and Chrwan-Jyh Ho. "Vendor Capacity Planning: An Approach to Vendor Scheduling." *Production and Inventory Management* (Fourth Quarter 1984): 63-73.

IBM. *Communications Oriented Production Information and Control System*. White Plains, NY: IBM Technical Publications Department, 1972.

Lankford, Raymond L. "Short-Term Planning of Manufacturing Capacity." *APICS Conference Proceedings* (1978): 37.

Orlicky, Joseph. *Material Requirements Planning*. New York: McGraw-Hill Book Co., 1975.

Plossl, George W., and Oliver W. Wight. "Capacity Planning and Control." In *Capacity Planning and Control*, 50-86. Falls Church, VA: American Production and Inventory Control Society, 1975.

Wallace, Thomas, ed. *APICS Dictionary*. 6th ed. Falls Church, VA: American Production and Inventory Control Society, 1987.

Wight, Oliver W. "Input/Output Control: A Real Handle on Lead Time." In *Capacity Management Reprints*, 107-129. Falls Church, VA: American Production and Inventory Control Society, 1984.

APPENDIX 13A
ROUGH CUT CAPACITY PLANNING
CALCULATIONS FOR STANDARD WIDGETS

In order to create a bill of labor, Sam Johnson took the routing data and lot size data from Tables 13-2 and 13-3 (reproduced below as Tables 13A-1 and 13A-2) and used it to compute the process time per part as shown in Table 13A-3.

Table 13A-1
Item Master Record Files for Standard Widget
as of Saturday, July 1, 1990

Item	Order Quantity	On Hand	On Order	Due Date	Lead Time	Allocated
100	LFL	0	250	7/3	1 week	0
110	400	500	400	7/10	2 weeks	0
121	2,400	1,500	2,400	7/10	3 weeks	0
122	6,000	2,500	6,000	7/10	4 weeks	0

Table 13A-2
Routing Files for Standard Widget

	Work Center	Setup Time/Lot	Run Time/Piece
Part 100	1	30 minutes	2.5 minutes
Part 110	2	10 minutes	0.75 minutes
	1	15 minutes	0.5 minutes
Part 121	3	15 minutes	0.3 minutes
	1	25 minutes	0.25 minutes
	2	15 minutes	0.25 minutes
Part 122	2	25 minutes	0.75 minutes
	3	30 minutes	0.15 minutes
	1	75 minutes	0.5 minutes
	3	30 minutes	0.75 minutes

Table 13A-3
Process Time Computation

(1) Part	(2) Opn.	(3) L.S.	(4) S.U.	(5) Run	(6) Process	(7) Qt/Part 100	(8) Total	(9) WC
100	1	200	30	2.50	2.650	1	2.650	1
110	1	400	10	0.75	0.775	2	1.550	2
110	2	400	15	0.50	0.538	2	1.076	1
121	1	2,400	15	0.30	0.306	6	1.836	3
121	2	2,400	25	0.25	0.260	6	1.560	1
121	3	2,400	15	0.25	0.256	6	1.536	2
122	1	6,000	25	0.75	0.754	10	7.540	2
122	2	6,000	30	0.15	0.155	10	1.550	3
122	3	6,000	75	0.50	0.513	10	5.130	1
122	4	6,000	30	0.75	0.755	10	7.550	3

In Table 13A-3 Column 1 gives the part number, Column 2 the operation number, Column 3 the lot size (Part 100 is an estimated average), Column 4 the setup time per lot, and Column 5 the run time per piece.

The process time per piece is calculated in Column 6 using Equation 1.

$$\text{Process Time/Piece} = \frac{\text{Setup Time/Lot}}{\text{Lot Size}} + \text{Run Time/Piece} \qquad (1)$$

A finished widget contains two subassemblies (Part 110) and a total of six component A's (Part 121) and ten component B's (Part 122). These quantities per end item are reflected in Column 7. Column 8 is process time times quantity per finished widget, yielding the total time spent on the operation for a finished widget. Column 9 shows the work center at which the operation is performed. In Table 13A-4, Table 13A-3 has been sorted by work center in order to obtain the total time in each work center. The rightmost column of Table 13A-4 is a bill of labor that has been extracted to form Table 13A-5.

Table 13A-4
Bill of Labor Computation

Part	L.S.	S.U.	Run	Process	Qt/Part 100	Total	WC	WC Total
110	400	15	0.5	0.538	2	1.076	1	
122	6,000	75	0.5	0.513	10	5.130	1	
121	2,400	25	0.25	0.260	6	1.560	1	
100	200	30	2.5	2.650	1	2.650	1	10.416
121	2,400	15	0.25	0.256	6	1.536	2	
110	400	10	0.75	0.775	2	1.550	2	
122	6,000	25	0.75	0.754	10	7.540	2	10.626
122	6,000	30	0.15	0.155	10	1.550	3	
122	6,000	30	0.75	0.755	10	7.550	3	
121	2,400	15	0.3	0.306	6	1.836	3	10.936

Table 13A-5
Bill of Labor for Standard Widget

Work Center	Time/Widget
1	10.416 minutes
2	10.626 minutes
3	10.936 minutes

Part
Five

Production
Activity
Control

14

PRODUCTION ACTIVITY CONTROL

The time arrives when plans must be executed, when material requirements planning and capacity requirements planning have been completed and the detail purchasing and production schedules must be determined and released for execution. The function of production activity control (PAC)—often called shop floor control (SFC)—is to have activities performed as planned, to report on operating results, and to revise plans as required to achieve desired results. Figure 14-1 shows the sequence of the various planning and control activities.

The PAC system also closes the control loop, as illustrated in Figure 14-1, by measuring actual output and comparing it to the plan. Thus, PAC is an essential component of closed-loop MRP. Although all PAC systems perform the same basic functions, individual systems differ because each manufacturing environment is unique. Each has a specific number of products, production processes, facility layouts, and relationships of available capacity of personnel and equipment to the required capacity.

SCHEDULING IN MANUFACTURING ENVIRONMENTS

Chapter 1 described the different types of production environments: continuous and repetitive flow lines, batch flow lines, manufacturing cells, job shop, and project (fixed site) processes. Each environment is distinctive. Scheduling continuous and repetitive flow lines is discussed in Chapter 18. Project scheduling is discussed in Chapter 16. This chapter discusses scheduling techniques for the traditional job shop and for batch flow production.

Figure 14-1
Production Activity Control Schematic

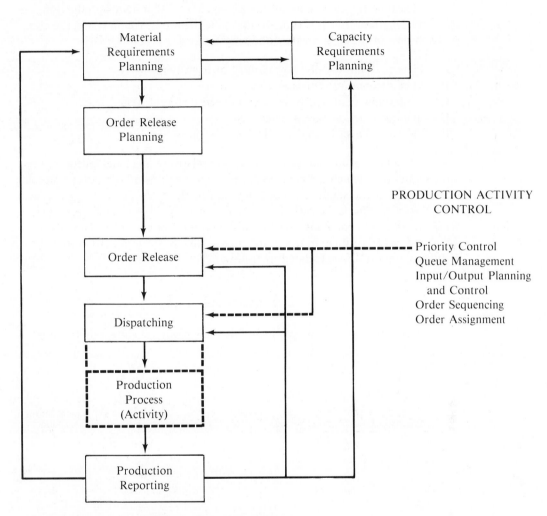

Scheduling for Batch Flow Lines

Batch flow lines exist in beverage companies, ice cream manufacturers, soap powder packaging facilities, and pharmaceutical plants. Typically, a group of similar items is manufactured on the batch line. As noted in Chapter 8, a family of items may be produced in batch quantities on the same line with some changes in the setup, a cleaning of the equipment, and changes in incoming materials. (If no time is required for switching from one item in the family to another, then the different items can be mixed in the same run and a mixed model line exists.) Thus, a primary production management objective is to reduce and eventually eliminate the time required for changing between items in a group. The smaller the changeover time, the greater the scheduling flexibility and the smaller the scheduling problem.

The quantity of an item produced depends on that item's production rate and the length of time it is run. Deciding the item to be run next and the quantity to be run depends on the following factors.

A. The on-hand (available) quantity of each item
B. The demand rate of each item
C. The times required to change between different items
D. The production rate of each item
E. The sequence, if any, in which items should be run

When the setup (changeover) times are relatively small and independent of the sequence in which the items are produced, the decision is relatively simple: the item with the smallest runout time is run first.

Runout time is the period existing inventory will last given forecast usage. For example, if a company uses (or sells) 20 printed circuits (Part No. 101) each day and has 80 of them in stock, the runout time of Part No. 101 is four days. Runout time (R) is calculated as follows:

$$R = \frac{\text{Units in Inventory}}{\text{Demand (Usage) Rate}}$$

Let's look at an example including four items, as shown in Table 14-1.

Table 14-1
Runout Time

Item	Inventory	Demand (units per day)	R (in days)	Scheduling Priority
A	80	20	4.0	1
B	100	10	10.0	2
C	150	12	12.5	3
D	60	4	15.0	4

Runout times in Table 14-1 are calculated using the equation above. For example, the runout time of Part B is:

$$R(B) = \frac{100 \text{ Units}}{10 \text{ Units per Day}} = 10.0 \text{ Days}$$

The items in Table 14-1 are scheduled according to their runout times.

If the setup times for the items in a group are relatively short and the production lot quantities are small due to relatively low demand rates and low setup costs, there is no problem. Sufficient time usually will exist to manufacture all items on schedule.

Let's look at another example. Table 14-2 shows runout times for three machined parts made on the same machine, a traditional machine tool with a larger setup time and corresponding larger production quantities.

Table 14-2
Runout Time

Item	Inventory	Demand (units per day)	R (in days)	Economical Production Quantity	Economical Production Time (in days)
A	80	80	1.0	400	2.0
B	150	75	2.0	400	2.0
C	60	30	2.0	300	1.5

The company has a problem. Items A, B, and C should be run immediately. Some of these items should have been manufactured last week. The purpose of this example is to point out that:

A. Manufacturing engineering should reduce the setup times and, thus, improve the production run quantities and time. A computer numerically controlled, (CNC), machine that can shift from one part to another with little or no setup time may be appropriate.
B. Proper timing of order releases is as important as the quantity decision.

In addition, the appropriateness of a model depends on the situation. Order quantity and order release decisions are more complicated when more than one group is run on the same equipment, when capacity is limited, or when items in a group must be run in a particular sequence to achieve minimum changeover times (for example first Item A, then B, C, and so on).

When sufficient inventory is available, personnel may be used for preventive maintenance, methods analysis, and setup time reduction to reduce lead time and improve quality rather than to produce unneeded parts. (These topics are discussed further in Chapter 17 as part of Just-in-Time concepts.)

Job Shop Scheduling

The physical layout of a job shop usually groups equipment performing similar functions in the same area. Typically, there are many different orders being processed in the plant at the same time and relatively few have the same routing (the department-by-department path through the plant). *Scheduling* is the assigning of starting and completion times to orders (jobs) and frequently includes the times when orders are to arrive and leave each department. *Sequencing* is the assigning of the sequence in which orders are to be processed, for example, do Order C first, then B, followed by D, and so on. However, in practice and in the literature, scheduling frequently refers to both the time schedule and the sequence of orders or jobs. The selection of a scheduling system, approach, or technique depends on the objectives of the schedule and the criteria by which its results will be measured.

Management policies and objectives are the basis for scheduling decisions. However, production management may define multiple and conflicting scheduling objectives in different ways, such as: minimize average lateness of orders, minimize maximum lateness, minimize manufacturing lead time (minimum average flow time), minimize work in process, and maximize utilization of bottleneck work centers. Fortunately, many of the objectives are mutually supportive. For example, reducing manufacturing lead time reduces work in process and increases the probability of meeting due dates.

Achievement of these scheduling objectives depends on the flexibility of the manufacturing equipment and personnel. The importance of achieving flexibility through methods improvement, facility layout, setup reduction, worker cross training, and the development of manufacturing cells cannot be overemphasized.

Priority Control

Many methods (sometimes called *priority rules*) exist for establishing the priority of orders. The priority, often expressed numerically, is used to determine the sequence in which the orders should be processed. The rules described in the following pages are probably the most common, but many variations and combinations of these methods exist. The list in Table 14-3 provides a good overview of the basic rules and their objectives.

To show how the rules in Table 14-3 are used to determine the priority of orders, let's consider a specific example. Table 14-4 shows data concerning four orders in a manufacturing plant in central Illinois. All orders were in the same department, which we call Department 7. The simplest priority rule to implement is earliest due date. For this example, the manufacturing sequence would be A, B, C, D. These jobs have due dates of 130, 132, 136, and 138, respectively. We now discuss the computation of slack and critical ratio rules.

Slack time (ST) is found by subtracting the present date (Day 125 in Table 14-4) and the total operation time remaining from the due date. That is,

$$ST = \text{Due Date} - \text{Present Date} - \text{Total Operation Time Remaining}$$

For Order A,

$$ST = 130 - 125 - 3.0 = 2.0$$

The critical ratio (CR) equals the difference between the due date and the present date divided by the manufacturing lead time remaining:

$$CR = \frac{\text{Due Date} - \text{Present Date}}{\text{Manufacturing Lead Time Remaining}}$$

Table 14-3
Common Priority Decision Rules

Rule	Objective
FCFS—First Come, First Served	Run the orders in the sequence in which they arrive at the work center. This "fairness" rule is especially appropriate in service organizations where most customers often either need or desire the completion of the service as soon as possible.
SPT, SOT—Shortest Processing (Operation) Time	Run the orders in the inverse order of the time required to process them (smallest time first) in the department. This rule usually results in the lowest work in process, the lowest average job completion (manufacturing lead time), and average job lateness. Unless this rule is combined with a due date or slack time rule, jobs (orders) with long processing times can be extremely late.
STPT—Shortest Total Processing Time Remaining	Run the orders in the inverse order of the total processing time remaining. The rationale of this rule is similar to the preceding one. It accomplishes similar objectives when most jobs follow a common process.
EDD—Earliest Due Date	Run orders with the earliest due date first. This rule works well when processing times are approximately the same.
FO—Fewest Operations	Run first the orders with the fewest operations remaining. The logic of this rule is that fewer operations involve less queue time and, as a result, the rule reduces average work in process, manufacturing lead time, and average lateness. However, jobs with a relatively large number of operations can take excessively long if another rule is not combined with this one.
ST—Slack Time	Run first the order with the smallest slack time and continue the sequence in the ascending order of their slack times. Slack time equals the due date minus the remaining processing time (setup plus run time). This rule supports the achievement of due date objectives. The slack time remaining per operation is a variation of this rule.
CR—Critical Ratio	For orders not already late (overdue), run first those orders with the lowest critical ratio. The critical ratio equals the due date minus the present date divided by the normal manufacturing lead time remaining.

Table 14-4
Scheduling Priority, Department 7, Day 125
(All times are in days.)

Order	Due Date	Current Operation Time	Total Operation Time Remaining	Manufacturing Lead Time Remaining*	Number of Operations Remaining	Slack Time	Critical Ratio
A	130	1.5	3.0	6.0	3	2.0	0.83
B	132	1.0	4.5	9.5	5	2.5	0.74
C	136	2.0	4.0	8.0	4	7.0	1.38
D	138	3.5	7.0	9.0	2	6.0	1.44

*Includes planned queue time

For Order D,

$$CR = \frac{138 - 125}{9.0} = 1.44$$

A CR of 1.0 indicates that the order is right on schedule; a CR greater than 1.0 indicates that the order is ahead of schedule; and a CR smaller than 1.0 indicates that the order is behind schedule. The smaller the CR, the higher the priority of the order. The CR index—as most priority criteria—should be used in conjunction with one or more other criteria. For example, Order X has 2 days left to delivery and 1 day of manufacturing lead time remaining; thus, its CR is 2.0 (2 ÷ 1). Suppose Order Y has a 1.11 CR: it has 10 days left until its due date and 9 days of manufacturing lead time remaining. On the basis of CR's, Order Y has the higher priority. Both have the same slack time, one day. However, the nearer due date of Order X argues strongly for giving it first priority.

In addition, the CR is not a good priority index for orders whose due date has passed. Priority indices for orders whose due dates have passed are described shortly.

Applying each of the priority rules in Table 14-3 (except FCFS) to the four orders in Table 14-4 gives the following processing sequences:

EDD (Earliest Due Date): A, B, C, D
SOT (Shortest Operation Time): B, A, C, D
STPT (Shortest Total Processing Time Remaining): A, C, B, D
FO (Fewest Operations): D, A, C, B
ST (Slack Time Remaining): A, B, D, C
CR (Critical Ratio): B, A, C, D

Although applying priority rules to any four orders at a given time in a specific department will produce different results, the above results are not unusual. Different rules produce different sequences, but certain patterns tend to appear in most. For example, Orders A and B are scheduled first or second by most rules. One factor that also should be considered is the status of the work center to which each order goes next. There would be little point in scheduling Order A first if its next operation was in a work center overloaded with higher priority orders.

An advantage of the SOT rule is that the data required to use it is readily available to the immediate supervisor, as should be the due date data. Operation and order due dates are very popular for establishing order priorities because of their simplicity, ease of understanding, and direct relationship to a primary objective of management—on time delivery. The other rules require calculations and considerably more data. Thus, they usually require a computerized shop floor control system that performs all calculations and prepares daily lists showing job priority.

Planning (determining) the priorities of orders is a prerequisite to effective production activity control. Priorities must reflect actual needs and be consistent among items going into the same assembly. Changing order priorities frequently will destroy their credibility.

Overdue Orders and Priority Indices. Overdue orders are of special interest because management is interested in minimizing the cost of late orders. Special priority indices are often used to manage overdue orders because, among other reasons, the CR technique gives confusing information when applied to overdue orders. The data in Table 14-5 illustrate the failure of CR in an overdue situation. Orders B and C both have a CR of 0.0 indicating identical priorities; but B is 10 days behind schedule and C is 8 days behind schedule. Clearly their priorities should not be the same. Order D has a CR of −2.5 which would indicate that it is in a poorer condition than Order E which has a CR of −1.25. This is not the case; Order E is further behind schedule than Order D.

Table 14-5
Critical Ratio for Overdue Orders
(Present date is Day 35.)

Order	Date Due	Actual Time Remaining	Manufacturing Lead Time Remaining*	CR	Days Behind or Ahead of Schedule
A**	40	5	2	2.5	+3
B	35	0	10	0.0	−10
C	35	0	8	0.0	−8
D	25	−10	4	−2.5	−14
E	25	−10	8	−1.25	−18

*Includes planned queue time
**Not overdue

The concept of slack time, the time ahead of or behind schedule, can be used to aid in determining priority for overdue orders. Slack time may be computed by different methods; manufacturing lead time and processing time remaining are the two most widely used. Managers may wish to minimize the *number* of late orders and decide to have one job very late. In this case, jobs that can be delivered on time are not delayed to process a job that already is late.

The manufacturing lead time remaining (MLTR) method of computing slack time computes the number of days ahead of or behind schedule by subtracting the manufacturing lead time from the actual lead time remaining. The priority is then computed based on the number of days behind or ahead of schedule. For example, Order E in Table 14-6 has highest priority because it is the farthest behind schedule on the basis of this method.

Table 14-6
Priority of Overdue Orders—Manufacturing Lead Time Remaining
(Present date is Day 35.)

Order	Date Due	Actual Time Remaining	Manufacturing Lead Time Remaining*	Days Behind or Ahead of Schedule	Priority
A**	40	5	2	+3	5
B	35	0	10	−10	3
C	35	0	8	−8	4
D	25	−10	4	−14	2
E	25	−10	8	−18	1

*Includes planned queue time
**Not overdue

The processing time remaining (PTR) method of computing slack time computes the number of days behind or ahead of schedule by subtracting the processing time remaining from the actual time remaining. These computations are shown in Table 14-7.

Table 14-7
Priority of Overdue Orders—Processing Time Remaining
(Present date is Day 35.)

Order	Date Due	Actual Time Remaining	Processing Time Remaining	Days Behind or Ahead of Schedule	Priority Rank
A*	40	5	2	+3	5
B	35	0	4	−4	4
C	35	0	5	−5	3
D	25	−10	1	−11	2
E	25	−10	3	−13	1

*Not overdue

The days behind schedule when computed using manufacturing lead time remaining as in Table 14-6 indicate that Order B is further behind schedule than Order C and thus has a higher priority. However, a ranking based on processing time remaining rather than total manufacturing lead time gives Order C a higher priority, as illustrated in Table 14-7. When queue and move time are a large but variable portion of manufacturing lead time, and the queue and move time can be compressed by priority sequencing, ranking is improved using days overdue plus processing time remaining rather than total lead time remaining.

Thus, for overdue orders, two priority rules are:

1. Run those orders first that have the greatest total of days behind schedule plus manufacturing lead time remaining.
2. Run those orders first that have the greatest total of days behind schedule plus processing time remaining.

Orders for safety stock and made-to-stock items should have lower priority than items being manufactured to fill a customer order with the same due date. This is in keeping with the philosophy that the customer always comes first. In addition, safety stock and finished goods stock are manufactured to meet probable but uncertain demands, while an actual order is a certainty.

Performance Measures.   Criteria for evaluating a priority control system can include the following:

1. Percentage of on time orders
   a. to customers
   b. to the assembly line
2. Average tardiness
3. Work in process
4. Idle time
5. Minimizing setup time
6. Energy conservation

One or two of the foregoing may be dominant over a short period. The planner must be able to recognize shifting criteria, or even different criteria in different parts of the plant, and to organize dispatch lists accordingly. A *dispatch list* is a document that lists the jobs in a work center and indicates the priority of each. Dispatching is discussed in detail later in this chapter.

QUEUE LENGTH MANAGEMENT

Queues consist of those items waiting to be processed at a work center. They usually are measured in hours of work required in the work center, that is, the length or size of the queue. The lengths of queues directly affect the value of work-in-process inventory and manufacturing lead times. In an ideal situation there are no queues and also no idle time: an item arrives exactly at the time scheduled for its processing and the work center has just become available to perform the operation. However, ideal conditions rarely exist in job shops and queues are planned to compensate for the uneven flow of incoming work and the variations in work center processing times. Chapter 17 describes how Just-in-Time concepts can reduce queues substantially. This section describes the management of queues prior to achieving the benefits of JIT.

The objective of queue length management is to control lead time and work in process and to obtain full utilization of bottleneck work centers. Material queues of only an hour's work or so may be planned in a flow line process to avoid downtime. In a job shop environment, determining the nature of queues at the critical work centers should be the first step. Meaningful queue length goals then can be established. First, we will examine queue length distributions. Then, we will investigate operation overlapping and operation splitting, two methods of managing queues and lead times.

Typical Queue Distributions

Figure 14-2 illustrates four different queue situations: (1) a controlled queue, (2) an excessive queue length, (3) an uncontrolled queue, and (4) substantial idle time due to a short queue.

Figure 14-2A illustrates a situation where the average queue length is 30 hours, the maximum length is 55 hours, and the work center is never idle because of lack of work and is seldom overloaded. On the other hand, the data in Figure 14-2B exemplify a queue whose length is never less than 45 hours. It is obvious that the length of this queue can be reduced by 45 hours without affecting idle time. This reduction can be accomplished by releasing work to the work center (controlling the input) at a reduced rate until the queue reduces.

Queue length also can be measured statistically with planned average lengths based on the probability of a stockout, a zero length queue. This approach calculates the planned average queue length by multiplying the standard deviation of the queue length observations by the number of standard deviations required to obtain the desired coverage. It assumes a queue length distribution on the basis of historical data and counts the item being machined as part of the queue. (Zero queue length corresponds to machine downtime.)

Let the queue in Figure 14-2B have a normal distribution with a 70-hour average length and a standard deviation of 9.7 hours. If management's objective is to have a material shortage less than 1 percent of the time (a 99 percent service level), the planned average queue length should be approximately 22.6 (2.33 × 9.7) standard hours. (The approximate number of standard deviations corresponding to 49 percent of the high side area under the normal curve is 2.33.)[1] Figure 14-3 illustrates the distribution of queue lengths.

The first approach to the queue in Figure 14-2B indicates that the average queue length can be reduced by up to 45 standard hours, and the statistical approach suggests that an average queue length of 22.6 standard hours (a reduction of 47.4 hours in the average queue length) will meet idle time objectives. Neither approach is exact and both should be applied with caution. Queue length distributions seldom are perfectly normal and shortening the length of a queue will, in itself, affect the distribution. In most cases, however, both

---

1. See Appendix A.

Figure 14-2
Typical Queue Lengths
(Time Series and Frequency Distributions)

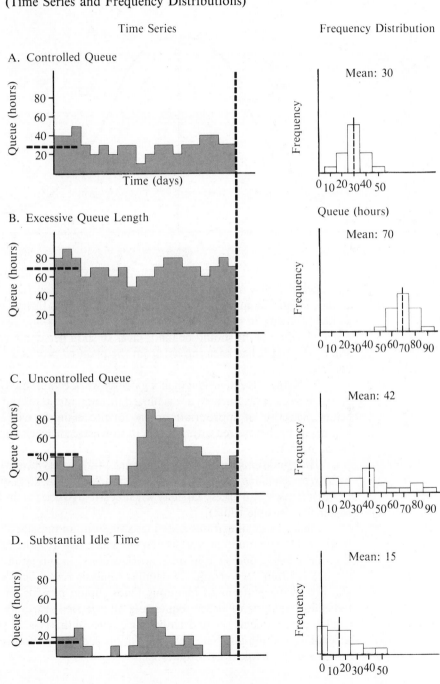

Figure 14-3
Distribution of Queue Lengths
(Standard Deviation = 9.7 Hours)

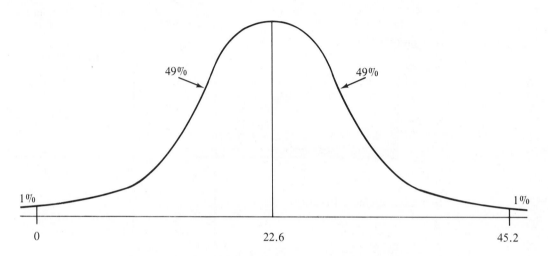

approaches clearly indicate when a queue can be shortened. In most cases the change should be made gradually to minimize shop adjustment problems. A sudden decrease in queue length can cause supervisors and operators to drag out available jobs. It should be made clear to shop personnel that the backlog still exists, but it has been moved from the plant to production planning and control.

Reductions in queue length at a gateway work center, the first work center at which work is performed, are achieved through input/output control at that center. Selection of appropriate orders for processing in earlier work centers will result in the desired adjustments in downstream work centers used later in the process.

The conditions represented by Figure 14-2D are typical of a work center with excess available capacity. Jobs at overloaded work centers should be moved to work centers with excess capacity when possible (when the underloaded work center is a feasible route).

Figure 14-2C illustrates a stickier situation, an uncontrolled queue. It is more likely to be found in work centers in which two or more preceding operations have been completed in other work centers. In this situation, the arrival of jobs is often very erratic. A detailed analysis revealing the major source and processing patterns of incoming loads should provide clues for possible remedies. Analysis of order sequencing alternatives also may reveal options available for reducing the unusually long queues in this type of situation. Finite scheduling techniques that have simulation capability often can be used to anticipate and avoid such situations.

Operation Overlapping (Transfer Batches)

Operation overlapping, schematically represented in Figure 14-4, is a technique used to reduce the total lead time of a production order by dividing the lot into two or more batches and linking at least two successive operations directly (one is performed immediately after the other). Operation overlapping is a common practice in manufacturing cells when setup is required.

Figure 14-4
Schematic of Operation Overlapping

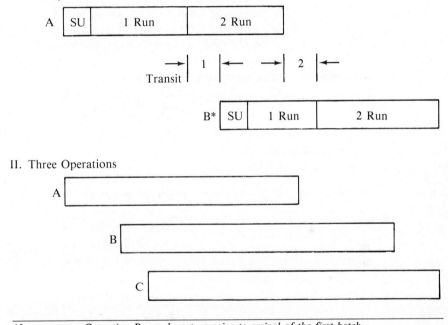

I. Two Operations

II. Three Operations

In some cases Operation B may be set up prior to arrival of the first batch.

Operation overlapping consists of the following:

1. A lot of parts is divided into at least two batches (transfer batches).
2. As soon as the first batch completes Operation A, it is moved to Operation B for immediate processing.
3. While Operation A is being performed on the second batch, Operation B is being performed on the first batch.
4. When Operation A has been completed on the second batch, it is moved immediately to Operation B.

If Operation B requires substantially shorter time per piece than Operation A, the first batch should be sufficiently large to avoid idle time at Operation B. Calculation of this minimum batch size is straightforward:

$$Q = Q_1 + Q_2$$

$$Q_1 P_B + T_{AB} + S_B \geq Q_2 P_A + T_{AB} \text{ (assuming } Q_2 \text{ is to be at}$$
Operation B before Operation B is completed on Q_1)

where Q = total lot size
Q_1 = minimum size of first batch
Q_2 = maximum size of second batch
S_B = setup time of Operation B
P_A = processing time per unit, Operation A
P_B = processing time per unit, Operation B
T_{AB} = transit time between Operations A and B

Solving the above equations for Q_1, gives:

$$Q_1 \geq \frac{QP_A - S_B}{P_B + P_A}$$

For example, if

$$Q = 100 \text{ units}$$
$$P_A = 10 \text{ minutes}$$
$$P_B = 5 \text{ minutes}$$
$$S_B = 40 \text{ minutes}$$
$$T_{AB} = 30 \text{ minutes}$$

then

$$Q_1 \geq \frac{100 \times 10 - 40}{10 + 5} = \frac{960}{15} = 64$$

The result is checked easily. The time required to process 64 units in Operation B is 320 (64 × 5) minutes of run time plus 40 minutes for setup, a total of 360 minutes. This is exactly the time required to process the second batch of 36 units at Work Center A. Move time is the same for both. If fewer than 64 units were in the first batch, Work Center B would be idle awaiting arrival of Batch 2.

If Operation B can be set up prior to the arrival of parts, consideration of setup time drops out of the equation defining the minimum size of the first batch. For example,

$$Q_1 \geq \frac{100 \times 10}{10 + 5} = 66.7 = 67 \text{ units}$$

Reduction of total manufacturing lead time by the reduction of the throughput time for Operations A and B is the benefit of operation overlapping, as illustrated in Figure 14-5. The disadvantages are the added cost of increased planning and control required by doubling the number of batches and material movements, plus the requirements that the first batch be moved immediately upon completion and that capacity be available at Work Center B when the first batch arrives. Time lost by not meeting these latter two requirements decreases the savings in lead time.

Figure 14-5
Comparison of Lead Time Without and With Overlapping

A. Lead Time Without Overlapping and No Queue

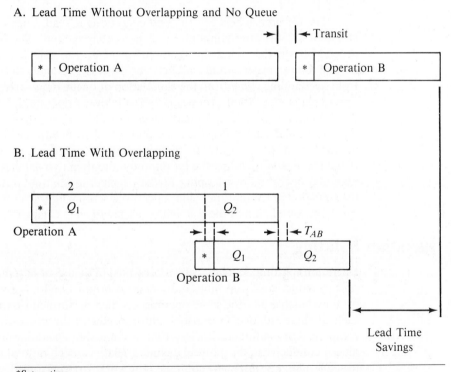

B. Lead Time With Overlapping

*Setup time

To calculate the difference between lead time without and with overlapping using the previous example, let:

$$
\begin{array}{ll}
Q = 100 \text{ units} & P_B = 5 \text{ minutes} \\
Q_1 = 66 \text{ units} & T_{AB} = 30 \text{ minutes} \\
Q_2 = 34 \text{ units} & S_A = 80 \text{ minutes} \\
P_A = 10 \text{ minutes} & S_B = 40 \text{ minutes}
\end{array}
$$

The manufacturing lead time (MLT) without overlapping and no queue equals the total time for Operation A (setup and run) plus transit time plus the total time for Operation B (setup and run). Thus,

$$MLT = 80 + 100 \times 10 + 30 + 40 + 100 \times 5 = 1,650 \text{ minutes}$$

The MLT with overlapping and prior setup of Operation B equals the time for Operation A on Batch 1 (setup and run) plus transit time from Operation A to Operation B plus the total time for Operation B (run only) on Batches 1 and 2. Batch 2 completes Operation A and is moved to Operation B while Batch 1 is being processed in B. Thus,

$$MLT = 80 + 67 \times 10 + 30 + 100 \times 5 = 1,280 \text{ minutes}$$

The difference between the two conditions in lead times is 370 minutes $(1,650 - 1,280)$, approximately a 22 percent reduction. The actual savings depend on whether parts are required to set up the machine as well as the normal time an order would wait between processes. Usually the major savings from overlapping come from the elimination of queue time—frequently several times greater than total processing time—between operations.

When the processing time of Operation B is greater than that of Operation A, similar calculations can be performed to determine the batch sizes required to maximize lead time savings under the constraint of only one additional movement (dividing the lot into no more than two batches). Chapter 17 examines operation overlapping further, including multiple transfer lots and the reduction of transit time. Since operation, setup, and transit times are rarely constants, simulation of these activities, as described in Chapter 23, is advisable.

Operation Splitting

Operation splitting, schematically represented in Figure 14-6, reduces total lead time by reducing the run time component. A production lot is divided into two or more batches and the same operation is then performed simultaneously on each of these sublots. Operation splitting reduces the processing (run time) component of manufacturing lead time at the cost of an additional setup. Conditions conducive to lot splitting include a relatively high ratio of total run time to setup time, idle duplicate equipment or work force personnel, and the feasibility of an operator running more than one machine. These conditions frequently exist. For example, in the cutting of large diameter ring gears, the setup time is small in comparison with the run time of a lot of 20 or more.

Lots also may be split in a "setup offset" manner as illustrated in Figure 14-6. After the first machine is set up and running, the operator sets up the second machine. For this approach to be feasible, the time required to unload one part and load the following part must be shorter than the run time per part. In addition, shop practices (and the labor contract) must allow an individual to run more than one machine. This approach reduces lead time and

Figure 14-6
Operation Splitting Impact on Manufacturing Lead Time

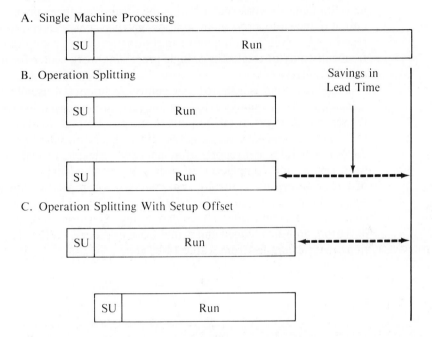

A. Single Machine Processing

B. Operation Splitting

C. Operation Splitting With Setup Offset

increases labor productivity. The appropriate mix of parts to equalize runout (see Chapter 8) or to meet cycle assembly requirements is committed as a group. Both overlapping and lot splitting are normal procedures in manufacturing cells.

INPUT/OUTPUT CONTROL

Input/output (I/O) planning and control is an integrated process that includes (1) planning the acceptable input and output performance ranges per time period in each work center, (2) measuring and reporting actual inputs and outputs (feedback), and (3) correcting out-of-control situations. Reporting systems are examined in a later section of this chapter and in Chapter 20.

Input/output control is an effective technique for controlling queues, work in process, and manufacturing lead time (the time from the release of an order to its completion). This section analyses actual inputs, outputs, and work in process. Input/output control enables the planner to determine what action is necessary to achieve the desired output, work in process, and manufacturing lead time objectives. We will examine the case of a single processing center and then the more complicated case of multiple work centers and many orders with different routings.

Single Work Center Processes

Some manufacturing processes have only one work center; others have a dominant (bottleneck) work center that is the focal point for controlling input and output to the entire process. In addition, gateway work centers, continuous and repetitive batch lines, and a uniform routing through a group of work centers frequently may be treated as a single processing work center for input/output analysis purposes.

Input/output is a short-range control technique; it usually is performed using daily rather than weekly time buckets. Input/output analysis compares the scheduled order (or task) inputs to the process and the scheduled outputs to the actual inputs and the actual outputs. This information comes from production schedules and reports of actual order releases, arrivals of orders in a work center, and completions of orders in a work center. The basic concept of I/O planning and control is that ending work in process equals beginning work in process plus input minus output, as illustrated by Figure 14-7. Further computations can provide the cumulative input deviation, the cumulative output deviation, and the planned and actual work in process (WIP). These computations, with examples from Table 14-8, are:

$$ICD_i = ICD_{i-1} - PI_i + AI_i$$
$$ICD_{26} = 0 - 16 + 12 = -4$$

$$OCD_i = OCD_{i-1} - PO_i + AO_i$$
$$OCD_{27} = 1 - 16 + 15 = 0$$

$$PWIP_i = PWIP_{i-1} + PI_i - PO_i$$
$$PWIP_{28} = 32 + 16 - 16 = 32$$

$$AWIP_i = AWIP_{i-1} + AI_i - AO_i$$
$$AWIP_{29} = 36 + 10 - 18 = 28$$

$$\text{Lead Time} = \frac{\text{Work in Process}}{\text{Output Rate}}$$

where
i = time period
PI = planned input
AI = actual input
PO = planned output
AO = actual output
ICD = input cumulative deviation
OCD = output cumulative deviation
$PWIP$ = ending planned work in process
$AWIP$ = ending actual work in process

Management can then develop various measures of process performances, including an acceptable level of input and output deviation and the acceptable

Figure 14-7
Input/Output Relationship of a Continuous
Process or Single-Operation Process

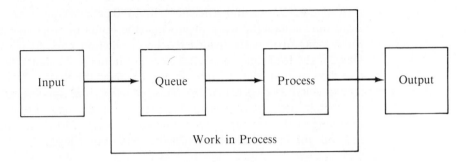

level of WIP. The following examples illustrate three different situations:
(1) a process in control, (2) the use of input/output to control and reduce
work in process and lead time, and (3) input/output controls under out-of-
control conditions.

In the first example, illustrated in Table 14-8, the situation is under control. Actual input and actual output differ little from the plan; the work in
process is never more than 5 hours different from the plan. Typically, management will establish an acceptable cumulative deviation, perhaps 20 hours of
work in process in this case for example, as acceptable due to random events.
Planned WIP is usually three to four times the standard deviation of the ending
WIP, resulting in virtually no time due to lack of work. Acceptable deviation
is about twice the standard deviation; beyond this, action is attempted to correct
the deviation. In Table 14-8, the planned WIP appears to be too high.

Table 14-8
Input/Output Control, Situation in Control

| | | Day | | | | |
	25	26	27	28	29	30
Input						
Planned (PI)		16	16	16	16	16
Actual (AI)		12	19	22	10	15
Cumulative Deviation (ICD)	0	−4	−1	5	−1	−2
Output						
Planned (PO)		16	16	16	16	16
Actual (AO)		17	15	17	18	15
Cumulative Deviation (OCD)	0	1	0	1	3	2
Work in Process (Ending)						
Planned (PWIP)		32	32	32	32	32
Actual (AWIP)	32	27	31	36	28	28

The second situation is illustrated in Table 14-9. Because planned WIP is excessive, a reduction in input beginning in Day 26 and constant output are planned to reduce work in process from 32 standard hours to 20 standard hours and to reduce lead time from two days (16-hour days, i.e., each day has two shifts and utilization and efficiency equal 100 percent) to two and a half shifts. Lead time equals the work in process (the hours of work in the queue plus those being processed) divided by the production rate. At the beginning of Day 26, the lead time equals 2.0 days (32 hours ÷ 16 hours per day). After five days, actual results approximate the plan; the WIP is 21 hours and the lead time is 1.31 days (21 ÷ 16). This reduction is reasonable only if 20 hours of work in process will sustain the production through normal variations in incoming work and output. Once the desired level of work in process has been reached, the input must be returned to the output level.

Table 14-9
Input/Output Control, WIP Reduction

		Day				
	25	26	27	28	29	30
Input						
Planned (*PI*)		14	14	14	13	13
Actual (*AI*)		12	17	16	9	14
Cumulative Deviation (*ICD*)	0	−2	1	3	−1	0
Output						
Planned (*PO*)		16	16	16	16	16
Actual (*AO*)		17	15	15	14	18
Cumulative Deviation (*OCD*)	0	1	0	−1	−3	−1
Work in Process (Ending)						
Planned (*PWIP*)		30	28	26	23	20
Actual (*AWIP*)	32	27	29	30	25	21

Typical out-of-control situations, possible causes, and corrective actions include the following:

1. Queues exceed upper limits. Possible causes include equipment failure, inefficient processing, and excessive input. Decreasing input or increasing process output is necessary to correct the situation.
2. Output is below the lower limit. Possible causes include equipment failure, inefficient processing, inadequate input, or the wrong input at assembly work centers.

Equipment failure and inefficient processing are manufacturing engineering problems. Inadequate, excessive, or the wrong input are I/0 problems that should be rectified by dispatching. I/O control is essential at critical (bottleneck) work centers whether they are gateway, intermediate, or the final work centers.

Table 14-10 illustrates an application of input/output control in an unanticipated situation. An equipment problem that began during Day 30 has decreased output and the work in process did not decrease as planned. The plan was to work 2 hours overtime in Days 31 and 32 to increase output by 25 percent to 20 hours, to hold input constant at 16 hours, and to reduce the work in process to 24 hours. However, the equipment performed erratically during Days 31 and 32 and output fell short as shown in Table 14-10. Solving the equipment problem is the first step in rectifying this situation. In the meantime, planned input and output should be reduced. Maintaining the present input level will only maintain the high work in process and hinder production. Planned output should be based on the actual capacity of approximately 16 standard hours per day. Excess work in process exists, so planned input for Day 33 is reduced to 12 hours to achieve planned work in process. Even if the work center performance returns to the normal 20 hours of output, sufficient work in process will be available with the planned input in Table 14-10.

Table 14-10
Input/Output Control, Unanticipated Event

		Day		
	30	31	32	33
Input				
Planned (*PI*)		16	16	12
Actual (*AI*)		16	16	
Cumulative Deviation (*ICD*)	0	0	0	
Output				
Planned (*PO*)		20	20	16
Actual (*AO*)		17	15	
Cumulative Deviation (*OCD*)	0	−3	−8	
Work in Process (Ending)				
Planned (*PWIP*)		28	24	28*
Actual (*AWIP*)	32	31	32	

*Based on AWIP at end of Day 32

Thus, as shown in Table 14-10, 12 hours of input are planned for Day 33 along with 16 hours of output, while working 2 hours overtime. If the equipment operates properly and produces 20 standard hours per day, sufficient work in process exists to prevent machine downtime due to lack of work.

Table 14-11 is an example of a situation in which input is insufficient to produce the planned output. This can result in late deliveries, poor customer service, poor profits in the short run, and the possibility of losing future orders. Measures should be taken to increase the actual input in Week 30, otherwise the work center will experience idle time. A work center that feeds this work center is probably causing this problem. The cause of the reduced input must be identified and corrected.

Table 14-11
Input/Output Control, Inadequate Input

		Day				
	25	26	27	28	29	30
Input						
Planned (*PI*)		16	16	16	16	16
Actual (*AI*)		12	12	13	12	
Cumulative Deviation (*ICD*)	0	−4	−8	−11	−15	
Output						
Planned (*PO*)		16	16	16	16	16
Actual (*AO*)		15	15	13	13	
Cumulative Deviation (*OCD*)	0	−1	−2	−5	−8	
Work in Process (Ending)						
Planned (*PWIP*)		20	20	20	20	20
Actual (*AWIP*)	20	17	14	14	13	

The principles of input/output control are:

1. The planned output should be realistic and should represent labor and equipment capacity.
2. A planned or actual input greater than the realistic output will increase WIP, hinder production, and increase manufacturing lead time.
3. All significant deviations from planned input and planned output indicate operational problems that must be identified and solved.

Multiple Work Centers

Work flow through multiple work centers is often represented schematically. Two formats are commonly used, the flow-by-order format and the rate-of-flow format. Figure 14-8 is a schematic representation of four possible order flow patterns in a job shop with ten work centers. Work Centers A1 and A2 are *gateway* work centers. The first operation is performed in one of these two work centers. Work Centers B1, B2, B3, C1, C2, and C3 are *intermediate* work centers, and D1 and D2 are the *finishing* or *final* work centers. All work centers in which processing is performed following processing in a given work center are called *downstream* work centers. Those work centers in which processing is performed prior to a given work center are *upstream* work centers. We will examine I/O control at each type of work center.

Figure 14-9 is a schematic of the rate-of-flow patterns found in a large complex job shop (Kettner and Bechte 1981). Although this schematic does not show separate orders, it does use the width of the channels to show the proportional rate-of-flow between work centers.

Figure 14-8
Flow Patterns in a Job Shop

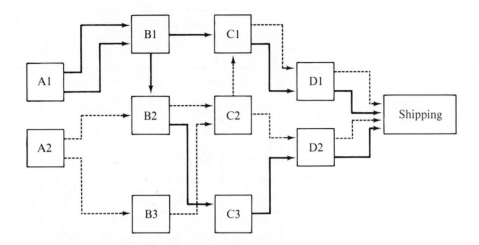

Gateway Work Center Control. Management of the release of orders controls the input, queues, and WIP at gateway work centers. If the work center is running smoothly, output also is controlled. The input to the gateway work centers also influences inputs to downstream work centers. There is little reason to have a long queue at a gateway work center. Keeping gateway queues at a minimum enables the dispatcher to use the latest available information when establishing order priorities. It also reduces WIP and expediting.

Downstream Work Center Control. The input and queues at downstream work centers are controlled by dispatching (order sequencing) at upstream work centers in the process flow. For example, if Work Center C3 in Figure 14-8 is running short of work, while there is a relatively large queue at Work Center C2, priority in Work Center B2 should be given to orders going to C3 next. This requires that order release decisions recognize the needs of downstream work centers as well as gateway work centers. Of course, other factors such as due dates and manufacturing inventory not required must also be considered.

Final Work Center Control. The output of final work centers influences shipments, due date commitments, billings, accounts receivable, and cash flow. Final output usually is one of the dominant measures of production management performance. Controlling final work center input is necessary to achieve the desired output. This involves coordinating the flow of parts, items, and subassemblies required in final assemblies. Dispatching is concerned with achieving control of the volume and specific items entering the final work centers. In some complex job shops, large-scale computer simulations are used to provide completion oriented priority control that extends backward from the final work center to gateway operations (Lankford 1978).

Figure 14-9
Rate-of-Flow Schematic

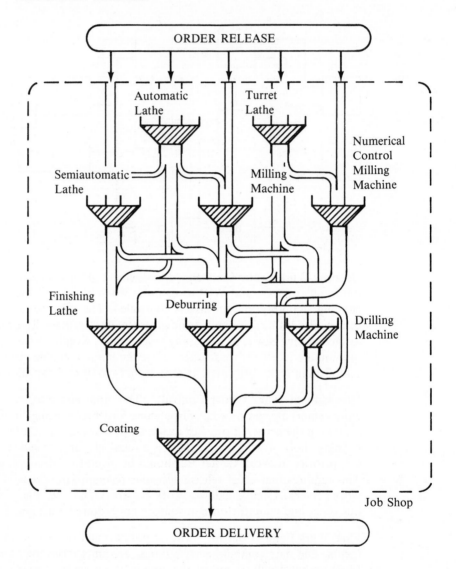

Bottleneck Work Centers.   When the capacity required exceeds the capacity available, a bottleneck exists. Often this condition either is short lived or can be solved by using the flexiblity of the work force and the equipment to increase capacity. Eliminating bottlenecks with flexible capacity is one of the primary objectives of the JIT approach and is necessary to compete in world markets. Chronic bottlenecks can occur even with the best planning and, therefore, should receive the special attention of planners. A bottleneck work center limits output, and an hour lost at such a work center is an hour of output lost. Thus, the scheduling of work in bottleneck work centers is critical to achieving production objectives. (See Chapter 19.) As a result, measures should be taken to provide flexible and sufficient capacity to eliminate bottlenecks when designing and developing production facilities. The objective of the theory of constraints is to manage bottlenecks.

Load Order Manufacturing Control.　　This is an input/output control method developed at the University of Hannover and implemented successfully at more than 20 manufacturing companies in Europe. It uses statistical analysis of the time-phased relationships of order releases, manufacturing process work center requirements, and loads at downstream work centers to develop order release priority rules and guidelines for specific environments. It has had noteworthy success in reducing queues, work in process, and manufacturing lead time in an orderly, practical, and systematic manner. (Bechte 1988; Wiendahl 1987).

TRADITIONAL PAC INFORMATION SYSTEMS

Production activity control (PAC) procedures include order release, dispatching, and production reporting (see Figure 14-1). Queue length management, input/output control, and priority control are interwoven and mutually supportive. Their principles and techniques are applied jointly in making order release and dispatching decisions. (JIT and theory of constraints concepts and approaches are discussed in Chapter 17, 18, and 19.)

Flow Line Processes

In both repetitive (discrete units) production and continuous process type production, the PAC system has requirements slightly different from the job shop. The salient differences are that (1) daily run schedules are used to authorize and control production rather than job orders and (2) control is executed by counts at key points in the flow.

In flow line manufacturing environments (continuous, repetitive, or manufacturing cell production), the consumption of ingredients, such as chemicals, powders, or component parts and subassemblies, may be recorded automatically when the production of the finished product is recorded. Component parts, materials, and subassemblies used in reaching a given stage in the production process are deducted from the inventory on hand by exploding the bill of material and multiplying the quantities of each required by the number of assemblies produced. This is called *backflushing*. For example, if 5 pounds of ammonia-nitrate are used in each 25 gallon container of a specific fertilizer, the number of such containers produced is multiplied by 5 pounds to determine the amount of ammonia-nitrate to be subtracted from the inventory of that ingredient. This occurs either at key completion stages in the process or at the final point in the process. A single-level backflush deducts only the items used in the last assembly or mixing process and is usually used when backflushing takes place more than once in a process. A *superflush* accounts for all items down to the lowest level in the bill of material and is appropriate when the process is relatively brief and backflushing takes place only after the final process is completed.

Backflushing reduces the amount of data capturing and processing but requires system integrity, accurate reporting of completed items, accurate measures of yield, and special reporting of unusual situations such as a batch that must be discarded (scrapped). It also results in inventory records for materials and components showing larger quantities of inventory on hand than actually is the case, for at least a short time.

Job Shops

A PAC system in a job shop must be capable of the following:

1. Releasing orders to the production department on schedule (per the order release plan), having verified materials, information (blueprints and manufacturing processes), tooling, personnel, and equipment availability
2. Informing the production department of the scheduled start and completion dates of steps (individual operations) in the production process as well as the scheduled completion date of the order
3. Informing the production department of the relative priorities of the orders released
4. Recording actual performance of steps in the production process and comparing actual performance to the schedule
5. Revising order priorities on the basis of performance and changing conditions
6. Monitoring and controlling input and output, lead times, work center queues, and work in process
7. Reporting work center efficiency, personnel attendance, operator times, and order quantity counts for planning, payroll, department efficiency, and labor distribution reports

Order Release

Order release initiates the execution phase of production; it authorizes production and/or purchasing. The planned order becomes a released (open) order. Placement of a purchase order or the initiation of manufacturing follows shortly. Order release planning may take place until the moment of order release. Authorization of order release is based first on the planned orders in the MRP output, the current priority, the availability of materials and tooling, and the loads specified by I/O planning. Release of an order triggers the release of the following:

1. Requisitions for material and components required by the order. If some of these items are not required immediately and have not been allocated previously, they are allocated now.
2. Production order documentation to the plant. This documentation may include a set of both engineering drawings and manufacturing specifications and a manufacturing routing sheet.
3. Requisitions for tools required in the first week or so of production. Tooling, including tapes for numerically controlled machines, required in later operations is reserved for the appropriate period. Tooling can be included in the master production schedule and the bill of material. Its availability is thus coordinated with material and equipment availability.

The time required to deliver production order documentation, tooling, and materials to the first operation is included in the normal planned lead time for the order. An order is released by adding it to the dispatch list.

Dispatching

Dispatching informs first-line supervision of the released orders and their priority, that is, the sequence in which orders should be run. This information can be transmitted via a hard copy (handwritten, typed, or computer printout) or via video output on a cathode ray tube (CRT). Telephone and face-to-face conversations also can be used but do not document the decisions. In a job shop a dispatch list should be prepared for each work center with the frequency of updating depending on the typical order-processing time. If orders take a day or less to process, dispatch lists usually are prepared daily. If orders take a few days, lists may be prepared weekly with midweek revisions handled on an exception basis with on-line processing. In a flow line process environment, a single list indicating the rate of flow (or in a batch flow line, the sequence in which orders are to be started) will control work on the entire line, which may be viewed as a single work center. Table 14-12 is an example of simple dispatch list information. It identifies the date, the plant, and the work center; it includes the work center capacity; and it lists the orders, their quantity, their capacity requirements, and their priority. Orders usually are listed in descending priority for a specified period.

The list also may include jobs at upstream work centers to provide the supervisor with information concerning orders that will arrive shortly and an indication of their priority upon arrival. A computerized system may produce relative rankings on the basis of criteria such as critical ratio and earliest due date, as described earlier, but review by a planner is required to determine if other considerations are overriding.

Table 14-12
Dispatch List Information

| Plant 02 | | | | | Capacity 85 hours/day | |
| Date 8/1 | | | | | | |
Part Number	Order Number	Quantity	Standard Hours per Unit	Total Standard Hours	CR Priority	Due Date
9706	S-4276	200	0.3	60	1.4	8/1
B1319	S-4518	100	0.8	80	2.1	8/2
H4276	S-4625	60	1.5	90	2.8	8/3

The planner determines the final dispatch list ranking of orders on the basis of multiple criteria including a formal priority index such as the critical ratio or the due date, input control at downstream work centers, the availability of tooling, the status of other parts required in the same assembly, energy consumption patterns, and sequencing and assignment criteria. For example, if the next operations for Orders S-4276 and S-4518 are at work centers heavily loaded with high priority orders while the next operation for Order S-4625 is at an idle work center, Order S-4625 may be processed first in spite of its CR or due date on this operation. Such situations should not occur, but they do occasionally, even in well-managed organizations. In addition, environments in which the energy consumption costs of production are relatively high can foster scheduling rules incorporating constraints on energy consumption peaks (Baker 1979).

Dispatch List Revisions.   The due dates and priorities of orders may change because of such developments as forecast revisions, cancellation of orders, and the scrapping of another lot of the same item at a later stage in the production process. For example, suppose the following events occur after the dispatch list, shown in Table 14-13, is released on August 1.

1. The customer has cancelled his order, S-4276, for Part 9706.
2. The completion date for Order S-4609, Part M3563, has been moved back one week due to a delay in receiving other parts required in their common next assembly.
3. The due date of Order S-4625, Part H4276, has been advanced two weeks to fill requirements that were to be met by another order that was scrapped at a later operation.

The dispatcher must exercise judgment in informing shop supervision of revised priorities. If Order S-4276 is in process, there may be no point in revising its priority in Work Center M3. The priority can be changed in its next work center. Revising the priorities and listings of Orders S-4609 and S-4625 seems appropriate. However, continual revision of order priorities will destroy the credibility of dispatch lists.

The dispatch list also may include orders that are due to arrive in the department shortly, as illustrated in Table 14-13. This enables supervisors to include these orders in their planning.

Table 14-13
Dispatch List Information with Lookahead

Plant 02 Date 8/1	Department 27		Work Center M3	Capacity 85 hours/day	
Part Number	Order Number	Quantity	Standard Hours per Unit	Total Standard Hours	(Priority) Due Date
9706	S-4276	200	0.3	60	8/1
B1319	S-4518	100	0.8	80	8/2
H4276	S-4625	60	1.5	90	8/3
Orders Arriving Tomorrow					
B7849	S-4429	60	0.7	42	8/4
M3563	S-4609	50	0.4	20	8/5

Few dispatching decisions can be made in a programmed automatic fashion. A computer can provide valuable assistance by keeping an accurate record of order status. It also can provide an inquiry capability, responding to the requests of managers and planners concerning the status of any order. However, the dispatcher must exercise judgment in balancing operating costs and customer service when determining the final priority of orders. Often local rules, or heuristics, are developed to simplify and structure order release policies.

Organization.   Dispatching may be organized in a centralized or decentralized manner. Centralized dispatching exists when decisions are made in a single location and communicated to supervisors throughout the plant. Centralization facilitates monitoring the progress of orders, coordinating the priority of orders required in the same assembly, and auditing the counts of lot quantities. Its advantage is that it can improve communications among dispatchers.

Decentralized dispatching exists when order sequencing decisions are made in the department. It has the advantage of decision making at the scene. The dispatcher may have a better grasp of the department's capabilities and efficient order sequencing. Wherever they are located, dispatchers must be aware of actual conditions in the work center and overall plant objectives and developments.

The development of computers, automatic counters, and electronic data collection devices has supported the adoption of centralized dispatching approaches. Management's desire to give more responsibility to first line supervision has supported the adoption of decentralized dispatching. Such considerations often lead to the adoption of hybrid systems. Overall order status is kept in a central location that issues sequencing recommendations, and supervisors possess the authority to alter sequences within certain limits to achieve production efficiencies.

Production Reporting

Reports describing actual production status are necessary for control. Dynamic response to changing conditions is possible only if timely, accurate, and adequate information is available. The information must enable management to take meaningful corrective action concerning production schedules.

The production environment influences the design of the production reporting system. Reporting in a line flow environment with long production runs, such as Wellco Carpet, may take place on an exception basis with feedback occurring only when the output rate falls below an acceptable level. In a custom design and manufacturing environment, such as Kickham Boiler, that has project management and fixed site manufacturing, emphasis is on reporting the status of activities on the critical path (see Chapter 16). All reporting systems should have an exception reporting capability to inform management whenever machine failure, material shortages, or similar events threaten planned output.

Parts fabrication in a job shop environment requires more data collection for control than continuous processes or repetitive manufacturing of discrete parts. Once a flow process is initiated, it will continue smoothly unless machine failure, employee absenteeism, scrap, a materials shortage, or production inefficiencies occur. Exception reporting usually works well in these circumstances. Flow in a job shop is more complex, and order status estimates are less certain. Thus, the processing and movement of orders does not automatically follow their release into the production stream as do orders in a flow process. Control in a job shop usually requires information concerning the following:

1. The release of orders
2. The beginning and completion of operations
3. The movement of orders
4. The availability of processing information, tooling, and material
5. The queues in each work center

Exception reporting is frequently adequate for controlling the availability of information required for processing, tooling, and material. Reporting both the beginning and completion of operations is appropriate when the total operation times are relatively long. For example, if the estimated completion time of processing a lot of parts through a particular operation is four days, reporting initiation of the operation makes sense. On the other hand, if an operation requires only an hour and a half, reporting its completion should be sufficient.

Data Collection.   On-line reporting systems directly report events as they occur, usually via a data terminal or other device capable of electronically transmitting the data to a centralized recording station. Such information is called *real time* since the records are updated instantaneously. Whether an organization requires real time information as provided by on-line processing or whether periodic reporting (by shift, day, or week) is sufficient for the desired control depends on the situation.

In some cases the operator reports the initiation or completion of an operation, order movement, etc., via a data terminal or by completing an operation reporting form included in the job packet. Figure 14-10 is an example of a reporting ticket. In other cases the supervisor or timekeeper is responsible for reporting this information.

Figure 14-10
Reporting Ticket

ML605	30				
Part No.	Oper. No.	Quantity	Start	Finish	
95620		29			
Order No.	Operator No.	Dept.	Scrap	Supervisor	

(Some information is preprinted on a form; other information is added by operator. Frequently, supervisor checks accuracy of information.)

Typical Reports. The status of WIP, inventory availability, and work center queues and utilization influences dispatching and order release decisions. When an on-line, real time reporting system with inquiry capability exists, management, dispatchers, and planners can obtain current status information virtually instantaneously. The response to their inquiry may be presented on a video output device and/or produced on a hard copy output. When an on-line, real time reporting system exists, daily status reports are required in most cases. In all cases, periodic summary reports are required to evaluate production performance.

The following information should be available to planners on either a real time or periodic basis.

1. Released order status (see Table 14-14). This report gives the status of every order that has been released physically to the plant and includes part number, description, quantity, order release date, order due date, operations completed, order location, quantity scrapped, and quantity good.
2. Unreleased order status (see Table 14-15). This report lists all orders whose release is past due. It also notes the cause of the delayed release, such as long queues of higher priority orders at gateway work centers, lack of required tooling, or lack of required material or parts.
3. Dispatch list-priority scheduling report (see Table 14-13 on page 477). This report lists in priority sequence all orders in each department plus those expected to arrive shortly—perhaps in the next day. Standard hours required for processing also are listed.

Table 14-14
Released Order Status Report

Date: 275

Part Number	Description	Order Number	Quantity On Order	Quantity Complete	Planned Release Date	Planned Due Date	Actual Release Date	Actual Completion Date	Location (Work Center)	MLTR*
P865	pin	952931	80	—	270	290	270	—	17	15
B6803	bushing	956735	160	—	275	292	270	—	21	10
R6027	ring gear	959063	40	—	260	294	265	—	9	29

*MLTR—manufacturing lead time remaining (days).

Table 14-15
Unreleased Order Status Report

Date: 275

Part Number	Description	Order Number	Type	Order Quantity	Planned* Release Date	Planned* Due Date	Cause**
SA9502	value assembly	957021	M	100	270	280	LOC
SA6807	switch assembly	968052	M	250	265	275	WCOL
ES3750	gear	968090	P	500	270	290	VOL
B6750	bracket	970211	M	200	250	280	TNA

*Gregorian dates have been converted to shop calendar dates.
**Typical codes: LOC—lack of component; WCOL—work center overload; VOL—vendor overloaded; TNA—tooling not available.

4. Weekly I/O by department (see Tables 14-8, 14-9, 14-10, and 14-11 on pages 467-470).

5. Exception reports. These should be designed to meet the needs of the organization. Possible exception reports, illustrated in Table 14-16, include a scrap report, a rework report, and a late orders report. A review of scrap reports will reveal if quality problems are recurrent with a particular item, operation, or operator. Scrap reports also can trigger the release of new orders or a quantity increase on unreleased orders for the same item. Rework reports also can alert management of quality problems and unplanned capacity requirements. The purpose of a late orders report is to inform management of orders that require expediting and possibly of customers who should be informed of late delivery. If the late orders list is extensive, the possibility of a capacity problem or an unrealistic MPS should be investigated. The late orders report should focus on a number of orders that can be expedited efficiently and that have high priority.

6. Performance summary report. The performance summary report should state the number and percentage of orders completed on schedule during a specific period—week or month—and the lateness of late orders. A late orders aging report, similar to an accounts receivable aging report, will reveal the magnitude of any delivery problems. Performance also should be reported in terms of volume (tons, units, feet, etc.) or dollars. The causes of late orders also should be tabulated.

Table 14-16
Exception Reports (Examples)

A. Scrap Report (weekly, daily, or by exception)

Order Number	Part Number	Quantity	Operation	Cause
M7240	2784	12	30	Operator error
M6843	6813	5	60	Welding fixture out of alignment

B. Rework Report (items requiring rework)

Order Number	Part Number	Quantity	Operation(s)	Cause
M6927	B8315	30	40 and 50	Eng. change
M7435	B8316	40	40 and 50	Eng. change

C. Late Orders Report (or Delayed Orders Report)

Date: 5/7 Order Number	Part Number	Quantity	Due Date	Operation Time Remaining	Queue Time Remaining	Cause
6895	R7516	100	5/7	2	2	Matl. late
6743	C8319	75	5/14	4	3	Scrap
7013	67059	120	5/17	6	6	Machine down
6985	28076	40	5/20	8	8	Tool late

The types of reports possible are many and varied. This chapter has included only some of them; the readings contain other examples. Too many reports diminish the value of each. Different situations require different information and different organization of that information.

PAC INFORMATION SYSTEM REQUIREMENTS

Certain data and files are required for a PAC system. In a manufacturing firm these usually are organized in the following files:

1. Planning files:
   a. Part (item) master file
   b. Routing file
   c. Work center file
2. Control files:
   a. Production order master file
   b. Production order detail file

Planning Files

The part master file is required for many activities, including material requirements planning (MRP), inventory management, cost estimating, and PAC. This file has a record for each part. Each record is identified by a part number and contains relevant data such as inventory status and standard cost. In addition, the record for each item includes the following data required for PAC:

1. Part number—the unique item number assigned to the part
2. Part description—the name of the item
3. Manufacturing lead time—the normal time required to produce the item in the typical lot quantity. This information may also be in the routing file.
4. On-hand quantity—the number of units of this part in stock
5. Allocated quantity—the number of units of this item that has been assigned to previously planned future orders
6. Available quantity—the difference between the on-hand quantity and the allocated quantity
7. On-order quantity—the total number of units due on all outstanding orders for this part
8. Lot-size quantity—the normal number of units of this item produced at one time (the order quantity)
9. Substitute items—the part numbers of items (or materials) that may be used in place of this item

The routing file and the work center file are used for capacity requirements planning (CRP).

Control Files

The production order master file contains a record of each active production order. The purpose of the file is to store summary data describing the nature, status, and priority of each order. It contains the following data required for PAC:

1. Production order number—the number assigned to uniquely identify each order or batch
2. Order quantity—the number of units (e.g., pounds, gallons) to be produced on this order
3. Quantity completed—the number of units (or volume) reported through the last operation and final inspection
4. Quantity scrapped—the total number of units (or volume) scrapped at any point in the production of this order. Separate records of the quantity scrapped during setup and the quantity scrapped when running the item at each work center may be kept.
5. Material disbursed—the quantity of each item of materials or component parts released from stores for the production of this order
6. Due date (original)—the initial date on which this order was scheduled for completion
7. Due date (revised)—if rescheduled, the new date on which this order is scheduled for completion
8. Priority—the value used to rank this order relative to all other orders
9. Balance due—the order (or batch) quantity minus the sum of the quantities completed and scrapped. If some units are scrapped, the material requirements system will determine if another order is necessary to meet requirements.

In a job shop environment, there is a production order detail file for each order. The file contains a record for each operation required by the production process for that order. The record for each operation typically contains the following data:

1. Operation number—the number uniquely identifying the operation
2. Description—a brief description of the operation
3. Setup time reported—the number of hours reported for setting up the equipment for this operation on the given order
4. Run time reported—the number of hours reported for performing this operation on the given order
5. Quantity reported complete—the accounted number of units meeting quality requirements on completion of this operation
6. Quantity reported scrapped—the number of units that were reported scrapped on inspection during or immediately following this operation
7. Due date (revised)—if rescheduled, the new date on which this order is scheduled for completion

CONCLUSIONS

PAC is concerned with converting plans into action, reporting the results achieved, and revising plans and actions as required to achieve desired results. Thus, PAC converts plans into action by providing the required direction. This requires the appropriate prior master planning of orders, work force personnel, materials, and capacity requirements.

Order release, dispatching, and progress reporting are the three primary functions of PAC. Dispatching is the activation of orders per original plans. Dispatching decisions are affected by queue management, I/O control, and priority control principles and techniques which are intertwined and mutually supportive. They are useful in the management of lead time, queue length, work center idle time, and scheduled order completion. Reports on the status of orders, materials, queues, tooling, and work center utilization are essential for control. Many report types with various information are possible. Examining a given situation will reveal which reports and information are required.

EXERCISES

1. Five items (A, B, C, D, and E) are run on a production line, with minor adjustments in the line required for each. The plant is producing Item E, and the supervisor asks which item to run next. There is no technological requirement to run the items in a particular sequence.

   a. Which item should be run next given the following information? Why?

   b. Place the other items in priority order.

Item	Present Inventory	Daily Demand
A	1,600	100
B	1,000	40
C	200	10
D	1,200	80

2. The following orders are in queue at Work Center 112. The following data are available:

Present Date is Day 50. Order	Due Date	MLT Remaining (days)
129	65	12
133	78	32
137	59	10
138	85	30

   a. Determine the relative priorities of these four orders on the basis of their CR.

   b. Determine their relative priorities on the basis of their due dates.

3. The following data describe the status of four orders in Department 795.

Present Date is Day 95.			
Order	Day Due	MLT Remaining*	Processing Time Remaining*
151	85	12	5
160	86	20	9
157	90	25	7
165	92	30	11

*In days

a. Calculate the number of days each is behind schedule (days overdue + MLT).
b. Calculate the days overdue plus processing time remaining for each order.
c. Why would the critical ratio not be a good measure of priority in this case?
d. In what order would it be best to process these orders? Justify your answer.

4. The planning department makes a work sampling study of queue lengths at six work centers over a four-week period of normal operation. The following data are obtained.

Idle Time	Percentage of Time					
Consecutive Hours Without Work (hours)	Work Center					
	101	102	103	104	105	106
>40	—	—	—	—	—	—
32-40	—	2	—	—	—	—
24-32	—	2	—	—	—	—
16-24	—	4	—	—	—	—
8-16	—	2	—	3	6	—
0-8	—	14	—	5	4	—
Queue Length Hours						
0-8	—	10	30	10	10	20
8-16	—	30	40	12	30	50
16-24	—	10	25	20	20	25
24-32	20	20	5	20	15	5
32-40	30	4	—	10	15	—
40-60	40	2	—	10	—	—
>60	10	—	—	10	—	—

a. Draw a queue length frequency distribution chart for each work center.
b. In which work centers do the queues seem to be controlled?
c. Which work centers have uncontrolled queues?
d. In which work center can the queue be reduced substantially and by how many hours without affecting capacity utilization?

5. The planning department makes a work sampling study of four departments over a four-week period of normal operation. They obtain the following data concerning queue lengths:

Work Center	Statistical Parameters of Queue Length
201	Normal distribution, Mean = 42.1 hours, Standard Deviation = 8.6 hours
202	Normal distribution, Mean = 20.7 hours, Standard Deviation = 6.5 hours
203	Rectangular distribution, approximately equal percentage in 0-8 hours idle; 0-8, 8-16, 16-24, 24-32, and 32-40 hours of queue
204	Normal distribution, Mean = 12.2 hours, Standard Deviation = 3.0 hours

  a. Draw an approximate queue length frequency distribution for each work center.

  b. Which work center(s) has (have) an excessive queue and/or idle time?

6. A planner at the Ajax Manufacturing Company states that "The shop should always have more work scheduled per day than it has performed in the past; it is the only way we will find out what they can really do." How would you respond?

7. Planners have an order for which they are considering operation overlapping to reduce the manufacturing lead time. The following data are available:

Lot size = 500 units
Processing time Operation A = 8 minutes
Processing time Operation B = 6 minutes
Minimum transit time, Operation A to Operation B = 40 minutes
Setup time Operation B = 1.5 hours
Assume parts will be processed immediately on Operation B.

  a. If Operation B cannot be set up until the parts arrive, what is the minimum size of the transfer lot that should be run on Operation A before moving parts to B? The goal is that there be no idle time on Operation B.

  b. What is the minimum size of the transfer lot if Operation B can be set up prior to the arrival of parts?

  c. Disregarding queue time, how much time will be removed from the MLT in each of the above cases?

  d. If the queue time at Operation B is normally 16 hours, how much total time will be removed from the MLT in a and in b?

8. A third operation, C, follows Operations A and B of Exercise 7. The following data concern it:

    Processing time = 4 minutes
    Setup time = 0.8 hours
    Minimum transit time, Operation B to Operation C = 40 minutes

    a. If Operation C cannot be set up until the parts arrive and there is to be no idle time at Operation C, what is the minimum size of the transfer lot that should be run on Operation B before moving parts to Operation C?
    b. How much operation time will be removed from the MLT in this case?
    c. If Operation C processing time is 12 minutes and the planners desire to have no more than two sublots, what is the minimum size of the transfer lot they should run on Operation B before moving parts to Operation C?
    d. If Operation C is 12 minutes and it is immediately adjacent to Operation B (no transit of parts is required), how many parts must be processed in B before Operation C can begin?

9. To remain competitive, an organization must reduce manufacturing lead time for an item to which the following data apply. They are considering operation overlapping.

    Lot size = 800 units
    Processing time Operation A (first operation) = 6 minutes
    Processing time Operation B (second operation) = 8 minutes
    Minimum transit time, Operation A to Operation B = 20 minutes
    Setup time Operation B = 1.5 hours
    Assume parts will be processed immediately on Operation B.

    a. If the lot is divided into two transfer lots and Operation B cannot be set up before the parts arrive, what is the minimum size of the transfer lot that should be run on Operation A before moving parts to B? The goal is that there be no idle time on Operation B.
    b. What is the minimum size of the transfer lot if Operation B can be set up prior to the arrival of parts?
    c. Disregarding queue time, how much time will be removed from the MLT in each of the above cases?
    d. If the queue time at Operation B is normally 16 hours, how much total time will be removed from the MLT in a and in b?

10. Regarding Exercise 9, plant engineering has agreed to move Work Center B immediately adjacent to Work Center A. What transfer lot size do you suggest now? What is the MLT that results?

11. A planner also is considering operation splitting (parallel scheduling) for the item described in Exercises 7 and 8. The data follow:

Lot Size = 500 units		
Operation	Setup Time (hours)	Operation Time (minutes)
A	1.0	8
B	1.5	6
C	0.8	4

a. By how much is MLT reduced if each operation is split between two machines with no setup offset?
b. By how much is MLT reduced if each operation is split between two machines and setups are offset?

12. A department has a normal capacity of 30 units of output a day. It is operating at full capacity and normal machine and worker utilization. The following performance data are given:

	Day			
	1	2	3	4
Input	30	30	30	35
Output	31	29	30	
WIP	39	40	40	

Beginning WIP = 40

a. What do you expect the WIP and output in Day 4 to be?
b. What should the input be in Day 4 if you desire to decrease WIP by 5 units? You believe that this will not affect output.

13. The following data concern two gateway work centers at two different plants. They have similar equipment and perform similar operations:

	Work Center A1 Day				Work Center A2 Day			
	1	2	3	4	1	2	3	4
Input								
Planned	80	80	80	80	80	80	80	80
Actual	75	85	80	82	82	76	80	82
Output								
Planned	80	80	80	80	80	80	80	80
Actual	85	75	80	82	77	75	83	84
WIP								
Actual	210	215	215	215	85	86	83	81
	Beginning WIP = 200				Beginning WIP = 80			

a. If there is no idle time in either work center, what planned input do you recommend for each in Day 5? Why?

b. If there is no idle time in Work Center Al, but about 0.5 hour idle time occasionally due to material shortages in Work Center A2, what input do you recommend?

14. The following data are available concerning four orders in Work Center A. All four require approximately the same processing time in Department A. C is the finishing department.

Order	Processing Sequence
128	A-B1-C
131	A-B2-C
133	A-C
141	A-B1-B2-C

Present Queue in Hours			
Work Center			
A	B1	B2	C
20	40	10	5

a. If all the orders in Work Center A have the same priority, in what order will you schedule them? (Most of the orders presently in Work Center B1 go to B2 next.)

b. Suppose the queue is 5 hours in Work Center B1 and 25 hours in both B2 and C. How will you schedule the orders in Work Center A?

15. The following is the parts list for a lamp assembly manufactured on an assembly line. Backflushing is used to update inventory records every four hours. Four hundred assemblies were produced in the most recent four-hour period. Calculate the number of units to be deducted from the on-hand quantity of each item and determine the new on-hand balance of each item.

	LA100 Lamp Assembly		
Part Number	Description	Quantity	On Hand
B100	Base assembly	1 each	2,220
1100	Finished shaft	1 each	1,815
2100	3/8″ Steel tubing	26 inches	49,276
1200	7″-Diameter steel plate	1 each	1,345
1300	Hub	1 each	1,222
1400	1/4-20 Screws	4 each	5,745
S100	14″ Black shade	1 each	3,099
A100	Socket assembly	1 each	1,689
1500	Steel holder	1 each	599
1600	One-way socket	1 each	987
1700	Wiring assembly	1 each	1,038
2200	16-Gauge lamp cord	12 feet	6,783
2300	Standard plug terminal	1 each	549

16. A company produces private label items to customer orders and its own brand to finished goods inventory on the same assembly line. It has an order for each with the same due date. Which would normally have the higher priority? Why?

MINI-CASE

Archway Manufacturing is a supplier of components and subassemblies to its parent company, a major truck equipment manufacturer. Archway's management has hired you as a consultant.

The company has approximately 60 employees organized as shown in the following figure. There are 4 people plus the president in the office and usually 50 or so in the shop.

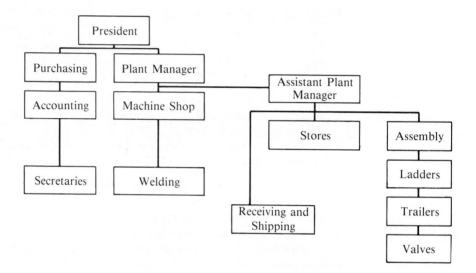

The president receives a major portion of his income in the form of a bonus based on monthly dollar volume of output.

The men in the shop belong to the machinists union. Labor relations are good and work habits seem good. Most workers have been with Archway for more than 10 years. There is no measure of plant productivity. The president and the plant manager also are the process engineers. The process instructions are brief, and most of the men know what to do.

The company has a reputation for quality and for meeting customers' needs through custom design and configurations. Archway's output is products for truck body and truck equipment manufacturers. It includes:

—Pins, shafts, collars
—Large and medium sized machined grey iron castings, forgings, and weldments
—Hydraulic manifold and valve assemblies made from purchased parts
—Utility pole trailers made from manufactured and purchased components
—Telescopic ladders, two or three sections, for electrical contractors and utilities, assembled from manufactured and purchased components

Archway's management has noted the following problems:

1. Some orders are completed way ahead of schedule, but many are late. This delays final assembly of truck bodies at the main plant.
2. Sales of the parent company are suffering due to price and poor delivery. Profits are suffering due to increased costs and poor sales.
3. Costs have forced the company to have a larger price differential (a higher price than competitors).
4. There is a large queue at the vertical turret lathes (VTL's); everybody agrees that this is a bottleneck.

In addition, Archway management has provided the following manufacturing information:

1. The plant is organized on a functional basis (job shop).
2. There are two VTL's with one operator per machine on each of two shifts five days a week. The president of this subsidiary is considering purchasing a third machine, used but in top condition, for $104,000.
3. A capacity analysis of the vertical turret lathes using annual requirements and actual setup and run times reveals that available capacity is 1.75 times required capacity.
4. The plant manager also serves as the scheduling department; he determines order quantities and priorities.
5. Hydraulic valve manifolds are purchased in sections and assembled. Final assemblies use some basic components but vary widely in configuration. Quantities per type run from 1 to 10 for 98 percent of all orders. An order for 30 or more occurs about once a year.
6. Requirements on pins, rings, and other lathe processed items are 10 to 20 annually for 20 percent of these items and 100 to 200 annually for the other 80 percent.
7. The plant usually has open (released) orders for 12 month's of forecasted requirements of the parent company. Rarely do they have less than 3 month's notice of requirements (due dates and quantities) for standard items. All orders the company has are released to the shop and available to the plant manager for processing as soon as they are received.

a. What policy do you suspect Archway's president has established for processing orders; that is, what is the basis for order quantity and priority?
b. What changes in operating procedures would you recommend immediately?
c. What changes do you recommend in the next six months? In the next one to three years?

SELECTED READINGS

APICS Shop Floor Control Reprints. Falls Church, VA: American Production and Inventory Control Society, 1986.

Baker, Eugene F. "Flow Management, the 'Take Charge' Shop Floor Control System." *APICS Conference Proceedings* (1979): 169-174.

Bechte, Wolfgang. "Load Oriented Order Control." *APICS Conference Proceedings* (1988): 148-152.

Bechte, Wolfgang. "Theory and Practice of Load Oriented Manufacturing Control." *International Journal of Production Research* 26, no. 3 (1988): 375-395.

Edwards, Bill, and Margaret O'Neill. "Checks and Balances in Job Shop Control." *APICS Conference Proceedings* (1978): 165-176.

Garwood, Dave. "Delivery as Promised." *Production and Inventory Management* 12, no. 3 (1971).

Hoffmann, Thomas R., and Gary D. Scudder. "Priority Scheduling With Cost Considerations." *International Journal of Production Research* 21, no. 6 (1983): 881-889.

Jones, William J. "The Integration of Shop Floor Control into the Materials System." *APICS Conference Proceedings* (1978): 133-141.

Kettner, Von Hans, and Wolfgang Bechte. "Neue Wege der Fertigungssteuerung durch belastungsorientierte Auftragsfreigabe." *VDI-Z (Society of German Engineers Journal)* 123, no. 11 (1981): 459-466.

Lankford, Raymond L. "Scheduling the Job Shop." *APICS Conference Proceedings* (1973): 46-65.

Lankford, Raymond L. "Short-Term Planning of Manufacturing Capacity." *APICS Conference Proceedings* (1978): 37-68.

Melnyk, Steven A., *Production Activity Control* (Shop Floor Control). Homewood, IL: Dow Jones-Irwin, 1987.

Melnyk, Steven A., and Phillip L. Carter. "Identifying the Principles of Effective Production Activity Control." *APICS Conference Proceedings* (1986): 227-231.

Melnyk, Steven A., and Gary L. Ragatz. "Order Review/Release and Its Impact on the Shop Floor." *Production and Inventory Management* 29, no. 2 (1989): 13-17.

Perreault, Alphedor. "The Bottom Line of Shop Floor Control Begins with a Good Data System." *APICS Conference Proceedings* (1977): 103-111.

Putnam, Arnold O., R. Everdell, D. H. Dorman, R. R. Cronan, and L. H. Lindgren. "Updating Critical Ratio and Slack-Time Priority Scheduling Rules." *Production and Inventory Management* 12, no. 4 (1971).

Wassweiler, William R. "Fundamentals of Shop Floor Control." *APICS Conference Proceedings* (1980): 352-354.

Wassweiler, William R. "Shop Floor Control." *APICS Conference Proceedings* (1977): 386-391.

Wiendahl, Hans P. *Belastungorientierte Fertigungssteuerung*. Munich, Vienna: Carl Hanser Verlag, 1987.

Wight, Oliver W. "Input/Output Control: A Real Handle on Lead Time." In *Capacity Management Reprints*, 107-129. Falls Church, VA: American Production and Inventory Control Society, 1984.

15

PURCHASING MANAGEMENT

Purchasing is important because of two factors. First, purchasing plays a key role in achieving the operations planning and control system objectives concerning delivery, flexibility, quality, and cost. Second, purchased items constitute 30 to 60 percent of the cost of goods sold in most manufacturing firms and a greater percentage in merchandizing firms. Whether in a merchandising operation such as Marvin's with little or no manufacturing, or in a build to custom design manufacturer such as Kickham Boiler and Engineering, or in a manufacturing to stock firm such as Wellco Carpet or Hewlett Packard, planning and control of purchasing is as important as planning and control of internal production activities.

The integration of purchasing in planning and control activities begins in the long range and continues through the execution and post production follow-up and control phases. In the long-range resource planning stage, purchasing's task is to establish relationships with reliable suppliers that have sufficient capacity to produce good quality parts at reasonable prices and that are able to deliver them on schedule. As the master production schedule and the resulting MRP is developed for purchased parts, purchasing's task is to communicate this information to suppliers in a timely manner and to verify that they have the capacity to fulfill these requirements.

Communication with suppliers is essential to adequate integration of suppliers in the production chain. Today, direct computer linkage between purchasers and suppliers is not uncommon and can be a considerable aid in achieving the desired integration. For example, when a supplier has the material requirements plan (MRP) for the items it supplies, the planned orders in that record provide a forecast of the orders they will receive.

Purchasing's role in planning and controlling priorities and capacities is very similar to the role of production activity control (PAC). While PAC closes the planning and control loop with respect to shop management, purchasing closes it with respect to supplier management, as illustrated in Figure 15-1.

Purchased parts and materials constitute 30 to 60 percent of the cost of goods sold in most manufacturing firms. Thus, a small percentage decrease in the cost of purchased items can result in a much larger percentage increase in profits. For example, if the cost of purchased materials is 50 percent of sales and profit is 10 percent of sales, decreasing the cost of those same purchased materials to 48 percent of sales will increase profits by 20 percent, as illustrated in Figure 15-2. Sanford Volsky (1981) has reported how Lubriquip saved $140,000 in the cost of purchased items through a formal program focused on several high dollar product groups. Since purchasing is also crucial in achieving product quality and delivery schedules, a study of purchasing policies, procedures, and decisions can be rewarding.

Figure 15-1
Relationship of Purchasing to Other
Planning and Control Activities

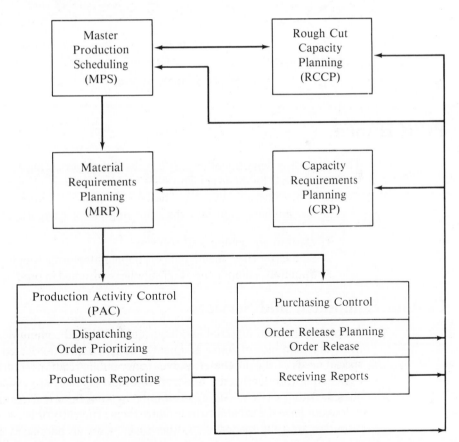

Figure 15-2
Purchasing Costs and Profits as a Percentage of Sales Income

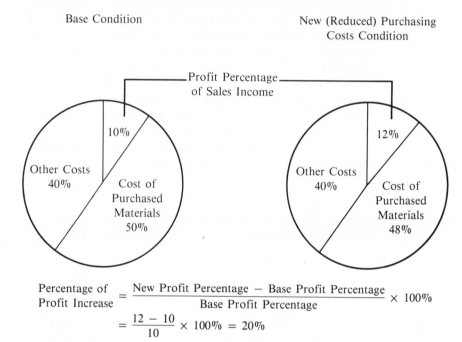

$$\begin{aligned} \text{Percentage of} \atop \text{Profit Increase} &= \frac{\text{New Profit Percentage} - \text{Base Profit Percentage}}{\text{Base Profit Percentage}} \times 100\% \\ &= \frac{12 - 10}{10} \times 100\% = 20\% \end{aligned}$$

PURCHASES

The purchasing department usually has the task of procuring all the goods and services required by the organization. Thus, its activities account for a greater portion of the cost of sales than the cost of materials alone indicates.

Items purchased fall into the following major categories:

1. Custom equipment and services
2. Standard office, maintenance, and manufacturing supplies and services
3. Materials, components, and supplies consumed in producing a product

Custom Equipment and Services

Process equipment, material handling equipment, and communications equipment are examples of items frequently designed and fabricated to meet the special needs of the purchaser. Advertising, public relations, market research, engineering (product) tests, and software development are examples of purchased custom services. An organization purchases these services either because it does not have the capability to produce them efficiently or because its internal resources are fully loaded with other tasks. Custom purchases usually begin with a funding request that states the need and justifies the expense. Since the department requesting the equipment or service usually possesses greater knowledge of the technical requirements and the supplier's capabilities than the purchasing department, purchasing often plays a supporting role, overseeing the paperwork and advising the technical experts of conditions or factors they might have overlooked. Each case may be different, and purchasing's cognizance of these differences and how they should be handled contractually can reduce misunderstandings and future difficulties. For more complex and costly expenditures, the legal department may take an active role in either developing or approving the final contract.

Standard Supplies and Services

Envelopes, paper clips, paper towels, and light bulbs are just a few of the many office and general supplies purchased. These are C items, commercially available for the most part. Once a reliable source of acceptable quality and cost is found, purchasing is a clerical function interrupted by a periodic, perhaps annual, review of the supplier's performance. Technological changes may also trigger a review. As is the case with most C items, it is better to have extra on hand than to be waiting for an order to arrive. The cost of a stockout is usually more expensive than carrying an ample safety stock.

Manufacturing supplies, such as cutting oil, drill bits, cutting tools, and welding rods, are also C items and should be managed accordingly. Standard hardware items, such as rivets, washers, and fasteners (pan stock), are kept in trays or pans on the shop floor readily available for use. Thus, they are managed not by a perpetual record system but by a visual review two-bin system (see Chapter 7).

Manufacturing Material, Components, and Supplies

The bulk of purchasing expenditures is for material, components, and supplies that become part of the final product. Management of these items directly affects the flow of incoming cash, production efficiency, inventory costs, and return on investment and, thus, the achievement of the primary goals of the organization. Determination of order quantities and order timing must be coordinated closely with manufacturing planning. Because of this relationship, this chapter is concerned primarily with the management of these purchases. Some organizations have combined the positions of inventory planner and buyer of manufacturing material and components to achieve this coordination.

Many types of equipment have components that are subject to failure. Since downtime of manufacturing equipment and material handling equipment often disrupts production, delays deliveries, and is very expensive, spare components usually are purchased and stocked. Spare tires, belts, pumps, motors, actuators, and solenoids are examples. The manufacturing and maintenance engineering departments should decide which and how many of each spare component to stock. These decisions should be based on manufacturing engineering estimates of failure rates, the impact of failure on production, and the cost of spares.

PURCHASING MATERIALS AND COMPONENTS

The objectives of purchasing materials and components are (1) to maintain a continuity of supply in keeping with a schedule, (2) to provide material and components that meet or exceed a specified level of quality, and (3) to obtain the required items at the lowest possible total cost consistent with delivery and quality requirements. These objectives are gained through activities such as the following:

1. Evaluating and approving vendors
2. Requesting quotations
3. Negotiating price and delivery
4. Preparing purchase orders
5. Determining purchase cash commitments
6. Tracking planned and open purchase orders
7. Determining order quantities and order release timing
8. Processing of receipts accurately
9. Handling receipts with discrepancies
10. Monitoring releases against blanket orders, systems contracts, and other special contractual arrangements
11. Analyzing variances in item and vendor prices, deliveries, and quality

Long-standing relationships of purchasers and suppliers often minimizes formal quotations and negotiations as described later in this chapter and in Chapter 17.

MAKE-OR-BUY DECISIONS

Make-or-buy decisions concern material, components, assemblies, and services. They take place during long-, medium-, and short-range planning. For example, the management of an automobile manufacturing company may decide to purchase an engine rather than build a new engine manufacturing line. A contract may be signed with a consulting firm to develop an integrated CAD/CAM system including a manufacturing control subsystem. At the same time, a one-year contract for part programming may be given to a software house due to the heavy initial programming load. Committing to use a given capacity per month to produce rather than to purchase a specific product during the next 12 months is another example of a medium-range make-or-buy decision—make in this case. In the short range, a local machine shop may be employed to produce some gear blanks rather than having the lathe department run overtime during the next two weeks.

All companies find it necessary to purchase some material and components. Paint, raw material, rivets, bolts, castings, and commercial electronic components are common purchases. Vertical integration is economically feasible only to a point. Factors that make some items readily recognized as purchase items include:

A. The purchaser's lack of the required technical capability
B. Patents or trade secrets possessed by the supplier
C. Cost advantages of the supplier due to many customers
D. The manufacturing superiority of the supplier in a particular technology

For other items, the decision of whether to manufacture or purchase is not as easily made. Many metal fabricators are faced with the decision, for example, of machining special gears themselves or having them machined by a firm specializing in gear machining (a gearhouse). Metal cutting and forming, plastics molding, diecasting, heat treating, and plating capability, for example, can also be found in relatively small firms in most geographic regions. These firms develop expertise in one or two of the above areas and frequently provide a viable alternative source of components or specific processing capability. When the potential purchaser possesses comparable capability, the make-or-buy decision is more complex.

Make-or-buy decisions affect a wide variety of services. They extend from services such as design engineering, tool design, advertising, and public relations to more mundane services such as janitorial, lawn care, and printing.

Factors that influence make-or-buy decisions include:

A. The relative quality
B. Capabilities of the purchaser
C. Capacity available
D. The marginal costs of the items or skills involved
E. Lead time
F. Supplier relations

To merit consideration, both the internal and external sources of supply must produce adequate quality. If the output of any one source far exceeds minimum quality at no additional cost, it is obviously preferable. If a purchaser has the capability but its capacity is fully utilized, overtime may be the only alternative to purchasing. If, on the other hand, both personnel and equipment are not fully utilized and a no-layoff policy exists, the marginal costs of producing an item internally are the costs of material only.

The lead time and the reliability of delivery promises are also important considerations. The forte of many suppliers is reliable short lead times and good quality—at a price. Whereas some suppliers thrive on producing small quantities on short notice at irregular intervals, others require a more stable relationship that involves purchase commitments for weeks or months at a lower unit cost. Thus, the supplier's preferred role and the existing purchaser-supplier relationship and commitment influence the make-or-buy decision. Because of their importance, the relationships with suppliers are discussed next.

SUPPLIER RELATIONS

Suppliers are as important to most manufacturers as the manufacturer's own production capability. The customer-supplier relationship affects the quality and cost of the purchaser's product as well as the purchaser's customer service capability. Relations with suppliers involve or primarily concern:

A.   Overall approach
B.   Part design
C.   Quality
D.   Schedule (quantity)
E.   Pricing
F.   Communication

The Overall Approach

Nakane and Hall (1981) have pointed out that many Japanese firms consider suppliers as relatives. Trust and loyalty dominate the relationship that emphasizes mutual assistance to strengthen the production capabilities of both companies. Such relationships also exist in the United States although to a much lesser extent. For example, automobile owners value highly the mechanic on whom they can depend. Such relationships usually provide quality and service resulting in lower total costs than those found in a *caveat emptor* environment.

Part Design

In some cases the nature of the item or the relative design engineering strengths of the purchaser and supplier naturally lead to the purchaser providing detailed specifications. In other cases the purchaser may provide only the interface design requirements (mechanical, electrical, and hydraulic connections, for example) and the general functional requirements. Thus, the supplier performs part of the design function to achieve quality and cost objectives. This is obviously true in the case of commercial items purchased from catalogs. When suppliers and customers view final product quality and cost as common objectives, design modification to achieve these objectives may originate two or more levels below the final product manufacturer. The firm making the mold for a plastic component, for example, may suggest a change in the component's design to the component manufacturer who, in turn, suggests it to the firm assembling the final product. In brief, design improvements and value analysis (discussed later in this chapter) are not limited to the firm performing the final assembly.

Quality

The consumer does not distinguish between the quality of purchased components and the quality of items manufactured by the firm from whom the final product is purchased. Both are equally important. When, for example, a solenoid in a dishwasher fails, the consumer holds the dishwasher manufacturer responsible. Thus, many organizations require that the quality control system as well as the manufacturing and financial capability of a potential supplier be approved prior to issuing any purchase orders to the supplier. There is more than a grain of truth in the adage that many people would not eat in their favorite restaurant if they observed what goes on in the kitchen. Continual improvement in supplier quality is an important result of the "we're in this together" attitude of the proper customer-supplier relationship. This attitude is manifested by the purchaser providing technical assistance to overcome production difficulties at the supplier, clearly delineating the critical from the not-so-critical characteristics, and providing immediate feedback of poor quality.

The Schedule

Nakane and Hall (1981) note that certain supplier capacity characteristics are important in the Just-in-Time environment. These capabilities, knowledge of which is important to the purchaser in any environment, include:

1. Capacity: An overall rate of production capacity commitment to the purchaser
2. Flexibility: The ability to respond to production rate changes and to product mix changes, and thus, the ability to respond to planning lead times required by the supplier and to revised commitments

With this knowledge, the purchaser can avoid making unrealistic demands of the supplier. Purchasers should treat suppliers' schedules in the same manner as they treat their internal master production schedule (MPS). Planning fences should be established for such things as delivery requirements, parts fabrication, and material purchases. In addition, the purchaser should work with suppliers and advise them how to reduce lead time and increase production flexibility.

Pricing

The cost to the purchaser may be based on a competitve bid, a cost-plus contract, a specified percentage of the cost (usually in the case of experimental or development work), or a negotiated figure. Negotiated costs are sometimes based on target costs, which in turn are based on learning curves and competitive factors. Long-term quality suppliers develop only under profitable conditions, and purchasers survive and prosper only with quality and cost competitive purchased parts.

Communication

The importance of communication is evident in all of the above. In some companies, the planner and buyer is a combined position, thus simplifying communication between planning and suppliers. Suppliers should be able to contact design engineers at the purchaser and in some cases expect aid in developing or improving manufacturing processes. Surprises should be a rare occurrence. The supplier should be informed of the relative importance of the purchaser's requirements, and the purchaser should have a clear picture of the supplier's capabilities.

Electronic data interchange (EDI), an electronic communication system between one or more installations of the same or different organizations, enables a purchaser to inform a supplier immediately of purchase authorization, to provide the supplier with direct access to those areas of the MPS that affect the supplier, to communicate shipments immediately, and to provide new information to the supplier immediately. Thus, with satellite technology, a carpet manufacturer in the Netherlands can be informed daily of the quantity of each carpet sold not only in Holland but also in England, France, and virtually the entire world. For a further discussion, see Emmelhorne (1986).

SUPPLIER PERFORMANCE RATINGS

Supplier performance can be tracked and quantified. The supplier performance rating model and process described below is similar to the one used at the Kingston-Warren Corporation as reported by Allison F. Gray (1984).

Let

$$SPR = W_1 \times QL + W_2 \times DL + W_3 \times QN + W_4 \times FL + W_5 \times TC$$

where SPR = supplier performance rating
   W_i = weight assigned to performance characteristic i
   $\Sigma W_i = 1.0$
   QL = quality rating
   DL = delivery rating
   QN = quantity rating
   FL = flexibility rating
   TC = technical contributions rating

The values of the weights (W_i's) depend on the purchaser's objectives. For example, in some cases little technical support from the supplier is desired, and W_5 would be relatively low, say 0.05. In other cases, design, performance, and reliablility improvements by the supplier may be crucial in supplier evaluations, and W_5 would be relatively high, say 0.25. The following are examples of how quality, delivery, quantity, and flexibility can be evaluated.

Quality

Quality is usually measured in terms of the percentage of items that meet the quality specifications. In the not too distant past a 99.9 percent quality performance was perceived as excellent in most situations. Today an expectation of less than five bad parts per million, a 99.9995 percent quality performance is not uncommon in high volume production situations. The following are two possible measures.

$$QL = \frac{\text{Units Accepted}}{\text{Units Received}}, \text{ or}$$

$$QL = \frac{\text{Lots Accepted}}{\text{Units Accepted}} \times \frac{\text{Samples Accepted}}{\text{Samples Rejected}}$$

Delivery

Good delivery performance means arrival of an order at the exact minute, hour, or day required. In some cases late delivery may be totally unacceptable and may result in a supplier being eliminated as an approved source. For example, late deliveries that shut down production at the purchaser's plant may negate both quality and price advantages of a supplier. Thus, the assignment of points to different levels of delivery performance depends on the situation. The following is only one possibility.

$$DL = \frac{\text{Sum of Points Earned}}{\text{Sum of Possible Points}}$$

Points are earned on the following basis:

Orders: Late (Early)	Points
On time (to 3 days early)	100
1 to 2 days late (4 to 6 days early)	80
3 to 5 days late (7 to 15 days early)	50
6 to 10 days late (16 or more days early)	30
More than 10 days late	0

Quantity

Suppliers may deliver on time but deliver more or less than ordered. Some deviation may be acceptable, especially for C items. Thus, a range (tolerance) within which the quantity received is considered as accurate often exists. Tolerances may vary for different types of materials and components. For example, at a custom manufacturer, such as Kickem Boiler and Engineering, there is a zero tolerance on expensive items required for special steel or fittings required only for a specific customer.

$$QN = \frac{\text{Sum of Points Earned}}{\text{Sum of Possible Points}}$$

Orders	Points
Within tolerance	100
±5 percent deviation	80
±6 to 10 percent deviation	50
±11 to 20 percent deviation	30
>20 percent deviation	0

Flexibility and Technical Competence

The flexibility evaluation is based on a supplier's ability to adjust to changes in design specifications, delivery dates, and quantities. Evaluations of technical competence are based on improvements in the manufacturing process and design that result in improved performance or cost. Suppliers may be classified as excellent, good, fair, or poor on each of these attributes.

VALUE ANALYSIS

The *APICS Dictionary* (1987) defines value analysis as "the systematic use of techniques which serve to identify a required function, establish a value for that function, and finally to provide that function at the lowest overall cost. This approach focuses on the functions of an item rather than the methods of producing the present product design." Because of the high cost of purchased items, value analysis is often applied as part of the purchasing function. In this context its objective is to find lower cost, alternative ways of performing the functions of currently purchased items.

Many people consider the terms *value analysis* and *value engineering* as synonymous; however, we agree with Carlos Fallon (1971, 13), a former president of the Society of Value Engineering, in believing that the term *value engineering* tends to tie the definition to a particular function and that marketing, engineering, manufacturing, and purchasing all play important roles in the analysis of value. *Value analysis* consists of the following sequence of tasks: (1) selection, (2) data gathering, (3) analysis, (4) innovation (simplification), (5) evaluation (comparison and choice), and (6) implementation.

Selection

The value analysis task group should select projects on the basis of the expected improvement per cost and time involved. Thus, high priority may be given to a task that promises small improvement but that can be accomplished in a short time and have results implemented at minimum cost. In other cases the need for improvement may be figuratively screaming for analysis. The difficulty, of course, is that the ease of and the time required to develop an improvement and the cost of implementation can only be estimated. In any event, the necessary information for analysis must be available or obtainable. First priority belongs to critical situations, those which if not remedied can destroy the company, division, or product line.

Data Gathering

A properly constituted value analysis task group inherently has a vast amount of diverse information concerning most projects. The first step is to document and organize that information. More important, organization of the available information should reveal what the group does not know. Organizing the task group's ignorance is essential to analysis and improvement. Once the voids in the data bank are identified, the priority and difficulty of filling each void can be established. Other members of the organization, consultants, suppliers, and subject area bibliographies are excellent sources. Many libraries and professional societies have computerized bibliographic reference sources. Seldom are all the facts available or necessary. Necessary information must be obtained and verified. Fallon (1971) aptly describes the data gathering dilemma with a figure similar to Figure 15-3.

Figure 15-3
Horns of the Information Dilemma

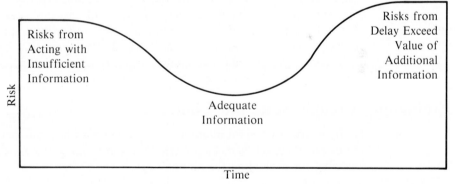

Analysis

The purpose of analysis is to define the function of an item, to determine its cost, and to ascertain its value (what it should cost). The function should be described simply such as:

Item	Primary Function
nut	hold wheel on
tube	conduct hydraulic fluid
knob	adjust volume
rivet	secure strap

Since an item may have a secondary function, secondary functions should be recognized and included in the cost and value analyses. For example, the rivet on a shoulder strap may also be decorative. The basic question is, "What does it do?" An item's value is the lower of two values: the minimum cost at which its essential functions can be fulfilled and the maximum price the customer will pay for the item. Customers, of course, usually do not buy components; they purchase end products. Thus, the latter measure of value (customer's willingness to pay) is not directly applicable to individual items, but is applicable to the total costs of the items in an end product.

Innovation

There is not a clear distinction between analysis and innovation. Thorough analysis itself usually leads to suggested improvements. Better, simpler, and more functional designs and methods are fostered by environments (colleagues and supervisors) that welcome new and different ideas and approaches. Thomas J. Peters and Robert H. Waterman, Jr. (1982) have described how the 3M Company provides an environment that not only welcomes but protects creativity in its research laboratories. Creativity is encouraged at 3M by budget policies and procedures that provide substantial latitude in the expenditure of time and money within the overall constraints. In brief, practices that require written proposals for approval of each expenditure of, say, $500 or more and approval of irregular working hours tend to stifle developments. Accurate accounting and aggregate budget control is essential; beyond that, the value analysis task group should feel free to work on various studies and experiments with relatively free rein. A dominating fear of failure and blowing a few dollars will minimize the chances of success. Simplification and other improvements in product design, manufacturing processes and setups, material handling, and distribution practices can reduce costs, capacity requirements, and manufacturing lead time while improving customer service.

Evaluation, Comparison, and Choice

The time arrives when the alternatives suggested must be evaluated, compared, and one or none selected. Fallon (1971) recommends a process similar to the following for evaluating the alternatives:

1. Identify the requirements and the expected benefits on the basis of functional analysis.
2. Assign weights to the different requirements.
3. Establish lower and upper bounds for each of the requirements.
4. Evaluate (score) each of the alternatives relative to each of the requirements.
5. Determine the aggregate score for each alternative.
6. Eliminate any alternative that does not meet the minimum requirement in any category.

7. Select the most desirable alternative based on one of the following criteria:
   a. The best set of improvements within a given cost (resource expenditure) constraint.
   b. The best set of improvements to cost (resource expenditure) ratio. The tendency is to object to the type process described above as ". . . attempting to measure the unmeasurable." This concern has some justification. For example, occasionally all involved (the entire value analysis task group) will agree that the alternative ranked third by the scale is the most desirable, rather that the first. This only reveals that either the listed requirements or the assigned weights are not accurate representations and should be changed. Chapter 20 describes the application of a similar rating procedure to software packages.

Implementation

This phase has many of the characteristics of management information systems implementation. First, another selection takes place. At any one time, a value analysis task force may have the results of two or more projects. Thus, they must rank the implementation of these recommendations. The criteria used are very similar to those for evaluating recommended information system changes. They include:

1. How critical is the present situation? Situations that severely damage a product's customer appeal or price competitiveness usually have highest priority.
2. What are the time and resource requirements of the change? Improvements that can be implemented in a relatively short time and at a small cost have a higher priority than those requiring a lengthy and costly implementation.
3. The probability of success and the value of the improvement also influence the priority. The product of these two factors is, by definition, the expected value of the change.

In addition, the "down side" risk must be considered. A change whose failure would bankrupt the company is undesirable unless no change also would destroy the firm. Thus, the need for improvement, probability of success, expected savings, time requirements, resource requirements, and the results of failure must be considered.

The Plan

Implementation plans should include explicit recommendations describing who is to perform the necessary tasks, what is to be done, and when it is to be done. Successful implementation requires commitment of management in writing to both the substance of the change and the resources required to accomplish it. Support of those directly responsible for implementing a change as well as those who will use it on a regular basis is enhanced substantially if they or their representatives participate in its development. Education of users concerning the reasons for the change and its benefits, along with training in any revised procedure or processes, also is essential.

The Value Analysis Team

History is replete with stories of solitary individuals working diligently and successfully to solve a problem that larger groups of experts had failed to master. Creativity still exists and impressive innovations occur in laboratory environments where design engineers, manufacturing engineers, and machinists experiment with little direct supervision but with a clear picture of general goals. Nonetheless, the team approach has proven productive in value analysis. Although the composition of the team depends on the nature of the organization, it usually includes members from design engineering, marketing, manufacturing engineering, and inventory planning and purchasing. As specific problems are considered, experts are added from each of the above areas and others. Suppliers may be invited to participate and external consultants can provide valuable assistance. The objective of the group is to obtain synergistic results—results that are better than the sum of the results of the individuals working within their normal confines. The objective is to have the interactive process stimulate creativity that focuses on corporate objectives and is unfettered by departmental interests. Group dynamics can be a source of energy and enthusiasm in a value analysis task group.

THE PURCHASING CYCLE

The purchase of raw materials and components can be viewed as having three phases: (1) prior to the order, (2) the order itself, and (3) after the order. During the time prior to the order, purchasing should be concerned with developing, evaluating, and selecting suppliers. Occasionally, engineering will develop requirements for a material or component not available in the marketplace. Purchasing and engineering must work with suppliers, perhaps funding research, in developing such items. Purchasing also should be adding to its list of acceptable suppliers for specific materials and components. Strikes, fires, floods, other calamities, and changes in vendor pricing or manufacturing practices can disrupt a heretofore reliable supplier. The supply chain frequently has many links, and the purchasing office may have to develop contacts with suppliers of their suppliers.

Evaluation of a potential supplier is based on the supplier's manufacturing process, product quality, management, financial health, lead time, price, and capacity. The manufacturing process is a major determinant of product characteristics, such as appearance, performance, reliability, and life expectancy. Poor management or inadequate financing can lead to a short life span for a supplier and to disruptions of deliveries. Unusually long or undependable delivery lead times decrease the competitive position of any supplier—as well as that of the purchaser. An assessment of vendor capacity is necessary to determine what proportion of the requirements the vendor can handle and if additional suppliers are necessary. Supplier evaluations frequently involve a visit to the vendor's facility to examine the production and quality control management systems as well as the manufacturing process. Many organizations have a formal vendor qualification process (vendor certification) that must be completed before a supplier's quotations will be accepted.

Supplier development and selection usually is a medium-range planning activity. During the same time period, purchasing should participate in establishing the master production schedule (MPS). The purchaser's role in the MPS is similar to that of the production planner. Using the production capacity and lead time of the supplier, the purchaser should confirm that the MPS is realistic in terms of supplier lead time and capacity. If an MPS requires more capacity than a supplier has available, the result will be either premium costs for overtime and transportation or else late deliveries, disrupted production, other inventory sitting around, and perhaps idle work centers.

Whenever possible, purchasing should negotiate for future capacity from vendors that furnish more than one item. This policy gives both supplier and purchaser a long-term commitment for a specific volume of a product family. The relationship remains flexible because the purchaser does not have to specify the quantity or item until required by the supplier's short-range time fence. Burlingame and Warren (1974) reported on such a relationship between Twin Disc Inc. and the Neenah Foundry Company. Carter and Monczka (1978) reported a similar relationship that Steelcase, Inc. has with its supplier of plywood seats and backs and its suppliers of fabric and yarn.

A supplier's flexibility in adapting to engineering, quantity, and schedule changes is also important; it is measured by monitoring the supplier's performance. The evaluation of suppliers continues through the control process.

Purchasing is primarily an execution activity—as opposed to planning and control—with the dominant elements being order placement and receipt. Thus, we will examine the order placement and receiving phases in detail.

ORDER PLACEMENT

An order can be initiated in several different ways. A periodic review of inventory, an item reaching its order point, the arrival of the planned order release date in a material requirements planning (MRP) system, or a Kanban trigger in a JIT system may reveal the need for additional purchased items and trigger a purchase requisition (see Figure 15-4). A computerized system may generate a purchase requisition automatically on the planned order release date or when the inventory of an item is reduced to or below its order point. The planner-buyer

Figure 15-4
The Purchasing Process: Order Placement and Receipt

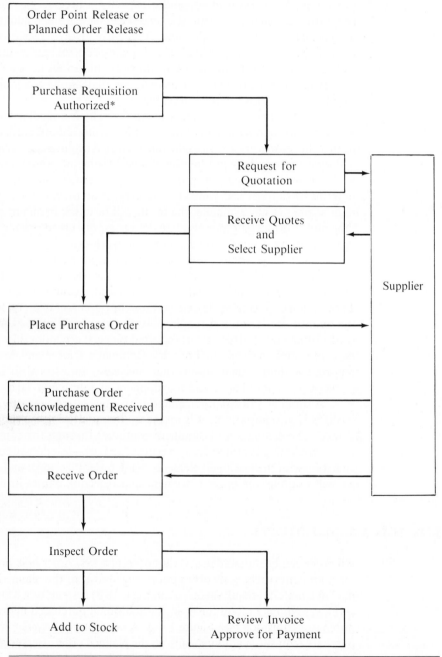

In many cases, the organization has selected the primary and secondary suppliers in the order planning phase.

then may edit the requisition before placing the purchase order. This is another situation where ABC analysis may be applied (see Chapter 6). For example, purchase orders for A and B items may be reviewed while those for C items are processed automatically. Each requisition is identified by number and usually contains the item number, item name, date, quantity, buyer's name, due date, and supplier's number and name. Since there is not a standard requisition form suitable for all companies, this information may vary. For example, the purchase requisition may also include the price and the account to be charged. Requisition control may be achieved by a system capable of reporting purchase requisitions for which purchase orders have not been prepared and the reason.

Timing the release of a requisition requires that all segments of lead time be considered. These segments include the planner's time, the buyer's time, the time required by the supplier to process and ship the order, receipt and inspection of the product, and movement of the order to the required work center. If quotations are required prior to order placement, additional time is required. In most cases, however, the price of raw materials and components used repetitively is known prior to the required order release.

Purchasing Contract Arrangements

A blanket order is probably the most common contract arrangement between a purchaser and a supplier. A *blanket order* is a contract to purchase a minimum quantity during a specific period, usually a year. Purchasing negotiates the initial contract, which may involve a fixed price, a price range, or a price tied to another base such as the cost of labor or raw materials. The minimum and maximum quantities that may be ordered over a given subperiod, say every 30 days, may also be specified. Once a blanket order is contracted, production and inventory control may send requisitions directly to the supplier, requesting shipments of specified quantities by given dates. Purchasing is involved only in establishing and, if necessary, renegotiating the contract.

A *standing order*, sometimes called a supply contract, is a blanket order for an indefinite period. It may specify a given quantity of an item to be shipped at fixed intervals or it may call for delivery only on receipt of a requisition with the quantity allowed to vary within a given range during specified intervals.

Blanket and standing orders are advantageous to both the buyer and the seller. The buyer receives a price discount because of the quantity commitment and eliminates the cost of repetitive purchase orders. The seller, in turn, receives a guarantee of sales for a relatively long period. Additionally, if the seller's capacity planning and production economics warrant it, the seller can produce the required items early without the normal risks of building to stock. These contracts frequently contain provisions governing the notice required for revising or canceling the contract as well as the costs of termination.

As noted earlier, when more than one item produced on the same equipment is purchased from a supplier, the buyer may place an initial blanket order for a supplier's capacity only. Later orders will specify which items are to be produced with this capacity. Both parties must agree to the lead time for the orders and define which items are to be produced.

Even when a blanket order does not exist, orders for B and C items may be placed with the assumption that the catalog or last quoted price is still applicable. A purchase order acknowledgement sheet or ticket may be made part of the purchase order. The vendor must use this ticket to inform the purchaser if there have been any changes in price, delivery, or other specifications. The magnitude of the order and the probability of a change or misunderstanding determine whether or not the purchaser will follow up with the supplier until an acknowledgement agreeing to the terms of the purchase order is received.

Systems and distributor contracts were described by Friessnig (1981) as follows:

> *Systems contracts*: Under a systems contract, vendors maintain, at their facilities, backup supplies of materials, and periodically inventory and replenish materials at your facility. A special order form is completed by the supplier which replaces and serves the function of the purchase order, receipt acknowledgment, and the invoice. Hardware, stationery and operating supplies are typical commodities covered by a systems contract. In the service environment, many retailers establish systems contracts with vendors in such areas as breads, candies, and photographic supplies.
>
> *Distributor contracts*: Under a distributor contract, vendors normally maintain, at their facilities, predetermined quantities of specific materials dedicated for your use. Purchase order releases are made against the master contract.

Just-in-Time inventory management procedures have encouraged the use of systems and distributor contracts (see Chapter 17). Such contracts usually require shipment within a given time period, e.g., three days. If the supplier is unable to ship, the purchaser has the right to obtain the merchandise from a second supplier. Fines for noncompliance often exist in these circumstances.

Prerequisite Data

Purchasing activities require that certain data be available to the planner-buyer. This information may be kept on 3″ × 5″ cards, in notebooks, or, more typically today, in a computer file. Commonly, data is kept in five files: (1) the item (part) master file, (2) the vendor file, (3) the requisition file, (4) the open purchase order file including a master file and a detail file, and (5) the purchase history file.

The item master file is used in many activities including MRP, inventory management, and cost estimating. There is much similarity between the part master file of manufactured items (described in Chapter 12) and the item (part) master file for purchased items. The item master file contains a record for each purchased item. The data in each record may be divided into general data and supplier data. Typical items in the general data portion include item number, item description, value classification, on-hand quantity, allocated quantity, available quantity, on-order quantity, lot-size quantity, ordering rules, type of demand, and substitute items. The supplier data of the item master file will include the supplier number, address, telephone number, supplier's item number, price, and lead time. The supplier information will be available for each approved supplier. Most item master files contain additional data to meet the needs of a given environment and for use in other activities.

The vendor (supplier) file contains a record for each supplier. Each record contains data describing the supplier performance, the location of the supplier, and the principal products obtained from the supplier. Typical data that might be included in such a file include:

1. A number uniquely identifying the supplier
2. The supplier's name
3. The supplier's address
4. The supplier's telephone number
5. The product or products sold by the supplier
6. The total units purchased this year to date—by item
7. The total dollars spent with the supplier this year
8. Information similar to 6 and 7 for one or more previous years
9. A measure of the supplier's quality performance—by item
10. A measure of item performance in service
11. A measure of delivery performance, such as average lead time and standard deviation
12. The current price
13. The method of payment
14. The discount schedule
15. The payments due
16. The unfilled (outstanding) purchase orders

It would not be unusual to find additional information in the vendor file. The data items listed above, however, are most of those usually required.

The open purchase order file contains a record of each released order. Since two or more items may be ordered on the same purchase order, the purchase order record frequently contains a master (or header) section and a detail section for each item. The master section of the file includes information such as the following:

1. The purchase order number—a unique number usually serially assigned to successive purchase orders
2. The order status—a code indicating whether partial shipments have been received, the total order has been received, the order has been cancelled, or the order has been closed (filled)

3. The purchase requisition number
4. The purchase requisition date
5. The supplier number
6. The buyer number
7. The number of shipments—a code indicating whether the order is for a single shipment, multiple shipments, a blanket order, a standing order, or any other special arrangement
8. An acknowledgement code—an indication of whether or not an acknowledgement is expected. (If one is expected, other data fields are required in the record to reveal the status of the acknowledgement.)
9. The total cost of the order
10. Special charges for transportation, special handling or packaging, insurance, expediting, etc.

The purchase order detail file contains information such as the following:

1. The item number (with applicable engineering changes)
2. The item name
3. The item line number on the purchase order
4. The unit of measure
5. The unit price
6. The requisition number
7. The requisition date
8. The quantity ordered
9. The date required
10. Various other dates, such as first and latest promised delivery dates, estimated delivery dates, shipping date, and date received
11. A location code revealing whether the item is at the supplier, in transit, in receiving, in inspection, in material review, or in stores
12. The receiving report number
13. The quantity received
14. The quantity accepted by inspection

Other data concerning the disposition of rejected items by the material review board also may be included.

A separate file, the purchase history file, may exist for closed purchased orders since they are voluminous and the data they contain is not accessed as often as open order data. The records in this file may be identified by item (part) number, supplier number, and/or purchase order number. The purchase history file typically includes quotation data, unit price, other costs, terms, relevant dates, quantities, the buyer, scheduled delivery dates, delivery dates, scrap quantities, deviations from specifications, and rework.

The list of data included in the files just described is not exhaustive. Many other data may be required to achieve all the goals of purchasing in a given situation.

Requisition Control

Release of a planned order should result in the preparation of the requisition. Requisitions for selected items, say A items and emergency orders, may be edited and expedited or may be delayed by the buyer. However, a computerized system may prepare a purchase order automatically for some inventory items (firm planned purchase orders, for example) on their planned order release date. The computer system should minimize the time planner-buyers spend on routine activities and allow them to concentrate on the A items that are critical because of their cost, delivery problems, or quality problems.

The computer system must allow the planner-buyer to determine the status of all requisitions. The system should have the capability of listing requisitions of a given or higher priority for which purchase orders have not been prepared. Priority may be based on the age of the requisition, a critical ratio, the order receipt due date, or some combination.

Wight (1974, 140-144) and Benson (1981) both report on the combination of the traditionally separate roles of the planner and the buyer into one position, the planner-buyer. We have used the term *planner-buyer* in this text to represent either that situation or the traditional separation of the planner and the buyer. Combining the roles of the planner and buyer into a single position makes sense when a formal order release system generates valid due dates and when contact with each supplier can be maintained by a single planner-buyer.

Supplier Lead Time and Delivery

MRP, capacity requirements planning (CRP), and input/output (I/O) planning and control aid in achieving desired supplier lead time and delivery. Providing suppliers with the planned requirements by period gives them valid priorities and reduces the surprises common when using order point systems. Using CRP and I/O planning to regulate the flow of orders to a supplier reduces the likelihood that orders will exceed the supplier's production capacity.

Supplier lead times are dynamic; they change as demand for the supplier's products vary, as the supplier increases or decreases capacity, and with the priority the supplier assigns to the purchaser's order. The planner-buyer should be sensitive to changes in the vendor's lead time and update the purchasing information system by revising the lead time in item and vendor records as these changes occur. Providing suppliers with long-term visibility of requirements and valid short-term priorities aids in controlling lead times. Morency (1977) reported on the excellent results by Bausch and Lomb Inc. in controlling supplier lead time and managing supplier capacity through the development of an MPS, MRP, and contract purchasing.

The Purchase Order Quantity

Chapters 4, 7, and 8 included detailed treatments of how to calculate order quantities. Those chapters dealt with, among other topics, the impact of dependent and independent demand, discrete order quantities, economic order quantities, order-up-to quantities, joint replenishment, and quantity discounts. This section describes a more complex order quantity situation and ranking of quantity discount opportunities. The planner-buyer should ascertain the dominant factor when determining the quantity of an item to be purchased. Supplier packaging, transportation costs, quantity discounts, and production requirements can affect the purchase order quantity.

Let's analyze the following example. The MRP calls for 60 units of a purchased item for each of the next 12 weeks. Estimated requirements beyond that period are also 60 units per week. The company operates 50 weeks a year. The purchaser estimates that the cost of preparing a purchase order is $50. The supplier packages the item in crates holding 150 units and charges an extra $20 for purchases of less than a full crate. The items cost $100 each at the supplier's dock. The supplier offers a 4 percent discount on orders for 600 or more units. The purchaser estimates it costs $100 for the truck to pick up one partial or full crate and deliver it to the plant. Carrying additional crates on the same trip costs an estimated $10 per crate. (Alternate shipping methods are more expensive.) The purchaser uses an inventory carrying cost rate (k) of 0.30 per year. What is the most economical order quantity?

The lot-for-lot (L4L) order quantity approach results in a weekly order for 60 units. Applying the basic economic order quantity (EOQ) model without consideration of the transportation costs, partial crate charges, or quantity discount gives an order quantity of 100 units. If we add the flat $100 transportation cost to fixed cost of an order (the order preparation costs), the EOQ model gives an order quantity of 173 units. None of these approaches, however, considers the reduced transportation cost per unit when two or more crates are combined in one shipment. Nor do these approaches consider the quantity discount.

The total costs for the different likely order quantities are tabulated in Table 15-1. Total costs include the unit costs, carrying costs, ordering costs, partial crate costs, and transportation costs. These costs are calculated as follows:

Total Unit Cost = Cost per Unit (C) × Annual Requirements (R)
$$= CR$$

Carrying Cost = Carrying Cost Rate (k) × Cost per Unit (C) × Order Interval (t, expressed in years by dividing the number of weeks by 50) × Number of Orders per Year (N) × one-half the Order Quantity ($Q \div 2$)
$$= kCtNQ \div 2$$

(Note: tN equals 1.0 by definition when the period of analysis is one year.)

Ordering Cost = Number of Orders per Year (N) × Preparation Cost per Order (S)
$$= NS$$

Partial Crate Cost = Charge per Partial Crate (C_p) × Number of Orders per Year (N)
$$= C_p N$$

$$\text{Transportation Cost} = \text{Number of Shipments per Year } (N) \times \text{Cost of}$$
$$\text{Transportation } (C_t)$$
$$= NC_t$$

where $C_t = \$100 + \$10(M - 1)$
$M = $ number of crates per shipment

Table 15-1
Tabulation of Total Costs per Order Quantity ($Nt = 1.0$ in all cases)

Lot For Lot: $Q = 60$ units; $N = 50$

Unit Costs = $100 × 3,000	=	$300,000
Carrying Costs = 0.3 × $100 × 60 ÷ 2	=	900
Ordering Costs = 50 × $50	=	2,500
Partial Crate Costs = $20 × 50	=	1,000
Transportation Cost = $100 × 50	=	5,000
		$309,400

Simple EOQ: $Q = 100$ units; $N = 30$

Unit Costs = $100 × 3,000	=	$300,000
Carrying Costs = 0.3 × $100 × 100 ÷ 2	=	1,500
Ordering Costs = 30 × $50	=	1,500
Partial Crate Costs = $20 × 30	=	600
Transportation Costs = $100 × 30	=	3,000
		$306,600

One Crate: $Q = 150$ units (one crate); $N = 20$

Unit Costs = $100 × 3,000	=	$300,000
Carrying Costs = 0.3 × $100 × 150 ÷ 2	=	2,250
Ordering Costs = 20 × $50	=	1,000
Partial Crate Costs = none	=	0
Transportation Costs = $100 × 20	=	2,000
		$305,250

Two Crates: $Q = 300$ units (two crates); $N = 10$

Unit Costs = $100 × 3,000	=	$300,000
Carrying Costs = 0.3 × $100 × 300 ÷ 2	=	4,500
Ordering Costs = 10 × $50	=	500
Partial Crate Costs = none	=	0
Transportation Costs = $110 × 10	=	1,100
		$306,100

Price Break Quantity: $Q = 600$ units; $C = \$96$; $N = 5$

Unit Costs = $96 × 3,000	=	$288,000
Carrying Costs = 0.3 × $96 × 600 ÷ 2	=	8,640
Ordering Costs = 5 × $50	=	250
Partial Crate Costs = none	=	0
Transportation Costs = $130 × 5	=	650
		$297,540

The data in Table 15-1 reveal that the quantity discount is the dominant factor in this lot-size decision. Purchasing in order quantities of 600 units results in an annual savings of $7,710 over the next best method. Since average inventory investment, computed as $QC \div 2$, increases from $7,500 to $30,000 when we purchase 600 units rather than 150 in one order, the rate of return, computed as the savings divided by the incremental investment, on our investment equals $7,710 divided by ($30,000 − $7,500) or approximately 0.34. Depending on the investment opportunities of the firm and the rates of return available, this may be a wise investment.

Quantity Discounts

The unit price of many items varies with the quantity purchased; a lower unit cost exists for larger purchase quantities. Chapter 8 described the process for determining the minimum cost order quantity for individual items with a quantity discount schedule. However, analyzing quantity discounts only on an individual item basis can lead to excessive inventory. Purchasing larger than the basic order quantity is often economically justified for many individual items. Purchasing the larger quantity for all such items can result in overcrowded stockrooms and in an inventory investment exceeding financial resources. The buyer must be able to select the most advantageous discount opportunities given total storage availability and financial capacity.

This selection can be based on a rate of return approach when opportunities concern items whose use is anticipated for the foreseeable future. When the opportunities concern items with different periods of anticipated usage, a present value approach is preferable. Let's examine the rate of return approach.

The rate of return approach ranks discount opportunities on the basis of their annual rate of return. Beginning with the highest rate of return opportunity and calculating the cumulative added inventory investment as the next highest rate opportunity is added in rank order sequence, the planner can determine the best selection of opportunities under a given investment constraint.

The annual rate of return (ROI) earned by purchasing a discount quantity equals the annual net savings divided by the increased inventory investment. Annual net savings equal the annual decrease in total unit costs due to the price discount plus the annual ordering cost savings due to the reduced number of orders per year minus the increased inventory carrying costs. The increased investment equals one-half the cost of a discount order quantity minus one-half the cost of the economic order quantity, given that usage is constant throughout the period.

That is, expressed as a mathematical model:

$$\text{Total Savings } (TS) = \text{Unit Cost Savings } (UCS) + \text{Ordering Cost Savings } (OCS) - \text{Increased Inventory Carrying Costs } (ICC)$$

where $UCS = D \times A$

$$OCS = S\left(\frac{A}{EOQ} - \frac{A - D \times A}{DOQ}\right)$$

$$ICC = k\left(\frac{DOQ}{2} - \frac{EOQ}{2}\right)$$

D = discount expressed as a decimal percentage
A = annual requirements in dollars—without discount
S = cost of placing an order
EOQ = economic order quantity in dollars
DOQ = discount order quantity in dollars
k = annual carrying cost rate

Thus,

$$TS = D \times A + S\left(\frac{A}{EOQ} - \frac{A - D \times A}{DOQ}\right) - k\left(\frac{DOQ}{2} - \frac{EOQ}{2}\right)$$

and the rate of return on investment is calculated as follows:

$$\text{ROI} = \frac{TS}{\dfrac{DOQ}{2} - \dfrac{EOQ}{2}}$$

Let's calculate the rate of return obtained from the discount for Item 1 in Table 15-2. From the table we have:

$A = \$54,800$	$D = 0.02$	$EOQ = \$3,160$
$S = \$32$	$k = 0.35$	$DOQ = \$5,000$

Annual Unit Cost Savings $(UCS) = D \times A$
$$= 0.02 \times \$54,800 = \$1,096$$

The annual ordering cost savings (OCS) equals the cost of ordering times the decrease in the number of orders per year.

$$OCS = \$32\left(\frac{\$54,800}{\$3,160} - \frac{\$54,800 - \$1,096}{\$5,000}\right)$$
$$= \$32 \times 6.6 = \$211$$

The annual increased inventory carrying costs (ICC) equals the annual carrying cost rate times the increase in average inventory investment.

$$ICC = 0.35\left(\frac{\$5,000}{2} - \frac{\$3,160}{2}\right)$$
$$= \$322$$

Total net savings is given by

$$TS = \$1,096 + \$211 - \$322 = \$985$$

The rate of return on investment equals the total savings divided by the increased inventory investment.

$$ROI = \frac{\$985}{\dfrac{\$5,000}{2} - \dfrac{\$3,160}{2}} = 1.071 \text{ or } 107.1\%$$

Similar data and the results of similar calculations are recorded in Table 15-2 for each of nine items. The increase in inventory investment due to the larger order size depends on the usage pattern. This example assumes a steady usage rate typical of independent demand, and the increase is estimated as one-half the difference between the normal and discount order quantities. Thus, for Item 1 the increased inventory investment equals $0.5 \times \$5,000 - 0.5 \times \$3,160 = \$920$. When those units that are added to the order quantity to obtain a discount likely will be held for a relatively long period of little or no usage, estimate the increased investment as a higher proportion, say 0.75, of the difference between the order quantities.

The next step is to list all discount opportunities in rank order with ranks based on the rate of return, as illustrated in Table 15-3. These calculations and tabulations aid management in answering questions such as: If a maximum of $5,000 can be added to inventory, which discounts should be taken? What additional investment is required to obtain all discounts with a rate of return greater than 30 percent?

The rates of return, annual discount, and average increase in inventory listed in Table 15-3 in ranking order reveal that the discounts on Items 5, 1, 3, 8, and the first discount on Item 2 have a rate of return greater than 30 percent. The data in Table 15-3 also reveal that the discounts on Items 5, 1, and 3 are the best discount opportunities if there is a $5,000 limit on the added inventory investment for this group of items. When available space limits increased purchase quantities, a similar ranking may be used to select the most desirable increases.

PURCHASING CONTROL

Purchasing should exercise control over individual purchase orders, purchase commitments, and vendor performances. Control of individual purchase orders begins with the control of the requisitions as described previously.

Purchase Order Control

Purchasing should be able to determine the status of each order including whether it is currently a planned order, a firm planned order, placed (open), acknowledged, received, or closed. Acknowledgement may be required only if

Table 15-2
Evaluation of Quantity Discounts, Rate of Return Approach
Ordering costs (S) equal approximately $32. The carrying cost rate (k) is 0.35.

Item	Annual Requirements A	EOQ	Discount D	Discount Order Quantity DOQ	Annual Discount UCS	Ordering Cost Savings OCS	Increase in Average Inventory	Increase in Carrying Costs ICC	Total Net Savings TS	Rate of Return ROI
1	$54,800	$3,160	0.02	$ 5,000	$1,096	$211	$ 920	$ 322	$ 985	107.1%
2	48,635	2,976	0.018	6,000	875	266	1,512	529	612	40.4
3	32,408	2,430	0.05	7,500	1,620	294	2,535	887	1,385	54.6
4	28,620	2,282	0.052	10,000	1,488	314	3,859	1,351	448	11.6
5	22,987	2,040	0.115	5,000	2,643	230	1,480	518	2,355	159.1
6	18,453	1,850	0.045	6,000	830	227	2,075	726	331	16.0
7	11,008	1,418	0.062	4,500	682	176	1,441	504	354	24.6
8	7,431	1,160	0.09	3,000	669	131	920	322	478	52.0
9	1,650	545	0.075	1,200	124	54	378	132	46	12.2

Table 15-3
Ranking Discount Opportunities by Rate of Return

Item	Rank	Return	Added Inventory	Cumulative Added Inventory
5	1	159.1	$1,480	$ 1,480
1	2	107.1	920	2,400
3	3	54.6	2,535	4,935
8	4	52.0	920	5,855
2	5	40.4	1,512	7,367
7	6	24.6	1,441	8,808
6	8	16.0	2,075	10,883
9	9	12.2	378	11,261
4	10	11.6	3,859	15,120

the supplier requests a change in order price, quantity, or product specification. Purchasing can request acknowledgements for orders to new suppliers or for orders with an unusual quantity, product specification, or shipping instructions. The purchasing information system should provide the capability of monitoring acknowledgements and following up on those acknowledgements not received in the prescribed time.

Purchase Commitments

Purchase orders call for deliveries that generate accounts payable and thus, negative cash flow. Controlling the cash commitments begins with the MPS, the MRP, and the resulting planned purchase orders. The planned order release dates, delivery lead times, and payment schedules determine when payment is due. Adding the cash commitments of the planned purchase orders from a given MPS enables management to evaluate the effect of purchases on projected cash requirements. Balancing projected cash requirements with budgeted available cash may require revisions in the MPS and planned purchase order releases. Working capital budgets may necessitate more frequent purchase orders for smaller quantities. Analysis of these cash commitments is part of the MRP II process of analysing the financial requirements of the production plan. MRP II continues this process by performing a similar analysis when the MPS is developed.

As purchase orders are released, actual cash commitments should be tabulated and compared to planned commitments. If significant variances exist, analysis can determine if they are due to price, quantity, or delivery changes. Accounting and finance can use actual purchase order cash commitments in controlling short-term cash flow.

The data in Figure 15-5 illustrate this process. For example, in Figure 15-5, the scheduled receipts and planned order receipts have been computed using the standard MRP process. The cash commitments in a specific period are obtained by multiplying the receipts quantity by the cost per unit. In Week 23 the cash required (Projected $) equals the 40 units to be received times the unit cost of $5.00 or $200.00, for example. This is based on payment required immediately upon receipt. If payment was required within 15 days, the $200.00 cash outflow would be shown in Week 25 instead of Week 23. The cash requirements in the other weeks are calculated in the same manner.

Capacity Commitments

Figure 15-6 illustrates how an MRP system report can aid the planner in evaluating a supplier's capacity relative to purchase order requirements. For example, it reveals that the supplier has insufficient capacity to manufacture all the units requested in Week 19, but will recover in Week 20 and have sufficient cumulative capacity from that point.

Figure 15-5
The Firm Planned Order with Cash Commitments

Planner-Buyer: Garcia; Item: A20; Lead Time: 3; Safety Stock: 0
6 Mo./Service Level: 87%; Cost: $5.00; Inventory Turns: 5.0

							Week							
	19	20	21	22	23	24	25	26	27	28	29	30	31	32
Gross Requirements				30		40	25		50		10		40	35
Scheduled Receipts			35		5				40					
On Hand	35	35	35	5	5	45	20	20	10	10	0	0	-40	-75
Planned Order Receipts											35F		35F	
Planned Order Releases								35F		35F	5			5
Projected $						200			200		175		175	25

Item	Firm	Quantity			Firm	Quantity	
P1951	ACME	20	Week 23	F*	ACME	20	Week 28
P1957	BEST	20	Week 23	F	BEST	15	Week 28
P1951	ACME	20	Week 26	F	ACME	20	Week 30
P1957	BEST	20	Week 26	F	BEST	15	Week 30

*F designates a firm planned order.

Figure 15-6
Time-Phased Vendor Record

Planner-Buyer: Tanaka; Vendor: ACME

Peg to	Week													
	19	20	21	22	23	24	25	26	27	28	29	30	31	32
A20					200			200		175		175		
A51		100		100		100		100		120		120		120
D84			360				290				350			
M02	350					350		300					350	
Scheduled Receipts	350	100	360	100	200	100								
FPO Receipts	350	100	360	100	200	350	290	300	270	295	350	295	350	120
Total Flow	350	100	360	100	200	450	290	300	270	295	350	295	350	120
Vendor Capacity	270	270	270	270	270	270	270	270	270	270	270	270	270	270
Over/Under	+80	−170	+90	−170	−70	+180	+20	+30	−270	+25	+80	+25	+80	−150
Cumulative Deviation	+80	−90	0	−170	−240	−60	−40	−10	−280	−255	−175	−150	−70	−220

ORDER RECEIPT AND RECEIVING

Receiving and purchasing activities are tied together by their very nature. Receiving plays a crucial role in purchasing control. Shipments from suppliers arrive at receiving. Receiving must record the date of arrival; identify the supplier, the item, and the quantity; inspect as required; forward the item to the proper location; and inform purchasing, inventory control, quality control, and accounting of these actions. Because all items may not require a detailed inspection of physical and performance characteristics, purchasing should assure that receiving knows the appropriate inspection procedures for all items. Receiving should confirm that the items are labeled properly and correspond to the purchase order. Receiving then must decide whether to send items directly to a manufacturing work center or to a given storage location. This requires prior instructions from either purchasing or planning. Movement to the wrong location can result in production delays and lost items. Receiving may have a list of critical items that should be expedited through receiving and sent immediately to manufacturing. Also, receiving normally should notify the planner-buyer and manufacturing of the arrival of critical items.

Receiving should inform purchasing of partial shipments as well as quantities that exceed the overshipment tolerance. The buyer then can follow up on items still due and decide whether or not the excess quantity should be returned to the supplier. Items that do not meet inspection requirements may be sent to a material review area. Representatives of quality control, engineering, purchasing, manufacturing, and sometimes the supplier then will decide on the disposition of the rejected items. Some may be reworked, others may be accepted as a usable variation, and others will be returned to the vendor.

Just-in-Time (JIT) purchasing requires suppliers to deliver components to the purchaser's receiving dock, or sometimes directly to the production line, as they are required. This approach is used widely in Japan and has been implemented at the Kawasaki Plant in Lincoln, Nebraska, as reported by Schonberger, Sutton, and Claunch (1981). Suppliers often are located near the purchaser, usually have a long-term contract (for a year or the production season), and deliver once or twice daily. This approach reduces the purchaser's work in process.

Purchasing control is the final stage in the preorder, order, and post order purchasing cycle. Purchasing activities have a substantial impact on material costs, availability, and quality. Effective purchasing can decrease inventory investment, increase customer service, and improve profits dramatically.

CONCLUSIONS

Purchasing has many responsibilities. Those that relate directly to production and inventory management concern order quantities, order release, the cost of purchased items, vendor capacity, the lead time of purchased items, the vendor's flexibility in adjusting to engineering and schedule changes, and vendor delivery performance. Planning and control of vendor deliveries are as crucial to achieving organizational objectives as planning and control of production. Techniques useful in controlling production also are useful in controlling vendor deliveries. Purchasing's role extends across the long-, medium-, and short-range planning horizons. New methods exist for extending capacity planning and control to encompass suppliers' facilities and to improve their delivery performance.

EXERCISES

1. Istvan Maygar, manager of purchasing for the Downhome Cookware Company, contends that the purchasing departments efforts in his company are sabotaged by an unrealistic master production schedule. If the MPS does often call for a output larger than capacity, explain why he probably has a valid contention.

2. Sean O'Malley is a production planner and Lars Henrickson is in purchasing at the Tarsh Stencil Company in Dubuque. They are responsible for items going into the same final assemblies. Over the years Sean and Lars have learned the value of close communication concerning the status of component and end item orders. Recently they have jointly proposed that they switch jobs for a six-month period just to add variety. What do you think of this idea?

3. The manager of purchasing, Nigel Underthink, does not encourage evaluating a supplier's capacity. He contends that it is the supplier's problem to fill the order or not accept it. How should you respond?

4. A company's sales last year were $60 million, profit was $12 million, and the cost of purchases was $30 million. If the rate of inflation is zero and sales volume remains the same, how much must the cost of purchased items be reduced to increase profits by 10 percent?

5. A small telecommunications equipment manufacturer produces a FAX unit. The demand for the unit averages 100 units per week, and forecasts of future demand are also for a continuing stable demand of 100 units per week. The company assembles the units at a rate of 100 units per week. It purchases a subassembly used in the FAX product for $200 each. The company estimates its cost of ordering as $75 per order, and uses a carrying cost rate of 30 percent. The supplier charges an additional $100 per order for ordered quantites less than 400 units. Transportation costs per delivery are $100. Calculate the total annual costs for a lot-for-lot (weekly) ordering policy and the EOQ approach. Use 50 weeks per year. How might a blanket or standing order approach be used to reduce costs in this situation?

6. The planned order receipts for an item follow. The item costs $42. Payment is required within four weeks of receipt. Calculate the time-phased cash commitments. (There are no planned reciepts in the weeks not shown.)

		Week	
	2	10	18
Planned Order Receipts	250	300	275

7. The planned order receipts for four items follow. The item costs are also given. Payment is required within two weeks of receipt. Calculate the time-phased cash commitments.

		Planned Order Receipts by Week							
Cost	Item	1	2	3	4	5	6	7	8
$18	A	10	10	10	10	10	10	10	10
31	B	0	17	0	17	0	17	0	17
7	C	33	0	46	18	0	25	30	25
75	D	8	7	21	16	0	12	18	12

8. The Wonarm Vending Machine Company purchases five items, all manufactured on the same equipment, from Sterling Products Ltd. Industry capacity for these items is in short supply and Sterling asks for a three-month lead time. The projected demand for the next six months (Months 1 through 3 are already under contract) for these items and the capacity required for each follows.

	Projected Requirements by Month						Capacity Required
Item	4	5	6	7	8	9	(hours/unit)
A	200	200	200	200	200	200	0.20
B	150	80	60	200	40	100	0.10
C	60	60	60	75	75	75	0.15
D	40	40	40	40	40	40	0.25
E	25	25	25	40	40	50	0.30

Since the actual product mix may vary slightly, Wonarm decides to purchase capacity based on the projected requirements plus 5 percent. Calculate the number of hours they should purchase for each month.

9. The requirements and present on-hand inventory for the five items discussed in Exercise 8 follow:

		Requirements by Week						
Item	On Hand	1	2	3	4	5	6	7
A	60	50	0	100	100	0		
B	25	20	40	40	0	60		
C	10	30	30	0	0	40		
D	5	0	0	0	20	20		
E	50	25	25	0	25	0		

a. In what order should they tell the supplier, Sterling Products, to run these items?
b. Calculate the capacity required by Sterling during each of these five weeks.

10. The promised delivery lead times and the actual delivery lead times of five suppliers are as follows (each supplies a different item).

Supplier	Promised Lead Time (days)	Actual Lead Time of the Last Ten Shipments (oldest orders first)
A	6	9, 7, 6, 9, 5, 9, 8, 9, 10, 10
B	10	12, 12, 11, 10, 10, 9, 10, 11, 10, 9
C	15	14, 15, 13, 17, 17, 16, 14, 15, 13, 15
D	20	20, 18, 19, 22, 22, 21, 24, 24, 26, 28
E	25	30, 29, 31, 29, 28, 30, 28, 31, 32, 28

Evaluate the performance of each supplier using the SPR system described in the text. Is the system adequate in this case or should it be revised?

11. The forecast demand for an item is a relatively stable 250 units per month for the next year. The cost of placing and receiving an order is $90, shipping costs are a flat $50 per shipment, and the company uses an annual carrying cost rate of 0.30 percent. The supplier has the following price schedule for the item.

Quantity	Price (each)
0-99	100
100-999	90
>1,000	80

a. Calculate the annual costs of an order quantity equal to:
   (1) the monthly requirement
   (2) the EOQ
   (3) 500 units
b. What is the least cost order quantity?
c. What would you suggest to the buyer?

12. All the facts of Exercise 11 remain the same except that the supplier now offers free delivery (they have added many other customers in the area). Calculate the least cost order quantity under these conditions.

13. All the facts of Exercise 11 remain the same except that the supplier now packs 100 items per crate and charges $200 per each partial crate. Calculate the least cost order quantity under these conditions.

14. The following purchase discount opportunity is available to a company. The company uses a carrying cost rate of 0.30.

Item	Annual Requirements	EOQ $ Quantity	Discount Percentage	Discount $ Order Quantity
1	$27,400	$1,500	4.0	$5,000

a. Calculate the savings and the rate of return if ordering costs are not a factor.
b. Calculate the savings and the rate of return if ordering costs are $75 per order.

15. The following purchase discount opportunities are available to a company. The company uses a carrying cost rate of 0.30. (Ordering costs are not a factor.)

Item	Annual Requirements	Order $ Quantity	Discount Percentage	Discount $ Order Quantity
1	$27,400	$1,500	4.0	$ 5,000
2	50,000	3,000	3.0	8,000
3	64,000	4,860	5.0	20,000
4	12,000	1,500	6.0	15,000
5	7,450	550	10.0	3,000
6	1,500	100	5.0	300

a. If the company only takes advantage of discount opportunities with a rate of return greater than 25 percent, determine which it will take.
b. Financial conditions prevent the company from investing more than $3,500 in purchase discounts for this group of items. Which opportunities should it take?

16. Use the data in Exercise 15 and an order cost of $50 to calculate the savings and rate of return on the different discount opportunities.
a. If the company only takes advantage of discount opportunities with a rate of return greater than 25 percent, determine which it will take.
b. Financial conditions prevent the company from investing more than $3,500 in purchase discounts for this group of items. Which opportunities should it take?

17. Describe how a purchasing planner might use input/output planning and control to monitor a supplier's deliveries and control releases of orders to a supplier.

18. An organization is planning to establish a direct computer linkage with many of its suppliers. The suppliers will receive the MRP reports of the items they supply. A purchasing agent states, "I won't have anything to do before long." Comment.

19. See Exercise 8 and describe the advantages to Sterling Products of the "purchasing capacity" arrangement.

20. The Maximillion Company is initiating a JIT program and intends to reduce its supplier base. They have reached consensus on the evaluation of suppliers of a group of valves that they presently purchase from any of four suppliers all of which have essentially the same price structure. Each

supplier has been evaluated as follows on five weighted characteristics. Rank the suppliers based on this evaluation.

Supplier Evaluations					
			Supplier		
Characteristic	Weight	Ajax	QRD	Wirth	Elco
Quality	0.40	9	9	10	7
Delivery	0.30	9	8	8	10
Quantity	0.10	10	8	9	10
Flexibility	0.10	6	7	9	9
Technical Contributions	0.10	5	6	8	9

21. Maximillion has also decided that a supplier must receive a minimum evaluation of 8 in quality and delivery to be acceptable. How does this affect the evaluations? What do you recommend?

22. After evaluating a group of suppliers by the purchasing organization's formal supplier evaluation procedure, a purchasing agent disagrees strongly with the relatively low rating of one of the suppliers. Describe some of the ways that the buyer might justify this objection and some of the errors the agent might be making.

23. A critical task of the purchasing department is the evaluation and selection of suppliers. What areas of a potential supplier's operation should be analysed before the supplier is granted the status of an approved supplier?

24. What is a blanket order? How does it differ from a standing order? What are the advantages of blanket orders and standing orders?

25. How does the computing of cash commitments relate to MRP II?

26. An old-timer in the purchasing department states, "We have been using Just-in-Time for years by our blanket orders." To what extent is the agent probably correct, and in what ways is he likely overlooking some of the important aspects of JIT? (See Chapter 17.)

27. Compare and contrast systems contracts and distributor contracts.

SELECTED READINGS

Benson, Randall J. "Can Purchasing Supply Tomorrow's Factory?" *APICS 24th Annual International Conference Proceedings* (1981): 355-359.

Burlingame, L. James, and R. A. Warren. "Extended Capacity Planning." *APICS 17th Annual International Conference Proceedings* (1974): 83-91.

Carter, Philip L., and Robert M. Monczka. "Steelcase, Inc.: MRP in Purchasing." In *Case Studies in Materials Requirements Planning*, 105-129. Falls Church, VA: American Production and Inventory Control Society, 1978

Emmelhorne, Margaret A. *Guide to Purchasing: Electronic Data Interchange*. Oradell, NJ: National Association of Purchasing Management, 1986.

Fallon, Carlos. *Value Analysis to Improve Productivity*. New York: John Wiley & Sons, Inc., 1971.

Friessnig, Rudy. "In Line—Real Time Procurement." *APICS 24th Annual International Conference Proceedings* (1981): 363-365.

Gray, Allison F. "Educating and Schdeluling the Outside Shop: A Case Study." In *Readings in Production and Inventory Control Interfaces*, 48-50. Falls Church, VA: American Production and Inventory Control Society, 1984.

Monczka, Robert M., and Phillip L. Carter. "Productivity and Performance Measurement in Purchasing." *APICS 19th Annual Conference Proceedings* (1976): 6-9.

Morency, Richard R. "A Systems Approach to Vendor Scheduling under Contract Purchasing." *APICS 20th Annual Conference Proceedings* (1977): 458-467.

Nakane, Jinichiro, and Robert W. Hall. "Transferring Production Control Methods Between Japan and the United States." *APICS 24th Annual International Conference Proceedings* (1981): 192-194.

Peters, Thomas J., and Robert H. Waterman, Jr. *In Search of Excellence*. New York: Harper & Row, Publishers, Inc., 1982.

Schnor, John E., and Thomas F. Wallace. *High Performance Purchasing*. Essex Junction, VT: Oliver Wight Publications, Ltd., 1986.

Schonberger, Richard J., Doug Sutton, and Jerry Claunch. "KANBAN (Just-in-Time) Applications at Kawasaki USA." *APICS 24th Annual International Conference Proceedings* (1981): 181-191.

Volsky, Sanford L. "Purchasing's Inflation Fighter: The Computer." *APICS 24th Annual International Conference Proceedings* (1981): 360-362.

Wallace, Thomas, ed. *APICS Dictionary*. 6th ed. Falls Church, VA: American Production and Inventory Control Society, 1987.

Wight, Oliver W. *Production and Inventory Management in the Computer Age*. Boston, MA: Cahner Books, 1974.

16

PROJECT MANAGEMENT (PERT/CPM)

Certain characteristics distinguish those projects that are most suitable for the application of project management techniques. These characteristics include the following:

1. Projects have a definite beginning and end. The building of a new plant, the hiring and training of an additional labor crew, the design and fabrication of tooling for a new product, and the installation of a new (substantially redesigned) PIM system are examples of projects that possess this characteristic. Whereas installing a new assembly line and producing the first acceptable lot constitutes a project, running that assembly line for the next month or year is more appropriately viewed as an ongoing, repetitive nonproject activity.

2. Project activities are one-at-a-time activities for the most part, isolated by either time or space. The fabrication of a single large pressure vessel might be planned and controlled using project management techniques; planning and controlling the fabrication and assembly of ten such vessels at the same facility within the same time requires increased application of the principles and techniques discussed in the chapters concerning medium- and short-range planning.

3. Projects can be subdivided into activities that have definite beginnings and ends; that is, the nature of the process does not require that activities be initiated immediately on completion of the preceding activity. In the case of certain refining processes, the next step must begin immediately due to the inability of the material to retain a chemical or physical property for any period without incurring substantial additional expense during a holding phase. Thus, the making of steel, the refining of gasoline, and the production of ice cream are not suited for the application of project management techniques. However, the launching of a space shot, the construction of a nuclear submarine, and the teardown, cleaning, and restarting of a bottling line are.

4. The activities that must be performed to complete the project have a definite sequential relationship. There are known technological factors that require certain activities to be completed before others and that allow other activities to be performed simultaneously. Thus, each activity can be defined with respect to every other activity as preceding, succeeding, or independent. Two activities that are independent may be performed in any order with respect to each other.

5. An estimate of the time required to complete each activity is available. These times are based on an assumed rate of the use of material, personnel, and equipment. For example, a time estimate to "fabricate assembly fixture" is based on the use of personnel and equipment with certain capabilities, the availability of the material, and the information required for fabrication.

Two project management techniques—project evaluation and review technique (PERT) and critical path method (CPM)—have received acclaim and acceptance across the entire industrial spectrum. The primary reasons for this broad and enthusiastic reception are:

1. The principles underlying the procedure followed in applying these techniques are clear.
2. The techniques provide an integrated approach to project planning, scheduling, and control that works.
3. Plans and schedules can be developed in the detail warranted by the complexity of the project and by the degree of control desired.
4. The principles and procedures are applicable to projects of all types including such diverse activities as research, engineering design, construction, fabrication of an assembly line, preparation of a dinner, major surgery, the rebuilding of a blast furnace, installation of a new management information system such as material requirements planning (MRP), and the increase of production output by the addition of a second shift.

In manufacturing, project management techniques are especially useful in planning and controlling the production of items that are custom designed around basic models to meet the special requirements of individual customers. The production cycle for such items usually includes design and production engineering activities as well as fabrication processes. This situation is common in the production of large equipment items such as material handling systems, truck bodies for utility companies, and industrial cleaning equipment.

Project management techniques are also helpful in the following PIM activities:

1. Short-range planning—crew changes, equipment start-ups and tear-downs
2. Increasing capacity—reducing planned maintenance time

3. Calculating manufacturing lead time—based on critical path of purchasing, fabrication, and assembly
4. Reducing work in process—reducing critical path of fabrication and assembly

BACKGROUND

PERT was developed jointly by members of the Booz, Allen and Hamilton consulting firm and the Navy's Special Project Office while planning the research, design, fabrication, and testing necessary for the production of the first nuclear submarine. They studied existing project management techniques and found none adequate for such a complex project. Application of PERT to the Polaris submarine project was one of the key factors for it being completed two years prior to the originally scheduled due date.

At about the same time, J. E. Kelley, Jr. of the Univac Division of Remington Rand and Morgan Walker of DuPont, working independently of the Polaris group, developed CPM as a result of a study concerning the planning and control of chemical plant maintenance. There are many similarities between PERT and CPM in their original forms and some essential differences that we will discuss later. Real world applications frequently incorporate features of both techniques in a hybrid fashion as desired by project management.

The forerunner of PERT and CPM was the Gantt chart developed by Henry Gantt around 1910. As illustrated in Figure 16-1 (which is based on activities listed in Table 16-1), the Gantt chart, or bar graph as it is sometimes called, is a graph with time on the horizontal axis and activities on the vertical axis. The following example used to illustrate these techniques has been taken from a real world situation with minor changes for the sake of simplicity. No changes have been made in essential characteristics.

DEVELOPING A NETWORK PLANNING MODEL

The firm whose activities are described in Table 16-1 and Figure 16-1 produces material handling systems. Some are standard assemblies fabricated to catalog specifications, while others are custom designed and fabricated to meet customer requirements. The activities described in Table 16-1 are required to complete the fabrication of a specific custom designed order. Figure 16-1 is a Gantt chart for these activities. We use this situation to illustrate the process of developing a network model.

In general, the starting point of each activity corresponds to the finishing point of the activity that directly precedes it. However, if an activity has more than one preceding activity, care must be taken in preparing a Gantt chart. Perhaps the most critical step, the one in which planning errors occur most frequently, is accurately recording the starting points of activities that have

Figure 16-1
Gantt Chart
Design, Fabrication, and Assembly
Material Handling System

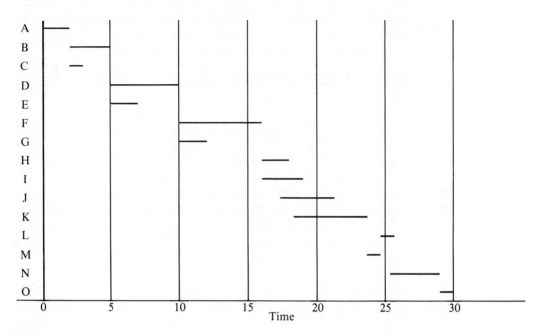

Table 16-1
Planning Data
Material Handling System
Design, Fabrication, and Assembly

Symbol	Activity Description	Activities Preceding	Activities Concurrent	Activities Following	Requirements (weeks)
A	Mechanical Design (1)	None	None	B, C	2
B	Mechanical Design (2)	A	C	E, D	3
C	Electrical Design (1)	A	B, E	D	1
D	Electrical Design (2)	B, C	E	F, G	5
E	Mechanical Fabrication (1)	B	C, D, F, G	H, I	2
F	Mechanical Fabrication (2)	D	E, G	H, I	6
G	Electrical Fabrication (1)	D	E, F, I	H	3
H	Electrical Fabrication (2)	E, F, G	I	J, K	2
I	Mechanical Subassembly (1)	E, F	H, G, J	K	3
J	Mechanical Subassembly (2)	H	K, I	M	4
K	Electrical Installation (1)	H, I	J	M	5
L	Electrical Installation (2)	M	None	N	1
M	Piping Installation (1)	J, K	None	L	1
N	Piping Installation (2)	L	None	O	3
O	Start-up, Test, and Ship	N	None	None	1

more than one preceding activity. For example, Activity H cannot begin until Activities E, F, and G have been completed. The temptation is to chart H immediately on completion of G, rather than waiting for Activity F, the last of the predecessors to be completed.

The Gantt chart is a powerful aid in planning relatively simple projects, although it does not provide the insight of the PERT and CPM network planning models. The Gantt chart does however reveal the normal length of the project: 30 weeks in the case of the example in Figure 16-1.

The advantages of network scheduling models incorporating the concepts and techniques of PERT and CPM over the Gantt chart and other similar techniques are as follows:

1. The sequential relationship between the activities that must be performed to complete the project is explicitly represented.
2. The critical path, i.e., the longest path (connected sequence of activities) from the beginning to the end of the project, is easily determined.
3. The individual activities whose completions on schedule are not critical to completion of the entire project on schedule are easily determined.
4. The impact on project completion of the probability of different activities being completed in less or more time than the most likely time estimate can be determined.

First, we will develop a network with attributes common to both CPM and PERT, then we will describe those characteristics that differentiate these two techniques. As noted earlier, features of both can be combined in real world applications as long as the required data and information-processing capabilities are available. The steps in building a network planning model are to (1) obtain the necessary input data, (2) construct the network model, and (3) determine the critical path.

Data Requirements

The necessary input data include a list of the activities that constitute the project, the time required to complete each activity, and the sequential relationships of the activities. The CPM approach uses deterministic (fixed) activity times. The PERT method, as shown later, uses stochastic (variable) activity times. Table 16-1 illustrates the input data required to construct a network model. As might be expected, the efficacy of the planning and control decisions that result from the use of the network model are directly affected by the accuracy and completeness of the input data. Grossly inaccurate or incomplete data lead to inadequate and unrealistic plans.

It is not unusual to reorganize input data when developing the network. For example, the original data sheet for the material handling system included all mechanical design activities under one activity. Discussions between planning and engineering representatives working together on development of the network revealed that electrical design activities could begin at a point where mechanical design activities were only partially complete. This led to the decision to divide mechanical design into two activities: Mechanical Design (1) and Mechanical Design (2). Developing the network model frequently provides added understanding and improved planning and execution of the project.

Constructing the Network

A network model is formed by connecting the symbols (arrows in this case) representing sequential activities in accordance with the input data. The arrows are connected to numbered nodes (junctions) that represent events, the completion of one activity and the beginning of another. Figure 16-2 includes the various symbols used in activity-on-the-arrow (AOA) networks. The activity-on-the-node (AON) method will be briefly discussed later.

Figure 16-2
Network Modeling Symbols and Conventions

Symbol	Description

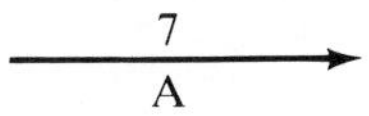

Activity: a job or task. Number on top of the arrow is an estimate of the time required to complete the task. Letter on the bottom is its identification.

Node: event, the beginning or end of an activty.

Dummy activity: used to accurately represent relationships of activities. No task time or resources are required.

Activity A must be completed before Activity B begins.

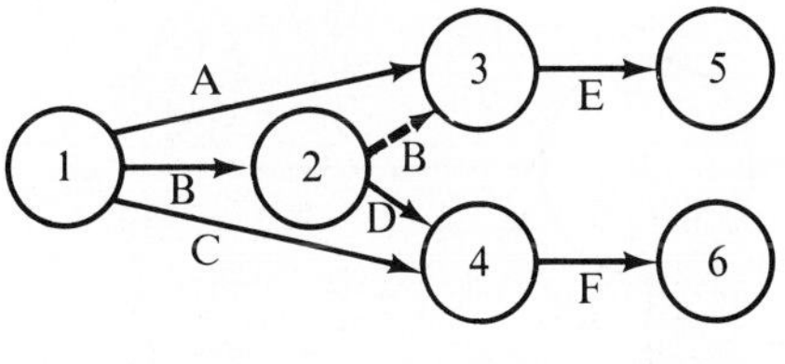

Subject Activity:	Activities that must be completed before subject activity can begin:
A, B, & C....	None
D	B
E..........	A and G, and thus B also.
F..........	C and D, and thus B also.

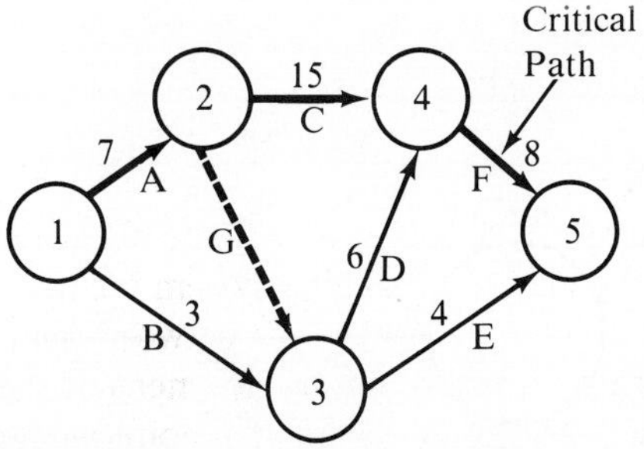

Network: connection of activities and events depicting the sequence they must follow for completion of the project. Nodes are numbered so that the beginning of an activity always has a smaller number than the end. The longest time path through the network is designated by a heavy line or special color. (See Activities A, C, and F in network schematic.)

Constructing the network begins with identification in Table 16-1 of the activity (or activities) that has no predecessors and connecting it to the activities that follow it immediately (as illustrated in Figure 16-3). Activity A has no predecessors, and Activities B and C follow it immediately. The next step is to add the arrows for those activities that immediately follow the followers of the initial activity. Table 16-1 reveals that Activity B immediately precedes Activities D and E and that Activity C is also an immediate predecessor of D. These relationships require the use of an additional symbol, a dummy arrow, as illustrated in Figure 16-4.

Figure 16-3
Initiation of a Network

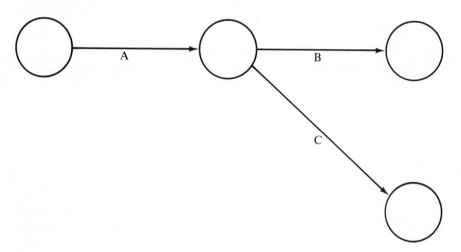

Figure 16-4
Network Development Continued

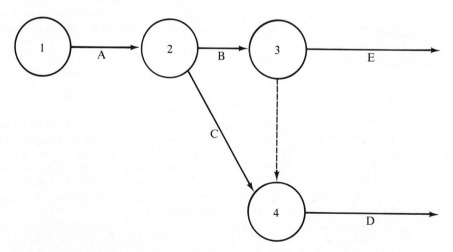

Dummy activities do not represent a task; they do not require any time and they do not use any resources. They are used to represent precedence requirements accurately, and uniquely identify activities. Without the dummy activity, for example, the network in Figure 16-5 might be interpreted to mean that both Activities B and C must be completed before either D or E can begin. This is inaccurate.

Figure 16-5
The Network without a Dummy Activity
(An Inaccurate Representation)

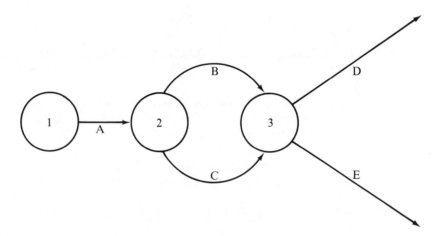

Construction of the network follows in this fashion until all activities are represented. A number is then assigned to each node so that the node at the start (tail) of each activity (arrow) has a smaller number than the node at the finish (head). This rule is important in using computer programs that identify activities by their node numbers (i, j—where i represents the start and j the finish of each arrow), and whose logic is based on i being less than j. For example, A is denoted by (1,2). If one cannot assign the numbers in this manner, there is an inconsistency in the stated precedence relationships and they should be reviewed to determine the error. Note that the dummy activities have also been labeled.

Determining the Critical Path

Complete development of the network per the data contained in Table 16-1 is shown in Figure 16-6. The time estimate for each activity has been added on top of each arrow to facilitate determination of the critical path.

Determination of the critical path involves defining each possible path from the start of the project to its finish, then calculating the length of each path, and, finally, determining the longest path. The longest path is the critical

Figure 16-6
Network Model
Design, Fabrication, and Assembly
Material Handling System

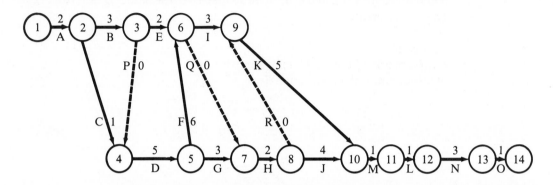

path because the completion of activities on this path determines whether or not the project is completed on schedule. On the other hand, activities not on the critical path may fall behind schedule and completion of the project within the schedule is still possible.

Table 16-2 lists the different paths that can be followed from the start to the finish of the project illustrated by the network model of Figure 16-6. Comparing the lengths of these paths reveals that the critical path consists of Activities A, B, P, D, F, I, K, M, L, N, and O and has a length of 30 weeks.

Table 16-2
Activity Paths in Figure 16-6 and Their Lengths

Number	Description (activities)	Length (weeks)
1	A, B, E, I, K, M, L, N, O	21
2	A, B, E, Q, H, R, K, M, L, N, O	20
3	A, B, E, Q, H, J, M, L, N, O	19
4	A, B, P, D, G, H, J, M, L, N, O	25
5	A, B, P, D, G, H, R, K, M, L, N, O	26
6	A, B, P, D, F, Q, H, J, M, L, N, O	28
7	A, B, P, D, F, Q, H, R, K, M, L, N, O	29
8*	A, B, P, D, F, I, K, M, L, N, O	30
9	A, C, D, G, H, J, M, L, N, O	23
10	A, C, D, G, H, R, K, M, L, N, O	24
11	A, C, D, F, Q, H, J, M, L, N, O	26
12	A, C, D, F, Q, H, R, K, M, L, N, O	27
13	A, C, D, F, I, K, M, L, N, O	28

Critical Path

Two other things also are immediately apparent. First, Activities A, M, L, N, and O are on every path and, thus, must be part of the critical path. If the path lengths were being calculated manually, these activities could be omitted until the longest length of the other segments was determined. They would then be added to determine the critical path length. The second obvious conclusion is that even in relatively simple situations, such as this example, there can be many possible paths. As the complexity of the project increases, the calculations required to determine the critical path increase at an even greater rate. Use of a computer program facilitates determination of the critical path and such attributes as slack (float) time per activity.

Latest and Earliest Start and Finish Times

The earliest and latest start and finish times can be calculated for each activity. The earliest start time (ES) of an activity is the sum of all the activities on the longest path to that activity. It is the earliest time an activity can begin, given that all preceding activities on this path begin as early as possible. Referring to the network in Figure 16-6, the ES for Activity I, (6,9), is 16 weeks from the beginning of the project. This is based on the time to complete Activities A, B, P, D, and F, the longest path to I.

The earliest finish time (EF) of an activity is equal to its earliest start time plus its activity time. For example, the earliest finish time for Activity I is 19 weeks.

The latest finish time (LF) of an activity is equal to the scheduled project completion time minus the time requirements of the longest path from the end of that activity to the completion of the project. For example, the LF for Activity B is 5 (30 − 25) and the LF for Activity C is also 5.

The latest start time (LS) for an activity is the latest time it can be started without delaying completion of the project. The LS of an activity is equal to the scheduled project completion time minus the time requirements of the longest path from the end of that activity to the completion of the project and the activity time. Or, more simply, it is the latest finish time minus the activity time. Referring again to the network in Figure 16-6, the LS of Activity B is 2 (30 − 28), where 30 is the length of the critical path and 28 is the time required to complete Activities B, P, D, F, I, K, M, L, N, and O. The ES, EF, LS, and LF of all activities in Figure 16-6 are listed in Table 16-3.

Slack (Float) Time

The term *slack* describes the amount of delay an activity can experience without affecting project completion. Whenever the desired project completion time is equal to the time requirements of activities on the critical path, as is the case in the example illustrated in Figure 16-6, all activities on the critical path have zero slack.

Table 16-3
Activity, ES, LS, EF, LF, and Slack Times
Design Fabrication and Assembly
Material Handling System

Activity	ES	LS	EF	LF	Total Slack	Free Slack
A	0	0	2	2	0	0
B	2	2	5	5	0	0
C	2	4	3	5	2	2
D	5	5	10	10	0	0
E	5	14	7	16	9	9
F	10	10	16	16	0	0
G	10	14	13	17	4	3
H	16	17	18	19	1	0
I	16	16	19	19	0	0
J	18	20	22	24	2	2
K	19	19	24	24	0	0
L	25	25	26	26	0	0
M	24	24	25	25	0	0
N	26	26	29	29	0	0
0	29	29	30	30	0	0
P	5	5	5	5	0	0
Q	16	17	16	17	1	0
R	18	19	18	19	1	1

There are two types of slack, total slack and free slack. *Total slack* is the amount of time that completion of an activity can slip and the project still be completed on schedule—given all the other activities are completed on schedule. It is equal to LS − ES and to LF − EF. Total slack may include free slack and slack shared with another activity. *Free slack* is defined as the amount of time the completion of an activity can slip and not delay the start of any subsequent activity.

For example, the total slack of Activity G in Figure 16-6 is 4 (17 − 13). Note that one week of Activity G's four weeks of slack is shared with Activity H. If the actual completion of G slips four weeks, H has no slack and must be completed without slippage to reach Node 9 in 19 weeks (the LF of Activity I). If, however, the completion of G slips three weeks or takes place on schedule, then Activity H has one week of slack. Thus, Activity G has four weeks of total slack and three weeks of free slack.

An alternative method of determining the critical path makes use of the concepts of ES and LS. By examining Figure 16-6, the ES for each activity can be computed by moving from left to right through each node, assuming the project starts at time zero. Then the LS for each activity can be computed by moving from right to left, assuming the last event takes place at project completion time. The critical path is then noted as the sequence of activities for which the earliest and latest start times are equal, i.e., those that have zero slack. The following summarizes this:

Critical Path = longest path through the network

Earliest Start (ES) = longest path to an activity

Earliest Finish (EF) = ES + activity time

Latest Finish (LF) = project completion time − time of the longest path to project completion

Latest Start (LS) = LF − activity time

Total Slack = LS − ES, or LF − EF (LS − ES = LF − EF)

Free Slack = ES of any subsequent activity − EF

Critical Path = those activities with ES = LS

Calculation of each activity's free and total slack informs project management of those activities whose completion can be delayed (and how much each can be delayed) without affecting project completion and the amount of delay an activity can experience without affecting the ES of another activity. This information is valuable in scheduling project activities in a limited resource or time environment. In some cases, the time from the start of a project to its desired completion date may be greater than the length of the critical path. All activities have slack in such situations. Each activity on the critical path has total slack equal to the difference between the critical path length and the time from the beginning until the desired completion of the project. For example, if the desired completion of the example project was in Week 32 instead of Week 30 and the job was scheduled to begin in Week 0, then all activities would have an additional two weeks of slack.

An example of a computer printout for this problem is given in Figure 16-7. The printout gives information for both events and activities. The events are sequentially numbered and the earliest occurrence and latest occurrence of the event is shown. The event is labeled as critical if the critical path activities pass through it. The activities are indicated with letters and the precedence relationships are shown by the start and finish nodes. The total slack is computed and, if 0, the activity is identified as critical. Free slack is also indicated.

In summary, a network planning model represents the activities of a project according to sequence and duration. It assists in the identification of the critical path and in the amount of total and free slack. Thus, the project manager can identify key milestones toward the completion of a project and the location and amount of available slack in activities that may be completed late without affecting project completion time.

Figure 16-7
Sample Computer Output

```
Normal Event Times

           Early         Late
  Event    Occurrence    Occurrence

   1          0             0          Critical
   2          2             2          Critical
   3          5             5          Critical
   4          5             5          Critical
   5         10            10          Critical
   6         16            16          Critical
   7         16            17
   8         18            19
   9         19            19          Critical
  10         24            24          Critical
  11         25            25          Critical
  12         26            26          Critical
  13         29            29          Critical
  14         30            30          Critical


Normal Activity Time

              Event                    Total    Free
  Activity    Precedence    Actual     Slack    Slack

   A            1-2           2          0        0
   B            2-3           3          0        0
   C            2-4           1          2        2
   D            4-5           5          0        0
   E            3-6           2          9        9
   F            5-6           6          0        0
   G            5-7           3          4        3
   H            7-8           2          1        0
   I            6-9           3          0        0
   J            8-10          4          2        2
   K            9-10          5          0        0
   L           11-12          1          0        0
   M           10-11          1          0        0
   N           12-13          3          0        0
   O           13-14          1          0        0
   P            3-4           0          0        0
   Q            6-7           0          1        0
   R            8-9           0          1        1
```

PROGRAM EVALUATION AND REVIEW
TECHNIQUE (PERT)

The distinguishing characteristic of PERT is its ability to encompass the inherent uncertainty of estimated activity completion times in certain types of projects. Although one may predict with relative certainty the time requirements of activities performed frequently in the past and with little variation in the time required, the time estimates of activities required to develop new technology or to perform a new and different task are inherently less certain. Thus, it is not surprising that a PERT approach frequently is adopted for research and design projects and that network models without provisions for measuring uncertainty are used in the management of many construction, equipment rebuilding, and assembly projects.

Time Estimates

PERT achieves a probabilistic estimate of project completion by obtaining three estimates for each activity, describing the statistical distribution of possible times for each activity, and determining the standard deviation of each activity time and also of the project completion time. The three PERT time estimates for each activity are:

1. The optimistic time (A)—the time required to complete the task if all goes especially well
2. The pessimistic time (B)—the time required to complete the task if things go wrong
3. The most likely time (M, the mode)—the time required to complete the task in most cases

The A and B times are estimated on the basis that the probability of an actual time falling outside their range is about one in one hundred. The expected activity time and its variance calculation are based on the assumption that the distribution of activity times approaches that of a beta distribution.

Figure 16-8 illustrates the general shapes of two beta distributions. In Curve 1 the distribution is skewed to the right and the B time estimate is a greater distance from the M time than the A time estimate is, and the expected time (t_{e1}) is greater than the M time. Curve 1 reflects the belief that difficulties that delay the project are most likely to occur.

In Curve 2 just the opposite is true. Curve 2 is skewed to the left and the A time estimate is a greater distance from the M time than the B time estimate is,

Figure 16-8
Profiles of Beta Distributions

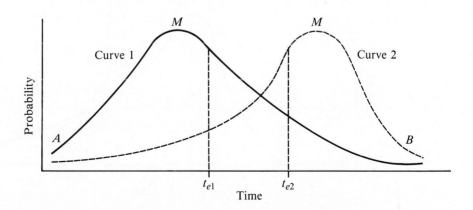

and the expected time (t_{e2}) is less than the M time. Curve 2 reflects a higher probability that few, if any, problems will occur.

The estimates of the expected activity time (t_e) and its variance (σ_t^2) are as follows:

$$t_e = \frac{A + 4M + B}{6}$$

$$\sigma_t^2 = \left(\frac{B - A}{6}\right)^2$$

For example, let the three time estimates for Activity K from the earlier example be the following:

$$A = 4 \qquad M = 5 \qquad B = 8$$

Then,

$$t_e = \frac{4 + 20 + 8}{6} = 5.33$$

$$\sigma_t^2 = \left(\frac{8 - 4}{6}\right)^2 = \frac{4}{9} \text{ or } 0.44 \qquad \sigma_t = \frac{2}{3} \text{ or } 0.67$$

These values indicate a distribution of activity times similar to that illustrated in Figure 16-9. Table 16-4 lists the optimistic, most likely, and pessimistic time estimates for the activities of the material handling system example discussed previously. These time estimates permit the calculation of expected times and variance estimates for each activity (also contained in Table 16-4).

Figure 16-9
Distribution of Times for Activity K

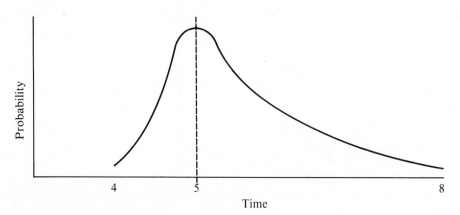

Table 16-4
Three Time Estimates, t_e, and σ_t^2 for Activities
Design, Fabrication, and Assembly
Material Handling System

| Activity | Time Estimates in Weeks | | | | |
	A	M	B	t_e	σ_t^2
A	1.6	2.0	2.4	2.0	0.018
B	2.0	3.0	4.6	3.1	0.188
C	0.9	1.0	2.0	1.15	0.034
D	3.0	5.0	7.0	5.0	0.444
E	0.6	2.0	2.8	1.9	0.134
F	4.6	6.0	7.4	6.0	0.218
G	2.5	3.0	3.5	3.0	0.028
H	2.0	2.0	3.0	2.17	0.028
I	2.0	3.0	5.0	3.17	0.250
J	2.0	4.0	6.0	4.0	0.444
K	4.0	5.0	8.0	5.33	0.444
L	1.0	1.0	1.0	1.0	0.000
M	0.8	1.0	2.0	1.13	0.040
N	2.8	3.0	3.6	3.07	0.018
O	1.0	1.0	3.0	1.33	0.111

The expected length of any path through a network is the sum of the expected lengths of the activities on the path. The longest such path is, of course, the critical path. Although the average time estimates of many activities differ slightly from the deterministic estimates given earlier, in this case the critical path is still that path consisting of Activities A, B, P, D, F, I, K, M, L, N, and O. However, the estimated project (critical path) length is now 31.13 weeks instead of 30 weeks due to the slightly longer average time estimates for Activities B, I, K, M, N, and O. This difference is not uncommon because deterministic estimates of activity times tend to be the M time rather than the expected time, and activity time distributions tend to be skewed to the right. In many cases, the small differences between these two methods of estimating total time and the negligible variances of activity times do not justify the added costs of developing a PERT network. However, in cases with substantial activity time variances or substantial costs associated with late project completion, the development of a PERT network and calculation of the probability of completing the project on schedule justify the added expense.

Project Completion Probability Distribution

Since the time required to complete each activity is a random variable, the expected time to complete the entire project (the sum of critical path expected times) is also a random variable. The variance of the expected time is equal to the sum of the variances of the activities on the critical path. Thus,

$$T_E = \sum_{i=1}^{k} t_{ei} \quad \text{and} \quad \sigma_T^2 = \sum_{i=1}^{k} \sigma_{t_i}^2$$

where T_E = expected time required to complete the project
        σ_T^2 = variance of the distribution of estimated project completion time
        $\sigma_{t_i}^2$ = variance of completion time for Activity i
        t_{ei} = estimated average element time to complete Activity i
        i = activities on the critical path
        k = number of activities on the critical path

In our example, the critical path consists of Activities A, B, P, D, F, I, K, M, L, N, and O. Using the data contained in Table 16-4, T_E and σ_T^2 can be calculated as follows:

$$T_E = 2.0 + 3.1 + 0 + 5.0 + 6.0 + 3.17 + 5.33 + 1.13 + 1.0 + 3.07 + 1.33$$
$$= 31.13$$
$$\sigma_T^2 = 0.018 + 0.188 + 0 + 0.444 + 0.218 + 0.25 + 0.444 + 0.04 + 0$$
$$\quad + 0.018 + 0.111$$
$$= 1.731$$

Since the standard deviation is equal to the square root of the variance, $\sigma_T = \sqrt{1.731} = 1.316$.

Due to what is known in statistics as the central limit theorem, the distribution of a sum of random variables follows a normal, bell-shaped distribution, regardless of the distribution of the components of the sum. This enables us to use the table of areas under the normal curve to calculate the probability of the project being completed within specific time frames.

To begin with, we know that there is a 50 percent probability that the project will be completed within 31.13 weeks, the expected time, and a 50 percent chance that it will take longer. But what is the probability that it can be completed in 30.0 weeks or in 35.0 weeks? To answer this type question, we must calculate the number of standard deviations a desired completion time is from the average completion time. The following formula is used:

$$z = \frac{T_D - T_E}{\sigma}$$

where T_D = desired completion time
        z = number of standard deviations separating T_D and T_E

Thus,

$$z = \frac{30 - 31.13}{1.316} = -0.86$$

Appendix A shows that the area of the curve from the mean to 0.86 standard deviations is equal to 0.3051. Figure 16-10 illustrates the relationship of T_{D30}, T_{D35}, and T_E, in addition to the probability of their occurrence. In the case of T_{D30}, T_D is less than the average. Thus, the probability represented by the area between T_E and T_D is subtracted from 0.50 to determine the probability, $P(T_D)$, of completing the project on or before T_D. Thus,

$$P(T_D \geq 30) = 0.50 - 0.3051 = 0.1949$$

Figure 16-10
Relationship Between Completion Times,
Standard Deviations, and Probabilities

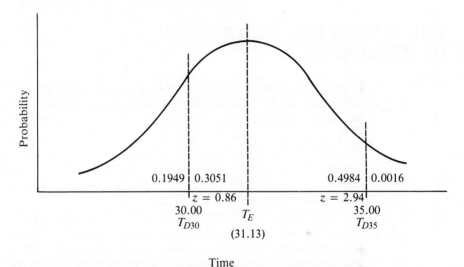

When T_D equals 35.0 weeks, we get the following value for z:

$$z = \frac{35 - 31.13}{1.316} = 2.94$$

Referring again to Appendix A, we find that the area of the curve between the mean and 2.94 standard deviations is 0.4984. Because T_{D35} is greater than T_E, the probability represented by the area between T_E and T_D is added to 0.5 to determine the probability, $P(T_D)$, of completing the project on or before T_D. Thus,

$$P(T_D \leq 35) = 0.50 + 0.4984 = 0.9984$$

Our calculations indicate that there is a 99.84 percent probability that the project will be completed within 35 weeks. This is slightly misleading because it assumes a 100 percent probability of completing the activities on all other paths within 35 weeks. Calculating the exact probability of completing a project within a time period greater than T_E is not straightforward. Subtracting the sum of the probabilities of the different paths requiring a time greater than T_D from 1, i.e., $1.0 - \Sigma P(T_{Ei} > T_D)$, will give a conservative probability estimate due to the interdependence of the paths. One clear indication that a second path may take the place of the critical path is if a near critical path has a high variance. Simulation (see Chapter 23) may also be used to estimate the probability of T_D when $T_D > T_E$.

In summary, our time estimates and calculations indicate that it is almost certain that the project will be completed within 35 weeks and that there is slightly more than a 19 percent (19.49) probability that the project will be completed within 30 weeks.

THE SCHEDULED ALLOCATION OF RESOURCES

Completion of the critical path network is a necessary planning step prior to scheduling. Decisions concerning which resources, workers, and machines will be assigned to tasks during a given period also are influenced by other factors, such as the total resources available, other projects competing for the same resources, penalties for late completion, bonuses for early completion, and the relationship of the time available to the time required for completion of the project. The final schedule must be developed in concert with capacity requirements planning as discussed in Chapter 13.

Up to this point, discussions of activity times were predicated on resources being allocated to activities at a normal rate (usually defined as the most efficient rate). However, in most cases management has the options of applying additional resources to decrease the duration of an activity (that is, *crashing* the activity) or of reducing the resources to a below normal rate to increase the duration of the activity. For example, a contractor responsible for the construction of a building may have determined a 58-week estimated completion time for the building. Two incentives normally would encourage the contractor to finish the project ahead of schedule. First, the contractor must pay fixed overhead costs, such as equipment rental, for each week on the job site. Second, the contract may specify a bonus for each week that the project is completed ahead of schedule. Thus, the contractor is encouraged to bear extra costs for critical path activities to reduce the total time on the project. Note that incurring these costs makes sense only for critical path activities or, in some cases, activities on a path whose length approaches that of the critical path. Typically, overtime, expedited shipment or production, and more costly subcontracting would be techniques that the project manager could use to crash the project, but the cost would be greater than normal.

Recognition of the relationship of activity time durations to the allocation of resources was discussed first in literature concerning deterministic

CPM models. However, the possibility of allocating resources to alter activity duration also exists in projects managed with the assistance of a PERT model; the distribution of possible activity times merely shifts. (In fact, other parameters in addition to the mean may change; but we will consider only changes in T_E).

Likely scheduling objectives include reduction of the project duration, cost minimization, and smoothing resource requirements over time. The typical real world project schedule usually requires that some balance be achieved between specific objectives in each of these areas. First, we will examine a case where resources are unlimited and the project duration must be shortened to a specific length with minimum additional costs.

Figure 16-11 illustrates the most typical relationship of activity times and resources allocation. This is the case in which an activity can be completed in normal time (t_n), at normal cost (C_n), or with the expenditure of additional resources in crash time (t_c), at a crash cost (C_c). It also may be completed in all times between t_c and t_n at the corresponding costs between C_c and C_n. Whether a single approximation of the slope is satisfactory or not depends on the degree of curvature.

Figure 16-11
Total Cost Versus Activity Duration
(A Typical Relationship)

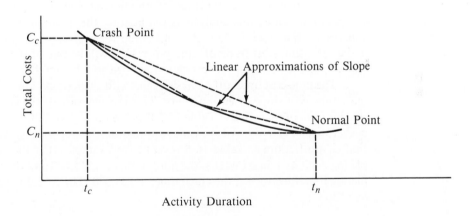

Extending the time may increase the total costs due to drawn-out inefficiencies or the costs may remain essentially the same. For example, if the normal procedure is to have four workers on an assembly, reducing the number to three will increase total costs only if some of the assembly operations are performed more efficiently by four persons working as a team. Increased costs associated with shortened activity times are the result of such things as overtime, additional setup and learning costs when the job is split among more workers, and the use of less skilled workers or less efficient machines.

Cost Minimization

Project completion costs usually are a minimum when resources are expended at the normal, most efficient rate. If, however, the aggregate organizational demand for resources is unusually low at a particular time, surplus resources requiring no additional out-of-pocket expense may be applied to a project even when shortening its length is not a priority. In such a case the recorded costs of a particular project may increase due to inefficiencies, but total corporate expenditures will not increase and resources will be freed in a later period for which additional demand may materialize. For example, labor may be committed to maintenance ahead of schedule because it is more readily available during the off-season than during peak production.

Shortening Project Length

There are many occasions when it is desirable to complete a project in less than normal time. Bonuses for early completion, penalties for late completion, weather problems anticipated beyond a certain date, a combination of relatively light aggregate demand in proximate periods and heavy demand in later periods, and accelerated revenue generation are some of the possible justifications for attempting to complete a project early.

Resources must be available when required if a modified project schedule is to be implemented successfully. As illustrated shortly, analysis of project time-cost trade-offs will provide the information indicating when these resources are required. Thus, this analysis is initiated on the assumption that such resources are available. If there is competition for such resources, as frequently is the case, time-cost trade-off analysis results will be one of the inputs to the capacity allocation decision process described in Chapter 13.

The time-cost trade-off analysis begins with a determination of the approximate time-cost slope of each activity. This is a measure of the cost to shorten the duration of an activity. Table 16-5 lists the normal and the crash times and costs for each activity. All the times approximate actual values, while the cost figures are fictitious. Table 16-5 reveals, for example, that the cost of completing Activity F in six weeks, the normal time, is $15,600 and the cost of completing it in three weeks, the crash time, is $20,000. The cost slope is calculated as follows:

$$\text{Cost Slope} = \frac{C_c - C_n}{t_n - t_c}$$

Thus, the cost slope for Activity F equals $\frac{\$20,000 - \$15,600}{6 - 3} = \$1,467$ per week.

The following example illustrates how management can use cost slope and related information in resource allocation decisions required during project planning. If management desires to complete the design, fabrication, and assembly of the material handling system in 27 weeks rather than the normal 30 weeks, additional resources must be allocated to selected activities on the critical path. (Reduction of the duration of activities not on the critical path will not reduce the time required to complete the project.) In some cases it may be necessary to reallocate resources within the project, and in other cases it may be possible and desirable to obtain additional resources (external to the project).

If internal reallocation is required, additional resources should be sought from those activities where slack is greatest and applied to an activity or activities where they will have the greatest impact. For example, Activity E, Mechanical Fabrication (1), has nine weeks of slack. If some of the personnel and machines normally assigned to Activity E can be reallocated to Activity F, Mechanical Fabrication (2), the length of the critical path can be reduced.

Table 16-5
Normal and Crash Times and Costs for Activities
Design, Fabrication, and Assembly
Material Handling System

Activities*	Events	t_n**	t_c***	C_n	C_c	Cost Slope ($ per week)
A	1-2	2.0	1.5	$ 4,800	$ 5,600	$1,600
B	2-3	3.1	2.6	7,680	8,500	1,640
C	2-4	1.15	0.80	3,100	3,600	1,429
D	4-5	5.0	3.0	13,500	18,000	2,250
E	3-6	1.9	0.9	4,940	6,000	1,060
F	5-6	6.0	3.0	15,600	20,000	1,467
G	5-7	3.0	2.0	4,200	5,000	800
H	7-8	2.17	1.2	3,025	4,000	1,005
I	6-9	3.17	1.17	4,100	4,400	150
J	8-10	4.0	2.5	5,200	5,600	267
K	9-10	5.33	3.0	3,730	4,500	330
L	11-12	1.0	0.6	700	1,100	1,000
M	10-11	1.13	0.8	790	1,000	636
N	12-13	3.07	2.0	2,015	2,400	360
O	13-14	1.33	1.0	2,100	2,700	1,818

*Critical path activities = A, B, D, F, I, K, L, M, N, and O.
**Normal time values are the same as the average time values in Table 16-4.
***Crash times are also averages from a distribution similar to that of t_e.

Guidelines for applying additional resources to the reduction of the critical path include the following:

1. Additional resources should be applied to critical path activities and also to those noncritical paths whose lengths approach that of the critical path. Resources, where transferable, should be taken from activities

that have the greatest amount of total slack. This approach will reduce the likelihood of creating a new critical path.

2. Additional resources should first be applied to activities with the smallest cost slope. This will minimize the costs of reducing the project length.

3. Additional resources should be applied to activities required relatively early in completion of the project. Once opportunities to reduce the project length are foregone, they cannot be regained. Should unplanned difficulties arise in early activities, later opportunities still will be available to compensate for unplanned delays.

Of the activities on the critical path, Activity I has the smallest cost slope, $150 per week. The project duration can be reduced 2 weeks ($3.17 - 1.17$) merely by investing an additional $300. Yet a total savings of 3 weeks is required to reduce the project to 27 weeks. Since a 2-week reduction is achieved by applying additional resources to Activity I, another week reduction must be found. Candidate activities on the critical path, in ranking order of their cost slopes, are:

Rank	Activity	Cost Slope	Possible Reduction (weeks)
1	K	$ 330	2.33
2	N	360	1.07
3	M	636	0.33
4	L	1,000	0.4
5	F	1,467	3.0
6	A	1,600	0.5
7	B	1,640	0.5
8	O	1,818	0.33
9	D	2,250	2.0

Selecting Activity K for the planned application of an additional $330 will reduce the duration of Activity K by 1 week, but unless H or J (which go on in parallel) are reduced, no reduction can be achieved.

Considering that it costs $1,005 to shorten Activity H by 1 week, but that Activity H can only be shortened by 0.97 weeks, it technically should not be considered further. Activity J can be shortened by 1 week for $267. Thus, the total cost to shorten Activities K and J simultaneously is $330 + $267 = $597.

A less costly alternative could be found. Activity N costs $360 per week to crash, and can be crashed for the required 1 week. However, it is much later in the project completion sequence. Thus, the scheduler has the option of crashing Activities K and J, an earlier and less risky, but more costly option, or Activity N, a less costly, but possibly more risky alternative.

It is not uncommon for planned shortening of project length to increase the number or activities that are critical. It is also true that many possible options must be examined before selection of the one that best meets management's criteria is found. It is difficult to keep track of all the interactions in evaluating alternatives. However, this resource allocation problem can be formulated and solved as a linear programming problem as discussed in Chapter 22.

Other Cost Slopes

Not all activities possess one of the cost slopes illustrated in Figure 16-12. Many, however, do. Discontinuous cost slopes, for example, can exist in the case of purchased equipment that may be delivered in, say, two weeks if shipped by truck or rail and in a day or two if shipped by air. Nothing in between is possible for practical purposes. Some activities inherently develop very slowly (gestational) and applying additional resources does not affect the time required to complete the activity. Physical growth, aging, fermentation, and some chemical processes cannot be shortened. Knowledge inputs, such as those required by research and design activities, also fall into this category on some occasions, as may product testing and evaluation. Decreasing the time requirements of such activities beyond a certain point may require an additional capital investment—as illustrated by a step increase in cost—to obtain the required additional personnel or machine capacity. Other cost slopes are also possible. The point is that the costs related to the possible durations of each activity must be analyzed to determine which cost slope adequately represents the cost-time relationship of each activity.

Figure 16-12
Other Cost Slopes

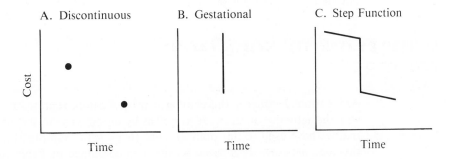

PROJECT CONTROL

The greatest benefit of network planning models is the improved insight they provide concerning project completion status. For example, activities behind schedule, but with sufficient slack to still complete the project on schedule, do not require corrective action. However, a behind schedule activity on the critical path with negative slack would demand corrective action.

Successful project completion requires timely monitoring of work completion and comparison to scheduled completion. Control of projects is based on the same principles that control ongoing, nonproject type activities. Although these principles are covered in other chapters, it is worth repeating some of them here.

1. Plans should be realistic and not reflect an overstated estimate of capacity.
2. Control of the planning activity itself requires:
   a. Management commitment to the objectives of the plan and the availability of the resources
   b. Agreement (preferably in writing) by the appropriate managers and supervisors that the precedence relationships, time estimates, and costs are realistic.
3. A performance reporting system with adequate, accurate, and timely information should exist. Most project completion situations are dynamic. Changing conditions and actual performance initiation and completion may change priorities.
4. Procedures should exist for evaluating performance on a regular basis, for determining what, if any, corrective action is required, and for revising schedules and operating plans accordingly.

Daily, or at least weekly, reports of performance to date are necessary to implement control. These reports should list revised, early, and late start and finish dates, activity slack, expected project completion, and activities to be initiated in the current period.

ACTIVITY-ON-THE-NODE (AON) NETWORKS

As mentioned earlier in this chapter, a project can be represented by a network with the activities on the node as well as by the activity-on-the-arrow approach that we have used to this point. Figure 16-13 is an example of an activity-on-the-node network. It is based on the data contained in Table 16-1 and is the counterpart of the activity-on-the-arrow network in Figure 16-6.

Examination of Figure 16-13 reveals the advantages of the activity-on-the-node approach. Dummy activities are not required; manual network construction and modification are simpler. At one time there was a scarcity of available computer software packages for activity-on-the-node applications, but that is no longer the case. Either deterministic or probabilistic (PERT type) models can be used with either activity-on-the-arrow or activity-on-the-node representations. Selection between these two approaches depends primarily on local conditions and preferences.

Figure 16-13
Activity-on-the-Node Network Model
Design, Fabrication, and Assembly
Material Handling System

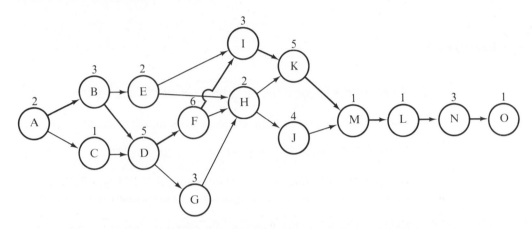

Network models have been widely accepted as valuable aids in planning and controlling project type activities. They are especially useful in defining the relative priorities of the tasks that constitute the project, estimating the probability of completing the project within specified time periods, scheduling resources for specific tasks, and determining if task completion times require either a revision of the schedule or a reallocation of resources.

CONCLUSIONS

PERT and CPM are widely used methods to assist in the management of projects. Because they show the critical path and the impact of slack, they are an improvement over previously used Gantt charts. The methodology permits numerous variations, including deterministic or statistical data input, activity-on-the-arrow or activity-on-the-node models, and crashing to achieve various objectives. Although available computer programs readily solve the algorithm, there is a great deal of judgmental interaction required of the program manager.

Accurate estimation of activity times and full understanding of the activity interaction are essential. Computations to several decimal places are highly dependent on the accurate estimation of activity durations (in the case of CPM) or of optimistic, most-likely, and pessimistic times (in the case of PERT). Yet, the very nature of the project, as a unique and one-time series of activities, makes estimation difficult and unreliable. For this reason, the most important contribution of the PERT/CPM process is probably to make the management decision issues visible to the project manager. The identification of the critical and near critical paths, the computation of slack associated with each activity, the evaluation of crashing opportunities and crashing cost slopes all focus the activity planning issues for the project manager. Subsequently, scheduling and the allocation or reallocation of resources is much easier.

EXERCISES

1. What are the major differences between PERT and CPM?

2. Explain the difference between total slack and free slack.

3. What are dummy activities, and why are they used?

4. Describe the advantages of a network model (CPM and PERT) over a Gantt chart. Under what conditions is a Gantt chart appropriate?

5. Explain why a planner would apply added resources to shorten an activity early on the critical path rather than applying added resources to a later activity on the critical path, even though the later activity could be shortened by the desired amount for less cost.

6. The precedence relationships and estimated times for the activities required to complete a project are given below.
   a. Construct an activity-on-the-arrow (AOA) network for this project.
   b. Determine the critical path and its length.
   (Hint: Requires a dummy activity.)

Activity	Preceeding Activities	Estimated Time (weeks)
A	—	3
B	—	5
C	A	4
D	B, C	10
E	A, G	7
F	D, E	14
G	—	6

7. Construct an activity-on-the-node (AON) network for the project described in Exercise 6.

8. The additional data given below is received for the project described in Exercise 6.
   a. Calculate the critical path and its length on the basis of these data.
   b. Calculate the probability of completing the project in 33 weeks.
   c. Calculate the probabilty of completing the project in 30 weeks.

	Time Estimates		
Activity	A	M	B
A	1	3	5
B	4	5	7
C	2	4	5
D	8	10	12
E	7	8	9
F	14	14	14
G	1	6	7

9. Solve (determine the critical path and its length) the following CPM problem for both normal and full crash conditions.

	Events		Normal		Crash	
Activity	Preceding	Following	Time	Cost	Time	Cost
A	1	2	4	140	2	230
B	2	3	5	210	3	370
C	1	4	2	130	2	130
D	4	5	7	250	6	375
E	3	6	7	230	4	400
F	5	6	3	150	2	195

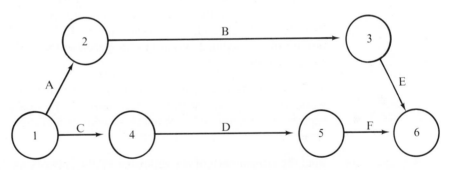

10. What is wrong with the following network?

Activity	Preceding Activities	Following Activities
A	—	A
B	—	E
C	F, I	—
D	J, H	I, E
E	B, C	H
F	G	C
G	A	F, J
H	E	D
I	D	C
J	G	D

11. Find the ES, LS, EF, LF, slack, and critical path for the following network.

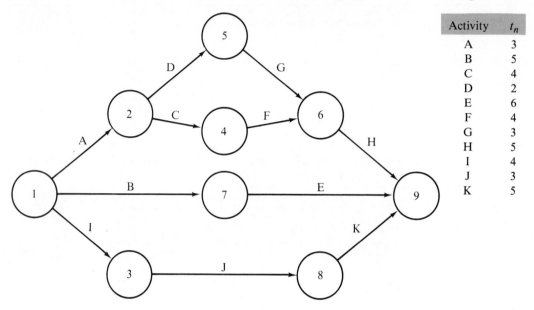

Activity	t_n
A	3
B	5
C	4
D	2
E	6
F	4
G	3
H	5
I	4
J	3
K	5

12. In Exercise 11, after one week (five days) a progress report is made: Activities A, C, D, and I are finished, B is 60 percent completed, work on Activity J will start on Day 6, as will work on F. The rest have not started nor are they scheduled. What has happened to the critical path and the slack for each activity?

13. The following time estimates are available for an activity in a PERT network: $A = 4$ weeks, $M = 8$ weeks, and $B = 11$ weeks. Calculate the expected time required to complete the activity and the variance and the standard deviation of the completion time.

14. Find the critical path of the following PERT network and determine the probability that the project will be completed in 28 days.

Activity	Time Estimates A	B	M
A	3	7	5
B	2	5	3
C	5	10	7
D	5	10	8
E	3	6	4
F	3	8	5
G	2	3	2
H	4	9	6
I	3	6	4
J	2	5	3
K	5	9	7

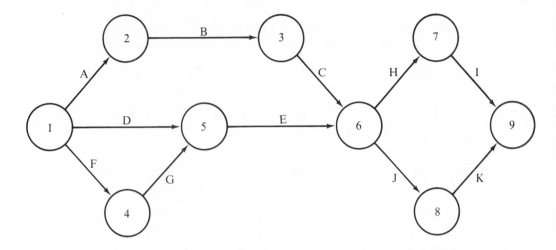

15. Find the critical path for both normal and full crash conditions. Assuming normal time operations cost $40 per day, what are the costs of each solution?

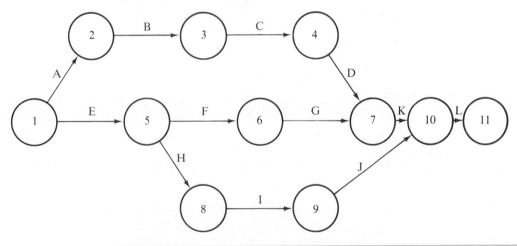

Activity	Preceding Activities	t_n	t_c	C_c per day
A	—	4	3	$ 60
B	A	6	4	100
C	B	5	4	50
D	C	3	3	—
E	—	7	4	85
F	E	6	3	55
G	F	6	4	65
H	E	7	6	120
I	H	3	3	00
J	I	4	3	80
K	D, G	5	4	90
L	K, J	3	2	45

16. Find the critical path and cost for both normal and full crash situations for the following network. Assume normal cost of $40 per day.

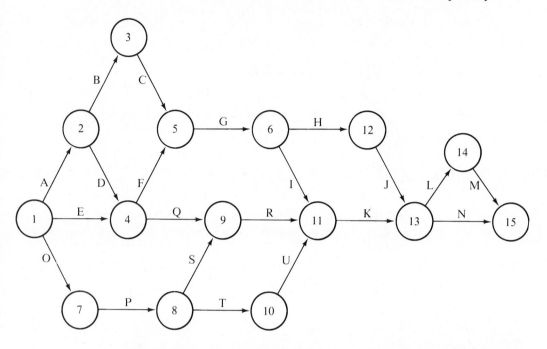

Activity	Preceding Activities	t_n	t_c	C_c per day
A	—	3	2	$ 65
B	A	5	3	105
C	B	4	3	120
D	C	7	5	65
E	—	11	7	90
F	D, E	4	3	45
G	C, F	3	3	—
H	G	6	5	40
I	G	5	2	65
J	H	5	3	105
K	I, R, U	7	4	45
L	J, K	3	3	—
M	L	2	1	110
N	J, K	3	2	60
O	—	9	7	75
P	O	2	2	—
Q	D, E	4	3	65
R	Q, S	6	5	95
S	P	3	2	55
T	P	5	3	80
U	T	3	1	60

17. Construct a precedence diagram (activity on the node) for the following relationships.

Activity	Preceding Activities	Succeeding Activities
A	None	C
B	None	C, D
C	A, B	E
D	B	E, F
E	C, D	C
F	D	H
G	E	None
H	F	None

18. After doing the initial planning in Exercise 9, we find that an additional activity, G, must be done before E or F can proceed and must follow A and C. G's normal time is 6 at a cost of $220, and it can be crashed to 5 at an additional cost of $100. Draw the revised network diagram and solve for the new critical path for both normal and crash conditions.

SELECTED READINGS

Burgess, A. R., and James B. Killebrew. "Variation in Activity Level on a Cyclical Arrow Diagram." *Journal of Industrial Engineering* 13, no. 2 (March-April 1962): 76-83.

Clingen, C. T. "A Modification of Fulkerson's PERT Algorithm." *Operations Research* 12, no. 4 (July-August 1964): 629-631.

Elmaghraby, Salah E. "On Generalized Activity Networks." *Journal of Industrial Engineering* 17, no. 11 (November 1966): 621-631.

Elmaghraby, Salah E. "On the Expected Duration of PERT Type Networks." *Management Science* 13, no. 5 (January 1967): 299-306.

Elmaghraby, Salah E. "The Theory of Networks and Management Science, II." *Management Science* 17, no. 2 (October 1970): 54-71.

Fulkerson, D. R. "Expected Critical Path Lengths in PERT Networks." *Operations Research* 10, no. 6 (November-December 1962): 808-817.

Kelley, James E. "Critical Path Planning and Scheduling, Mathematical Basis." *Operations Research* 9, no. 2 (May-June 1961): 296-320.

Klingel, A. R., Jr. "Bias in PERT Project Completion Time Calculations for a Real Network." *Management Science* 13, no. 4 (1966): 194-201.

Levin, Richard I., and Charles A. Kirkpatrick. *Planning and Control with PERT/CPM.* New York: McGraw-Hill Book Co., 1966.

Levine, Harvey A. *Project Management Using Microcomputers.* Berkeley, CA: Osbourne/McGraw-Hill, 1986.

Levy, Ferdinand K., Gerald L. Thompson, and Jerome D. Wiest. "The ABC's of the Critical Path Method." *Harvard Business Review* (September-October 1963): 98-108.

Malcolm, D. G., J. H. Roseboom, C. E. Clark, and W. Fazar. "Application of a Technique for Research and Development Program Evaluation." *Operations Research* 7, no. 5 (September-October 1959).

MacCrimmon, Kenneth R., and Charles A. Ryavec. "An Analytical Study of the PERT Assumptions." *Operations Research* (January-February 1964): 16-37.

Moder, Joseph J., and Cecil R. Phillips. *Project Management with CPM and PERT*. 2d ed. New York: Litton Educational Publishing, Inc., Van Nostrand Reinhold Co., Inc., 1970.

Posner, Barry Z. "What It Takes to Be a Good Project Manager." *Project Management Journal* 18, no. 1 (March 1987): 51-54.

Shaffer, L. R., J. B. Ritter, and W. L. Meyer. *The Critical Path Method*. New York: McGraw-Hill Book Co., 1965.

Van Slyke, Richard M. "Monte Carlo Methods and the PERT Problem." *Operations Research* 11, no. 5 (September-October 1963): 839-860.

Wiest, Jerome D. "Heuristic Programs for Decision Making." *Harvard Business Review* (September-October 1966): 129-143.

Wiest, Jerome D., and Ferdinand K. Levy. *A Management Guide to PERT/CPM*. 2d ed. Englewood Cliffs, NJ: Prentice-Hall, Inc., 1977.

Part
Six

The Just-in-Time
Approach

17

THE JUST-IN-TIME (JIT) APPROACH

To prosper—and often even to survive—manufacturing companies must provide value at least equal to that of competitors. Today, manufacturing competition includes plants located in many different parts of the world. For example, some refrigerators sold at major department stores in Canada are assembled in Wroclaw, Poland, using a condenser manufactured in Sao Paulo, Brazil. Much of the world is one big market, with goods crossing many different types of boundaries.

Although international trade always has existed, it has exploded in the last few decades. Improved communication and transportation have been contributing factors, but the primary cause has been dramatically improved manufacturing productivity—with emphasis on both quality and cost. Although Japan has been in the forefront of this advance, South Korea, Taiwan, Malaysia, Singapore, and Thailand have made remarkable strides. Progress is also taking place in Mexico and Brazil, and most Western European countries have continued to improve their industrial capability. In addition, it is not unreasonable to expect that Eastern European countries will improve their competitive position as they revise their economic policies.

These developments and a benign neglect of manufacturing by top management in many North American firms caused foreign trade balance deficits and a lower productivity growth in the United States during the 1960s and 1970s than in many other countries. Some U.S. companies lost market share and others lost markets. The MIT commission on industrial productivity reported a large and increasing balance of trade deficit in automobiles, consumer electronics, machine tools, semiconductors, and textiles (Dertouzos et al. 1989). Continuation of such a pattern can have dire consequences for the quality of life in any country. Foreign debt, currency devaluation, and loss of markets and profits eventually not only affect the ability of consumers to purchase material goods such as toasters and automobiles but also limit a nation's ability to support health care, the arts, education, and recreation activites. In brief, the standard of living can decrease dramatically. For example, Argentina was a relatively prosperous country at the turn of the century, but today its economy is in shambles. Nearly all citizens suffer when such a change occurs.

The MIT commission observed:

> A large continental economy like the United States will not be able to function primarily as a producer of services in the foreseeable future. One reason is that it would have to rely on exports of services to pay for its imports, and this does not seem realistic. In 1987 gross U.S. exports of services, excluding income from overseas investments and overseas sales of government services, were worth $57 billion, whereas the total value of goods and services imported into the United States was about $55 billion. . . . The United States thus has no choice but to continue competing in the world market for manufactures. The ultimate scale of American manufacturing is not known, but it will not be trivial. The important question is not whether the United States will have a manufacturing industry but whether it will compete as a low-wage manufacturer or as a high-productivity manufacturer. (Dertouzos et al. 1989, 39-40)

Clearly it is preferable to compete as a high-productivity manufacturer.

These considerations led many organizations in the United States, Canada, and other countries to examine successful manufacturing organizations in North America and throughout the world to identify the operating characteristics and practices of companies capable of competing in the present worldwide market. The essential characteristics of a such a company are that it produces high quality products at low cost and that it responds quickly to customer requests for delivery, changes in design, and changes in volume. When a company has achieved these goals, it can compete with anybody, anywhere. It is important to understand that both high quality and low cost are relative terms; continuous improvement is needed to maintain high relative quality and low relative cost. Referring to the degree of change needed to achieve world class status in *Thriving on Chaos* (1987), Tom Peters notes:

> Radical changes in organizational structure and procedures are called for. Layers of management must be reduced in most big firms by 75 percent. Product development time and order lead time must be slashed by 90 percent. Electronic/telecomunication linkups to customers and suppliers must be developed posthaste. Just listening to customers and dealers needs to become the norm—and as yet it is not.

Different terms are used to identify the process of improving manufacturing productivity with emphasis on high quality and low cost: the Just-in-Time (JIT) approach, zero inventory, total quality management, world class manufacturing, and the search for excellence. We are using JIT because it seems to have been the first, and all of the essential concepts are inherent to it. The title of the process is not important; adopting the philosophy and pursuing its operating objectives are. This chapter includes concepts, approaches, and practices that may have originated under the aegis of programs with each of the different labels and titles given to various productivity improvement programs.

THE PHILOSOPHY OF JIT

JIT is a philosophy embodying various concepts that result in a different way of doing business for most organizations. The basic tenets of this philosophy include:

A. All waste, anything that does not add value to the product or service, should be eliminated. Value is anything that increases the usefulness of the product or service to the customer or reduces the cost to the customer.
B. JIT is a never ending journey, but with rewarding steps and milestones.
C. Inventory is a waste. It covers up problems that should be solved rather than concealed. Waste can gradually be eliminated by removing small amounts of inventory from the system, correcting the problems that ensue, and then removing more inventory.
D. The customers' definitions of quality, their criteria for evaluating the product, should drive product design and the manufacturing system. This implies a trend toward increasingly customized products.
E. Manufacturing flexiblity, including quick response to delivery requests, design changes, and quantity changes, is essential to maintain high quality and low cost with an increasingly differentiated product line.
F. Mutual respect and support based on openness and trust should exist among an organization, its employees, its suppliers, and its customers.
G. A team effort is required to achieve world class manufacturing capability. Management, staff, and labor must participate. This implies increasing the flexibility, responsibility, and authority provided to the hourly worker.
H. The employee who performs a task often is the best source of suggested improvements in the operation. It is important to employ the workers' brains, not merely their hands.

JIT is a very eclectic approach. It includes many old ideas and some new ones and relies on basic concepts from many disciplines, including statistics, industrial engineering, production management, and the behavioral sciences. But first and foremost, it is pragmatic and, thus, empirical. Discovering "what works" and why it works requires that plant operations be studied thoroughly. This requires the collection and analysis of relevant data concerning the plant's operation and its performance. This pragmatism causes the manufacturing process and its environment to be viewed as a research laboratory, similar to a university hospital, in that the primary task may be to produce quality output but another important goal is to learn how to do it better the next time.

Traditionally, inventory has been viewed as an asset, one that can be converted to cash. The Just-in-Time view is that inventory does not add value but instead incurs costs, and thus is a waste. Holding inventory is analogous to not receiving any interest for a deposit in a bank and, furthermore, paying to keep it there. Traditionally, holding inventory was seen as being less costly than correcting the production and distribution inefficiencies that inventory overcame. For example, large lot sizes spread the cost of expensive setups across many parts. JIT takes a different view.

JIT views inventory as a symptom of inadequate management, a method of hiding inefficiencies and problems, as shown in Figure 17-1. Inefficiencies that cause inventory include: long and costly setups, scrap, lengthy and widely varying manufacturing lead times, long queues at work centers, inadequate capacity, machine failure, lack of worker and equipment flexibility, variations in employee output rate, long supplier lead times, and erratic supplier quality. JIT emphasizes that solving each of these problems will reduce the need for inventory and improve productivity. It strives to have the right material, at the right time, at the right place, and in the exact amount. Thus, the name "Just-in-Time" is used by many to designate an organized and continuing program to improve operations productivity.

Figure 17-1
Obstacles to Material Flow

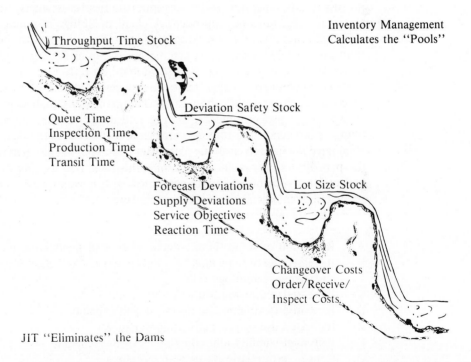

JIT "Eliminates" the Dams

In *Kaizen* (1986), Masaaki Imai argues that the most important aspect of JIT is a philosophy of continuous improvement. He explains that although Westerners and Japanese both ascribe to improvement, he has discovered that the two cultures have different concepts of what this term means. Westerners think of improvement as a step function—a change represents a marked increase in performance. That level of performance is held until the next performance leap is introduced. The Japanese view continuous improvement as an upward sloping line—driven by numerous incremental improvements. Each improvement is in itself imperceptible, but collectively the changes made in a few months will represent a great deal of progress.

This difference in culture can be seen in the management of suggestions. Western companies offer large rewards for suggestions that substantially reduce company costs. In a typical year a few hundred suggestions may be received, a small percentage of which actually are implemented. Toyota, by contrast, offers a small, fixed fee—less than $1—per suggestion. They receive hundreds of thousands of suggestions each year and implement more than 90 percent of them. Imai contends that the total improvement achieved by emphasizing incremental improvement is greater than that achieved by emphasizing dramatic improvement. Certainly the performance of Toyota in recent years represents a strong case for Imai's point of view.

The Japanese do not neglect dramatic improvement, either. The books of Shigeo Shingo (1985, 1986, 1988) explore from an engineer's perspective the process of analyzing operations for opportunities for dramatic improvement. One story illustrates his approach. A client of Shingo's, a manufacturer of engraved brass plates, was seeking a way to efficiently remove the lubricating fluid used to cool the engraving pen, because cleaning the engraved plate represented the largest single process cost. Shingo, on reflecting on the purpose of the fluid—cooling plus debris removal—suggested the use of a focused stream of compressed air rather than fluid. The company's management felt that air would not properly protect the pen and would shorten the pen's life. On Shingo's insistence, the company tried it and found that the method not only eliminated the need to clean the plate after engraving but also actually extended the pen life by 30 percent. This story illustrates two aspects of continuous improvement—careful analysis combined with a willingness to try new approaches, even when they seem unpromising.

The JIT approach includes the following:

A. Reduction of setup times to achieve smaller production lot sizes
B. Increased use of sequential flow processes such as dedicated assembly lines and group technology cells
C. Increased use of multifunction workers
D. Increased flexibility of equipment and capacity
E. Increased use of preventive maintenance
F. Increased stability and consistency in the schedule
G. Longer term relationships with suppliers
H. More frequent deliveries from suppliers
I. Improved technical support of suppliers
J. Employee involvement programs such as quality circles
K. Statistical process control (SPC)
L. The stop production prerogative
M. Cause and effect analysis

Although this new philosophy affects all areas of a business, major changes take place in manufacturing management, purchasing, human resources management, and quality management.

MANUFACTURING MANAGEMENT—A GENERAL OVERVIEW

Large work-in-process inventories can be the result of a number of difficulties, including: lengthy setups, long queues at work centers, material waiting to be moved to the next operation, long distances between work centers, uneven loads from one period to the next, equipment and workers with limited flexibility, unexpected equipment failure, and large safety stocks to cover possible scrap. Let's consider how the JIT approach can solve some of these difficulties.

Setups

Reduced setup times have two important benefits. First, they allow lot sizes to be reduced without any setup cost penalty. Second, because of the increased ability to switch production between different items, manufacturing can respond quickly to different customer demands. There are a host of principles and guidelines for reducing setup times. Many of them apply to specific types of equipment; however, a few are universally applicable. The most prominent of these guidelines is that setup operations should be divided into internal elements (those that must be done when the machine is not operating) and external elements (those that can be performed when the equipment is operating). Performing as many of the setup activities as possible while the machine is operating can often reduce setup time substantially. Shingo (1985) estimates that setup time can be reduced 30 to 50 percent merely by separating internal and external procedures. Other universal guidelines include:

A. Modify equipment by the use of standard die height, locator pins, etc. to eliminate the need for adjustments.
B. Be sure all needed material and tools are available when the setup is scheduled to begin.
C. Videotape the setup operation for analysis and training.
D. Study the setup process in order to design a standard setup process. Prepare setup process sheets that list the elemental tasks in each setup. List elements according to their priority for future improvements using Pareto's (ABC) analysis.
E. Color code all connections: air, hydraulic, water, electrical, etc. Use quick disconnects.
F. Involve tool and die designers in setup reduction programs so that all new designs incorporate quick changeover concepts.

G. For large dies, improve transportation time by using a standard table to roll the die into position. Standardize machine bed heights so the die can easily slide from the table to the machine bed.

H. For small tools (e.g., hand power drills), use duplicate tooling to avoid setup.

I. Involve the people that do the work and know the equipment.

J. Make improvements as they develop—including the small ones.

See Shingo (1985), Hall (1983), and Schonburger (1987) for a further discussion of setups. The above recommendations point out the importance of "Housekeeping."

Housekeeping

It would seem obvious that an organized and uncluttered work place is conducive to efficient and effective manufacturing. Visiting some plants reveals that not everyone is sufficiently convinced. Poor housekeeping includes random location of tools, dirty equipment, poorly lighted areas, and cutting oil, material remnants, and chips on the floor. These lead to lost and damaged tools, accidents, and slower than necessary setups, and reflect an attitude that accuracy, appearance, and quality are not important. In general, poor housekeeping sends the message that: "What takes place here is not important." The effect of this message on effective operations may be greater than just the physical obstacles of poor work place organization. Few would argue that good housekeeping is a prerequisite to JIT. A few basic rules for housekeeping include:

1. Keep tools clean, lubricated, calibrated, sharp, and in their designated location.

2. Clean, inspect, and repair tools during or immediately after teardown (end of setup).

3. Classify tools, jigs, attachments, and supplies on the basis of the frequency of their use and store accordingly.

4. Store materials and supplies in designated locations. Mark each location so that what belongs there is clearly visible, both when the spot is empty and when it is occupied. Visibility is crucial for identification of parts, tools, and supplies.

5. Avoid the "Call Housekeeping" syndrome. Let each employee or small group be responsible for the order and cleanliness in an area. This motivates everyone to keep things clean and in order and also raises the importance of housekeeping.

Although housekeeping is not the most exciting topic, the improved quality and productivity that often follow improved housekeeping can be very exciting.

Total Preventive Maintenance

Total preventive maintenance (TPM) includes both preventive maintenance (PM) and continual analysis of and improvements to equipment, tooling, and the work place organization. TPM increases flexibility, reduces material handling, and improves flow. TPM is discussed in greater detail in Chapter 18.

When equipment fails, work in process increases at upstream work centers as queues increase, and downstream work centers are idle due to the lack of incoming parts. In addition, deliveries are delayed, and scrap is often produced before the operation is stopped. One advantage of preventive maintenance over repair maintenance is that PM can be scheduled when the machine is not needed. Repair cannot. Furthermore, if PM is performed properly, there is less total maintenance effort required than when each component failure is repaired in isolation. Much lip service has been paid over the years to the value of PM. More often than not PM was practiced in the breach rather than on a regular basis.

Preventive maintenance is essential in many types of equipment, from an automobile to a commercial airliner. Both the failure of the braking system in the former and the failure of a hydraulic system in the latter can produce disastrous results. JIT stresses PM using statistical analysis and the knowledge of the operator. Statistical analysis has revealed when fan belts and hoses on an automobile should be replaced to avoid a breakdown. In the same way, it can reveal that specific adjustments and component replacements must be made on many types of equipment after so many hours of operation (or number of items processed) to avoid failure during processing.

Preventive maintenance begins with simple housekeeping procedures. For example, if equipment is kept clean, signs of trouble, such as oil leaks can be spotted before seals fail completely. And, just as the experienced driver can foresee potential failures by sensing unusual noises and vibrations or spotting a fluid leak, the experienced operator often can sense potential equipment failures by closely observing the behavior of equipment. When a worker is responsible for maintaining a machine, he or she tends to correct problems when they occur. When a maintenance person is responsible for repairing the machine, the worker tends to let the machine continue to run until it fails catastrophically. The combination of the statistical analysis of the reliability and life expectancy of components, the alertness of experienced operators, and scheduled preventive maintenance can substantially reduce unplanned downtime. This reduces the need for some inventory and improves delivery performance.

Manufacturing Flexibility

The ability to rapidly shift production from one item to another is a function of many factors, including setup times, work rules, worker flexibility, and equipment flexibility. Setups were discussed previously. Recently, labor unions have been more receptive to changes in work rules that allow workers to perform operations previously restricted to a specific worker classification. These changes combined with training workers to perform various operations are essential to increased flexibility. Such training is well received by most workers when it is introduced by an education program that demonstrates its relationship to the survival and prosperity of the firm and, thus, their future employment. When production quantities do not justify dedicated equipment, equipment flexibility can often be increased substantially with minor equipment modification.

PROCESS FLOW AND LAYOUT

Job shops have traditionally been organized with equipment performing similar functions located in the same department. For example, drill presses, lathes, milling machines, and welding equipment would each be in a different location (department). Thus, each order must be moved from department to department as required by the manufacturing process. This brings about material handling, material waiting to be moved, occasional damage to material during movement, and personnel and workers invested in moving material. None of these activities add value. JIT aims at eliminating these activities by changing from a job shop process to a flow process.

Because major benefits of JIT usually are achieved as improvements in the process flow are made, we describe these changes and their benefits in detail using the following examples:

I.   Deterministic Simulation, One Product, Four Operations
 A.   Job shop
 B.   Operation overlapping
 C.   Sequential flow
II. Stochastic Simulation, Five Products, Varied Operation Sequences
 A.   Job shop
 B.   Dedicated flow lines: two products
 C.   Job shop: reduced setups and improved quality

Our first example reveals the benefits of operation overlapping. Our second example illustrates the advantages of moving to a sequential flow process and of reducing batch sizes where nonsequential flow remains.

Example 1—Deterministic Simulation, One Product, Four Operations

The first step in the movement from a job shop to a sequential flow process is often operation overlapping (see Chapter 14) followed by the application of group technology concepts and the development of manufacturing cells. This example portrays such a movement and its results. The process has four operations with the following operation, setup, queue, wait, and movement times. The lot size is 200 units.

Operation	Queue Time* (Q)	Setup Time* (S)	Operation Time/Part* (O)	Wait Time* (W)	Movement Time* (M)
1	480	90	4.5	240	15
2	480	60	5.0	240	15
3	480	75	5.5	240	15
4	480	90	6.0	240	—
	1,920	315	21.0	960	45

All times are in minutes.

A traditional measure of manufacturing efficiency (ME) is calculated by dividing the total of setup time and operation time by the total manufacturing lead time (MLT). Thus, for this example:

$$\text{Total Setup Time} + \text{Total Operation Time} = 315 + (200 \times 21)$$
$$= 4{,}515 \text{ minutes}$$

$$\text{MLT} = \Sigma Q + \Sigma S + (N \times \Sigma O) + \Sigma W + \Sigma M$$
$$\text{MLT} = 1{,}920 + 315 + (200 \times 21) + 960 + 45$$
$$= 7{,}440 \text{ minutes}$$

$$\text{ME} = \frac{4{,}515}{7{,}440} = 0.607 \text{ or } 60.7 \text{ percent}$$

This seems to be a rather good performance and is not surprising because the queue and wait times are relatively low for a traditional job shop. However, the 60.7 percent is misleading because 199 parts are in queue or waiting while each part is being processed, and all of this time is counted as processing time. A better measure is required.

Value Added Efficiency.   A more accurate measure of manufacturing efficiency is obtained by dividing the processing time, the only time when value is added, by the total manufacturing lead time of the part. We have chosen to designate this measure as the *value added efficiency* (VAE). In the example,

$$\text{VAE} = \frac{O}{\text{MLT}} = \frac{21 \text{ minutes}}{7{,}440 \text{ minutes}} = 0.0028 \text{ or } 0.28 \text{ percent}$$

This result is not very impressive, but it is an accurate measure of the percentage of time each part is being processed, that is, having its value increased.

Operation Overlapping.   Operation overlapping can increase the VAE substantially. For example, reducing the queue times to 30 minutes each and the waiting times to 15 minutes each and performing the setups prior to the operation as shown in Figure 17-2, gives the following transfer lot sizes for Operation 1. (See Chapter 14 for discussion of calculation of transfer lot sizes.)

$$Q_1 \geq \frac{Q \times O_1}{O_1 + O_2} \quad \text{and} \quad Q_2 = Q - Q_1$$

$$Q_1 \geq \frac{200 \times 4.5}{4.5 + 5.0} = 94.7 \text{ or } 95$$

$$Q_2 = 200 - 95 = 105$$

The transfer lot sizes for the other operations are calculated in the same manner.

Figure 17-2
Manufacturing Lead Time, Two Transfer Batches
(All times are in minutes.)

Operation	Transfer Lot Sizes Q_1	Q_2	Operation Time/Part (O)	$Q_1 \times O$	$Q_2 \times O$	Time (M)
1	95	105	4.5	427.5	472.5	15
2	96	104	5.0	480.0	520.0	15
3	96	104	5.5	528.0	572.0	15
4	200	—	6.0	1,200.0	—	—
				2,635.5		45

Processing Gantt Chart

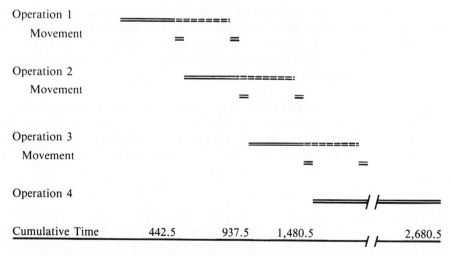

The analysis shown in Figure 17-2 reveals that the manufacturing lead time has been reduced to 2,680.5 minutes by processing the second transfer lot (Q_2) for each of the first three operations while the first lot (Q_1) is being processed in the next operation. This results in the following improved VAE.

$$\text{VAE} = \frac{21 \text{ minutes}}{2,680.5 \text{ minutes}} = 0.0078 \text{ or } 0.78 \text{ percent}$$

This is nearly three times the former value of 0.28 percent, a marked improvement but still not very good. Proceeding further with operation overlapping and dividing the lot into 20 transfer batches of 10 units each provides the data for the analysis shown in Figure 17-3. Note that each transfer batch arrives at the next operation prior to the completion of the previous batch.

Figure 17-3
Manufacturing Lead Time, 20 Transfer Batches of 10 Each
(All times are in minutes.)

Operation	Transfer Lot Sizes Q_1	$Q_2 - Q_{20}$	Operation Time/Part (O)	$Q_1 \times O$	$Q_2 \times O$	Time (M)
1	10	10	4.5	45.0	45.0	15
2	10	10	5.0	50.0	50.0	15
3	10	10	5.5	55.0	55.0	15
4	200	—	6.0	1,200.0	—	—
				1,350.0		45

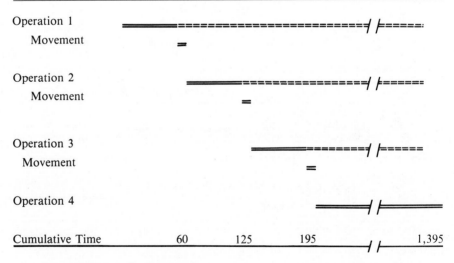

Processing Gantt Chart

The VAE is calculated as:

$$VAE = \frac{21 \text{ minutes}}{1,395 \text{ minutes}} = 0.015 \text{ or } 1.5 \text{ percent}$$

This is approximately double the previous performance, a noteworthy improvement. But there is still ample room, 98.5 percent, for further improvement.

Manufacturing Cells. Group technology and manufacturing cells can improve the VAE by identifying parts with similar processes and locating personnel and equipment dedicated to manufacturing these items in one location. Manufacturing cells reduce setup times and lot sizes by using common setups. The proximity of equipment reduces material handling, and parts completed in one operation are immediately available in many cases for processing in the next.

Now we examine a manufacturing cell with a transfer batch of 1 unit, material arriving every hour in standard containers holding 10 units, no movement between operations, and 10 finished units being moved every hour from the final operation to finished goods. In addition, the process has been redesigned so that the smallest operation time is now 5.0 minutes, the largest is 5.5 minutes, and 6.0 minutes are allowed for each operation. The total processing time is still 21.0 minutes. Figure 17-4 describes this situation.

Figure 17-4
Manufacturing Lead Time, Manufacturing Cell, Lot Size 1
(All times are in minutes.)

Operation	Lot Sizes $Q_2 - Q_{20}$	Operation Time/Part (O)	$Q_1 \times O$	Queue Time (Q)	Wait Time (W)
1	1	5.0	5.0	30.0	
2	1	5.0	5.0	—	
3	1	5.5	5.0	—	
4	1	5.5	5.5	—	30
		21.0	21.0	30.0	30

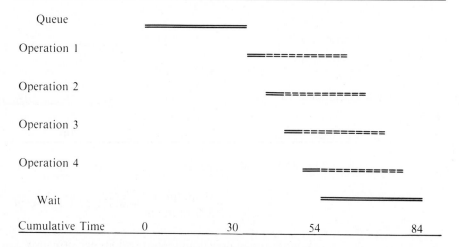

Processing Gantt Chart

Queue				
Operation 1				
Operation 2				
Operation 3				
Operation 4				
Wait				
Cumulative Time	0	30	54	84

Figure 17-4, based on the average queue and wait times, gives a manufacturing lead time of 84 minutes. This results in a VAE of 21 ÷ 84 = 0.25 or 25 percent. This performance is roughly one hundred times better than the performance of the job shop with which we began and roughly seventeen times better than the best operation overlapping performance. Improvement in actual situations depends on the present efficiency, the nature of the product and process, and the skills and creativity of those making the improvements.

Example 2—Stochastic Simulation, Five Products, Varied Operation Sequences

Example 1 purposely oversimplifies the situation for the sake of clarity. Now we use stochastic simulation to examine a more realistic example that has more than one product, different routings, scrap, and equipment failures. This example illustrates the advantages of moving to a sequential flow process and of reducing batch sizes where nonsequential flow remains.

Imagine a shop that has four departments, each with four machines. The shop produces five part types. The part routing, run time, and demand data are shown below:

Part	Daily Demand	Routing	Run Times
1	400	A-B-C-D	4.5, 5, 5.5, 6
2	200	B-D-A-C	4.5, 5, 5.5, 6
3	80	C-A-D-B	4.5, 5, 5.5, 6
4	80	D-C-B-A	4.5, 5, 5.5, 6
5	40	C-A-B-D	4.5, 5, 5.5, 6

Thus, Part 1 begins at Station A, where it requires 4.5 minutes per part to produce; it then proceeds to Station B, where it requires 5 minutes per part; then on to Station C for 5.5 minutes per part; and finally to Station D for 6 minutes per part. Part 2 is routed first to Station B then to Station D, and so on. In addition, assume Station A requires 90 minutes to change from one part to any other part, Station B requires 60 minutes, Station C requires 75 minutes, and Station D requires 90 minutes. Average daily demand for each part is shown above. Each part is made in batches of 100 each. On the average, a batch of 100 is released to the shop every 3 hours. The process of releasing individual batches to the shop can be modeled as a Poisson arrival process (i.e., time between release of batches follows a negative exponential distribution with a mean interarrival time of 3 hours).

Each of the five parts is subject to scrap. There is an inspection station immediately after the final operation for each part. There is a 4 percent chance that any given lot is scrapped. When a lot is scrapped, a replacement lot is started at the first operation for that part. Each of the 16 machines is subject to random breakdowns; each machine is available 95 percent of the time. The mean time to repair a machine ranges from 50 minutes for Work Center D to 400 minutes for Work Center A. In all cases, the mean time to failure is 19 times as large as the mean time to repair. Figures 17-5 and 17-6 show printouts of the simulation of the shop.

Figure 17-5
GEMS* Results, Job Shop Model

```
**** TIME AND ASSOCIATED NETWORK COST STATISTICS ****

BOX    NAME    STAT    NO. OF      MEAN      STD.DEV     MIN.        MAX.
NUM            TYPE    OBS.

       9 STOCK  INTV    19005     3232.849   840.536   2180.914    12638.870

**** QUEUE BOX STATISTICS ****

QUE    STAT. TYPE         MEAN        STD.DEV          MIN.              MAX.
NUM                                                   MEAN              MEAN

       WORK CENTER A                          NUMBER OF SERVERS=  4
3      NUMB BUSY SERVER    2.848      .073              2.665             2.991
3      QUEUE LENGTH         .615      .144               .369              .960
3      WAITING TIME      120.537      .000             78.660           183.306
3      BUSY %             96.959      .831             95.066            98.237
3      ENTITIES PASSED   659.533    16.490            621.000           693.000
3      MAX QUEUE LENGTH    7.000     1.661              5.000            12.000
       FINAL STATUS: Q-LENGTH    0 IDLE SERVERS    0

       WORK CENTER B                          NUMBER OF SERVERS=  4
4      NUMB BUSY SERVER    2.868      .078              2.691             3.008
4      QUEUE LENGTH         .580      .141               .357              .933
4      WAITING TIME      113.777      .000             75.071           178.284
4      BUSY %             97.048      .658             95.619            98.120
4      ENTITIES PASSED   658.733    17.235            617.000           696.000
4      MAX QUEUE LENGTH    6.600     1.276              5.000            11.000
       FINAL STATUS: Q-LENGTH    0 IDLE SERVERS    0

       WORK CENTER C            NUMBER OF SERVERS=   4
5      NUMB BUSY SERVER    3.079      .077              2.894             3.233
5      QUEUE LENGTH         .763      .168               .414             1.195
5      WAITING TIME      149.828      .000             86.777           228.711
5      BUSY %             97.946      .740             96.074            99.371
5      ENTITIES PASSED   659.133    16.858            620.000           692.000
5      MAX QUEUE LENGTH    7.200     1.215              5.000            10.000
       FINAL STATUS: Q-LENGTH    0 IDLE SERVERS    0

       WORK CENTER D            NUMBER OF SERVERS=   4
6      NUMB BUSY SERVER    3.140      .082              2.949             3.303
6      QUEUE LENGTH         .878      .213               .430             1.363
6      WAITING TIME      172.223      .000             89.971           260.536
6      BUSY %             98.466      .587             97.088            99.474
6      ENTITIES PASSED   659.133    17.192            616.000           693.000
6      MAX QUEUE LENGTH    7.667     1.768              5.000            12.000
       FINAL STATUS: Q-LENGTH    0 IDLE SERVERS    1

       MATERIAL HANDLING
7      NUMB BUSY SERVER     .610      .016               .572              .642
7      QUEUE LENGTH         .375      .034               .291              .447
7      WAITING TIME       18.412     1.339             15.248            20.869
7      BUSY %             61.026     1.563             57.217            64.241
7      ENTITIES PASSED  2636.267    67.609           2471.000          2775.000
7      MAX QUEUE LENGTH    5.733      .691              4.000             7.000
       FINAL STATUS: Q-LENGTH    0 IDLE SERVERS    1
```

*Generalized Manufacturing Simulator; see Chapter 23 for a description of the GEMS language. An explanation of
how to interpret the GEMS output is provided in Appendix 17A for those who desire to examine portions of the
output not discussed here.*

Figure 17-6
Distribution of Manufacturing Lead Time

```
                          0     2299   4597   6896   9194  COUNT
        FROM      TO  ..............................
        BELOW        .00  .       .      .      .      .   0
          .00   1000.00  .       .      .      .      .    0
      1000.00   2000.00  .       .      .      .      .    0
      2000.00   3000.00  .***************************.  9094
      3000.00   4000.00  .********************       .   8061
      4000.00   5000.00  .*****  .      .      .      .  1015
      5000.00   6000.00  .**     .      .      .      .   396
      6000.00   7000.00  .*      .      .      .      .   284
      7000.00   8000.00  .       .      .      .      .    93
      8000.00   9000.00  .       .      .      .      .    40
      9000.00  10000.00  .       .      .      .      .    16
     10000.00  11000.00  .       .      .      .      .     3
     11000.00  12000.00  .       .      .      .      .     2
     12000.00  13000.00  .       .      .      .      .     1
     13000.00  14000.00  .       .      .      .      .     0
     14000.00  15000.00  .       .      .      .      .     0
     15000.00  16000.00  .       .      .      .      .     0
     16000.00  17000.00  .       .      .      .      .     0
     17000.00  18000.00  .       .      .      .      .     0
        ABOVE  18000.00  .       .      .      .      .     0
```

As discussed for Example 1, a traditional measure of manufacturing efficiency (ME) is calculated by dividing the total of setup time and operation time by the total manufacturing lead time (MLT). The total of setup time and operation time for a batch of 100 is:

Setup Time + Operation Time = 315 + (100 × 21) = 2,415 minutes

The MLT for a batch of 100 was found by simulating the shop using GEMS. The average manufacturing lead time was found to be approximately 3,233 minutes. (In Figure 17-5, under Time and Associated Network Cost Statistics, find the row labeled "Stock" and the value labeled "Mean." This value represents the average time a batch spent from release to stock—the manufacturing lead time. The standard deviation of manufacturing lead time and the minimum and the maximum times also are shown.)

Thus,

$$ME = \frac{2,415 \text{ minutes}}{3,233 \text{ minutes}} = 0.747 \text{ or } 74.7 \text{ percent}$$

This seems to be a rather good performance and not surprising because the queue and wait times are relatively low for a traditional job shop. In fact, a scrutiny of Figure 17-5 reveals that only 557 minutes are spent waiting in queue. (In the section labeled "Queue Box Statistics," results are reported for five queues. Four of the queues are labeled "Work Center A," "Work

Center B," etc. Within the statistics reported for each queue is a row marked "Waiting time." In the column labeled "Mean" is the average waiting time for a batch of 100 parts. The average waiting time at Work Center A is approximately 121 minutes; at Work Center B, it is approximately 114 minutes; at Work Center C, it is approximately 150 minutes; at Work Center D, it is approximately 172 minutes. Adding these, one obtains an average time in queue of 557 minutes.) Each batch also spent 192 minutes being moved and waiting to be moved. (The queue labeled "Material Handling" reports a mean waiting time of 18 minutes. Actual move time averaged 30 minutes. The total of 48 minutes per move times 4 moves yields 192 minutes of move time.) There is a maxim that a job processed by a traditional job shop spends 90 percent of its time waiting in queue. For this job to spend 74.7 percent of its time actually being worked on is exceptional.

However, the 74.7 percent is misleading because 99 parts are in queue or waiting while each part is being processed, and all of this time is counted as processing time. As noted earlier, a more accurate measure of manufacturing efficiency is the value added efficiency (VAE), obtained by dividing the processing time, the only time when value is added, by the total manufacturing lead time of the part. In the example,

$$\text{VAE} = \frac{O}{\text{MLT}} = \frac{21 \text{ minutes}}{3{,}233 \text{ minutes}} = 0.0065 \text{ or } 0.65 \text{ percent}$$

This result is not very impressive, but it is an accurate measure of the percentage of time each part is being processed, that is, having its value increased. A second problem is revealed if one studies the standard deviation of manufacturing lead time together with the minimum and maximum lead times. Note that there is a very high variation to lead time, including a maximum of more than 12,000 minutes. (These data were collected by measuring time from release until the batch, or its replacement, was completed. During 30 simulations of 90 days each, more than 19,000 batches were released. Of these, roughly 4 percent or 760 batches were rejected. Of the 760 replacement batches, roughly 4 percent of them also were rejected. Thus, about 30 batches were rejected twice. Of these 30, 4 percent were rejected, yielding an expected value of 1 batch rejected three times. The maximum of 12,000 minutes, which from Figure 17-6 occurred for only one batch, is consistent with an average lead time of 3,200 minutes times 4 batches required to finally have a batch accepted.) Although the number of batches having exceptionally long lead times is quite small relative to the total, to the individual customer whose batch is delayed inordinately, the delay may be a major problem. Each batch that is delayed a substantial length of time represents a potential lost customer.

Thus, the traditional job shop approach suffers from the fact that lead times are both long and highly variable. Notice especially the COUNT column on the right of Figure 17-6. The distribution of lead times is right skewed, that is, has a number of observations to the right of the mean that are quite far from the mean while no comparable events occur to the left of the mean. The existence of right skewness in the manufacturing lead time distribution suggests that a few jobs will consistently be very late. Furthermore, for most of the lead time, more than 99 percent in this case, the individual piece is merely sitting, waiting to be worked on.

Flow (Sequential) Process with Dedicated Lines.   Now let's consider a JIT approach to this situation. Recall from the problem description that there are four machines in each of the four work centers and that Part 1 is responsible for 50 percent of the demand and Part 2 is responsible for 25 percent of the demand. A JIT solution would be to move two machines out of each work center and set up two parallel lines dedicated to the production of Part 1. JIT would continue by moving one more machine from each work center to a third dedicated line, this one making only Part 2. The remaining four machines would produce the remaining three parts in a job shop fashion. The JIT approach immediately solves the problem of large batch size for Parts 1 and 2. Since both parts are manufactured continuously, no setup occurs. Manufacturing lead time is minimized because each part is passed to the next station as soon as it is completed. Figure 17-7 reports results from the three dedicated lines.

Figure 17-7
Results from Dedicated Lines

BOX NUM	NAME	STAT TYPE	NO. OF OBS.	MEAN	STD.DEV	MIN.	MAX.
31	LINE 1 & 2	INTV	19396	62.428	28.360	13.174	397.651
37	LINE 3	INTV	9085	107.203	70.211	14.476	617.948

Distribution of Manufacturing Lead Time

```
               0     2032    4064    6096    8127 COUNT
FROM      TO   ..................................................
BELOW    .00   .        .       .       .      .    0
  .00   25.00  .**      .       .       .      .  368
25.00   50.00  .***************************.6506
50.00   75.00  .****************************.8027
75.00  100.00  .********      .       .      .2240
100.00 125.00  .*******.      .       .      .1793
125.00 150.00  .**      .       .       .      .  273
150.00 175.00  .        .       .       .      .   68
175.00 200.00  .        .       .       .      .   53
200.00 225.00  .        .       .       .      .   30
225.00 250.00  .        .       .       .      .   26
250.00 275.00  .        .       .       .      .    5
275.00 300.00  .        .       .       .      .    4
300.00 325.00  .        .       .       .      .    2
325.00 350.00  .        .       .       .      .    0
350.00 375.00  .        .       .       .      .    0
375.00 400.00  .        .       .       .      .    1
400.00 425.00  .        .       .       .      .    0
425.00 450.00  .        .       .       .      .    0
ABOVE  450.00  .        .       .       .      .    0
```

Note that lead time for Lines 1 and 2 averaged 62 minutes and that lead time for Line 3 averaged 107 minutes. VAE for Lines 1 and 2 is thus

$$VAE_1 = \frac{21 \text{ minutes}}{62 \text{ minutes}} = 0.339 \text{ or } 33.9 \text{ percent}$$

VAE for Line 3 is

$$VAE_3 = \frac{21 \text{ minutes}}{107 \text{ minutes}} = 0.196 \text{ or } 19.6 \text{ percent}$$

The VAE for Lines 1 and 2 is more than 50 times the former value of 0.65 percent. The VAE for Line 3 is about 30 times the old value. (The observant student may be wondering why Line 3 does not have the same manufacturing lead time as Lines 1 and 2 since the operation times are the same. The answer is that machine type A has the longest mean time to repair and, thus, is going to delay the part more, on average, than the other machines. For Part 1, machine A has the shortest processing time of the four machines. For Part 2, machine A has the next to longest time. Thus, parts are delayed considerably longer at machine type A in Line 3 than in Lines 1 and 2.)

An interesting question is: Why does a dedicated line not achieve a VAE of 1? To achieve a VAE of 1, a part would have to be worked on 100 percent of the time, that is, move time must be zero and there must be no delay in a queue. In this model, arrivals of jobs to the line are constant, one every 7.2 minutes. If machine times were constant and if machines never broke down and if parts were never scrapped, a job would never wait. But the machines are down 5 percent of the time. This causes upstream machines to be blocked, since any queue will accept only five jobs. Also, because of scrap, a replacement part and a new part may arrive at the first station in line almost simultaneously, causing one to wait. Finally, machine times are random variables, so although average machine time may be only 5.5 minutes or 6 minutes for a given station, any single machine time may exceed the 7.2 minute cycle time.

Nondedicated Cell with Reduced Setup.   Let's now consider what JIT would do with the remaining four machines and three parts. We should first note that setup times may be reduced for some machines by the mere fact that there are only three parts to be produced rather than five. For example, some machines have a tool magazine that will hold a fixed number of tools. Suppose the magazine holds 10 tools and that each of the five parts requires 3 distinct tools. Then for the original situation, the arrival of a new part might require that one or more tools be added to the tool magazine, requiring several minutes of setup time. However, with only three parts, the 9 tools may stay in the magazine all the time, and the setup is avoided.

The experience of many American firms that have adopted JIT is that about 75 percent of the setup time can be eliminated, without spending money to modify the equipment, by taking two steps. The first step is to separate tasks into internal task time and external task time, performing all external setup tasks while the machine is producing. The second step is to perform a methods improvement analysis on the setup and develop a standard setup methodology. (By traditional standards, setup time does not represent enough total time to warrant methods improvement analysis, so most setups have never been studied when a firm begins to implement JIT.) We assume each of the four setups is quickly reduced by 90 percent and, as a consequence, the batch size for the three jobs that continue to be produced in batches now is 10. The result of this simulation is presented in Figure 17-8.

Figure 17-8
Results of the Job Shop Portion of the Modified Plant

BOX NUM	NAME	STAT TYPE	NO. OF OBS.	MEAN	STD.DEV	MIN.	MAX.
9	STOCK	INTV	5175	1182.856	647.692	232.045	5894.738

```
               Distribution of Manufacturing Lead Time

                    0     252    504    756   1007 COUNT
       FROM    TO ........................................

       BELOW     .00 .        .       .       .       .   0
         .00  250.00 .        .       .       .       .   6
       250.00  500.00 .***************                .   533
       500.00  750.00 .**************************      .   957
       750.00 1000.00 .**************************      .   957
      1000.00 1250.00 .*******************.            .   725
      1250.00 1500.00 .****************                .   632
      1500.00 1750.00 .*************.                  .   459
      1750.00 2000.00 .************  .                 .   400
      2000.00 2250.00 .******.                         .   178
      2250.00 2500.00 .****  .                          .   89
      2500.00 2750.00 .****  .                          .   88
      2750.00 3000.00 .***   .                          .   64
      3000.00 3250.00 .**    .                          .   43
      3250.00 3500.00 .*     .                          .   20
      3500.00 3750.00 .      .                          .   6
      3750.00 4000.00 .      .                          .   5
      4000.00 4250.00 .      .                          .   7
      4250.00 4500.00 .      .                          .   0
      ABOVE  4500.00 .      .                          .   6
```

Note that average manufacturing lead time now is approximately 1,183 minutes, and

$$VAE = \frac{21 \text{ minutes}}{1,183 \text{ minutes}} = 0.0178 \text{ or } 1.78 \text{ percent}$$

While this result is almost three times as large as the original value, it is somewhat disappointing, especially when one considers that setup time was reduced by 90 percent and batch size was reduced by 90 percent. This result emphasizes the value of getting the batch size down to 1 (at least the transfer batch, the number of parts required to be built at one station before parts are transferred to the next). One might also note from Figure 17-8 that the maximum manufacturing lead time is almost five times as large as the average time, emphasizing that the maximum lead time is strongly influenced by the scrap rate. (Recall that the maximum lead time typically occurs on an order that has a batch rejected, the replacement batch rejected, etc.)

Nondedicated Cell with Improved Quality and Reduced Setup.   Figure 17-8 understates the effect on the manufacturing lead time of going from five parts to three parts using a job shop or nonsequential flow method. The figure assumes that going to JIT has no effect on product quality. Let's consider the effect JIT has on how often a part is made. Parts 3 and 4 have a demand of 80 units each per day. Part 5 has a demand of 40 units. When these parts are made in batches of 100, the part is released to the shop about once each day or two. When there are four machines in each work center, any single machine operator sees a part once every four to eight days on the average. When a worker processes a part only once a week, a learning process is required to regain top form in producing the part. This learning process almost certainly influences the scrap rate. When the batch size is reduced to 10, all three parts are built every day. Further, when only one machine is present in each work center, every machinist builds every part every day. No learning is needed to recall how to do something that is done every day for an extended period. Thus, from the learning effect alone, scrap should be reduced.

The use of standard die heights and locator pins to eliminate adjustments also improves quality. When die heights vary, there is a certain amount of guesswork concerning how a press should be set up to deliver maximum pressure to the desired point. In the absence of locator pins, there is also guesswork concerning the ideal positioning of the die on the press bed. The usual procedure is to use trial and error, expecting several defective parts to be made in the adjustment process. Once a good part is made, manufacture begins in earnest. Thus, the advantage of the JIT approach is that in addition to saving setup time, considerable scrap is eliminated almost immediately.

Let's examine the effect of reducing scrap from 4 percent to 2 percent, as shown in Figure 17-9. Note that both the maximum lead time and the mean lead time are reduced by about 25 percent. Maximum lead time is reduced because the likelihood of a job being rejected two or three times in a row is reduced substantially. (The chance of being rejected twice is reduced from 0.16 percent for 4 percent rejects to 0.04 percent for 2 percent rejects. The chance of being rejected three times is reduced from 0.00064 percent for a 4 percent rate to 0.00008 percent for a 2 percent rate.) The average is influenced quite a lot by extremely large values. Reducing the number of jobs that pass through the shop two or three times reduces the mean considerably. Another factor that reduces the mean is the fact that the smaller rejection rate also leads to slightly smaller queues and, hence, slightly smaller waiting times throughout the entire facility.

Figure 17-9
The Revised Job Shop Model with 2 Percent Defectives

```
**** TIME AND ASSOCIATED NETWORK COST STATISTICS ****

BOX    NAME      STAT    NO. OF    MEAN     STD.DEV    MIN.      MAX.
NUM              TYPE    OBS.

  9 STOCK        INTV    5420   775.035   360.036   228.271   3931.364

              Distribution of Manufacturing Lead Time

                   0      425      849     1274    1698 COUNT
        FROM    TO  ..............................

        BELOW    .00  .        .        .        .        .       0
          .00  250.00  .        .        .        .        .      15
        250.00  500.00  .*********************        .    1303
        500.00  750.00  .***************************  .    1598
        750.00 1000.00  .*********************        .    1306
       1000.00 1250.00  .************ .        .        .    698
       1250.00 1500.00  .***** .        .        .        .    268
       1500.00 1750.00  .*** .        .        .        .      127
       1750.00 2000.00  .** .        .        .        .       71
       2000.00 2250.00  .* .        .        .        .        18
       2250.00 2500.00  .        .        .        .        .    8
       2500.00 2750.00  .        .        .        .        .    2
       2750.00 3000.00  .        .        .        .        .    3
       3000.00 3250.00  .        .        .        .        .    0
       3250.00 3500.00  .        .        .        .        .    2
       3500.00 3750.00  .        .        .        .        .    0
       3750.00 4000.00  .        .        .        .        .    1
       4000.00 4250.00  .        .        .        .        .    0
       4250.00 4500.00  .        .        .        .        .    0
        ABOVE 4500.00  .        .        .        .        .    0
```

The net effect of changing to a one-machine-per-station job shop handling three jobs with a scrap rate of 2 percent is the following:

$$\text{VAE} = \frac{21 \text{ minutes}}{775 \text{ minutes}} = 0.027 \text{ or } 2.7 \text{ percent}$$

This VAE is approximately four times the original 0.65 percent. Computing a weighted average for Lines 1 to 3 and the job shop yields

$$\text{VAE} = (0.5)(33.9\%) + (0.25)(19.6\%) + (0.25)(2.7\%) = 22.5\%$$

Effect on Lead Time.   Another way to express the benefit gained from moving to JIT is the reduction in lead time. In the original model, manufacturing lead time was 3,323 minutes or 55 hours. In the revised model, lead time for the most popular part is 1 hour; for the next most popular, it is 2 hours; and for the last three parts, it is about 12.9 hours. There can be a large competitive advantage to promising delivery of a part in one or two hours, or at most one day, rather than promising delivery in three days.

The value of work in process inventory is greatly reduced in the Just-in-Time example. Consider Figure 17-5, the original model. Examine the row marked "Queue Length." For Work Center A, this has a value of 0.615. This value is a time weighted value over the entire simulation. The simplest way that this value might arise is that 61.5 percent of the time there is a batch waiting to be processed, and 38.5 percent of the time there is not. There are also more complicated situations that achieve the same result. At any rate, since each batch represents 100 parts, there are 61.5 parts waiting to be processed, on the average, at Work Station A. Furthermore, there are an average of 2.848 operators busy at Work Station A. Each busy operator represents another 100 pieces. For each of the four stations, there is a positive value for queue length and busy servers. To determine total work in process, one must add queue length and busy servers for each of the four work centers and for material handling. These ten numbers add to 15.76 batches or 1,576 parts waiting to be processed or moved at any given time. By comparison, the JIT model results in an average work in process of 134 pieces, a 91.5 percent reduction in work in process.

Is our JIT example realistic? The Hewlett-Packard plant in Cupertino, California, actually did achieve a 94 percent reduction in work-in-process inventory when it implemented JIT (as did several others). Although an actual shop processes hundreds to thousands of parts rather than five, our example is not unrealistic. Typically, 5 percent of the parts account for some 60 percent of the product volume. Thus, most plants can move a few high volume parts into dedicated sequential flow lines. For the remaining parts, very often a number of medium volume parts have similar material content and part geometries (i.e., all are cylinders or all are spheres or all are plates that require holes to be drilled, etc.). By moving all parts having material and geometry similarities into an area dedicated to only that family, much of the efficiency of a dedicated line can be achieved. There are several intermediate shop forms between the purely nonsequential flow and the purely sequential flow. For example, a family of parts may share three or four operations in the same sequence. An area may be created to process sequentially a portion of the operations, while the remaining operations are performed nonsequentially in another area of the plant. This arrangement provides the benefit of sequential flow for part of the routing, greatly reducing the lead time for the part and, hence, reducing the average WIP.

Taken all in all then, this example is quite realistic both in terms of the types of actions JIT would cause to be taken in moving from a pure nonsequential process shop to a JIT shop and in terms of the magnitude of WIP and lead time reduction.

Uniform (Level) Flow

An objective of JIT is to have a smooth, relatively constant flow of work and material with a synchronized movement of small lots through the plant. However, a level load, day-in and day-out, is often difficult to achieve because of changing demand patterns, the mixed requirements that different level (smoothed) final assembly schedules place on upstream departments, and the necessity for freezing the final assembly and master production schedules for a month or so. Even when the load on the final assembly department is level, the corresponding load on the subassembly and parts fabrication departments may not be level. The following example from a major supplier of the automobile industry describes the objectives, benefits, and challenges of attaining uniform flow.

A major supplier of automobile subframes receives a schedule, usually frozen for at least a month, for three subassemblies. The subassemblies are manufactured (primarily welded) on a synchronized line that includes automatic welders, automatic movement, and a few manual operations. The representative data in Table 17-1 is used to describe the present operation, typical of many similar situations. At present the firm produces one lot of each of the three items each month. (They are working aggressively at implementing JIT concepts and have achieved substantial results in many parts of the plant.)

Table 17-1
Loading: One Lot Each per Month, 22 Working Days in Month

Part No.	Requirements for the Month	Production Plan	Planned Output
F-11	35,000	First 14 days @ 2,500/day	35,000
F-12	2,500	Day 15: 2,500	2,500
F-13	17,500	Last 7 days @ 2,500/day	17,500

Because the assembly plant uses each of these parts at virtually a uniform rate, the subassembly manufacturer is carrying a little less than one-half month's inventory of each. (The actual amount can be estimated using the information concerning production lot size inventories described in Chapter 6.) The level loading policy shown in Table 17-2 eliminates nearly all this inventory and the resulting expense.

Table 17-2
Uniform Loading: One Lot Each per Day, 22 Working Days in Month

Part No.	Requirements for the Month	Production Plan	Planned Output
F-11	35,000	1,591 each day	35,002
F-12	2,500	114 each day	2,508
F-13	17,500	795 each day	17,490

Changeover (setup) time usually is the impediment to producing the same amount of each item each day—even when only three items are involved. When it takes five hours to change production from one item to another, manufacturing each item each day would require three shifts to produce the output they now accomplish in one. Clearly the challenge is to improve the design of the part, the line, and the changeover process to reduce setup requirements. The first objective is to make the improvements necessary to halve the lot sizes, especially for F-11 and F-12. The beauty of JIT is that it points out the inefficiency of the present changeover requirements.

Pull Production Control

Push systems are the traditional method of controlling orders and material in a plant. When an order is completed at one work center it is sent (pushed) to the work center where the next operation will be performed. A push system assumes the next work center will be ready to process the order. In a pull system, the parts are not forwarded to the next operation until they are requested.

A pull system works well in a sequential flow process environment because the source of incoming material is always the same work center. As variations in the process flow increase, implementation of a pull system becomes more difficult. For example, if the material at a work center arrives from a limited number of work centers (say two or three) in a constant pattern, a pull system may work effectively. However, if the master production schedule and the resulting schedules for individual items call for the arrival of parts from many different work centers in an irregular pattern, a JIT pull system usually is not feasible. (In the next chapter, a different type of pull system that pulls materials from several locations to a critical control point is described.)

Many different methods may be used in a pull system to authorize a supplying work center to send parts. Returning empty containers is a common method; other methods include cards and tokens of various types. Another method requires the supplying department to observe the status of inventory in the receiving department and to forward material whenever the incoming material in the receiving department is reduced to a specified level. Using this method, the receiving department has specific shelves or locations on the shop floor that are designated for incoming material and are clearly visible to the supplying department. Thus, empty shelves or empty floor spaces authorize the movement of material.

The objectives of a pull system are to:

A. Synchronize the movement of material throughout the manufacturing and distribution system at the rate of withdrawal of material from the system.
B. Limit the total inventory in the system.
C. Facilitate analysis, process improvements, and further reductions in inventory.

Because the Kanban pull system of Toyota is the best known pull system, pull systems are sometimes called Kanban systems.

Let's consider an example of a simple pull system that exists between a department manufacturing components and the assembly line it feeds. Standard containers, each holding 10 items, are used to move components to the final assembly line. As the last of 10 components in a container is used, the container is returned to the parts fabrication department where its arrival authorizes the fabrication of another 10 components. On completion of the 10 components, the container is sent immediately to the assembly department. The advantages of this type of system are apparent. The upstream (supplying) department cannot flood the assembly department with unneeded parts. Furthermore, if the need at the assembly department increases, it becomes apparent immediately to the supplying department because the containers are returned sooner and at a faster rate.

The number of containers required for the system to function properly between two departments depends on the demand rate (the production rate of the assembly line in this case), the movement time between the two departments, the time the container waits to be moved, and the processing time. This relationship is represented by the following model.

$$N \geq \frac{D(M + P)(1.0 + S)}{Q}$$

where N = an integer, the number of movement cards (containers) required
   D = demand per hour (the rate at which the user department requires the parts)
   M = average wait time (wait time includes the processing time at the user department) and move time required. Thus, M is the total round trip time from the source (parts producing work center) to the user (assembly line) and back.
   P = average setup, run, and inspection time required to manufacture the parts in a container
   S = the safety factor, expressed as a percentage to compensate for varying rates of production and the efficiency of the producing department
   Q = quantity of parts held by each container

In this example the demand rate of the assembly department is 20 parts per hour; the move time is 15 minutes (0.25 hours); the assembly time is 30 minutes (0.50 hours); the total processing time for a container of parts in the parts fabrication department is 24 minutes (0.40 hours); the safety factor is 0.05; and there are 10 parts in each container. The number of cards is then calculated as follows:

$$N = \frac{20(0.75 + 0.40)(1.0 + 0.05)}{10}$$
$$= 2.415 \text{ or } 3 \text{ containers}$$

A Gantt chart analysis of the movement of containers in this situation will reveal that three containers is the minimum that can be used to keep the assembly department operating at all times. This is based on the containers not being returned until all the incoming parts have been used in the assembly process. Since the safety factor used to estimate the number of Kanbans cannot be determined with precision, in reality the number of Kanbans are determined by trial and error.

HUMAN RESOURCE MANAGEMENT

If there is a single key to attaining JIT objectives, it is a genuine respect for fellow human beings, for their aspirations, capabilities, and integrity. This requirement is the foundation of the recommendations concerning the treatment of customers, employees, and suppliers.

It is not surprising that changes in this area present the greatest challenges to Western companies. This is especially true for companies in which the work force and management have a long-standing adversarial relationship. Adopting JIT requires that all personnel—management, staff, and labor—must perceive changes as enhancing their personal goals as well as the goals of the organization. Employees must be confidant that improvements will not jeopardize their employment and that they will share in the resulting benefits.

The following are critical in winning the trust, participation, and wholehearted support of all employees:

A.   Employees must be convinced that the improvements they suggest will not result in their unemployment.
B.   Orientation, education, and training programs must exist so that employees understand the objectives and policies of the company and the rationale of related programs. Furthermore, they must be given the opportunity to increase their skills and to participate more fully in the improvement activities.
C.   Employees must be given more responsibility as decision making is driven downward in the organizational structure.
D.   Formal procedures must be developed for tapping the experience and knowledge of all employees through improvement suggestions. A system must exist for evaluating suggestions quickly and rewarding them fairly.
E.   Employees must be united, team spirit must be developed, and performance evaluations and rewards must be based on the performance of functional groups and the whole organization. In many cases this requires the development of a new organizational culture. Developing a new and pervasive culture takes commitment, leadership, patience, and time.

Companies with seasonal demand and a tradition of seasonal production and layoffs face a substantial challenge. Developing a flexible work force capable of performing equipment and plant maintenance during normally dormant demand periods can reduce the need for layoffs. Dormant periods can also be profitably used for employee education and training. The Sunnen Corporation of St. Louis has followed this approach successfully for many decades.

Quality circle programs, productivity improvement programs, and other similar programs have been used successfully by many companies. Such programs have a twofold effect. First, they generate cost savings and profit improvements. Equally important, they go a long way in convincing employees that management does value employee ideas and competence. These programs, combined with opportunities for skill development, are an indication of an organization's true respect for its employees. Most employees respond positively when they perceive themselves as being treated as important in a company's operation. A few isolated and fragmented projects have little value; a continuing and ever-present management attitude supporting teamwork and employee participation can work wonders. Case studies of JIT implementations are contained in Crawford, Cox, Blackstone (1988) and Sepehri (1986).

PURCHASING AND SUPPLIERS

The relationship between purchaser and supplier often has been one of mutual suspicion. The phrase *caveat emptor* (buyer beware) was the watchword of the purchaser. On the other hand, suppliers were often treated unfairly. For example, a supplier might provide excellent products on time and at a reasonable cost only to lose the next order due to a 10 cent lower bid by a competitor.

Under JIT, emphasis is on developing long-term relationships with suppliers. The relationship is based on mutual trust with quality the main objective. The supplier, and the supplier's supplier, are viewed as links in the industrial chain meeting the needs of the customer. If any link fails to perform satisfactorily, the final product is unsatisfactory and the entire system fails. The objective is to reduce costs and increase quality and productivity by:

1. Involving the supplier in the product design effort in order to take advantage of the supplier's specific competencies
2. Reducing the number of suppliers and the continual bidding process
3. Increasing the technical support provided to suppliers
4. Providing the schedule of order releases in a time frame that encourages the supplier to commit resources to improving quality, delivery, and cost
5. Lowering costs through the increased learning curve effects that result from the long-term relationship
6. Increasing communications through electronic transmission of engineering changes and delivery schedules
7. Locating suppliers nearby to reduce average delivery times and their variance, to increase frequency of deliveries (daily if possible), and to reduce lot sizes

8. Aiding suppliers in establishing statistical process control to improve quality
9. Reducing inspection requirements as quality levels increase
10. Improving product design through the supplier's innovations that result from increased experience and commitment
11. Increasing detection and correction of defects through the supplier's frequent deliveries
12. Using standard containers and simplifying the count of incoming parts
13. Obtaining dollar volume discounts through larger purchase commitments

These improvements do not occur overnight or automatically; they result from consistent and painstaking analyses with a sprinkling of failures and false starts.

TOTAL QUALITY MANAGEMENT

The conventional wisdom concerning quality has been that as the quality of a product was increased, the cost of manufacturing it increased exponentially. This contention was debunked by Phil Crosby (1979) who is credited with the statement, "Quality is free." Dave Garwood (1988), among others, illustrates this graphically by what is known as the "Mount Fuji Effect." (See Figure 17-10.) According to this concept, the cost of quality increases up to a point, the top of the mountain, and then the net costs decrease dramatically—they go down the other side of the mountain—as the benefits of good quality exceed the costs. The point is that conventional wisdom overlooked both the costs of poor quality and the value of good quality, as given in Table 17-3.

Table 17-3

Costs of Poor Quality	Benefits of Good Quality
Scrap	Increased demand
Rework	Customers willing to pay more
Late deliveries	Increased production
Scheduling replacements	
Lower demand	
Customers willing to pay less	
Warranty costs	
Product liability costs	

Total quality management (TQM) differs from traditional quality control in a number of other important ways. They are:

A. Quality begins at the source, namely the product design, the design of the manufacturing process, and the supplier in the case of purchase parts.

Figure 17-10
Mt. Fuji Effect

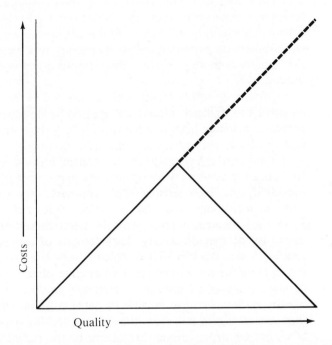

B.   Operators are responsible for the quality of their output. Inspection is
     not left until the batch is completed or the product completes the final
     operation.
C.   Statistical process control (SPC) is used to spot trends in output that
     presage tool wear or equipment requiring adjustment before unacceptable
     output is produced.
D.   A supplier's processes and its statistical process control system is evaluated
     before the supplier is certified as an approved supplier.
E.   Preventive maintenance, based on statistical analysis of past performance
     and output characteristics, is emphasized.

        Some of these approaches have existed in many companies for some time.
It is the synergistic effects of all of them combined with a corporate culture
giving top priority to quality that makes the difference. Certain methods including SPC, stop production authority, mistake-proofing, preventive maintenance, and fishbone analysis, are used to achieve the goals of TQM. These
terms are discussed briefly here and in greater detail in Chapter 18.
        Statistical process control (SPC) is based on a prior analysis that deter-
mines those process characteristics that are critical in producing a quality product. Measurement and analysis of these process characteristics in relationship
to their acceptable averages and variances alerts management to the likelihood
of out-of-control processing conditions before they occur.

Stop production authority (jidoka) permits an employee to stop the production process, an entire line if appropriate, when a quality defect occurs. The problem is analysed immediately, with the assistance of manufacturing and equipment engineers if necessary. The objective is to eliminate quality problems before they multiply and before additional work is performed at downstream work centers on parts that are already scrap. It is consistent with the attitude that quality is more important than output quantity and that bad parts are unacceptable.

Mistake-proofing (poka-yoke) is targeted at the process design stage in an attempt to eradicate mistakes. There may be limit switches that automatically prevent a machine from moving too far in a given direction or other devices that physically prevent the mistake from occurring.

Cause and effect analysis is an excellent method for analysing defects and for educating employees concerning the importance of different product and process design characteristics. This approach uses a schematic diagram resembling a fishbone, and thus, it is often called *fishbone analysis*. In Figure 17-11, the bone structure represents the hierarchical relationship of contributing causes to the specific quality characteristics of a release product. A *release product* is any label or sticker which is sold fixed to a carrier, but which is pulled from the carrier and stuck to another object. Preprinted price stickers or mailing labels are examples of release products. Quality control for the release product is critical because the label must have a weak enough adhesive (not very sticky) to pull from the carrier (backing paper) without tearing the label, yet be strong enough to adhere to the recipient object surface. This measure of stickiness is called the release value.

The fishbone diagram shows four principle contributors to defective release values: strength of the label paper, strength of the release adhesive, coating of the carrier paper, and surface of the recipient object (i.e., envelope or paper on which the label is placed). Once the quality problem has been isolated to one of the four principle contributors to defective release values, possible secondary reasons are pursued by the analysis. For example, if the strength of the release adhesive were found faulty, secondary reasons would be evaluated, including: humidity, temperature, speed of application rollers, chemical formulation of the adhesive, electron dryer mechanism, and consistency of the mixture. The fishbone diagram is very useful in quality diagnosis of complex processes because it encourages a logical analysis to sequentially isolate quality problems.

JIT AND COSTS

JIT can affect the bottom line in a variety of ways. Improvement in quality and delivery times can increase demand and, thus, revenue. Costs are also affected; the JIT philosophy contends that inventory reduction and increased quality reduce costs. Traditional cost accounting systems often make it difficult

Figure 17-11
Fishbone Diagram for Release Products

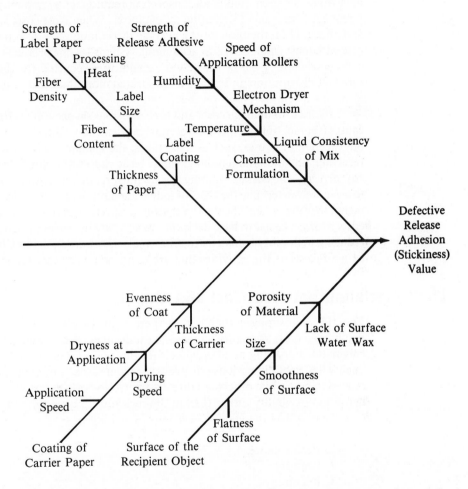

to measure the effects of changes except in very aggregate terms. One of the tenets of JIT is to account for these effects more accurately.

Cost Accounting Systems

Costs are a major factor in PIM decisions. Unfortunately, traditional cost accounting systems often do not tell the decision maker how much a specific decision will affect actual expenditures. This is due to overhead costs being hidden by the allocation methods. For example, overhead costs usually are allocated to departments (cost centers) rather than to activities, such as setup, and inspection and maintenance operations. In addition, allocation based on the material or direct labor required to manufacture an item ignores the fact that different items are in different stages of their life cycles. Thus, different items may have different manufacturing, engineering, and tooling costs, may have quite different quality and inspection requirements, and may require different marketing and distribution expenditures. When these costs are aggregated and allocated on the basis of the average direct labor cost of a part—as is the case with most traditional cost accounting systems—some products are allocated costs considerably below the actual expenditures required for their manufacture and distribution and others are allocated more than their true cost. Thus, decisions often are based on inaccurate information.

In order to manage costs and base decisions on accurate information, the causes (source) of the expenditures must be identified. Chapter 5 discussed various expenditure causes, such as setup times, shop and purchase order processing, receiving, and material handling. These basic causes of indirect costs are called *cost drivers*. The cost accounting system must report the cost of these activities to accurately determine the costs of indivividual products. Such reporting enables manufacturing management to treat setup, inspection, receiving, and transaction costs as direct costs, to base decisions on accurate information, and to focus on reducing high cost elements. An ABC analysis, as described in Chapter 5, can be used to select the activities that are appropriate for cost reduction studies.

The Correlation Between Cost and Quality

The JIT philosophy contends that there is an inverse relationship between quality and cost: as quality increases, cost declines. While some find this belief enigmatic, a growing number agree with this notion. Garvin (1988) notes that quality has eight dimensions. He posits that some aspects of quality are inversely related to cost while others are directly related to cost. People disagree in their definition of quality rather than in the relationship between cost and quality.

Garvin lists the eight dimensions of quality as:

1. Performance
2. Features
3. Reliability
4. Conformance (to specifications)
5. Durability
6. Serviceability
7. Aesthetics
8. Perceived quality

Garvin found empirical evidence that reliability and conformance are inversely related to cost. He found no empirical evidence supporting either an inverse or a direct relationship between cost and any of the other six quality dimensions. Garvin argues that the Japanese (JIT) viewpoint arises from a strong emphasis on reliability and conformance in defining quality.

Reliability—the mean time to first failure (and for repairable items, the mean time between failures)—heavily determines warranty cost and product liability cost. Conformance is the inverse of scrap and rework percent, a measure of "doing it right the first time." It is not surprising that Garvin found evidence supporting inverse relationships between cost and reliability and between cost and conformance.

However, Garvin's thesis that the inverse relationship between cost and quality extends only to reliability and conformance ignores the JIT emphasis on designing for ease of manufacture. Designing for ease of manufacture is intended to produce a high quality, low cost product by (1) reducing options and (2) avoiding requirements beyond the capability of available equipment.

Reducing the number of options reduces cost by reducing inventory. For this strategy to work, the model choices must each please a large number of consumers. Pleasing consumers requires listening carefully—a Japanese design engineer spends much more time with customers than does an American designer. Once the most popular options have been determined, they can be made standard features at a much lower cost than the cost of providing for each as options. The Toyota Cressida at one time sold with a standard luxury package—leather seats, impressive sound system, maximum use of electronics, etc.—for thousands of dollars less than a comparably equipped American or German luxury car.

A very strong argument can be made that by designing for ease of manufacture, there can be an inverse relation between cost and features, aesthetics, and perceived quality. Because design influences durability, there may also be an inverse relationship between cost and durability (largely offset by a higher material cost to build in durability). Because only a few firms today truly design for ease of manufacture, it is not surprising that Garvin was unable to find empirical support for this relationship.

High quality, low cost items will be essential if a company is to compete in future world markets. These items require a strong emphasis on product design and manufacturing process design and a high degree of cooperation between product design and process design teams. The product design must emphasize performance, features, aesthetics, serviceability, durability, and perceived quality, while enabling inexpensive manufacture. The process design must emphasize conformance and, hence, reliability, durability, and perceived quality.

Low manufacturing cost also requires the realization of economies of scale-volume production. To achieve world class production volume requires worldwide markets. Unfortunately, many American firms do not emphasize export and lack the skills needed to customize products for foreign markets. Manufacturing cannot propel a company to world class status by itself—dramatic change is also required in marketing. But that's another topic.

PERFORMANCE MEASUREMENT

In a survey of JIT implementation to identify problems, Crawford, Blackstone, and Cox (1988) found that the largest single problem was failure to change to an appropriate performance measurement system before JIT was introduced to the shop floor. In a follow-up study, Crawford, Cox, and Blackstone (1988) identified appropriate JIT performance criteria as follows:

Raw Materials: Inventory dollar days, raw material stockouts, raw material reduction, vendor delivery, vendor quality

Equipment: Machine breakdowns, preventive maintenance, setup reduction

Facility: Space requirements

Employee: Morale, education and training acquired, labor effectiveness

End item: Cost of goods sold, customer service, schedule flexibility, inventory dollar days, inventory reduction, lead time, output per employee, scrap, rework

Transformation: Cycle efficiency, process improvement, lot-size reduction, material stockouts, WIP reduction

Most companies reported the use of relative measures rather than absolute measures, i.e., what mattered was the improvement and the trend, not the level that existed when the improvement process began. Most companies displayed results graphically in the work center area so that workers could take pride in their accomplishments.

Crawford, Cox, and Blackstone report the following performance measure system principles:

1. The performance measurement system should have multiple criteria.
2. The primary purpose of the performance measurement system should not be to reward or to punish.
3. Performance-to-schedule measures must use group, not individual, results.
4. Specific goals must be established for performance-to-schedule criteria and must be revised when met.
5. Specific goals are not necessary for inventory and quality criteria; improving trends are needed.
6. Performance measures must be understood by those who are being evaluated.
7. Performance data should be collected by the person being evaluated.
8. Graphs should be the primary reporting method.
9. Performance data should be available for constant review.
10. Schedule performance should be reported daily.
11. Inventory and quality performance should be reported monthly.
12. The performance system must include frequent performance review sessions.
13. Suppliers should be evaluated on quality and delivery.

IMPLEMENTATION

Implementation of JIT involves six phases: organization, education, evaluation, planning, execution, and review. A prerequisite to success is top management's long-term commitment. Employees quickly sense when management is half-hearted or not fully convinced of the ultimate benefits and will quickly relegate JIT to the burial grounds that hold many previous "panaceas of the month."

Organization

A broadly based steering committee should be formed with representation from purchasing, design and manufacturing engineering, manufacturing management, production control, industrial engineering, quality control, maintenance, and operations. The leader should be the champion of change and have an under-standing of the requirements for, and preferably some experience in, implement-ing change. The members should possess a certain discontent with the present yet be able to express this discontent and support change in a constructive manner. In addition, including a facilitator, often someone from outside the firm, aids in providing a broader frame of reference and overcoming those blind spots that naturally develop in most firms due to long-accepted ways of operating.

Education

The development of knowledge, understanding, confidence, and trust through-out the organization begins in the organization phase and is solidified in the education phase. Although education is continual in a JIT mode of operation, it is most intense and crucial in the beginning. It should begin with top manage-ment and cover virtually everyone in the organization. JIT must be understood and appreciated throughout the organization to achieve its full benefits. Nothing will work on the plant floor unless the workers are convinced of its benefits; and it will not reach the plant floor if staff and middle level managers do not support it. First, the education should cover the basic objectives and philosophy of JIT and its importance to all employees (their livelihood and development). It should stress that JIT is not a "microwave" program; benefits do not come overnight. Patience is required. It is an evolution not a revolution, and not all changes will be success stories. Education should also encompass basic concepts concerning such areas as the importance of the customer, quality, the cost of inventory, lead time, and productivity.

After the initial education program, specific and focused education train-ing programs concerning topics such as setup reduction, working with suppliers, statistical process control, and group technology are appropriate.

Evaluation and Assessment

Because organizations have different environments and are at different stages in developing their manufacturing activities, each should make a thorough assessment of its environment, decide on its strategic objectives relative to JIT, and evaluate its present status relative to the major operating objectives of JIT. Assessment of the present status is a prerequisite for deciding the priority of proposed improvement activities. Ken McGuire (1984) recommends that three teams perform independent assessments. The reconciliation of these assessments then provides a consensus final assessment that serves as a basis for selecting initial JIT activities.

Figure 17-12 is an adaptation of the chart McGuire proposes for rating and ranking areas for improvement. It assesses each area on the basis of its importance relative to the success of the firm, the current operating effectiveness of the area, the resources required to improve it substantially, and the time required to complete the improvement. This method of assessment is similar to that often used in establishing the priority of information system improvement projects. Clearly, an area that is critical to the success of the firm, whose present performance is inadequate, and which can be improved with little investment and in a relatively short time would likely be attacked first. Although it would seem that there are few such opportunitites, there are usually at least a few substantial and visible improvements that can be made. For example, Miller Fluid Power of Bensonville, Illinois, reorganized the assembly area for one of its product lines by dedicating specific lines to assemblies that require many common parts and that use the same assembly fixtures and by stocking the appropriate parts next to each line. These changes in layout, allocation of lines, and stocking locations reduced lead time from approximately two weeks to one day, reduced inventory levels, and released space for other uses. On the other hand, A. O. Smith in Granite City has heavy presses that cannot be relocated easily. In this case, provisions were made for rapid movement of smaller transfer batches to the next manufacturing operation. Manufacturing cells with cross training of workers were established in other areas. The point is that each firm must work within the constraints and opportunities of its environment.

Outside assistance is often very helpful in providing perspective and objectivity and in gaining a consensus concerning the present status and the priority of different potential actions. The objective is to begin with low risk, high yield tasks—those that have a high probability of success.

The Plan

The initial plan begins by obtaining the commitment of top management and is followed closely by the introductory education programs for the entire work force. Different programs may be appropriate for different groups. Evaluation and assessment provide the basis for developing the plan for the initial improvement activities.

A strong case can be made for stressing quality improvement early in a JIT program (Hall 1983). An analysis of quality requires a study of the customers' requirements. Improved quality inherently reduces inventory requirements,

Figure 17-12
JIT Assessment Process, Rating and Ranking of Critical Areas

Criterion

1. Critical Issue to Business Success in JIT . . . . Rate A, B, C, D

2. Current Status and Operating Condition . . . . Rank 1-10

3. Resources Required to Improve Significantly . . . . Rate A, B, C, D

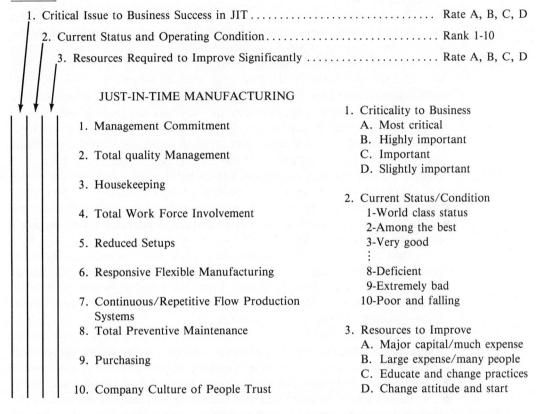

JUST-IN-TIME MANUFACTURING

1. Management Commitment

2. Total quality Management

3. Housekeeping

4. Total Work Force Involvement

5. Reduced Setups

6. Responsive Flexible Manufacturing

7. Continuous/Repetitive Flow Production Systems

8. Total Preventive Maintenance

9. Purchasing

10. Company Culture of People Trust

1. Criticality to Business
   A. Most critical
   B. Highly important
   C. Important
   D. Slightly important

2. Current Status/Condition
   1-World class status
   2-Among the best
   3-Very good
   ⋮
   8-Deficient
   9-Extremely bad
   10-Poor and falling

3. Resources to Improve
   A. Major capital/much expense
   B. Large expense/many people
   C. Educate and change practices
   D. Change attitude and start

reduces scheduling problems, and improves personnel and equipment capability. Good housekeeping should be considered a prerequisite, and improvements should be initiated post haste, if required.

Most people respond to performance measures: Students want to know what the exam will cover, and production personnel act to achieve good scores on their performance measures. Early replacement of inappropriate performance measures is essential. For example, if a manager's performance is measured by output volume alone rather than by completion of the right products (orders) at the right time, the manager will be hard pressed to take JIT seriously. Department heads and workers, who for years have been encouraged to keep equipment utilization high and output volume high and have been measured on that basis, will continue to produce unneeded parts at nonbottleneck work centers unless their performance is measured in terms of improved processes, reduced setup times, reduced work in process, reduced lead times, improved quality, and an improving percentage of deliveries right on schedule.

RESULTS

The following results have been reported by American companies applying JIT to American plants:

The Apple Macintosh factory, 18 months into JIT, reported that rejects were reduced from 28 percent to 1 percent, inventory turns were twice the industry average, space requirements were reduced 35 percent, labor productivity was increased 60 percent (Sepehri 1986).

Omark Industries, in the first year, reduced inventory 25 percent ($20 million), increased productivity 30 percent, reduced lot sizes, shortened lead times, and improved quality. Later into the program, raw material was reduced 95 percent and WIP 96 percent. In the case of WIP, the reduction was from 100,000 pieces on the floor at any given time to 4,000 pieces, with an eventual goal of 1,000. The consequences of this reduction to material scheduling and control are that material can be much more tightly controlled. (Sepehri 1986)

Harley-Davidson reports a 50 percent inventory reduction, a 50 percent reduction in scrap and rework, a 32 percent productivity increase, an increase in inventory turns from 5 to 17, and a decrease in warranty claims despite a longer warranty period (Sepehri 1986).

IBM's plant in Raleigh, North Carolina, which makes terminals for mainframe computers, while not reporting numeric results did report that manufacturing costs were greatly reduced, inventory turns increased, mean time between failures was reduced, and cycle time from product inception to customer availability was reduced (Sepehri 1986).

JIT's applicability is not limited to discrete parts manufacturers or to large companies. ChemLink, a small petroleum processor, reports that inventory was reduced by 21 percent, sales grew by 9 percent, obsolete inventory was reduced by 30 percent, and transportation cost was reduced 8 percent (Crane 1989).

Hay (1988) estimates the range of improvement possible for a western JIT implementer to be about 83 to 92 percent reduction of lead time, 5 to 50 percent reduction of direct labor, 21 to 60 percent reduction of indirect labor, 26 to 63 percent reduction in the cost of poor quality, 6 to 45 percent decrease in purchased material costs, 35 to 73 percent reduction in purchased materials, 70 to 89 percent reduction in work in process, 0 to 90 percent reduction in finished goods inventory, 75 to 94 percent reduction in setup time, and 39 to 80 percent reduction in space requirements.

SUMMARY

JIT presentations often employ the analogy of a stream when describing proper inventory management. Well managed systems achieve a flow of inventory from raw material to the customer like a smooth river, unimpeded by shoals of scrap or machine breakdown or other problems. This concept did not originate with the Japanese; Henry Ford's River Rouge plant regularly converted iron ore into a Model T in four days. However, in recent years, especially the 1970s,

American business has not improved its manufacturing capability quickly enough to maintain a competitive position in cost or quality or market responsiveness or flexibility.

In 1983 APICS began a zero inventory crusade—strongly advocating JIT. Firms such as GM, Ford, Chrysler, Bendix, Harley-Davidson, IBM, Hewlett-Packard, AT&T, and others began the journey even earlier. There has been much progress on regaining competitiveness in recent years, as evidenced by some of the successes presented in the previous section. This progress has been achieved by emphasizing continuous improvement, reduced inventories, expanded roles for hourly workers, fewer levels of management, longer term relationships with customers and suppliers, and an emphasis on providing value to the customer. Many American firms are once again at or near world class status. We should remember, however, that complacency is the principle barrier to maintaining world class status. We must adopt the philosophy of Kaizen, continuous improvement. The Japanese underscore the urgency of maintaining competitiveness with a phrase taught to every schoolchild, "Export or Die!" In yesterday's world, export or die was a truism for any island economy. In today's global village, export or die is a truism for all economies.

EXERCISES

1. Describe the benefits of JIT for the operating employee.

2. Name and describe the JIT methods that have been implemented in an organization with which you are familiar.

3. The Ajax Company supplies plastic components, including agitators, to a major manufacturer of automatic washing machines—the type found in most homes. They have agreed that they will both operate using a JIT approach. Specify what the manufacturer of washing machines must do to facilitate implementation of JIT at the components manufacturer.

4. Planners have an order for which they are considering operation overlapping to reduce the manufacturing lead time (MLT). The following data are available (see Chapter 14):

   Lot size = 500 units
   Processing time, Operation A = 8 minutes
   Processing time, Operation B = 6 minutes
   Minimum transit time, Operation A to Operation B = 40 minutes
   Setup time, Operation B = 1.5 hours
   Assume parts will be processed immediately on Operation B.

   a. If Operation B cannot be set up until the parts arrive, what is the minimum size of the transfer lot that should be run on Operation A before moving parts to B? The goal is that there be no idle time on Operation B.

b. What is the minimum size of the sublot if Operation B can be set up prior to the arrival of parts?

5. Calculate the VAE for each of the situations described in Exercise 4, beginning with no overlapping.

6. Use the information in Exercise 4 to answer the following.
   a. Disregarding queue time, how much time will be removed from the MLT in each of the cases in Exercise 4?
   b. If the queue time at Operation B is normally 16 hours, how much total time will be removed from the MLT in each of the cases in Exercise 4?

7. Calculate the VAE for each of the situations described in Exercise 6.

8. A third operation, C, follows Operations A and B in Exercise 4. The following data concern Operation C:

Processing time = 4 minutes
Setup time = 0.8 hours
Minimum transit time, Operation B to Operation C = 40 minutes

   a. If Operation C cannot be set up until the parts arrive and there is to be no idle time at Operation C, what is the minimum size of the sublot that should be run on Operation B before moving parts to Operation C?
   b. How much operation time will be removed from the MLT in this case?
   c. If Operation C processing time is 12 minutes and the planners desire to have no more than two sublots, what is the minimum size of the sublot they should run on Operation B before moving parts to Operation C?
   d. If Operation C is 12 minutes and it is immediately adjacent to Operation B (no transit of parts is required), how many parts must be processed in B before Operation C can begin?

9. Calculate the VAE for each of the situations described in Exercise 8.

10. A planner also is considering operation splitting (parallel scheduling) for the item described in Exercises 4 and 8. The data follow:

| Lot size = 500 units | | |
Operation	Setup Time (hours)	Operation Time (minutes)
A	1.0	8
B	1.5	6
C	0.8	4

   a. By how much is MLT reduced if each operation is split between two machines with no setup offset?
   b. By how much is MLT reduced if each operation is split between two machines if setups are offset?

11. Prepare a graphical analysis of the units in inventory for one month operating under the plan in (a) Table 17-1 and (b) Table 17-2.

12. Given the following costs, calculate the average value of the units in inventory for one month operating under the plan in (a) Table 17-1 and (b) Table 17-2.

Part	Cost
F-11	$125.00
F-12	148.00
F-13	127.00

13. Using the data in Exercises 11 and 12, calculate the annual inventory carrying cost savings if the company changes from operating per Table 17-1 to Table 17-2. The annual carrying cost rate is 0.30.

14. A small manufacturer produces hats for a branch of the U.S. military. The manufacturer contends that implementing JIT is not appropriate for this firm because it receives payment for material as soon as it arrives in the plant. Respond to this contention.

15. A company that has made considerable progress in reducing work in process and manufacturing lead time never calculates the number of move (kanban) cards to use. Instead, its practice is to start with more than enough cards and gradually reduce the number. What do you think of this approach?

16. A process has 12 operations. A manufacturing cell that will include Operations 3 through 9 is proposed. Two production planners are discussing the merit of the proposal. One contends that it does not make much sense to reduce lead time in only part of the process. A colleague believes that progress must be made a step at a time.
   a. Take and justify a position on this matter.
   b. Describe the factors that would influence the appropriate decision in a given situation.

SELECTED READINGS

Ansari, A., and Jim Heckel. "JIT Purchasing: Impact of Freight and Inventory Costs." *Journal of Purchasing and Materials Management* (Summer 1987): 24.

Ansari, A., and Batoul Modarress. "Just-in-Time Purchasing: Problems and Solutions." *Journal of Purchasing and Materials Management* (Summer 1986): 11.

Celley, Albert F., William H. Clegg, Arthur W. Smith, and Mark A. Vonderembse. "Implementation of JIT in the United States." *Journal of Purchasing and Materials Management* (Winter 1986): 9.

Conway, Richard, William L. Maxwell, John O. McClain, and Steven L. Worona. *User's Guide to XCELL + Factory Modeling System*. Redwood City, CA: The Scientific Press, 1987.

Crane, Daniel. "Organizing and Implementing TQC/JIT in a Process Industry: A Case Study." *JIT Seminar Proceedings*. Falls Church, VA: American Production and Inventory Control Society, 1989.

Crawford, Karlene M., John H. Blackstone, Jr., and James F. Cox. "A Study of JIT Implementation and Operating Problems." *International Journal of Production Research* (1988).

Crawford, Karlene M., James F. Cox, and John H. Blackstone, Jr. *Performance Measurement Systems and the JIT Philosophy: Principles and Cases*. Falls Church, VA: American Production and Inventory Control Society, 1988.

Crosby, Philip B. *Quality is Free: The Art of Making Quality Certain*. New York: McGraw-Hill Book Co., 1979.

Deming, W. Edwards. "The Roots of Quality Control in Japan: An Interview with W. Edwards Deming." *Pacific Basin Quarterly* (Spring/Summer 1985).

Dertouzos, Michael L., Richard K. Lester, Robert M. Solow, and the MIT Commission on Industrial Productivity. *Made In America: Regaining the Productive Edge*. Cambridge, MA: The MIT Press, 1989.

Dilworth, James D. *Information Systems for JIT Manufacturing*. Wheeling, IL: Association for Manufacturing Excellence, 1987.

Feigenbaum, A. V. *Total Quality Control: Engineering and Management*. New York: McGraw-Hill Book Co, 1961.

Garvin, David. *Managing Quality*. New York: Free Press, 1988.

Garwood, Dave, and Michael Bane. *A Jumpstart to World Class Performance*. Marietta, GA: Dogwood Publishing, 1988.

Gelb, Thomas A. "The Material as Needed Program at Harley-Davidson." *Proceedings 1985 Annual Conference*. Association for Manufacturing Excellence: 49-64.

Goddard, Walter, and Associates. *Just-in-Time: Surviving by Breaking Tradition*. Essex Junction, VT: Oliver Wight Publications Ltd., 1986.

Green, Donald R. "Direct Pegging, MRP/JIT Bridge." *P&IM Review* (April 1987).

Hall, Robert W. *Attaining Manufacturing Excellence*. Homewood, IL: Dow Jones-Irwin, 1987.

Hall, Robert W. "Measuring Progress: Management Essential." *Target* (Summer 1987): 5-13.

Hall, Robert W. *Zero Inventories*. Homewood, IL: Dow Jones-Irwin, 1983.

Hay, Edward J. *The Just-in-Time Breakthrough: Implementing the New Manufacturing Basics*. New York: John Wiley & Sons, Inc., 1988.

Imai, Masaaki. *Kaizen: The Key to Japan's Competitive Success*. New York: Random House Business Division, 1986.

Just-in-Time Seminar Proceedings July 24-26. Washington, DC: American Production and Inventory Control Society, 1989.

Just-in-Time Reprints. Revised Ed. Falls Church, VA: American Production and Inventory Control Society, 1989.

Masaracchia, Philip. "TQC—The 'Quality' Component of J-I-T." *P&IM Review* (April 1987): 44.

McGuire, Kenneth J. *Impressions From Our Most Worthy Competitor*. Falls Church, VA: American Production and Inventory Control Society, 1984.

O'Neal, Charles R. "The Buyer-Seller Linkage in a Just-in-Time Environment." *Journal of Purchasing and Materials Management* (Spring 1987): 7.

Ouchi, William G. "Theory Z: An Elaboration of Methodology and Findings." *Journal of Contemporary Business* II, no. 2: 27-41.

Pascale, Richard T., and Anthony G. Athos. *The Art of Japanese Management*. New York: Simon & Schuster, Inc., 1981.

Peters, Thomas J. *Thriving on Chaos*. New York: Harper & Row, Publishers, Inc., 1987.

Peters, Thomas J., and Robert H. Waterman. *In Search of Excellence*. New York: Harper & Row, Publishers, Inc., 1982.

Powell, Cash. "Refocusing Materials Management with JIT." *APICS 31st Annual Conference Proceedings* (1988): 509-513.

Powell, Cash. "Workshop Report: Cincinnati Milacron-Electronics System Division." *Target* (Summer 1987): 28-33.

Quinlan, J. "Just-in-Time at the Tractor Works." *Material Handling Engineering* (June 1982): 62-65.

Riopel, Robert J. "JIT: Evolutionary Revolution." *Manufacturing Systems* (July 1986): 44.

Rohan, Thomas M. "The Empire Strikes Back." *Industry Week* (April 15, 1985): 40-48.

Sandras, William A., Jr. "JIT/TQC Changes in Thinking for Information Systems." *P&IM Review* (April 1987): 33.

Schonberger, Richard J. *Japanese Manufacturing Techniques: Nine Hidden Lessons in Simplicity*. New York: Free Press, 1982a.

Schonberger, Richard J. "Some Observations on the Advantages and Implementation Issues of Just-in-Time Production Systems." *Journal of Operations Management* 3, no. 1, (November 1982b): 5.

Schonberger, Richard J. *World Class Manufacturing Casebook: Implementing JIT and TQC*. New York: Free Press, 1987.

Sepehri, Mehran. *Just-in-Time, Not Just in Japan: Case Studies of American Pioneers in JIT Implementation*. Falls Church, VA: American Production and Inventory Control Society, 1986.

Shingo, Shigeo. *A Revolution in Manufacturing: The SMED System*. Cambridge, MA: Productivity Press, 1985.

Shingo, Shigeo. *Non-Stock Production: The Shingo System for Continuous Improvement*. Cambridge, MA: Productivity Press, 1988.

Shingo, Shigeo. *Zero Quality Control: Source Inspection and the Poka-yoke System*. Cambridge, MA: Productivity Press, 1986.

Taguchi, Genichi. *Introduction to Quality Engineering: Designing Quality into Products and Processes*. White Plains, NY: Asian Productivity Organization, 1986.

Wildemann, Horst. "JIT Progress in West Germany." *Target* (Summer 1987): 23-27.

Wordsworth, Albert G. "Survival." *Proceedings 1985 Annual Conference*. Association for Manufacturing Excellence: 49-64.

APPENDIX 17A
GEMS SIMULATION RESULTS

This appendix presents the GEneralized Manufacturing Simulator (GEMS) output report for Example 2. The simulation was executed for 144,000 minutes with statistical arrays cleared and statistics collected after 14,400 minutes, at which point steady state was assumed. The simulation was replicated 30 times.

Shown below are the actual statistics furnished by GEMS, except for a preamble that shows date, time, length of simulation, and whether the simulation was completed or was terminated abnormally.

```
**** TIME AND ASSOCIATED NETWORK COST STATISTICS ****
```

BOX NUM	NAME	STAT TYPE	NO. OF OBS.	MEAN	STD.DEV	MIN.	MAX.
9	STOCK	INTV	19005	3232.849	840.536	2180.914	12638.870

The above results appear because we requested that each job be timed from leaving box 1 to entering box 9. The statistics were collected at box 9, STOCK, and they represent an interval statistic. There were 19,005 jobs processed in total in the 30 replications. These jobs had a mean time in the shop of 3,232.849 minutes with a standard deviation of 840.536 minutes. The minimum time in the shop was 2,180.914 minutes and the maximum time in the shop was 12,638.870 minutes. The inspection box (box 8) sends a rejected lot back to box 2; box 2 sends a replacement to the job shop; the time this job entered the shop is retained on the replacement batch. The history of the job achieving the maximum time was not captured in these results, but the job was probably rejected three times. The expected number of jobs rejected three times given 19,005 jobs completed in the shop is $19,005 \times 0.043 = 1.22$.

GEMS provides a wealth of information about each queue box when multiple replications of a model are performed. The MEAN column provides

```
**** QUEUE BOX STATISTICS ****

QUE   STAT. TYPE          MEAN    STD.DEV    MIN.       MAX.      TIME
NUM                                         MEAN       MEAN      SHOT

      WORK CENTER A
+                                           NUMBER OF SERVERS=      4
3     NUMB BUSY SERVER    2.848     .073    2.665      2.991
3     QUEUE LENGTH         .615     .144     .369       .960
3     WAITING TIME      120.537     .000   78.660    183.306
3     BUSY %             96.959     .831   95.066     98.237
3     ENTITIES PASSED   659.533   16.490  621.000    693.000
3     MAX QUEUE LENGTH    7.000    1.661    5.000     12.000
      FINAL STATUS:  Q-LENGTH       0   IDLE SERVERS      0
```

results averaged over the 30 replications. Queue number 3, above, represents Work Center A. Work Center A averaged 2.848 workers busy, the average queue waiting to be worked on was 0.615, the average waiting time was 120+ minutes. At least one of the workers was busy 96.959 percent of the time. Each replication averaged 659.533 batches. The longest queue waiting to be worked on during any one replication averaged 7 batches. Note that $659.533 \times 30 =$ 19,785.99 batches, representing 19,005 that passed and 781 that were rejected or were still in process when the simulation ended. 19,005 times 4 percent reject yields 760, so the number of rejects is right on target (some of the 781 were jobs not completed at the end rather than rejects). The three columns to the right of the column labeled MEAN represent the standard deviation between the 30 replications, the minimum value obtained for an entire replication among the 30, and the maximum value obtained for an entire replication among the 30. Thus, the number of busy servers averaged 2.848 with a standard deviation of 0.073. The smallest value observed for an entire replication was 2.665, the largest 2.991. To obtain a confidence interval estimate of the mean, one needs the standard error (the standard deviation divided by the square root of the sample size). In this case the standard error of estimate would be 0.0133. The FINAL STATUS line at the bottom of each queue statistic set gives the number of lots waiting to be processed when the last replication completed and the number of busy servers at the end of the last replication.

18

TOTAL QUALITY CONTROL AND TOTAL PREVENTIVE MAINTENANCE

Two prerequisites to Just-in-Time system implementation are high process yields and infrequent machine breakdowns. In a Just-in-Time system, the inventory buffer that protects each activity from quality and performance problems of related activities is removed. Each station, therefore, becomes quite sensitive to fluctuations that occur at other stations. A few rejected parts or a breakdown of moderate duration can cause a domino effect that leads to the shutting down of many work stations. It is therefore imperative that excellent quality control and equipment maintenance be implemented before the inventory buffer is reduced. The efforts to improve quality and machine reliability often are called *total quality control* (TQC) and *total preventive maintenance* (TPM). The names reflect the concept that quality and productivity are everybody's business.

Quality is a very difficult concept to define. What comes to mind when your hear the phrase "quality automobile"? How about "good, reliable transportation"? Did you picture a Cadillac, a Rolls Royce, or a Mazerati for the first phrase and something like a 15-year-old Ford pickup, a 25-year-old Volkswagen, or a 10-year-old Honda Civic for the second? Do your expectations concerning the quality of an item vary with its price? Quality is often defined as *fitness for use*, that is, the degree to which an item performs as a consumer expects it to perform. Thus, one difficulty in defining quality is the subjective nature of consumer expectations. Once the performance expectations of a consumer are understood, there remains the difficulty of translating these expectations into product characteristics.

Figure 18-1 describes fitness for use in terms of a set of measurable parameters. On a gross level, quality may be measured by the quality of the product design, the quality of component conformance to design specifications, the quality of integration of components into an assembly, the availability of

Figure 18-1
Quality Parameters

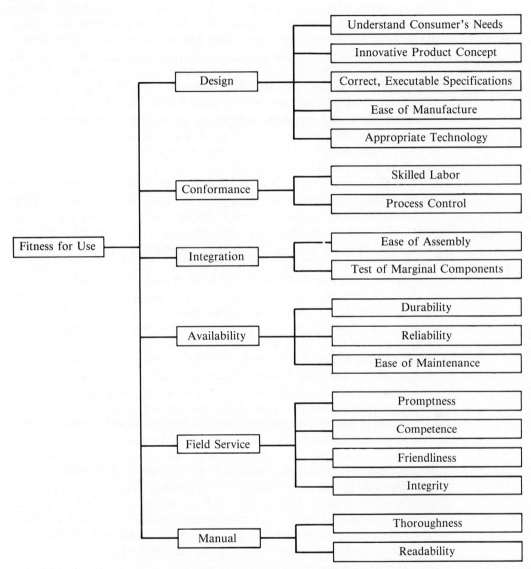

Modified from Juran, Joseph M., ed., *Quality Control Handbook*, Figure 2-1.

the product over time after purchase, the quality of the field service provided to support and maintain the product, and the quality of the owner's manual provided to assist the consumer in assembly or use of the product.

In this chapter, we focus on quality control as it affects the manufacturing process. That is, we are primarily interested in issues of conformance and integration, on how well the product design can be translated into physical reality. A prerequisite of excellent manufacturing quality is designing for ease of manufacture. That is, the product designer must understand the capabilities and limitations of his or her company's machines and personnel; the product design must not require capabilities that the manufacturing facility lacks.

To manufacture components that conform to design specifications sometimes requires the purchase of new technology. For example, as integrated circuits get smaller and smaller, their manufacture is shifting from a technology based on photography to one based on the use of lasers. The older technology lacks the precision required by the smaller circuits. Thus, while design for current capabilities is an important consideration, the ability to produce products that have competitive performance characteristics is a more important consideration.

As the manufacturing process becomes increasingly complex, a greater degree of skill is required from operators. The ability to hire, train, and retain skilled workers is an important aspect of quality. But good machines and good people alone will not guarantee the conformance of products to design specifications. Later in the chapter we discuss two techniques to control conformance: statistical process control and mistake-proofing.

A frequently overlooked aspect of product quality is product integration, that is, how well the components function as an assembly. For example, consider the components that go into an automobile's engine and transmission. Assume that when the engine is bored, the cylinders are, by chance, as large as they can be and still be within specifications. Assume further that the pistons are also barely within specifications, but the pistons are as small as they can be and still be within specifications. Because of slightly oversized cylinders and undersized pistons, there will be an excessive escape of energy along the perimeter of the piston. Therefore, the engine will not deliver quite as much power as it is rated to deliver. Now suppose that two interacting gears within the transmission are barely within specifications, with one being as large as possible and one as small as possible, but both still within specifications. As a result of imperfect mesh, a small decrease in the energy transmitted to the wheels occurs. Will the resulting automobile satisfy the customer in its ability to climb a steep hill when fully loaded? How many combinations such as this exist within a complex assembly? How many combinations need to be tested to determine how well the components integrate into a properly functioning assembly? The Taguchi method provides a series of experimental designs that permit such questions to be answered.

Designing for ease of maintenance is almost as important for products with long life spans as is designing for ease of manufacture. Some automobiles have repair and maintenance costs that are much higher than the norm because a part is particularly difficult to remove and/or install. For products that normally are not repaired, ease of maintenance is not as important as durability—the length of time the product will survive under use. Both ease of maintenance and durability are important aspects of availability—the extent to which the product is available for the customer's use over its expected life span. The lonely Maytag repairman who appeared in television commercials was a good example of how the availability aspect of quality can be a major competitive weapon for a manufacturer.

For products that must be serviced, the quality of the field service is an important aspect of quality. The degree of friendliness, promptness, competence, and integrity of field service personnel has a major impact on perceived product quality and on the loyalty of customers to a particular manufacturer.

Finally, perhaps the most overlooked aspect of quality is the manual that accompanies the product. Have you ever tried to learn a new computer software package using the manual provided? Were you pleased or disappointed with the manual? How did your reaction to the manual influence your perception of product quality?

During the 1950s, statistically based methods of quality control gained a wide popularity. In the late 1950s, a countermovement emphasized nonstatistical approaches such as designing for ease of manufacture and 100 percent inspection. This countermovement was given the name *total quality control* by Feigenbaum (1961). As the name implies, the total quality control movement demands that quality be an aspect of all parts of the design, manufacture, distribution, and field service process. The total quality control concept is illustrated in Figure 18-2. Total quality control, as previously stated, is an important part of the Just-in-Time philosophy.

In this chapter we review the Just-in-Time philosophy as it relates to quality and maintenance. We begin by contrasting the Just-in-Time viewpoint with the techniques traditionally employed in western industrial companies. Next we look briefly at the contributions of quality experts such as Shewhart, Deming, Juran, Dodge, Crosby, Ishikawa, Taguchi, and Shingo. Finally, we look at preventive maintenance comments from various authorities. We end the chapter with a brief discussion of total preventive maintenance.

TRADITIONAL VERSUS JUST-IN-TIME APPROACHES TO QUALITY

The traditional approach to quality control, used in Japan until the 1950s and in the United States until the 1980s, is to determine an "optimal" level of inspection effort. This optimization is based on the trade-off between the cost of inspection and the cost of defects, as illustrated in Figure 18-3. The JIT approach considers this trade-off thinking to be shortsighted. The trade-off representation presents a static view of product quality. The Just-in-Time philosophy requires continuous improvement. One should identify and correct the causes of defective units to prevent their recurrence. By tracing the chain of cause and effect and finding a correctable cause, one continually increases the fraction of units built right the first time. The Just-in-Time philosophy insists on a goal of zero defects. As we eliminate the causes of defects, we

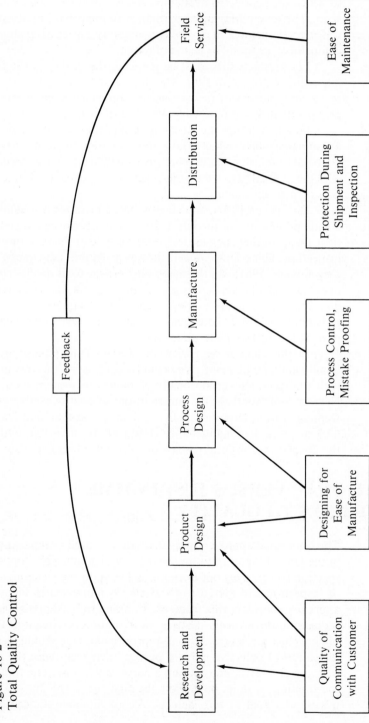

Figure 18-2
Total Quality Control

reduce the total cost of quality. In Philip Crosby's book *Quality is Free* (1979), he notes that quality not only is free, it pays dividends by cutting scrap, rework, and warranty costs. The best Japanese, American, and European firms now use TQC.

Figure 18-3
Costs of Inspection Effort

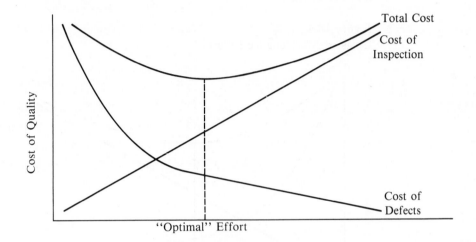

Frequency of Inspection

TRADITIONAL VERSUS JUST-IN-TIME APPROACHES TO MAINTENANCE

The traditional approach to preventive maintenance was to accept some minimum level of breakdowns as optimal, as illustrated in Figure 18-4. The trade-off this time is between the cost of performing the preventive maintenance and the cost of breakdown maintenance, i.e., the cost of repairing the broken machine. The Just-in-Time approach notes that this trade-off thinking does not properly consider how the effect of a breakdown interacts with production as a whole. For example, if a worker is trained to perform his or her own preventive maintenance, that maintenance often can be performed during periods when the worker otherwise would be idle. On the other hand, a breakdown occurs when the machine is operating, which is by definition a time when the machine should be working. Therefore, the true cost of preventive maintenance is difficult to estimate. Furthermore, when a machine breaks down, it sometimes is down for a long time. Unless a large buffer of material is provided to decouple related work stations, a breakdown at one station soon affects several. The extent to which a breakdown at one station affects other stations is a function of the level of work in the shop, the distribution of breakdown times, and the buffer policy. Work levels change with demand shifts, breakdown distributions change with machine age and treatment, and buffer policies change occasionally. Thus, the determination of the effect of a breakdown on all other stations is difficult. Finally, if the ultimate cause of a breakdown is sought and corrected, the frequency of breakdown can be dramatically reduced. Just-in-Time aims to keep material moving; it views breakdown maintenance as being expensive, wasteful, and avoidable.

Figure 18-4
Costs of Maintenance Effort

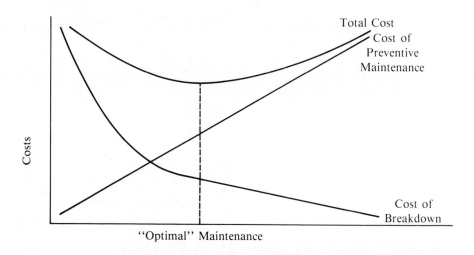

A second aspect of maintenance is the issue of when to replace a machine. The traditional western thought is that there comes a time when maintenance is too expensive and it is cheaper to buy a new machine. Shingo (1986) states that if a machine is maintained properly, it appreciates in value rather than depreciates. The increase in value comes from alterations made to the machine over time to customize it to the company's needs.

QUALITY DEFINED

Garvin (1984) lists five types of definitions of quality: the transcendent definition (quality is an ideal), the product-based definition (quality is based on a product attribute), the user-based definition (quality is fitness for use), the manufacturing based definition (quality is conformance to requirements), and the value-based definition (quality is bang for buck). Garvin (1987) ascribes the existence of multiple definitions to the fact that quality has eight attributes:

1. Performance
2. Features
3. Reliability
4. Conformance
5. Durability
6. Serviceability
7. Aesthetics
8. Perceived quality

Garvin (1984, 35) also notes that the debate about the cost of quality is a function of how quality is defined. If quality is defined in terms of features and performance, the product is likely to carry a large price and, as a result, a small market share. However, if the definition of quality is simply fitness for use, then of two products having the same price, the one with higher quality will sell more.

CONTRIBUTORS TO QUALITY CONTROL THEORY AND PRACTICE

In this section, we briefly profile the persons who are credited with significant contributions to the development of quality control theory and practice. The techniques themselves are mentioned in this section and are described in the section following this one. It is interesting to note that a very large portion of the techniques described here were developed during the 1920s and 1930s in one location: AT&T's Hawthorne Works of the Western Electric Company. This facility was headed by W. A. Shewhart and included H. F. Dodge and J. M. Juran. W. E. Deming was also employed by the Hawthorne works during this period, but his responsibilities were not quality related. (Juran 1989)

Walter A. Shewhart

Dr. Shewhart developed the Shewhart statistical process control chart at AT&T's Bell Laboratories in 1924. This chart permits the detection of a drift in machine performance before defective units are created. Shewhart's 1931 text, *Economic Control of Quality of Manufactured Product*, was reproduced by the American Society for Quality Control in 1980. Shewhart also conceptualized what is now called the Deming cycle (Deming 1986). Shewhart developed the concept of an assignable cause of poor quality, i.e., a problem to be identified and corrected.

W. Edwards Deming

Dr. Deming lectured in Japan in 1950. Together with Joseph Juran, he is credited with instilling an awareness of the importance of quality into Japanese management practices. Deming has a 14-point plan for improving quality, shown in Figure 18-5, that focuses on continuously improving the process.

Figure 18-5
Deming's 14-Point Plan for Quality

1. Create constancy of purpose for improvement.
2. Adopt the new approach.
3. End reliance on inspection as the sole quality control tool.
4. Stop selecting vendors on the basis of price alone.
5. Continuously improve every aspect of production.
6. Train the workers.
7. Lead.
8. Eliminate fear.
9. Eliminate line/staff communication barriers.
10. Eliminate slogans.
11. Eliminate production quotas.
12. Eliminate barriers to pride of person.
13. Institute self-improvement programs.
14. Implement this program universally.

Deming received the Shewhart medal from the American Society for Quality Control in 1956. The Union of Japanese Science and Engineering (JUSE) annually awards the Deming Prize for product quality and dependability. The Deming Prizes were established from royalties earned on a book created from the lectures Deming gave on the 1950 tour. The Deming Application Prize is awarded to a company for exceptional performance in statistical quality control. Deming is the author of *Out of the Crisis* (1986).

Joseph M. Juran

Dr. Juran lectured in Japan in 1954. Ishikawa (1985) credits Juran's visit for moving the objective of quality control from the level of the shop floor to the level of the total organization. Juran is editor of the *Quality Control Handbook* (1979) and has authored several books on quality, the most recent of which is Juran on *Leadership for Quality* (1989).

Juran argues that managers cause at least 80 percent of all quality problems. For a firm to achieve high quality production, managers must recognize that the firm's product quality determines its competitive position. Juran's five point program is as follows:

1. Convince others that the firm needs an attitudinal breakthrough.
2. Identify the vital few projects.

3. Organize for a breakthrough in knowledge.
4. Conduct an analysis to discover the cause(s) of the problem.
5. Determine the effect of the proposed changes on the people involved, and find ways to overcome resistance to these changes.

Juran also argues that quality is fitness for use, as determined by the customer. Therefore, it is vital that the manufacturer have close contact with the customer, understand exactly how the product is used, and design the product to serve well in actual usage. According to Juran (1989), "Product satisfaction has its origin in product features and is why clients buy the product. Product dissatisfaction has its origin in nonconformances and is why customers complain. There are many products that give little or no dissatisfaction; the products do what the supplier said they would do. Yet the products are not salable because some competing product provides greater product satisfaction."

Juran defines a trilogy consisting of quality planning, quality control, and quality improvement. *Quality planning* includes identifying the customers, determining their needs, developing product features that respond to those needs, and developing processes capable of producing those products and features. *Quality control* consists of evaluating actual performance, comparing this to the company's goals, and taking action. *Quality improvement* includes establishing an improvement infrastructure, identifying key improvement projects, establishing a project team for each project that has clear responsibility for successfully concluding the project, and providing the resources, training, and motivation needed to successfully complete the project.

Harold F. Dodge

Together with Harold G. Romig, Dodge developed the technique of acceptance sampling as a replacement for 100 percent inspection (Juran 1989). Acceptance sampling became the preferred method of quality control in the United States, in contrast to Japan which emphasized statistical process control. Many American companies used both acceptance sampling and statistical process control. However, Japan's wider use of statistical process control is generally credited as the source of Japan's present high reputation for quality.

Philip B. Crosby

Crosby, a former vice-president of ITT, is author of *Quality is Free* (1979) and *Quality Without Tears* (1984). He operates the Quality College in Winter Park, Florida.

Crosby defines quality as conformance to requirements. His philosophy is "loose tolerances tightly enforced." Many production managers feel that engineers arbitrarily set tolerances that are too tight, i.e., parts that are slightly outside the specified limits will function perfectly well. Accepting parts that are marginally outside specification limits destroys the tolerance limit. The company is operating without tolerance limits. Crosby believes there must be an agreed limit that is acceptable to marketing (the customer), product design, and manufacturing, and that is enforced without exception. He also emphasizes defect prevention, pointing out that it is impossible for an inspector to miss a nonexistant defect.

Kaoru Ishikawa

Dr. Ishikawa is credited with the Ishikawa diagram, also known as the *fishbone diagram*, and with the concept that, for a worker in a manufacturing facility, the customer is the next process. The Ishikawa diagram extends the concept of assignable cause, created by Shewhart, to the identification and correction of underlying causes. The diagram is a formalization of the "five whys," i.e., the practice of asking *why* an event occurred until the ultimate source of the problem is identified. Ishikawa is author of *What is Total Quality Control? The Japanese Way* (1985).

Genichi Taguchi

Dr. Taguchi created the Taguchi methods of analysis of product design and the concept of a quality loss function. The Taguchi methods are a sophisticated analysis of how well a set of components will function as a total assembly. The loss function measures the cost to society of poor quality as a function of the variability of the manufacturing process. (Schonberger 1985)

Shigeo Shingo

Dr. Shingo introduced the concepts of source inspection and mistake-proofing. Briefly, Shingo believes that statistical process control is a good start for the quality control process, but one that assumes that errors are unavoidable. Shingo's techniques are built around the concept that it is possible to modify equipment in order to physically prevent certain motions that would cause a defect to occur. Utah State University annually awards the Shingo Prize to the American company making the greatest contribution to quality control.

QUALITY CONTROL TECHNIQUES

In this section we discuss some common quality control techniques, including Pareto analysis, fishbone diagrams, the house of quality, quality control circles, inspection, acceptance sampling, statistical process control, and mistake-proofing. These techniques by no means exhaust the important subject of quality control. They do, however, represent some of the more important techniques, especially for companies seeking to achieve the level of quality attained by the Japanese.

Pareto Analysis

To attain continuous improvement in quality, the ultimate cause of serious uality problems must be determined and corrected. However, the time required to investigate the ultimate source of a single quality problem is quite large. It is clearly impossible to have every single problem completely checked and corrected. However, there are probably a small fraction of the quality problems that are responsible for the majority of all defects. The concept that a small part of any population is responsible for most of anything one cares to measure is known as the *80-20 rule*, or *Pareto analysis*. Pareto, an economist, first applied the rule to income distribution.

How does one decide which quality problems constitute the significant set? A common Just-in-Time practice is to have operators inspect items and pull any defective items. The operator should also record the immediate cause of the defect. The most frequently recurring problems can be attacked first. The principle of identifying and attacking the most frequently occurring problems is quite simple. However, it cannot be overemphasized that to be effective, one must concentrate on identifying and correcting the most serious problems.

Fishbone Diagram

A fishbone diagram (see Chapter 17) shows cause and effect for commonly occurring problems. The main line of the chart represents the process, the first branches are immediate causes of problems, and smaller branches represent underlying causes. Thus, the fishbone diagram can shorten the time required to root out the underlying problem.

House of Quality

The house of quality technique is really a communications device for use by engineering design and process design teams. A slogan used almost as frequently as "Total Quality Control" is "Quality at the Source," meaning that quality must be designed into the product. But because there are eight dimensions to quality, quality objectives often conflict with one another. For example, in designing the door of a luxury automobile, it may be desirable for the power window to operate quickly and also for the door to be light and easy to open and shut. Because faster window operation is likely to require a heavier, more powerful motor, these two objectives may be in conflict.

The house of quality technique is a grid that charts the various quality improvement objectives and notes those that are complementary and those which are in opposition. This technique highlights the places where trade-offs may be required and where good communication within the design team is needed concerning the relative importance of meeting each objective, etc.

While the importance of good product and process design cannot be overemphasized, design is the realm of the engineer. This book is for production and inventory managers and management students. For that reason, we focus on techniques relating to inspection, acceptance sampling, statistical process control, and mistake-proofing.

Quality Control Circles

Quality circles are groups of employees, usually with 5 to 15 members who meet regularly to discuss and suggest remedies for quality problems within their department. There are approximately 125,000 registered quality circles in Japan, containing more than 1.1 million employees. There is speculation that when unregistered circles are included, employee involvement is likely to exceed 2 million workers. Quality circles became very popular in the United States in the early 1980s. At present, they appear to be losing popularity here. The philosophy of continuous improvement and universal involvement really demands that quality circles or some other form of employee involvement be extended throughout the company.

Western disillusionment with quality circles is either because of a misunderstanding of their purpose or because they have multiple, often conflicting, purposes. Basically, quality circles can be formed to solve problems *or* to improve management-employee relations, but should not be used to do both.

Inspection

Suppose you are the manufacturer of a steel cylinder that is supposed to have a diameter of 0.75″, with a tolerance of ±0.003″ permitted (i.e., diameters from 0.747″ to 0.753″ are acceptable). You are also to take an existing, larger cylinder and bore a cylindrical hole 0.755″ in diameter in it. The larger cylinder has a tolerance of ±0.001″. An example of such cylinders is illustrated in Figure 18-6. The 0.75″ cylinder is then to be fitted into the 0.755″ hole to form an arm for a piece of robotic equipment. How would you go about making the determination that a particular cylinder met these specifications?

Figure 18-6
Cylinder Specifications

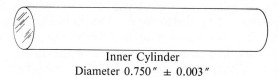

Inner Cylinder
Diameter 0.750″ ± 0.003″

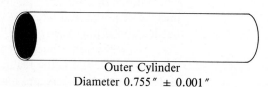

Outer Cylinder
Diameter 0.755″ ± 0.001″

The Just-in-Time philosophy is to have the machine operator inspect every piece whenever possible. For example, suppose the inner cylinder is machined on a lathe from a piece of bar stock. The operator could be furnished with a go/no go gauge like the one in Figure 18-7. This particular gauge has two holes bored in it. The innermost hole is bored to a diameter of 0.747″, the outermost to 0.753″. Both the inner and outer dimensions must be very precise for the go/no go gauge to be useful. The operator could then take each cylinder completed on the lathe and attempt to insert it into the go/no go gauge. If the piece being inspected meets specifications, it will pass through the outer hole bored into the gauge and not pass through the inner hole. Parts that will not go into the first hole must be larger than 0.753″. Parts that will go into the second hole are smaller than 0.747″. As the operator places the cylinder into the go/no go gauge, he or she can scan the cylinder for surface defects.

Figure 18-7
Go/No Go Gauge for Inner Cylinder

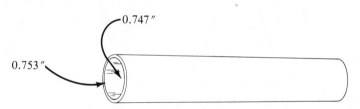

Suppose that the outer cylinder is bored at a boring machine, whose operator has been furnished a go/no go gauge like the one in Figure 18-8. In this example, the gauge itself is to be placed into the cylinder. Recall from Figure 18-6 that the specification for the outer cylinder was 0.755″ ± 0.001″. If the cylinder has been bored to the correct dimensions, the tip of the gauge, which measures only 0.754″, should fit within the cylinder, but the bulk of the gauge, measuring 0.756″, will not fit into the cylinder.

Figure 18-8
Go/No Go Gauge for Outer Cylinder

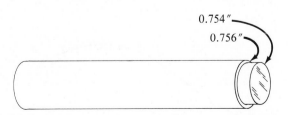

A go/no go gauge is an example of one way that a policy of 100 percent inspection of completed parts can be performed with little cost to the company.

Most of the company's cost comes from the creation and storage of the gauges themselves. The operator can remove a recently completed piece, load a second piece and start the machine, then test the first piece while the second piece is being machined.

Why is inspection of a part necessary in the first place? As is shown in Figure 18-9, the diameter of a cylinder machined for a specific time on a specific lathe may vary because of differences in steel hardness, tool wear, the condition of the machine itself, and the condition and ability of the machine operator. The variances that occur because of each of these factors sum to yield the variance of the part diameter itself.

Figure 18-9
Sources of Cylinder Diameter Variability

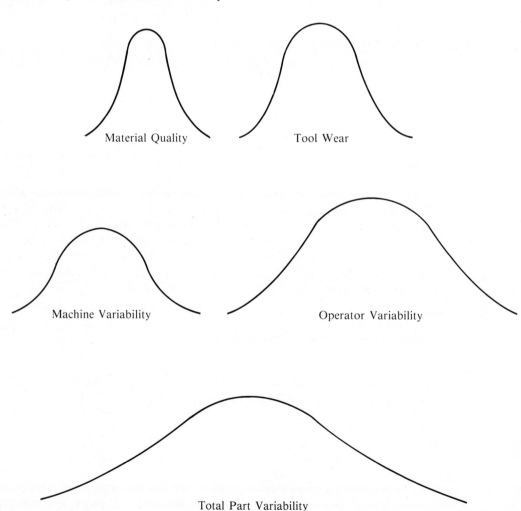

Material Quality   Tool Wear

Machine Variability   Operator Variability

Total Part Variability

Let's consider an example of part variance. Suppose that the diameter of the cylinders is normally distributed, that the average inner cylinder diameter is 0.75″ and that the standard deviation of cylinder diameter is 0.001″. What is the probability that any given cylinder will pass the go/no go gauge test (i.e., is within specifications)? Figure 18-10 illustrates the distribution of cylinder diameters that should be produced if the lathe is functioning properly.

Figure 18-10
Distribution of Inner Cylinder Diameters

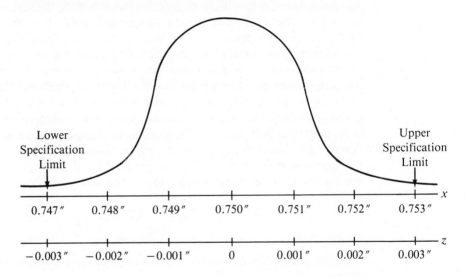

The problem stated is identical to a two-tailed test of hypothesis:

$$H_o: \text{diameter} = 0.75''$$
$$H_a: \text{diameter} \neq 0.75''$$

So we would expect to use a procedure analagous to a test of hypothesis. Since we know we are testing a normally distributed random variable for which the mean and standard deviation both are known, we can test by converting the diameter to a standard normal distribution (i.e., one having a mean of 0 and standard deviation of 1) by the following equation:

$$z = \frac{X - \mu}{\sigma}$$

where X = diameter of a hypothetical part
μ = expected diameter
σ = standard deviation of the parameter

In this case, to find the probability that any given diameter, X, is larger than 0.753", one takes $z = \dfrac{0.753 - 0.750}{0.001} = 3$. We now need to find $z = 3$ on a standard normal table, such as the one in Appendix A. From this we find a value of 0.4986, meaning that of the portion of the normal curve between $z = 0$ and $z = \infty$, which has an area of 0.5000, a total of 0.4986 lies between $z = 0$ and $z = 3$. Thus, an area of $0.5000 - 0.4986 = 0.0014$ lies between $z = 3$ and $z = \infty$. For a diameter smaller than 0.747", an identical area, 0.0014, lies between $z = -3$ and $z = -\infty$. Thus, the probability that a given part has a diameter that is out of specification is 0.0028, the sum of the areas in the two extremes of the distribution, or approximately 3 in 1,000. From Figure 18-10, it certainly appears that we have a good manufacturing situation and should experience considerably less than a 1 percent rate of rejection of parts.

Suppose after cylinder manufacture has proceeded for some time, the operator notices that 2 or 3 parts in every 100 is too small and that almost no parts are too large. The part rejection rate is between 2 and 3 times as large as the pessimistic estimate of 1 percent. What would account for this change in the pattern of part diameters? Something has happened to cause the distribution of part diameters to shift to the left, as shown in Figure 18-11. The new true population mean is 0.749". The probability of finding a part to be too small is found by finding the area under a standard normal curve to the left of

$$z = \frac{0.747 - 0.749}{0.001} = -2$$

while the probability of finding a part to be too large is found by the area to the right of

$$z = \frac{0.753 - 0.749}{0.001} = 4$$

From the table in Appendix A, the probability of being too small is 0.0228, while the probability of being too large is almost 0. Thus, if the control limits are set to a value of $\pm 3\sigma$ from the specification, a slight shift in process mean causes a significant loss of yield from the process. Ideally, control limits are about $\pm 6\sigma$ from the specification.

Acceptance Sampling

In the previous section, we considered two scenarios for the manufacture of steel rods. In the first scenario, quality was excellent, with only 3 parts in 1,000 being out of specification. In the second scenario, a slight shift in the production process caused the error rate to increase to about 23 parts in 1,000. The diameter of the rod is only one factor that influences its quality. There is also the length, the uniformity, the appearance, and the tensile strength. It is not

Figure 18-11
Distribution of Cylinder Diameters Shifts to Left

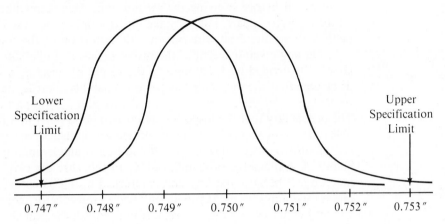

economically feasible to test all of the aspects of quality on every unit. For example, testing tensile strength requires destruction of the part. Given that we cannot fully inspect every unit, how can we ensure that the product we ship to the customer has the quality we desire? Acceptance sampling is a technique that was created to judge the quality of a batch of parts without inspecting every part.

The procedure for acceptance sampling is to select a random sample of items from a large batch, to test the selected items, and to accept the batch for shipment if and only if the number of defective units in the sample is equal to or less than some threshold value. For example, suppose we have a batch of 1,000 steel rods like those described in the previous section. Suppose we only want to ship these rods if the percent defective is less than 1 percent. Our acceptance sampling procedure might be to select 50 rods at random from the batch of 1,000 and to ship the batch only if there are 0 defective items found in the sample. If one or more defects are found, the batch will be 100 percent inspected and only the good units shipped.

Acceptance sampling is an easy technique to administer. The inspector only needs to select 50 units at random from the batch, inspect all 50, and pass the batch if and only if there are no defectives found. The difficult part of acceptance sampling is to design a reasonable plan. There are two risks that cannot be avoided in any acceptance sampling plan. The first risk is that a lot with too many defectives is shipped. The second risk is that a lot with an acceptable number of defectives is not shipped. Each of these risks is unavoidable because only a small fraction of the lot is tested and there is no way to be certain that the random sample has exactly the same proportion of defects as the entire batch.

Suppose that there are exactly 15 defective units in the batch of 1,000. This batch should be rejected, but, of course, the inspector does not know that.

What is the probability that the inspector will reject the lot? We will assume that when the inspector finishes inspecting one unit, he or she replaces that unit in the batch before selecting the second unit. This seems like a silly action on the inspector's part, but we make the assumption because it simplifies the mathematics quite a bit with only a little distortion of the results.

On any given inspection, the inspector has a probability of 0.985 (985 good units divided by 1,000 units in the batch) of selecting a good part. Let us assume that the inspector has perfect reliability, that is, he or she always recognizes a defective part as being defective and a good part as being good. The probability that the inspector selects two good parts in a row is 0.985×0.985. (Perhaps you recall from an elementary statistics course that the intersection of two independent events, A and B, is found by multiplying the probability of A times the probability of B. In this case the two inspections are independent because the first unit is returned to the batch before the second unit is randomly chosen. If you haven't had an introductory course in statistics, you may wish to verify these assertions.) In general, the probability that n good parts in a row are selected is 0.985^n. The probability that 50 good pieces will be found in a sample of 50 is 0.985^{50} or 0.46969.[1]

The implication of the preceeding paragraph is that a batch that contains 1.5 times the maximum acceptable level of defects has a probability of acceptance of 0.46969. A risk of this type is known as a consumer's risk, because the consumer receives a bad batch that should have been rejected and 100 percent inspected. The probability the batch will be rejected is $1 - 0.46969 = 0.53031$. In this particular example, the only way to reduce the consumer's risk is to take a larger sample size. To determine how large the sample size should be, the company must first decide how large a consumer's risk it is willing to tolerate. One can then find the proper sample size.[2]

Now let's consider the second type of risk that is unavoidable in acceptance sampling. Suppose a batch of 1,000 has exactly 6 defective units. Using the procedure outlined above, we can determine that the probability of accepting the batch is approximately 74 percent. Thus, the probability of incorrectly rejecting the batch is 26 percent. An error of this type is known as a producer's risk because the effect of the error is to cause the producer to 100 percent inspect a batch that should have been accepted and shipped. If the sample size is increased while no defectives are tolerated in order to decrease the likelihood of accepting a batch with 15 defectives, the likelihood of accepting a batch with 6 defectives also decreases. Thus, to lower the probability of making an error of the first type we increase the probability of making an error of the second type.

---

1. If we change assumptions so that the inspection is done without replacement of the inspected part, the probability becomes 0.460712.
2. For this example, the formula $0.985^n = a$, where a is the acceptable consumer's risk and n is the sample size, must be solved for n.

The example above illustrates a major limitation of acceptance sampling, the inability to eliminate sampling error (making the wrong decision because the sample randomly selected happened to be unrepresentative of the batch). The existence of sampling error is one reason the JIT philosophy prefers statistical process control to acceptance sampling. A second reason is that when the defect rate gets very low, such as a few defects per million units as the Japanese now claim for some processes, the sample size required for effective acceptance sampling approaches 100 percent inspection, which defeats the purpose of acceptance sampling.

Statistical Process Control

Statistical process control (SPC) charts were created by Dr. Walter Shewhart and others at Bell Laboratories early in the 1930s. Leading American companies have used the technique for a long time. W. Edwards Deming and Joseph Juran, both of whom worked for Bell Laboratories at some point in their careers, introduced SPC to Japan in the early 1950s. Many people credit SPC for Japan's surge in quality. Shigeo Shingo, a Japanese quality consultant, disagrees with this viewpoint. Shingo suggests using SPC but claims that one must use source inspections and mistake-proofing to achieve results like those achieved by leading Japanese companies.

Statistical process control charts are available for means, ranges, proportion defective, and number of defects per unit. We will explore the theoretical underpinnings of the process control chart for means and then briefly examine other control charts. The bases of a statistical process control chart for means are (1) the central limit theorem and (2) the statistical test of hypothesis. The central limit theorem says that, given a sufficient sample size, the distribution of sample averages will be normal. That is, if we were to make a bar chart of the result of several sample averages, the chart would roughly resemble Figure 18-12, which is an example of a normal distribution. We can also chart each sample mean on a scatter diagram, as shown in Figure 18-13. By charting the mean values of sequential samples, we expose trends that indicate the process is slipping out of control. We can prevent defects by spotting process problems before we produce defective units.

To demonstrate that sample means tend to be normally distributed even when the values being sampled are not normally distributed, we will perform an experiment that can be replicated with an electronic worksheet. Figure 18-14 shows a bar graph taken from 6,000 random numbers, each number coming from a uniform distribution having the range 0 to 1. You can create this graph in the following fashion. First, enter @**RAND** into cell A1 of a worksheet. (Commands are given in Lotus 1-2-3 format and may differ for other spreadsheets.) Then copy cell A1 to cells A1 to L500. You now have 6,000 random variables. To fix the value of these variables, extract the values in cells A1 to L500 to a new worksheet and then retrieve the new worksheet. You now have

Figure 18-12
Distribution of Sample Means
Taken from 12 Uniformly Distributed Values

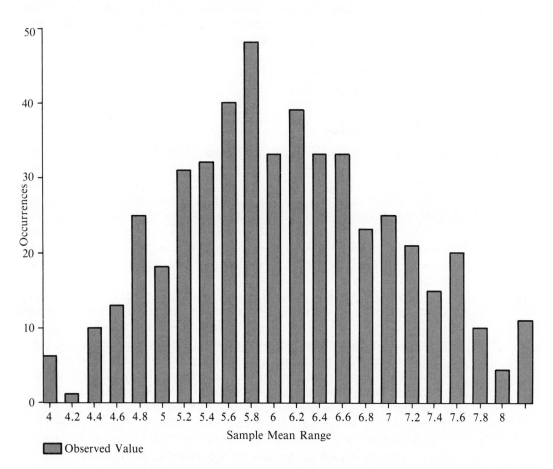

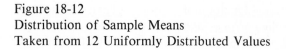 Observed Value

6,000 random values that will not change. To produce the graph, first enter the values 0.1, 0.2, . . ., 1.0 into cells N1 to N10. Next, issue the command sequence / **Data Distribution A1.L500 N1.N10**. This command sequence tells Lotus 1-2-3 to count the number of entries in the area enclosed by cells A1 to L500 that fall within each of the ranges identified (0 to 0.1, 0.1 to 0.2, etc.). To make the graph, enter the command sequence / **Graph Type Bar X N1.N10 A O1.O10 View**. The result should be somewhat like Figure 18-14, that is, with each bar averaging about 600 entries with some variability between bars. Figure 18-14 shows that the individual random numbers are distributed uniformly.

Now place the cursor in cell M1 and enter the formula @SUM(A1.L1). Copy this formula to cells M2 to M500. You now have the sum of 12 random numbers. Place the cursor in cell M1 and enter the values 4 to 8 in steps

Figure 18-13
$\overline{X}$-Chart

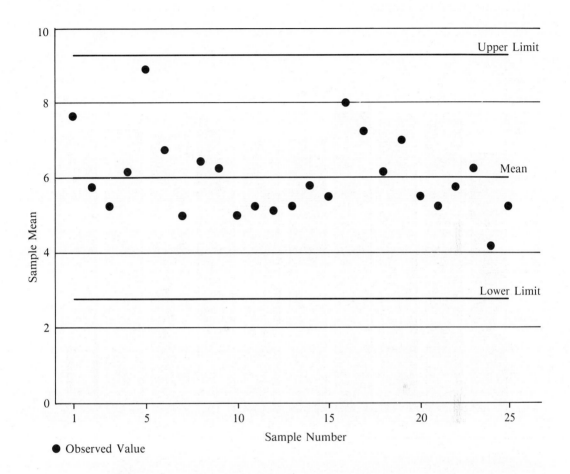

● Observed Value

of 0.2 in cells N1 to N21. Issue the command sequence / **Data Distribution M2.M500 N1.N21**. To make the graph, issue the command sequence / **Graph Type Bar X N1.N21 A O1.O21 View**. The result should look somewhat like Figure 18-12, which resembles the bell-shaped distribution one expects from a normally distributed random variable. Since the average is merely the sum divided by a constant (12 in this case), the average will have the same distribution shape as the sum.

To this point we have demonstrated that sums of random variables tend to be normally distributed, even if the underlying population is not normal. We will now make use of the property that sample means are normally distributed to draw certain inferences concerning a process control chart. An example of a statistical process control chart is shown in Figure 18-13. This chart was created by plotting the first 25 sample means from the spreadsheet used

Figure 18-14
Distribution of Sample Values
Uniform 0-1 Random Variables

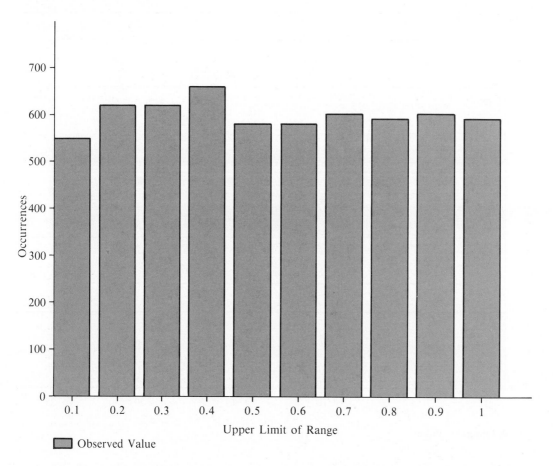

Observed Value

to create Figure 18-12. The mean of 12 0-1 uniform random variables clearly should be 6. The standard deviation from the sample of 6,000 was a little more than 1.1. A control chart for sample means usually shows the mean as a line, and also has lines at the mean plus 3 standard deviations (a value of 9.3 in this case) and at the mean minus 3 standard deviations (a value of 2.7 in this case). If a process is acting properly, all observations should lie within the control limits, the "typical" value should be close to the mean, and there should be few extreme values, i.e., values more than 2 standard deviations from the mean. Figure 18-13 conforms in all respects. Note that most values are quite close to 6, none exceed the control limits and only one observation, the fifth in the sequence, is greater than 2 standard deviations from the mean. If any of the above are not true, then the process is probably out of control and we should try to find an assignable cause for the abnormal pattern.

Let's return to the example of machining the piston or inner cylinder shown in Figure 18-6. The pistons are supposed to be 0.75″ in diameter. The tolerance limits for an acceptable piston are 0.747″ to 0.753″. If the diameter is greater than 0.753″, the piston is too large and either will not fit in the chamber or will fit so tightly that excessive friction is created. If the diameter is less than 0.747″, the piston is too small and will allow too much of the energy from the exploding fuel to dissipate without performing useful work. Suppose also that when the process that machines the pistons is in control, the pistons are machined to a mean diameter of 0.750″ with a standard deviation of 0.0005″. Figure 18-15 illustrates the distribution of piston diameters that will be created when this process operates exactly as it is designed to operate.

Figure 18-15
Distribution of Piston Diameters

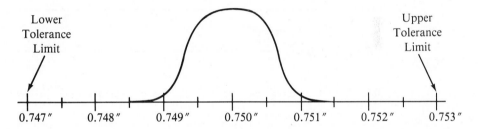

Suppose that from a particular hour's production run of pistons a sample of size 4 is taken. The mean of the sample is expected to be 0.750″, the population's target mean. The standard error of a sample of size 4 taken from this distribution is 0.00025″, i.e., the population standard deviation divided by the square root of the sample size. Since the underlying population of piston diameters is known to be normally distributed, the distribution of sample means will be normally distributed in spite of the small sample size. Figure 18-16 shows the distribution of sample means.

Figure 18-16
Distribution of Sample Means, Sample Size = 4

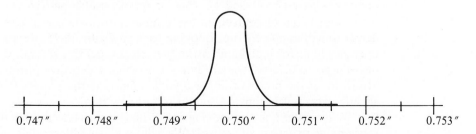

A possible SPC chart for this process is shown in Figure 18-17. Note that the desired mean value, 0.750″, is placed in the middle of the chart and that

Figure 18-17

Normal Distribution Superimposed on a Hypothetical $\overline{X}$-Chart

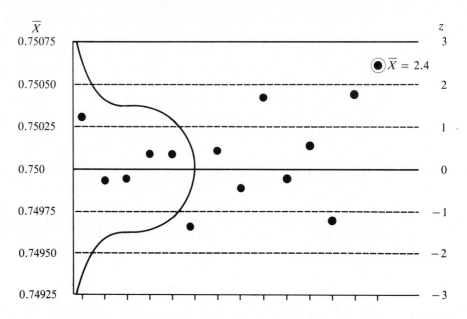

control limits are set at z-values of ± 3 that correspond to sample mean values of 0.74925″ and 0.75075″. The present sample has a mean of 0.7506″ which translates to a z-value of 2.4. This point is circled on Figure 18-17. If we were to make a decision on whether or not to shut down the process based on one sample, we would probably have to decide to shut the process down because the z-score is quite high. But when we look over the past dozen or so samples taken, we find that two of the five previous sample means were below the desired setting, that roughly as many samples have been below the mean as above (the normal distribution is symmetric, so we expect 50 percent of the sample means to be above the desired setting), and that most of the sample means have been within one standard error of the desired setting (68 percent of the distribution should be within one standard error; in this case 8 of 13 points are between -1 and 1). There is no discernible pattern that indicates the process is out of control, so based on all information available to us, we decide to let the process run. Looking back to Figure 18-15, we note that the tolerance limit for individual piston diameters is 0.753″, so even if the mean has slipped to 0.7506″, we are not yet producing defective pistons. We can afford to let the process run for a while longer. If the process is producing slightly oversized pistons we should soon know it.

What patterns are we looking for? What patterns indicate that the process is beginning to get out of control? We will list seven patterns and then discuss each one.

1. Nine points in a row on one side of the mean.
2. Six points in a row steadily increasing or decreasing.
3. Fourteen points in a row alternating up and down.
4. Two out of three points beyond the two standard error limit on the same side of the mean.
5. Four out of five points beyond the one standard error limit on the same side of the mean.
6. Fifteen points in a row between $z = -1$ and $z = 1$.
7. Eight points in a row on both sides of the center with no points between $z = -1$ and $z = 1$.

All seven patterns have a probability of about 0.003 of observing the pattern due to pure chance when the process operates exactly as it should. For example, Test 1 corresponds in likelihood to tossing a fair coin nine times and getting nine straight heads. It is possible, but the probability of it happening is 0.5^9 or 0.00195. This is slightly less than 0.003. If we were to set the limit at eight in a row, the probability would be 0.0039. The probability of erroneously stopping the process on the other six tests is more difficult to compute, but all are set to be less than 0.003.

Test 1 is based on the fact that if the process mean has slipped, we are more likely to find several observations on one side of the mean. Test 2 is based on the belief that most processes slip out of control rather than jump out, so we may find an increasing or decreasing trend. Test 3 checks for a recurrent problem that causes the mean to vacillate regularly. Test 4 and Test 5 check for substantial shifts in the mean. Test 6 checks for improper control limits. We expect to find some observations outside of 1 standard error. If we have none we probably made an arithmetic mistake in calculating the standard error. Test 7 may also be due to an arithmetic error in calculating the standard error; it may also indicate that the process *variance* has increased while the mean is unaffected.

If the process variance or standard deviation were to increase, we could begin producing defective items even though the mean value is unchanged. Figure 18-18 illustrates the situation in which, for some reason, the process standard deviation has increased from 0.0005 ″ to 0.001 ″. Notice that in the original example almost no defective parts were produced when the process was in control. Now, however, the best case is that the mean setting is perfect and 0.3 percent of all parts are defective. Because 99.7 percent of a normal curve is within three standard deviation of the mean, to eliminate defects requires tolerance limits about six standard deviations from the process mean, as shown in Figure 18-15. Achieving and maintaining such limits may require the purchase of machines capable of tighter tolerance than those presently owned.

To minimize manufacturing problems, the normal tolerance limits of the process should be substantially larger than the tolerance limits of the product. For best results, the tolerance limits of the process being controlled should be ±6 standard deviations from the mean. If the product is not fit for use with

Figure 18-18
Distribution of Piston Diameters, $\sigma = 0.001$

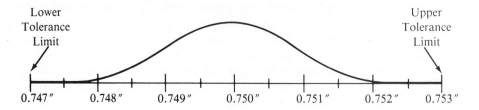

Lower Tolerance Limit   Upper Tolerance Limit

0.747″   0.748″   0.749″   0.750″   0.751″   0.752″   0.753″

tolerance limits of this magnitude, then a way must be found to reduce the process standard deviation or a machine capable of less deviation must be purchased. Shingo discusses numerous ways to reduce the process standard deviation.

There are three ways in which statistical process control is being mis-applied in industry. First, as Deming points out, the process must be known to be in control when the procedure is implemented for it to have any use. It is not sufficient simply to put a chart on the floor; one must first verify that the process is in control. Second, SPC is often used when the tolerance limits are less than ±6 times the population standard deviation. While there is still some benefit from using SPC, the number of defects will not be reduced to a few defects per million parts until tolerance limits are at least six standard deviations. Finally, too often when the process slips out of control, the process merely is recalibrated without asking *why* the process went out of control. Perhaps the pistons are too large because the cutting blade is dull, because the blade is not being replaced often enough, or because the machine is being operated at the wrong speed. Correcting the cause of the problem can prevent the problem from recurring, which is the real objective.

As mentioned earlier, there are SPC charts other than the SPC chart for means. Recall that a process can go out of control by having the variability of the process increase. The process variability can be estimated by the sample *range*, i.e., the largest value minus the smallest value. This chart commonly is called an *R-chart*. One can check process variability by plotting the sample range on a control chart and looking for increasing trends.

Sometimes no attribute of a part is measured; the part is simply classified as acceptable or defective. In this case, a *P-chart* for proportion defective can be used. As with the *R*-chart for sample range, one is looking for an increasing trend.

Mistake-Proofing

An area of disagreement between Deming and some other experts, particularly Shingo, is on the role of statistically based techniques such as statistical process control in the quality control process. Deming maintains that everyone needs a good background in statistics to manage quality properly. He states that it is naive to think that complex problems have simple solutions. Shingo contends that expecting line workers and supervisors to understand the mathematical complexities of statistics and probability theory is asking too much of line workers and supervisors. Shingo recommends the use of mistake-proofing techniques, which he contends we can develop simply and inexpensively. Both experts have valid points. Middle and upper level management certainly need to have a much better understanding of statistics. With proper understanding at the middle management level, middle managers should be able to design quality improvement systems that do not require line workers and supervisors to understand the underlying theory.

In his book, *Zero Quality Control: Source Inspection and the Poka-yoke System* (1986), Shingo recounts that after years of study and application of the statistical process control concepts of Deming, he reluctantly concluded that more action was necessary to prevent defects. In 1961, Shingo visited Yamada Electric in Nagoya. There, he heard of an annoying quality problem. One of the operations performed involved the assembly of a simple push-button device for Matsushita Electric, in Kyushu. The device had two buttons, under each of which was a small spring. Occasionally, the assembler would forget to put in a spring. When Matsushita Electric discovered a switch without a spring, Yamada had to send an inspector all the way to Kyushu to check every switch that was delivered. Shingo realized that to expect the operator never to forget was to expect superhuman performance. He realized that what was needed was a type of checklist. Shingo had the company apply the concept of a checklist to the assembly operation by adding a dish, into which the worker first put two springs for assembly from a large box of springs. After completing the switch assembly, the worker checked the dish. If a spring remained in the dish, the worker knew he had omitted a spring from the switch. This simple checklist approach eliminated the problem and caused Shingo to consider ways to build mistake-proofing into other operations. After more than 25 years of work in this area, Shingo has concluded that given enough resourcefulness one can inexpensively mistake-proof any operation.

Shingo also contends that statistical process control alone will only take a company down to a few percent defective. To move from two or three percent defective down to defect rates of a few parts per million, one must use mistake-proofing to prevent errors.

Shingo notes that there are three types of inspection. First, there is sampling inspection, which is designed to accept or reject a batch of goods and/or to separate the good products from the bad. Second, there is information inspection, i.e., the results of the inspection are fed into a statistical process control chart in order to determine and correct occasions when the manufacturing process is not working as it should. Third, there is what Shingo calls a *source inspection*. By source inspection, Shingo means an inspection that is carried out automatically on 100 percent of all products immediately following some operation. If a defective unit is discovered, the source inspection will usually, but not in all applications, cause the production process to stop until the cause of the defective unit is uncovered and corrected.

Western managers have long considered 100 percent inspection to be too costly to be economically feasible. Shingo contends that it is not. In his book *Zero Quality Control: Source Inspection and the Poka-yoke System* (1986), Shingo relates his experience in putting numerous 100 percent inspection devices into place inexpensively and effectively. The book contains well over 100 pages of examples of specific examples. The subject is really too complex to discuss in this chapter. The interested reader should consult Shingo directly.

THE IMPORTANCE OF QUALITY

We would be remiss if we ended the discussion of quality control without emphasizing the importance of quality to competing in today's world. Every researcher who has examined the reason for American companies losing market share at home and abroad has identified poor quality as the most important factor. There is also a strong relationship between quality and return on investment, as shown in Table 18-1, adapted from a study by Miller and Camp (1985). The high return on investment is not surprising when one examines surveys of consumers' willingness to pay more for perceived quality. A 1985 Gallup survey conducted for the American Society of Quality Control revealed that consumers say they would pay one-third more for a quality car, 50 percent more for a quality dishwasher, and roughly 70 percent more for a quality television or sofa. This data reinforces Crosby's contention—quality is not free, it pays! We must cease discussing the *cost* of quality and begin discussing the *profit potential* of quality.

Table 18-1
Return on Investment as a Function of Quality and Price

Price Category	Quality Classification			
	Low	Medium	High	Average
High	17	18	34	23
Medium	9	2	16	9
Low	15	11	36	21
Average	14	10	29	17

TOTAL PREVENTIVE MAINTENANCE

Imagine an assembly line that produces bicycles and that has 15 stations. Between each pair of stations, there is room for one assembly. Therefore, when any operator finishes with an assembly and finds the space between his or her station and the next already occupied, the operator must stop. This phenomenon is known as *blocking*. Blocking is not uncommon in a Just-in-Time environment because of the low inventory that is permitted. Now further imagine that the time required to complete the work at each station averages 7 minutes. Each station exhibits some process time variability, the standard deviation of process time is 0.7 minutes. Assume the assembly line operates 24 hours per day, 7 days per week. Then the expected output of the line would be 1,440 units, which is 10,080 minutes per week divided by 7 minutes per operation.

The result of this essentially deterministic model is easily verified using a simulation model. This model represents the Just-in-Time ideal, a low work-in-process, low-variation environment. Suppose, however, that as the machines used to assist in the assembly process begin to age, each of the 15 stations breaks down approximately 20 times per week for an average of 20 minutes, repair time being negative exponentially distributed. An example of a negative exponential distribution having a mean of 20 is shown in Figure 18-19. How many bicycles would you expect this shop to produce?

A very simplistic answer would be that since each machine is down an average of 20 times for an average of 20 minutes, the shop will produce for $10,080 - (20)(20) = 9,680$ minutes. At an average of 7 minutes per bicycle, production would be 1,382 units. This answer is simplistic because it ignores the effect of blocking and starvation. Whenever any station breaks down for a long time, the stations upstream to the broken station become blocked because there is no place to put the completed work. The stations downstream from the break run out of work (known as *starvation*). In a simulation of this scenario, we obtained an output of about 1,140 bicycles per week, substantially less than predicted by the simplistic model. Figure 18-20 shows the relationship between output and the number of outages per week for the 15 station case.

Figure 18-20 illustrates the importance of preventive maintenance in a Just-in-Time environment. Any breakdown of a machine during operation will cause a chain reaction due to blocking and starvation. Preventive maintenance is intended to prevent the machine from failing in operation. In addition to routinely cleaning and oiling a machine, preventive maintenance requires that parts that wear out be replaced as they reach the end of their predicted life span, rather than waiting for the part to fail in usage. From the point of view of productivity and maintaining the daily shipping rate, total preventive maintenance is as important to Just-in-Time as total quality control. However, total preventive maintenance is not as complex a topic as total quality control.

The traditional approach to managing production is not to use extensive preventive maintenance but rather to decouple the 15 stations. The stations are placed quite far apart and a large buffer of inventory is placed at each station. With sufficient inventory at each station, each will operate independently and the process will average a bicycle every 7 minutes. The difficulty with this approach is that the buffer required to achieve this decoupling amounts to several days' supply at each station. Lead time through the whole system is about 75 working days. Thus, the traditional approach solves the problem at the expense of a large amount of inventory held at all times, long manufacturing

Figure 18-19
Distribution of Repair Times, Negative Exponential Repair, Mean = 20

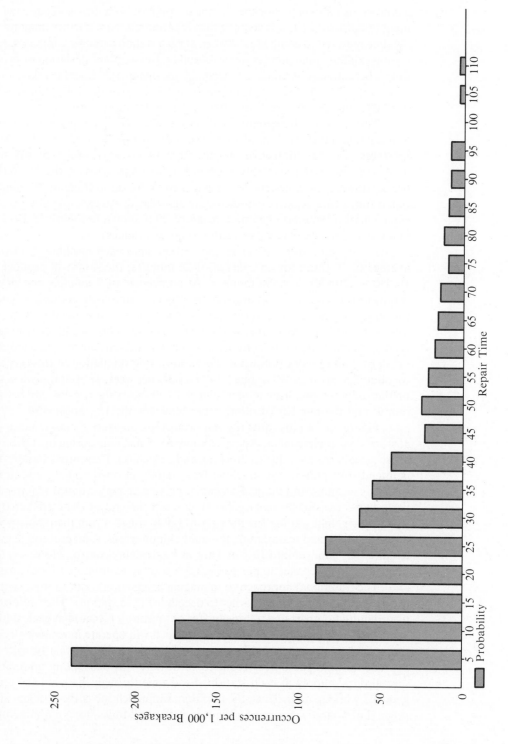

Figure 18-20
Relationship Between Availability and Output
15 Machines, Serial Assembly, 1 Unit of Inventory Permitted Between Machines

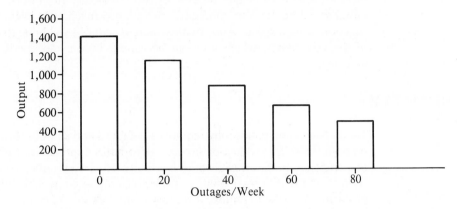

lead times, and consequently, poor response to changing market conditions. Fortunately, the situation is changing in many companies that have or are implementing JIT, TQC, and TPM.

The Just-in-Time philosophy removes the inventory, shortens the lead time, and enhances responsiveness to the market. However, if a company attempts to simply reduce inventory without first removing the variability in output that caused the inventory to be created, the result will be a substantial loss in output. Therefore, it is imperative that a good preventive maintenance system be put in place before the inventory is removed, so that output can be sustained while the inventory is being reduced.

The total preventive maintenance (TPM) philosophy also recommends lessening the strain on machines by running them at speeds below their maximum rated speed. This helps avoid the creation of machines that are breakdown prone. Overworked machines are also more prone to produce defective parts. Thus, running at maximum speed in order to increase departmental efficiency may cause a loss of output due to rejected parts and machine breakdowns.

Seiichi Nakajima recently published *Introduction to Total Preventive Maintenance* (1988), which is a very thorough introduction to the subject. Nakajima calls the approach total *productive* maintenance, to emphasize the relationship between machine availability and output that was demonstrated in Figure 18-20. Nakajima identifies five elements of TPM. First, the goal is to maximize equipment effectiveness, or the productive output of the machines. Second, there must be a system of preventive maintenance over the entire life span of every machine. Third, preventive maintenance implementation must involve engineering, operations, and maintenance. Fourth, the concept of total preventive maintenance must be understood by all employees. Fifth, the notion of small group improvement activities must be extended from the quality function (quality circles) to include the improvement of maintenance activities.

Nakajima identifies five obstacles to the effective use of equipment. First, there is equipment failure, which was explored in Figure 18-20. Second, setups and adjustments require time that otherwise could be used productively. Third, there are minor stoppages because of tool breakage, etc. Fourth, there is reduced speed because an improperly maintained machine is beginning to malfunction at high speed. And, finally, there is reduced yield due to the creation of defective parts, which also can be caused by an improperly maintained machine.

SUMMARY

The Just-in-Time philosophy requires a balanced and smooth flow of material through the entire production process. Before this approach is feasible, sources of disruptions to the schedule must be eliminated. Two significant and pervasive sources of disruption are quality problems (scrap and rework) and breakdown problems. In order to remove inventory from the system and maintain the flow of material, it is necessary to implement total quality control and total preventive maintenance to largely eliminate these problems. This chapter briefly discussed some techniques associated with quality improvement and machine availability improvement.

EXERCISES

1. Discuss the reasons TQC and TPM are prerequisites to JIT implementation.

2. Discuss the phrase "You cannot inspect quality into a product."

3. How does preventive maintenance affect product quality?

4. How does product quality affect company productivity?

5. Discuss the difference between reliability and durability.

6. Why is serviceability an aspect of quality?

7. Compare and contrast Crosby's approach to quality with Deming's.

8. Compare and contrast Deming's approach to quality with Shingo's.

9. Define poka-yoke.

10. Do all quality experts agree with the goal of zero defects? Discuss.

11. Discuss the relationship between fitness for use and conformance to specifications.

12. Compare Deming's 14 points to Juran's quality trilogy.

13. A process produces ball bearings that have a mean diameter of 5″ and a standard deviation of 0.004″. If samples of size 16 are used, what should be the upper and lower control limits of a SPC chart?

14. Assume the process chart developed in Exercise 13 is used to control bearing manufacture. The last 20 sample means are as follows:

Sample	Mean	Sample	Mean
1	4.9972	11	5.0015
2	4.9993	12	5.0021
3	5.0011	13	5.0019
4	5.0014	14	5.0001
5	4.9982	15	5.0022
6	5.0029	16	4.9999
7	5.0023	17	5.0028
8	5.0014	18	5.0016
9	5.0016	19	5.0015
10	4.9992	20	5.0019

Is the process in control?

SELECTED READINGS

Crosby, Philip B. *Quality is Free: The Art of Making Quality Certain*. New York: McGraw-Hill Book Co., 1979.

Crosby, Philip B. *Quality Without Tears: The Art of Hassle-Free Management*. New York: McGraw-Hill Book Co., 1984.

Deming, W. Edwards. *Out of the Crisis*. Cambridge, MA: The MIT Press, 1986.

Feigenbaum, A.V. *Total Quality Control: Engineering and Management*. New York: McGraw-Hill Book Co., 1961.

Garvin, David A. "Competing on the Eight Dimensions of Quality." *Harvard Business Review* (November-December 1987): 101-109.

Garvin, David A. 'What Does 'Product Quality' Really Mean?'' *Sloan Management Review* (Fall 1984).

Ishikawa, Kaoru, and David Lu. *What is Total Quality Control?* Englewood Cliffs, NJ: Prentice-Hall, Inc., 1985.

Juran, Joseph M. *Juran on Leadership for Quality: An Executive Handbook*. New York: Free Press, 1989.

Juran, Joseph M., ed. *Quality Control Handbook*. New York: McGraw-Hill Book Co., 1979.

Miller, Alex, and Bill Camp. "Exploring Determinants of Success in Corporate Ventures." *Journal of Business Venturing* (Winter 1985): 87-105.

Nakajima, Seiichi. *Introduction to Total Productive Maintenance*. Cambridge, MA: Productivity Press, 1988.

Sage, Lee A. "Just-in-Time: Elements and Applications." *Just-in-Time Reprints*. Annandale, VA: American Production and Inventory Control Society, 1987.

Schonberger, Richard J. *Operations Management: Productivity and Quality*. Plano, TX: Business Publications, Inc., 1985.

Shingo, Shigeo. *Non-Stock Production: The Shingo System for Continuous Improvement*. Cambridge, MA: Productivity Press, 1988.

Shingo, Shigeo. *The Sayings of Shigeo Shingo, Key Strategies for Plant Improvement*. Cambridge, MA: Productivity Press, 1987.

Shingo, Shigeo. *Zero Quality Control, Source Inspection and the Poka-yoke System*. Cambridge, MA: Productivity Press, 1986.

Taguchi, Genichi. *Introduction to Quality Engineering: Designing Quality into Products and Processes*. Asian Productivity Organization, 1986.

Part Seven

Production Systems Design and Operation

19

THEORY OF CONSTRAINTS

Thus far we have examined two approaches to production planning and control system design, material requirements planning (MRP) and Just-in-Time (JIT). In this chapter we examine a third approach, the theory of constraints (TOC). Developing a production planning and control system would be simple except for the existence of seemingly random problems (machine breakdowns, tool breakages, worker absenteeism, lack of a component, scrap, rework, customers who change their order timing or quantity, etc.) and the fact that operations are linked, with Operation A dependent on Operation B (the output of Operation B is all or part of the input into some Operation A). Henceforth, we shall refer to these problems as the problem of random fluctuations and dependent events.

The traditional, or MRP, approach to the problem of random fluctuations and dependent events is to eliminate the dependence by having a large inventory buffer at every work station. The JIT approach is to eliminate the random problems by seeking out the root cause of each problem and correcting it. For example, machine breakdown may be eliminated by the use of preventive maintenance.

Both MRP and JIT practitioners believe that an ideal plant is a balanced plant, i.e., one in which every resource has the same output capability relative to the plant's need. The TOC approach is to accept the existence of an unbalanced plant, one in which some resource has less relative output capability than the others. The most limited resource is called the *constraint*. TOC breaks dependencies by creating a material buffer, but TOC buffers *only* the constraint. Nonconstraint stations have a capacity buffer, i.e., excess capacity. Nonconstraints usually do not need a material buffer in addition to the existing capacity buffer. To add inventory to a nonconstraint station causes lead time to increase (a cost) and work-in-process inventory to increase (a cost) while providing little tangible benefit. TOC thus agrees with JIT that inventory is waste, if the inventory is planned at a nonconstraint station. However, by buffering the constraint from random problems at other stations, therefore permitting the constraint to work all the time, *an inventory buffer at the constraint does add value and hence is not waste.*

TOC does not try to eliminate all problems, only those that threaten the constraint in spite of the constraint's inventory buffer. To use JIT terminology, excessive effort in problem elimination is a waste. There must come a point when it is much less expensive to provide a small buffer against a problem at the constraint than it is to eliminate the problem. The constraint buffer also frees management time to solve problems against which no buffer can be provided.

SIMULATION MODEL COMPARING MRP, JIT, AND TOC

The following discussion is intended to illustrate the differences in the traditional, JIT, and TOC approaches. An extremely simple shop was simulated so that it is easier to explore the implications of each approach.

Consider a shop that has a two-station assembly line and produces one product. Station 1 can produce either 2, 3, or 4 units of product each day; each outcome is equally likely. Station 2 has an identical capacity. There can be a maximum of 2 units of work in process between Station 1 and Station 2. Station 1 has an unlimited supply of raw material. There are presently 2 units of WIP between the stations. The shop is to operate for 200 days. What is the expected output of this system? How can the system be improved?

It might surprise you to learn that the expected output from this system is 2.806 units per day.[1] You can estimate this result using Lotus 1-2-3 to simulate the shop.[2] When we simulated this shop, we obtained approximately 2.80 units per day, averaged over the 200 days. Results of 10 replications of 200 simulated days are shown in Table 19-1. Single replication results varied from a low of 2.72 units to a high of 2.91 units and averaged 2.80 units. Since each station is capable of averaging 3 units per day of output, our results are about 7 percent below what we expect to produce. Traditional thought, JIT, and TOC have different approaches to solving this problem. The traditional approach would add WIP between stations, JIT would reduce variability at each station, TOC would unbalance the line, add WIP at one station, and reduce variability slightly. Let's explore the implications of each of these approaches.

Table 19-2 shows a portion of the spreadsheet used to perform the Monte Carlo simulation. This particular spreadsheet was used only to prepare this example and is not one of the 10 replications reported. Random numbers determine the production output for each station. A random number between 0 and 0.33 yields an output of 2, one between 0.33 and 0.67 yields a 3, and one between 0.67 and 1 yields a 4. In the first row of the main body of the table,

---

1. It is possible to find a closed form solution to this problem using the Markov chain approach. Students familiar with the basics of matrix algebra may wish to examine this methodology, which is presented in Appendix 19A.
2. See Appendix 19B for details of how to perform all simulations presented in this section using Lotus 1-2-3.

Table 19-1
Original Distribution of Output from the Two-Station Line*

Replication	Station 1	Station 2	Line
1	2.96	3.01	2.78
2	2.92	2.89	2.72
3	3.01	2.97	2.82
4	2.88	3.04	2.74
5	3.02	3.00	2.81
6	2.98	2.98	2.79
7	3.08	3.14	2.91
8	2.92	3.06	2.80
9	2.93	3.01	2.76
10	3.03	3.03	2.87

The values shown under the columns labeled Station 1 and Station 2 represent the values obtained by the random variables representing the potential of that one station for the day to be simulated. An output less than the station's potential may actually be achieved.

Station 1 drew a random number of 0.519239, so Station 1 has a possible production of 3. There are 2 units of inventory available (beginning condition). Station 2, therefore, has 5 units of inventory potentially available. Station 2 drew a random number of 0.006+, yielding an output of 2 (because it is between 0 and 0.33). The output of the line is 2, the output of Station 2 is 2, and the actual output of Station 1 is limited to 2 since there is not room to store the additional potential unit between the stations. However, for collecting data for the Station 1 column, the value 3 is used. The unused inventory available for the next trial is 2. You may wish to verify the next line, in which Station 1's output is 3, Station 2's is 4, and the output of the line is 4. The inventory available for the third trial therefore drops to 1.

To understand how Station 2's output may be limited, assume at a given time no WIP exists between stations and Station 1 draws a potential of 2 while

Table 19-2
A Portion of the Monte Carlo Model

Trial example	Line 1 2.97		Begin 2	Line 2 3.045	Plant Average 2.792929		
Station 1	Output	Unused	Potential	Station 2	Output	Plant	Average
0.519239	3	2	5	0.006113	2	2	2.00
0.356443	3	2	5	0.979778	4	4	3.00
0.561540	3	1	4	0.594740	3	3	3.00
0.747586	4	1	5	0.223032	2	2	2.75
0.771711	4	2	6	0.039914	2	2	2.60
0.694519	4	2	6	0.939549	4	4	2.83
0.413725	3	2	5	0.932463	4	4	3.00
0.380023	3	1	4	0.244712	2	2	2.88
0.053727	2	2	4	0.592990	3	3	2.89
0.479721	3	1	4	0.913273	4	4	3.00

Station 2 draws a potential of 4. Then the output of the line would be 2, because Station 2 is furnished only 2 units to process, despite its own potential to process 4 units. The output of the line would be 2, the value recorded for Station 1 would be 2, and the value recorded for Station 2 would be 4.

Observe in Table 19-1 that, in isolation, both Station 1 and Station 2 produced the theoretical average of 3 units per day, with some minor fluctuation around these averages for most replications of the simulation. However, the output of the line was consistently about 2.8 units per day because of the interaction of random fluctuations and the station dependencies.

Traditional Approach and Results

The traditional approach to production and inventory system design would eliminate the limit of 2 units of WIP between the two stations. (For convenience of notation, we will designate this traditional approach the MRP approach, although no MRP logic is actually present in the example.) Assume we permit an unlimited amount of WIP and begin the simulation by having 5 units of WIP available between the two stations. The results are shown in Table 19-3. Average line output is up to about 2.96 units per day, not quite to the theoretical average of 3.00 units. This result may be surprising, but it is correct. It would take much more than 5 units of WIP in position initially to completely decouple the two stations. Note that ending inventory fluctuates quite a lot, implying that lead times also fluctuate quite a lot. In Table 19-1, ending inventory was not shown because ending inventory was limited to 2 pieces and would therefore have to be 0, 1, or 2. Ending inventory can fluctuate substantially only when we relax the policy that at most 2 units of WIP are permitted.

Table 19-3
Output Given No Limit on WIP*

Replication	Station 1	Station 2	Line	Ending Inventory
1	2.91	2.98	2.92	6
2	3.03	3.02	2.96	20
3	2.97	3.00	2.91	17
4	3.04	3.15	3.05	6
5	2.96	3.09	2.94	10
6	2.91	3.02	2.92	5
7	3.02	3.00	3.00	11
8	3.06	2.96	2.96	28
9	3.00	2.97	2.97	13
10	2.90	3.00	2.93	3

*The values shown under the columns labeled Station 1 and Station 2 represent the values obtained by the random variables representing the potential of that one station for the day to be simulated. An output less than the station's potential may actually be achieved.

As WIP increases, at some point, according to theory, Station 2 is decoupled from Station 1. The line output should then equal the output of Station 2. As can be seen from Table 19-3, the average line output was 2.96 units per day, varying from a low of 2.91 to a high of 3.05. It appears that an initial WIP much higher than 5 is necessary to completely decouple Stations 1 and 2. Only 2 of the 10 replications achieved an average of 3 units per day output.

To achieve the traditional approach, the only change made to the simulation is that the limitation of 2 that was placed on the inventory column is relaxed; inventory is permitted to vary without limit. A negative side effect of the traditional decoupling approach is that lead times become highly variable. Note that ending inventory at the end of the 200th trial varied from 3 units to 28 units, which implies that lead time for a job entering the system varies from 1 day to 10 days. Fluctuating lead times make it difficult to establish the time to order needed raw materials and/or the time to promise delivery to specific customers.

Thus, the traditional approach does not quite achieve the desired output and has a highly undesirable side effect. If you ponder the implications of the variation in ending inventory to managing lead times and producing a specific order to a specific due date, perhaps you will comprehend why many western managers believe their shop is controlling them rather than vice versa.

JIT Approach and Results

The JIT approach to production and inventory management would greatly reduce the variability of the system, attacking causes of variability (breakdown, scrap, etc.) at both stations while maintaining the WIP at only 2 units between stations. Assume JIT is able to reduce variability to the point that there is an 80 percent chance of getting exactly 3 units from each station, with a probability of 10 percent of getting only 2 units and a probability of 10 percent of getting 4 units. WIP between stations is limited to 2 units. The results of this simulation are shown in Table 19-4. Note that the average output of the line is about 2.94 units per day, slightly below the traditional approach, but with minimal in-process inventory and a consistent one day lead time. (If we produce 3 units per day and there are 2 units in process, a new unit will start at Station 1 on one day and complete Station 2 the next day.)

Note from Table 19-4 that the JIT approach greatly reduces the variability of line output. Line output is in a narrow band around the average of 2.94, with a low of 2.92 and a high of 2.97. WIP varies from 0 to 2, so lead time is always one day or less; a unit may enter this morning and finish this afternoon. Unfortunately, JIT achieves a smaller average output than the traditional approach. Also, quite a lot of effort may be required to achieve the reduction in variability at both stations. For example, variability may be due to scrap, the scrap may be a function of incoming raw material variability, and the incoming raw material variability may be inherent (for example, mineral ores and other natural resources have inherent variabilities that cause the number of

Table 19-4
Output Using JIT Approach and a Maximum of Two Units WIP Permitted*

Replication	Station 1	Station 2	Line
1	3.05	2.97	2.94
2	2.98	3.02	2.95
3	3.01	3.02	2.97
4	2.98	3.04	2.94
5	3.06	2.98	2.94
6	2.99	3.00	2.92
7	3.00	3.00	2.93
8	3.00	2.98	2.93
9	2.97	3.02	2.92
10	3.00	3.02	2.95

*The values shown under the columns labeled Station 1 and Station 2 represent the values obtained by the random variables representing the potential of that one station for the day to be simulated. An output less than the station's potential may actually be achieved.

defects to vary). Output variability may be due to having an occasional worker absent due to illness, vacation, or other unavoidable event.

Despite the high cost of reducing variability, when system predictability is considered, the JIT approach seems clearly superior to the traditional approach for this simple two-station, one-product situation.

TOC Approach and Results

TOC's approach to production and inventory system design is somewhat of a hybrid of the traditional and the JIT approaches. TOC would declare one of the two stations to be a constraint, buffer that station, eliminate the worst of the variability at the constraint, and try to expedite at the nonconstraint whenever the constraint buffer becomes small. The concept of what TOC is doing is quite simple. The details of how this is accomplished can be a bit confusing.

Assume TOC declares Station 2 to be the constraint. (The choice is arbitrary. In this instance, choosing Station 1 would actually produce better results.) TOC would reduce the variability of Station 2, but not to the extent JIT does. Assume TOC is able to reduce variability at Station 2 so that there is a 60 percent chance of getting 3 units, a 20 percent chance of getting only 2 units, and a 20 percent chance of getting 4 units. Because TOC permits more variability than JIT, TOC requires somewhat more WIP. Assume WIP is permitted to go to a maximum of 4 units, with 4 units initially in the system.

Since Station 2 is the constraint, TOC tries to prevent the constraint from being idle. As the traditional results demonstrate, having 5 units of WIP initially is not enough to prevent Station 2 from being idle if the output of Station 1 is not changed. TOC would therefore expedite material at Station 1 whenever the buffer at Station 2 becomes small (i.e., whenever Station 2 is threatened with lack of work). Assume the following strategy is employed: If WIP is 3 or 4, no expediting is performed at Station 1. Output is therefore 2, 3, or 4 units, each equally likely (the original situation). However, if only 1 or 2 units of WIP exist at the beginning of a day, additional management attention is placed on Station 1. For that day, for Station 1 only, there is a 50 percent probability of getting 3 units and a 50 percent probability of getting 4 units. Finally, if WIP ever hits 0, more attention is given to Station 1 so that 4 units of output are guaranteed from Station 1.

As Table 19-5 shows, the TOC approach achieves the theoretical average of 3 units per day output while maintaining a reasonably steady two-day lead time ($\frac{1}{3}$ day at Station 1, $\frac{4}{3}$ day in queue, $\frac{1}{3}$ day at Station 2).

Table 19-5
Output Using TOC Approach*

Replication	Station 1	Station 2	Line
1	3.27	3.12	3.10
2	3.22	2.94	2.94
3	3.22	3.02	3.02
4	3.20	2.98	2.98
5	3.19	2.97	2.96
6	3.19	3.01	3.00
7	3.14	2.88	2.87
8	3.18	2.97	2.96
9	3.14	3.04	3.03
10	3.24	3.00	3.00

The values shown under the columns labeled Station 1 and Station 2 represent the values obtained by the random variables representing the potential of that one station for the day to be simulated. An output less than the station's potential may actually be achieved.

The TOC approach is to unbalance the line. As Table 19-5 shows, the average capacity at Station 1 is up to about 3.2 units per day, because on days when Station 2's WIP is less than 3, Station 1's average output increases to 3.5 or 4.0. The result of increasing Station 1's capacity is to maintain sufficient buffer to decouple Station 2 from Station 1. TOC thus achieved the theoretical capacity of Station 2, approximately a 2 percent increase in output compared to JIT. TOC also required less effort than JIT at Station 2, where variability was not reduced as much. (Recall that initially the outcomes 2, 3, and 4 had probabilities of 0.333, 0.333, and 0.333, respectively; JIT changed these to 0.1, 0.8, and 0.1, respectively, while TOC changed them to 0.2, 0.6, and 0.2, respectively.) Not only is the change in variability due to TOC about half that of the change due to JIT, but if you assume that the easiest sources of variability to change were attacked first, you can argue that the work required to achieve the TOC result at Station 2 must be much less than half of the effort required to achieve the JIT result.

The relative effort required to change Station 1 is less clear. How much effort does it require to eliminate a result of 2 units output on a few critical days? Does that require more or less effort than that needed to reduce the probability of getting only 2 units to 0.1 on *all* days? Let's assume the change made at Station 1 by TOC requires the same effort as the change made at Station 1 by JIT. TOC still requires less overall effort because there is clearly less effort needed at Station 2. Thus, TOC improves the results obtained by JIT by about 2 percent while requiring less effort.

But are the TOC results superior to the JIT results? Probably so. An additional 2 units of WIP and one day of lead time seems a small price to pay for 2 percent additional output. This example actually distorts the difference in WIP that JIT and TOC would achieve. TOC has more WIP at constraints but less at nonconstraints. A system with several stations will still have only one constraint station, so for a line with four or more stations, TOC probably has less WIP than JIT in addition to its other benefits.

An important secondary point is that both MRP and JIT agree that this assembly line is well balanced, because both stations have identical characteristics. TOC does not agree with this notion; it insists that a balanced plant is inefficient. Note that most assembly lines have more than two stations. An interesting exercise would be to simulate a three or more station line for one or more of the cases and compare the output of the three-station line to the two-station results. You will find that the three-station line consistently achieves less output and that the longer the line the less the output.[3]

Clearly TOC requires more effort than the traditional approach. But in addition to increasing output by slightly more than 1 percent compared to the results of the traditional approach, TOC also stabilized the amount of WIP in the system and, hence, stabilized the due date performance. There is a definite competitive advantage to having a short lead time as well as to having a consistent lead time.

This simulation illustrates the philosophical differences between the traditional, the JIT, and the TOC approach to dealing with the problem of random fluctuations and dependent events. The traditional approach is to buffer everything, which leads to high inventory costs and long lead times. The JIT approach is to eliminate the random fluctuations. The superiority of the JIT approach compared to the traditional approach for situations in which one product is manufactured continuously is evident in this simulation. From this simulation, it is evident why repetitive manufacturers in the West are rapidly changing to the JIT approach. At the same time, it appears from this simulation that TOC can offer some improvements to the JIT approach to managing a line. TOC reduces some of the fluctuations, buffers only the constraint, and expedites elsewhere when the constraint buffer is less than it should be. TOC produced greater output with less effort and only marginally greater inventory

---

3. Extending the output to three or more stations simply requires replicating the logic for Station 2, including the interstation WIP, for the third and later stations. The output of the line is equal to the output of the final station.

than JIT. For larger plants, TOC requires less WIP than JIT because JIT maintains a small buffer between every station while TOC focuses the buffer at the constraint and permits less WIP than JIT at all other stations.

In the remainder of this chapter we discuss the theory of constraints: We present a brief history of the development of TOC. We define constraint and delineate the five steps of the theory of constraints. We describe the scheduling technique TOC uses for job shops, known as drum-buffer-rope. We describe the use of buffer status information as the shop floor control information system. We discuss performance measurement in a TOC system. We discuss the implementation of TOC via the Socratic method. Finally, we briefly describe the results achieved by some companies that are using TOC.

DEVELOPMENT OF THE THEORY OF CONSTRAINTS

The creation of the theory of constraints is primarily the effort of one man, Eliyahu Moshe Goldratt. Goldratt is a physicist by education who became involved with production system design to help a friend who operated a plant that made chicken coops. The friend asked Goldratt to design a scheduling system. His system *tripled* the output of the plant (Jayson 1987). Goldratt eventually marketed the scheduling system in the United States under the trade name OPT.

OPT was effective, but controversial. The controversy arose from the fact that a plant had to execute the OPT schedule without understanding it, because Goldratt refused to release details of his scheduling algorithm. Because many of the schedules were counterintuitive, some plants had difficulty getting supervisors to perform tasks in the sequence called for by the schedule. In an effort to alleviate this problem, Goldratt wrote a book, *The Goal: A Process of Ongoing Improvement* (1986), which explains the philosophy underlying the algorithm in the form of a novel.

With the publication of *The Goal* came the issue of what to call the philosophy underlying the scheduling algorithm. At first the term *OPT Thoughtware* was used, but this resulted in confusion between the philosophy and the proprietary software. Then the term *Synchronous Production* was used, but that terminology proved confusing also because there are other approaches that occasionally are called synchronous production. The term that finally emerged is *theory of constraints*. The theory of constraints represents a refinement of the ideas presented under the names OPT Thoughtware and Synchronous Production. Despite the name changes, the philosophy itself has remained basically the same, although refinement has occurred as experience with the philosophy in a variety of environments has created feedback on how the methods might be improved.

The theory of constraints is being refined and expanded at the Avraham Y. Goldratt Institute (named after Dr. Goldratt's late father) and elsewhere. The Goldratt Institute publishes *The Theory of Constraints Journal* on an irregular, approximately quarterly, basis. Most transfer of the theory to industry occurs through a series of seminars provided by Goldratt, Bob Fox, Dale Houle, and Donn Novotny. At the time of this writing, the institute had entered into agreements with the University of Georgia and Lehigh University to offer theory of constraint courses as continuing education courses on campus. More universities were expected to participate. Other major contributors to the development of the theory include Alex Klarmon, Eli Schreigenheim, and Avraham Mordoch. Other sources of written material on the theory include chapters in books by Blackstone (1989), and Cohen (1988), and a book by Umble and Srikanth (1989). Portions of the theory of constraints have not yet appeared in print, but are transmitted through workshops. Some of the material in this chapter is based on material not documented elsewhere.

THE FIVE STEPS OF THE THEORY OF CONSTRAINTS

In order to define the theory of constraints, it is first necessary to define the concept of a constraint. A *constraint* may be defined as anything that prevents a system from achieving a higher performance relative to its goal. This definition indicates that the theory of constraints may have a wider application than simply production planning and control systems. It also begs that we define what we mean by "goal" and how we measure performance. The goal of any business is to make more money, now and in the future. A finance professor might say that the goal of a business is to maximize the net present value of stockholders' wealth. The two definitions are essentially the same, especially if you recognize that the finance definition requires the estimation of the amount of money to be made in the future. The performance measures needed are both absolute and relative, e.g., net profit (absolute) and return on investment (relative).

There are three broad categories of constraints, internal resource constraints, market constraints, and policy constraints. Each of these can be illustrated using the simple two-station assembly line described earlier. Suppose for a moment that the demand for the single product made on the line is 4 units per day. Then using the theory of constraints approach to managing the line, Station 2 is an *internal resource constraint*. Station 2 has a capacity of 3 units per day, which is less than both Station 1 (3.2 units per day) and the market (4 units per day). When an internal resource constraint exists, it dictates the pace to be used for all resources in the plant. If, on the other hand, market demand is only 2.5 units per day, there is a market constraint. A *market constraint* exists when the market demand for an item is less than the capacity of the machine having the least capacity available to produce that item. When the market is the constraint for an item, the market should dictate the pace of production. In the simulation results shown in Table 19-1, there is a *policy constraint*. The constraint is the policy of permitting only 2 units of WIP between the two stations. As Tables 19-2 to 19-4 illustrate, changing this policy results in increased throughput for the system.

The five steps of the theory of constraints are as follows:

1. *Identify* the constraint.
2. Decide how to *exploit* the constraint.
3. *Subordinate* everything else to the action taken in 2.
4. *Elevate* the constraint. (The term *elevate* is used in TOC to mean to make possible a higher performance relative to the goal, usually by acquiring additional capacity at the constraint.)
5. WARNING: If in Step 4 the constraint is eliminated, do not let *inertia* become the new constraint.

To illustrate the five steps in action, assume that we are operating the facility with the conditions that produced Table 19-1, a simple assembly line with an output averaging 2.81 units per day, and that market demand is 3.10 units per day. We are operating the line permitting only 2 units of WIP. Having learned a little about TOC, we decide to move to the TOC approach. In Step 1, we identify the constraint to be Station 2. In Step 2, we decide to exploit this constraint by protecting the constraint with a buffer of material, by reducing the variability at Station 2, and by increasing the capacity of Station 1 by selective expediting. Recall that we expedite at Station 1 whenever Station 2's queue drops below 3 units.

In Step 3, we subordinate Station 1's output to Station 2. This is accomplished by forcing Station 1 to go idle whenever Station 2's queue is full. If we did not subordinate Station 1 to Station 2's pace, Station 1 would continue to build inventory so that the WIP awaiting Station 2 would grow without limit.

Step 4 usually requires the acquisition of additional resources by buying a new machine, subcontracting work outside the plant, or rerouting work within the plant. Suppose that we are able to subcontract work to another vendor who delivers to us 1 unit of the finished item every other day. The output of the entire plant is thus raised by 0.5 units per day to an average of 3.5 units per day. Step 5 now becomes important because by elevating the constraint from 3.0 units per day to 3.5 units per day, the new constraint becomes the market (3.1 units per day). If we continue to let Station 2 dictate the pace, we will accumulate finished goods inventory at the rate of 0.4 units per day. Since accumulating this inventory adds cost but does not add value, we have allowed inertia to limit our profitability. It is important to recognize that the way a plant is operated, even a simple two-station assembly line, changes when the constraint moves from an internal resource to the market.

A few generalizations can be made regarding the five steps for a firm that has never implemented the theory of constraints. Most facilities have policy constraints that need to be eliminated before the identification of resource constraints begins. The most common policy constraints are the use of work station utilization or efficiency as a performance measure and the use of individual incentives based on output. Since the pace of work will be dictated by the slowest station or by the market, whichever is smaller, almost all work stations will have a certain amount of planned idle time. To attempt to utilize this idle time by building products would result in excess inventory. Workers will not willingly be idle, however, if their performance evaluation will suffer as a result of the idleness. Workers certainly will not willingly be idle if they lose incentive pay as a result. Any policy that is in conflict with having planned idle time at nonconstraint resources must be changed before the constraint begins to dictate the pace of work.

A plant may or may not have an internal resource constraint. A resource is an internal constraint if and only if the resource can produce less output than the market will demand when the resource is working 24 hours per day 7 days per week. A plant that can increase output by adding a shift or working overtime does not have a resource constraint. Many production planners claim that their plants have many constraints and that the location of the constraint changes as the product mix changes. This claim is rarely, if ever, true. Very often a plant appears to have many constraints simply because every station *attempts* to work all the time because of performance measures and/or incentive bonuses. Also, the existence of large lots or batches may create temporary bottlenecks as the large lot is processed at first one station and then a second. To determine whether a plant truly has a constraint it may be necessary to eliminate machine utilization as a performance measure and to implement drum-buffer-rope scheduling, described in the next section, as though the market were the constraint. If a true resource constraint exists, it will quickly be identified by the amount of work that accumulates at the station.

Step 2 is to decide how to exploit the constraint. If the market is the constraint, we should exploit the fact that we have excess capacity. With excess capacity we should be able to eliminate almost all work in process, which will cause lead times to diminish. With shorter lead times, we should be able to aggressively pursue additional business. We are *exploiting* the fact that we have a market constraint. Whenever a true internal resource constraint is found, we exploit that constraint by operating it at all times and by protecting the constraint from problems at other stations by means of an inventory buffer. Another way to protect the constraint is to perform an inspection immediately prior to the constraint operation, so the constraint never wastes time on a part that already is defective. Another way to exploit the constraint is by adjusting our product mix to recognize the constraint. Most firms decide what to produce based on profitability per unit. TOC points out that if Item A has a profit of $2 per unit and requires 5 minutes of constraint time while Item B has a profit of $1 per unit but requires 1 minute of constraint time, then Item B is more profitable than Item A.

Consider the following example. Suppose the market for Item A is 1,000 units per week while the market for Item B is 8,000 units per week. Suppose Item A requires $2 of raw material and sells for $4 while Item B requires $1 of raw material and sells for $2. Both A and B require a single operation. Item A requires 5 minutes of machine time while Item B requires 1 minute. In any week there are 10,000 minutes of machine time available. If we consider Item A to be the more profitable, we can build all 1,000 units of A plus 5,000 units of B for a total revenue of $14,000 and a profit of $7,000. If, however, we recognize that B is more profitable *per constraint minute*, we will produce 8,000 units of B and 400 units of A for a revenue of $17,600 and a profit of $8,800. The two alternative product mixes are summarized in Table 19-6.[4]

Table 19-6
Detailed Calculations

Option	A's	Time/A	Total	B's	Time/B	Total	Sum
		Computation of Capacity Requirements					
1	1,000	5	5,000	5,000	1	5,000	10,000
2	400	5	2,000	8,000	1	8,000	10,000

Option	A's	Profit/A	Total	B's	Profit/B	Total	Sum
		Computation of Profit					
1	1,000	2	2,000	5,000	1	5,000	7,000
2	400	2	800	8,000	1	8,000	8,800

An interesting feature of theory of constraint implementation is that a firm can realize an almost instantaneous increase in profitability by (1) achieving an increase in output by buffering the constraint properly, as shown in the two-station line example, or (2) slightly altering the product mix, as shown in the Product A and B example.

Step 3 is to subordinate everything else to the decision made on how to exploit the constraint. This means that the schedule of work is determined by the constraint and that a buffer is created to protect the constraint. Material release is dictated by the needs of the constraint. Early release of material to prevent a nonconstraint from going idle must be prohibited. The workers on nonconstraint machines must be educated that they are working at nonconstraints. They should use time not needed for production to maintain the machine, cross train on a second machine, improve quality, or any other useful nonproductive tasks. Expediting is performed only when the condition of the buffer indicates that expediting is needed. Expediters should regularly check the status of the material in the constraint buffer. If a significant amount of work is missing from the constraint buffer, the expeditor should locate the

4. The same result could be obtained by using linear programming. However, many firms do not use linear programming at all and few, if any, firms use linear programming to perform production scheduling. Furthermore, if only one constraint exists, linear programming is not needed since the use of a simple ratio, as in this example, suffices. Finally, if there are two interacting constraints, the linear programming solution will be optimistic because of the existence of random fluctuations and dependent events, as illustrated in the simple two-station assembly line case.

material, expedite its production, and then try to identify why the material was late and, if possible, correct the cause of the delay. By eliminating the largest causes of delay of material moving to the constraint buffer, one can eventually reduce the size of the constraint buffer. Thus, the effort to improve the shop floor is subordinated to the constraint as well as the effort to schedule and control the shop floor.

Step 4 is to elevate the constraint. This step should be taken with caution, because when the constraint shifts, the way in which the shop is operated must also shift. Everyone affected (which means everyone in the plant) should know in advance that the constraint will shift, and therefore the way in which the shop will operate will also shift. Many firms have found that their constraint is their newest, most expensive, and most highly automated piece of equipment. This machine is the constraint because a great deal of work was moved to it in order to eliminate lengthier operations on other equipment. Sometimes the older equipment may even be moved into storage. Once the fact that this machine is a constraint is recognized, the jobs with the least profit per constraint minute often can be moved back to older equipment, which now is recognized to be a nonconstraint. By shifting work from the constraint to a nonconstraint, the revenue generated by the shop is increased with little or no increase in operating expense. At a recent conference of theory of constraint implementors, most attendees reported eliminating all internal constraints within one to six months of TOC implementation. Many eliminated the internal constraints without investing in additional capacity. This result is not surprising when you realize that many operations can be performed on alternate equipment and that when constraints and nonconstraints have been identified, it is a fairly simple matter to offload some of the work currently performed at the constraint onto nonconstraint stations.

DRUM-BUFFER-ROPE SCHEDULING

Drum-buffer-rope scheduling has one distinctive feature that must be emphasized—a process batch size that is not equal to the transfer batch size. A *process batch* is defined to be the number of units run after a station sets up to produce some Part A and before the station sets up to produce some other Part B. A *transfer batch* is defined to be the number of units of an item physically transported from some Work Station X to some other Work Station Y. In most job shop operations the transfer batch and the process batch are the same, i.e., an entire process batch is completed at one station and then materials handling personnel are called to transfer the job to the next station on the routing. It is not at all uncommon for a job requiring one hour of work at each of three stations to require a three-week lead time—roughly one week in queue and one hour in process at each station. The long queue time is due to the large amount of work in process maintained at each station. However, if the plant manager decides to put this job on a truck in two hours, the job can be completed. All three stations set up for the job and pieces are carried from station to station whenever one piece is completed. In this situation the transfer batch is one and the process batch is the order size. The third station is able to complete its operation a few minutes after the first station completes the last piece, with a little over one hour elapsed, total.

TOC assumes that a transfer batch of one is used whenever it is needed. Because most operators work at nonconstraints, there is no reason not to have the worker pull material forward from feeding stations whenever the worker runs out of work. Each station is furnished with a schedule of work that should be coming through the station in the near future. It is therefore a relatively minor task for an idle worker to check possible feeding stations for completed work and to bring forward any items that are ready to be transferred. In this situation the transfer batch is usually variable—however many happen to be ready when the next operator checks. The process batch size usually is equal to the order size. The transition to a smaller transfer batch can be made with no change in plant layout—provided one recognizes that nonconstraint workers can move materials. However, Shigeo Shingo (1987) has several comments on shop layout that might be helpful.

The TOC approach raises two interesting questions. First, the JIT approach advocates reducing setup time until a shop can afford a process batch of one. If the transfer batch has been lowered to one unit to speed the order through the shop, what additional benefit is to be gained by reducing the process batch down to one unit? Second, since the order will be shipped to the customer as a batch, does it ever make sense to have the process batch be less than the order size (or the delivery size in the case of a blanket order with several deliveries)? Unless there is some clear benefit to be obtained by continuing to reduce the setup time beyond that needed to support a process batch equal to the order size for all orders, JIT is creating wasted effort by forcing the transfer batch to equal the process batch.[5]

The concept of drum-buffer-rope is as follows: Ideally, all nonconstraint stations preceding the constraint on a part's routing should begin production of the part as soon as the part is released to the first station on its routing. Thus, parts move very quickly from material release to the constraint buffer. The parts then wait for an indeterminate time in the constraint buffer until the constraint begins to process the part. Once the constraint begins to process the part, ideally all nonconstraints on the routing between the constraint and the shipping dock should also set up for the part, so the part is moved one unit at a time to the shipping point. Thus, drum-buffer-rope schedule development consists of two stages. First, develop a detailed schedule for the constraint itself, this schedule is called the *drum*. Second, determine how much time is to be

---

5. In a one card kanban operation, the kanban authorizes production and transport, so the process batch clearly equals the transfer batch. In a dual card kanban operation, the number of production kanbans usually equals the number of transport kanbans, which implies a transfer batch equal to the process batch, even though this implication is never stated.

allowed for material to move from material release to the constraint and, for each end item, how much time should be allowed for material to move from the constraint to shipping. This time offset is called the *rope*, because it links material release to the constraint so the constraint can pull forward the material as it needs it. A rope also pulls material forward from the constraint to shipping (or, in the case of a good that does not require processing at the constraint, the rope pulls material from release to shipping). The material that is scheduled to be at the constraint at any point in time is called the *constraint buffer*. Material that is scheduled to be at shipping at any point in time is called the *shipping buffer*. This description should make clear the origin of the name drum-buffer-rope.

The unit of measurement for the constraint buffer is standard time, i.e., time estimated to be required for the constraint to process all items in the buffer. The time represented by the internal constraint buffer is equal to the lead-time offset of the rope connecting the constraint to material release. Because of the assumption of a transfer batch of one, TOC assumes that all non-constraint stations will begin processing material as soon as it is released, so the delay in moving to the constraint buffer is minimal. TOC recognizes that some time is required to move from material release to the constraint buffer, so material is not considered to be overdue until a time equal to one-half the buffer size has passed. If material that should be in the first half of the buffer is missing, corrective action will be taken to expedite material and to determine and correct the cause for the delay.

There is a second rope that pulls material from the constraint to the shipping dock. The length of this rope is equal to the length of the shipping buffer, which is a buffer maintained to protect the shipping schedule. Although each product may have a distinct shipping buffer size, there is usually only one internal constraint and, hence, only one internal constraint buffer size. The unit of measure for the shipping buffer is units of end item.

Drum-buffer-rope scheduling thus reduces to: (1) identify the constraint, (2) sequence jobs on the constraint, (3) decide on the size of the constraint buffers (which fixes the length of the rope from the constraint to material release), and (4) decide on the size of the shipping buffers (which, in effect, forward schedules material from the constraint to shipping and fixes the promise date to the customer). The job of shop scheduling, thought by most researchers to be extremely complex, is thus reduced to a simple single machine scheduling problem. The simplicity of the problem is conditional on the shop having one or no internal constraints.

A common objection to theory of constraints is the notion that there are many interacting constraints in a shop. This notion really is not true. Although most companies that have implemented TOC *initially* believed they had many constraints, all have found that they had few resource contraints, that they rarely interacted, and that moving the constraint to the market is much simpler than they thought.

If demand can be forecast with accuracy over the planning horizon (and all scheduling procedures make this assumption), then the load required from every resource can be predicted. One resource will be more heavily loaded than all others. This statement can be made with confidence, since it is extremely unlikely that two or more resources will have exactly the same load. The most heavily loaded resource is treated as the constraint; all other resources are subordinated to it. If a shop has a highly seasonal demand for several items, such that the most heavily loaded resource shifts from season to season, then the planning horizon should be one year. By having a one-year planning horizon, the effect of seasonality is eliminated and the most heavily loaded resource for the entire year is selected as the constraint. Of course, an unanticipated shift in *product mix* may cause the constraint to move. But such a shift would cause replanning in *any* system.

The schedule created by drum-buffer-rope is entirely feasible provided that the constraint is never permitted to go idle and the efficiency and utilization of the constraint are approximately as predicted. Buffer management, discussed in the next section, is intended to insure the constraint is used as planned, assuring schedule performance.

BUFFER MANAGEMENT

There are three types of buffers present in the theory of constraints, two of which have been discussed. The constraint buffer protects the constraint; the shipping buffer protects the promised due date delivery. There is also an assembly buffer, which stages nonconstraint parts at assembly points with constraint parts so that constraint parts are never delayed for lack of nonconstraint parts. If all buffers in the shop have the correct material in them at all times and never have material that is not supposed to be there, the shop must be operating on schedule. Any schedule deviation will cause expected material to be missing from the buffer. Management using the theory of constraints is a type of management by exception that reacts only when material is missing from the buffer.

Suppose the constraint is scheduled to produce the following parts in the next week:

Part	Time	Units
A	7.5 hours	150
B	8.5 hours	200
C	7 hours	100
D	17 hours	300

Suppose further that the constraint buffer is set to 16 hours. Then, at present, all 150 units of A and all 200 units of B should be in the buffer.

For buffer management purposes, the buffer is logically divided into thirds. At present, one-third of the buffer is about 5 hours. We might choose to call Region I 5 hours, Region II 6 hours, and Region III 5 hours. We could represent this buffer as a visual display as shown in Figure 19-1.

Figure 19-1
Hypothetical Constraint Buffer

Minutes	60	AAAAA	AABBBB	BBBBB
	45	AAAAA	AABBBB	BBBBB
	30	AAAAA	AAABBB	BBBBB
	15	AAAAA	AAABBB	BBBBB
Hours:		12345	678901	23456
Region		I	II	III

In Figure 19-1, the vertical axis shows minutes, each letter represents a vertical distance of 15 minutes; the horizontal axis shows hours, the numbers on the next to last row represent hours in the future, from 1 to 16. Note that the hours 10 through 16 are identified only by the last digit. Figure 19-1 indicates that for the next 7.5 hours the constraint will process A and for 8.5 hours after that it will process B, consistent with the schedule presented earlier. Assume that the letter (A or B) is colored green if the required material is present in the buffer and red if the material has not yet been reported as being present at the buffer.

Note that this visual could be kept up to date at all times simply by having a PC or a terminal in the constraint area and having the material handler log material in and out as material is moved. Then anyone walking by the constraint area and glancing at the display could determine in a glance whether the constraint was properly protected. For that matter, with the computer at the constraint hooked to a network of PCs or to a central computer, it would be possible for anyone in the plant having access to a PC or a terminal to check the status of the constraint buffer at any time.

A red letter occurring in Region I of the buffer would literally raise a red flag that immediate expediting is required. A red letter occurring in Region II indicates material is taking somewhat too long to move to the constraint. Investigative and corrective action is required, although expediting is not yet indicated. In theory of constraints terminology a *hole* in the buffer occurs whenever material that should be in the buffer is missing.

The shipping buffer and assembly buffer can be created and managed in a fashion analogous to the constraint buffer. The size of the buffer is a function of the degree of variability that exists within the shop and of the extent to which nonconstraints are loaded. If the shop has some machines with long setup times, others that break down quite frequently, and nonconstraint machines that are loaded quite heavily, then a large buffer is required to protect the constraint and to permit ample time for jobs to move from shipping to the constraint. Whenever a hole occurs in Region I or Region II of the buffer, the cause of the hole is investigated and recorded. Those problems that most frequently appear on the list of causes, such as long setups at Machine X or long breakages at Machine Y, are high priority items for corrections.

Like JIT, TOC advocates continuous improvement, but TOC wishes to focus the continuous improvement effort on those things that cause the most frequent and most severe holes in the buffer. Once these problems are eliminated, so that a hole in Region I of the constraint has not occurred for some time, then the size of the buffer can be reduced. Note the sequence of events. JIT removes inventory and then attacks the problems that surface. TOC uses buffer management information to identify the most critical problems, corrects the problem, and then reduces the inventory. It therefore seems logical that one should get more output from a TOC-run plant as problems are corrected than from an identical plant run by JIT. A JIT-run plant causes disruptions in flow in order to identify problems; a TOC plant identifies potential disruptions in flow and attempts to correct them before flow is actually disrupted. Because of continuous flow, other things being equal, the TOC plant should have more output.

It is also important to note that buffer management is a complete shop floor control system, provided that nonconstraint stations are evaluated on their ability to keep material moving on schedule into the buffers. In the next section we discuss the use of local performance measures that are consistent with global objectives.

PERFORMANCE MEASUREMENT

As has been noted, the present system of performance measurement used by most western companies is not consistent with either TOC or JIT operations. The most common problem is machine utilization and efficiency measures at nonconstraint stations. Because we desire nonconstraint stations to produce only what is needed to support the schedule, nonconstraints must have some idle time. However, if the machine utilization performance measure is retained, the machine operators and their supervisors will literally beg, borrow, and steal material to prevent idle time. Thus, machine utilization must be eliminated as a performance measure. Anything that would cause an operator to want to be busy, such as incentives based on the number of pieces produced, must also be eliminated.

A logical question then becomes: What performance measures should be used by a company operating under the theory of constraints? It is easy to criticize existing measures, but some performance measure is necessary so that management can properly do its job. The most important performance measure is performance to schedule. Performance to schedule implies that pieces are not made early and they are not made late. Therefore, two performance measures are required, one to measure things done ahead of schedule and a second to measure things done behind schedule. The theory of constraints suggests inventory dollar days as a measure of things done ahead of schedule (and hence inventoried) and throughput dollar days as a measure of things done behind schedule.[6]

---

6. See Volume 1, Number 3, *The Theory of Constraints Journal*, for a more detailed discussion.

A dollar day is simply one dollar held for one day. If you borrow money from a bank to finance your education or a car, you pay for the use of that money on the basis of the amount you borrowed and the length of time you held the money—dollar days. It makes sense to value inventory that is built ahead of schedule on the basis of dollar days. In essence, the company has loaned the using department the resources needed to make the inventory. The department should repay the company based on the dollars tied up in inventory and the length of time the money is held as inventory. It also makes sense to measure shipments that are delayed on the basis of dollar days. The delay in shipment will probably result in delay in payment. The cost to the company of receiving payment late is measured by the size of the payment and the number of days that payment is delayed because of late shipment.

Both inventory dollar days and throughput dollar days are measured relative to a buffer. Let's first consider the shipping buffer. To consider the shipping buffer in isolation, assume the market is the constraint so that only a shipping buffer exists. Inventory dollar days would be accrued if material is present at the shipping dock (or finished goods inventory) and the material is not required by the shipping buffer. This material should not yet have been released to the floor. Having been released, it should not have been processed by any station since all stations should have noted that the material was not being pulled into the shipping buffer. Thus, the stockroom that released the material and every station that processed the material is charged with inventory dollar days equal to the cost of the material held in inventory times the length of time until that material will be needed. As time passes, the time until needed will diminish and so the penalty will diminish.

Note that this process has two important features. First, the measure is consistent with the actual cost to the company for the mistake that was made. Second, as the problem becomes corrected, the penalty for the mistake is eliminated. Consistency is important so that decisions made on the basis of local interest do not have a negative impact on the entire company. The problem with machine utilization as a measure at nonconstraint stations is that it is not consistent; there is incentive for the station to produce inventory that is not needed. The elimination of the penalty as the mistake is eliminated is important because it provides an incentive for the work station to operate efficiently whenever there is work available.

The effect of using inventory dollar days and throughput dollar days on a nonconstraint is as follows: When work arrives, the worker will verify that the job appears on one of the buffer documents. As long as the job appears on one of the buffer documents, the worker will not be charged inventory dollar days for processing it. Throughput dollar days are computed from the midway point in the buffer. If the work on hand has not reached the midpoint of the time buffer, the worker can avoid any dollar day penalty by processing the job and passing it along before the halfway mark is reached. If the work has reached the halfway mark, the worker is charged throughput dollar days until the work is passed to the next station. The worker has incentive to work quickly either to avoid throughput dollar days or to eliminate an existing dollar day charge.

The use of inventory dollar days is particularly effective in eliminating a tendency on the part of workers to get material early in order to avoid idle time. This tendency is a habit in most shops that have been evaluated on the basis of machine utilization, and the habit will require some effort to break. With the new measure, the worker should soon realize that not only is it not good to work ahead of schedule but that such action will actually incur a penalty.

A worker also has incentive to work carefully. If work is done improperly, the station causing the defect is charged throughput dollar days until the defect is corrected or a replacement unit can be made. If a part that has constraint time embedded in it is scrapped, that part can never be replaced. The constraint has no time to spare to devote to the replacement part. Thus, throughput dollar days can be charged to some arbitrary future point in order to arrive at a finite penalty that emphasizes the cost to the firm of losing a part that has been processed by the constraint.

Sometimes a worker will have two jobs in the station at the same time. Throughput dollar days will cause the worker to process the job that is closest to its due date first (assuming approximately equal order value). If the worker acts in a manner to minimize the throughput dollar day charge to the local station, he or she is doing precisely what top management wants done. A consistent performance measure provides excellent shop floor control without the need for management intervention.

If a constraint exists, the constraint station will be provided with a schedule. The use of throughput dollar days and inventory dollar days encourages the constraint operator to keep precisely to the schedule and to produce with perfect quality. If the station for some reason runs out of work, the station is not charged with throughput dollar days while it is idle; the station holding the material needed is charged. However, when work arrives, the operator has an incentive to work quickly and carefully. The constraint operator has a double incentive to do work in the proper sequence: If a job is done early, that job creates inventory dollar days while throughput dollar days accrue on the job that should have been processed.

To summarize this section, throughput dollar days and inventory dollar days provide an incentive for workers to follow the schedule and to work quickly and carefully. They are consistent performance measures in that if the performance of a particular station improves with respect to a measure, the performance of the entire shop must also improve. The performance measures would also work well with an MRP system or a JIT system provided that all workers are made aware of the schedule to be followed.

IMPLEMENTATION TECHNIQUES

A doctrine of the theory of constraints is that any person responsible for decision making in a particular area is a potential constraint. The chief of purchasing can become the constraint by ordering the wrong material; the chief of personnel can become the constraint by hiring the wrong type of workers; marketing can become the constraint by emphasizing the wrong product(s); many different sections of manufacturing can become the constraint by processing jobs in the wrong sequence or the wrong quantity. It is therefore important for the decision makers to feel a sense of ownership of the global decision-making process. This can best be accomplished by having each decision maker invent the specific system to be used in his or her area.

At the same time, it is important that all areas of a firm are pulling in the same direction, that is, all areas must agree on what constraints exist and what should be done to exploit or elevate the constraints.

To accomplish both goals simultaneously, theory of constraint implementation should proceed from the top of the organization down. At each level, a manager who has just received education on the theory of constraints makes a presentation of an implementation plan for his or her area of responsibility to a superior. Unless some gross error in identifying the nature of the constraint has been made, the superior will accept the plan and request the manager to provide for education in the theory of constraints for any subordinate decision makers. This implementation procedure is called *Socratic* because, like Socrates, the manager must ask questions, not provide answers. It is often difficult for a manager to avoid the temptation to "correct" a subordinate's implementation plan. Nevertheless, this temptation must be avoided. If a manager changes the solution, the implementation becomes the manager's, not the subordinate's. The feeling of ownership is lost. The feeling of ownership is far more important than the precise sequence in which improvement actions are taken. If the manager has patience, the subordinate will eventually find the correct solution—and retain ownership of the solution.

The theory of constraints emphasizes a continual process of improvement. Improvement should be focused on the constraints so that improvement proceeds as rapidly as is practical. Every decision maker should therefore know what the constraints are, how his or her area of responsibility interfaces with the constraints, what the next constraints are expected to be if a given constraint is broken, and how his or her area interfaces with the anticipated constraints. With this knowledge, the decision maker should be able to identify the set of problems experienced by his or her area that have the greatest impact on the business.

In a sense, the theory of constraints makes the decision-making process much easier. Most managers have an almost endless set of data to track and potential improvement efforts to consider. By identifying those problems that have the greatest impact on the constraint, a manager can limit the amount of data that must be monitored and also postpone consideration of certain improvement efforts. At the same time, the amount of information that must be passed around the organization can be reduced, as a lot of detail concerning nonconstraint activities can simply not be transmitted.

The theory of constraints provides two useful techniques for use in developing and refining implementation plans. The first is effect-cause-effect and the second is a cloud diagram.

Effect-Cause-Effect

In order to create a good implementation plan, it is necessary to identify those problems that create or contribute to constraints and to understand their underlying causes. For example, the market for a product might be a constraint. When analyzing performance versus competition, we might note that although we are competitive on cost, we have poorer quality and longer lead time than the competition. We should therefore identify the causes of the poor quality and/or long lead time. The long lead time might be caused by a lack of certain components at assembly. It should be easy to verify that assembly jobs are often held due to lack of a full set of components. There are many reasons that components might be missing. One is that a constraint exists in the system. A second is that workers may be taking components allocated to one assembly in order to complete a second assembly. Another is that the inventory records are poor and the component never existed in the first place. In order to find a solution we need to understand why the parts are missing. If inventory records are the problem, we need a much different implementation plan than if a constraint is the problem.

At this point we have three hypothesized causes of the problem, any one of which could take quite a bit of time to pursue. Are any of the hypothesized causes worth pursuing? Here is where effect-cause-effect comes in. If any of the three hypothesized causes of the problem really is the cause, there should be some subsidiary effect that exists and that we can verify. For example, if inventory records are the problem, we should find that many of the components do not have correct on-hand quantities recorded. We can verify this subsidiary effect by identifying several components, counting the on-hand quantity, and determining whether the count is correct. If all of the parts tested have accurate counts, it is unlikely that poor inventory records are causing a persistent problem with missing parts. If there is a constraint in the system, a subsidiary effect would be that several of the parts that are supposed to be at the assembly area are sitting at the constraint awaiting processing. We could check this by examining the routings of the missing parts for common stations, then checking the stations that appear on all or most routings to see if one of them has a lot of the missing parts. If there is no concentration of parts at any one station, we are less comfortable pursuing the notion that a constraint exists than if one station has all the parts.

The key feature of effect-cause-effect is that before we spend a lot of time tracing cause and effect we find a way to test whether or not a hypothesized cause is a likely candidate. If we can find no verifiable subsidiary effect, we are likely to waste time by pursuing the present hypothesized cause. Our search is likely to be more effective if we give further thought to possible causes and find one that has subsidiary effects that can be verified. The use of a testable hypothesis is a technique of scientific method that is taught to scientists but, for some reason, is not a standard part of the manager's tool kit. Because it is important for a manager to make effective use of problem solving time, the use of effect-cause-effect to avoid spending time on dead ends is recommended.

Cloud Diagrams

Once the cause of a problem is understood, its solution may not be obvious. The cloud diagram is a useful technique for trying to identify a solution to an intractable problem. For example, the most common topic of articles discussing inventory management is the topic of batch size, indicating that there is no agreement on the ideal batch sizing procedure. Figure 19-2 shows a cloud diagram of the batch sizing decision. The first task is to identify the objective of the decision to be made. In this case, we wish to find a way to minimize inventory costs. Since inventory costs are composed of the costs associated with holding inventory and the costs associated with processing orders, two requirements for minimizing inventory costs are minimizing holding costs and minimizing order processing costs.

Figure 19-2
Cloud Diagram

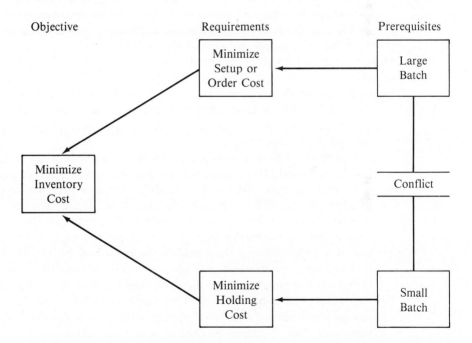

To complete the cloud diagram it is necessary to identify the prerequisite(s) of each requirement. To minimize our holding costs, a prerequisite is that we order in small batches. To minimize our order processing costs, a prerequisite is that we order in large batches. A conflict exists because we cannot both order in large batches and order in small batches. The usefulness of the cloud diagram as a problem solving technique is that it forces us to understand the nature of the problem. To understand that we cannot order in both small batches and large batches is to achieve a much better understanding of the problem than merely to understand that we should minimize inventory costs but that we need inventory.

Once we have clarified the nature of the problem, we can check that the assumptions used in defining the problem are appropriate. The task of determining underlying assumptions is the most difficult and the most critical part of the cloud diagramming process. It is easy to identify a trivial assumption that merely restates a requirement. For example, we might say that it is necessary to minimize inventory holding costs because holding inventory costs money. That is not an underlying assumption; it merely restates the requirement. If we cannot find the true underlying assumption, the technique will be useless. To find the underlying assumption, ask why is this requirement a requirement? Why does it absolutely have to be? In this case, a good statement of the assumption relating holding cost to inventory cost is that we assume that we must pay our vendor for our material before our customer will pay us. Note that this way of stating the assumption does not merely restate the requirement, it truly explains the requirement. If we could find a way to get our customer to pay for the raw material, we wouldn't care how much inventory we kept. (As the amount of inventory held by defense contractors that are paid on a progress payment basis amply demonstrates!)

Figure 19-3 gives the cloud diagram with an underlying assumption for each of the five arcs. There must exist at least one assumption per arc. If any of the assumptions can be shown to be invalid, the conflict disappears, and the problem is solved. As was mentioned in the previous paragraph, if a contractor can have the customer agree to pay the vendor, the contractor is happy to work with large batches.

The other assumptions present in the usual batch sizing model are now briefly explained. The requirement to minimize setup or order costs assumes that setup costs are variable, that is, the cost varies directly with the number of setups or orders. For a manufactured part this assumption may or may not be true. There is always a real setup cost at the constraint. There often is not a setup cost at a nonconstraint, although there may sometimes be an expediting cost if a setup causes a deep hole in the constraint buffer. Order cost also may not be a variable cost. We usually include in the order cost the cost of filling out the paperwork for the order and the cost of offloading the truck and storing the goods received. One might ask whether the offloading and storage costs are a function of annual volume or a function of the size of shipments. One can make an argument that the cost is a function of annual volume and is independent of the size of an individual shipment. The process of filling out the paperwork is largely computerized and perhaps is more correctly treated as a fixed cost. The cost of negotiating the purchase may also be fixed. Many firms negotiate a blanket purchase order once a year. For a firm having setup or order costs that virtually are fixed costs, the use of small batches, as JIT advocates, is clearly indicated.

The notion that a large batch is a prerequisite to a small setup cost (accepting the assumption that setup costs are variable) assumes that there is an

Figure 19-3
Evaporating the Cloud

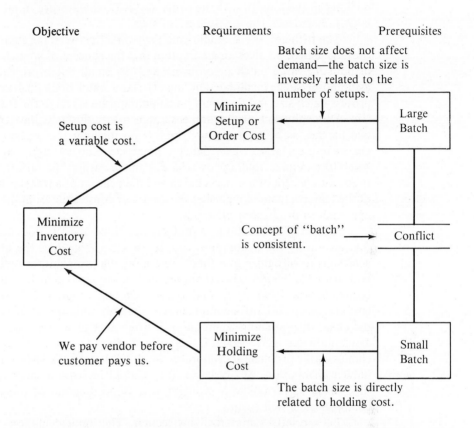

inverse relationship between the batch size and the number of setups. This assumption is expressed explicitly in the total cost equation used to derive the economic order quantity. The total cost equation has a term stating that the total setup cost is equal to the cost of setup times the annual demand divided by the batch size. Annual demand is assumed to be a constant, independent of batch size. One could argue that the batch size determines the lead time, the longer the lead time the less demand there will be, and therefore the batch size should be chosen based on annual volume considerations, not on setup cost considerations. The Japanese essentially used this line of reasoning to arrive at the practice of JIT and then took their reasoning a step further: Given that volume considerations determine the batch size, let's force the setup cost down to something that is consistent with the desired batch size.

The notion that a small batch is a prerequisite to minimizing holding cost involves a similar assumption—that the batch size is directly related to the holding cost. Again the economic order quantity formula makes the assumption explicit: Holding cost is equal to one-half the batch size times the unit cost times the holding cost percentage. In this instance, the assumption seems unassailable. A change in volume does not affect the average on-hand quantity in the long run. If the order size is Q, the average number on hand is $Q \div 2$, independent of the rate of sales.

The fifth arc, the arc indicating the conflict between the small batch and the large batch, involves an assumption that the concept of a batch is the same in both the large batch prerequisite and the small batch prerequisite. This assumption can be invalidated because the large batch prerequisite refers to the process batch size and the small batch prerequisite refers to the transfer batch size. Although batch production environments traditionally have treated these two batches as being the same, there is no inherent reason that we cannot choose to use a large process batch to minimize setup cost and a small transfer batch to minimize holding cost. As was stated earlier, the differentiation between the concept of a process batch and the concept of a transfer batch is one of the features that distinguishes the theory of constraints from the traditional approach to production planning.

The act of diagramming a problem in a cloud diagram does not guarantee that an underlying assumption can be broken. Sometimes the best one can achieve is to recognize that there are conflicting prerequisites and accept the best available compromise. (Compromise is the approach that underlies the economic order quantity formulation—accepting a trade-off between holding cost and setup cost.) If a compromise is the only solution, so be it. However, the cloud diagramming technique will often expose an unstated, underlying assumption that is erroneous. The process of exposing the erroneous assumption eliminates the problem; it evaporates the cloud. Because exposing an erroneous hidden assumption usually leads to a marked increase in performance, the time taken to formulate a problem as a cloud diagram before accepting a compromise is well spent.

Let's briefly summarize this section. The implementation process for the theory of constraints relies on managers at each level creating an implementation plan. This approach is used because of a belief that a feeling of ownership of the plan is more important than the short run specifics of the plan. In order to implement, a manager needs to understand the five steps and to understand where the firm's constraints presently are and where they are likely to go in the foreseeable future. Two problem solving techniques, known as effect-cause-effect and the cloud diagram, are useful to managers preparing an implementation plan.

REPORTED RESULTS

Because the theory of constraints is quite new, only a few firms are actively using the concepts and only a portion of those have reported results. Firms that have reported results, discussed briefly below, include General Motors, DuPont, and AT&T. The reason we have elected to report on a technique that is still quite young and not thoroughly tested is that it appears to offer a method of moving the Just-in-Time philosophy of keeping material moving, never idle, from the sequential flow environment to the batch production environment. By having a small transfer batch, a large process batch can be moved through a shop rather quickly. A necessary consequence is that some machines have idle time. We accept that we cannot perfectly balance an assembly line. Perhaps we should also accept an unbalanced shop and learn to exploit the constraint rather than trying to create interacting constraints.

The plant that has reported the most complete set of statistics concerning theory of constraint implementation is GM's Windsor, Ontario, trim plant. Their results were reported in an article in *Automotive Industries* (Callahan 1989). Windsor calls their approach to production planning *synchronous manufacturing*, which they describe as an amalgam of theory of constraints and Just-in-Time concepts. Synchronous manufacturing implementation began in 1986, at which time the company was achieving 17.3 inventory turns per year. Their goal was to achieve 35 turns. By December 1988 the plant had achieved 50.4 turns. The company also achieved a 94 percent reduction in lead time and a \$23 million reduction in annual costs, while increasing output by 16.8 percent.

An interesting aspect of these numbers is that lead time was reduced by 94 percent while inventory was reduced by 68 percent. For most companies employing JIT, the lead time reduction is usually one percentage point different, at most, from the inventory reduction. The reason for the difference is that JIT uses a transfer batch equal to the process batch while TOC does not.

AT&T's microelectronics division reports results achieved with what they call *common sense manufacturing* (CSM) at their Reading plant (Cannon and Kapusta 1989). Common sense manufacturing is described as including an end-to-end pull system, strategic buffers, constraints management, drum-buffer-rope scheduling, and total employee involvement. Like GM, AT&T's approach apparently is to merge the theory of constraints and Just-in-Time concepts. The Reading plant's reported results include a 50 percent reduction in inventory, a 70 percent reduction in lead time, a 60 percent increase in rework, and a five-fold increase in turnover. They do not report their change in output, however, since turns are defined as annual sales divided by inventory, and since inventory went down only 50 percent, for turns to increase five-fold, annual sales must have increased by 250 percent. They do report, "The results left no doubt that CSM techniques did, in fact, work—and work well beyond our greatest expectations."

DuPont reports some short-term results achieved early into a theory of constraints implementation (Davis and Fox 1989). The implementation team identified the constraint and proceeded to implement the five steps. First, they noticed that the operator was manually counting parts, delaying the machine. A counter was moved from an unused machine, saving one hour per eight-hour shift. Next, the team noted that part of the time the constraint was performing rework for a nonconstraint machine. This activity probably made sense using traditional cost accounting but it made no sense from a theory of constraints perspective. The rework activity was moved back to the nonconstraint. This change freed another hour per eight-hour shift. Next, the team noted that the three operators (one per shift) had quite different methods. A conference was held and a standard method was agreed on and implemented. Within five weeks the output of the constraint had moved from 3,000 units per shift (on average, varying from 2,000 to 4,000) to 8,000 units per shift. The production rate was then backed down to 5,000 units per shift, with little variation, to meet the needs of the market. The original constraint was broken and the market is pacing production, with a different machine than the original constraint identified as the next constraint.

SUMMARY

The theory of constraints is a new philosophy that has a lot in common with Just-in-Time but also has some critical differences. There are two basic differences. The first is that the theory of constraints accepts the existence of a constraint, at least temporarily, and focuses the improvement effort on the constraint and related work stations. The second is that the theory of constraints uses overlapped production (transfer batch not equal to the process batch) to schedule work through a batch production environment, while Just-in-Time provides no scheduling mechanism for a batch environment. Thus, the theory of constraints scheduling approach has wider applicability than Just-in-Time (although Just-in-Time's continuous improvement philosophy and quality emphasis clearly is applicable to batch production environments).

There are five steps to the theory of constraints: identify the constraint, exploit it, subordinate everything else to it, elevate the constraint, and avoid inertia when the constraint shifts. In exploiting the constraint, the drum-buffer-rope scheduling technique and buffer management are used. In finding ways to elevate the constraint, the techniques of effect-cause-effect and the cloud diagram often are useful.

EXERCISES

1. Discuss the process that JIT advocates for setting priorities for problems to be addressed. How would you modify this process for use with TOC?

2. Use a six-sided die to simulate the two-station line described in this chapter. If the die roll results in a one or two, pass two counters (chips, matches, pennies) to the next location. If the die yields a three or four, pass three; if the die yields a five or six, pass four. Begin with two counters awaiting Station 2. On each turn, Station 1 rolls first, then Station 2. Roll for 20 trials and record the results. Repeat the experiment using three stations. Record the average output per trial for each line length.

3. Repeat Exercise 2 using a microcomputer to perform the experiment. An electronic spreadsheet or the Basic compiler are both good choices for model development. Perform 200 trials of each line. Determine the mean and standard deviation of the output per turn.

4. Repeat Exercise 3 with the three-station line using a beginning and maximum WIP of 10 units. Before conducting the experiment, record the number of units you think you will obtain. Compare the actual results to your estimate.

5. How might the experiment in Exercises 2 and 3 be modified to unbalance the assembly line while retaining an expected output of three units per day? Change the experiment using whatever method you derive and repeat it twice, first using a buffer of size two, then a buffer of size four. Which buffer size do you recommend? Discuss how an actual plant would decide which station should be the constraint and how large the buffer should be.

6. List and discuss three likely reasons material might be missing from a constraint buffer. What actions can be taken to correct these problems?

7. Modify the experiment in Exercise 2 or 3 so that there is a 5 percent chance that any single item completing Station 1 is scrapped. Repeat the experiment with a 5 percent scrap at Station 2 only. Discuss the implications of scrap at constraint and nonconstraint stations.

8. Suppose an operation requires 10 minutes to complete on Machine A and 5 minutes to complete on Machine B. Both Machine A and Machine B have charge rates of $0.40 per minute. On which machine should you make the part? Now suppose you find that Machine B is the constraint and that profit per constraint minute is $3 for the least profitable item. On which machine would you make the part? What would the accounting department be likely to say about your decision?

9. Assume a three-station plant makes three products, as follows:

Product	Weekly Demand	Sales Price	Material Cost	WC1	WC2	WC3
A	500	$100	$40	5	3	8
B	800	90	40	6	7	3
C	900	80	35	4	2	4

The times shown for WC1, WC2, and WC3 are in minutes. There are 10,080 minutes per week available at each work center. What product mix should this plant produce? How much time will WC1, WC2, and WC3 work? What will be the effect of having all produce output for 10,080 minutes?

10. Given the information in Exercise 9, suppose the next jobs to be processed by WC1 are:

Job	Requirement	Present
B	50	50
A	100	80
C	120	0
B	60	0

By present, we mean the number of items presently available in the buffer. Suppose further that WC1 is the constraint and that the constraint buffer is 16 hours. Should expediting be performed? Should other action be taken?

11. Given the following two-station, four-product line:

Product	Demand	Price	Material	WC1	WC2
A	800	$30	$10	10	3
B	400	$50	$20	6	8
C	900	$25	$15	2	3
D	300	$70	$30	15	8

The times shown for WC1 and WC2 are time required in minutes, price is the selling price, material is the material cost, and demand is weekly demand. What should the product mix be? Suppose that management requires production of at least 200 of each of the four products. What is the cost of this policy? Why would this requirement be imposed?

12. George borrows $2,400 to buy a microcomputer. He agrees to repay the loan in 12 monthly installments of $200 plus simple interest of 1 percent per month on the outstanding balance. How many dollar days are accumulated? How much interest does George pay? What is the relationship between dollar days and interest paid?

13. Create a cloud diagram of the problem of identifying the frequency with which machine maintenance should be performed. Indicate the assumption underlying each arc and possible ways to invalidate each assumption.

SELECTED READINGS

Blackstone, John H., Jr. *Capacity Management*. Cincinnati: South-Western Publishing Co., 1989.

Callahan, Joseph M. "GM's Plant Saver." *Automotive Industries* (March 1989).

Cannon, Joseph J., and Gary Kapusta. "Just-in-Time at AT&T's Reading Works." *Just-in-Time Seminar Proceedings* (July 24-26, 1989).

Cohen, Oded. "The Drum-Buffer-Rope (DBR) Approach to Logistics." In *Computer-Aided Production Management*, edited by A. Rolstadas, New York: Springer-Verlag, 1988.

Davis, Neal S., and George Fox. "JIT Case Study: DuPont Powder Metal." *Just-in-Time Seminar Proceedings*, (July 24-26, 1989).

Goldratt, Eliyahu M. "An Unbalanced Plant." *Proceedings of the 24th Annual APICS Conference* (October 1981).

Goldratt, Eliyahu M. "Cost Accounting: The Number One Enemy of Productivity." *Proceedings of the 26th Annual APICS Conference* (October 1983).

Goldratt, Eliyahu M. *The Theory of Constraints Journal* 1 (1989).

Goldratt, Eliyahu M., and Jeff Cox. *The Goal: A Process of Ongoing Improvement*. Croton-on-Hudson, NY: North River Press, Inc., 1986.

Goldratt, Eliyahu M., and Robert Fox. *The Race: For a Competitive Edge*. Croton-on-Hudson, NY: North River Press, Inc., 1986.

Jayson, Susan. "Goldratt & Fox: Revolutionizing the Factory Floor." *Management Accounting* (May 1987): 18-22.

Shingo, Shigeo, *Non-Stock Production: The Shingo System for Continuous Improvement*. Cambridge, MA: Productivity Press, 1988.

Umble, M. Michael, and M. L. Srikanth. *Synchronous Manufacturing: Principles for World Class Excellence*. Cincinnati: South-Western Publishing Co., 1989.

APPENDIX 19A

This appendix explains the closed form solution to the problem of determining the expected output of a line consisting of two stations, each station having the potential to produce 2, 3, or 4 units per day, each outcome being equally likely, with work-in-process inventory between Stations 1 and 2 limited to two units. The technique employed to perform this analysis, Markov chains, is commonly taught in industrial engineering programs but is less common to business programs. Those wishing an in-depth coverage of Markov chains should consult Cinlar, *Introduction to Stochastic Processes*. The Markov chain approach requires the multiplication of matrices. Although an attempt is made to explain these results using a technique that avoids the matrix algebra, those not familiar with matrix algebra may wish to omit this appendix.

Consider the possible outcomes of one day of work on the two-station line: Station 1 may produce 2, 3, or 4 units; Station 2 may produce 2, 3, or 4 units; ending WIP inventory may be 0, 1, or 2 units. Station 1 has three states, Station 2 has three states, ending inventory has three states. Thus, at first glance it would seem that there are 27 possible states for this system: $3 \times 3 \times 3 = 27$. However, some of the 27 combinations are not possible. For example, if Station 1 produces 2 units and Station 2 produces 4 units, ending WIP is 0. To obtain an ending WIP of 1 or 2 units would require a beginning WIP of 3 or 4 units, violating the constraint of 2 units of WIP. In all there are 19 feasible states, which are shown in Figure 19A-1.

Figure 19A-1
Output by Beginning and Ending State

State	State Number	State Number																	
		1	2	3	4	5	6	7	8	9	10	11	12	13	14	15	16	17	18	19
(2,2,0)	1	2	0	0	2	0	2	2	0	3	0	0	3	0	2	3	0	4	0	0
(2,2,1)	2	0	2	0	0	2	2	3	0	0	3	0	0	3	3	4	0	0	4	0
(2,2,2)	3	0	0	2	0	2	2	0	3	0	0	3	0	3	4	0	4	0	0	4
(3,2,1)	4	0	2	0	0	2	2	3	0	0	3	0	0	3	3	4	0	0	4	0
(3,2,2)	5	0	0	2	0	2	2	0	3	0	0	3	0	3	4	0	4	0	0	4
(4,2,2)	6	0	0	2	0	2	2	0	3	0	0	3	0	3	4	0	4	0	0	4
(2,3,0)	7	2	0	0	2	0	2	2	0	3	0	0	3	0	2	3	0	4	0	0
(2,3,1)	8	0	2	0	0	2	2	3	0	0	3	0	0	3	3	4	0	0	4	0
(3,3,0)	9	2	0	0	2	0	2	2	0	3	0	0	3	0	2	3	0	4	0	0
(3,3,1)	10	0	2	0	0	2	2	3	0	0	3	0	0	3	3	4	0	0	4	0
(3,3,2)	11	0	0	2	0	2	2	0	3	0	0	3	0	3	4	0	4	0	0	4
(4,3,1)	12	0	2	0	0	2	2	3	0	0	3	0	0	3	3	4	0	0	4	0
(4,3,2)	13	0	0	2	0	2	2	0	3	0	0	3	0	3	4	0	4	0	0	4
(2,4,0)	14	2	0	0	2	0	2	2	0	3	0	0	3	0	2	3	0	4	0	0
(3,4,0)	15	2	0	0	2	0	2	2	0	3	0	0	3	0	2	3	0	4	0	0
(3,4,1)	16	0	2	0	0	2	2	3	0	0	3	0	0	3	3	4	0	0	4	0
(4,4,0)	17	2	0	0	2	0	2	2	0	3	0	0	3	0	2	3	0	4	0	0
(4,4,1)	18	0	2	0	0	2	2	3	0	0	3	0	0	3	3	4	0	0	4	0
(4,4,2)	19	0	0	2	0	2	2	0	3	0	0	3	0	3	4	0	4	0	0	4

Figure 19A-1 shows the line output by beginning and ending state. At any arbitrarily selected time, the plant may be in any of the 19 feasible states. On the next day, only 9 of the 19 possible states can be reached. Because beginning WIP is known with certainty, each of the 9 combinations of Station 1 and Station 2 results has but one possible ending WIP. For example, if today we achieved the result (3,3,1), meaning Station 1 had a potential of 3, Station 2 had a potential of 3, and we began the day with 1 unit of WIP, then we must end the day with 1 unit of WIP. If tomorrow Station 1 draws a potential of 2 while Station 2 draws a potential of 4, the ending state is (2,4,0) indicating all existing WIP was used up. The output of the line is 3 units, because Station 2 is furnished only 3 units to work on in this scenario. Note in Figure 19A-1 that the state (3,3,1) is state 10 while the state (2,4,0) is state 14. The body of the table represents the output achieved when one starts in state A and ends in state B. Looking in row 10, column 14, one finds a value of 3, the value we just derived. Each of the rows of Figure 19A-1 contains 10 zeroes, representing the 10 states that cannot be reached from the beginning state shown in the row margin. Each row also contains 9 nonzero values, representing the 9 possible ending states corresponding to that beginning state.

Figure 19A-2 shows the probability of going from any beginning state i to any other state j in one step (one day in our case). As we have just reasoned, only 9 ending states are possible for any given beginning state. Furthermore, the 9 possible ending states are equally likely, since Station 1's potential is independent of Station 2's potential and both are independent of ending WIP. (Actual output is not independent of ending WIP, but what we have chosen to call potential, i.e., what the station would have done given unlimited WIP, is independent of ending WIP.) Thus, the probability of going from any state i to any other state j is either 0, if the transition cannot be done in one step, or $\frac{1}{9}$. Although Figure 19A-2 shows a value of 0.11 for $\frac{1}{9}$, Lotus 1-2-3, used to perform these calculations, was furnished a figure of $\frac{1}{9}$, which it carries internally to several decimal places. Each entry in the rightmost column contains the sum of the 19 probabilities contained within that row. Each sum is 1, indicating that each row is a proper probability distribution function. Having rows that sum to 1 is a requirement of proper Markov chain formulation. Figure 19A-2 has just been shown to meet the requirements of a Markov chain.

In matrix notation, Figure 19A-1 presents a 19 × 19 matrix, as does Figure 19A-2. Figure 19A-3 was created by multiplying each cell in Figure 19A-1 by the corresponding cell in Figure 19A-2 and storing the product in the corresponding cell in Figure 19A-3. That is, if we designate the matrix in Figure 19A-1 as A, the matrix in Figure 19A-2 as B, and the matrix in Figure 19A-3 as C, then

$$c_{ij} = a_{ij} \times b_{ij}$$

In probability notation, the value a_{ij} represents some outcome, x, of an experiment; x is the value obtained when the starting state is i and the ending state is j and refers to the production obtained by the line. The value b_{ij} represents the probability that x occurs, given that the starting state is i. We usually write the probability that x occurs as $p(x)$. Thus, c_{ij} could be written as $xp(x)$. The value of $xp(x)$ in isolation has no meaning. However, the figure that appears in the final column of row 1 of Figure 19A-3 represents the expected value, $E(x)$, of the output of the line *given that* the starting state was (2,2,0).

Recall that the expected value of x, $E(x)$, is defined as $\Sigma xp(x)$, which is precisely how each of the values in the final column of Figure 19A-3 is found. Each of the values thus represents the average output given the starting state. Actually, average output should only be a function of beginning WIP, it should be independent of yesterday's potential. If you examine the $E(x)$ column carefully, you will see that in fact only three values are possible, 2.55, when beginning WIP is 0, 2.88, when beginning WIP is 1, and 3, when beginning WIP is 2.

Figure 19A-2
Probability of Attaining Ending State by Beginning State

State	State Number																				
		1	2	3	4	5	6	7	8	9	10	11	12	13	14	15	16	17	18	19	
(2,2,0)	1	0.11	0	0	0.11	0	0.11	0.11	0	0.11	0	0	0.11	0	0.11	0.11	0	0.11	0	0	1
(2,2,1)	2	0	0.11	0	0	0.11	0.11	0.11	0	0	0.11	0	0	0.11	0.11	0.11	0	0	0.11	0	1
(2,2,2)	3	0	0	0.11	0	0.11	0.11	0	0.11	0	0	0.11	0	0.11	0.11	0	0.11	0	0	0.11	1
(3,2,1)	4	0	0.11	0	0	0.11	0.11	0.11	0	0	0.11	0	0	0.11	0.11	0.11	0	0	0.11	0	1
(3,2,2)	5	0	0	0.11	0	0.11	0.11	0	0.11	0	0	0.11	0	0.11	0.11	0	0.11	0	0	0.11	1
(4,2,2)	6	0	0	0.11	0	0.11	0.11	0	0.11	0	0	0.11	0	0.11	0.11	0	0.11	0	0	0.11	1
(2,3,0)	7	0.11	0	0	0.11	0	0.11	0.11	0	0.11	0	0	0.11	0	0.11	0.11	0	0.11	0	0	1
(2,3,1)	8	0	0.11	0	0	0.11	0.11	0.11	0	0	0.11	0	0	0.11	0.11	0.11	0	0	0.11	0	1
(3,3,0)	9	0.11	0	0	0.11	0	0.11	0.11	0	0.11	0	0	0.11	0	0.11	0.11	0	0.11	0	0	1
(3,3,1)	10	0	0.11	0	0	0.11	0.11	0.11	0	0	0.11	0	0	0.11	0.11	0.11	0	0	0.11	0	1
(3,3,2)	11	0	0	0.11	0	0.11	0.11	0	0.11	0	0	0.11	0	0.11	0.11	0	0.11	0	0	0.11	1
(4,3,1)	12	0	0.11	0	0	0.11	0.11	0.11	0	0	0.11	0	0	0.11	0.11	0.11	0	0	0.11	0	1
(4,3,2)	13	0	0	0.11	0	0.11	0.11	0	0.11	0	0	0.11	0	0.11	0.11	0	0.11	0	0	0.11	1
(2,4,0)	14	0.11	0	0	0.11	0	0.11	0.11	0	0.11	0	0	0.11	0	0.11	0.11	0	0.11	0	0	1
(3,4,0)	15	0.11	0	0	0.11	0	0.11	0.11	0	0.11	0	0	0.11	0	0.11	0.11	0	0.11	0	0	1
(3,4,1)	16	0	0.11	0	0	0.11	0.11	0.11	0	0	0.11	0	0	0.11	0.11	0.11	0	0	0.11	0	1
(4,4,0)	17	0.11	0	0	0.11	0	0.11	0.11	0	0.11	0	0	0.11	0	0.11	0.11	0	0.11	0	0	1
(4,4,1)	18	0	0.11	0	0	0.11	0.11	0.11	0	0	0.11	0	0	0.11	0.11	0.11	0	0	0.11	0	1
(4,4,2)	19	0	0	0.11	0	0.11	0.11	0	0.11	0	0	0.11	0	0.11	0.11	0	0.11	0	0	0.11	1

Figure 19A-3
Expected Output Given Beginning State

State Number	State	1	2	3	4	5	6	7	8	9	10	11	12	13	14	15	16	17	18	19	$E(x)$
1	(2,2,0)	0.22	0	0	0.22	0	0.22	0.22	0	0.33	0	0	0.33	0	0.22	0.33	0	0.44	0	0	2.55
2	(2,2,1)	0	0.22	0	0	0.22	0.22	0.33	0	0	0.33	0	0	0.33	0.33	0.44	0	0	0.44	0	2.88
3	(2,2,2)	0	0	0.22	0	0.22	0.22	0	0.33	0	0	0.33	0	0.33	0.44	0	0.44	0	0	0.44	3
4	(3,2,1)	0	0.22	0	0	0.22	0.22	0.33	0	0	0.33	0	0	0.33	0.33	0.44	0	0	0.44	0	2.88
5	(3,2,2)	0	0	0.22	0	0.22	0.22	0	0.33	0	0	0.33	0	0.33	0.44	0	0.44	0	0	0.44	3
6	(4,2,2)	0	0	0.22	0	0.22	0.22	0	0.33	0	0	0.33	0	0.33	0.44	0	0.44	0	0	0.44	3
7	(2,3,0)	0.22	0	0	0.22	0	0.22	0.22	0	0.33	0	0	0.33	0	0.22	0.33	0	0.44	0	0	2.55
8	(2,3,1)	0	0.22	0	0	0.22	0.22	0.33	0	0	0.33	0	0	0.33	0.33	0.44	0	0	0.44	0	2.88
9	(3,3,0)	0.22	0	0	0.22	0	0.22	0.22	0	0.33	0	0	0.33	0	0.22	0.33	0	0.44	0	0	2.55
10	(3,3,1)	0	0.22	0	0	0.22	0.22	0.33	0	0	0.33	0	0	0.33	0.33	0.44	0	0	0.44	0	2.88
11	(3,3,2)	0	0	0.22	0	0.22	0.22	0	0.33	0	0	0.33	0	0.33	0.44	0	0.44	0	0	0.44	3
12	(4,3,1)	0	0.22	0	0	0.22	0.22	0.33	0	0	0.33	0	0	0.33	0.33	0.44	0	0	0.44	0	2.88
13	(4,3,2)	0	0	0.22	0	0.22	0.22	0	0.33	0	0	0.33	0	0.33	0.44	0	0.44	0	0	0.44	3
14	(2,4,0)	0.22	0	0	0.22	0	0.22	0.22	0	0.33	0	0	0.33	0	0.22	0.33	0	0.44	0	0	2.55
15	(3,4,0)	0.22	0	0	0.22	0	0.22	0.22	0	0.33	0	0	0.33	0	0.22	0.33	0	0.44	0	0	2.55
16	(3,4,1)	0	0.22	0	0	0.22	0.22	0.33	0	0	0.33	0	0	0.33	0.33	0.44	0	0	0.44	0	2.88
17	(4,4,0)	0.22	0	0	0.22	0	0.22	0.22	0	0.33	0	0	0.33	0	0.22	0.33	0	0.44	0	0	2.55
18	(4,4,1)	0	0.22	0	0	0.22	0.22	0.33	0	0	0.33	0	0	0.33	0.33	0.44	0	0	0.44	0	2.88
19	(4,4,2)	0	0	0.22	0	0.22	0.22	0	0.33	0	0	0.33	0	0.33	0.44	0	0.44	0	0	0.44	3

We now know the expected output given the beginning state for each of the 19 states. If we knew the probability of each of the 19 states, we could find an expected value in the manner just explained. It is tempting to assume that each of the three WIP values is equally likely; however, that happens to be a false assumption. It turns out that both 0 and 2 are somewhat more likely than 1 as an ending WIP value. The Markov chain approach permits us to find the steady state probability of obtaining each of the 19 states.

We have chosen to call the Markov chain, Figure 19A-2, matrix B. Each cell in matrix B represents the probability of going to some beginning state, i, to some ending state, j, in one step. If we multiply B by itself, to get B^2, the result is a matrix of probabilities of going from some beginning state i to some ending state j in two steps. For example, we could find the probability of going from state (2,2,2) to state (3,3,1) in two steps. Note that it is impossible to go from (2,2,2) to (3,3,1) in one step. To make the transition in two steps, we must have a beginning inventory of 1 at the beginning of the second step. That means the result of the first step must be $(x,y,1)$. Possible values for the first step are thus (2,3,1) and (3,4,1). Therefore, the probability of going from (2,2,2) to (3,3,1) in two steps is $\frac{2}{9} \times \frac{1}{9} = \frac{2}{81}$, and we should find the decimal value of $\frac{2}{81}$ in the appropriate cell of B^2.

If we square B^2 to get B^4, we have in each cell the probability of going from state i to state j in 4 steps. If we keep squaring B, we reach a point where every value in a given column becomes identical. At that point, the probability of being in a given state is a function only of the state, not of the initial condition. When that occurs, each row gives us the steady state probability of being in a particular state at an arbitrary point in time, precisely the information we need.

The adventuresome may wish to type Figure 19A-2 into an electronic spreadsheet having matrix multiplying capability and continue multiplying the matrix times itself until steady state is reached. It took us about seven steps to achieve steady state.

In Figure 19A-4, the third column, labeled $p(x)$, represents the steady state probability of the state shown in the first column occurring. The expected output of that state is shown in Column 2. Multiplying Column 2 times Column 3 and adding thus yields the expected outcome of any one turn, which is 2.80554.

APPENDIX 19B

In this appendix, we discuss the creation of a Lotus 1-2-3 model to perform the simulations described in this chapter. The model is shown in Figure 19B-1.

Figure 19A-4
Determining Expected Output

State	x	$p(x)$	$xp(x)$
(2,2,0)	2.55556	0.04167	0.1065
(2,2,1)	2.88889	0.02778	0.08025
(2,2,2)	3	0.04166	0.12498
(3,2,1)	2.88889	0.04167	0.12039
(3,2,2)	3	0.06944	0.20831
(4,2,2)	3	0.11111	0.33333
(2,3,0)	2.55556	0.06945	0.17749
(2,3,1)	2.88889	0.04166	0.12035
(3,3,0)	2.55556	0.04167	0.1065
(3,3,1)	2.88889	0.02778	0.08025
(3,3,2)	3	0.04166	0.12498
(4,3,1)	2.88889	0.04167	0.12039
(4,3,2)	3	0.06944	0.20831
(2,4,0)	2.55556	0.11111	0.28395
(3,4,0)	2.55556	0.06945	0.17749
(3,4,1)	2.88889	0.04166	0.12035
(4,4,0)	2.55556	0.04167	0.1065
(4,4,1)	2.88889	0.02778	0.08025
(4,4,2)	3	0.04166	0.12498
		$\Sigma p(x) = 1$	$\Sigma xp(x) = 2.80554$

Figure 19B-1

Trial example	Line 1 2.97	Begin 2	Line 2 3.045	Plant Average 2.792929		
Station 1	Output	Unused	Inventory	Station 2	Output	Plant	Average

Station 1	Output	Unused	Inventory	Station 2	Output	Plant	Average
0.519239	3	2	5	0.006113	2	2	2.00
0.356443	3	2	5	0.979778	4	4	3.00
0.561540	3	1	4	0.594740	3	3	3.00
0.747586	4	1	5	0.223032	2	2	2.75
0.771711	4	2	6	0.039914	2	2	2.60
0.694519	4	2	6	0.939549	4	4	2.83
0.413725	3	2	5	0.932463	4	4	3.00
0.380023	3	1	4	0.244712	2	2	2.88
0.052727	2	2	4	0.592990	3	3	2.89
0.479721	3	1	4	0.913273	4	4	3.00
0.837216	4	0	4	0.728147	4	4	3.09
0.316938	2	0	2	0.097137	2	2	3.00
0.165298	2	0	2	0.864391	4	2	2.92
0.384584	3	0	3	0.845236	4	3	2.93
0.362397	3	0	3	0.632100	3	3	2.93
0.697070	4	0	4	0.759582	4	4	3.00
0.881963	4	0	4	0.895764	4	4	3.06

For the moment, ignore the top two rows of Figure 19B-1, which we will explain later. The first column, Station 1, is a set of random numbers. Each cell in the column is created by the function **@RAND**. Column 2 is obtained by performing the following table lookup:

Random Number	Station Output
<0.33	2
0.33 to 0.67	3
>0.67	4

Assume the first cell under the word "output" is cell B5, then the formula for cell B5 is **@IF(A5<.3333,2,@IF(A5<.6667,3,4))**.

The third column represents the unused inventory from the previous day. The first value is a special case, since initial beginning WIP is input data. There are three cases for unused inventory, depending on the relation Station 1's output has to Station 2's:

Case 1: Station 1's output exceeds Station 2's: The second row is obtained by taking the unused inventory value from the previous row plus the Station 1 output in the previous row minus the Station 2 output from the previous row. Unused inventory is limited to 2.

Case 2: Station 1's output equals Station 2's: Unused inventory does not change.

Case 3: Station 1's output is less than Station 2's: The second row is obtained by taking the unused inventory value from the previous row plus the Station 1 output from the previous row minus the Station 2 output from the previous row. Unused inventory cannot be negative.

Thus, the formula for cell C6, second row of the chart, is

@IF(B5>F5,@MIN(2,C5+B5−F5),@IF(B5=F5,C5,@MAX(0,B5+C5−F5)))

The **@MIN** function limits unused inventory to 2 while the **@MAX** function says unused inventory can never be negative.

The fourth column, labeled "inventory," is simply the sum of Station 1's output and unused inventory from the previous day. This value is the inventory potentially available to Station 2 if it needs it.

The fifth column, Station 2, is a column of **@RAND** functions. The sixth column is identical to the second, except that the random number comes from the fifth column. Since the formula in cell B5 uses relative addresses, the formula can be copied from cell B5 to cell F5 and will be correct.

The seventh column, plant output, is the minimum of Column 4 or Column 6, the inventory available to Station 2 or Station 2's own potential. Cell G5 contains the formula **@MIN(D5,F5)**. The eighth column is a running average. Cell H5 contains the formula **@AVG(F5.F5)**. When copied down the column, this formula fixes the starting point of the average at the first observation and moves the ending point of the average to the current row, yielding the desired average.

We can now explain the top two rows. The top row is labels, the second row contains values or formulas. The leftmost item is labeled "Trial." Whenever any number is changed in a Lotus 1-2-3 spreadsheet, every **@RAND** gets a new value (provided recalculation is automatic). This statement is not true for Quattro and may or may not be true for other electronic spreadsheets. It is a necessary feature for the experiment as described, although with minor modification the spreadsheet can be made to run in Quattro. The effect of having every random number change whenever any cell changes is that by changing the trial number, you get a new trial. Thus, to perform the 10 simulations we merely entered the number 1, wrote the values under the labels "Line 1," "Line 2," and "Plant Average" down on paper, entered the number 2, entered the results, and continued until 10 trials were complete. We could have used a one-way data table to accomplish the same thing but decided we could get the results more simply by just writing them down.

To modify the basic spreadsheet after the initial results were compiled, we did the following (in each case the modification described is a modification of the *original* spreadsheet):

1. For the MRP case, the **@MIN** restriction on the unused inventory was removed.
2. For the JIT case, the formulas in the Output columns were changed to read

$$\textbf{@IF(X < .1,2,@IF(X < .9,3,4))}$$

where **X** refers to the cell to the left of the cell in question.
3. For the TOC case, the formulas in the Output columns were changed to read

$$\textbf{@IF(X < .2,2,@IF(X < .8,3,4))}$$

where **X** refers to the cell to the left of the cell in question. The unused inventory column was changed to read

$$\textbf{@IF(BY > FY,@MIN(4,CY+BY FY),@IF(BY=FY,CY,@MAX(0,BY+CY FY)))}$$

where **Y** is the row number above the row in question.

20

PRODUCTION AND INVENTORY MANAGEMENT SYSTEMS

Manufacturing facilities can be classified in several dimensions. Some facilities produce low-volume, high-variability, discrete items; others produce medium-volume items in economic batches; others produce high-volume, low-variability items repetitively; and still others produce continuous products and package the products in a variety of ways. The design and operation of the facility is often a function of the strategy employed in marketing the product. The product may compete on the basis of quality, price, availability, field service, ease of maintenance, durability, or other performance features. The manufacturing facility may be labor intensive or capital intensive. The facility may employ only a few people or it may employ thousands. The philosophy implemented in organizing and operating the facility may be traditional, Just-in-Time, or theory of constraints. Each of these dimensions helps determine the way in which the production management system is defined. The production management system, in turn, influences the design of the management information system. A requisite for successful production and inventory management (PIM) is an information system that provides the information needed for decision making without overwhelming the manager with data of minor interest.

In this chapter we relate production and inventory management systems development to the factors that drive it and to the design of the supporting information systems. The chapter, of necessity, interleaves manufacturing planning and control system design concepts and manufacturing information system design concepts. We begin by discussing systems concepts in general, then move to production management system and management information system development. The chapter provides the following:

1. Definitions of relevant terms
2. Descriptions of basic systems concepts and their relationship with information systems

3. Descriptions of management system and management information system development and design
4. Examination of the essential ingredients of a PIM information system, its implementation concepts and techniques, and the importance of monitoring the system's performance
5. Technological choices available to management

DEFINITIONS

Definitions of relevant terms follow. By their very nature these terms serve as an introduction to many of the concepts. A clear understanding of these terms is usually an excellent aid in problem solving and information system design activities.

The Systems Approach

The systems approach is a group of concepts, methods, and techniques used for problem solving, decision making, organizational analysis, management process design, and organizational performance evaluation. It encompasses all the definitions, concepts, and techniques described in this chapter.

System

A system is a group of elements working in an interrelated fashion toward a set of objectives. A system's elements may be personnel, machines, or nonmaterial entities such as energy and information. A system is a goal-directed activity that often is viewed as inputs being transformed into outputs.

Systems Analysis

Systems analysis is a somewhat formal methodology for the following:

1. Defining the problems of management as decision-making situations with constraints, resources, alternative courses of action available, and criteria by which to measure decision results
2. Analyzing the decision situation to determine the relationship of controlled and uncontrolled variables to the decision results and developing models that describe these relationships
3. Running the model by inserting different values for the variables controlled by management, calculating the results, evaluating the alternatives, and identifying preferred courses of action

The study of the relationships described by the models leads to decision rules and decision guidelines. The creation of such rules and guidelines is facilitated by identifying cause and effect relationships between the controlled variables and the uncontrolled ones. However, in complex systems understanding cause and effect is often difficult, so rules and guidelines often are based on correlations observed rather than on an understanding of cause and effect.

Information Systems

Once the criteria, decision rules, and guidelines for making decisions have been selected, means of gathering, recording, processing, and communicating the required information to the proper decision makers at the right time must be developed. These methods of gathering, recording, processing, and communicating constitute the information system.

SYSTEM CONCEPTS

This section contains an overview of rudimentary system concepts necessary for a full understanding of management planning, directing, and control systems. It deals with the elements of a system and with adaptive systems.

System Elements

Figure 20-1 illustrates the concept that a system consists of five essential elements: inputs, processes, outputs, feedback, and a control unit. Inputs are all the resources consumed in the process. For example, raw materials, labor, and purchased parts are inputs in a manufacturing system, while information such as demand requirements, stock balances, lead times, unit costs, and the manufacturing processing sequence are inputs to a manufacturing information system.

Figure 20-1
Block Diagram of System Elements

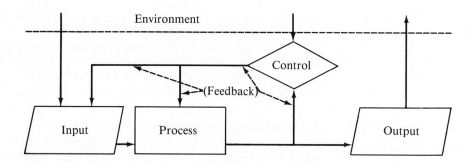

The process consists of all the activities that transform inputs into outputs. For example, machining of parts, heat treating, plating, painting, and packaging are all part of the process. In an information system the process is the changing of input data into information that can be used for decision making. It involves sorting, collating, tabulating, multiplying, etc.

Feedback includes the monitoring of system performance, determining the actual output of the system, and transmitting that data to the control unit. Feedback also includes the transmission of directives from the control unit to the individuals or mechanisms that control the inputs and processes.

The control unit is the decision-making unit. It receives the measures of actual results through the feedback channels and then compares the actual results with the desired results. If actual results differ from desired results by more than an acceptable margin, the control unit directs that inputs or the process or both be changed to bring actual results into closer alignment with desired results. The control unit must have a model describing the relationship of the inputs, processes, and outputs. Otherwise, changes would be based on random guesses.

Systems that operate in this fashion immediately come to mind. When the thermostat in a home heating system senses that the temperature has dropped below a desired level it immediately activates the furnace, resulting in a warmer home. Physicians observe the progress of patients and continuously evaluate the efficacy of the therapy being employed. In a kitchen the chef decides to add seasoning on the basis of taste. The machinist adjusts a machine tool if parts are beginning to exceed or approach a tolerance limit. Students are encouraged to devote more time to their studies when they are obtaining unsatisfactory grades. Few individuals go through a day without comparing the results of some activity to desired results and deciding that certain changes should be made. Such activities frequently can be described and understood better when they are viewed as a system.

In PIM, decisions made to bring actual results into closer alignment with desired results include reassigning shop order priorities, recommending overtime, and revising order quantities.

Adaptive Systems

Let's look at some examples differentiating internal and external levels of analysis using the systems concept. Take the case, circa 1907, of the general manager of a manufacturing organization that has just experienced its best annual sales and profit. As you might suspect, it is producing within desirable unit cost limits, achieving the desired quality, and shipping orders on schedule. It is in great shape at the internal level of analysis; it is achieving its objectives. Now let it be revealed that its business is horse-drawn carriages. Our hindsight view of the environment tells us that the outputs of this organization will fill the needs of society to a lesser degree each year. Some carriage manufacturers realized this; others did not. It all depended on how well the system functioned at the external level. History is replete with examples of governments, manufacturing organizations, service organizations, and academic institutions that either were ignoring information received from the environment or did not evaluate the information properly.

The contrasting expansion policies of Sears and Montgomery Ward after World War II are classic examples. The extraordinary expansion of Sears is history. Montgomery Ward, however, had plenty of company in its conservative approach, including literally hundreds of school boards that did not anticipate the burgeoning school populations—sometimes even after the children had been born. Today's world is no less dynamic than the immediate post-World War II period. In fact, it is difficult to disagree with Alvin Toffler's contention in *Future Shock* (1971, 19-35) that the greatest challenge to individuals, organizations, and society itself will be the ability to cope with an ever-increasing rate of change in technology and human behavior. Today, for example, Sears is struggling to compete with the aggressive marketing strategies of K-Mart and Wal-Mart.

An organization that has the ability to measure the impact of environmental developments on the organization and to change its operation so as not only to survive but to thrive is designated an *adaptive system*. The industrial enterprise that changes its products and services to meet the changing needs of society while continuing to earn a profit can be described as an adaptive organization. Such organizations must not only revise their inputs and processes to meet immediate objectives, but they also must continually evaluate their objectives and processes in order to remain competitive.

What is the relevancy of the foregoing to the production and inventory control manager? The relevancy is that constant assessment of developments in PIM concepts and techniques for continual application in the organization are necessary if the firm is to survive.

MANAGEMENT INFORMATION SYSTEMS: THEIR DEVELOPMENT AND DESIGN

Management information systems do not spring out of the blue. At least, they should not if we expect them to contribute to PIM effectiveness and corporate productivity. There are rational approaches for developing an individual system and for planning the development of a group of related systems or systems modules. We will make just a few comments concerning the relation of systems analysis, models, decision rules, information systems, and the role of production inventory managers.

Individual System Development

The development, design, and implementation of the individual information system begins with systems analysis. As mentioned previously, the objective of systems analysis is to examine a decision situation and determine how the controllable variables relate to the results obtained. Systems analysis usually begins with the recognition that a problem exists. The problem can be either of two types: (1) desired results are not being obtained or (2) a decision must be made and no rules or guidelines have been established. An organization that continually misses due dates on many of its orders yet has an inventory investment well above the target level has the first type problem. The necessity either to build inventories or to cut production in an economic downturn without any corporate guidance is an example of the second type problem. In the first case, we assume that some system of decision making exists but is not working well. In the second case, no decision-making procedures exist. In both cases, systems analysis is appropriate and consists of the following steps, which are illustrated in Figure 20-2:

1. Define the problem.
2. State the objectives of the decision. (For example, what profit level, inventory investment level, and manufacturing lead time are desired?)
3. Identify the available resources and the existing constraints.
4. Determine the uncontrollable and controllable variables and how they relate to the results.
5. Develop a model of the relationship of these variables to the decision outcome by describing that relationship verbally, mathematically, or graphically.
6. Determine the alternate courses of action that may be followed, i.e., the choices available to the decision maker.
7. Use the model of the real world to evaluate the different decisions that can be made.
8. Establish decision rules or guidelines for making the decision on the basis of the results obtained by running the model.
9. Evaluate the performance of the system in the real world and revise the model and decision rules as required.

Systems analysis is not a one-shot affair. The results of actual operating systems must be reviewed after implementation to determine if the expected results are being obtained.

Management Information Systems

Recurring types of decisions are most amenable to systems analysis and the development of decision rules that constitute a management system. The ordering of material and the scheduling of jobs are two examples of recurring PIM decisions. If decisions are to be made on the basis of a decision rule that evaluates the facts in relation to management objectives, an information system must exist to capture relevant data, to convert raw data into information, and to present this information to the decision maker in a timely manner.

Some decision situations are well structured, and the relation of controlled variables to results is very clear. For example, if 3 valves of a particular type are required for a hydraulic assembly and we plan to fabricate 30 such assemblies, then 90 valves are required—assuming no rejects or pilferage. Other decision situations are not well structured, and the relationship of controlled variables to desired results is not clear. For example, it may be difficult to

Figure 20-2
Information Systems Analysis Schematic

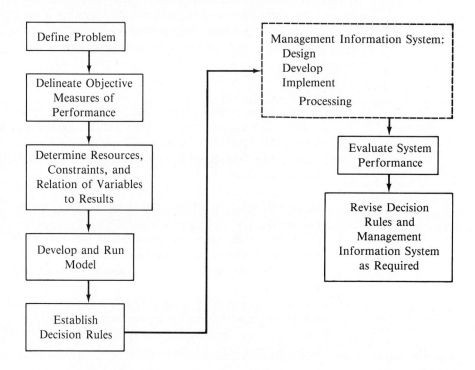

decide which of three late orders for three different preferred customers should receive priority. For the most part, in well-structured situations, decisions can be made by the computer or the clerk. In less structured situations either computer or clerk may gather the facts but the manager is stuck with the decision making.

It is not our purpose here to cover the principles and techniques of designing information systems in detail. Rather, it is our purpose to emphasize that the decision rules determine the input, process, storage, and output requirements of the information system. One cannot design, select, or approve of an information system without at least implicitly agreeing that the model underlying the decision rules encompassed in that information system is applicable to the situation.

Management should strive to have decisions in recurring, well-structured situations handled by an approved processing system, whether it be manual, mechanical, or electronic. This allows management to devote its attention to the nonrecurring, less structured, exceptional activities. These activities include developing management systems, determining staffing and staff development, establishing performance objectives and criteria, and evaluating performance. In order to delegate decision making in recurring, well-structured sitiuations, the nature of the recurring situation and the appropriate responses must be clearly articulated.

The Modular Approach to Systems

A systems module consists of a single set of inputs, processing, and outputs along with the necessary files, as illustrated in Figure 20-3. A subsystem consists of one or more modules to carry out a particular function such as forecasting, material requirements planning (MRP), or capacity requirements planning. The modular approach develops the subsystems in the sequence required by technological factors and existing conditions. The bill of material (BOM) subsystem, for example, usually is developed prior to the MRP subsystem. Many subsystems commonly found in a PIM system are listed in Table 20-1. These titles in themselves, however, do not delineate exactly what the input, process, and output are, but give a general indication of the area of application.

Figure 20-3
A Systems Module, Stock Status Example

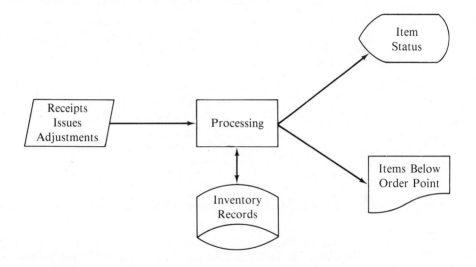

Table 20-1
Some Common PIM Subsystems

Production Planning	Operation Scheduling
Resource Requirements Planning	Shop Floor Control
Forecasting	Dispatching
Master Production Scheduling	Work-in-Process Control
Rough Cut Capacity Planning	Purchasing
Order Entry	Vendor Performance Analysis
Bill of Material Processing	Receiving
Inventory Management	Distribution Requirements Planning
Materials Requirements Planning	Product Costing
Tool Control	Job Costing
Capacity Requirements Planning	Labor Reporting
Order Release Planning	

Files and the Data Base

The simplest and least costly file structure to design and implement is one in which each subsystem, such as MRP or shop floor control, has its own files. This approach, however, creates many problems since the same data is stored in many different locations. For example, the item master file may be used in the forecasting, inventory management, MRP, and production activity control systems. Recording of an event, such as the completion of a shop order or an engineering change, requires recording in each of these files. Maintaining accuracy in each file and consistency among the different files is difficult. Implementing inquiry and search capabilities in such a system also is relatively difficult.

A data base system combines all files—in a logical and operational sense—into one master file with many subdivisions. These subdivisions are combined temporarily as required to fit the application. This combining is accomplished by data base management software, and files that are separated physically are joined logically. Table 20-2 lists some of the files required by PIM information systems.

Table 20-2
Some Common PIM Files

> Forecasts
> Item Master Record
> Master Production Schedule
> Routing
> Work Center Master
> Customer
> Vendor
> Production Order
> Purchase Order

Several data base systems may be developed with each serving two or more subsystems, or one data base system may be developed to serve all PIM subsystems. In some cases, the PIM subsystems may be only one of the subsystems served by the data base. Figure 20-4 illustrates how some of these files might be handled by a data base management system.

Distributed Data Processing (DDP)
and Microcomputers

Data processing can take place primarily at a central location with data entered and output received via remote terminals. Or some of the processing, data storage, and control can take place at the remote terminal sites. The advent of powerful and relatively inexpensive microcomputers along with data base management techniques has made DDP feasible and appropriate in some cases. Figure 20-5 illustrates a DDP system with a distributed data base.

Figure 20-4
Simplified Illustration of Data Base Management System

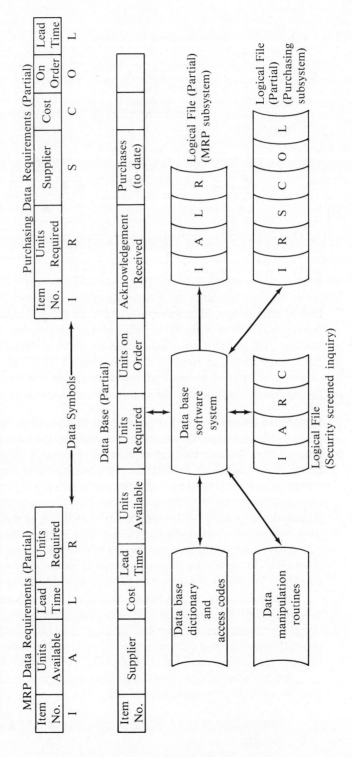

Figure 20-5
Distributed Data Processing with Distributed Data Base

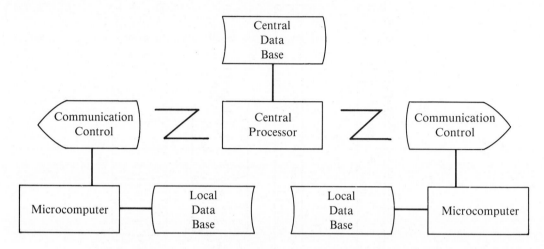

Microcomputers. Microcomputers with the power of third generation main-frame computers are available today at a small fraction of the cost of main-frames. This enables an organization to perform systems processing at the plant, warehouse, or field service site without tying up or depending on the central computer. The local microcomputer can handle data applicable to a given location and processing required to manage daily activities.

Distributed Processing. The assignment of systems activities depends on the needs of the users, the computing and storage capability required, and the capability of the users and the local equipment. Leland R. Kneppelt (1980) recommends that forecasting, production planning, resource requirements planning, master production scheduling (MPS), and rough cut capacity planning be performed at the central site. Since planning activities relate to overall management objectives and policies, and since plans frequently are prepared monthly or quarterly, this recommendation makes sense. The MRP and capacity requirements plan also can be processed centrally due to computer capacity requirements and the need to integrate the effects of usage at all warehouses and production at all plants. Aggregate inventory reports also would be processed centrally.

Distributed processing (local microcomputer processing) would include shop floor control reports and scheduling, customer order processing, and local inventory management processes. Thus, in general, short-range priority and capacity planning and control are performed at the local site, and long- and medium-range planning and control activities are centralized.

Advantages of distributed data processing and data base management systems using microcomputers include:

1. The failure of one processor (computer) does not shut down the entire system.

2. Greater throughput is possible since some tasks are allocated to local microcomputers.
3. Functions not economical for processing centrally can be added at local sites.
4. Greater cost-effectiveness due to the increasing power and lower cost of microcomputers results.
5. Consistent data exist throughout the system.

Some disadvantages or problems include:

1. Control of access to computers is more difficult.
2. Monitoring of local data entry and systems development activities to assure appropriate internal controls and systems integrity is more difficult.
3. Development of applications at local sites may be haphazard.

James M. Venglarik (1979) points out that the installation of distributed data processing should be based on all factors and not only on computer technology considerations. The data processing system should be consistent with the system objectives and with the capability of personnel.

PIM INFORMATION SYSTEMS

Since there is no one set of decision techniques applicable to all organizations, it follows that there is no single PIM information system that is appropriate for all manufacturing firms. As Buffa and Miller (1979, 700-703) have pointed out, the process technology, product positioning, product structure, organization structure and capability, organization goals, and costs and benefits determine the nature of the appropriate information system.

Process Technology

Process technology often is broken into three broad categories: job shop production, batch production, and mass production. Each category has distinctive information system needs, although basic PIM principles apply to all. A fourth category is beginning to emerge—customized mass convenience—which occupies the high-volume, high-variety niche. The information needs of all four will be discussed.

Engineer-to-Order. The information needs of an engineer-to-order firm revolve around the customer. First, the functions a customer desires must be listed, along with any other requirements (size, color, etc.). From this, a design must be created and approved by the customer. Often, the design stage requires several revisions before a satisfactory blueprint is developed. After the blueprint is accepted, a prototype is built. For orders of one unit, the prototype is the unit. For orders involving several units, the prototype often is field-tested and perhaps redesigned, and then several units are built.

Prior to the widespread application of computer aided design (CAD), there was little advantage provided to an engineer-to-order firm by computerizing its information. Manual systems were more the norm than the exception. Today, however, it is possible to design a part on a CAD system, print the design using a plotter or laser printer, transmit the design electronically, and receive approval electronically. On approval, the CAD system in some instances has the capability of automatically creating a bill of material and passing the data electronically to the inventory control system. CAD systems exist that can transfer designs into motions for activities in which two dimensions only are critical, such as picking chips from a roll containing hundreds and placing them properly on the surface of a printed circuit board. Research is proceeding on the development of CAD systems that can translate designs into motions where three dimensions are critical. Thus, CAD is leading many small, engineer-to-order firms into computerized information systems.

Batch Production.   A shop that engages in batch production has a wide variety of standard parts that are manufactured in batches either to order or to stock. Because of batching, precise timing and sizing of component lots is essential to control of inventory and production. Such shops traditionally have used MRP systems, as described in Chapter 10. For such firms, MRP is the manufacturing information system. A firm using drum-buffer-rope as a scheduling procedure still needs an information system. Most such firms retain their existing MRP system as the information system.

Mass Production.   Mass production can be further subdivided into continuous process production and high-volume, low-variety repetitive production. Continuous process production usually is used when the object is processed in a liquid or molten state. Examples include breweries, refineries, and primary metal mills. A continuous process is also used in creating cloth and other textiles. High-volume, low-variety repetitive production is used in making popular consumer goods, such as automobiles, televisions, personal computers, other consumer electronics, toys, games, dolls, and so on. Each of these technologies has distinct information system requirements.

Continuous Process Industries.   Sam Taylor (1980) has pointed out that continuous process industries are capital intensive whereas fabrication and assembly industries are materials intensive. As a result, substantially different management information systems are required in process industries and in fabrication and assembly industries. Finch and Cox (1987) identify factors influencing process industry PIM system and manufacturing information system design. R. Leonard Allen (1980) has reported on the application of standard manufacturing software to primary metals processing. R. T. Rowan and J. A. Wellendorf (1980) have reported on the applicability and customization of commercial software packages in process industries.

Repetitive Manufacturing. Production and inventory control systems for repetitive manufacturing have different requirements than project manufacturing, job shop, or flow manufacturing in process industries. Repetitive manufacturing deals primarily with the mass production of discrete units and less with fluids, powders, and chemical change processes. The following are some of the characteristics of repetitive manufacturing that create data collection, data processing, and information requirements different from the typical job shop (Hall 1982):

1. The mass production configuration of the physical facilities plant requires MPS's that authorize runs for specific time periods.
2. Daily run schedules, not job orders, are used to authorize and control production.
3. Production control is executed by kanbans and by counts at key points in the flow.
4. The status of raw material and purchased parts inventory is accomplished by backflushing, i.e., calculating the inventory withdrawn from stores by exploding the BOM applicable to the point of the count and multiplying each item by the count.
5. MPS's frequently are stated in cumulative values for the month or year. Cumulative values are used for control of incoming material, flow through key points, and finished production output.
6. The use of feeder plants supplying components often requires multiplant production planning.
7. Many items produced by repetitive manufacturing are produced to stock and have national or international distribution systems. This requires a close linking of the MPS and the distribution plan. Production and distribution may occur in different nations and perhaps on different continents.
8. Capacity planning is especially challenging in multiplant, multiproduct environments.

The foregoing covers many of the salient PIM problems of repetitive manufacturing, and documents the need for manufacturing control systems different from those found in the single plant job shop environment.

Customized Mass Convenience. Harvard's Earl Sasser (1988) believes the customers in the future will demand customized mass-produced products that can be ordered electronically and delivered to the home. He calls this phenomenon customized mass convenience (CMC). CMC is driven by the increasing trend toward two-worker families and by the increased value placed on leisure time. Leading indicators of this trend are increased mail-order volume and the creation of electronic shopping capabilities, such as Home Shopping Network on cable television.

The first industry to exploit this trend is the magazine industry, which is moving from customizing products by region to customizing by individual.

The technology needed to create this customization is a standard product, readily customizable by computer-controlled production, and the ability to access a customer data base.

The Japanese now produce robots that can tailor clothes. Controlling such robots by a computer that has access to customers and customer order data is all that is required to realize Sasser's prediction in the apparel industry.

Organization and Organization Goals.   The assignment of tasks, duties, and decision-making authority within the organization defines who needs what information. The capabilities of users influence the complexity and sophistication of the system. In all cases the process and the output should be transparent to the user. The user needs to understand clearly how the data were obtained, the process they underwent, and what the output information means, that is, what action, if any, should be taken.

W. Skinner (1974) has noted that different firms emphasize different strategies to maintain and improve their competitive positioning. A firm may emphasize quality, delivery, price, flexibility (the willingness to modify the product or normal sales quantity requirement), or a combination of these. Emphasis on delivery requires a strong PIM system that emphasizes the availability of items and that has more than adequate capacity. An emphasis on price, on the other hand, demands minimum inventory and high resource utilization.

System Design Specification

Developing the overall PIM system design specification begins with responses to a group of broad questions. This group of questions includes, but is not limited to, the following:

1. What is the product positioning strategy of the firm? Does it make to stock, make to order, assemble to order, or a little of each?
2. What is the organizational structure of PIM activities? Should it be changed? If so, is an organizational change likely?
3. What is the process technology of the company? Is it a continuous process, repetitive discrete parts, discrete batch fabrication and assembly shop, job shop, or project manufacturing type organization? Perhaps it includes features of two or more of these types.
4. How do present organizational personnel resources compare with the resources required by the systems development activity? Should additional individuals be hired? If so, when? Should outside resources be hired to assist?
5. What data processing capabilities exist? If they are inadequate, are financial resources available to improve them?
6. How complete and accurate are existing data resources?

Most of these questions concern the general nature and status of the business. Many other examples can be given. After answering such general questions, decisions concerning the overall design of the PIM information system must be made. These include the following:

1. What type of management systems (planning and control techniques) are required? For example, should master production schedules be material oriented or capacity oriented?
2. What outputs (reports) are required? When?
3. What data need to be available for inquiry? for search?
4. What system module structures (subsystems) are feasible? Which data base structure options are available? How do they relate? Which combination is preferable?
5. After the overall systems design is determined, in what order will the subsystems be developed?

The answers to these questions are used to develop a statement of system requirements in terms of specific output information, the time when it is needed, and by whom. Furthermore, the priority of the different requirements and the costs and benefits of each should be documented. Successful systems development and operation require the following:

1. Documentation
2. Forming a project team
3. Planning and controlling design and development
4. Software decisions
5. Planning and controlling the implementation
6. Monitoring and refining the system

Systems Implementation

Implementation involves more than conversion. Adequate documentation is a prerequisite; training and education are key elements; different types of testing are required; and equipment, procedures, inputs, files, output, and performance measures all may change.

The need for documentation exists from the inception of the project, the development of functional requirements. Completely developing user and operations documentation prior to training and implementation is essential to adequate training and a reasonable expectation of success.

Education. The transition from one method of operation to another requires the education and training of people in many different positions. This is especially true when a company is switching from a primarily informal system to a formal one. Top management, managers, and staff personnel all require training. Education and training cover the why in addition to the how. Production planning and inventory management techniques may change; therefore, all in-volved personnel need to understand the objectives of these techniques and how they work. Education is discussed at length in Chapter 21.

Testing. The computerized information system, programs, and I/O devices all require testing. Programs are run using either historical data, fabricated data representing all possible permutations of input data and processing runs, or live data in order to verify the functional results of the programs and systems. Systems modules, frequently developed in the required technological sequence, are tested to verify that they interface properly.

Installation. New systems may require changes in data processing equipment, functional systems, forms, data recorded, information provided, and, perhaps most importantly, the organization structure and the way the company does business. Thus, orientation, training, and testing are essential. Final responsi-bility for successful implementation belongs to the users; they are the crucial factor in a system's operation and must live with its results daily. Therefore, they should participate in its development.

Monitoring System Performance

Once a system is installed successfully, a new task arises—monitoring the system to assure that it is being used properly and is achieving the desired results. Even under the best conditions there is a tendency for the enthusiasm and attention to the necessary detail to wane once a system has been installed. In addition, some users may make unilateral decisions to improve the system by changing the input data or the process at a local site. There is a need to verify that actual practice conforms to the documented, prescribed method. If it does not, deter-mine why. Perhaps a bootlegged change is justified and should be formalized throughout the system.

Monitoring system performance involves not only checking that users and data processing personnel are following the proper procedures, but also deter-mining that the system is achieving management objectives. Has inventory, for example, been reduced to the amount expected? Has manufacturing lead time decreased? Has customer service improved? New systems do not achieve their objectives in a week or two; it usually takes six months or longer, depending on the company's production, distribution, and sales cycle. Harvey N. Rose (1978) recommends an in-depth operational audit of the PIM systems at least every two years.

CURRENT DEVELOPMENTS

Computers have been a major factor in altering production management policies and practices during the last two decades. Computer-related developments will continue to be a major cause of change in PIM. Two such developments already evident are microcomputers and the enhanced aid of computers in design and manufacturing. Blackstone and Cox (1988) reported that MRP is now feasible on microcomputers due to the advent of 32-bit technology and high-capacity Winchester hard disks. Hardware in the $3,000 range and systems and MRP software estimated at less than $2,000 provide the small manufacturer with data processing capability at an affordable price. If history is any guide, these costs will decline in the next decade. Blackstone and Cox found, however, that most small manufacturers were quite far from having adequate data to support MRP.

Computers are being used extensively in engineering design and manufacturing. Computer aided design (CAD) is used not only in design engineering analysis and product design, but also in calculating material layout and in specifying cutter location and tool paths for machining. Computer-Aided Manufacturing International, a nonprofit association of computer hardware and software developers, has developed a software system called CAM-I Automated Process Planning. This system generates standard routings on the basis of part characteristics determined according to a standard classification table. The process then is modified by the process engineer to match the requirements of a specific part. (Johnson 1982)

Computer aided manufacturing (CAM) usually refers to a broad range of techniques for discrete parts production including paper tape, numerically controlled (NC) machine tools; dedicated computer, numerically controlled machine tools (CNC); direct numerical control (DNC) of more than one machine by a single computer; and computer controlled robots. Computer aided inspection and automatic (computerized) storage and retrieval systems also exist. Computers additionally are used to control continuous manufacturing processes.

While some companies are beginning to explore the potential of CAD and CAM, others have a decade or more of experience. This experience has been diverse, dealing with a variety of problems in design and manufacturing. Integration of different computerized systems has, at best, been partial in most organizations. The challenge is to combine computerized systems and PIM in an integrated computer aided manufacturing system. (Len 1981)

Group technology (GT) and cellular manufacturing are two approaches that partially integrate design and manufacturing systems. GT involves identifying items with either similar design or similar manufacturing process characteristics and grouping them into families of like items. Coding and classification schemes are used to record item attributes such as function, material, shape (internal and external dimensional relationships, e.g., length/diameter), surface finish, tolerances, weight, demand rate, processing operations, and their sequence in a computerized data base.

Analysis of the designs of items in the same group frequently leads to the discovery of some items with identical designs and others with very similar designs. Redundant designs can be eliminated and similar designs combined on a single drawing. Savings result in engineering and manufacturing. Analysis of similar designs and similar manufacturing processes can lead to the development of standardized processes and setups with minor modifications for each item. The development of such processes combined with the development of manufacturing cells usually generates larger cost reductions than parts coding alone.

Cellular manufacturing, frequently considered an integral part of group technology, is the organization of a small group of workers and machines in a repetitive production flow layout to manufacture a group of similar items. It achieves economies due to the modified equipment dedicated to the group, special tooling, reduced setup and run time, reduced material handling, shorter throughput time, and reduced WIP.

CAM and cellular manufacturing both can result in smaller lot sizes and, thus, reduced cycle stock. The production of a group of items on dedicated equipment presents problems in scheduling order releases and calculating lot sizes; multilevel requirements exacerbate these problems. Michael Spencer (1989) reported on the success of combining MRP, GT, and JIT to overcome these problems.

Clearly the integration of computerized systems, GT, MRP, JIT, and TOC is a major task facing manufacturing management. Increased computer capacity per dollar and continual improvements in software present manufacturing management with the task of developing manufacturing policies and strategies that recognize these developments. Technological choices and computer integrated manufacturing are discussed in depth in the next section.

TECHNOLOGICAL CHOICES

Manufacturers constantly seek the right balance or combination of process characteristics that will give them a competitive edge. With the dynamics of changing process developments, product technology, information management, and product distribution methods, numerous technologies are emerging. The computer is playing an increasing role at all levels of production and distribution process design.

The realization of computer integrated manufacturing (CIM) is not straightforward. Computer aided design, computerized scheduling and material control packages, computer controlled machines and robots, and computer aided instruction all arose independently. Often these technologies exist on machines that do not share a common file format for data or for communication. CAD was developed on dedicated CAD work stations. Computerized scheduling is most frequently performed on plant or departmental minicomputers. Computerized equipment usually has an on-board microprocessor, which may not have been designed for communication with a larger computer. Computer aided instruction was developed for education and is only now developing popularity as a means of customer service. Finally, the company's accounts payable and receivable records may well be on a mainframe computer at a central location far removed from the manufacturing facility. Therefore, a company must decide which of these technologies, if any, is appropriate for the company. Each technology is explored in more detail in this section.

Electronic Data Interchange (EDI)

EDI refers to the electronic exchange of standard documents, such as requests for quotation, purchase orders, notifications of delivery or receipt, and invoices. This interchange is not straightforward for two reasons. First, there are two formats for data storage in a computer, known as ASCII and EBCDIC. A computer that uses ASCII does not recognize an EBCDIC file and vice versa. Second, most data reside in data base management programs, each of which has its own idiosyncrasy concerning the definition of fields, etc. Two computers that utilize ASCII may have different data base management programs and be unable to exchange data. The work in electronic data interchange is primarily devoted toward the development of industry standards. Standardization is common in consumer items. If audio compact disk players had no standardization, a consumer who owned a Sony player would have to have a different compact disk from one who owned a Pioneer, who in turn would need a different disk from one who owned a Kenwood. Because computer companies have developed data base management software to operate on their hardware, standardization does not exist for most electronic information.

Even after the industry adopts standards, a company whose existing data is largely in nonstandard format faces a difficult choice in deciding when and how to move toward standardization. As more firms become fully integrated within the corporation and with suppliers and customers, there will be immense competitive pressures toward a "paperless" operation. On the other hand, a truism of data processing is that you do not want to pioneer a technology (unless pioneering the technology is part of the firm's strategic plan for competition). At the time of this writing, EDI and much of CIM are still in the pioneering stage.

Computer Aided Design (CAD)

CAD systems have resulted in tremendous productivity increases for design engineers. A CAD system has the ability to rotate a drawing of a part through three dimensions, to zoom onto a particular portion of the drawing to provide needed detail, and to pan to a full view of the product. In addition, the CAD system can access previous part drawings, permitting a designer to perform a computer-assisted search for the existence of a particular part. The designer can then merge the existing part into the new design. Prior to CAD, companies commonly had extensive duplication among parts performing the same function, because it was much easier for a design engineer to design a new part than to determine if it already existed. Plants might often stock 15 different 3/8″ screws. Of course, the proliferation of part numbers led to a proliferation of inventory, especially obsolete inventory because the part might not be reused in new designs. Given CAD, this part proliferation is inexcusable. CAD systems easily pay for themselves in inventory saving and in designer productivity.

Computer Aided Process Planning (CAPP)

Because a CAD system is used in designing the part, it would seem a small step to having the computer design manufacturing instructions that a robot or direct numerically controlled machine can use. CAPP is a reality where the operation is critical in only two dimensions. For example, pick-and-place robots are used to remove a chip from a roll of chips and place it in the proper position on the surface of a printed circuit board. (The chip is later fixed in position by passing over a wave solder machine that simultaneously solders all chips placed on the board.) At the time of this writing, there are still problems in having a CAD system develop instructions in three dimensions for cutting, drilling, or grinding of parts.

Another aspect of process planning is choosing which among several existing machines should be used to make a part. The choice is a function of quality and of the cost of using a particular machine. Software to make this choice is functioning in a number of companies.

Computer Aided Scheduling and Material Planning (CAS&MP)

The traditional approach to scheduling and material planning is to use a material requirements planning (MRP) package to plan component and material purchases and production. The MRP package must be furnished a master product schedule that gives the quantity and timing of finished product delivery. The development of a master production schedule is discussed in Chapter 4; MRP is the subject of Chapter 10. An MRP system also must have a bill of material listing the components of a finished product. Today, most CAD systems have the ability to automatically generate a bill of material. Unfortunately, few CAD systems can transmit the bill of material electronically to the computer that performs material planning. The MRP system must also have a routing, i.e., a list of the operations to be performed, the work center to perform the operation, and the time usually required to set up the work center and to produce a part after setup. Today, most routing information is developed manually. We presume that companies that are developing CAPP systems are developing them to transmit the routing data to the CAS&MP system.

Computer Aided Instruction (CAI)

The advantage of CAI is that, unlike human instructors, a computer never becomes bored or irritable with a student. The disadvantage is that many people are intimidated by computers. Use of a compact disk with interactive video for training in the proper use and maintenance of a product has the advantages of CAI without the disadvantage of requiring what the user perceives as a computer. (There are several microprocessors in the typical home entertainment center.) It is therefore not surprising that CAI technology is expected to move to CDI (compact disk-interactive) and to become very popular in the future.

Computer Aided Manufacturing (CAM)

CAM exists at several levels. At the simplest levels are robots and computer numerically controlled machines that have microprocessors (small, independent, special purpose computers) that are not controlled by a central computer. At a more complex level, there are robots and direct numerically controlled machines that are programmable from a central computer to perform a variety of tasks. At the most complex level, there is the flexible manufacturing system (FMS). This system contains several direct numerically controlled (DNC) machines, a computer controlled part storage and retrieval system, and an automatic guided vehicle that carries parts between machines and storage. In theory, the FMS permits parts to be produced without being touched by humans.

Manufacturing Cells

Cellular manufacturing is the organization of a small group of workers and machines in a production flow layout, frequently a U-shaped configuration, to produce a group of similar items. Reduced production costs result from the modified equipment dedicated to the group, special tooling, reduced setup and run time, reduced materials handling, shorter throughput time, and reduced work in process. Colin New (1977), for example, reported a 70 percent average reduction in throughput time for a group of U.K. firms using cellular manufacturing. Another example is at John Deere's Waterloo, Iowa, engine plant where manufacturing cells reduced the inventory of diesel engines required for final assembly (Spencer 1980).

Manufacturing cells are generally differentiated into two types: (1) those requiring setup time when changing from one item to another and (2) those where no setup time is required when switching between items. This latter type of manufacturing cell is usually called a flexible manufacturing system (FMS).

Flexible Manufacturing System (FMS)

The ability to avoid a new setup each time a different item is processed is the differentiating characteristic of an FMS. The absence of setup requirements allows manufacturing to switch from one item to another without an economic penalty for the setup. Thus, the system has great flexibility.

The typical FMS is an automated cell (integrating materials handling and processing equipment) used to produce a group of parts or assemblies. Although all items require similar manufacturing processes, the sequence of operations is not necessarily the same in each case. A nonautomated production line that can switch from one product to another without any setup time is also an FMS. For example, an assembly line that can switch production between any of several different but similar cylinders is technically an FMS. Such lines exist at Miller Fluid Power in Bensonville, Illinois.

In an automated FMS, either computers or operators or both might perform the required functions as follows:

1. Computers control the:
   a. Machine tools
   b. Materials handling equipment
   c. Integration of the activities of the machine tools and materials handling equipment
2. Operators:
   a. Perform emergency and preventive maintenance
   b. Enter data, such as part numbers
   c. Enter new or revised programs
3. Either the operators or the computer-controlled, automated equipment can:
   a. Load materials (rough castings for example) into the materials handling system
   b. Unload completed parts from the materials handling system
   c. Remove or add tools to the tool magazines of different machines

An FMS is dedicated to manufacturing a family of items. In an ideal situation, each item in the family is designed with a standard set of mounting bosses (lugs, holes, or ears, for example) or is mounted on a standard plate or frame. Thus, all items in a group are secured to the table, bed, or faceplate of a machine tool in the same manner. As a result, it is not necessary to change fixtures or holding devices when switching from one item to another. Because there is no setup time, a process batch size of one is economically feasible. In some situations different mounting fixtures may be required, but automatic sensing devices can recognize these variations and, through the computer, instruct the equipment to make the necessary adjustments.

In addition to product mounting, setup time may also include adjustments to control the length and depth of a cut. This is not necessary in an FMS, as each machine tool performs the programmed operation with an accuracy matching or surpassing that of the best operator. The computer controlling the machine's operation accesses the program for machining the particular item and follows that program. The machine also may have the capability to read a coded identification on an item and verify its identity. Thus, the use of computers and software in the FMS provides an *economy of scope*, which is the ability to produce many different items automatically and economically in small lot sizes. This is sometimes called *soft automation*. In contrast, *hard automation* can produce only one item in a large volume very efficiently, and is thus associated with *economies of scale*.

Setup costs still exist, however, just as the need for human skill and ingenuity exists. The cost of programming the process instructions for each item is a fixed setup cost. In an FMS it is spread across many production lots (frequently one unit each) and is not incurred each time a lot is produced. Further, just as the efficiency of a traditional job shop depends on the art and craft of the setup operator, the efficiency of an FMS depends on the skill of the programmer. System design and programming of the direction, monitoring, and control of the integrated materials handling and machining processes are also key factors in the efficiency of the FMS. Thus, the setup (software) costs must be considered when deciding to establish an FMS. Other factors affecting the decision are quality, lead time reductions, and reduced inventory.

Computer Integrated Manufacturing (CIM)

CIM is a natural extension of FMS. It is an application of computer technology to take full advantage of both hardware and software developments in conjunction with manufacturing technology and management control systems. It combines these to provide greater flexibility by integrating product design and manufacturing processes, producing small lot sizes, and switching among items in a family economically. It is discussed further in Chapter 17. Today, an FMS is economical only for items with a high enough volume to justify the complexity of producing programs for the DNC machines. If CIM progresses to the point that CAD systems can produce machine instructions in three dimensions automatically, then the use of an FMS for unique or low-volume parts is possible.

Computer integrated manufacturing presents a path for integrating the various computers already in use in most manufacturing facilities in order to improve their collective productivity. CIM is inevitable, but may be decades in reaching completion because of the cost of converting existing hardware and software. CIM should be adopted as part of the overall strategic direction of a company. Adopting CIM generally reduces material and/or information lead time. A company needs to know precisely what benefits will accrue from shortening these lead times before adopting CIM. (Swann, 1989)

Swann (1989) summarizes CIM as follows:

> What is CIM? Whatever you can cost justify, but basically CIM is JIT for information.
>
> Why does it cost $40 million? Because we have hidden behind "the cost system is broken" instead of insisting that CIM investments be justified on a basis of costs and benefits.
>
> CIM is an area that no manufacturer can ignore, because his competitors are very likely to be exploring it. But it can be tackled by:
>
> —understanding the information needs of users
> —defining an overall strategy for CIM investment
> —developing candidate CIM scenarios
> —analyzing the cost/benefit of CIM alternatives
> —actively pursuing a course of action that is strategically correct, and fiscally sound

A common fallacy is to assume that problems with people can be avoided by automation. In fact, to realize the full benefits of computer integrated manufacturing, people and automation must be integrated. Careful job analysis is a first step toward planning that integration. Prudent managers should make long-term forecasts of job requirements before introducing automation.

In summary, PIM management systems run from the simple to the very complex. Developments in computer technology enable PIM to explicitly manage its interfaces with marketing, accounting and finance, product design, and manufacturing engineering.

EXERCISES

1. Prepare a list of the key PIM system functions for the following types of firms. If you believe that critical information is lacking, make assumptions as consistent as possible with available information.

    a. A small ($4,000,000 sales annually) high-precision gear manufacturing company has a gear blanking department and five different gear-cutting departments, each for a special type of gear. Machinists are nonunion, highly paid, and each can operate most equipment. The company builds to order. The rank-ordered priority of objectives is quality, delivery, and price. There are three supervisors who also serve as dispatchers, an operations manager who is the master scheduler, and the company president who is director of manufacturing, engineering, and marketing.

    b. A medium-sized specialized truck body manufacturer:
        (1) Manufactures 20 percent—in dollars—of its final product, components, and subassemblies to stock.
        (2) Builds most final assemblies of major items to order. The competitive strength of the company lies in its ability to produce high quality final products with engineering modifications to the customer's specification.
        (3) Has approximately 400 shop employees, 15 departments, and 10 distributors where final mounting of truck bodies on chassis sometimes is performed.
        (4) Annually sells 25 to 50 percent of its product to the export market.
        (5) Experiences problems with delayed delivery from chassis manufacturer when truck bodies are mounted on the chassis at the plant.
        (6) Has wandering bottlenecks in the plant and in engineering as the mix of orders and order processing shifts.

    c. A small process industry company produces one item, a gel-like soap for industrial use. It packs the soap in three different size containers and sells to one private label distributor, directly to local plants through its own three-agent sales force, and directly to tool and supply peddlers who contact gas stations and small plants in the area.

    d. A medium-sized ($50,000,000 annual sales) specialty machine tool and replacement tooling manufacturer produces to stock with emphasis on delivery and quality. Of all orders, 95 percent are shipped within 24 hours. It has two or three competitors, but estimates that it has 60 to 70 percent of the market. It sells its products from central warehouses—one on the West Coast and one in Canada. It has a no-layoff policy, subcontracts some work in high-demand years, and has a labor agreement that allows personnel to be moved from department to department. Many components are manufactured as joint orders.

2. For each of the firms in Exercise 1, list the logical files required.

3. The Ajax Manufacturing Company produces to stock and sells from a central warehouse and five regional distribution centers. Each of the distribution centers has three to six company-owned warehouses that it serves. The company is planning to switch from its present pull system of distribution, which is based on weekly batched reports of sales and orders, to a push allocation distribution system.
    a. Discuss the advantages and disadvantages of having microcomputers at the regional centers and at each warehouse.
    b. Develop an implementation plan including all the steps required.

4. Visit a local company that uses a PIM package and determine its strengths and weaknesses.

5. Which records probably are required in the item master file of the company in Exercise 1d?

6. The company described in Exercise 1d decides to use a data base system.
    a. Describe the data base down to the record level of detail.
    b. Illustrate how three different logical files might use the same items from the data base.
    c. What advantages does this company achieve from a data base? What, if any, disadvantages does it encounter?

7. The company described in Exercise 1d implements a file-oriented system over a two-year period. List the steps to be followed and measures to be applied in monitoring its systems.

8. A local repetitive process manufacturing company provides original equipment parts for the automobile industry. It is interested in monitoring the PIM system. Develop a plan listing the steps to be followed and measures to be applied in monitoring its systems.

9. Another company, similar to that described in Exercise 8, manufactures automotive parts for the replacement market only. How would monitoring the PIM system for this company differ from that described in Exercise 8?

SELECTED READINGS

Allen, R. Leonard. "The Applicability of Standard Manufacturing Software to Primary Metals Processing." *APICS 23d Annual Conference Proceedings* (1980): 85-89.

Blackstone, John H., Jr., and James F. Cox. "MRP Design and Implementation Issues for Small Manufacturers." *Production and Inventory Management* (Third Quarter 1988): 65-76.

Bolander, Steven F., Richard C. Heard, Samuel M. Seward, and Sam G. Taylor. *Manufacturing Planning and Control in Process Industries.* Falls Church, VA: American Production and Inventory Control Society, 1981.

Bourke, Richard W. "Selecting Software Smartly: The Early Steps." *Production and Inventory Management* (May 1981): 13-16.

Bourke, Richard W. "Surveying the Software." *Datamation* (October 1980): 101-107.

Buffa, Elwood S., and Jeffrey G. Miller. *Production-Inventory Systems: Planning and Control* 3d ed. Homewood, IL: Richard D. Irwin, Inc., 1979.

Cook, Milton E. "Developing a Successful P&IC Training Program." *APICS 23d Annual Conference Proceedings* (1980): 6-8.

Cook, Milton E. "How to Evaluate Software Packages." *APICS 24th Annual Conference Proceedings* (1981): 126-130.

DeSantis, Gerald F. "Implementation Considerations in Systems Design." *APICS 20th Annual Conference Proceedings* (1977): 210-216.

Dickson, Gary W., James A. Senn, and Normal L. Chervany. "Research in Management Information Systems: The Minnesota Experiments." *Management Science* (May 1977).

Finch, Byron J., and James F. Cox. *Planning and Control System Design: Principles and Cases for Process Manufacturers.* Falls Church, VA: American Production and Inventory Control Society, 1987.

Fogarty, Donald W. "Change and the Materials Manager, or Is Your System Open?" *APICS 15th Annual International Conference Proceedings* (1972): 260-374.

Gray, Max, and Keith R. London. *Documentation Standards.* New York: Brandon/Systems Press, Inc., 1969.

Groover, Mikell P. *Automation, Production Systems, and Computer-Aided Manufacturing.* Englewood Cliffs, NJ: Prentice-Hall, Inc., 1987.

Gunn, Thomas G. *Computer Applications in Manufacturing.* New York: Industrial Press, Inc., 1981.

Hall, Robert W. "Repetitive Manufacturing." *Production and Inventory Management* (Second Quarter 1982): 78-86.

Hoyt, George S. "The Art of Buying Software." *APICS 18th Annual Conference Proceedings* (1975): 316-320.

Hoyt, George S. "Successes and Failure in MRP User Involvement." *APICS 20th Annual International Conference Proceedings* (1977): 204-209.

Johnson, Jan. "Pushing the State of the Art." *Datamation* (February 1982): 112-114.

Kneppelt, Leland R. "Real Time, On-Line Distributed in the Manufacturing Systems Environment." *APICS 23d Annual Conference Proceedings* (1980): 58-60.

Len, John J. "CAD/CAM-Productivity Tools for MRP Record Accuracy." *APICS 24th Annual International Conference Proceedings* (1981): 374-377.

Murphy, Robert H., Jr. "Assuring Cost-Effective Manufacturing Systems." *APICS 23d Annual Conference Proceedings* (1980): 70-73.

New, C. Colin. "MRP & GT, A New Strategy for Component Production." *Production and Inventory Management* 18, no. 3 (1977): 50-62.

Paul, Lois, ed. "Benefits of Packaged Software Called Myths." *Computerland* (January 25, 1982).

Pennente, Ernest, and Ted Levy. "MRP on Microcomputers." *Production and Inventory Management Review* (May 1982): 20-25.

Pinella, Paul, and Eric Cheathan. "In-House Inventory Control." *ICP INTERFACE Manufacturing and Engineering* (Winter 1981): 18-21.

Rose, Harvey N. "Auditing of P&IC Systems: The Necessary Ingredient." *APICS 21st Annual Conference Proceedings* (1978): 436-454.

Rowan, R. T., and J. A. Wellendorf. "Implementing Manufacturing Control Software Package in a Process Industry." *APICS 23d Annual Conference Proceedings* (1980): 81-84.

Sasser, Earl. Presentation to Atlanta Harvard Club, January 1988.

Skinner, Wickham. "The Focused Factory." *Harvard Business Review* (May-June 1974): 113-121.

Spencer, Michael S. "Lessons from the JIT Journey: A Case Study." *Just-in-Time Reprints*. Falls Church, VA: American Production and Inventory Control Society, 1989.

Swann, Don. "What is CIM, and Why Does it Cost $40 Million." *P&IM Review* (July 1989): 34.

Taylor, Sam G. "Are Process Industries Different?" *APICS 23d Annual Conference Proceedings* (1980): 94-98.

Toffler, Alvin. *Future Shock*. New York: Bantam Books, Inc., 1971.

Venglarik, James M. "Distributed Processing by Means of Minicomputer Networks." *APICS 22d Annual Conference Proceedings* (1979): 58-60.

Vollum, Robert B. "Integrated Data Base: Solid Foundation or Deep Hole." *APICS 22d Annual Conference Proceedings* (1979): 48-51.

Yost, Gary S. "Inventory through Timesharing." *ICP INTERFACE Manufacturing and Engineering* (Winter 1981): 18-21.

21

MANAGING PIM

This chapter concerns the overall management of production and inventory planning and control activities, functions, and systems. Overall production and inventory management (PIM) begins with establishing a set of objectives that supports the organizational goals. Attaining these objectives requires the following basic management activities:

1. Planning all PIM activities
2. Coordinating and integrating PIM activities with marketing, finance, accounting, manufacturing management, industrial engineering, and manufacturing engineering
3. Developing an organizational structure consistent with the manufacturing process and corporate goals
4. Managing human resources
5. Executing the plan
6. Establishing policies and procedures for controlling PIM activities
7. Being cognizant of developments in PIM technology, evaluating them, and determining how those that are appropriate can best be implemented in the organization's production and marketing environment

Maintaining production output and keeping inventory within targets while evaluating and implementing developments in PIM technology is the challenge to PIM managers. This is not a new challenge. During the last quarter century or so, the production and inventory manager has had to achieve current operating objectives while evaluating, implementing, and then sometimes discarding various techniques. Today the manager must determine how, where, and when to implement the principles and techniques of JIT and TQC in an organization's unique and changing production-marketing environment.

This chapter briefly discusses operating objectives and then examines the application of basic management concepts to managing PIM.

PERFORMANCE OBJECTIVES AND MEASURES

Management needs to establish operating performance objectives in measurable (quantitative) terms.[1] These objectives are a basis for planning. Manufacturing and marketing management establish customer service objectives (delivery lead time and desired achievement levels) to meet or surpass competition. PIM determines the aggregate inventory investment and production output required to support these objectives. PIM also establishes subsidiary objectives that are consistent with and support the general management goals. A possible set of PIM objectives for a company that manufactures components to stock and assembles final products to order is listed in Table 21-1.[2]

Table 21-1
Examples of PIM Objectives

Customer Service
Ship 95 percent of orders within 48 hours of receipt.
Ship 90 percent of backorders within 5 days.
Ship 100 percent of backorders within 2 weeks.

Inventory Investment
Aggregate inventory investment should be less than $15,000,000.
The inventory turnover rate on components and raw materials should be greater than 15.0.

Operating Efficiency
Overtime costs should not exceed $200,000 per quarter.
Lot sizes of 90 percent of all production runs for Product Group A should be within 10 percent of the planned quantity.
JIT and TQC concepts and techniques are to be applied to the manufacturing of Product Group B.
Total quality management concepts will be applied.

Human Resource Management
The policy is no involuntary layoffs.
All employees will be given the opportunity to develop to their full capability.
A minimum 5 percent of work force time will be scheduled for productivity improvement (quality circle) meetings.

These objectives are based on corporate marketing (product positioning and customer service), labor relations (retaining a highly skilled, well-compensated labor force with a productivity-oriented attitude buttressed by

---

1. Possible measures have been discussed throughout the text and especially in Chapters 5 and 7.
2. These objectives exist at a company with which one of the authors is familiar.

profit sharing), and productivity. They lead to subsidiary objectives that support their achievement. Some typical subsidiary objectives are:

1. Developing a manufacturing cell for Product Group B
2. Reducing all setup times on Product Group B by 50 percent
3. A 100 percent accuracy on 90 percent of components in cycle counting (There is no annual physical inventory.)
4. A 100 percent accuracy and completeness in the bill of material (BOM)
5. Production of 90 percent of orders within the planned lead time
6. A 100 percent fulfillment of the master production schedule (MPS) in 10 out of every 13 weeks in the quarter

Many other subsidiary objectives can be added to this list. Such additions might concern purchase commitments, the value of receipts, downtime due to material or tool shortages, and raw material and work-in-process (WIP) investment. The point is that establishing realistic objectives provides employees a target at which to aim and a measure of their performance. A set of overall PIM objectives and subsidiary objectives requires internal consistency, but objectives will differ depending on the nature of the organization. A company manufacturing final assemblies to stock, for example, will not have the same set of objectives as a firm manufacturing custom items to order. And because sales volume, product lines, and manufacturing processes change, PIM objectives need to be reviewed periodically.

PIM objectives include not only operating objectives, such as customer service and inventory investment, but also those concerning planning, organization, staffing, training, and information systems, the attainment of which will support the achievement of operating objectives. The implementation of JIT and TQC, the development of a manufacturing control systems group, and the completion of JIT education and training sessions by all employees are examples.

PLANNING

PIM needs to develop master plans of the organization structure, human resources management, and management systems it intends to have in order to achieve its performance objectives. (These plans are in addition to the operating plans concerning production and inventory.) The organization plan should define the departments, the subgroups, and their functions. It needs to reveal the relationship of these units to other functions such as marketing, engineering, and the shop.

The human resources management plan includes a specification of the policies, the capabilities, and the education and training required to manage and carry out the various activities. A project manager, for example, with successful JIT and TQC experience may be required to manage the development and implementation of such approaches.

The Management System Plan

This plan specifies all the requirements of the information systems modules plus a description of each module's objectives, inputs, processes (design techniques), and outputs. This plan describes the data base, files, decision processes (such as the capacity planning methods and inventory management systems to be employed), and the reports and information included in each. The technological precedence of these modules is included, represented perhaps by a schematic. These plans constitute a blueprint of what is to be.

Development and Implementation Plan

This is a schedule of the various steps required to achieve the desired organization, staffing, and management systems. Education and training activities may be added to this plan. This plan recognizes the major tasks and their relationships, frequently describing them by a network model, as illustrated in Figure 21-1. Such a plan clearly indicates priorities and can serve as the basis for determining required resources, such as space, recruiting, training, equipment, systems, software, and the data required to accomplish the plan. Estimating the costs of these resources provides the necessary information for developing a time-phased budget for top management approval.

Obtaining top management's written approval of the plan and its development, including the budget, is an essential step. It greatly increases the probability that top management will understand the objectives, approaches, and requirements of the plan. Management commitment is crucial because organization, staffing, education and training, and PIM systems affect most functional areas in the business; changes in operating procedures are required throughout the organization; substantial resources frequently are required to accomplish the changes; and transfer of key personnel from daily operating decisions to detailed planning and implementation of any changes may be required.

ORGANIZATION

Organizing consists of grouping individuals to perform assigned tasks and of establishing both the relationships among the groups and the flow of authority. Most groups (departments) have line duties that require the performance of specified tasks and staff duties that require providing information, advice, and support to other groups for the performance of their tasks. Basic principles of organization design include the following:

1. Form should fit function.
2. More than one PIM organization structure may work well in a given situation.

Figure 21-1
Systems Development Plan

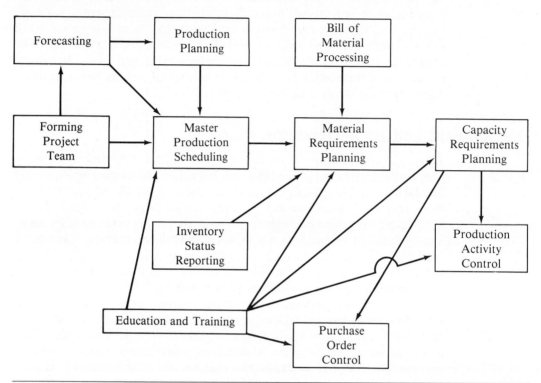

Note: *This is a partial plan. For example, acquiring necessary personnel and computer hardware should be added.*

3. For the organization to operate at its full potential, there must be a match between the capabilities and talents of individuals and the positions they occupy.
4. Reorganizing of itself rarely solves a problem.
5. Good morale, a team effort, realistic measurable objectives, and a good formal system can overcome a deficient organizational structure in many instances.
6. "The simplest organization structure that will do the job is the best one." (Drucker 1974, 601)

Peter Drucker (1965) states that organization design begins with the following type questions:

1. What are the truly important roles of the department? Which goal(s) is (are) dominant?
2. In which functions of PIM is excellence required to achieve these goals?
3. In which PIM functions would inadequate performance jeopordize attainment of these goals?

Organization Structure

The traditional organization of production and inventory planning and control activities is similar to the organization described in Figure 21-2. The inventory control department and production control department are separate and distinct. The former works with a relatively formal system to plan and control inventories. One of its main tasks is to launch orders. The production control department is concerned primarily with getting the orders through the plant. In many firms it has traditionally relied heavily on informal systems and expediting. (Wight 1974, 224-229; Motwane 1981, 347-350)

Figure 21-2
Traditional PIM Organization

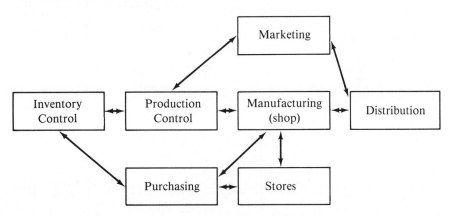

The deficiencies of the traditional organization are obvious. Inventory control and production control have inherent obstacles to control beginning with checking the feasibility of the production plan. For example, if production control does not control the release of production orders, it hardly controls production. If it does not control the release of purchase orders for manufacturing materials and components, it does not control those inventories.

Organizing PIM in a structure consistent with planning and controlling activities, as illustrated in Figure 21-3 and 21-4, is a more rational approach. (Many companies have developed systems that, in effect, reorganize production and inventory management without formally documenting the reorganization.)

The differences between job shops and flow production, either repetitive manufacturing of discrete parts or continuous processing of liquids and powders, have been discussed earlier. Relatively little has been written directly concerning any differences between PIM organization structures in process flow manufacturing and job shop manufacturing. However, some points can be made.

Preventive maintenance of equipment is crucial in flow manufacturing. If one machine is down, the entire line is down. Thus, planning and scheduling preventive maintenance is a task of the production planning group and is blended into production schedules. Flow manufacturing typically exists in a make-to-stock environment with distribution an important part in providing

Figure 21-3
Functional PIM Organization Activity Flow

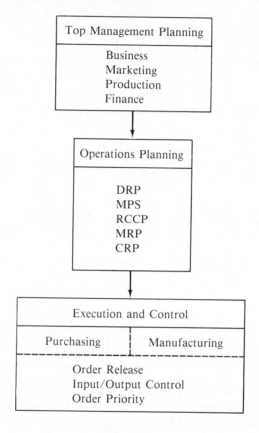

customer service. The need to coordinate purchasing, inventory control, production, and distribution in this type situation is apparent and has been mentioned often in previous chapters.

The Master Scheduler

The master scheduler, a key individual in a PIM organization, is the link between marketing, distribution, manufacturing, and planning. Oliver Wight (1974, 68-69) stated that the tasks of the master scheduler include the following:

1. Check the sales forecast for reasonableness and work with marketing to resolve questions.
2. Convert the sales forecast into a production plan.
3. Be sure that the MPS correlates with the production plan, shipping budget, inventory investment planning, and marketing plans.
4. Give delivery promises on incoming orders and match actual requirements with the master schedule as they materialize.

Figure 21-4
Functional Organizational Structure

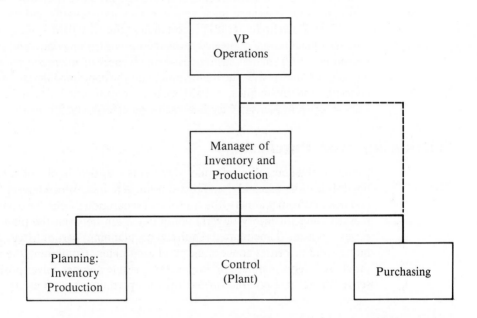

Whether or not a firm has someone formally designated as the master scheduler, the tasks are essential. Combining them under the jurisdiction of one individual improves the likelihood that they will be coordinated and managed properly. Most important, it provides a focal point for the required coordination of marketing, manufacturing, distribution, and planning as well as a place to look when things are not going well. The position of master scheduler has been established in many different types of firms with beneficial results.

The Manufacturing Control Systems Group

The design and implementation of a PIM information system is a major effort that usually consumes months. System evaluation, maintenance, and refinement are also substantial tasks. The user should be responsible for system maintenance and refinement, just as in design and development. Managing the system and planning (or controlling) production and inventory are two full-time jobs in most organizations. Attempting to do both simultaneously will likely lead to neither task being performed well.

A major system development and implementation project usually requires the formation of a project team with full-time participation and, usually, management by PIM personnel. This is a natural launching point for a manufacturing control systems group. In small organizations, only one or two individuals may be required. In a large company, the group may include systems designers and programmers. Corporate systems and data processing provide the policies and general procedures under which the group operates. Its tasks include development, implementation, and training tasks. Users are the primary source of systems improvements and refinements since they work with the system daily and, thus, are most familiar with its strengths and weaknesses.

Cash Powell, Jr., (1981) recommends that the PIM systems group have the task of evaluating requested refinements, controlling data, and training new personnel. With the increasing cost-effectiveness of microcomputers, the networking of micros with the mainframe, and the continued development in PIM concepts and techniques, a PIM systems group will be kept busy. Marion Laboratories in Kansas City has used one effectively for years.

Relationship with Purchasing

Planning and controlling supplier shipments is critical in planning and controlling fabrication, assembly, and distribution activities. When buyers are separate and distinct from planners (the traditional separation of purchase part inventory planners and inventory buyers) communication between the planner and the buyer is crucial. Time-phased requirements planning, part of MRP, can give the buyer valid priorities concerning purchased items. Combining the roles of the purchased items planner and buyer into a single planner-buyer position makes sense whenever a reliable formal priority planning system exists.

Service Parts and New Products

Service parts sales contribute substantially to the profits of many firms. They typically are more profitable than finished goods sales. This is not surprising. Availability and delivery of service parts is more important to the typical customer than the price of the service part, because an hour or two of equipment downtime may be more costly than the service part. Thus, healthy prices on service parts frequently do not affect sales (sales are price inelastic over a considerable range), but availability and delivery are crucial.

Planning and controlling service parts delivery performance justifies assignment of this task to one or a group of individuals in many firms. This group needs to work closely with the master scheduler in planning for service parts and adjusting the schedule to meet unusual requirements. When service parts planning and the master scheduler do not work in concert, schedule disruption becomes common. Parts are bootlegged or removed from stores by "midnight requisitions" to meet service requirements. This usually is not discovered until the final assemblies are at the production line and parts shortages are discovered. Coordinating service parts requirements formally through the master scheduler will eliminate such costly experiences.

Products being developed, experimental models, and pilot models may be entirely revised final assemblies costing tens or hundreds of thousands of dollars or they may involve relatively minor changes. Some firms have relatively stable product designs. Other firms use an ability to develop new products or customized final assemblies as their competitive edge, (Powell 1981). The latter situation warrants the existence of a new product manager to take care of the following:

1. Planning and controlling engineering design activities
2. Coordinating engineering design and the sales (product) specification (Production planning and manufacturing engineering personnel usually participate in the development of proposed cost and production schedules.)
3. Developing and releasing complete BOM's for new and or modified products
4. Obtaining sources for new materials
5. Developing a realistic master production schedule by working with engineering, marketing, and the master scheduler
6. Coordinating the implementation of engineering changes

Thus, an organization structure similar to that in Figure 21-5 is necessary for firms with a dynamic product design and substantial service parts sales.

THE MANAGEMENT OF CHANGE

Kenneth Boulding (Toffler 1970, 13) asserts that the world of today is as different from the world of 1900 as the world of 1900 was different from the world of Julius Caesar. Peter Drucker (1974, 518-609) has noted that ". . . change is the order of things." Rapid social and technological change is the hallmark of modern society and of production management. For example, MRP, distribution requirements planning (DRP), push allocation distribution systems, I/O planning and control, JIT, application of mathematical programming and simulation to production planning and scheduling problems, and the digital computer have arrived since 1950. Automated fabrication processes, automated material handling and warehouse control, increased foreign competition, group technology and cellular manufacturing, the use of microcomputer networks linked to the mainframe, and the increased cost of capital are examples of relatively recent dramatic changes in operating conditions.

Many managers, pressed with short-term problems of performance and survival, become firefighters, too busy coping with day-to-day operations to anticipate the challenges and opportunities of tomorrow. Their organization has only one mode of activity, the operational.

Kurt Lewin (1951) was the first to articulate the three phases of change management, namely: unfreezing, changing, and freezing. Bell and Burnham (1987a, 1987b) have more aptly called these phases preparing for change, implementing change, and stabilizing the change. They, along with White (1980) and Taylor, Hills, and Davis (1979), have reported the success of using this model as a basis for change implementation.

Figure 21-5
PIM Organization Structure
Dynamic Product Design and Substantial Service Parts Sales

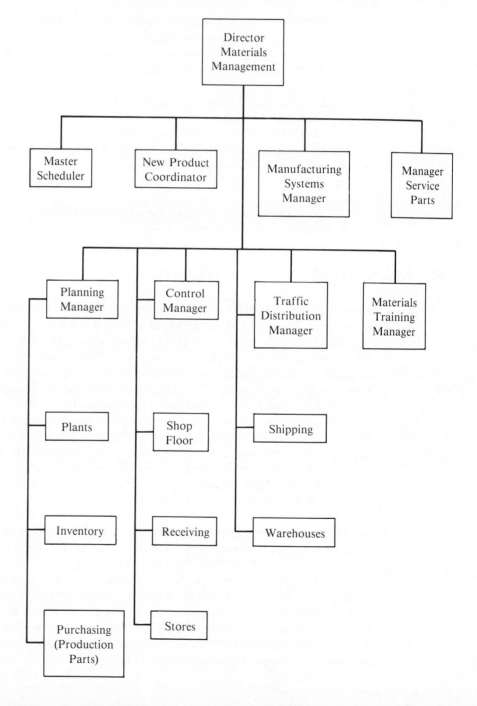

Phase I: Preparing for Change

We have noted the importance of preparing for change by establishing an environment in which change is viewed as not only acceptable but desirable and normal, and in which fear of failure does not dominate. As Peters and Waterman (1982) have noted, developing a substantial tolerance for failure is crucial in establishing the willingness to risk the implementation of new ideas. The world market in which most manufacturing firms exist requires that manufacturing personnel manage today's production with the best technology available while searching for improved processes and methods to manage tomorrow's production. Thus, the first task of manufacturing management is to develop an organization culture that both formally and informally rewards employees for attempting to improve productivity. This is the key to unfreezing present attitudes, norms, and behavior patterns and overcoming resistance to change in manufacturing management policies and techniques. Management must be committed to the change, employees must be educated concerning the relationship of productivity, competitiveness, and profit, and performance must be evaluated in terms of the new behavior objectives.

Phase II: Implementing Change

Selecting changes for intensive investigation and study is the first step in implementation. The second step is determining the advisability of implementing specific changes. Both steps occur continually and concurrently in most organizations.

Taking an inventory of the departmental capabilities, practices, and systems enables PIM management to focus change activities rationally. Without this capability inventory, innovations may be incorporated on the basis of present fashion or the special interests of staff members or supervisors. A companion piece to the capability inventory is an inventory of techniques—management systems, software packages, hardware development, and other tools available for use in PIM. Such an inventory reveals the approaches, policies, and techniques the department is aware of, those that have been evaluated, and those that seem relevant given its competitive strategy and market and process environment. The manufacturing control systems group is usually well suited to develop these inventories.

Evaluating present operations and defining areas of possible improvement precede selection of an area for intensive study. Candidate areas can be evaluated on a rational basis. For example, whether the department should assign priority to improving its procedures for a specific area can be based on the following:

1. How vital is the system or area?
2. How effective is the present approach, method, or system?
3. What are the expected costs in terms of personnel-hours, equipment, and software to design and successfully implement any changes?
4. What are the expected benefits of the change?
5. What is the probability of a sucessful change?

6. How long will it take to complete the study and implementation phases?
7. Can the organization make the study and carry out likely change recommendations?

Selection of Study Area.   If the PIM system is failing in a vital area—all other things being equal—that problem should have highest priority. For example, if shortages of raw materials and purchase parts are occurring frequently and stopping production for relatively long periods, this problem likely deserves top priority. Expediting, rescheduling, and the usual firefighting type activities that are used to solve a single occurrence are complemented by an investigation of the entire situation to find an approach that will eliminate the chronic problem.

Development of the required data base frequently receives top priority. For example, implementation of MRP requires an accurate and complete BOM, forecasting techniques require knowledge of past demand, and capacity planning needs the estimated times of the production processes for each item. When attempting to change a somewhat stagnant organization into a dynamic one receptive to change, initial changes should have a high probability of success and the value of the change should be highly visible. An ABC analysis can be used to classify those changes with relatively easy and clearly visible success for early implementation. This will encourage innovators and stimulate skeptics. (Bell and Burnham 1987a)

Decision to Implement.   A cost/benefit analysis may serve as a guide to the choice among the alternative areas but also can be misleading. The largest cost may be the long-run cost of not making the change. The major benefit is often the enhanced competitve posture of the firm. Improvements that begin in small numbers can snowball and change a barely surviving organization to one that is a leader in world markets.

The costs involved include both initial and operating costs. Initial costs include the cost of the study itself, the training of personnel for the new procedures, the development and debugging of the systems and programs, the design of forms, the development of a data base, and the cost of electronic data processing equipment. There are also costs for more mundane items, such as file cabinets, card holders, and wall-mounted charts. Other initial costs are associated with the personnel time required to reduce the confusion that is possible with change implementation and to overcome the resistance to change. Operating costs include those associated with forms administration, data capturing, computer processing, report preparation, report utilization, report storage, and system and software surveillance. The ability to estimate these costs grows exponentially with experience in change evaluation and implementation.

The ability to quantify the benefits depends to a large extent on the nature of the resulting improvement. For example, the benefit of a new inventory management system that reduces inventory investment by 10 percent or the implementation of a revised shop floor procedure that reduces queue time and WIP by specific percentages is less difficult to quantify than the benefit of a change that improves customer service.

Implementation. Successful change implementation includes convincing those affected of the merits of the change, involving leaders in its selection and implementation, proper training, surveillance, occasional confrontation, and recognition of failure possibilities. Personnel who will be responsible for executing new procedures should be involved in the evaluation of those procedures. Their knowledge of operating conditions aids in evaluating prospective changes. Their involvement and knowledge of adopted changes usually reduce their resistance to the change. Including the leaders, both formal and informal, in the change selection and analysis activities is especially important in obtaining their commitment and in the success of the change.

All those involved in the use of the technique or equipment should be thoroughly trained in its application prior to its implementation. In addition, all departments whose cooperation is required in executing the change need to be included in orientation and training. This training is usually interlaced with the selling of the change. Many a good idea has gone down the drain because the precise method of application was not understood and not followed.

Phase III: Stabilization of Change

Full acceptance of the new policies and methods is important. This is aided by recognizing and rewarding successes. The effects of a change should be monitored and the results analyzed until all difficulties have been overcome and the change is clearly a profitable one. Minor modifications and adaptations to the particular circumstances of an organization are often required. In addition, the procedures should be audited to ascertain that the changes are being followed properly. Few changes generate an immediate payoff. In fact, many changes are costly in the beginning because things frequently get worse before they get better. For example, seldom does a revised inventory management system reduce inventory in the short run. The time required to reap the benefits of the change should be clear to all involved. Learning curve and other transitional effects should not be minimized.

HUMAN RESOURCES MANAGEMENT

Fogarty, Hoffmann, and Stonebraker (1989, 34) note that human resources management (HRM) includes:

1. Management policies and attitudes that recognize basic human needs and create an environment supporting those needs
2. A system for determining personnel needs by skill and profession under different marketing and production plans
3. A system that develops employee capabilities, skills, potentials, interests, and development opportunities
4. An explicit policy of rewards that recognizes employee interests and objectives and is based on both group and individual performance. This

should encourage all employees to act as if they are part of a research group searching data for suggested productivity improvements.

5. Integration of recruitment and selection policies, personnel levels, capacity requirements, aggregate plans, and processes employed

HRM policies should develop an environment in which change is viewed as a normal event and in which occasional failures and mistakes due to new methods are accepted as a small price to pay for improved productivity.

Personnel Requirements

The number of individuals required by a firm depends on its size, manufacturing process, product positioning, number of plants, distribution system, and span of PIM activities. Many companies back into a workable level of personnel through implicit trial and error. However, personnel requirements are related directly to the functional requirements of the PIM information system and the educational needs assessment described later in this chapter. These requirements reveal the knowledge and skills required by PIM personnel. Traditional industrial engineering techniques of job and workload analysis are useful in measuring personnel requirements.

Capability Assessment

The knowledge and capability of present personnel also need assessment. The numerous and wide range of individuals participating in PIM seminars, conferences, and training and the increasing number of Certified Practitioners and Fellows are evidence of the quantum leap in the knowledge level of the profession. However, there is a continual influx of new people in the field who have little PIM education or experience. The capability of personnel in the firm can be determined by reviewing personnel files and by individual interviews. Certification at the Practioner Level is prima facie evidence of an understanding of the basic concepts. Certification at the Fellow Level generally indicates a deep and broad understanding of the principles, concepts, and techniques. One-on-one interviews can aid in determining individual experience and needs and in establishing individual professional growth objectives.

EDUCATION AND TRAINING

Charles G. Andrew (1980) points out that learning objectives include knowledge, skills, and attitude. Education is concerned primarily with knowledge and understanding, training is concerned with skills and understanding, and both have attitude formation goals. John Burnham's (1980) in-depth study of seven manufacturing firms documented the need for education and training. He found a direct relationship between a lack of continuing pragmatic education in PIM and a failure to grasp and deal with the major manufacturing control problems facing an organization.

Education should begin with top management; middle management personnel in related areas such as marketing, purchasing, engineering, and manufacturing; and key PIM personnel. Education of these individuals stresses the objectives, the rationale and approach of revised decision techniques, the benefits, the costs, and the specific cooperation that is required from each area. The necessity of marketing's participation in the integration of the MPS and the distribution plan is an example of the last mentioned requirement—specific cooperation required from each area. A clear understanding of the role of the master scheduler and his or her interface with marketing, manufacturing, and distribution is crucial. Approval of a planned system calling for this integration through the master scheduler might be the time to select marketing, manufacturing, and distribution representatives to work with the scheduler.

Inventory planners-buyers, production planners, storeroom, receiving, and purchasing personnel, shop supervisors, and shop floor control personnel (dispatchers) also must be trained. They do not need to know about the details of computer programs or file structures in most cases. They should understand the mechanism used to convert data to the information used for management. For example, they should know how the available-to-promise is calculated in order to use the information correctly. The collection of data, data input, information output, format, and timing are important to them. The education and training of these individuals, which encourages their critical evaluation of the planned system, has two benefits. First, it provides an opportunity for explaining why their criticisms are invalid or, if they are valid, it enables the system designers to revise the system prior to implementation. The daily users frequently spot detailed operating problems that systems design and PIM personnel have overlooked. Second, and equally important, they appreciate the recognition of their competence and are more likely to be supportive of the system when it is implemented. The best of systems can fail in a nonsupportive user environment. George S. Hoyt (1980) notes some very practical applications to training based on his experiences at Sundstrand. He points out the value of training that takes place after implementation, including returning errors to the originator for correction.

Education is expensive; it may involve preparing films, booklets, and instructions as well as many personnel hours spent in training sessions. Lack of adequate education and training is frequently more expensive than training, however. Knowledgeable, trained, and committed people are the key to successful implementation. User commitment means the assuming of responsibility for proper functioning of the system. Approval of the system by a written sign-off by all user departments is a good idea. The difference between involvement and commitment is illustrated well by the analogy of a ham-and-eggs breakfast in which the chicken is involved, but the pig is committed.

Needs Assessment

Planning requires objectives, and determination of objectives begins with an assessment of needs. Peter Grieco (1981) recommends using a competency model similar to that shown in Figure 21-6 for determining education and training needs. The functional requirements of the management information systems will provide a basis for determining the specific knowledge and skill required for successful operation and continued development of a company's PIM activities and systems. When specific capabilities are required depends on the plans for systems development and implementation. Knowledgeable users are a valuable aid in system development and design. Providing education after the system is designed can result in user dissatisfaction with approaches and techniques previously adopted. Top management and key PIM managers certainly should be well versed in modern PIM technology prior to any major specific system design and development commitment. Training, on the other hand, is appropriate immediately prior to and during system installation.

In most firms educational needs range from the broad and general principles of PIM (the relationship of major functions such as production planning, master production scheduling, resource planning, rough cut capacity planning) to details concerning how and why shop order priorities are determined. The broad knowledge required by corporate and production management is provided by many organizations with established performance records. Active participation in the APICS Certification Program is the best approach for PIM personnel to develop and solidify their knowledge of the discipline, as noted by many, including Charles Andrew (1980), George S. Hoyt (1980), and Peter F. Ryan (1980). The intrinsic value of the program is the learning that occurs while preparing for the examination. Training in the details of managing and operating the firm's PIM system follows. Each step is crucial in a successful education and training program. The early educational programs provide the stimulus, attitudes, and management and user commitments required for success of the educational program and the system. Training is essential if the system is to work.

Objectives and Performance Criteria

The true objective of education and training is improved PIM performance. Better customer service, decreased inventory, reduced lead times, lower work in process, etc., are the true objectives of the program. Attendance at seminars, participation in in-house training, certification, and demonstrated skill are important, but only to the extent that they are steps to improved operating performance. Thus, the education and training program must emphasize the objectives and operating details of an individual firm's system as well as the general principles and techniques of the field. The program also plays a role in developing a positive attitude toward the system and the opportunities it presents.

Figure 21-6
Competency Model for Determining Knowledge and
Skill Requirements per Position (abridged)

POSITION

COMPETENCY AREAS	Production Planner	Senior Planner	Planning Supervisor	Master Scheduler	Inventory Planner	Inventory Manager	Dispatcher	General Manager
Master schedule	2	1	1	1	2	1	2	2
BOM	1	1	1	1	1	1	2	3
MRP	1	1	1	1	1	1	2	3
CRP*	1	1	1	1	1	1	2	3
Lead time	2	1	1	1	1	1	1	3
Order release	2	1	1	1	1	1	1	3
Order quantities	2	1	1	1	1	1	1	3

The competency required is defined by the following (these are illustrative and requirements will be different in different environments):

1. Requires knowledge of concepts, principles, and techniques plus the ability to apply them to routine and nonroutine decisions (expertise).
2. Requires knowledge of concepts, principles, techniques and the ability to apply them to routine decisions (a working knowledge of the field).
3. Requires knowledge of concepts, principles, and techniques to the extent necessary to understand how and why decisions are made by others and how they relate to other areas of the firm.

Capacity Requirements Planning

Motivation

The value and importance of career-oriented education would seem to be self-evident. Many participants, however, have attended programs that they believe provided few tangible benefits. In addition, many believe that their years of experience, an occasional professional meeting, and browsing through a journal now and then have kept them current.

If the training concerns a new approach such as JIT or TQC, having someone from a similar organization report on the benefits the approach has provided his or her firm is a good beginning. Working with each member of the department to develop a personalized professional growth and career development path is appropriate in the management of any group of professionals but is especially necessary in a dynamic field and in a firm with increasing productivity requirements due to competitive pressures. A self-graded evaluation examination frequently will point out personal deficiencies without embarrassment to an employee.

Certification and successful completion of education and training courses are a valid basis for salary increments and promotions. Most successful programs have explicit learning objectives and use testing to measure the achievement of those objectives. Knowledge deficiencies, outside sources that the student may pursue on his or her own, and the obligations of both the company and the employee are documented in these contracts. Broadly based user participation in establishing systems goals and competency requirements normally will lead to peer pressure to attain the objectives and to their acceptance.

Managing Education

Education and training need to be more than occasional fireworks displays. Both need to be continuing activities with direction and leadership. In relatively large organizations a full-time director of training usually is needed. In some companies the director of the PIM training position is combined with the manufacturing control systems manager position. The point is that a specific person should have this task. This responsibility is best shared by a steering committee with representatives from top management, marketing, engineering, finance, data processing, and manufacturing, in conjunction with a project team whose members are from PIM, data processing, and other areas such as distribution and engineering. The steering committee provides overall management guidance and support. The project team consists of users; many of these people will be on the project team guiding systems design and implementation activities. Different training project leaders may exist for different functional areas such as JIT and manufacturing cell development. The project team needs to play an active role in planning the entire program, conducting the program, evaluating it, and making necessary changes. An education and training plan might be charted as illustrated in Figure 21-7.[3]

Education of PIM personnel alone will not do the job. Top management's understanding of the significance of production and inventory management to the firm's success provides a solid base for their commitment. New approaches frequently mean discarding traditional philosophies and methods and, in brief, mean a new way of doing business. This is especially true in the adoption of JIT concepts. Engineering, marketing, purchasing, and manufacturing also are

---

3. See Peter L. Grieco's presentation (1981) for further treatment.

Figure 21-7
Education and Training Activity Plan

Activity	Time Periods									
	1	2	3	4	5	6	7	8	9	10
Assess needs	X									
Evaluate competence	X	X								
Develop preliminary plan		X								
Prepare budget		X								
Obtain management support		X								
Develop steering committee	X									
Develop project team		X	X							
Outline course plan			X							
Develop program measurement techniques			X							
Train the trainers			X							
Hold pilot model courses				X						
Schedule education courses					X					
Schedule training courses					X					
Offer course*					X	X	X	X	X	X
Measure results (knowledge and skills)					X	X	X	X	X	X
Measure PIM performance results							X	X	X	X
Revise program as required								X	X	X

Sequence course offerings consistent with time-phased requirements of competency requirements.

affected by the change. Their cooperation is essential to its success. Education must include management personnel from all functional areas.

Much has been said and written about PIM training and education in the last few years. These presentations and articles contain proposed basic education and training concepts, principles, and techniques as well as many experiential anecdotes. The latter, to their credit, include stories of failure as well as success. There is, fortunately, a consensus on principles, concepts, and valuable techniques including the following:

1. Educational activities should encompass almost everyone in the firm. Changes in PIM technology change the way most firms do business. Successful implementation and continuing execution of this technology requires understanding, cooperation, and performance from a broad range of individuals.
2. Planning education and training programs requires a professional approach. This begins with an analysis of the needs of the organization.

3. Specific education and training goals should be established.
4. The results of education and training should be measured formally and explicitly.
5. Project teams headed by an overall manager or coordinator have worked well in achieving successful program designs and results.
6. Motivation for participant development and self-education is an important part of the program.
7. People are the key to successful PIM.
8. Management commitment is essential.
9. Education is expensive; but the benefits usually outweigh the costs.

EXECUTION

Execution of organization, systems, human resource, and education and training plans requires application of the principles and techniques of production activity (shop floor) control. The plans must be realistic in terms of the capacity, budget, and personnel available to attain them. Valid priorities for the activities must be established to recognize the sequential requirements of each. Implementing new information systems, for example, is not realistic prior to the required training and education. Release of directives (orders) to perform management tasks requires an estimate of lead time, input/output planning and control, a measurement of capacity and load, and a control of priorities. This is accomplished through formal priorities and their control. Thus, just as the vice-president of sales or engineering may not change the priority of a shop order without working through the formal system, revising the PIM organization structure or its information systems must be done through the formal system. Overloading the systems group with design projects or the department with a variety of training projects can have the same effect as overloading the shop with orders. Priorities become confused, activities become inefficient, and many tasks are not completed on schedule. Proper execution requires adequate planning, control, and application of the basic concepts and techniques of order release and sequencing.

CONTROL

Control closes the management loop of planning, execution, evaluation, and corrective action. Control of PIM is concerned with the following:

1. Assuring that PIM performance objectives, policies, and procedures support the organization's strategic objectives and are consistent with strategic plans
2. Evaluating planned organization and management system developments relative to state-of-the-art developments; to changes in the structure of the firm's market, products, or processes; and to changes in

the availability of personnel and supporting services in education and counseling

3. Comparing actual organization and management system developments with planned developments
4. Comparing education and training results with planned results
5. Taking the corrective actions suggested by the evaluation performed in the preceding steps
6. Determining not only that personnel know and understand the new concepts but also that they are applying them

Operational controls are discussed throughout this text; they include the many techniques for controlling forecasts, inventory, order releases, capacity, order sequencing, lead time, and so on. Management controls concern aggregate measures of performance such as inventory investment, production output, customer service, employment levels, personnel utilization, and overtime. Control should be an integral part of the management system. Limits may be established on the absolute value of inventory, the inventory turn ratio, overtime, or percentage of orders backordered, for example, with exception reports to PIM whenever a limit is exceeded. Periodic meetings, perhaps biweekly, might be held to review performance against all major objectives.

Organization development and management system development also require control. The first step in this control is a realistic plan specifying the different steps and milestones on the path to achieving a revised organization structure, better educated and trained employees, or a new or revised management system (as described in the planning section of this chapter). Actual organization changes, systems development, human resosurce management, and training accomplishments then are compared to plans on a periodic basis.

Management audits are an essential element of management control. The management audit provides an evaluation of the overall performance of PIM. It usually is performed by experts from outside the company. The use of external personnel is meant to increase the likelihood of an objective assessment and to provide some fresh inputs. The management audit may evaluate the following:

1. The contribution of the PIM organization to attaining the firm's objectives
2. The effectiveness and efficiency of PIM communication with other functional areas such as marketing, finance, and manufacturing ▸
3. The department's performance objectives, their measurement, and the degree of attainment
4. The department's research and development activities (Does the department have an organized approach to learning and assessing new ideas and approaches?)
5. The capability of department managers (What is the contribution of each? Do they work together as a team?)

6. The efficiency of the present PIM systems
7. The department's organization structure, personnel, and related plans (Are they consistent with the department's task and resources?)
8. The management information systems, their effectiveness relative to user needs, and their efficiency in terms of hardware, software, and ease of user interaction
9. Top management's commitment to the PIM function in terms of interest, time, and resources

Management audits are not weekly or even quarterly routines, but they are appropriate every two to three years. It is not a bad idea to perform a partial audit each year using internal personnel.[4]

All elements of management are important, but planning and control are particularly important. Without a plan or control, chances of attaining desirable goals decrease substantially. Firmness and consistency in monitoring progress toward goals convert plans into results.

SUMMARY

Production and inventory managers must be able to plan, organize, manage human resources, execute, and control as well as manage change. The goals of PIM must support the overall organization objectives and their attainment must be measurable in quantitative terms. Change pervades industry and PIM in particular. Recognition of change and strategies for dealing with change are crucial in the management of PIM.

EXERCISES

1. Prepare a set of finished goods customer service goals that will be appropriate for a make-to-order, large equipment company.

2. Why does performance measurement itself affect motivation and behavior?

3. Identify at least two PIM activities to which a network model (see Chapter 16) might be applied for planning and control purposes.

4. Visit a local firm and determine the hierarchy of objectives beginning with profit and ROI and working down through various PIM goals.

5. Name at least two different organization strategies that directly affect PIM. Explain why.

---

4. See the articles by John Burnham (1980) and Harvey Rose (1978) for further treatment of PIM audits.

6. How are the PIM organization structure, available personnel, and management system related? Describe a situation in which the plans in these areas must be coordinated.

7. What is the value of a well-defined organization structure?

8. List the characteristics of an organization and its environment that should have a major influence on the design of an organization.

9. Some companies have different PIM organizations in different divisions. What is a rational explanation of this situation?

10. Name two companies that exemplify the types of firms that do not require a service parts department within PIM. Name two that exemplify types of firms that do.

11. A medium-sized manufacturer of specialty farm equipment builds components to stock and final assemblies to order. Its WIP inventories are high and customer service (meeting promised delivery dates) is poor. A proposal has been made to solve these problems by changing the present traditional organization to one that assigns the planning and control function to different groups. Comment.

12. In what type firm would you recommend that the scheduling of plant maintenance be part of the PIM planning task?

13. List the conditions under which a manufacturing control systems group is most likely to be cost-effective.

14. The vice-president of manufacturing at a local firm contends that the firm does not need a master scheduler. She says that the production control manager knows what is going on and adding a master scheduler would only increase the payroll. Comment.

15. The materials manager of an expanding multiplant firm that produces tools and equipment for the oil exploration and mining industries has proposed the addition of systems analyst and programmer positions as the nucleus of a systems group within PIM. The manager of corporate data processing objects to the change; he views it as redundant staffing. Comment.

16. How would you expect PIM staffing requirements to differ among the following types of firms:
   a. A manufacturer of components for the automobile industry
   b. A relatively small gear manufacturer
   c. A multiplant, multiwarehouse manufacturer of small tools
   d. A small chemical company that produces industrial strength hand soaps

17. The three individuals in a production and inventory planning group contend that they are overloaded with work and require additional personnel. What procedure would you follow to evaluate their claim?

18. The director of manufacturing at a local plant whose inventory and shipping performances are below par contends that educational programs will be of little value to his PIM staff since the programs are too general and do not recognize the specific problems of his firm. Comment.

19. What is the difference between education and training in PIM?

20. How should education and training programs relate to management information systems plans?

21. Why are quantifiable performance objectives essential for control?

22. Give two examples of how exception management controls may be used in controlling PIM management activities.

23. Explain how the first stages of control take place long before any execution begins.

24. Materials management is convinced that a push allocation distribution system will be more effective than the present traditional order point system. Where do you believe the most resistance to this change will exist? Why? What steps do you recommend to overcome the resistance?

SELECTED READINGS

Andrew, Charles G. "Certification-RX for Effective MRP Education." *APICS 23d Annual International Conference Proceedings* (1980): 1-5.

Bell, Robert R., and John M. Burnham. "Managing Change in Manufacturing." *Production and Inventory Management* 28, no. 1 (1987a): 106-115.

Bell, Robert R., and John M. Burnham. "The Politics of Change in Manufacturing." *Production and Inventory Management* 28, no. 2 (1987b): 71-78.

Burnham, John M. "The Operating Plant—Case Studies and Generalizations." *Production and Inventory Management* 21, no. 4 (1980): 63-94.

Drucker, Peter F. *Landmarks of Tomorrow*. New York: Harper & Row, Publishers, Inc., Colophon Books, Montclair, NJ, 1965.

Drucker, Peter F. *Management: Tasks, Responsibilities, Practices*. New York: Harper & Row, Publishers, Inc., 1974.

Fogarty, Donald W., Thomas R. Hoffmann, and Peter W. Stonebraker. *Production and Operations Management*. Cincinnati: South-Western Publishing Co., 1989.

Grieco, Peter L. "The ABC's of Training." *APICS 24th Annual International Conference Proceedings* (1981): 430-432.

Hall, Robert W. "Repetitive Manufacturing." *Production and Inventory Management* (Second Quarter 1982): 78-86.

Hoyt, George. "Effective In-House MRP Training." *APICS 23d Annual International Conference Proceedings* (1980): 26-30.

Lewin, Kurt. "Field Theory in Social Science." In *Field Theory*, by D. Cartwright. New York: Harper Brothers, 1951.

Motwane, Aman A. "How to Organize a Production Planning Department." *APICS 24th Annual International Conference Proceedings* (1981): 347-350.

Peters, Thomas J., and Robert H. Waterman, Jr. *In Search of Excellence*. New York: Harper & Row, Publishers, Inc., 1982.

Plossl, George W. *Production and Inventory Control Applications*. Atlanta, GA: George Plossl Educational Services, 1983.

Powell, Cash, Jr. "MRP System-MRP Organization." *APICS 24th Annual International Conference Proceedings* (1981): 339-343.

Powell, Cash, Jr. "Systems Planning/Systems Control." *Production and Inventory Management* 18, no. 3 (1978): 15-25.

Rose, Harvey N. "Auditing of P&IC Systems: The Necessary Ingredient." *APICS 21st Annual Conference Proceedings* (1978): 436-454.

Ryan, Peter F. "Training and Education in Production/Material Control (Management's Survival Kit)." *APICS 23d Annual International Conference Proceedings* (1980): 19-22.

Skinner, Wickham. "The Focused Factory." *Harvard Business Review* (May-June 1974): 113-121.

Taylor, Bernard, III, Fredrick S. Hills, and K. Roscoe Davis. "The Effects of Change Factors on the Production Operation and the Production Manager." *Production and Inventory Management* 20, no. 3 (1979): 18-32.

Toffler, Alvin. *Future Shock*. New York: Random House, Inc., 1970.

White, Edna M. "Implementing an MRP System Using the Lewin-Schein Theory of Change." *Production and Inventory Management* 21, no. 1 (1980): 1-12.

Wight, Oliver W. *Production and Inventory Management in the Computer Age*. Boston, MA: Cahner Books, 1974.

Part
Eight

Technical
Topics

22
MATHEMATICAL PROGRAMMING

Mathematical programming is a set of methods for solving linear, nonlinear, integer, geometric, goal, stochastic, 0-1, and mixed integer problems, as well as the transportation problem, the assignment problem, and others. Each of these techniques uses a model of some process or situation and the determination of a best or optimal (maximum or minimum) solution (in terms of profits, costs, or other measure or measures of merit) through the proper allocation of limited resources.

The fundamental concepts were developed in the 1940s and 1950s and have been continuously expanded and refined. Many practical problems involve prodigious amounts of computation. As a result, the rise in usefulness of mathematical programming has paralleled the growth in computer power and the reduction in its cost. Many texts are devoted exclusively to one or more of these techniques and lengthy users' manuals exist for standard computer packages. Our purpose here is only to acquaint or refresh the reader with the basic models and solution techniques, particularly as they are found in applications related to production and inventory control. Such applications include optimal blending of raw materials into final product, aggregate planning, optimal critical path method (CPM) schedules, capital budgeting, and other resource constrained, complex problems.

LINEAR PROGRAMMING AND THE SIMPLEX SOLUTION TECHNIQUES

At the heart of linear programming (LP) is a model of the real world expressed in linear equations; that is, all variables are to the first power (e.g., X, Y, etc., not X^2 and not products like XY). Furthermore, none of the variables can take on negative values and they must be continuously divisible; i.e., they can take on values like 0.5 or 3.167 as well as 4. Finally, there is no uncertainty in the coefficients or values in the model. (The various other mathematical programming techniques relax these conditions to obtain more realistic models, as in nonlinear and stochastic programming. Or they impose additional conditions to handle real world situations more accurately, as in integer and goal programming. The solution procedures are generally more complex as a result.) Although these conditions (linearity, nonnegativity, continuity, and certainty) limit the value of these models in some situations, they have proved not to hinder their successful application in many settings.

The general form of a linear programming problem is a set of linear relationships defining the trade-offs for each resource that is to be allocated and a single objective function that gives the contribution of each decision variable. Mathematically, this general form resembles the following:

$$5X + 6Y \leq 27.75$$

Constraints or Requirements $\quad 4X + 2Y \leq 13$

$$3.6X + 8.1Y \geq 23$$

Objective $\quad$ Maximize $1.8X + 2Y$

(Note: The nonnegativity constraint is usually not shown explicitly, nor is it required, since the solution procedure guarantees its existence.)

In a problem such as this one that has only two variables, the system of equations can be easily graphed and the solution obtained by inspection. Few real world problems are this simple. However, the graphical solution illustrates the innate features of any mathematical programming problem, so it is worthwhile examining it briefly before going on to a purely mathematical procedure, the simplex technique.

Graphical Representation and Solution

The first equation in the system above, $5X + 6Y \leq 27.75$, represents an area (technically a half plane) bounded by and including the line $5X + 6Y = 27.75$. Note that the inequality ($\leq$) distinguishes the line from the area bounded by the line. Since both X and Y must be positive, the area is further bounded by the X and Y axes (the first quadrant). This is shown in Figure 22-1. We now add the constraint $4X + 2Y \leq 13$, which, since any feasible solution must simultaneously satisfy both constraints, effectively chops off a corner of the first area (see Figure 22-2). Finally, the requirement that $3.6X + 8.1Y \geq 23$ confines the solution space to the area lying above $3.6X + 8.1Y = 23$, as illustrated in Figure 22-3.

The objective is to maximize the value of $1.8X + 2Y$. This equation defines a family of straight lines all parallel to each other and so having the same slope $(-\frac{1.8}{2})$. Our task is to find the one that has the largest sum and still intersects the solution space. In Figure 22-4 several lines have been drawn that intersect the feasible region at various places. One of the important discoveries of the theory of linear programming is that the optimal solution will always lie on a corner (vertex) of the constrained space or on an edge connecting two corners. This means that instead of having to search the entire area defined

Figure 22-1
Area Bounded by $5X + 6Y = 27.75$ and the X and Y Axes

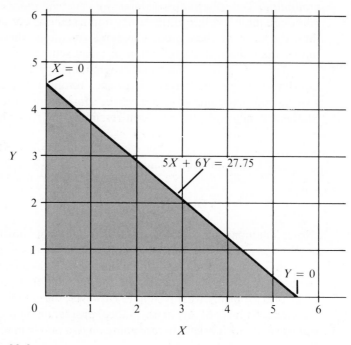

Figure 22-2
Area Further Bounded by $4X + 2Y \leq 13$

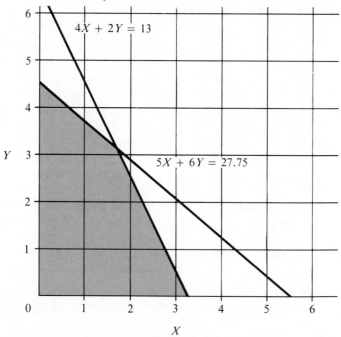

Figure 22-3
Area with all Constraints in Place

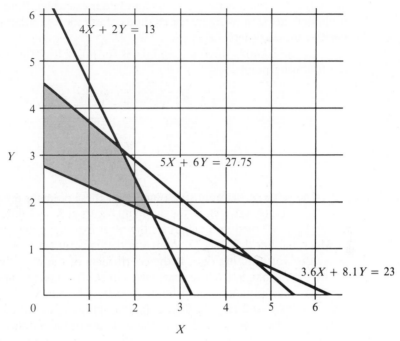

Figure 22-4
Constrained Area with Intersecting Lines

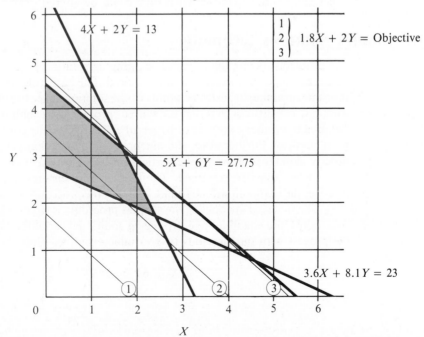

by the constraints, we need only look at the corners in order to find the optimal solution. There are an infinite number of points in the area, but there are only a finite number of corners (four in our example). Purely mathematical techniques are simply organized methods of examining, either implicitly or explicitly, these corners.

In our example the four candidates for possible optimal solutions are at the following points:

X	Y
0	2.839
0	4.625
1.607	3.286
2.353	1.794

The value of the objective function at these points is 5.678, 9.25, 9.465, and 7.823, respectively. Thus, the optimum occurs at $X = 1.607$ and $Y = 3.286$, as can be confirmed graphically as the most extreme point (from the origin) at which the line $1.8X + 2Y$ intersects the constrained area.

It is worth noting that, if the coefficients of the objective function had a ratio of less than 5 to 6 (the coefficients of the first constraints), for example, 1.6 to 2, the optimum would be at $X = 0$, $Y = 4.625$. If the ratio rose to greater than 4 to 2 (e.g., 1.8 to 0.8), the optimum would be at $X = 2.353$, $Y = 1.794$. This sort of analysis of the structure of the problem and the impact of changes to the coefficients is referred to as postoptimality or sensitivity analysis and is commonly done when the real world coefficients have some uncertainty about them or when they could be altered.

The Simplex Solution Technique

For problems having many variables, graphic solution procedures are inadequate, and algebraic techniques are required. The basic rule, however, remains the same: examine the extreme points of the solution space to find the optimum solution. The difference is that for simplex problems the solution space is not a flat area but rather a volume or hypercube. Therefore, the corners are referred to as vertices. Furthermore, the algebraic simplex technique proceeds in an orderly manner to examine the vertices in such a way that each one does not have to be explicitly examined. The mathematics ensures that variables stay positive, the optimum will be found, and that the procedure will then terminate.

The first step in applying the simplex procedure is to convert the inequality constraints into equalities by introducing additional variables. We can illustrate the process with our previous two variable example. Thus,

$$5X + 6Y \leq 27.75$$

becomes

$$5X + 6Y + S_1 = 27.75$$

Where S_1 takes on whatever slack value is necessary for given X and Y values in order that the sum will equal 27.75 exactly. Similarly,

$$4X + 2Y + S_2 = 13$$

If we only included a slack variable in the third equation,

$$3.6X + 8.1Y \geq 23$$

to yield

$$3.6X + 8.1Y + S_3 = 23$$

then S_3 would have to be negative and that would violate the nonnegativity constraint. Instead, we introduce an artificial variable with a positive coefficient and a slack variable with a negative coefficient:

$$3.6X + 8.1Y + A_3 - S_3 = 23$$

Now we must incorporate these additional variables into the objective function. Since the slack variables contribute nothing to the cost or profit, their coefficients are zero. The artificial variable, on the other hand, is just that, and while the simplex procedure needs it to get started, we do not want it in the final solution. To accomplish that we simply assign it a large negative profit coefficient, often referred to as "big M" where M is a very large number. Thus, the objective is to maximize

$$1.8X + 2Y + 0S_1 + 0S_2 - MA_3 + 0S_3$$

Subject to

$$
\begin{array}{llllll}
5X & + 6Y & + S_1 & & & = 27.75 \\
4X & + 2Y & & + S_2 & & = 13 \\
3.6X & + 8.1Y & & & + A_3 - S_3 & = 23
\end{array}
$$

Now, for convenience, this can be converted to matrix form by just writing down the numeric values and remembering that those in the first column apply to X, the second column to Y, and so forth.

Objective	1.8	2	0	0	$-M$	0	
Subject to	5	6	1	0	0	0	27.75
	4	2	0	1	0	0	13
	3.6	8.1	0	0	1	-1	23

For an initial solution, we can assume both X and Y are zero and let $S_1 = 27.75$, $S_2 = 13$, $A_3 = 23$, and $S_3 = 0$. That choice for X and Y does not yield a good objective value, but the equations are satisfied and we have an initial feasible solution. In order to keep track of everything we will establish the following format (or tableau as it is sometimes called):

C_j		1.8	2	0	0	$-M$	0	
		X	Y	S_1	S_2	A_3	S_3	Solution quantities
0	S_1	5	6	1	0	0	0	27.75
0	S_2	4	2	0	1	0	0	13
$-M$	A_3	3.6	8.1	0	0	1	-1	23
Z_j		$-3.6M$	$-8.1M$	0	0	$-M$	M	$-23M$
$C_j - Z_j$		$1.8 + 3.6M$	$2 + 8.1M$	0	0	0	$-M$	

The C_j row (j is the column number) at the top contains the coefficients of the objective function. The C_j column at the left contains the objective coefficients of the variables in the solution (whose names appear in the second column). The values in the Z_j row are the sum of the products of the C_j column of coefficients with the jth column of coefficients in the body of the table. For example, $Z_1 = 0 \times 5 + 0 \times 4 + 3.6(-M) = -3.6M$. The $C_j - Z_j$ row is used to determine which variable to next bring into the solution in order to get the greatest improvement in the objective function. To do this we look for the largest positive value ($2 + 8.1M$) and find it under Column Y. This is referred to as the key column. Next we see which variable must go out when Y comes in. To do this we compute the ratio of the solution quantities (in the right-hand column) to their respective coefficients in the key column and identify the smallest of these that is nonnegative. In our case the ratios are: $27.75 \div 6 = 4.625$, $13 \div 2 = 6.5$, and $8.1 \div 23 = 0.352$. The smallest of these is the last one and so row three is the key row. This means that we are going to bring into our solution Y in place of Z_3. While the basic process is very similar to the usual Gaussian elimination procedure normally used in solving simultaneous equations, it is convenient here to compute the new table of coefficients with the following formula. (All of these processes are consistent with the basic laws of matrix algebra.)

$$\text{New Value} = \text{Old Value} - \frac{\text{Corresponding Value in Key Row} \times \text{Corresponding Value in Key Column}}{\text{Key Number}}$$

where the key number is the number at the intersection of the key row and key column (8.1 in our example). Thus, the new value in the X column, first row (the one with S_1 in it) is computed as:

$$\text{New Value} = 5 - \frac{3.6 \times 6}{8.1}$$

$$= 2.333$$

The new tableau is thus computed as follows:

C_j		1.8	2	0	0	$-M$	0	Solution quantities
		X	Y	S_1	S_2	A_3	S_3	
0	S_1	2.333	0	1	0	-0.741	0.741	10.713
0	S_2	3.111	0	0	1	-0.247	0.247	7.321
2	Y	0.444	1	0	0	0.123	-0.123	2.840
Z_j		0.888	2	0	0	0.246	-0.246	5.680
$C_j - Z_j$		0.912	0	0	0	$-0.246 - M$	0.246	

Repeating this procedure, we find the largest value is 0.912 in the column headed by X and the key row is the S_2 one with a ratio of $7.321 \div 3.111$. The new matrix is tabulated, then, as follows:

C_j		1.8	2	0	0	$-M$	0	Solution quantities
		X	Y	S_1	S_2	A_3	S_3	
0	S_1	0	0	1	-0.750	-0.556	0.556	5.222
1.8	X	1	0	0	0.321	-0.079	0.079	2.353
2	Y	0	1	0	-0.143	0.159	-0.159	1.794
Z_j		1.8	2	0	0.292	0.176	-0.176	7.823
$C_j - Z_j$		0	0	0	-0.292	$-0.176 - M$	0.176	

Repeating the procedure once again, the largest $C_j - Z_j$ is 0.176 under the column headed S_1, and the smallest ratio is $5.222 \div 0.556$ for the row labeled S_1. The next matrix is thus:

C_j		1.8	2	0	0	$-M$	0	Solution quantities
		X	Y	S_1	S_2	A_3	S_3	
0	S_3	0	0	1.800	-1.350	-1.00	1	9.400
1.8	X	1	0	-1.43	0.429	0	0	1.607
2	Y	0	1	0.286	-0.357	0	0	3.286
Z_j		1.8	2	0.314	0.057	0	0	9.464
$C_j - Z_j$		0	0	-0.314	-0.057	$-M$	0	

Examination of this $C_j - Z_j$ row shows that none of the values is positive and, therefore, no further improvement in the objective function can be made. The optimal solution is therefore $X = 1.607$ and $Y = 3.286$. This is, of course, the same solution we found earlier by graphical means. The advantage of the algebraic simplex technique is that a great deal more information can be obtained from this final matrix, and we are not limited to just two (or three) variables as we are for graphical presentations.

While extensive development of postoptimality or sensitivity analysis is beyond the scope of this text, an indication of some of the additional insights that can be gained from this technique is seen by looking at the meaning of the $C_j - Z_j$ row values. These are the so-called shadow costs (or shadow prices) and give the marginal change that would occur in the objective function for each unit of a variable that would enter the solution. For example, looking at the second solution matrix, page 751, we observed a shadow cost of 0.912 for X. This means that the objective function will increase by 0.912 for each unit of X we bring into the solution. Because of the constraints we could only bring in $7.321 \div 3.111$ units and, hence, the objective function increased by $0.912 \times 2.353 = 2.146$. This is confirmed as $7.823 - 5.680$, the difference between the objective function values for the successive solutions. (The slight difference in the last digit is due to rounding.) Similar computations allow one to state the range of values for each constraint under which the solution will not change, or to predict the sensitivity of the solution to possible changes in the cost or price coefficients.

Obviously the amount of computation for this procedure is very large; hence, computer programs have been developed to minimize the computational burden. Because of the ready availability of these programs, the difficulty in applying linear programming is not in solving such problems, it is in formulating—that is, stating—the problems in linear equations. The following section describes several such formulations.

EXAMPLE FORMULATIONS OF PRACTICAL PROBLEMS

As pointed out earlier, the basic practicality of LP is in its ability to model complex real world situations. The decision maker can confront problems in production and inventory management with greater confidence by using LP. The constant competitive conditions prevailing in business, industry, and government necessitate the use of tools that help in the decision-making process. Many have found LP to be such a tool.

The Linear Programming Aggregate Planning Problem

The first example of the use of linear programming is found in the aggregate planning problem. The problem is to schedule varying levels of production over some set planning horizon so as to minimize costs (see Chapter 4). Simple to very complex formulations of the problem have been developed. A possible formulation of this situation begins by defining the variables:

D_i = predicted demand in Period i
i = 1, 2, or 3 (model limited to three-period time horizon)
P_i = scheduled regular time production in Period i
P_i^* = maximum regular time production that can be scheduled in Period i
O_i = overtime scheduled in Period i
O_i^* = maximum overtime that can be scheduled in Period i
r = regular time cost per unit
s = overtime cost per unit
c = inventory carrying charge per unit per period
h_i = cost of increasing production by one unit of output (hiring cost)
f_i = cost of reducing production by one unit of output (firing cost)
I_i = increase in production level in Period i
R_i = reduction in production level in Period i

For each time period:

$$P_i \leq P_i^* \quad \text{and} \quad O_i \leq O_i^*$$

The inventory constraints are as follows:

$$P_i + O_i \geq D_i$$

This assumes that the initial inventory is zero. The inventory at the end of Period 1 will be:

$$P_1 + O_1 - D_1$$

and so for Period 2:

$$P_1 + O_1 - D_1 + P_2 + O_2 \geq D_2$$

Rearranging terms we next obtain:

$$P_1 + P_2 + O_1 + O_2 \geq D_1 + D_2$$

or

$$\sum_{i=1}^{2} P_i + \sum_{i=1}^{2} O_i \geq \sum_{i=1}^{2} D_i$$

This can be extended easily by analogy to Period 3 as:

$$\sum_{i=1}^{3} P_i + \sum_{i=1}^{3} O_i \geq \sum_{i=1}^{3} D_i$$

Next we examine the hiring and firing constraints. These, respectively, are simply:

$$I_i \geq P_i - P_{i-1} \quad \text{and} \quad R_i \geq P_{i-1} - P_i$$

By rearranging terms we have the following:

$$I_i - P_i + P_{i-1} \geq 0 \quad \text{and} \quad R_i + P_i - P_{i-1} \geq 0$$

Specifically for Period 1,

$$I_1 - P_1 \geq -P_0 \quad \text{and} \quad R_1 + P_1 \geq P_0$$

So much for the constraints. Our objective is to minimize costs: costs of production, costs due to work force level changes, and inventory carrying costs. For the first period we have, respectively:

$$(rP_1 + sO_1) + (hI_1 + fR_1) + c(P_1 + O_1 - D_1)$$

For the second period we have similar production and change costs. The inventory costs are:

$$c(P_1 + O_1 - D_1 + P_2 + O_2 - D_2)$$

The third period is a simple extension of these. The total cost can then be summarized as:

$$r\sum_{i=1}^{3} P_i + s\sum_{i=1}^{3} O_i + h\sum_{i=1}^{3} I_i + f\sum_{i=1}^{3} R_i + c\sum_{i=1}^{3} \sum_{j=1}^{i} (P_j + O_j - D_j)$$

As an example consider the following case.

Month	D_i	P_i^*	O_i^*
1	3,400	3,200	900
2	4,500	3,200	900
3	3,750	3,000	700

$$r = \$17 \text{ per unit}$$
$$s = \$25 \text{ per unit}$$
$$h = \$30 \text{ per unit}$$
$$f = \$12 \text{ per unit}$$
$$c = \$4 \text{ per unit}$$
$$P_0 = 3,000$$

The constraint equations are:

$$P_1 \leq 3,200$$
$$P_2 \leq 3,200$$
$$P_3 \leq 3,000$$
$$O_1 \leq 900$$
$$O_2 \leq 900$$
$$O_3 \leq 700$$
$$P_1 + O_1 \geq 3,400$$
$$P_1 + P_2 + O_1 + O_2 \geq 7,900$$
$$P_1 + P_2 + P_3 + O_1 + O_2 + O_3 \geq 11,650$$
$$I_1 - P_1 \geq -3,000, \text{ or } P_1 - I_1 \leq 3,000$$
$$I_2 - P_2 + P_1 \geq 0$$
$$I_3 - P_3 + P_2 \geq 0$$
$$R_1 + P_1 \geq 3,000$$
$$R_2 + P_2 - P_1 \geq 0$$
$$R_3 + P_3 - P_2 \geq 0$$

The objective function is:

$$17 \sum_{i=1}^{3} P_i + 25 \sum_{i=1}^{3} O_i + 30 \sum_{i=1}^{3} I_i + 12 \sum_{i=1}^{3} R_i + 4 \sum_{i=1}^{3} \sum_{j=1}^{i} (P_j + O_j - D_j)$$

The solution, obtained with a standard LP computer program, is:

Month	P_i	O_i	I_i	R_i
1	3,075	900	75	0
2	3,075	900	0	0
3	3,000	700	0	75

Examination of the solution shows that not all regular time capacity is used in the first two periods and yet overtime is used fully. At first glance this may seem wrong, but not when the cost of hiring is recognized. It is common for companies to resort to overtime or subcontracting when hiring costs are substantial.

This formulation of the aggregate planning problem is not very complex relatively. Other concepts such as subcontracting, underutilization of work force, and backorders or shortages might be included (Shore 1973).

The Feed Mix Problem

Another classic linear programming problem is the feed mix problem. This problem could also arise in determining the optimal ingredients in grass seed manufacture, cereal making, or sausage formulation.

Suppose the Super Chicken Production Company can purchase and mix one or more of three different grains, each containing different amounts of four nutritional elements. The production manager specifies that any feed mix for the chickens must meet certain minimal nutritional requirements and at the same time be as low in cost as possible. Grains can be bought and mixed on a weekly basis at known prices to meet known total nutritional requirements during that week.

The following table lists the requirements of each nutritional ingredient, the contribution of each grain to the requirement, and the cost of each grain. The manager must decide how to combine these grains to meet the minimum requirements at the minimum cost.

Nutritional Ingredient	Contribution/Unit Weight			Minimum Total Requirements
	Grain 1	Grain 2	Grain 3	
A	1	0	1	1,200
B	3	2	0.5	4,000
C	5	7	9	5,500
D	0	3	4	750
Cost/Unit Weight	$30	$37	$45	

We will use the following variables:

X_1 = amount of Grain 1 to include in mix
X_2 = amount of Grain 2 to include in mix
X_3 = amount of Grain 3 to include in mix

Then, the requirements for Nutritional Ingredient A are:

$$X_1 + X_3 \geq 1,200$$

For Nutritional Ingredient B:

$$3X_1 + 2X_2 + 0.5X_3 \geq 4,000$$

For Nutritional Ingredient C:

$$5X_1 + 7X_2 + 9X_3 \geq 5,500$$

And for Nutritional Ingredient D:

$$3X_2 + 4X_3 \geq 750$$

These must be satisfied while minimizing:

$$30X_1 + 37X_2 + 45X_3$$

The solution to this problem is to use 1,180.64 units of Grain 1, 224.19 units of Grain 2, and 19.36 units of Grain 3 at a total cost of \$44,385.48 for the entire feed mix.

The Fluid Blending Problem

The fluid blending problem is a variation of the feed mix problem. The fluid blending problem was one of the first formulated as a linear programming problem, and variations of it are in wide use today in refineries, foundries, and chemical plants. Although the problem is similar to the feed mix problem, this problem is more complex because a set of output blends are to be derived from a set of inputs. Let:

X_{ij} = number of gallons of Input i to be used in Output Blend j

Assuming two inputs are to be blended into three outputs, the first constraints are:

$$X_{11} + X_{12} + X_{13} \leq S_1 \text{ (the available supply of Input 1), and}$$
$$X_{21} + X_{22} + X_{23} \leq S_2$$

The second set of constraints relates to the demand (D_j) for each output and is as follows:

$$X_{11} + X_{21} \geq D_1$$
$$X_{12} + X_{22} \geq D_2$$
$$X_{13} + X_{23} \geq D_3$$

Suppose further that each Input Chemical i contains a critical constituent (a), the proportion of which in each input is a_i. A constraint is that Output 1 must have at least a fraction, r_{a1}, of that constituent. These proportions can be related as:

$$\frac{a_1 X_{11} + a_2 X_{21}}{X_{11} + X_{21}} \geq r_{a1}$$

This equation can be rewritten as:

$$a_1 X_{11} + a_2 X_{21} \geq r_{a1} X_{11} + r_{a1} X_{21}$$

Combining terms to get a simple linear equation we have:

$$(a_1 - r_{a1})X_{11} + (a_2 - r_{a1})X_{21} \geq 0$$

Similarly, Output 2 must have at least a proportion r_{a2} of constituent a. The corresponding equation is as follows:

$$\frac{a_1 X_{12} + a_2 X_{22}}{X_{12} + X_{22}} \geq r_{a2} \quad \text{or} \quad (a_1 - r_{a2})X_{12} + (a_2 - r_{a2})x_{22} \geq 0$$

Similarly, for Output 3 we have the following:

$$(a_1 - r_{a3})X_{13} + (a_2 - r_{a3})X_{23} \geq 0$$

A second critical constituent (b) might be constrained to be no more than proportions r_{b1}, r_{b2}, and r_{b3} in their respective outputs. This results in similar equations, as follows:

$$(b_1 - r_{b1})X_{11} + (b_2 - r_{b1})X_{21} \leq 0$$
$$(b_1 - r_{b2})X_{12} + (b_2 - r_{b2})X_{22} \leq 0$$
$$(b_1 - r_{b3})X_{13} + (b_2 - r_{b3})X_{23} \leq 0$$

Assume that Output 1 sells for $\$O_1$ per gallon, Output 2 sells for $\$O_2$ per gallon, and Output 3 sells for $\$O_3$ per gallon, and that Inputs 1 and 2 cost $\$I_1$ and $\$I_2$, respectively. The objective is to maximize profits, so,

$$(O_1 - I_1)X_{11} + (O_1 - I_2)X_{21} + (O_2 - I_1)X_{12} + (O_2 - I_2)X_{22}$$
$$+ (O_3 - I_1)X_{13} + (O_3 - I_2)X_{23}$$

As an example, suppose we have available 12,000 gallons of Input 1 and 8,000 gallons of Input 2. Fluid 1 is 20 percent phosphorous, and Fluid 2 is 15 percent phosphorous. Fluid 1 is also 75 percent inert ingredients, and Fluid 2 is 80 percent inert ingredients. We wish to make 5,000 gallons of each of three outputs. The first is to be at least 17 percent phosphorous and not more than 77 percent inert ingredients. For the second the figures are 18 percent and 76 percent, and for the third the figures are 19 percent and 78 percent. Output 1 sells for $20 per gallon, Output 2 sells for $17 per gallon, and Output 3 sells for $22 per gallon. Inputs 1 and 2 cost $12 and $15 per gallon, respectively. The set of equations would be as follows:

$$X_{11} + X_{12} + X_{13} \leq 12{,}000$$
$$X_{21} + X_{22} + X_{23} \leq 8{,}000$$
$$X_{11} + X_{21} \geq 5{,}000$$
$$X_{12} + X_{22} \geq 5{,}000$$
$$X_{13} + X_{23} \geq 5{,}000$$
$$0.03X_{11} - 0.02X_{21} \geq 0$$
$$0.02X_{12} - 0.03X_{22} \geq 0$$
$$0.01X_{13} - 0.04X_{23} \geq 0$$
$$-0.02X_{11} + 0.03X_{21} \leq 0$$
$$-0.01X_{12} + 0.04X_{22} \leq 0$$
$$-0.03X_{13} + 0.02X_{23} \leq 0$$

The objective is to maximize:

$$8X_{11} + 5X_{12} + 10X_{13} + 5X_{21} + 2X_{22} + 7X_{23}$$

The optimal solution uses all Fluid 1 ($X_{11} = 3{,}000$, $X_{12} = 4{,}000$, and $X_{13} = 5{,}000$) and 4,250 gallons of Fluid 2 ($X_{21} = 2{,}000$, $X_{22} = 1{,}000$, and $X_{23} = 1{,}250$) and achieves a profit of $114,750. Note that only Output 3 is produced above its minimum requirement of 5,000 gallons.

The Project Duration Reduction Problem

In Chapter 16 the problem of reducing project duration was introduced and examined. As was described, the analysis and determination of which activities to crash and by how much is quite complicated. It is difficult to enumerate all the possibilities because the number is quite large. If we assume, as we did in the example in Chapter 16, pages 552-555, that the cost slope is linear between normal and crash times, then this problem can be formulated as a linear programming problem.

Consider Figure 22-5, a revision of Figure 16-11. The i and j refer to event numbers, and C_{ij} would thus be the cost of the activity that lies between Events i and j. The t_{ij} are the activity times. C_{ij}^c is the crash cost, t_{ij}^c is the crash time, C_{ij}^n is the normal cost, and t_{ij}^n is the normal time.

Figure 22-5
Activity Cost Versus Activity Duration

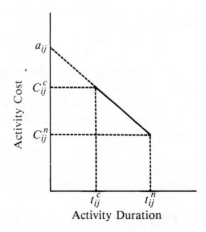

The slope (b_{ij}) of the cost trade-off line is:

$$b_{ij} = \frac{C_{ij}^c - C_{ij}^n}{t_{ij}^n - t_{ij}^c}$$

Hence, the cost (C_{ij}) is as follows:

$$C_{ij} = a_{ij} - b_{ij}t_{ij}$$

The objective function is to minimize the sum of the C_{ij}'s within the constraints of not reducing the t_{ij}'s below their minimums (crash times) while remaining within the precedence relationships of the activities. This can be expressed as follows.

$$\text{minimize } \Sigma C_{ij} = \text{minimize } \Sigma(a_{ij} - b_{ij}t_{ij}), \text{ or}$$

$$\text{minimize } \Sigma - b_{ij}t_{ij}, \text{ or maximize } \Sigma b_{ij}t_{ij}$$

subject to:

1. $\qquad t_{ij} \leq t_{ij}^n$
2. $\qquad t_{ij} \geq t_{ij}^c$
3. $x_i + t_{ij} - x_j \leq 0$
4. $\qquad x_e - x_1 \leq T$

where x_i = time of occurrence of Event i
$\qquad x_e$ = ending event

and $T_c < T < T_n$, where T_c = the total time if all activities are crashed and T_n = the total normal time.

The first equation constrains the actual times not to exceed the normal times. The second equation constrains the actual times not to be less than the crash times. The third equation defines the precedence relationships, and the fourth equation sets the elapsed time goal. There is one equation of Types 1, 2, and 3 for each activity.

When the problem in Table 16-5, page 553, is thus formulated and solved, the optimal solution is to crash Activities I, J, K, and N to 2.17, 3.27, 3.27, and 2.0 weeks, respectively, at a cost of \$1,409.91.

If, instead of aiming for a particular date to finish on, a bonus is offered for each week ahead of normal that the project is completed, then a slight modification of the previous formulation will yield an optimum solution. To the objective function add $-Bx_e$, where B is the weekly bonus and x_e is the time of the last event. Also, replace Equation 4 with $x_1 = 0$. If the bonus is \$500 a week, then it only pays to crash to Week 28 since the incremental cost of crashing one more week exceeds \$500. (Only Activities I, K, and N are crashed.)

THE TRANSPORTATION ALGORITHM

Certain types of linear programming problems result in a set of equations that have a unique form. Because of this unique form a special algebraic technique is possible that both reduces and simplifies the computations necessary to solve the problem. One such class of problems arises when the problem is to find the assignment of quantities and routes by which to transport a commodity from a set of origins to a set of destinations in such a manner as to minimize transportation costs.

If we have a simple problem involving two origins (A and B) and two destinations (X and Y), we might have a shipping cost table like the following:

	To	
From	X	Y
A	3	7
B	8	9

Where, for example, it costs $7.00 a unit to ship from A to Y. Assume A can supply 15 units and B can supply 12 units. Also assume X needs 17 units and Y needs 8 units. Then the linear programming problem could be framed as follows.

Let Q_1 = quantity shipped from A to X
Q_2 = quantity shipped from A to Y
Q_3 = quantity shipped from B to X
Q_4 = quantity shipped from B to Y

Minimize $3Q_1 + 7Q_2 + 8Q_3 + 9Q_4$

Subject to
$$Q_1 + Q_2 \leq 15$$
$$Q_3 + Q_4 \leq 12$$
$$Q_1 + Q_3 \geq 17$$
$$Q_2 + Q_4 \geq 8$$

Notice that all the coefficients of the constraints are one. Furthermore, there is a pattern of sets of ones (this would be more apparent if the problem had more sources and destinations). Notice also that the number of variables is $m \times n$ (m = number of sources and n = number of destinations), while the number of constraints is $m + n$. (Actually one of these is not needed because it is automatically satisfied if the others are.) This problem formulation results in a very large linear programming problem for a relatively small transportation problem. Fortunately, there is an alternative solution technique for this type of problem.

Consider the following situation:

Source	Capacity		Destination	Demand
S_1	37		D_1	18
S_2	75		D_2	12
S_3	128		D_3	30
			D_4	83
			D_5	97

Cost Table

From \ To	D_1	D_2	D_3	D_4	D_5
S_1	21	16	7	23	15
S_2	15	8	12	9	21
S_3	25	19	15	12	17

To use the transportation algorithm (procedure), we need an initial, feasible solution. Later a good technique for finding an initial solution will be illustrated, but for now just assume we have the following:

Initial Solution

From \ To	D_1	D_2	D_3	D_4	D_5	Supply
S_1	18		19			37
S_2		12		63		75
S_3			11	20	97	128
Demand	18	12	30	83	97	

The cost of this solution is:

$$18 \times 21 + 12 \times 8 + 19 \times 7 + 11 \times 15 + 63 \times 9 + 20 \times 12 + 97 \times 17$$
$$= 3,228$$

Now consider how we might improve this solution. As an example, if we shipped to D_5 from S_1 instead of from S_3, it would appear to save some cost ($15 per unit versus $17). If we did this we would not be able to ship as much to either D_1 or D_3, but we also would not have to ship as much from S_3 to D_5. Therefore, we could make up the shortfall for D_3 from S_3. To compute the impact we need only add 15, subtract 7, add 15, and subtract 17 (the respective unit shipping costs of each affected route) to get a result of 6. This means that it costs $6 more for each unit shipped via this new route. A similar analysis can be done for each unused (empty square) route in the current solution. The problem with this is that it needs to be systematized so as to make sure the computations are done correctly. A common way of doing this is with the modified distribution (MODI) technique. While on the surface it does not appear to be the same as our what-if procedure, it is logically equivalent and results in the same values. Its advantage is that it is very orderly, and, if followed, guarantees obtaining the lowest cost solution.

To see how it works, we first construct a matrix containing the unit costs (C_{ij}) corresponding to the routes we have selected.

From \ To	D_1	D_2	D_3	D_4	D_5
S_1	21		7		
S_2		8		9	
S_3			15	12	17

Now we associate a value R_i ($i = 1, 2, 3$) with each row and a value K_j ($j = 1, 2, 3, 4, 5$) with each column. These values are chosen such that $R_i + K_j = C_{ij}$. Because of the nature of this type of problem, we can arbitrarily set any one of the R or K values equal to zero and then compute the rest. For example, if $R_3 = 0$, then K_3 must equal 15 so that $R_3 + K_3$ will equal C_{33}, which is 15. If K_3 is 15, then R_1 must be $7 - 15 = -8$. Thus, K_1 must be $21 - (-8) = 29$, etc. This can be shown in tabular form as follows:

From \ To	D_1	D_2	D_3	D_4	D_5	R_i
S_1	21		7			-8
S_2		8		9		-3
S_3			15	12	17	0
K_j	29	11	15	12	17	

The next step is to use these R and K values to compute the missing C_{ij} values. For example, $C_{21} = R_2 + K_1 = -3 + 29 = 26$. Similarly, $C_{14} = -8 + 12 = 4$. The result of this is the following:

From \ To	D_1	D_2	D_3	D_4	D_5	R_i
S_1	21	3	7	4	9	-8
S_2	26	8	12	9	14	-3
S_3	29	11	15	12	17	0
K_j	29	11	15	12	17	

To complete the evaluation, we now subtract these values from the original cost matrix, cell for cell. The result follows:

From \ To	D_1	D_2	D_3	D_4	D_5
S_1	0	13	0	19	6
S_2	-11	0	0	0	7
S_3	-4	8	0	0	0

These are now the shadow costs just as in the corresponding simplex problem. Since we are minimizing cost, the meaning of these values is that the total cost would decrease by, for example, $11 for each unit shipped from S_2 to D_1. Since this is the greatest per unit savings we can achieve, let's use it. What, however, is the maximum we can ship this way? If we put an X in Row 2, Column 1 of the shipping table, it will help us to visualize the needed changes.

From \ To	D_1	D_2	D_3	D_4	D_5
S_1	18		19		
S_2	X	12		63	
S_3			11	20	97

If we ship X units from S_2 to D_1, we will not need to ship X units from S_1 to D_1. That means we will have X more available to ship from S_1 to D_3. Thus, we do not need the X units from S_3 to D_3, so they can now be shipped to D_4. This means we can compensate at D_4 by not shipping X units to D_4 from S_2. This just balances our original need for X units from S_2 to D_1. On the shipping matrix this is shown as follows:

From \ To	D_1	D_2	D_3	D_4	D_5
S_1	7		30		
S_2	11	12		52	
S_3				31	97

This is a new solution, having a cost of $11 \times (-11) = \$121$ less than the previous solution. It must be evaluated in the same manner as the first one. If none of the shadow costs are negative, then it must be the optimal solution. If there are negative costs, then an improved solution must be developed as was done above. The process is repeated until all the shadow costs are nonnegative.

In our case:

From \ To	D_1	D_2	D_3	D_4	D_5	R_i
S_1	21		7			21
S_2	15	8		9		15
S_3				12	17	18
K_j	0	-7	-14	-6	-1	

From \ To	D_1	D_2	D_3	D_4	D_5	R_i
S_1	21	14	7	15	20	21
S_2	15	8	1	9	14	15
S_3	18	11	4	12	17	18
K_j	0	-7	-14	-6	-1	

From \ To	D_1	D_2	D_3	D_4	D_5
S_1	0	2	0	8	-5
S_2	0	0	11	0	7
S_3	7	8	11	0	0

From \ To	D_1	D_2	D_3	D_4	D_5
S_1	$7 - x$		30		x
S_2	$11 + x$	12		$52 - x$	
S_3				$31 + x$	$97 - x$

From \ To	D_1	D_2	D_3	D_4	D_5
S_1			30		7
S_2	18	12		45	
S_3				38	90

From \ To	D_1	D_2	D_3	D_4	D_5
S_1			7		15
S_2	15	8		9	
S_3				12	17

From \ To	D_1	D_2	D_3	D_4	D_5	R_i
S_1			7		15	0
S_2	15	8		9		-1
S_3				12	17	2
K_j	16	9	7	10	15	

From \ To	D_1	D_2	D_3	D_4	D_5	R_i
S_1	16	9	7	10	15	0
S_2	15	8	6	9	14	−1
S_3	18	11	9	12	17	2
K_j	16	9	7	10	15	

From \ To	D_1	D_2	D_3	D_4	D_5
S_1	5	7	0	13	0
S_2	0	0	6	0	7
S_3	7	8	6	0	0

Since none of these shadow costs is negative the new solution is optimal.

Because the number of iterations for a problem such as this is related to how good the initial solution is, it is worthwhile considering how to obtain a good solution quickly. One of the best known and most reliable methods is known as Vogel's Approximation Method (VAM). The following is a somewhat simplified version that seems to give as good results. To illustrate it we will apply it to our sample problem.

Set up a matrix with only the marginal supply and demand figures (as shown next) and, then, referring to the original cost matrix for each column, calculate the difference between the two lowest costs in that column.

From \ To	D_1	D_2	D_3	D_4	D_5	Supply
S_1						37
S_2						75
S_3						128
Demand	18	12	30	83	97	
Cost Difference	6	8	5	3	2	

In the column having the largest difference, select the lowest cost and enter a quantity to be shipped equal to the smaller of the demand or supply for that column and row. In this case Column 2 has the largest cost difference, and the minimum cost is in Row 2. The demand is smaller than the supply so the quantity assigned is 12 units. Cross off that column (or row if the supply is exhausted), reduce the available supply (or demand if not completely satisfied) by the assigned amount, and repeat this procedure until all the demands are satisfied. In our case the next two matrices would be as follows:

From \ To	D_1	D_2	D_3	D_4	D_5	Supply
S_1						37
S_2		12				63
S_3						128
Demand	18	X	30	83	97	
Cost Difference	6	X	5	3	2	

From \ To	D_1	D_2	D_3	D_4	D_5	Supply
S_1						37
S_2	18	12				45
S_3						128
Demand	X	X	30	83	97	
Cost Difference	X	X	5	3	2	

Continuation of this process leads to an initial solution, which, when evaluated by the MODI technique, is found to be optimal. While this is not always the case, at least the solution will reduce the number of MODI iterations required compared with an arbitrary initial solution.

Several computational complexities—chiefly so-called degeneracy or a related phenomenon, e.g., alternate optimal solutions—may arise in these types of problems. Treatment of such issues is left to an operations research text.

APPLICATION OF THE TRANSPORTATION FORMULATION TO AGGREGATE PLANNING

Besides the obvious application of the transportation technique to shipping problems, it can also be used to solve a simple aggregate planning problem. If the costs of changing levels of production from period to period are not significant, that is, there are no hiring and firing costs to be considered, then we can consider each period of regular and overtime production to be a source and each period of demand to be a destination in the transportation matrix. Thus, the rows are labeled P_1, O_1, P_2, O_2, P_3, O_3 (using the same symbols as in the earlier aggregate planning example in this chapter). The columns are demand in each period. The result follows:

Production	Period 1	Period 2	Period 3	Maximum Available
Regular Time 1				3,200
Overtime 1				900
Regular Time 2				3,200
Overtime 2				900
Regular Time 3				3,000
Overtime 3				700
Demand	3,400	4,500	3,750	

Now the costs of producing and carrying inventory are used in arriving at the shipping costs. For Row 1, Column 1 that is just r ($r = \$17$). For Row 1, Column 2 it is $r + c$ ($r + c = 17 + 4 = \$21$). The result follows:

Production	Period 1	Period 2	Period 3	Maximum Available
Regular Time 1	17	21	25	3,200
Overtime 1	25	29	33	900
Regular Time 2	X	17	21	3,200
Overtime 2	X	25	29	900
Regular Time 3	X	X	17	3,000
Overtime 3	X	X	25	700
Demand	3,400	4,500	3,750	

The X's indicate impossible activities, that is, production after demand. (A modified formulation would allow backorders, in which case the X's would reflect production costs plus backorder costs and a feasible activity.) In order to apply the solution procedure, simply assign an arbitrarily very high cost to these routes. Also, since the total maximum available exceeds total demand, we add a slack column to achieve balance and assign zero cost to using these routes.

An optimal solution is:

Production	Period 1	Period 2	Period 3	Slack	Maximum Available
Regular Time 1	2,750	450			3,200
Overtime 1	650			250	900
Regular Time 2		3,150	50		3,200
Overtime 2		900			900
Regular Time 3			3,000		3,000
Overtime 3			700		700
Demand	3,400	4,500	3,750	250	11,900

The weakness of this formulation is that the cost structure is not realistic enough. One result is that there are many alternate optimal solutions to this problem, that is, there are many other allocations of the productive capacity that are equally inexpensive.

GOAL PROGRAMMING

One of the criticisms of linear programming is that there is room for only one objective function. Hence, the several objectives that a decision maker may have need to be expressible in a common measure (like dollars). Another difficulty arises because the constraints may not actually be as rigid as the solution procedure suggests. For example, a firm may wish to maximize profit, but it also wants to have stable employment, a diversified product line, and minimal pollution. These goals are not easily or naturally transformed into dollar measures, nor are they easily set as constraints while the profit equation is maximized.

An alternative linear equation approach to this type of problem is goal programming (GP). To use this procedure, it is necessary to consider both the structural or technological constraints (raw material and machine hour availability, for example) and the objectives. For each constraint, possible deviations are stated, and for each objective, a target level is set. The objective is to minimize stated constraint deviations and variations from the target levels. The GP procedure provides a methodology for minimizing these deviations and for dealing with them in the rank order specified while not violating the technological constraints.

To see how this works, let's reconsider the LP problem stated earlier as:

$$5X + 6Y \le 27.75$$
$$4X + 2Y \le 13$$
$$3.6X + 8.1Y \ge 23$$

with the objective of maximizing:

$$1.8X + 2Y$$

Deviations below the goal are symbolized by:

$$d_n^-$$

and those above are symbolized by:

$$d_n^+$$

Let's reconsider the problem as having the same constraints, but our goals are, first, to make just as much X as Y and, second, to maximize profit.

The constraints are restated as follows:

$$5X + 6Y + d_1^- = 27.75$$
$$4X + 2Y + d_2^- = 13$$
$$3.6X + 8.1Y - d_3^+ = 23$$

Note how these were constructed. Our less-than constraints allow a negative deviation (akin to the slack in an ordinary LP problem) and the greater-than constraint allows the subtraction of a positive deviation (a surplus). Our profit goal is added by setting some reasonably large value for the profit and allowing a negative deviation, e.g., the following:

$$1.8X + 2Y + d_4^- = 20$$

Now the equal production goal is constructed by allowing the difference between X and Y to be either positive or negative:

$$X - Y + d_5^- - d_5^+ = 0$$

Our objectives can then be stated as:

Priority 1: minimize $d_5^- + d_5^+$, and
Priority 2: minimize d_4^-

Before considering variations on this problem formulation, let's briefly look at the mechanics of the solution procedure. We begin by setting up a matrix similar to our original LP matrix (see Figure 22-6). There are several differences between Figure 22-6 and the matrix on page 750. Across the top, in place of the costs (C_j's) are the priority levels (P_n's). Note particularly that for $3.6X + 8.1Y \geq 23$, where an artificial variable is required in order to create a nonnegative basis, a priority of P_0 is established instead of the big M used in the LP simplex calculation. Below the matrix, in place of a single $C_j - Z_j$ row there are now several rows, one for each priority level. By convention, these rows are ordered downward in increasing levels of importance. The entries are computed in a manner similar to the LP simplex. For the column headed X:

$$C_j - Z_j = 0 - (5 \times 0 + 4 \times 0 + 3.6 \times P_0 + 1.8 \times P_2 + 1 \times P_1)$$
$$= -3.6P_0 - 1.8P_2 - P_1$$

These coefficients are then entered in their respective rows of the $C_j - Z_j$ priority levels.

Selecting a variable to enter into the solution proceeds as in the LP simplex, but with a slight modification. We start with the highest priority and select the most negative element. We continue working with that level until all its entries are zero or positive and then move to the next lower level and examine

Figure 22-6
Initial Goal Programming Matrix

$P =$		0	0	0	0	0	P_0	P_2	P_1	P_1	
	Basis	X	Y	d_1^-	d_2^-	d_3^+	A_3	d_4^-	d_5^-	d_5^+	RHS
0	d_1^-	5	6	1							27.75
0	d_2^-	4	2		1						13.0
P_0	A_3	3.6	8.1			−1	1				23.0 ←
P_2	d_4^-	1.8	2					1			20.0
P_1	d_5^-	1	−1						1	−1	0.0
	P_2	−1.8	−2								−20
$C_i - Z_j$	P_1	−1	1						2		0
	P_0	−3.6	−8.1								−23

its entries. We select the most negative element in that level, so long as no positive, nonzero $C_j - Z_j$ exists in that column for a higher priority level. We continue in this stepwise manner through all levels of priority.

The criterion for selecting the variable that leaves the solution is the same as in the LP simplex: Divide the RHS column entries by their respective positive coefficients in the selected entry variable column and choose the smallest. The remainder of the simplex computations are as illustrated previously.

Figure 22-7 shows the result of the first iteration. The entries in $C_j - Z_j$ for P_0 are all positive or zero, so we move on to the P_1 row. The most negative of these is in the column headed X, and the smallest ratio is 2.840 ÷ 1.444 in the row labeled d_5^-; so X replaces d_5^-. Note that even if the −0.123 in the column headed A_3 were the most negative it could not have been chosen because of the plus one in the row below it.

Figure 22-8 shows the next iteration. Since all P_1 entries are zero or positive, we move to P_2 and find we can improve P_2 by bringing in d_3^+ in place of d_2^- (as shown in Figure 22-9). Now the entry in the column headed d_5^- cannot be brought into the solution because to do so would reduce achievement of Goal P_1. Since all other entries in Row P_2 are positive, this represents the optimal solution, that is:

$$X - Y = 2.167$$

P_2 misses being achieved by 11.767 for a net profit of 20 − 11.767 or 8.233.

Figure 22-7
First Iteration Result

		0	0	0	0	0	P_0	P_2	P_1	P_1	
		X	Y	d_1^-	d_2^-	d_3^+	A_3	d_4^-	d_5^-	d_5^+	RHS
0	d_1^-	2.333		1		0.741	−0.741				10.713
0	d_2^-	3.111			1	0.247	−0.247				7.321
0	Y	0.444	1			−0.123	0.123				2.840
P_2	d_4^-	0.911				0.247	−0.247	1			14.321
P_1	d_5^-	1.444				−0.123	0.123		1	−1	2.840 ←
$C_j - Z_j$	P_2	−0.911				−0.247	0.247				−14.321
	P_1	−1.444				0.123	−0.123			2	−2.84
	P_0						1				0

Figure 22-8
Second Goal Progamming Iteration

		X	Y	d_1^-	d_2^-	d_3^+	A_3	d_4^-	d_5^-	d_5^+	RHS
0	d_1^-			1		0.940	−0.940		−1.615	1.615	6.126
0	d_2^-				1	0.513	−0.513		−2.154	2.154	1.205 ←
0	Y		1			−0.085	0.085		−0.308	0.308	1.966
P_2	d_4^-					0.325	−0.325	1	−0.631	0.631	12.530
0	X	1				−0.085	0.085		0.692	−0.692	1.966
$C_j - Z_j$	P_2					−0.325	0.325		0.631	−0.631	−12.53
	P_1								1	1	0
	P_0						1				0

Figure 22-9
Final Solution Matrix

		X	Y	d_1^-	d_2^-	d_3^+	A_3	d_4^-	d_5^-	d_5^+	RHS
0	d_1^-			1	−1.833				2.333	2.333	3.917
0	d_3^+				1.950	1	−1		−4.200	4.200	2.350
0	Y		1		−0.167				−0.667	0.667	2.167
P_2	d_4^-				−0.633			1	0.733	−0.733	11.767
0	X	1			0.167				0.333	−0.333	2.167
$C_j - Z_j$	P_2				0.633				−0.733	0.733	−11.767
	P_1								1	1	0
	P_0						1				0

Some Considerations and Limitations

It is well to note some of the considerations and limitations to GP. We still have linear equations and continuous variables. (Some research is being done on integer versions of GP.) Within any priority level the deviations must be commensurable (for example, dollars or pounds or hours), but different levels may be in different dimensions. It is possible to give different weights to the various deviations within a level; that is, we could weight a negative deviation with a factor of two and a positive deviation with a one if we were more concerned with the former. Postoptimality analysis is more complicated for GP than for LP.

Because GP opens up a broader way of looking at problems, it lends itself to finding solutions to sets of problems in a sort of what-if mode. Interchanging the order of goals one and two in the previous example results in a quite different solution; namely, the same solution as the plain LP formulation achieved. In more complex problems involving more goals, it is likely that the decision maker will want to explore a variety of goal structures and to consider the sensitivity of the solutions to any structure changes.

A Goal Programming Formulation of a Manufacturing Mix Problem

Let's consider an example of a standard linear programming illustration—the product mix problem. Among the many products a plant produces, there are two that tend to cause a bottleneck in their conflicting use of manufacturing resources. They are motors and compressors. The motors require 2.25 hours of machining each and the compressors require 1.5 hours each. The finishing operation requires 1.5 hours for each motor and 3 hours for each compressor. Storage is 1.5 cubic meters for each. Machining is limited to 13,500 hours, finishing is limited to 18,750 hours, and storage is confined to 11,250 cubic meters. The profit contribution of motors is $30 each, and for compressors it is $50 each. Determine how many motors and compressors to make in order to maximize profit.

Letting X_M be the production quantity of motors and X_C be the same for compressors, the problem can be formulated as follows:

$$\text{Maximize} \quad 30X_M + 50X_C$$
$$\text{Subject to} \quad 2.25X_M + 1.5X_C \leq 13,500$$
$$1.5X_M + 3X_C \leq 18,750$$
$$1.5X_M + 1.5X_C \leq 11,250$$

Calculation is straightforward and results in producing 2,500 motors and 5,000 compressors.

Suppose, however, we have some additional objectives. For example, suppose we want to maximize sales or to limit in-process inventory or to allow limited overtime or to restrict cash tied up in receivables. We can incorporate these objectives if we change the preceding problem to allow a GP approach.

First, assume that we want to sell at least 3,000 of each product. For in-process inventory, $200 is required for each motor and $375 is required for each compressor. The technological constraints of the linear programming formulation can be transformed as follows:

$$2.25X_M + 1.5X_C + d_1^- - d_1^+ = 13,500$$
$$1.5X_M + 3X_C + d_2^- - d_2^+ = 18,750$$
$$1.5X_M + 1.5X_C + d_3^- - d_3^+ = 11,250$$

If the limit on in-process inventory is $2 million, then

$$200X_M + 375X_C + d_4^- - d_4^+ = 2,000,000$$

For the sales goals:

$$X_M + d_5^- = 3,000 \quad \text{and} \quad X_C + d_6^- - d_6^+ = 3,000$$

The profit goal is the following:

$$30X_M + 50X_C + d_7^- - d_7^+ = 300,000$$

Next, we must rank the conflicting goals. A possible ordering is:

Priority 1: minimize d_4^+
Priority 2: minimize $d_5^- - d_6^-$
Priority 3: minimize d_7^+
Priority 4: minimize $d_1^- + d_2^- + d_3^-$

That is, in order, minimize the excess in-process inventory, make the sales goals, make the profit goal (if possible), and try not to exceed plant capacity.

The optimal solution is to make 4,375 motors and 3,000 compressors. Goals 1 and 2 are met, but profit is only $281,250 and capacity in both finishing and storage are exceeded.

If we interchange Goals 1 and 4, then the optimal solution is to make 3,000 motors and 4,750 compressors. This does not exceed plant capacity and it does meet sales goals. However, in-process inventory goes up to $2,381,250. In compensation for this 19 percent increase in inventory, there is also a 16 percent increase in profits to $327,500. Whether this is acceptable or not depends on financial constraints, but it certainly is worth exploring.

The other linear programming problems that were formulated could also be transformed into GP problems, and conflicting goals could be considered.

CONCLUSIONS

The techniques of mathematical programming are varied. The essence of mathematical programming is the creation of a mathematical model and rigorous manipulation of the model to secure an optimum solution to a real world problem. Since mathematical programming is designed to deal with complex problems having many variables, the models are often complex, albeit less complex than the real world. Since the modeling process involves extraction of the important from the complex, there is always some sort of simplification. In some problems there may be too much simplification, and the solution may not be optimal in the real world. But if the appropriate technique—linear programming, stochastic, or goal programming—is chosen, the process and solution should at least shed some light and provide some information.

EXERCISES

1. Reformulate the linear programming aggregate planning problem, pages 752-755, to include limited subcontracting and constrain overtime production to be a proportion of regular time production. Also include beginning and ending inventory levels.

2. Solve Exercise 1 assuming a modification of the example in the text to allow subcontracting at $27 per unit, not more than 200 units subcontracted per period, and overtime constrained to 25 percent of regular time production. Beginning and ending inventory is to be 300 units.

3. Reformulate and solve the transportation method aggregate planning problem, pages 767-769, assuming backorders are allowed. The added cost of a backorder is $3 per unit.

4. Reformulate and solve Exercise 3 if demand increases 20 percent in each period, and subcontracting at $25 per unit is allowed.

5. Pacific Hoist and Crane makes two models of a jib crane. Since each has a profit of $250, they have been making equal quantities of each. Manufacturing limits are as follows:

	Machining Hours/Unit	Welding Hours/Unit	Assembly Hours/Unit
Model 1051	5.25	1.75	5.25
Model 1348	3.00	3.00	7.00
Hours Available	48,870	23,750	61,670

a. If they stay with their equal-quantity rule, how much should they make to maximize profit?

b. If they simply want to maximize profit, how many of each model should they produce?

c. Because of a machine failure, machining capacity is reduced to 37,125 hours. How does this affect the solutions to a and b?

6. Suppose that in Exercise 5, in order to maintain a constant work force level, all the assembly capacity must be used exactly. At the same time, management wants to minimize overtime in machining and welding, maximize profits, and produce at least 9,000 units of Model 1051 and 3,000 units of Model 1348.

a. If the goals are ordered as stated here, what is the optimal solution?

b. If Goal 4 is placed above all the others, without changing their order, what is the solution?

7. Given the following aggregate planning data, what should the production be each month and how much inventory will be held each period? What will be the total cost?

Month	Demand	Maximum Production	
		Regular	Overtime
1	4,275	3,700	900
2	4,760	4,000	1,000
3	5,545	4,500	1,100
4	4,438	4,000	1,000

$$r = \$14/\text{unit} \qquad f = \$15/\text{unit}$$
$$s = \$21/\text{unit} \qquad c = \$3/\text{unit}$$
$$h = \$35/\text{unit} \qquad P_0 = 3,500$$

8. Solve the following linear programming problem graphically.

$$\text{Maximize} \quad 2X + Y$$
$$\text{Subject to} \quad 3X + 2Y \geq 12$$
$$X + 1.4Y \leq 7$$
$$3X + 16Y \geq 24$$
$$X \geq 0, \ Y \geq 0$$

9. Solve the following linear programming problem graphically.

$$\text{Maximize} \quad 0.6X + Y$$
$$\text{Subject to} \quad 3X + 2Y \leq 45.0$$
$$0.5X + Y \leq 62.5$$
$$X + Y \leq 5.0$$

10. Solve Exercise 9 by the simplex method.

SELECTED READINGS

Hillier, Frederick, and Gerald Lieberman. *Introduction to Operations Research.* 2d ed. Oakland, CA: Holden Day, Inc., 1974.

Lee, Sang M. *Goal Programming for Decision Analysis.* Pennsauken, NJ: Auerbach Publishers, Inc., 1972.

Plane, Donald, and Gary Kochenberger. *Operations Research for Managerial Decisions.* Homewood, IL: Richard D. Irwin, Inc., 1972.

Shore, Barry. *Operations Management.* New York: McGraw-Hill Book Co., 1973.

Wagner, Harvey. *Operations Research.* 2d ed. Englewood Cliffs, N.J.: Prentice-Hall, Inc., 1974.

23

STOCHASTIC SIMULATION

Throughout this text we discuss the use of models in making decisions. Most of these models employ deterministic data or data that is assumed to be deterministic. For example, in developing the economic order quantity model, we assume that the annual demand, the setup cost, and the holding cost are known with certainty. In other models we analyze probability distributions. For example, in developing a reorder point we usually assume demand during the lead time to be a normally distributed random variable with a known mean and a known standard deviation. We use the normal distribution to find the safety stock and the reorder point needed for a given level of customer service.

Sometimes a problem cannot easily be modeled using deterministic techniques or simple analysis of probability distributions. Sometimes we need to recreate important facets of the problem in a stochastic simulation model and to perform experiments with the model in order to establish an effective policy. Simulation models are simply models that mimic other processes in some fashion. Stochastic means random. Stochastic simulation models have several random variables, such as purchased part lead time, fraction scrapped, time of machine breakdown, etc., each of which has a unique probability distribution.

Three broad categories of simulation are Monte Carlo simulation, discrete event simulation, and continuous simulation. Monte Carlo simulation describes a probabilistic system that does not change over time. It is named after the principality that is world famous for its gambling casinos. For example, suppose we know that lead time is four days and we know the probability distribution for daily demand, but we cannot find the distribution of demand for four days analytically. We can still find a good order point by simulation. All we have to do is to generate four random numbers from the distribution of daily demand and add the four numbers to obtain one observation of demand during four days. We can repeat the four random draws hundreds of times until we obtain a good picture of the distribution of demand during four days.

The fact that we have placed an order with our vendor should have no effect on demand placed on us by our customers. Thus, it is reasonable to assume that the distribution of demand during any arbitrary four-day interval will hold during a four-day lead time period. We now have a mechanism to identify the probability of a stockout, a measure of our service level, during the reorder interval for any given reorder point. We can now determine the reorder point for our desired level of service. Monte Carlo simulation easily can be performed using an electronic spreadsheet, such as Lotus 1-2-3.

Discrete event simulations are used to model processes that employ probability distributions, such as time in queue, that change over time. Frequently, discrete event models describe queuing processes, such as the queue awaiting a teller at a bank or a checkout clerk at a store. These simulations are called discrete event because the only items of interest to the modeler are those events that cause the status of the system to change. In the queuing model, two events are significant, the arrival of a customer into the system and the departure of a customer from the system. Each event causes the number of persons in the system to change by one. Using a discrete event simulation we can answer such questions as "How long does a customer wait for service?" and "If I add one additional teller (or clerk), by how much will the average waiting time decrease? By how much will the maximum waiting time decrease?" Most simulation models used for production and inventory management are discrete event models. An example of a discrete event model is given in the next section.

Continuous simulation models are systems of equations that involve time as one of the variables. Processes that change continuously with time, such as acceleration and deceleration, require continuous simulation models for precise results. Continuous simulation models are often used by engineers in designing automated materials handling systems in order to determine how various independent components (e.g., several automatically guided vehicles) will interfere with one another. Physical scientists often use continuous simulation to model chemical reactions and other processes that change over time. Such detailed models are rarely needed for production and inventory management.

PROCEDURE AND RATIONALE

The procedure for creating a simulation is based on building a logical representation of a system, recognizing the input variables and their statistical variations, exercising the model to make it behave like the real world it represents, and observing the consequences. The specific steps are as follows:

1. Describe the decision to be studied and its objective. For example, determine the level of safety stock that minimizes the sum of stockout and inventory holding costs under stochastic demand conditions.
2. Construct a model that replicates reality and permits measurement of the objective function under different conditions.

3. Determine the frequency distribution of the uncontrollable events. Determination of more than one frequency distribution is necessary if more than one event is probabilistic.
4. Convert the frequency distribution(s) to cumulative probability distribution(s). The data may be fit to a theoretical distribution, such as the Poisson distribution, or to an anticipated actual distribution.
5. Establish the initial conditions.
6. Generate (obtain) sets of random numbers (RN's), one set for each event to be simulated.
7. For each RN, determine the corresponding value of the event (input) of concern.
8. Insert these values in the model measuring the decision effectiveness and compute the results.
9. Repeat Steps 6, 7, and 8 many times for each of the alternatives. Determination of the exact number of repetitions required to achieve a statistical confidence in the results of the simulation is beyond the scope of this book.
10. Apply controls. Compare the parameters (mean and variance) of the simulated events to the actual distribution parameters.
11. Select the particular course of action that achieves the best results on the basis of the preselected criteria and which is within control limits.

Two results of the procedure constitute its rationale: (1) the event values occur with the same relative frequency in the simulation as they do in reality and (2) the numerous repetitions of the procedure include the many possible sequential combinations and the actual outcome of each combination. The probability of occurrence of each sequence is the same as it is in reality. For example, if in the real world there is a 5 percent probability that one machine will fail during an eight-hour period, simulated history will have one failure per eight-hour day approximately 5 percent of the time. If, in addition, an eight-hour period with only one failure can be followed by an eight-hour period with a small number of failures, or a relatively large number, or an average number of failures, simulation will include each possible sequential pattern in the proportion that it occurs in the real world. It is this combination of probabilistic events and a wide variety of possible sequential combinations with widely varying effects on outcomes that analytical solution approaches cannot represent adequately.

Setting Up a Simulation—An Example

Consider the case of an organization, or a department within an organization, that receives a different number of orders each day. The orders vary in the time required for processing. The company is interested in determining how many machines it should have to minimize the combined cost of machine idle time and order waiting time. The company knows the cost of machine idle time, the cost of order waiting time, and the probability distributions for the number of orders each day and the number of hours required to process an order. The number of machines that will result in minimum total variable costs cannot be determined analytically because such approaches do not consider the sequential pattern of the hours required for processing. A stochastic simulation includes these sequential patterns.

This problem can be couched in a maintenance setting. Machine failure and repair time can be the probabilistic events rather than orders received and the time required for processing. Furthermore, our example can be expanded to include priority of processing rules such as first-come-first-served; a ratio of delivery time to lead time; and order profit. A first-come-first-served priority rule is used to keep the example simple.

The minimization of total variable costs—idle machine cost plus order-waiting cost—is the objective function. The company has calculated these costs as $3.00 an hour for idle machine time and $5.00 an hour for orders back-ordered. (Note: The model oversimplifies reality for purposes of illustration. The cost figures are hypothetical.)

The measure of effectiveness is as follows:

$$\text{Total Variable Costs} = \$3 \times \text{Idle Machine Hours} + \$5 \times \text{Hours}$$
$$\text{for Orders Backordered Each Day}$$

The determination of costs is a crucial step in any model-building procedure. The number of machines that minimizes these costs is the optimal number of machines (Steps 1 and 2).

The next step is to describe the frequency distribution of the probabilistic events. There are two such events: the number of orders per day and the number of machine hours required per order. Therefore, two frequency distributions are required. The frequency distributions for these inputs, based on historical data, and their cumulative probability distributions are shown in Figure 23-1 (Steps 3 and 4).

The initial conditions (the backlog of orders and machine status in this case) must be set. The example has an arbitrary initial setting of no backlog and all machines idle. Considerable study is required in most situations to determine realistic initial conditions (Step 5).

Tables 23-1 and 23-2 list the RN samples that determined the number of orders per day and the number of hours per order. The random numbers in Table 23-1 were obtained by selecting an arbitrary starting point in a random number table and taking that number and the next four two-digit numbers.[1] The random numbers in Table 23-2 were obtained in a similar way. The manner in which the number of orders and the hours per order are determined once

---

1. A random number table is given in Appendix B at the back of this text.

the corresponding random number is found is explained in a subsequent paragraph. Table 23-3 lists the summarized activity of the five days simulated in the one trial of this example. For the sake of brevity, only one trial of five days is made (Steps 6 and 7).

Figure 23-1
Probability Distribution

A. Number of Orders

No. of Orders	Probability	Cumulative Probability
0	0.10	0.10
1	0.15	0.25
2	0.25	0.50
3	0.30	0.80
4	0.15	0.95
5	0.05	1.00

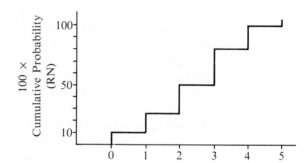

B. Number of Machine Hours per Order

Hours/ Order	Probability	Cumulative Probability
5	0.05	0.05
10	0.05	0.10
15	0.10	0.20
20	0.10	0.30
25	0.20	0.50
30	0.25	0.75
35	0.15	0.90
40	0.10	1.00

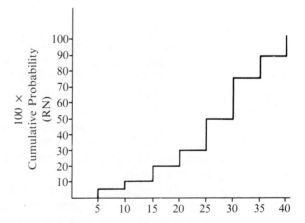

Table 23-1
Determination of the Number of Orders

Day	Random Number	Number of Orders
1	26	2
2	78	3
3	57	3
4	58	3
5	23	1

Table 23-2
Determination of the Number of Hours per Order

Order Number	Random Number	Hours per Order
1	85	35
2	75	30
3	74	30
4	28	20
5	40	25
6	69	30
7	60	30
8	11	15
9	74	30
10	15	15
11	04	5
12	21	20
13	97	40
14	66	30
15	42	25

A reasonable number of machines with which to begin the experiment is the number required for the average number of order hours per day. In the example, the average number of orders per day is 2.4 and the average hours per order is 26. Thus, the average number of order hours per day is 62.4 (2.4 × 26). Eight machines, providing 64 hours of available machine time per day, is a rational starting point. Total variable costs (TVC) are determined for operating with 8, 9, and 10 machines (see Table 23-3).

The TVC of operating with 9 machines is less expensive than operating with 8 or 10 machines. Since the cost curve is simple and well behaved, a minimum at this point indicates that the TVC's with 7 and 11 machines must be higher. Therefore, it is not necessary to calculate the TVC for 7 or 11 machines (Step 8).

The following is a brief explanation of how the first few days' simulation was run using 8 machines. All others were performed in essentially the same manner.

1. The RN's listed in Tables 23-1 and 23-2 were obtained from a table of random numbers. The table was entered at two different points: one to obtain the RN's for the number of orders per day and another to obtain the RN's for the number of hours per order.
2. To determine the number of orders per day, the first RN, 26, is compared to the cumulative probability distribution (Figure 23-1) and found to correspond to 2 orders (26 is greater than 25 and less than 50). In the same manner 78 corresponds to 3 orders for the second day (50 < 78 < 80).

Table 23-3
Trial One Five Days Simulated Activity
(TVC = Cost of Idle Time (CI) + Cost of Waiting Time (CW)
CI = $3 an hour of machine idle time
CW = $5 an hour of orders held over each day

A. Using 8 Machines—64 Hours of Available Machine Time/Day

Day	Order Hours Received	Total Order Hours To Be Processed	Hours Idle	Hours Backordered	CI	CW
1	65	65	0	1	$ 0	$ 5
2	75	76	0	12	0	60
3	75	87	0	23	0	115
4	50	73	0	9	0	45
5	20	29	35	0	105	0
					$105 +	$225 = $330 TVC

B. Using 9 Machines—72 Hours of Available Machine Time/Day

Day	Order Hours Received	Total Order Hours To Be Processed	Hours Idle	Hours Backordered	CI	CW
1	65	65	7	0	$ 21	$ 0
2	75	75	0	3	0	15
3	75	78	0	6	0	30
4	50	56	16	0	48	0
5	20	20	52	0	156	0
					$225 +	$ 45 = $270 TVC

C. Using 10 Machines—80 Hours of Available Machine Time/Day

Similar calculations render TVC = $345

3. The number of hours per order are determined in the same manner as described in Step 2 using the second set of RN's and the cumulative distribution for the hours per order (Figure 23-1).
4. Thus, on the first day of simulation, two orders arrived and they require 35 and 30 machine hours, respectively. This is a total of 65 hours, which is 1 hour more than capacity. Thus, 1 order hour is backordered at a cost of $5. The backlog initial condition was set at zero (Table 23-3).
5. Three orders arrive on the second day requiring 75 (30 + 20 + 25) machine hours. Adding these to the 1-hour backorder from Day 1 brings the total processing requirement to 76 hours. This is 12 hours more than capacity and the backorder cost is $60 (Table 23-3).
6. The simulated inputs and costs for all other days are determined in the same manner.

Simulation in Lotus 1-2-3

Performing a simulation using Lotus 1-2-3 is an advanced application for Lotus or any other electronic spreadsheet. Additional detail is given in Appendix 23A. The explanations given assume some familiarity with Lotus 1-2-3. Those who wish an in-depth discussion of the use of Lotus to perform simulations should consult Watson and Blackstone (1989) for an explanation using Lotus 1-2-3 that assumes no prior knowledge of electronic spreadsheets.

The example in the previous section is a Monte Carlo simulation model. A distinguishing characteristic of all Monte Carlo models is that the probability distributions involved do not change over time and are not dependent on the state of the system. Figure 23-2 shows a printout of a portion of a Lotus 1-2-3 spreadsheet that is designed to simulate the situation described in our example. At the top of the spreadsheet are the cumulative distribution functions for the number of orders and the processing hours per order. The cumulative distribution functions are presented with the columns transposed from the way you normally see them, i.e., the probability that a value x occurs is on the left and the value of x is on the right. Due to the way Lotus 1-2-3's @**VLOOKUP** function works, the value of x also appears one row above the cumulative probability that a randomly selected value is equal to or less than x. This condition also forces the final value of x to be listed twice.

Figure 23-2
Lotus 1-2-3 Version of Monte Carlo Simulation

Cum. Prob.	# of Orders	Cum. Prob.	Hours per Order	Number of Machines	FINAL RESULTS	Machines	Costs
0	0	0	5	11		Machines	Costs
0.1	1	0.05	10	Idle Cost		8	112374
0.25	2	0.1	15	6975		9	34720
0.5	3	0.2	20	BckOrd Co		10	15325
0.8	4	0.3	25	5790		11	12765
0.95	5	0.5	30	Total Cos		12	13045
1	5	0.75	35	12765		13	14180
		0.9	40				
		1	40				

Random Number	Number Orders	Total Time	Time Avail.	Hours Idle	Hours Bkordered	Cost Idle	Cost Bkorder
				0	0		
0.208302	1	40	88	48	0	144	0
0.144529	1	30	88	58	0	174	0
0.478230	2	50	88	38	0	114	0
0.152237	1	30	88	58	0	174	0
0.763165	3	85	88	3	0	9	0
0.589176	3	85	88	3	0	9	0

Now consider the bottom of Figure 23-2. The first column is a series of random numbers. These could be taken from a table of random digits and entered manually, however, they were in fact generated using the @**RAND** function built into Lotus 1-2-3. @**RAND** returns a uniform random number larger than 0 and smaller than 1. The column immediately to the right of the random numbers contains the number of orders, which was obtained by using the @**VLOOKUP** procedure. Assume the first entry under the Number Orders column is in cell B19. The random number 0.208302 is thus in cell A19. The specific argument in cell B19 is @**VLOOKUP(A19,A\$6.B\$12,1)**. This formula is interpreted as follows: Compare the value in cell A19 to the values in column A starting in cell A6 and continuing through A12. Each value in the column has a corresponding value in column B. Because the third argument is 1, i.e., offset from the search column by one column to find the return value, a value from column B will become the value for cell B19. When a value greater than the value in cell A19 is found in the range A6 to A12, the preceeding value in column B is returned. The cell references A\$6 and B\$12 are mixed references, indicating that although the A and B are permitted to change the 6 and 12 are not. The mixed reference is used so that when the formula is copied down column B to obtain several trials of the experiment, the location of the cumulative distribution function is preserved. The cell reference A19 is a relative reference, because when the formula is copied we wish the formula to be changed to always refer to the random number contained in the current row.

The test value, the value of cell A19 (0.208302), is first compared to the value of cell A6 (0). Cell A6 is the first cell in the area labeled "Cum. Prob." in the upper left of Figure 23-2. Because the value of cell A19 is larger, it is next compared to the value of cell A7 (0.1). Because the value of cell A19 is larger, it is next compared to the value of cell A8 (0.25). Because the value of cell A8 is larger than the test value, the procedure returns to the previous row (7) and offsets 1 column (the third argument of @**VLOOKUP(X,Y,Z)** in this case is 1) to column B. The value of cell B7 is 1, so cell B19 takes the value 1.

Take the test value used in the previous paragraph, 0.208302, and use it with Figure 23-1 to determine the number of orders you would obtain if you were to replicate Figure 23-1 manually. You should also obtain the value 1. Test each random number shown in Figure 23-2 versus Figure 23-1 to verify that the correct number of orders is selected. Thus, the @**VLOOKUP** function is working with a cumulative probability distribution just as we did in the manual example, although the arrangement of the cumulative probability distribution used by @**VLOOKUP** looks a bit odd when first encountered.

The column labeled "Total Time" in Figure 23-2 requires a bit of explanation. Consider Figure 23-3, which shows a set of random numbers used to generate the Total Time amount. Assume the value 40 located in the column labeled "One Order" is in cell H19. This value represents the total time required to complete the first order in this particular random draw. Cell H19 is defined by using the argument @**VLOOKUP(M19,D\$6.E\$14,1)**. This argument says to pull the number in the First RN column in the current row, look this value up in the appropriate cumulative distribution function that is contained in the area bounded by D6 and E14, pull the appropriate value from column E and return it. Note that the first random number is 0.9773 and that the proper value, 40, is returned. The area bounded by D6 and E14 is labeled "Cum. Prob." and "Hours per Order" in Figure 23-2. The first value contained in the column labeled "Two Orders" is the total time required by the first two orders. The time of the second order is found by looking up the value under Second RN in the cumulative probability distribution for hours per order and adding this time to the time of the first order. The time for the first three orders, first four orders, and all five orders is found in an analagous fashion. Thus, in the first trial, if one order is placed, it takes 40 hours; if two orders are placed, they take 45 hours; if three orders are placed, they take 80 hours; if four orders are placed, they take 120 hours; and if 5 orders are placed, they take 135 hours.

Figure 23-3
Random Numbers used with Figure 23-2

One Order	Two Orders	Three Orders	Four Orders	Five Orders	First RN	Second RN	Third RN	Fourth RN	Fifth RN
40	45	80	120	135	0.9773	0.0294	0.7816	0.9719	0.1011
30	65	95	115	140	0.6732	0.8726	0.5614	0.2974	0.4580
25	50	85	110	140	0.3495	0.3825	0.8407	0.3454	0.6572
30	65	105	120	160	0.7009	0.7553	0.9809	0.1510	0.9319
30	70	85	120	140	0.7313	0.9970	0.1235	0.8144	0.2161
35	70	85	120	140	0.8719	0.8936	0.1494	0.8441	0.2803

What remains is to use the number of orders placed in the first trial (which we previously determined to be 1 and which is located in cell B19) to define the Total Time for the trial, which will be stored in cell C19. Cell C19 could have been defined by using @**HLOOKUP**, the horizontal lookup function, as will be shown in the next example. In this case, however, we elected to use the @**IF** function. @**IF** contains three arguments @**IF(A,B,C)** and says if A is true use B else use C. It is perfectly legal to nest @**IF** statements, such as @**IF(A,B,@IF(C,D,E))** which says if A is true use B else if C is true use D else use E. In this instance, cell C19 reads

@**IF(B19 = 0,0,@IF(B19 = 1,H19,@IF(B19 = 2,I19,@IF(B19 = 3,J19,@IF(B1 = 4,K19,L19)))))**

which says if B19 indicates 0 orders the time required is 0, otherwise, if B19 indicates 1 order, the time required is shown in cell H19, otherwise if B19 indicates 2 orders the time required is shown in cell I19, otherwise if B19 indicates 3 orders the time required is shown in cell J19, otherwise if B19 indicates 4 orders the time required is shown in cell K19, otherwise the time required is shown in cell L19. Cell C19 implements the horizontal lookup function in an alternate format and also illustrates the usefulness of the lookup function.

The reader should now be able to verify that 40, the first value in the Total Time column, is properly defined. The reader may wish to use Figure 23-3 to verify each of the values in the Total Time column of Figure 23-2.

The remaining values at the bottom of Figure 23-2 were obtained exactly as in the manual computations used earlier. The hours available were obtained by multiplying the number of machines by 8 hours per machine per day. The hours idle are defined whenever the hours available exceeds total time required and are found by taking hours available minus hours required. Whenever total time exceeds hours available, hours backlogged is defined by taking total time minus hours available. Idle cost and backlog cost are defined by taking hours idle and hours backlogged and multiplying by their respective cost factors.

In the upper right portion of Figure 23-2, the result of 100 replications of the experiment with 8, 9, 10, 11, 12, and 13 machines is shown. The total cost is minimized when 11 machines are utilized. The result of the 100 replications for the 11 machine case is also shown. The reader may have noted that the 12 machine case shows little additional total cost and that the back-order cost for the 11 machine case is quite high. Before deciding to use 11 machines, management should carefully consider whether the cost of back-ordering is completely defined. There is very little difference, given the current data, between using 11 machines and using 12 machines, but the use of 12 machines would significantly lower the number of backorders compared to the 11 machine case.

The interested reader may wish to replicate this spreadsheet. The description given should be sufficient to completely replicate the spreadsheet. For 100 trials, worksheet recomputation requires approximately 10 to 15 seconds using a 16 MhZ 80386 machine with 80387 math coprocessor. This result implies a recomputation time of approximately 10 minutes for a first generation machine lacking a math coprocessor. The reader may, therefore, wish to use fewer than 100 replications.

Another Simulation Example

As a further example of a simulation problem, consider the following situation. A production process manufactures about 12 units per day when fully loaded; specifically, it manufactures 12 units 80 percent of the time, 11 units 10 percent of the time, and 13 units 10 percent of the time. Orders are received according to the following distribution:

Number of Orders/Day	Frequency
5	0.10
6	0.15
7	0.25
8	0.35
9	0.15

Demand that is not immediately satisfied is lost. Each order can be for one or more units. The distribution of order size is as follows:

Units/Order	Frequency
1	0.5
2	0.3
3	0.2

Some units not sold on a given day can be saved to satisfy demand the following day, but because of perishability we cannot save them a second day.

The company is considering expanding sales and wants to see what it has to do to production to handle various sales increases. The principal concern is with the service level. The new sales levels to be examined are for the following distributions:

Number of Orders/Day	Frequency
6	0.10
7	0.10
8	0.35
9	0.30
10	0.15

Units/Order	Frequency
1	0.2
2	0.5
3	0.3

The cases to be considered are (1) no increase in number of orders, but increased units per order; (2) increased orders, but no increase in size of orders; and (3) increase in both orders and size of orders. As a start, we will leave production as is or increase it by two units a day.

To facilitate analysis, the spreadsheet described in Appendix 23A has been developed. Using it we first simulate our current situation to see whether the simulated results resemble current practice. This test of the accuracy or validity of the simulation model is sometimes termed *face validity*. After all, if we cannot simulate the current situation, how can we have any confidence in our simulation of predicted situations? Another check on whether the simulation is working properly is to compare the theoretical means or averages of the distributions to the averages of the samples. Other tests may also be performed to verify that the simulation process is working properly. Since the service levels of the simulation are reasonably close to what we have observed, we can go on to explore the impact of increased sales.

Table 23-4 summarizes some of our simulation runs. Note that with no change in production and an increase in orders, service drops from 94 percent to 83 percent. To compensate for the increased orders, we must raise production by 2 units per day to get a satisfactory 97 percent service level. But with increased units per order as well, we must increase production to 17 units each day, on average, in order to have a 95 percent service level.

Table 23-4
Service Level Changes as a Function of
Demand and Production Changes

Demand Conditions	MPL*	Service Level
Current Level	12	94%
Increased Orders	12	83%
	14	97%
Increased Order and Units/Order	12	66%
	14	78%
	17	95%

Mean Production Level (units per day)

Pitfalls and Safeguards

Most mathematical models of real world systems greatly oversimplify because, as the simple model is modified to achieve greater correspondence with reality, the mathematical complexities increase at a much greater rate than the model's correspondence to reality. For instance, note that our first example does not consider the possibility of machine failure. Inclusion of that factor could have been accomplished with the addition of a third probability distribution defining the probability of machine failures. Although it was omitted to keep the example simple, its inclusion would be desirable if machine failures were relatively common.

In addition, there is the slight possibility that nonrepresentative inputs might be generated by simulation. In one run of only 100 repetitions, there is always the possibility that the average RN, and therefore the average event value, may be considerably above or below the expected 0.50 value. Should this occur, the simulation results could be misleading.

A method exists for avoiding this pitfall. Running the simulation more than once, say four or five times, substantially reduces the possibility of nonrepresentative event values. Each run must be made with a unique set of RN's. The average measure of effectiveness value of these runs is used to evaluate the effect of the specific values of the controlled variables (number of machines in the example) being compared.

The values in Table 23-4 are the result of having replicated each run three times. Three was deemed sufficient because the service levels differed only slightly between runs.

Sensitivity Analysis

After the initial solution of the problem is obtained, a sensitivity analysis is advisable. Such analysis evaluates the impact of changes in the parameters. For instance, would the optimum number of machines in our first example still be 9 if the cost of idle time were $3.50 instead of $3.00, or if the cost of backordering were $5.25 instead of $5.00, or if processing time were reduced by 10 percent across the board because of increased operating efficiencies, or if the number of orders turned out to be 15 percent higher than anticipated? Sensitivity analysis is performed by running the simulation with one or more of these factors changed to the alternate possibility and the resulting costs calculated.

Such an analysis enables us to evaluate how sensitive the decision is to variations in real world conditions. If changes similar to those described above have little or no effect on the decision, the situation is described as being insensitive relative to those factors. Each decision situation must be examined to determine its sensitivity to changes in specific parameters.

Building a Simulation Model

Each possible simulation situation must be studied before a model is developed for it. When a decision criterion, such as minimizing total costs or maximizing rate of return, has been selected, the designer of the simulation experiment must determine which variables influence the result and how they influence it. This requires that the designer possess adequate knowledge of and an insight into the real world situation. Without this capacity the odds are that the model will not tell it like it is. For example, the designer must decide whether to include the possibility of machine failure.

After the model has been developed, it must be validated. The model validation process begins with the usual questions: Does the model appear accurate? Does it provide reasonable answers? In short, does it have face validity? Do others familiar with the real world situation agree that the model is representative and the results reasonable? In addition, the model can be run using historical data and the results compared with actual results. For instance, does actual receipt of a specific number of orders and hours per order result in the same costs predicted by the model?

Computers

The digital computer's speed and accuracy has made the application of simulation concepts to industrial problems practical. A computer cannot construct a model of the real world, nor can it select the settings of controlled variables for the experiment. It cannot evaluate assumptions or estimate the extent the future will conform to the past unless given specific instruction how to do so. The designer still performs these vital functions.

Much of the early use of computers in simulation was performed using standard programming languages, such as FORTRAN and ALGOL. Though developing the FORTRAN program and running the simulation model on a digital computer was faster and more efficient than using a desk calculator, writing and debugging the program was a tedious and time-consuming task. The development of special simulation languages substantially reduced this task. Detailed descriptions and analyses of these languages are contained in the selected readings at the end of this chapter.

Network Based Languages

With the advent of the microcomputer, specialized simulation languages have become very sophisticated. Some of the most sophisticated permit a problem to be modeled by drawing the flow of events as a network. For example, Figure 23-4 shows a four-box network model of a bank with two tellers. Box 1 creates customers arriving at the bank. The time between arriving customers averages 40 seconds and follows a negative exponential distribution. As customers arrive, 60 percent choose the express teller, who handles small transactions, and 40 percent choose the regular teller window. Boxes 2 and 3 represent the two tellers and the queues of people awaiting service. Box 2 indicates that Teller 1 requires an average of 60 seconds, the standard deviation is 10 seconds, and the distribution is lognormal. Box 3 indicates that Teller 2 requires an average of 95 seconds per transaction, the standard deviation is 15 seconds, and the distribution is lognormal. Box 4 represents the customer leaving the bank. At Box 4, data is collected on the time each customer spends in the system.

Both the negative exponential distribution and the lognormal distribution are skewed to the right, indicating that the majority of entities are smaller than

Figure 23-4
GEMS Network of a Bank

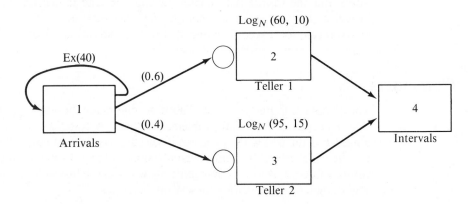

the mean value but a few entities are much larger than the mean value. The exponential distribution is frequently used to model arrival processes. The lognormal distribution is frequently used to model service processes.

Codes are not needed with network based languages; the information contained in the network diagram is simply translated into data input. The GEMS language provides an intelligent menu system from which one chooses the type box, the definition of arcs connecting boxes (a variety of options exist for routing arriving transactions), and the definition of the probability distribution employed at each box. Figure 23-5 shows both the GEMS model that is created by the namelist menu interactive portion of GEMS and the result of running the bank for 20 simulated days of 8 hours (28,800 seconds).

Interpretation of the GEMS Input Data is not important. The data set is presented primarily to show an example of a language that does not require programming. The $RUN data set describes the number of replications (passes), boxes, parameter sets, time to stop, and other values. The $PAR PSN1 line describes the arrival process. PSN2 describes Teller 1 while PSN3 describes Teller 2. (The extra parameters in the parameter sets are minimum and maximum legal values.) The $BOX ID = 1 card describes Box 1. It provides a name and the parameter set to be used, and defines the arcs to be taken. The ID = 2 and ID = 3 cards describe the two tellers. They define the parameter set and define the boxes as queue boxes. Because the maximum queue length and the queue discipline are not specified, the default values of infinite maximum queue and first-come-first-served queue discipline will be used.

The results show that more than 13,000 customers were serviced during the 20 simulated days and that each customer averaged just under 6 minutes (356+ seconds) in the bank. The shortest time in the bank was less than one minute (32+ seconds), while the longest time was 2,269+ seconds, nearly 40 minutes. The queue box statistics show that the express teller, Teller 1, was busy 88.3 percent of each day and processed an average of 423 customers. There was an average queue of 3+ people waiting for Teller 1, and the average wait was 211+ seconds. Teller 2 was busy 90.7 percent of the time and processed 274.3 customers per day on the average. The average queue for Teller 2 was 3.8 people. The average wait was 274+ seconds.

The queue information is quite useful to the manager. In the case of the bank, the average waiting time is slightly high, and the maximum time in the bank is quite high. The manager may wish to consider adding a third teller.

A bank was chosen for this example because the arrival pattern is more easily described than is the arrival pattern of jobs to a manufacturing work center. In a manufacturing work center, each batch might contain a unique number of parts to be worked on, and the distribution of time per part may also be unique to the type of part. A manufacturing facility is somewhat more complex to model than a bank, but the information the manager wants from the model, such as average busy percentage for the worker or average time in queue for the job, is very similar.

Figure 23-5
GEMS Model and Results for Bank Example

GEMS Input Data

```
$RUN NATRIB=2,NPASS=20,NBOX=4,NPARS=3,ISEED=1357,TSTOP=28800,QUE=T,NAMES=T,$END
$PAR PSN=1,DTYPE=EX,PARAM=40,5,1000,$END
$PAR PSN=2,DTYPE=LO,PARAM=60,1,1000,10,$END
$PAR PSN=3,DTYPE=LO,PARAM=95,1,1000,15,$END
$BOX ID=1,NAME=ARRIVALS,NFRL=0,PSN=1,PROB=.6,0,.4,0,IFOLL=2,1,3,1,$END
$BOX ID=2,NAME=TELLER 1,PSN=2,QBOX=T,IFOLL=4,$END
$BOX ID=3,NAME=TELLER 2,PSN=3,QBOX=T,IFOLL=4,$END
$BOX ID=4,NAME=INTERVALS,$END
$STAT IN=-3,1,4,9,0,
$END
```

GEMS Results

GEMS-II PROBLEM NUMBER 23-3
FINAL REPORT
FOR   20 PASS RUNS

**** TIME AND ASSOCIATED NETWORK COST STATISTICS ****

BOX NUM	NAME	STAT TYPE	NO. OF OBS.	MEAN	STD.DEV	MIN.	MAX.
4	INTERVALS	INTV	13954	356.831	301.312	32.438	2269.979

**** QUEUE BOX STATISTICS ****

QUE NUM	STAT. TYPE	MEAN	STD.DEV	MIN. MEAN	MAX. MEAN	TIME SHOT
	TELLER 1					
2	NUMB BUSY SERVER	.883	.032	.820	.937	
2	QUEUE LENGTH	3.175	1.248	1.418	6.184	
2	WAITING TIME	211.324	75.486	102.126	392.278	
2	BUSY %	88.272	3.241	81.966	93.724	
2	ENTITIES PASSED	423.400	16.330	398.000	454.000	
2	MAX QUEUE LENGTH	13.400	4.083	7.000	24.000	
2	NO. NONZERO WAIT	377.200	29.138	325.000	426.000	
2	NONZERO WAITING	238.132	78.242	125.693	419.045	
	FINAL STATUS: Q-LENGTH 1 IDLE SERVERS 0					
	TELLER 2					
3	NUMB BUSY SERVER	.907	.039	.813	.986	
3	QUEUE LENGTH	3.806	1.868	1.221	9.427	
3	WAITING TIME	384.871	173.544	139.572	904.991	
3	BUSY %	90.749	3.910	81.273	98.580	
3	ENTITIES PASSED	274.300	11.453	247.000	297.000	
3	MAX QUEUE LENGTH	13.150	3.870	6.000	24.000	
3	NO. NONZERO WAIT	252.400	24.803	197.000	307.000	
3	NONZERO WAITING	421.330	171.297	178.539	932.980	
	FINAL STATUS: Q-LENGTH 0 IDLE SERVERS 0					

Network languages such as GEMS, SLAM, and SIMAN are available on microcomputers and truly can simulate manufacturing facilities without programming. Because of the ease with which the shop can now be simulated and because of the low cost of microcomputers as well as microcomputer software, simulation is now affordable even by small plants. The SLAM language and the SIMAN language both have extensions permitting animated output of model results so a modeler can directly observe the systems behavior. For larger shops, network based languages are useful in modeling small portions of the shop and for rapidly prototyping simulation models of the full shop. Very large simulations are still quite often written in general purpose languages, especially FORTRAN, in order to achieve very fast execution. Simulation of large facilities remains an expensive proposition, although future developments in microcomputing, especially the Intel 80486 and 80586 chips, should make the simulation of very large facilities on microcomputers quite feasible.

Benefits of Simulation

Simulation is relatively inexpensive. The cost of simulating a production system and using the model to experiment with different policies (for example, different scheduling priority systems) is much lower than experimenting with the system in reality. Simulation also provides those involved with a better understanding of the situation. It is an excellent training device, since the individuals involved get a feel for the interaction of the controlled variables and their impact on decision results.

Some Applications. William Lee and Curtis McLaughlin (1974) reported on the development and implementation of a simulation model of the aggregate material management function in an $11 million firm. They evaluated decisions concerning work force size and stability, overtime, inventory fluctuations, and cash flow over given operating ranges of demand and capacity.

Stanley C. Gardiner (1988) studied the interaction of single stage lot-size models (EOQ, lot-for-lot, period order quantity, etc.) and dispatching rules (first-in, first-out, earliest due date, etc.) in a material requirements planning system. He examined various combinations of these rules under a master production schedule with slight instability. Gardner's article is typical of the research going on in this area. Earlier papers on MRP lot sizing are by David A. Collier (1980) and by Stephen H. Goodman, Stanley T. Hardy, and Joseph R. Biggs (1977). Their results examine these rules for various performance criteria.

Frederick C. Weston, Jr. (1980), looked at EOQ, reorder point, and exponential smoothing interactions in an elementary setting. He demonstrated, among other things, that the results of this type of system may be quite contrary to generally accepted theory.

SUMMARY

Stochastic simulation is a synthetic method of dynamically representing a decision system over time and of evaluating the alternate settings of controlled variables. It is quicker and less expensive than trial and error in the real world. It is especially useful when the complexity of a situation prevents application of an analytical model. Monte Carlo simulation works because (1) simulated event values occur with the same frequency as in the real world and (2) sequential combinations of event values have the same probability of occurrence as in the real world. The advent of the digital computer, with its capacity to accurately handle a large quantity of data through many mathematical steps in a relatively short period of time, has been a boon to the utilization of Monte Carlo simulation. The development of special simulation programming languages has reduced the cost of simulation. Simple Monte Carlo simulations can even be developed with an electronic spreadsheet. For very large models, languages such as FORTRAN are more cost effective.

The design of the simulation model and the experiment is the cornerstone of the process. Critical assumptions are always necessary: Will the future conform to the past? If historical data are not to be used, can a standard probability distribution be used to generate inputs? Inaccurate assumptions and sloppy experiments can generate misleading answers. Stochastic simulation is no panacea, but it is a valuable tool when applied properly.

EXERCISES

1. A common maintenance problem involves group replacement. For example, if a fluorescent light fixture contains three lights and one fails, should all of them be replaced? Group replacement of lights is a common practice in industry, due to the cost of having a maintenance person come out, climb the ladder, and replace the light. The correct policy depends on the service life distribution of the lights. The following table gives the observed service life distribution, in operating hours, for the light presently used:

Service Life	Probability
1,000	0.05
1,200	0.25
1,400	0.20
1,600	0.20
1,800	0.15
2,000	0.10
2,200	0.05

The cost of each light is $2. The cost to have a light fixture serviced is $15, independent of the number of lights replaced.

Simulate the process of replacing lights for a department that operates a single three-light fixture 24 hours per day, 365 days per year. Simulate an entire year (8,760 hours) five times. Determine which of the following policies has the lowest cost:

a. Replace only the light that fails.
b. Replace all lights when one fails.
c. When one light fails, replace all lights that have more than 1,200 hours of service.

2. Repeat the experiment in Exercise 1, except assume that the life of a light follows a negative exponential distribution with a mean time to failure of 1,000 hours. (Hint: A random deviate from a negative exponential distribution with mean X can be found by taking **-ln(rnd)*X**, where ln is the natural logarithm and rnd is a common random number such as that produced by the **RND** function in BASIC or the **@RAND** function in Lotus 1-2-3, i.e., a uniform, 0-1 random variable.)

3. Shown below is an activity on arc representation of a project having five activities. For each activity an optimistic, most likely, and pessimistic time has been estimated. Use the Monte Carlo simulation process to estimate the duration of the process. Use a sample of size 10 (100 if an electronic spreadsheet can be used).

	Time Estimates		
Activity	Optimistic	Most Likely	Pessimistic
A	1.6	2.8	4.3
B	3.4	4.6	6.0
C	0.8	2.0	2.8
D	1.4	2.5	3.5
E	2.1	2.9	4.2

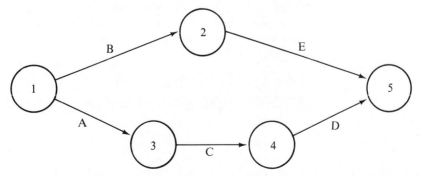

4. Some people advocate choosing the alpha factor for exponential smoothing by simulating past experience using different alpha factors and choosing that which minimizes the error. For the following data, what value of

alpha among the set (0.1, 0.2, 0.3, 0.4) minimizes the sum of the absolute values of the errors? If an electronic spreadsheet is available, create a one-way data table to perform this experiment.

Period	Demand	Period	Demand	Period	Demand
1	55	11	48	21	50
2	65	12	45	22	55
3	62	13	40	23	60
4	56	14	42	24	57
5	57	15	49	25	65
6	51	16	48	26	55
7	58	17	43	27	57
8	60	18	57	28	63
9	52	19	49	29	64
10	42	20	45	30	50

5. Create a spreadsheet like the one shown in Appendix 23A and use it to determine service level under the following conditions:

Number of Orders/Day	Frequency	Units/Order	Frequency
6	0.1	1	0.5
7	0.2	2	0.4
8	0.3	3	0.1
9	0.3		
10	0.1		

a. Produce 16 units each day.
b. Produce an average of 16 units, but 10 percent of the time produce 15 units and 10 percent of the time produce 17 units.

6. When equipment breaks down, the repairman must go to a tool crib to get necessary tools and parts. An expansion in the number of machines is expected, and to minimize downtime the company is considering having two clerks on duty to serve 50 percent more repairmen. But first it wants to simulate the situation to see how long repairmen wait under various assumptions. The distribution of time between arrivals is as follows:

Interarrival Time (minutes)	Probability	Service Time (minutes)	Probability
10	0.10	7	0.10
11	0.30	8	0.25
12	0.25	9	0.30
13	0.20	10	0.20
14	0.15	11	0.15

a. Perform a simulation for 50 arrivals, starting with no one at the crib, and compute the average wait, average number waiting, and average service time.

b. Now assume the arrival distribution becomes:

Interarrival Time (minutes)	Probability
7	0.10
8	0.25
9	0.30
10	0.20
11	0.15

Perform the simulation twice more, first with one clerk, then with two clerks, and compute the same statistics. (Assume the second clerk has the same service time distribution as the first.)

c. If the expansion occurs, should the company add a clerk?

7. A product is assembled in a three-station assembly line. Because of variability in the materials, the time at each station is a random variable. The following table gives the time distribution at each station.

Station 1		Station 2		Station 3	
Minutes	Probability	Minutes	Probability	Minutes	Probability
3.2	0.1	3.2	0.05	3.0	0.05
3.3	0.2	3.3	0.20	3.2	0.15
3.4	0.4	3.4	0.50	3.4	0.60
3.5	0.2	3.5	0.20	3.6	0.15
3.6	0.1	3.6	0.05	3.8	0.05

a. Assume no buffer stock is permitted between stations. Hence, Worker 2 must wait for Worker 1 to finish before Work Station 2 can start. A similar situation exists for Worker 3. How long will it take to process 20 jobs?

b. Assume one unit of buffer stock is permitted between stations, but the system starts with no inventory between stations. How long will it take to process 20 jobs?

c. Compare worker idle time for a and b.

In performing this simulation, use a network based language like SLAM or SIMAN or GPSS if one is available. Otherwise, perform the simulation manually.

SELECTED READINGS

Chorafas, D. N. *Systems and Simulation.* New York: Academic Press, Inc., 1965.

Collier, David A. "The Interaction of Single-Stage Lot Size Models in a Material Requirements Planning System." *Production and Inventory Management* 21, No. 4 (1980): 11-20.

Fishman, G. S. "Estimating Sample Size in Computer Simulation Experiments." *Management Science* 18, no. 1 (1971): 21-38.

Forrester, J. W. *Industrial Dynamics*. Cambridge, MA: The MIT Press, 1961.

Gardiner, Stanley C. "A Study of MRP Lot Sizing and Dispatching Rules With MPS Instability." Ph.D. diss., University of Georgia, 1988.

Goodman, Stephen H., Stanley T. Hardy, and Joseph R. Biggs. "Lot Sizing Rules in a Hierarchical Multistage Inventory System." *Production and Inventory Management* 18, no. 1 (1977): 104-116.

Gordon, Geoffrey. *System Simulation*. Englewood Cliffs, NJ: Prentice-Hall, Inc., 1969.

Gordon, Geoffrey. *The Application of GPSS V to Discrete System Simulation*. Englewood Cliffs, NJ: Prentice-Hall, Inc., 1975.

IBM. *Bibliography on Simulation Form 320-0924*. White Plains, NY, 1966.

Kiviat, P. J., R. Villanueva, and H. M. Markowitz. *The SIMSCRIPT II Programming Language*. Englewood Cliffs, NJ: Prentice-Hall, Inc., 1969.

Kiviat, P. J., R. Villanueva, and H. M. Markowitz. *The SIMSCRIPT II.5 Programming Language*. Los Angeles, CA: Consolidated Analysis Centers, Inc., 1973.

Lee, W. B., and C. P. McLaughlin. "Corporate Simulation Models for Aggregate Materials Management." *Production and Inventory Management* 15, no. 1 (1974): 55-67.

Maisel, Herbert, and Guiliano Gnugnoli. *Simulation of Discrete Stochastic Systems*. Chicago, IL: Science Research Associates, Inc., 1972.

McMillan, Claude, Jr., and Richard F. Gonzales. *Systems Analysis: A Computer Approach to Decision Models*. rev. ed. Homewood, IL: Richard D. Irwin, Inc., 1968.

Mize, J. H., and J. G. Cox. *Essentials of Simulation*. Englewood Cliffs, NJ: Prentice-Hall, Inc., 1968.

Naylor, T. J., J. L. Balintfy, D. S. Burdick, and Kong Chu. *Computer Simulation Techniques*. New York: John Wiley & Sons, Inc., 1966.

Pegden, C. Dennis. *Introduction to SIMAN*. State College, PA: Systems Modeling Corp., 1987.

Pritsker, A. A. B. *Introduction to Simulation and SLAM II*. New York: John Wiley & Sons, Inc., 1986.

Salvador, Michael S., et al. "Mathematical Modeling Optimization and Simulation Improve Large-Scale Finished Goods Inventory Management." *Production and Inventory Control Management* (Second Quarter 1975).

Shannon, Robert E. *Systems Simulation—the Art and Science*. Englewood Cliffs, NJ: Prentice-Hall, Inc., 1975.

Watson, Hugh J., and John H. Blackstone, Jr. *Computer Simulation*. New York: John Wiley & Sons, Inc., 1989.

Weston, Frederick C., Jr. "A Simulation Approach to Examining Traditional EOQ/EOP and Single Order Exponential Smoothing Efficiency Adopting a Small Business Perspective." *Production and Inventory Management* 21, no. 2 (1980): 67-83.

Wyman, F. P. *Simulation Modeling: A Guide to Using SIMSCRIPT*. New York: John Wiley & Sons, Inc., 1970.

APPENDIX 23A

In this appendix, we discuss the development of a Lotus 1-2-3 version of the simulation model for the second example in the chapter. The basic model is shown in Table 23A-1. For convenience of reference, standard Lotus 1-2-3 row and column designations (numbers for rows, letters for columns) have been added to the top and left margins of Table 23A-1.

Table 23A-1
The Basic Model

	A	B	C	D	E	F	G	H	I
1					Lotus 1-2-3 Version of Monte Carlo				
2					Simulation				
3			DEMAND DISTRIBUTIONS				SUPPLY DISTRIBUTION		
4		Cum.	# of	Cum.	Units per		Cum.	Units per	
5		Prob.	Orders	Prob.	Order		Prob.	Order	
6		0	5	0	1		0	12	
7		0.1	6	0.5	2		0.8	11	
8		0.25	7	0.8	3		0.9	10	
9		0.5	8	1	3		1	10	
10		0.85	9						
11		1	9						
12						SERVICE RATE:		0.94422	
13									
14									
15		Random	Number	Number	Random	Units	Units	Excess	Lost
16	Trial	Number	Orders	Units	Number	Produced	Sold	Units	Sales
17									
18	1	0.208302	6	12	0.177157	12	12	0	0
19	2	0.144529	6	13	0.954203	10	10	0	3
20	3	0.47823	7	10	0.351461	12	10	2	0
21	4	0.152237	6	11	0.147544	12	11	3	0

The area bounded by B6 and C11 contains the cumulative distribution function for the number of orders. For any given trial, the number of orders to be used in that trial is shown in column C, beginning in cell C18. The formula for cell C18 is **@VLOOKUP(B18,B$6.C$11,1)**. This function says to compare the random number in cell B18 to the probabilities in column B, beginning at B6, and locate the last number not larger than B18. Then return the value offset one column to the right of the appropriate cumulative probability value. B18 contains the value 0.20+. This is larger than 0.10 but smaller than 0.25 so the value 6 is returned. Once the number of orders for a given trial is known, this must be converted into the number of units ordered during the trial. The number of units is performed by applying a horizontal lookup to the data contained in Table 23A-2, which represents another area of the same spreadsheet.

Table 23A-2
Determining the Number of Units

	J	K	L	M	N	O	P	Q	R	S
	One	Two	Three	Four	Five	Six	Seven	Eight	Nine	Ten
15	Order	Orders	Orders	Orders	Orders	Orders	Orders	Orders	Orders	Orders
16										
17	1	2	3	4	5	6	7	8	9	10
18	3	4	6	9	11	12	13	15	18	19
19	2	5	7	8	11	13	14	16	19	21
20	1	2	5	6	7	8	10	11	12	13

The argument used for cell D18 is **@HLOOKUP(C18,J17.S117,A18)**. This says to find in the area from J17 to S17 the last value not larger than C18, and return the value contained in the row that is offset from row 17 by the value of A18. Since A18 is 1, the initial offset is one row. Cell C18 contains the value 6. This corresponds to the value of cell O17, so the value of cell O18, which is 12, is returned. There are, for this trial, 12 units ordered in 6 separate orders.

The number of units ordered is obtained by finding the number of units in the first order, then the first two orders, and so on through the tenth order. The random numbers used in each order are generated through the **@RAND** function and are shown in Table 23A-3. The formula for cell J18 is **@VLOOKUP(T18,D6.E10,1)**. This formula says to look up the random number in cell T18 in the cumulative distribution function shown in cells D6 to E10 and return the appropriate number from column E. The formula for cell K18 is **@VLOOKUP(U18,D6.E10,1)+J18**, which says look up the number of units ordered in the second order and add that to the number of units ordered in the first to obtain the number of units ordered in the first two orders. The formula for cell K18 can then be copied to cells L18 to S18.

Table 23A-3
The Random Numbers Used to Determine the Number of Units

	T	U	V	W	X	Y	Z	AA
15	First	Second	Third	Fourth	Fifth	Sixth	Seventh	Eighth
16	RN	RN	RN	RN	RN	RN	RN	RN
17								
18	0.9773	0.0294	0.7816	0.9719	0.5658	0.264798	0.467912	0.798573
19	0.6732	0.8726	0.5614	0.2974	0.9224	0.682418	0.22655	0.736083
20	0.3495	0.3825	0.8407	0.3454	0.3487	0.233784	0.782802	0.328414
21	0.7009	0.7553	0.9809	0.151	0.5554	0.20586	0.020486	0.322256

Once demand is known for the trial, supply is determined by finding the random number shown in column E in the cumulative distribution of supply located in columns G and H. For the first trial, the random number is 0.177, which is larger than 0 but smaller than 0.8, so a value of 12 is returned.

When row 18 is completely defined, cells A18 to AA18, this row (which defines the procedure) can be copied to the next 99 rows to obtain 100 trials. Note the use of mixed and absolute address references to fix the location of the probability distribution tables to be used by the lookup operations. In the first trial, supply is 12 and demand is 12, and there are no shortages or excess units. In Trial 2, 13 units are demanded but only 10 are produced, so there is a lost sale of 3 units. This process is continued for 100 trials to obtain a service rate slightly in excess of 94 percent, as reported in the text.

Once the basic spreadsheet has been established, it is a fairly simple matter to change the parameters. Table 23A-4 presents the same model except that the probability distributions have been changed to reflect the higher sales rate, and the operations have been improved to increase the number of units sold. With proper foresight in setting up the first version of the model, the other versions of the simulation can be executed merely by changing the data in the various probability distributions. As reported in the text, with a maximum production level of 14 and a higher demand rate, the service rate drops to about 78 percent.

Table 23A-4
The Expanded Sales Case with 14 Machines

Lotus 1-2-3 Version of Monte Carlo
Simulation for Example 23-2

DEMAND DISTRIBUTIONS				SUPPLY DISTRIBUTION	
Cum. Prob.	# of Orders	Cum. Prob.	Units per Order	Cum. Prob.	Units per Order
0	5	0	1	0	14
0	6	0.2	2	0.8	13
0.1	7	0.7	3	0.9	12
0.2	8	1	3	1	10
0.55	9				
0.85	10				
1	10		SERVICE RATE:	0.783922	

Trial	Random Number	Number Orders	Number Units	Random Number	Units Produced	Units Sold	Excess Units	Lost Sales
1	0.208302	8	19	0.177157	14	14	0	5
2	0.144529	7	16	0.954203	12	12	0	4
3	0.47823	8	18	0.351461	14	14	0	4
4	0.152237	7	15	0.147544	14	14	0	1

APPENDIX A
AREAS OF THE NORMAL CURVE

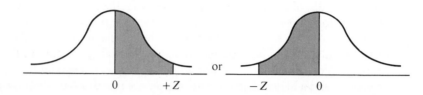

or

Z	0.00	0.01	0.02	0.03	0.04	0.05	0.06	0.07	0.08	0.09
0.0	0.0000	0.0040	0.0080	0.0120	0.0160	0.0199	0.0239	0.0279	0.0319	0.0359
0.1	0.0398	0.0438	0.0478	0.0517	0.0557	0.0596	0.0636	0.0675	0.0714	0.0753
0.2	0.0793	0.0832	0.0871	0.0910	0.0948	0.0987	0.1026	0.1064	0.1103	0.1141
0.3	0.1179	0.1217	0.1255	0.1293	0.1331	0.1368	0.1406	0.1443	0.1480	0.1517
0.4	0.1554	0.1591	0.1628	0.1664	0.1700	0.1736	0.1772	0.1808	0.1844	0.1879
0.5	0.1915	0.1950	0.1985	0.2019	0.2054	0.2088	0.2123	0.2157	0.2190	0.2224
0.6	0.2257	0.2291	0.2324	0.2357	0.2389	0.2422	0.2454	0.2486	0.2517	0.2549
0.7	0.2580	0.2611	0.2642	0.2673	0.2704	0.2734	0.2764	0.2794	0.2823	0.2852
0.8	0.2881	0.2910	0.2939	0.2967	0.2995	0.3023	0.3051	0.3078	0.3106	0.3233
0.9	0.3159	0.3186	0.3212	0.3238	0.3264	0.3289	0.3315	0.3340	0.3365	0.3389
1.0	0.3413	0.3438	0.3461	0.3485	0.3508	0.3531	0.3554	0.3577	0.3599	0.3621
1.1	0.3643	0.3665	0.3686	0.3708	0.3729	0.3749	0.3770	0.3790	0.3810	0.3830
1.2	0.3849	0.3869	0.3888	0.3907	0.3925	0.3744	0.3962	0.3980	0.3997	0.4015
1.3	0.4032	0.4049	0.4066	0.4082	0.4099	0.4115	0.4131	0.4147	0.4162	0.4177
1.4	0.4192	0.4207	0.4222	0.4236	0.4251	0.4265	0.4279	0.4292	0.4306	0.4319
1.5	0.4332	0.4345	0.4357	0.4370	0.4382	0.4394	0.4406	0.4418	0.4429	0.4441
1.6	0.4452	0.4463	0.4474	0.4484	0.4495	0.4505	0.4515	0.4525	0.4535	0.4545
1.7	0.4554	0.4564	0.4573	0.4582	0.4591	0.4599	0.4608	0.4616	0.4625	0.4633
1.8	0.4641	0.4649	0.4656	0.4664	0.4671	0.4678	0.4686	0.4693	0.4699	0.4706
1.9	0.4713	0.4719	0.4726	0.4732	0.4738	0.4744	0.4750	0.4758	0.4761	0.4767
2.0	0.4772	0.4778	0.4783	0.4788	0.4793	0.4798	0.4803	0.4808	0.4812	0.4817
2.1	0.4821	0.4826	0.4830	0.4834	0.4838	0.4842	0.4846	0.4850	0.4854	0.4857
2.2	0.4861	0.4864	0.4868	0.4871	0.4875	0.4878	0.4881	0.4884	0.4887	0.4890
2.3	0.4893	0.4896	0.4898	0.4901	0.4904	0.4906	0.4909	0.4911	0.4913	0.4916
2.4	0.4918	0.4920	0.4922	0.4925	0.4927	0.4929	0.4931	0.4932	0.4934	0.4936
2.5	0.4938	0.4940	0.4941	0.4943	0.4945	0.4946	0.4948	0.4949	0.4951	0.4952
2.6	0.4953	0.4955	0.4956	0.4957	0.4959	0.4960	0.4961	0.4962	0.4963	0.4964
2.7	0.4965	0.4966	0.4967	0.4968	0.4969	0.4971	0.4970	0.4972	0.4973	0.4974
2.8	0.4974	0.4975	0.4976	0.4977	0.4977	0.4978	0.4979	0.4979	0.4980	0.4881
2.9	0.4981	0.4982	0.4982	0.4983	0.4984	0.4984	0.4985	0.4985	0.4986	0.4986
3.0	0.4986	0.4987	0.4987	0.4988	0.4988	0.4988	0.4989	0.4989	0.4989	0.4990

APPENDIX B
RANDOM NUMBER TABLE

4456	6279	0305	1620	1871	5406	1315	5918	9499	3462
6827	2841	0852	5538	4694	9457	2850	6500	3441	0815
8476	3021	6176	8220	1936	8112	6989	0021	6311	8153
9866	4888	3717	2425	0091	7593	7956	5138	8154	7296
9680	9970	6153	8321	4040	7087	6707	3439	0846	2686
4357	9650	7224	1016	9475	6465	2768	8918	4670	6684
7201	2848	3692	9681	0528	8416	2839	7182	5694	2412
4868	1548	3740	7339	5393	6557	1459	8444	1798	0685
1551	3249	4640	2883	5281	3584	1557	0865	7636	0116
3672	1885	4978	9381	4502	6020	5203	3317	1361	1949
0398	1290	9270	5236	1993	4632	7360	9113	8421	3669
7780	7757	5275	7252	7104	2075	7959	4787	0233	7982
6851	0770	6808	7186	4954	1816	0109	0466	8055	6188
8469	3456	7379	5834	9173	4923	4750	0913	4867	7550
0240	6828	2466	1219	2332	3758	4560	8788	0572	8688
3316	4379	0727	9942	6889	4149	2443	4213	8327	9584
9395	6093	6976	3267	1951	0107	2388	7170	2323	5242
0725	3430	2227	1980	3668	7632	3033	1828	9821	4587
8431	9349	8617	6618	9577	6695	6728	4338	2756	0637
6967	9934	9536	2095	9695	2943	9425	8172	6729	8541
5026	6684	7749	8317	9694	3190	9199	3559	7693	0526
5700	1032	6849	0833	3951	1261	3712	0091	9139	9314
1206	5148	3842	8079	8791	3255	9437	4048	5115	4090
0009	5598	3171	4299	8749	3773	7956	4519	6871	5563
6622	8914	5009	9687	1139	7202	7129	4873	3445	9192
6932	0640	3107	1811	6764	0582	7473	8636	9016	8143
4333	1926	0038	4904	7071	7152	6539	1361	2323	0031
4496	0206	0134	6054	0561	2113	6612	2519	5963	4013
9089	3062	2922	9879	3769	4687	3546	4006	5893	7301
1244	6792	2391	5740	4631	3021	7037	4304	3931	2642
8109	3787	9888	4051	8541	1009	5168	9875	8583	0846
8267	5247	0956	0762	9919	8593	8506	7839	2000	4913
4365	8312	8933	1556	4602	9596	1599	6511	3383	4818
3738	9179	0625	9851	0858	3660	2155	2842	1642	4533
2362	6246	1853	5135	9358	1355	0738	8345	2630	5329
9939	9865	3200	0732	4896	3999	6278	7555	8755	1937
6420	7756	8771	2535	5185	2284	5219	5596	1289	0615
2797	7650	3263	2781	4532	0240	4609	3903	8190	0696
1454	1221	5176	5425	2712	3623	1946	5682	2732	3681
3912	5862	6462	2180	1844	4273	7101	5149	0784	6421

APPENDIX C
NONINSTANTANEOUS RECEIPT

Selected items produced internally to stock also can be grouped to obtain the economic benefits of joint replenishment. For example, a group of items produced on a screw machine may share a major setup with relatively minor adjustments required for individual items once the major setup is made. In the hot rolling of steel shapes (e.g., angle iron), changing the large mill rolls for a family of sizes is a very major setup. Yet switching from one size to another requires only minor adjustments of guides to direct the steel to the proper grooves in the rolls. Textiles or paper products may be identical except for color. A major setup is made for the entire group with, again, relatively minor changes required as the colors of the final product are changed progressively from light to dark.

Producing an aggregate lot of a group of items internally results in inventory being increased gradually rather than in one large lot at a point in time. Each lot enters inventory gradually as it is completed; in fact, the value of inventory increases hourly as labor is expended during the production period. Figure C-1 illustrates this relationship.

Average inventory in the case of noninstantaneous receipt of an aggregate order equals $\Sigma Q_{\$_i}(1 - \Sigma D_{\$_i} \div \Sigma P_{\$_i}) \div 2$, where $D_{\$_i}$ = demand rate of individual Product i in dollars and $P_{\$_i}$ = production rate of Product i in dollars.

The minimum cost aggregate lot size model in the case of noninstantaneous receipt is determined in the typical manner. The first derivative of the total period cost model is set equal to zero and solved for $Q_\$^*$ as follows:

$$TC' = \frac{(S + \Sigma s_i)A}{Q_\$} + k(\Sigma Q_\$)(1 - \Sigma D_{\$_i} \div \Sigma P_{\$_i}) \div 2$$

$$TC' = 0 = -\frac{(S + \Sigma s_i)A}{(\Sigma Q_\$^*)^2} + (k \div 2)(1 - \Sigma D_{\$_i} \div \Sigma P_{\$_i})$$

$$Q_\$^* = \left[\frac{2(S + \Sigma s_i)A}{k(1 - \Sigma D_{\$_i} \div \Sigma P_{\$_i})}\right]^{1/2}$$

$$Q_{\$_i}^* = (a_i \div A)\Sigma Q_\$^*$$

$$Q_i^* = Q_{\$_i}^* \div C_i$$

Figure C-1
Aggregate Production Lot Size Example Data and Graphs
(Stock on Hand Versus Time)

A. Data

Item	Production Rate (daily) $(P_{\$_i})$	Demand Rate (daily) $(D_{\$_i})$	$Q_{\$_i}^*$	Inventory Value per Item in Week 1	2	3	4	5	6	7
A	$ 8.00	$1.60	$40.00	8	0	32	24	16	9	0
B	4.00	0.80	20.00	8	4	0	16	12	8	4
C	2.00	0.40	10.00	6	4	2	0	8	6	4
	$14.00	$2.80		22	8	34	40	36	22	8

B. Graphs (The major setup precedes manufacturing of Item A; minor setup times are absorbed in the production rate for each item.)

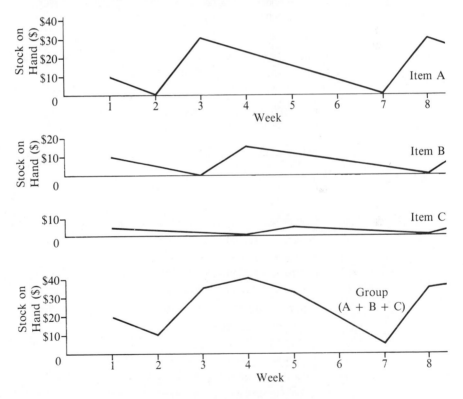

Table C-1, for example, contains data regarding a group of items manufactured on the same equipment with one major setup for the group and a minor setup for each item. Production and demand rates in dollars have been calculated by multiplying the unit cost of each item by its production and demand rates in units.

When determining the actual lot size, the results of the calculations in Table C-1 are combined with practical considerations such as container size, process yield, and the number of units that can be made from the normal unit of raw material. The actual lot sizes for Items 1 through 5 might be 900, 320, 700, 400 and 400, respectively.

Table C-1
Data, Aggregate Lot Size, Noninstantaneous Replenishment

Item (i)	Annual Demand (a_i)	Unit Cost (C_i)	Minor Setup Cost (s_i)	Daily Production Rate ($P_{\$_i}$)	($a_i \div A$)
1	$ 20,500	$2.00	$10	$ 500	0.1460
2	14,400	4.00	6	264	0.1026
3	48,000	6.00	4	860	0.3419
4	35,000	7.00	8	560	0.2493
5	22,500	4.50	12	360	0.1602
	$140,400		$40	$2,544	1.0000

Major setup costs, $S = \$80$; Holding cost rate, $k = 0.3$
Daily aggregate demand rate, $\Sigma D_{\$_i} = A \div$ days per year $= \$140,400 \div 250 = \$561.60$

$$Q_\$^* = \left[\frac{2(\$80 + \$40)(140,400)}{0.3(1 - \$561.60 \div \$2,544)} \right]^{1/2}$$

$$= \left[\frac{2(\$120)(140,400)}{0.3(1 - 0.22)} \right]^{1/2}$$

$$= \left(\frac{33,696,000}{0.234} \right)^{1/2}$$

$$= \$12,000$$

$Q_{\$_1}^* = 0.1460 \times \$12,000 = \$1,752.00$
$Q_{\$_2}^* = 0.1026 \times \$12,000 = \$1,231.20$
$Q_{\$_3}^* = 0.3419 \times \$12,000 = \$4,102.80$
$Q_{\$_4}^* = 0.2493 \times \$12,000 = \$2,991.60$
$Q_{\$_5}^* = 0.1602 \times \$12,000 = \$1,922.40$
$Q_1^* = \$1,752.00 \div \$2.00 = 876.00$
$Q_2^* = \$1,231.20 \div \$4.00 = 307.80$
$Q_3^* = \$4,102.80 \div \$6.00 = 683.80$
$Q_4^* = \$2,991.60 \div \$7.00 = 427.40$
$Q_5^* = \$1,992.40 \div \$4.50 = 427.20$

As noted in Chapter 11, this model is applicable to independent demand cycle stock but not to the production of anticipation inventory.

GLOSSARY*

ABC classification   Classification of the items in decreasing order of annual dollar volume or other criteria. This array is then normally split into three classes, called A, B, and C. Class A contains the items with the highest annual dollar volume and receives the most attention. The next grouping, Class B, receives less attention, and Class C, which contains the low-dollar volume items, is controlled routinely. The ABC principle is, that effort saved through relaxed controls on low-value items will be applied to improve control of high value items. The ABC principle is applicable to inventories, purchasing, sales, etc. Syn: distribution by value. See: Pareto's Law.

action message   An output of a system that identifies the need for and the type of action to be taken to correct a current or potential problem. Examples of action messages in an MRP system are "release order," "reschedule in," "reschedule out," "cancel." See: exception report.

adaptive smoothing   A term applied to a form of exponential smoothing in which the smoothing constant is automatically adjusted as a function of forecast error measurement.

aggregate inventory   The inventory for any grouping of items or products, involving multiple stockkeeping units.

AGVS   Abbreviation for automated guided vehicle system, vehicles equipped with automatic guidance equipment which follow a prescribed path, stopping at each machining or assembly station for automatic or manual loading and unloading of parts.

algorithm   A prescribed set of well-defined rules or processes for the solution of a problem in a finite number of steps; for example, the full statement of the arithmetic procedure for calculating the reorder point.

allocation   (1) In an MRP system, an allocated item is one for which a picking order has been released to the stockroom but not yet sent out of the stockroom. It is an "uncashed" stockroom requisition. (2) A process used to distribute material in short supply.

alpha factor   The smoothing constant applied to the most recent forecast error in exponential smoothing forecasting.

anticipation inventories   Additional inventory above basic pipeline stock to cover projected trends of increasing sales, planned sales promotion programs, seasonal fluctuations, plant shutdowns, and vacations.

---

*Adapted with permission from the *APICS Dictionary*, 6th ed. (American Production and Inventory Control Society, 1987).

assemble-to-order product   A make-to-order product where all components (bulk, semifinished, intermediate, subassembly, fabricated, purchased, packaging, etc.) used in the assembly, packaging, or finishing process, are planned and stocked in anticipation of a customer order. See: make-to-order product.

assembly   A group of subassemblies and/or parts which are put together and constitute a major subdivision for the final product. An assembly may be an end item or a component of a higher level assembly. See: component, subassembly.

automated storage/retrieval system   A high-density rack storage system with vehicles automatically loading and unloading the racks.

automatic rescheduling   Allowing the computer to automatically change due dates on scheduled receipts when it detects that due dates and need dates are out of phase. Ant: manual rescheduling.

available inventory   The on-hand balance minus allocations, reservations, backorders, and (usually) quantities held for quality problems. Often called beginning available balance.

available-to-promise   The uncommitted portion of a company's inventory or planned production. This figure is normally calculated from the master production schedule and is maintained as a tool for customer order promising.

average forecast error   The arithmetic mean of the forecast errors, or the exponentially smoothed forecast error. See: forecast error, mean absolute deviation.

backflush   The deduction from inventory of the component parts used in an assembly or subassembly by exploding the bill of materials by the production count of assemblies produced. Syn: post-deduct inventory transaction processing. See: single-level backflush, superflush.

backlog   All of the customer orders received but not yet shipped. Sometimes referred to as "open orders" or the "order board."

backorder   An unfilled customer order or commitment. It is an immediate (or past due) demand against an item whose inventory is insufficient to satisfy the demand. See: stockout.

back scheduling   A technique for calculating operation start and due dates. The schedule is computed starting with the due date for the order and working backward to determine the required start date and/or due dates for each operation.

balancing operations   In repetitive Just-in-Time production, trying to match actual output cycle times of all operations to the demand of use for parts as required by final assembly, and eventually as required by the market.

bar coding   A method of encoding data for fast and accurate readability. Bar codes are a series of wide or narrow, light or dark, vertically printed lines where the width of lines and spaces between lines is arranged to represent letters and numbers.

beginning inventory   A statement of the inventory count at the end of last period, usually from a perpetual inventory record.

bill of labor   See: product load profile.

bill of material (BOM)   A listing of all the subassemblies, intermediates, parts, and raw materials that go into a parent assembly showing the quantity of each required to make an assembly. There are a variety of display formats of bill of material, including single level bill of material, indented bill of material, modular (planning) bill of material, transient bill of material, matrix bill of material, costed bill of material, etc. May also be called "formula," "recipe," "ingredients list" in certain industries.

bill of material processor   A computer program for maintaining and retrieving bill of material information.

bill of material structuring   The process of organizing bills of material to perform specific functions. See: bill of material, planning bill.

bill of resources   See: product load profile.

blanket order   A long-term commitment to a vendor for material against which short-term releases will be generated to satisfy requirements. Often blanket orders cover only one item, with predetermined delivery dates.

blow-through   See: phantom bill of material.

bottleneck   A facility, function, department, etc., that impedes production—for example, a machine or work center where jobs arrive at a faster rate than they can be completed.

bottom-up replanning   In MRP, the process of using pegging data to solve material availability and/or problems. This process is accomplished by the planner (not the computer system) who evaluates the effects of possible solutions. Potential solutions could include: compress lead time, cut order quantity, substitute material, change the master schedule, etc.

bucketed system   An MRP, DRP, or other time-phased system in which all time-phased data are accumulated into time periods or "buckets." If the period of accumulation would be one week, then the system would be said to have weekly buckets. See: bucketless system, time bucket.

bucketless system   An MRP, DRP, or other time-phased system in which all time-phased data are processed, stored, and usually displayed using dated records rather than defined time periods or "buckets." See: bucketed system, time bucket.

business cycle   A seemingly recurring change in general business activity going from a low point (depression) to a high point (prosperity). While called a "cycle" it does not recur with clocklike regularity. Understanding of cycles is important to forecasting. See: random variation, seasonality.

CAD/CAM   The integration of computer aided design and computer aided manufacturing to achieve automation from design through manufacturing.

capacity   (1) In a general sense, refers to an aggregated volume of work load. It is a separate concept from priority. See: priority. (2) The highest reasonable output rate which can be achieved with the current product specifications, product mix, work force, plant, and equipment.

capacity control   The process of measuring production output and comparing it with the capacity requirement plan, determining if the variance exceeds pre-established limits, and taking corrective action to get back on plan if the limits are exceeded. See: input/output control, closed-loop MRP.

capacity requirements planning (CRP)   The function of establishing, measuring, and adjusting limits or levels of capacity. The term capacity requirements planning in this context is the process of determining how much labor and machine resources are required to accomplish the tasks of production. Open shop orders, and planned orders in the MRP system, are input to CRP which "translates" these orders into hours of work by work center by time period. See: infinite loading, closed-loop MRP, rough cut capacity planning.

carrying cost   Cost of carrying inventory, usually defined as a percent of the dollar value of inventory per unit of time (generally one year). Depends mainly on cost of capital invested as well as the costs of maintaining the inventory such as taxes and insurance, obsolescence, spoilage, and space occupied. Such costs vary from 10-35% annually, depending on type of industry. Ultimately, carrying cost is a policy variable reflecting the opportunity cost alternative uses for funds tied up in inventory. See: economic order quantity, cost of capital.

cause and effect diagram   A precise statement of a problem or phenomenon with a branching diagram leading from the statement to the known potential causes. Syn: fishbone chart, Ishikawa diagram.

cellular manufacturing   A manufacturing process which produces families of parts within a single line or cell of machines operated by machinists who work only within the line or cell.

centralized dispatching   Organization of the dispatching function into one central location. This often involves the use of data collection devices for communication between the centralized dispatching function, which usually reports to the production control department, and the shop manufacturing departments. See: decentralized dispatching.

changeover   The refitting of equipment to either neutralize the effects of the just completed production, to prepare the equipment for production of the next scheduled item, or both. See: setup.

changeover cost   The sum of the teardown costs and the setup costs for a manufacturing operation. See: idle time. Syn: turnaround costs, shutdown/startup costs.

CIM   Abbreviation for computer integrated manufacturing.

closed-loop MRP   A system built around material requirement planning and also including the additional planning functions of sales and operations (production planning, master production scheduling, and capacity requirements planning). Further, once this planning phase is complete and the plans have been accepted as realistic and attainable, the execution functions come into play. These include the manufacturing control functions of input-output measurement, detailed scheduling and dispatching, as well as anticipated delay reports from both the plant and vendors, vendor scheduling, etc. The term "closed loop" implies that not only is each of these elements included in the overall system but also that there is feedback from the execution functions so that the planning can be kept valid at all times. See: manufacturing resource planning.

commodity buying Grouping like parts or materials under one buyer's control for the procurement of all requirements to support production.

common parts bill (of material) A type of planning bill which groups common components for a product or family of products into one bill of material, structured to a "pseudo" parent item number. See: planning bill, modular bill, super bill.

component A term used to identify a raw material, ingredient, part, or subassembly that goes into a higher level assembly, compound, or other item. May also include packaging materials for finished items. See: assembly.

composite part A part which represents operations common to a family or group of parts controlled by group technology. Tools, jigs, and dies are used for the composite part and therefore any parts of that family can be processed with the same operations and tooling. The goal here is to reduce setup costs. See: group technology.

computer aided design (CAD) The use of computers in interactive engineering drawing and storage of designs. Programs complete the layout, geometric transformations, projections, rotations, magnifications, and interval (cross-section) views of a part and its relationship with other parts.

computer aided manufacturing (CAM) Use of computers to program, direct, and control production equipment in the fabrication of manufactured items.

computer integrated manufacturing (CIM) The application of a computer to bridge and connect various computerized systems and connect them into a coherent, integrated whole. For example, budgets, CAD/CAM, process controls, group technology systems, MRP II, financial reporting systems, etc., would be linked and interfaced.

computer numerical control (CNC) A technique in which a machine tool control uses a minicomputer to store numerical instructions.

consigned stocks Inventories, generally of finished products, which are in the possession of customers, dealers, agents, etc., but remain the property of the manufacturer by agreement with those in possession.

constraint A limitation placed on the maximization or minimization of a objective function. These usually result from scarcity of the resources necessary for attaining some objective. See: objective function. Syn: structural constraint, restriction.

continuous production A production system in which the productive equipment is organized and sequenced according to the steps involved to produce the product. Denotes that material flow is continuous during the production process. The routing of the jobs is fixed and setups are seldom changed. See: intermittent production.

control chart A statistical device usually used for the study and control of repetitive processes. It is designed to reveal the randomness or non-randomness of deviations from a mean or control value, usually by plotting these.

cost center   The smallest segment of an organization for which costs are collected, typically a department. The criteria in defining cost centers are that the cost be significant and the area of responsibility be clearly defined. A cost center may not be identical to a work center. Normally, it would encompass more than one work center. See: work center.

cost of capital   The cost of maintaining a dollar of capital invested for a certain period, normally one year. This cost is normally expressed as a percentage and may be based upon factors such as the average expected return on alternative investments and current bank interest rate for borrowing. See: economic order quantity.

critical path method (CPM)   A network planning technique used for planning and controlling the activities in a project. By showing each of these activities and their associated times, the "critical path" can be determined. The critical path identifies those elements that actually constrain the total time for the project. See: PERT.

critical ratio   A dispatching rule which calculates a priority index number by dividing the time to due date remaining by the expected elapsed time to finish the job.

$$\frac{\text{Time Remaining}}{\text{Work Remaining}} = \frac{30}{40} = 0.75$$

Typically ratios of less than 1.0 are behind, ratios greater than 1.0 are ahead, and a ratio of 1.0 is on schedule. See: dispatching rules.

cumulative lead time   The longest planned length of time involved to accomplish the activity in question. For any item planned through MRP, it is found by reviewing the lead time for each bill of material path below the item. Whichever path adds up to the greatest number defines cumulative lead time. Syn: aggregate lead time, stacked lead time, composite lead time, critical path lead time, and combined lead time.

curve fitting   An approach to forecasting based upon a straight line, polynomial, or other curve which describes some historical time series data.

cycle   (1) The interval of time during which a system or process, such as seasonal demand or a manufacturing operation, periodically returns to similar initial conditions. In inventory control, a cycle is often taken to be the length of time between two replenishment shipments. (2) The interval of time during which an event or set of events is completed. In production control, a cycle is often taken to be the length of time between the release of a manufacturing order and shipment to the customer or inventory. Syn: manufacturing cycle, manufacturing lead time.

cycle counting   An inventory accuracy audit technique where inventory is counted on a cyclic schedule rather than once a year. For example, a cycle inventory count is usually taken on a regular, defined basis (often more frequently for high-value fast-moving items and less frequently for low-value or slow-moving items). Most effective cycle counting systems require the counting of a certain number of items every workday with each item counted at a prescribed frequency. The key purpose of cycle counting is to identify items in error, thus triggering research, identification, and elimination of the cause of the errors. See: ABC classification.

cycle stock   One of the four main components of any item inventory, the cycle stock is the most active part; i.e., that which depletes gradually and is replenished cyclically when orders are received. See: lot size.

cycle time   (1) In industrial engineering, the time between completion of two discrete units of production. For example, the cycle time of motors assembled at a rate of 120 per hour would be 30 seconds, or one every half minute. (2) In materials management, it refers to the length of time from when material enters a production facility until it exits. Syn: throughput time.

data   Any representations such as alphabetic or numeric characters to which meaning can be assigned. See: information.

data base   A data processing file-management approach designed to establish the independence of computer programs from data files. Redundancy is minimized and data elements can be added to, or deleted from, the file designs without necessitating changes to existing computer programs.

decentralized dispatching   The organization of the dispatching function into individual departmental dispatchers. See: centralized dispatching.

dedicated capacity   A work center which is designated to produce a single item or a limited number of similar items. Equipment which is dedicated may be special equipment or may be grouped general purpose equipment committed to a composite part.

dedicated line   A production line "permanently" configured to run well-defined parts, one piece at a time from station to station.

delivery lead time   The time from the receipt of the customer order to the delivery of the product. Syn: delivery cycle. See: lead time.

delivery schedule   The required and/or agreed time or rate of delivery of goods or services purchased for a future period.

demand   A need for a particular product or component. The demand could come from any number of sources, i.e., customer order, forecast, interplant, branch warehouse, service part, or for manufacturing another product. At the finished goods level, "demand data" are usually different from "sales data" because demand does not necessarily result in sales, i.e., if there is no stock there will be no sale. See: dependent demand, independent demand.

demand filter   A standard which is set to monitor individual sales data in forecasting models. Usually set to be tripped when the demand for a period differs from the forecast by more than some number of mean absolute deviations.

demand management   The function of recognizing and managing all of the demands for products to ensure that the master scheduler is aware of them. It encompasses the activities of forecasting, order entry, order promising, branch warehouse requirements, interplant orders, and service parts requirements. See: master production schedule.

demand pull   The triggering of material movement to a work center only when that work center is out of work and/or ready to begin the next job. It in effect eliminates queue from in front of a work center, but it can cause queue at the end of a previous work center. See: pull.

demonstrated capacity   Proven capacity calculated from actual output performance data, usually number of items produced times standard hours per item. Syn: actual capacity. See: rated capacity.

dependent demand   Demand is considered dependent when it is directly related to or derived from the schedule for other items or end products. Such demands are therefore calculated, and need not and should not be forecast. A given inventory item may have both dependent and independent demand at any given time. See: independent demand.

detailed scheduling   The actual assignment of starting and/or completion dates to operations or groups of operations to show when these must be done if the manufacturing order is to be completed on time. These dates are used in the dispatching operation. Syn: operations scheduling. See: dispatching.

deterioration   Product spoilage, damage to the package, etc. One of the considerations in inventory carrying cost. See: obsolescence.

deviation   The difference, usually the absolute difference, between a number and the mean of a set of numbers, or between a forecast value and the actual datum.

direct cost   A variable cost which can be directly attributed to a particular job or operation. See: variable cost.

direct labor   Labor which is specifically applied to the product being manufactured, or utilized in the performance of the service.

direct material   Materials which become a part of the final product in measurable quantities. See: indirect materials.

discontinuous demand   A demand pattern that is characterized by large demands interrupted by periods with no demand, as opposed to a continuous or "steady" (e.g., daily) demand. See: lumpy demand.

discount   An allowance or deduction granted by the seller to the buyer, usually when certain stipulated conditions are met by the buyer, which reduces the cost of the goods purchased. A quantity discount is an allowance determined by the quantity or value of purchase. A cash discount is an allowance extended to encourage payment of invoice on or before a stated date which is earlier than the net date. A trade discount is a deduction from an established price for items or services, often varying in percentage with volume of transactions, made by the seller to those engaged in certain businesses and allowed regardless of the time when payment is made.

discrete manufacturing   Production of distinct items: automobiles, appliances, computers. See: process manufacturing.

dispatcher   A production control person whose primary function is dispatching.

dispatching   The selecting and sequencing of available jobs to be run at individual work stations and the assignment of these jobs to workers. See: centralized dispatching, decentralized dispatching, detailed scheduling, expediting.

dispatching rule   The logic used to assign priorities to jobs at a work center. See: critical ratio, due date rule, slack time.

dispatch list   A listing of manufacturing orders in priority sequence. The dispatch list is usually communicated to the manufacturing floor via hard copy or CRT display, and contains detailed information on priority, location, quantity, and the capacity requirements of the manufacturing order by operation. Dispatch lists are normally generated daily and oriented by work center. Syn: foremen's report. See: shop floor control.

distributed processing   A data processing organizational concept under which computer resources of a company are installed at more than one location with appropriate communication links. Processing is performed at the user's location generally on a smaller computer, and under the user's control and scheduling, as opposed to processing for all users being done on a large, centralized computer system.

distributed systems   Refers to computer systems in multiple locations throughout an organization, working in a cooperative fashion, with the system at each location primarily serving the needs of that location but also able to receive and supply information from other systems within a network.

distribution center   A warehouse with finished goods and/or service items. A company, for example, might have a manufacturing facility in Philadelphia and distribution centers in Atlanta, Dallas, Los Angeles, San Francisco, and Chicago. The term distribution center is synonymous with the term branch warehouse, although the former has become more commonly used recently. When there is a warehouse that serves a group of satellite warehouses, it is usually called a regional distribution center.

distribution requirements planning   The function of determining the needs to replenish inventory at branch warehouses. A time-phased order point approach is used where the planned orders at the branch warehouse level are "exploded" via MRP logic to become gross requirements on the supplying source. In the case of multi-level distribution networks, this explosion process can continue down through the various levels of master warehouse, factory warehouse, etc., and become input to the master production schedule. Demand on the supplying source(s) is recognized as dependent, and standard MRP logic applies. See: time-phased order point, physical distribution, push (distribution system).

double order point system   A distribution inventory management system which includes two order points. The smallest equals the original order point, which covers replenishment lead time. The second order point is the sum of the first order point plus normal usage during manufacturing lead time. It enables warehouses to forewarn on manufacturing of future replenishment orders.

downstream operation   Subsequent tasks to the task currently being planned or executed.

downtime   Time when a machine is scheduled for operation but is not producing for reasons such as maintenance, repair, or setup.

due date   The date when purchased material or production material is due to be available for use. See: need date, scheduled receipt.

due date rule   A dispatching rule which directs the sequencing of jobs by the earliest due date.

dynamic lot sizing   A lot-sizing technique that creates an order quantity subject to continuous recomputation. See: least total cost, least unit cost, part period balancing, period order quantity.

dynamic programming   A method of sequential decision making in which the result of the decision in each stage affords the best possible means to exploit the expected range of likely (yet unpredictable) outcomes in the following decision making stages.

earliest start date   The earliest date an operation or order can start. It may be restricted by the current date, material availability and/or management specified "maximum advance."

economic order quantity (EOQ)   A type of fixed order quantity, which determines the amount of an item to be purchased or manufactured at one time. The intent is to minimize the combined costs of acquiring and carrying inventory.

effective date   The date on which a component or an operation is to be added or removed from a bill of material or an assembly process. The effective dates are used in the explosion process to create demands for the correct items. Normally, bill of material and routing systems provide for an effectivity "start date" and "stop date," signifying the start or stop of a particular relationship. Effectivity control may also be by serial number rather than date.

efficiency   Standard hours earned divided by actual hours worked. Efficiency is a measure of how closely predetermined standards are achieved. Efficiency for a given period of time can be calculated for a machine, an employee, a group of machines, a department, etc.

ending inventory   A statement of on-hand quantities/money at the end of a period, often determined by a physical inventory. See: beginning inventory.

engineering change   A revision to a parts list, bill of material or drawings, authorized by the engineering department. Changes are usually identified by a control number and are made for "safety," "cost reduction," or "functionality" reasons. In order to effectively implement engineering changes all affected functions such as materials, quality assurance, assembly engineering, etc., should review and agree to the changes.

engineer-to-order   Products whose customer specifications require unique engineering design or significant customization. Each customer order then results in a unique set of part numbers, bills of material, and routings.

equal runout quantities   Order quantities for items in a group which result in an equal time supply for all items.

exception report   A report which lists or flags only those items which deviate from plan.

expected value The average value which would be observed in taking an action an infinite number of times. The expected value of an action is calculated by multiplying the outcome of the action by the probability of achieving the outcome.

expediting   The "rushing" or "chasing" of production or purchase orders which are needed in less than the normal lead time. See: dispatching.

expeditor   A production control person whose primary duties are expediting.

exponential smoothing   A type of weighted moving average forecasting technique in which past observations are geometrically discounted according to their age. The heaviest weight is assigned to the most recent data. The smoothing is termed "exponential" because data points are weighted in accordance with an exponential function of their age. The technique makes use of a smoothing constant to apply to the difference between the most recent forecast and the critical sales data, which avoids the necessity of carrying historical sales data. The approach can be used for data which exhibit no trend or seasonal patterns or for data with either (or both) trend and seasonality. See: first order smoothing, second order smoothing.

exposures   The number of times per year that the system risks a stockout. This number of exposures is arrived at by dividing the lot size into the annual usage.

external setup time   Elements of a setup procedure performed while the process is in production; the machine is running. See: internal setup time.

extrinsic forecast   A forecast based on a correlated leading indicator such as estimating furniture sales based on housing starts. Extrinsic forecasts tend to be more useful for large aggregations such as total company sales, than for individual product sales. Ant: intrinsic forecasts.

fabrication   A term used to distinguish manufacturing operations for components as opposed to assembly operations.

failsafe work methods   Methods of performing operations so that actions which are incorrect cannot be completed. Examples: Part without holes in the proper place cannot be removed from a jig. Computer systems which reject "invalid" numbers or require double entry of transaction quantities outside normal range. Called "poka-yoke" by the Japanese.

families   A group of end items whose similarity of design and manufacture facilitates being planned in aggregate, whose sales performance is monitored together, and occasionally whose cost is aggregated at this level.

feedback   The flow of information back into the control system so that actual performance can be compared with planned performance.

FIFO   Abbreviation for a first in, first out method of inventory valuation for accounting purposes. The assumption is that oldest inventory (first in) is is the first to be used (first out), but has no necessary relationship with the actual physical movement of specific items of materials. See: LIFO.

file An organized collection of records or the storage device in which these records are kept.

final assembly (1) The highest level assembled product, as it is shipped to customers. (2) The name for the manufacturing department where the product is assembled. Syn: erection department, blending department, pack-out department.

final assembly schedule (FAS) Also referred to as "finishing schedule" as it may include other operations than simply the final operations. It may also not involve "assembly" but only final mixing, cutting, packaging, etc. It is a schedule of end items to finish the product for specific customer orders in a "make-to-order" or "assemble-to-order" environment. It is prepared after receipt of a customer order as constrained by the availability of material and capacity and it schedules the operations required to complete the product from the level where it is stocked (or master scheduled) to the end item level. Syn: blending, schedule, pack-out schedule.

finite loading Conceptually the term means putting no more work into a work center than the work center can be expected to execute. The specific term usually refers to a computer technique that involves automatic shop priority revision in order to level load operation by operation. See: infinite loading.

firm planned order (FPO) A planned order that can be frozen in quantity and time. The computer is not allowed to automatically change it; this is the responsibility of the planner in charge of the item that is being planned. This technique can aid planners working with MRP systems to respond to material and capacity problems by forming up selected planned orders. Additionally, firm planned orders are the normal method of stating the master production schedule.

first-come-first-served rule A dispatching rule under which the jobs are sequenced by their arrival times. See: dispatching rule.

first order smoothing This phrase refers to single exponential smoothing. First order smoothing is best applied to forecasting problems where the data do not exhibit significant trend or seasonal patterns. Syn: single smoothing. See: exponential smoothing.

first-piece inspection A quality check on the first component run after a new setup has been completed.

fishbone chart See: cause and effect diagram.

fitness for use Involves the quality of a product, but also the appropriateness of its design characteristics as well.

fixed cost An expenditure that does not vary with the production volume; for example: rent, property tax, salaries of certain personnel. See: variable cost.

fixed interval reorder system A periodic reordering system where the time interval between orders is fixed, such as weekly, monthly or quarterly, but the size of the order is not fixed and orders vary according to usage since the last review. This type of inventory control system is employed where it is convenient to examine inventory stocks on a fixed time cycle, such as in warehouse control systems, in systems where orders are placed mechanically, or for handling inventories involving a very large variety of items under some form of clerical control. Also called fixed reorder cycle system. See: min-max system, fixed order quantity system.

fixed order quantity   A lot-sizing technique in MRP or inventory management that will always cause planned or actual orders to be generated for a predetermined fixed quantity in MRP, or multiples thereof if net requirements for the period exceed the fixed order quantity. See: economic order quantity, lot-for-lot, period order quantity.

fixed order quantity system   An inventory control method where the size of the order is fixed, but the time interval between orders depends on actual demand. The practice of ordering a fixed quantity when needed assumes that individual inventories are under constant watch. This system consists of placing an order of a fixed quantity (the reorder quantity) wherever the amount on hand plus the amount on order falls to or below a specified level (the order point or reorder point). See: two-bin system, fixed interval reorder system.

flexible manufacturing system (FMS)   A manufacturing process designed so that the production line may be rebalanced often, rapidly matching output to changes in demand. Involves mixed-model scheduling, multi-skilled operators, standardization of equipment for quick changeover times, and design of the production line to allow workers to do more than one job and to cut down on transportation time between lines.

floating order point   An order point which is responsive to changes in demand and/or to changes in lead time.

flow control   A term used to describe a specific production control system that is based primarily on setting production rates and feeding work into production to meet these planned rates, then following it through production to make sure that it is moving. Flow control has its most successful application in repetitive production. See: order control.

flow shop   A form of manufacturing organizations in which machines and operators handle a standard, usually uninterrupted material flow. The operators tend to perform the same operations for each production run. A flow shop is often referred to as a mass production shop, or is said to have a continuous manufacturing layout. The plant layout (arrangement of machines, benches, assembly lines, etc.) is designed to facilitate a product "flow." The process industries (chemicals, oil, paint, etc.) are extreme examples of flow shops. Each product, though variable in material specifications, uses the same flow pattern through the shop. Production is set at a given rate, and the products are generally manufactured in bulk.

fluctuation inventory   Inventories that are carried as a cushion to protect against forecast error. See: safety stock.

focus forecasting   A system that allows the user to simulate the effectiveness of numerous forecasting techniques, thereby being able to select the most effective one.

focused factory   A plant established to produce a limited number of products and/or employ a limited number of processes.

forecast   An estimate of future demand. A forecast can be determined by mathematical means using historical data; it can be created subjectively by using estimates from informal sources; or it can represent a combination of both techniques. See: extrinsic forecast, intrinsic forecast.

forecast consumption   The process of replacing the forecast with customer orders, or other types of actual demands, as they are received.

forecast error   The difference between actual demand and forecast demand, stated as an absolute value or as a percentage.

forward scheduling   A scheduling technique where the scheduler proceeds from a known start date and computes the completion date for an order usually proceeding from the first operation to the last. Dates generated by this technique are generally the earliest start dates (ESD) for operations. Ant: backward scheduling.

free slack   The amount of time that the completion of an activity in a project network can increase without delaying the start of the very next activity.

full pegging   Refers to the ability of a system to automatically trace requirements for a given component all the way up to its ultimate end item, customer, or contract number.

Gantt chart   A control chart especially designed to show graphically the relationship between planned performance and actual performance, named after its originator, Henry L. Gantt. Used for machine loading, where one horizontal line is used to represent capacity and another to represent load against that capacity, or for following job progress where one horizontal line represents the production schedule and another parallel line represents the actual progress of the job against the schedule in time. Syn: job progress chart.

gross requirement   The total of independent and dependent demand for a component prior to the netting of on-hand inventory and scheduled receipts.

group technology   An engineering and manufacturing philosophy which identifies the "sameness" of parts, equipment, or processes. It provides for rapid retrieval of existing designs and anticipates a cellular type production equipment layout.

handling cost   The cost involved in handling inventory. In some cases, the handling cost incurred may depend on the size of the inventory.

hard automation   Use of specialized machines to manufacture and assemble products. Normally, each is dedicated to one function, such as milling.

hedge   (1) In master production scheduling, a quantity of stock to protect against uncertainty in demand. The hedge is similar to safety stock, except that a hedge has the dimension of timing as well as amount. A typical example of a "product mix" hedge might be for a company that makes a box with either gold or silver handles (all else same). If 40% of the boxes usually took gold handles and 60% silver, a master production schedule for 200 would explode into 200 common boxes, 80 gold handles, and 120 silver handles. The mix hedge might be to carry 50 extra gold and 50 extra silver handles. If at some point in time 180 of the 200 boxes are sold, uncertainty only exists as to the remaining 20; any silver or gold handles above 20 can be rescheduled until the next uncertainty occurs. Another hedge is called the "volume" hedge, which would be for the common boxes in this example. This hedge is typically carried by the master production scheduler just beyond some time fence in the future such that rolling the hedge over the time fence will result in planned orders for major expense items to now be in the action time bucket. (2) In purchasing, any purchase or sale transaction having as its purpose the elimination of the negative aspects of price fluctuations.

heuristic   A form of problem solving where the results or rules have been determined by experience or intuition instead of by optimization.

idle time   Time when operators or machines are not producing product because of setup, maintenance, lack of material, tooling. Syn: downtime.

implode   Compression of detailed data into a summary-level record or report. Or tracing a usage and/or cost impact from the bottom to the top (end product) of a bill of material using "where-used" logic.

inbound stockpoint   A defined location next to the place of use on a production flow to which materials are brought as needed, and from which material is taken for immediate use. Used with a pull system of material control. See: Just-in-Time.

indented bill of material   A form of multi-level bill of material. It exhibits the highest level parents closest to the left side margin and all the components going into these parents are shown indented to the right of the margin. All subsequent levels of components are indented farther to the right. If a component is used in more than one parent within a given product structure, it will appear more than once, under every subassembly in which it is used.

independent demand   Demand for an item is considered independent when such demand is unrelated to the demand for other items. Demand for finished goods, parts required for destructive testing and service parts requirements are some examples of independent demand. See: dependent demand.

independent demand inventory system   The policies, methods, and procedures used to manage inventory items that have independent demand. See: independent demand, order point system.

indirect cost   Cost which is not directly incurred by a particular job or operation. Certain utility costs, such as plant heating, are often indirect. An indirect cost is typically distributed to the product through the overhead rates. See: direct cost.

indirect labor   Work required to support production in general without being related to a specific product. For example, floor sweeping.

indirect materials   Materials which become part of the final product but in such small quantities that their cost is not applied directly to the product. Instead their expense becomes a part of manufacturing supply or overhead costs.

infinite loading   Showing the work behind work centers in the time periods required regardless of the capacity available to perform this work. The term infinite loading is considered to be obsolete today, although the specific computer programs used to do infinite loading can now be used to perform the technique called capacity requirements planning. Infinite loading was a gross misnomer to start with, implying that a load could be put into a factory regardless of its availability to perform. The poor terminology obscured the fact that it is necessary to generate capacity requirements and compare these with available capacity before trying to adjust requirements to capacity. See: capacity requirements planning, finite loading.

information   The meaning derived from data which have been arranged and displayed in such a way that they can be related to that which is previously known. See: data.

input   (1) Work arriving at a production facility. (2) Data to be processed on a computer.

input/output control   A technique for capacity control where actual output from a work center is compared with the planned output as developed by capacity requirements planning and approved by manufacturing management. The input is also monitored to see if it corresponds with plans so that work centers will not be expected to generate output when work is not available. See: capacity control, closed-loop MRP.

instantaneous receipt   The receipt of an entire lot size quantity in a very short period of time.

interactive   Refers to those applications where a user communicates with a computer program via a terminal, entering data and receiving responses from the computer.

intermittent production   A form of manufacturing organization in which the productive resources are organized according to function. The jobs pass through the functional departments in lots and each lot may have a different routing. Syn: job shop. See: continuous production.

internal setup time   Elements of a setup procedure performed while the process is not running. Ant: external setup time.

interoperation time   The time between the completion of one operation and the start of the next. See: move time.

interplant demand   Items to be shipped to another plant or division within the corporation. Although it is not a customer order, it is usually handled by the master production scheduling system in a similar manner. See: demand management.

intransit inventory   Material moving between two or more locations, usually separated geographically. For example, the shipment of finished goods from a plant to a distribution center.

intrinsic forecast   A forecast based on internal factors, such as an average of past sales. See: extrinsic forecast.

inventory   Items which are in a stocking location or work in process and which serve to decouple successive operations in the process of manufacturing a product and distributing it to the consumer. Inventories may consist of finished goods ready for sale; they may be parts or intermediate items; they may be work in process; or they may be raw materials.

inventory buffer   See: fluctuation inventory.

inventory control   The activities and techniques of maintaining the stock of items at desired levels, whether they are raw materials, work in process, or finished products.

inventory investment   The number of dollars that are tied up in all levels of inventory.

inventory turnover   The number of times that an inventory "turns over," or cycles during the year. A frequently used method to compute inventory turnover is to divide the average inventory level into the annual cost of sales. For example, if average inventory were three million dollars and cost of sales were twenty-one million dollars, the inventory would be considered to "turn" seven times per year.

inventory usage   The value or the number of units of an inventory item consumed over a period of time.

inventory valuation   The value of the inventory at either its cost or its market value. Because inventory value can change with time, some recognition is taken of the age distribution of inventory. Therefore, the cost of value of inventory is usually computed on a first-in-first-out (FIFO), last-in-first-out (LIFO) basis, or a standard cost basis to establish the cost of goods sold.

Ishikawa diagram   See: cause-and-effect diagram.

issue   The physical movement of items from a stocking location. Often, also refers to the transaction reporting of this activity. See: planned issue.

item   Any unique manufactured or purchased part, material, intermediate, subassembly, or product.

item number   A number which serves to uniquely identify an item. Syn: part number, stock code.

item record   The "master" record for an item. Typically it contains identifying and descriptive data, control values (lead times, lot sizes, etc.) and may contain data on inventory status, requirements, planned orders, and costs. Item records are linked together by bill of material records (or product structure records), thus defining the bill of material.

jidoka   Practice of stopping the production line when a defect occurs.

JIT   See: Just-in-Time.

job order costing   A costing system in which costs are collected to specific jobs. This system can be used with either actual or standard costs in the manufacturing of distinguishable units or lots of products.

job shop   See: intermittent production.

job shop layout   The arrangement of equipment in functional areas.

joint order   An order on which several items are combined for the purpose of obtaining volume or transportation discounts. See: joint replenishment, group technology.

joint replenishment   Coordinating the lot sizing and order release decision for related items and treating them as a family of items. The objective is to achieve lower costs due to ordering, setup, shipping, and quantity discount economies. Applies equally to joint ordering (family contracts) and to composite part (group technology) fabrication scheduling.

Just-in-Time (JIT)   In the broad sense, an approach to achieving excellence in a manufacturing company based on the continuing elimination of waste (waste being considered as those things which do not add value to the product). In the narrow sense, Just-in-Time refers to the movement of material at the necessary place at the necessary time. The implication is that each operation is closely synchronized with the subsequent ones to make that possible. See: zero inventories.

kanban   A method of Just-in-Time production which uses standard containers or lot sizes with a single card attached to each. It is a pull system in which work centers signal with a card that they wish to withdraw parts from feeding operations or vendors. Kanban, in Japanese, loosely translated means "card," literally "billboard" or "sign." The term is often used synonymously for the specific scheduling system developed and used by Toyota Corporation in Japan.

kit   The components of a parent which have been pulled from stock and readied for movement to a production area.

latest start date   The latest date at which an operation order can be started in order to meet the due date of the order.

leading indicator   A specific business activity index that indicates future trends. For example, housing starts is a leading indicator for the industry that supplies builders' hardware. See: extrinsic forecast.

lead time   A span of time required to perform an activity. In a logistics context, the time between recognition of the need for an order and the receipt of goods. Individual components of lead time can include: order preparation time, queue time, move or transportation time, receiving and inspection time. See: manufacturing lead time, purchasing lead time.

lead-time offset   A technique used in MRP where a planned order receipt in one time period will require the release of that order in an earlier time period based on the lead time for the item.

learning curve   A planning technique particularly useful in the project-oriented industries where new products are phased in rather frequently. The basis for the learning curve calculation is the fact that workers will be able to produce the product more quickly after they get used to making it.

least squares method   A method of curve fitting which selects a line of best fit through a plot of data to minimize the sum of squares of the deviations of the given points from the line.

least total cost   A dynamic lot-sizing technique that calculates the order quantity by comparing the carrying cost and the setup (or ordering) costs for various lot sizes and selects the lot where these costs are most nearly equal. See: part period balancing.

least unit cost   A dynamic lot-sizing technique that adds ordering cost and inventory carrying cost for each trial lot size and divides by the number of units in the lot size, picking the lot size with the lowest unit cost.

level   Every part or assembly in a product structure is assigned a level code signifying the relative level in which that part or assembly is used within that product structure. Normally, the end items are assigned level "0" with the components/subassemblies going into it assigned level "1" and so on. MRP explosion process starts from level "0" and proceeds downward one level at a time.

level of service   A measure of the demand that is routinely satisfied by inventory, e.g., the percentage of orders filled from stock; the percentage of dollar demand filled from stock.

LIFO   Abbreviation for last in, first out method of inventory evaluation. The assumption is that the most recently received (last in) is the first to be used or sold (first out). Ant: FIFO.

LIMIT   Abbreviation for lot-size inventory management interpolation technique. A technique for looking at the lot sizes for groups of products to determine what effect economic lot sizes will have on the total inventory and total setup costs.

line   A specific physical space for manufacture of a product which in a flow plan layout is represented by a straight line. This may be in actuality a series of pieces of equipment connected by piping or conveyor systems.

linear production   Actual production to a level schedule, so that plotting actual output versus planned output is straight, even when plotted for a short segment of time.

line balancing   (1) An assembly line process can be divided into elemental tasks, each with a specified time requirement per unit of product and a sequence relationship with the other tasks. Line balancing is the assignment of these tasks to work stations to minimize the number of work stations and to minimize the total amount of idle time at all stations. (2) Line balancing can also mean a technique for determining the product mix that can be run down an assembly line to provide a fairly consistent flow of work through that assembly line at the planned line rate.

load leveling   Spreading orders out in time or rescheduling operations so that the amount of work to be done in sequential time periods tends to be distributed evenly and is achievable. See: finite loading.

locator file   A file used in a stockroom or where each item does not have a specific fixed location. The locator file records where the items have been selected to be stored.

logistics   In an industrial context, this term refers to the art and science of obtaining and distributing material and product. In a military sense (where it has greater usage), its meaning can also include the movement of personnel.

lot   A quantity produced together and sharing the same production costs and resultant specifications.

lot-for-lot   A lot-sizing technique which generates planned orders in quantities equal to the net requirements in each period. Syn: discrete order quantity.

lot number   A unique identification assigned to a homogenous quantity of material. Syn: batch number, mix number.

lot number control   Assignment of unique numbers to each instance of receipt and carrying forth that number into subsequent manufacturing processes so that, in review of an end item, each lot consumed from raw materials through end item can be identified as having been used for the manufacture of this specific end item lot.

lot size   The amount of a particular item that is ordered from the plant or a vendor. Syn: order quantity.

lot splitting   Dividing a lot into two or more sublots and simultaneously processing each sublot on identical (or very similar) work centers.

lot traceability   The ability to identify the lot or batch numbers of consumption and/or composition for manufactured, purchased, and shipped items. This is a federal requirement in certain regulated industries.

low level code   Identifies the lowest level in any bill of material at which a particular component may appear. Net requirements for a given component are not calculated until all the gross requirements have been calculated down to that level. Low level codes are normally calculated and maintained automatically by the computer software. See: level.

lumpy demand   A demand pattern with large fluctuations from one time period to another. Syn: discontinuous demand.

machine loading   The accumulation by work station(s), machine, or machine group of the hours generated from the scheduling of operations for released orders by time period. Machine loading differs from capacity requirements planning in that it does not use the planned orders from MRP but operates solely from scheduled receipts. As such, it has very limited usefulness. See: capacity requirements planning.

machine utilization   See: utilization.

maintenance repair and operating supplies (MRO)   Items used in support of general operations and maintenance such as maintenance supplies, spare parts, consumables used in the manufacturing process, etc.

major setup   The equipment setup and related activities required to manufacture a group of items in sequence, exclusive of the setup required for each item in the group. Ant: minor setup.

make-or-buy decision   The act of deciding whether to produce an item in house or buy it from an outside vendor.

make-to-order product   A product which is finished after receipt of a customer order. Frequently long lead-time components are planned prior to the order arriving in order to reduce the delivery time to the customer. Where options or other subassemblies are stocked prior to customer orders arriving, the term "assemble-to-order" is frequently used.

make-to-stock product   A product which is shipped from finished goods, "off the shelf," and therefore is finished prior to a customer order arriving.

manufacturing calendar   A calendar, used in inventory and production planning functions, which consecutively numbers only the working days so that the component and work order scheduling may be done based on the actual number of work days available. Syn: M-day calendar.

manufacturing lead time   The total time required to manufacture an item, exclusive of lower level purchasing lead time. Included here are order preparation time, queue time, setup time, run time, move time, inspection, and put-away time.

manufacturing order   A document, group of documents, or schedule identity conveying authority for the manufacture of specified parts or products in specified quantities.

manufacturing process   The series of activities performed upon material to convert it from the raw or semifinished state to a state of further completion and a greater value.

manufacturing resource planning (MRP II)   A method for the effective planning of all resources of a manufacturing company. Ideally, it addresses operational planning in units, financial planning in dollars, and has a simulation capability to answer "what if" questions. It is made up of a variety of functions, each linked together: business planning, sales and operations (production planning), master production scheduling, material requirements planning, capacity requirements planning, and the execution support systems for capacity and material. Output from these systems would be integrated with financial reports such as the business plan, purchase commitment report, shipping budget, inventory projection in dollars, etc. Manufacturing resource planning is a direct outgrowth and extension of closed-loop MRP. See: closed-loop MRP, material requirements planning.

manufacturing strategy   A collective pattern of decisions that act upon the formulation and deployment of manufacturing resources. To be most effective, the manufacturing strategy should act in support of the overall strategic direction of the business unit, and provide competitive advantage where called for.

marginal cost   The additional out-of-pocket costs incurred when the level of output of some operation is increased by one unit. See: marginal revenue.

marginal revenue   The additional income received when the level of output of some operation is increased by one unit. See: marginal cost.

master production schedule (MPS)   The anticipated build schedule for those items assigned to the master scheduler. The master scheduler maintains this schedule and, in turn, it becomes a set of planning numbers which "drives" material requirements planning. It represents what the company plans to produce expressed in specific configurations, quantities, and dates. The master production schedule is not a sales forecast which represents a statement of demand. The master production schedule must take into account the forecast, the production plan, and other important considerations such as backlog, availability of material, availability of capacity, management policy and goals, etc. Syn: master schedule. See: closed-loop MRP.

master schedule item   A part number selected to be planned by the master scheduler. The item would be deemed critical in terms of its impact on lower level components and/or resources such as skilled labor, key machines, dollars, etc. Therefore, the master scheduler, not the computer, would maintain the plan for these items. A master schedule item may be an end item, a component, a pseudo number, or a planning bill of material.

master scheduler   The job title of the person who manages the master production schedule. This person should be the best scheduler available as the consequences of the planning done here have a great impact on material and capacity planning. Ideally, the person would have substantial product and plant knowledge.

material planner   The person normally responsible for managing the inventory levels, schedules, and availability of selected items, either manufactured or purchased. In an MRP system, the person responsible for reviewing and acting upon order release, action and exception messages from the system.

material requirements planning (MRP)   A set of techniques which uses bills of material, inventory data, and the master production schedule to calculate requirements for materials. It makes recommendations to release replenishment orders for material. Further, since it is time phased, it makes recommendations to reschedule open orders when due dates and need dates are not in phase. Originally seen as merely a better way to order inventory, today it is thought of as primarily a scheduling technique, i.e., a method for establishing and maintaining valid due dates (priorities) on orders. See: closed-loop MRP, manufacturing resource planning.

materials management   The grouping of management functions supporting the complete cycle of material flow, from the purchase and internal control of production materials to the planning and control of work in process to the warehousing, shipping, and distribution of the finished product.

material usage variance   The difference between the planned or standard requirements for materials to produce a given item and the actual quantity used for this particular instance of manufacture.

material yield   The ratio of usable material from a given quantity of same. Syn: potency.

matrix bill of material   A chart made up from the bills of material for a number of products in the same or similar families. It is arranged in a matrix with components in columns and parents in rows (or vice versa) so that requirements for common components can be summarized conveniently.

mean   The arithmetic average of a group of values.

mean absolute deviation (MAD)   The average of the absolute values of the deviations of some observed value from some expected value. MAD can be calculated based on observations and the arithmetic mean of those observations. An alternative is to calculate absolute deviations of actual sales data minus forecast data. These data can be averaged in the usual arithmetic way or with exponential smoothing.

min-max system   A type of order point replenishment system where the "min" is the order point, and the "max" is the "order-up-to" inventory level. The order quantity is variable and is the result of the "max" minus available and on-order inventory. An order is recommended when the available and on-order inventory is at or below the "min."

minor setup   The incremental setup activities required when changing from one item to another within a group of items. See: major setup.

mixed-model production   Making several different parts or products in varying lot sizes so that a factory is making close to the same mix of products that will be sold that day. The mixed-model schedule governs the making and the delivery of component parts, including outside suppliers. The goal is to build every model, every day, according to demand.

modular bill (of material)   A type of planning bill which is arranged in product modules or options. Often used in companies where the product has many optional features, e.g., automobiles. See: planning bill, common parts bill, super bill.

Monte Carlo simulation   A subset of digital simulation models based on random or stochastic processes. See: simulation.

move card   In a Just-in-Time context, refers to a card or other signal indicating that a specific number of units of a particular item are to be taken from a source (usually outbound stockpoint) and taken to a point of use (usually inbound stockpoint). Syn: move signal. See: kanban, production card.

move order   The authorization to move a particular item from one location to another.

move ticket   A document used in dispatching to authorize and/or record movement of a job from one work center to another. It may also be used to report other information such as the active quantity or the material storage location.

move time   The actual time that a job spends in transit from one operation to another in the plant.

MPS   See: master production schedule.

MRP   See: material requirements planning.

MRP II   See: manufacturing resource planning.

multi-level bill of material   A display of all the components directly or indirectly used in a parent, together with the quantity required of every component. If a component is a subassembly, blend, intermediate, etc., all of its components will also be exhibited and all of their components, down to purchased parts and materials.

multi-level where used   A display for a component listing all the parents in which that component is directly used and the next higher level parents into which each of those parents is used, until ultimately all top-level (level 0) parents are listed.

need date   The date when an item is required for its intended use. In an MRP system, this date is calculated by a bill of material explosion of a schedule and the netting of available inventory against that requirement. See: due date.

net change MRP   An approach via which the material requirements plan is continually retained in the computer. Whenever there is a change in requirements, open order or inventory status, or bill of material, a partial explosion is made only for those parts affected by the change. Ant: regeneration MRP, requirements alteration.

net requirements   In MRP, the net requirements for a part or an assembly are derived as a result of applying gross requirements and allocations against inventory on hand, scheduled receipts, and safety stock. Net requirements, lot sized and offset for lead time, become planned orders.

netting   The process of calculating net requirements.

nominal capacity   See: rated capacity.

normal distribution   A particular statistical distribution where most of the observations fall fairly close to one mean, and a deviation from the mean is as likely to be plus as it is likely to be minus. When graphed, the normal distribution takes the form of a bell-shaped curve.

objective function   The goal or function which is to be optimized in a model. Most often it is a cost function which we are attempting to minimize subject to some restrictions or a profit function which we are trying to maximize subject to some restriction. See: constraint.

obsolescence   Loss of product value resulting from a model or style change or technological development. See: deterioration.

on-hand balance   The quantity shown in the inventory records as being physically in stock. See: available inventory.

on order   The stock on order is the quantity represented by the total of all outstanding replenishment orders. The on order balance increases when a new order is released and it decreases when material is received against an order, or when an order is cancelled. See: on-hand balance, open order.

open order   (1) A released manufacturing order or purchase order. Syn: scheduled receipt. (2) An unfilled customer order.

operating efficiency   A ratio of the actual output of a piece of equipment, department, or plant as compared to the planned or standard output.

operation description   The description of an operation to be performed. This is normally contained in the routing document and could include setup instructions, operating instructions (feeds, speeds, heats, pressure, etc.) and required product specifications and/or tolerances.

operation duration   The total time which elapses between the start of setup of an operation and the completion of the operation.

operation priority   The scheduled due date and/or start date of a specific operation for a specific job, usually as determined by the back scheduling process. See: back scheduling, dispatching, order priority.

operation sequencing   A simulation technique for short-term planning of actual jobs to be run in each work center based upon capacity, priority, existing manpower, and machine availability.

operation splitting   See: lot splitting.

operations sequence   The sequential steps for an item to follow in its flow through the plant. For instance, operation 1: cut bar stock; operation 2: grind bar stock; operation 3: shape; operation 4: polish; operation 5: inspect and send to stock. This information is normally maintained in the routing file.

operating start date   The date when an operation should be started in order for its operation and order due date to be met. It can be calculated based on scheduled quantities and lead times (queue, setup, run, move) or based upon the work remaining and the time remaining to complete the job.

optimization   Achieving the best possible solution to a problem in terms of a specified objective function.

order control   Control of manufacturing activities by individual manufacturing, job, or shop orders, released by planning personnel, and authorizing production personnel to complete a given batch or lot size of a particular manufactured item. Information to complete the order (components required, work centers and operations required, tooling required, etc.) is often printed on paper or tickets, and distributed to production personnel. These are often called shop orders or work orders. This sometimes implies an environment where all the components for a given order are picked and issued from a stocking location, all at one time, and then moved as a kit to manufacturing before any activity begins. Most frequently seen in job shop manufacturing. See: schedule control.

order entry   The process of accepting and translating what a customer wants into terms used by the manufacturer or distributor. This can be as simple as creating shipping documents for a finished good product line, to a more complicated series of activities including engineering effort for make-to-order products.

ordering cost   Used in calculating economic order quantities, and refers to the costs which increase as the number of orders placed increases. Includes costs related to the clerical work of preparing, releasing, following, and receiving orders, the physical handling of goods, inspections, and setup costs, as applicable. Syn: acquisition cost. Ant: carrying costs.

order multiples   An order quantity modifier applied after the lot size has been calculated that increments the order quantity to a predetermined multiple.

order point   A set inventory level where, if the total stock on-hand plus on-order falls to or below that point, action is taken to replenish the stock. The order point is normally calculated as: forecasted usage during the replenishment lead time plus safety stock. Syn: reorder point, trigger level. See: time-phased order point.

order point system   The method whereby replenishment orders are triggered (launched) at a calculated inventory level. See: order point, time-phased order point.

order priority   The scheduled due date to complete all of the operations required for a specific order. See: operation priority.

order promising   The process of making a delivery commitment, i.e., answering the question "when can you ship?" For make-to-order products this usually involves a check of uncommitted material and availability of capacity. Syn: order dating, customer order promising. See: available-to-promise.

order reporting   Recording and reporting the start and completion of the manufacturing order (shop order) in its entirety.

order up to level   See: target inventory level.

out-of-pocket costs   Costs which involve direct payments such as labor, freight, insurance, etc., as opposed to depreciation which does not. See: marginal cost.

output   (1) Work being completed by a production facility. (2) The result of a computer program.

overhead   Costs incurred in the operation of a business which cannot be directly related to the individual products or services produced. These costs, such as light, heat, supervision, and maintenance are grouped in several pools (department overhead, factory overhead, general overhead) and distributed to units of product, or service, by some standard method such as direct labor hours, direct labor dollars, direct materials dollars.

overlapped schedule   The "overlapping" of successive operations, whereby the completed portion of a job lot at one work center is processed at one or more succeeding work centers before the pieces left behind are finished at the preceding work center(s). Syn: lap-phasing, telescoping. Ant: gapped schedule.

overlap quantity   The amount of product which needs to be run and sent ahead to the following operation before the following "overlap" operation can being.

overload   A condition when the total hours outstanding at a work center exceed that work center's capacity.

paperless purchasing   A purchasing operation which does not employ purchase requisitions or hard-copy purchase orders. In actual practice, a small amount of "paperwork" usually remains, normally in the form of the vendor schedule. See: Just-in-Time, vendor scheduling.

parallel schedule   Use of two or more machines or job centers to perform identical operations on a lot of material. Duplicate tooling and setup are required.

Pareto's Law   A concept developed by Vilfredo Pareto, an Italian economist, which states that a small percentage of a group accounts for the largest fraction of the impact, value, etc. For example, twenty percent of the inventory items may comprise eighty percent of the inventory value. Syn: 20/80 rule. See: ABC classification.

part   Normally refers to a material item which is used as a component and is not an assembly, subassembly blend, intermediate, etc. See: component.

part number   See: item number.

part period balancing (PPB)   A dynamic lot-sizing technique that uses the same logic as the least total cost method, but adds a routine called "look ahead/look back." When the look ahead/look back feature is used, a lot quantity is calculated and before it is firmed up, the next or the previous periods' demands are evaluated to determine whether it would be economical to include them in the current lot. See: least total cost.

part type   A code for a component within a bill of material may be defined as regular, phantom, reference, etc.

past due   An order that has not been completed on the date scheduled. Syn: delinquent.

pegged requirement   A requirement that shows the next level parent item (or customer order) as the source of the demand. See: pegging.

pegging   In MRP, pegging displays for a given item the identity of the source of its gross requirements and/or allocations. Pegging can be thought of as "live where used" information.

performance efficiency   A ratio, usually expressed as a percentage, of actual output to a benchmark or standard output.

performance standard   A criterion or benchmark against which actual performance is compared.

periodic inventory   A physical inventory taken at some recurring interval, e.g., monthly, quarterly, or annual physical inventory.

periodic replenishment   A method of aggregating requirements to place deliveries of varying quantities at evenly spaced time intervals, rather than variably spaced deliveries of equal quantities.

periodic review system   See: fixed interval reorder system.

period order quantity   A lot-sizing technique under which the lot size will be equal to the net requirements for a given number of periods (e.g., weeks) into the future. Syn: days' supply, weeks' supply. See: fixed order quantity, lot-for-lot.

perpetual inventory   An inventory record-keeping system where each transaction in and out is recorded and a new balance is computed. See: physical inventory, on-hand balance.

perpetual inventory record   A computer record or manual document on which each inventory transaction is posted so that a current record of the inventory is maintained. See: on-hand balance.

PERT   Abbreviation for program evaluation and review technique. This is a project planning technique similar to the critical path method. It includes obtaining a pessimistic, most likely, and optimistic time for each activity from which the most likely completion time for the project along the critical path is computed. See: critical path method.

phantom bill of material   A bill of material coding and structuring technique used primarily for transient (non-stocked) subassemblies. For the transient item, lead time is set to zero and the order quantity to lot-for-lot. This permits MRP logic to drive requirements straight through the phantom item to its components, but usually retains its ability to net against any occasional inventories of the item. This technique also facilitates the use of common bills of material for engineering and manufacturing. Syn: transient bill of material, blow-through.

physical distribution   The activities associated with the movement of material, usually finished products or service parts, from the manufacturer to the customer. These activities encompass the functions of transportation, warehousing, inventory control, material handling, order administration, site/location analysis, industrial packaging, data processing, and the communications network necessary for effective management. In many cases, this movement is made through one or more levels of field warehouses. See: distribution requirements planning.

physical inventory   (1) The actual inventory itself. (2) The determination of inventory quantity by actual count. Physical inventories can be taken on a continuous, periodic, or annual basis. See: cycle counting.

picking   The process of withdrawing from stock the components to make the products, or the finished goods to be shipped to a customer.

pipeline stock   Inventory to fill the transportation network and the distribution system including the flow through intermediate stocking points. The flow time through the pipeline has a major effect on the amount of inventory required in the pipeline. Time factors involve order transmission, order processing, shipping, transportation, receiving, stocking, review time, etc.

planned issue   A disbursement of an item predicted by MRP through the creation of a gross requirement or allocation.

planned load   The standard hours of work required by MRP recommended (planned) production orders. See: planned order.

planned order   A suggested order quantity, release date, and due date created by MRP processing, when it encounters net requirements. Planned orders are created by the computer; exist only within the computer; and may be changed or deleted by the computer during subsequent MRP processing if conditions change. Planned orders at one level will be exploded into gross requirements for components at the next lower level. Planned orders, along with released orders, also served as input to capacity requirements planning, to show the total capacity requirements in future time periods. See: firm planned order, open order, scheduled receipt.

planned receipt   A receipt against an open purchase order or open production order.

planning bill (of material)   An artificial grouping of items and/or events, in bill of material format, used to facilitate master scheduling and/or material planning. See: common parts bill, modular bill, super bill.

planning horizon   The span of time from the current to some future point for which plans are generated.

poka-yoke   Mistake-proofing techniques, such as manufacturing or setup activity designed in a way to prevent an error from resulting in a product defect. For example, in an assembly operation, if each correct part is not used, a sensing device detects a part was unused and shuts down the operation, thereby preventing the assembler from moving the incomplete part on to the next station or beginning another one. Sometimes spelled poke-yoke.

primary work center   The work center wherein an operation on a manufactured part is normally scheduled to be performed. Ant: alternate work center.

priority   In a general sense, refers to the relative importance of jobs, i.e., the sequence in which jobs should be worked on. It is a separate concept from capacity. See: capacity, scheduling.

priority control   The process of communicating start and completion dates to manufacturing departments in order to execute a plan. The dispatch list is the tool normally used to provide these dates based on the current plan and status of all open orders.

priority planning   The function of determining what material is needed and when. Master production scheduling and material requirements planning are the elements used for the planning and replanning process in order to maintain proper due dates on required materials.

probability distribution   A table of numbers or a mathematical expression which indicates the frequency with which each of all possible results of an experiment should occur.

process flow production   A production approach with minimal interruptions in actual processing in any one production run or between production runs of similar products. Queue time is virtually eliminated by integrating the moving of the product into the actual operation of the resource performing the work.

process manufacturing   Production which adds value by mixing, separating, forming, and/or chemical reactions. It may be done in either batch or continuous mode.

process sheet   Detailed manufacturing instructions issued to the plant. The instructions may include speeds, feeds, temperatures, tools, fixtures, machines, and sketches of setups and semifinished dimensions. See: routing.

process time   The time during which the material is being changed, whether it is a machining operation or a hand assembly. Syn: residence time.

procurement lead time   The time required by the buyer to select a supplier, and to place and obtain a commitment for specific quantities of material at specified times. See: purchasing lead time.

product family   A group of products with similar characteristics, often used in sales and operations (production) planning.

product group forecast   A forecast for a number of similar products.

production card   In a Just-in-Time context, it refers to a card or other signal for indicating that items should be made for use or to replace some items removed from pipeline stock. See: kanban, move card.

production control   The function of directing or regulating the movement of goods through the entire manufacturing cycle from the requisitioning of raw material to the delivery of the finished products. See: inventory control.

production cycle   The lead time to produce a product. See: cycle.

production forecast   A predicted level of customer demand for an option, feature, etc., of an assemble-to-order product (or finish-to-order product). It is calculated by netting customer backlog against an overall family or product line master production schedule and then factoring this product "available-to-promise" by the option percentage in a planning bill of material.

production line   A series of pieces of equipment dedicated to the manufacture of a specific number of products or families.

production plan   The agreed-upon plan that comes from the sales and operations (production) planning function, specifically the overall level of manufacturing output planned to be produced. Usually stated as a monthly rate for each product family (group of products, items, options, features, etc.). Various units of measure can be used to express the plan: units, tonnage, standard hours, number of workers, etc. The production plan is management's authorization for the master scheduler to convert it into a more detailed plan, that is, the master production schedule. See: sales and operations planning.

production schedule   A plan which authorizes the factory to manufacture a certain quantity of a specific item. Usually initiated by the production planning department. See: work order, manufacturing order.

productivity   Refers to a relative measure of output per labor and/or machine input. An overall measure of production effectiveness which is composed of two factors: efficiency (how well a resource is performing) and utilization (how intensively a resource is being used). It is calculated (1) as the product of the efficiency and utilization factors or (2) as the ratio of the output achieved as measured in standard hours to the total clock time scheduled for production for a given time period.

$$\text{productivity} = \text{efficiency} \times \text{utilization}$$

or

$$\text{productivity} = \text{standard hours of output/clock time scheduled}$$

product layout   See: continuous production.

product load profile   A listing of the required capacity and key resources required to manufacture one unit of a selected item or family. Often used to predict the impact of the item scheduled on the overall schedule and load of the key resources. Rough cut capacity planning uses these profiles to calculate the approximate capacity requirements of the master production schedule and/or the production plan. Syn: bill of labor, bill of resources, resource profile.

product mix   The proportion of individual products that make up the total production and/or sales volume. Changes in the product mix can mean drastic changes in the manufacturing requirements for certain types of labor and material.

product structure   The way components go into a product during its manufacture. A typical product structure would show raw material converted into fabricated components, components put together to make subassemblies, subassemblies going into assemblies, etc.

projected available balance   In MRP, the inventory balance projected out into the future. It is the running sum of on-hand inventory minus requirements plus scheduled receipts and planned orders. See: projected on hand.

projected on hand   Same as projected available balance, except excludes planned order.

pull (system)   (1) In production, it refers to the production of items only as demanded for use, or to replace those taken for use. (2) In a material control context, it refers to the withdrawal of inventory as demanded by the using operations. Material is not issued until a signal comes from the user. (3) In distribution, it refers to a system for replenishing field warehouse inventories wherein replenishment decisions are made at the field warehouse itself, not at the central warehouse or plant. Ant: push system.

purchase order   The purchaser's document used to formalize a purchase transaction with a vendor. A purchase order, when given to a vendor, should contain statements of the quantity, description, and price of the goods or services ordered; agreed terms as to payment, discounts, date of performance, transportation, and all other agreements pertinent to the purchase and its execution by the vendor.

purchase part   An item source from a vendor.

purchase requisition   A document conveying authority to the purchasing department to purchase specified materials in specified quantities within a specified time.

purchasing capacity   The act of buying capacity or machine time from a vendor. This allows a company to use and schedule the capacity of the machine or a part of the capacity of the machine as if it were in their own plant.

purchasing lead time   The total lead time required to obtain a purchased item. Included here are order preparation and release time, vendor lead time, transportation time, receiving, inspections and put-away time.

push (system)   (1) In production, it refers to the production of items at times required by a given schedule planned in advance. (2) In material control, it refers to the issuing of material according to a given schedule and/or issued to a job order at its start time. (3) In distribution, it refers to a system for replenishing field warehouse inventories wherein replenishment decision making is centralized, usually at the manufacturing site or central supply facility. Ant: pull system.

quality   Conformance to requirements.

quality at the source   A producer's responsibility to provide 100% acceptable quality material to the consumer of the material. The objective is to reduce or eliminate shipping/receiving quality inspections and line stoppages as a result of supplier defects.

quality circle   A small group of people who normally work as a unit and meet frequently for the purpose of uncovering and solving problems concerning the quality of items produced, process capability or process control. Syn: quality control circle.

quality control   The function of verifying conformance to requirements.

quantity discount   An allowance determined by the quantity or value of a purchase.

quarantine   The setting aside of items from availability for use or sale until all required quality tests have been performed and conformance certified.

queue   A waiting line. In manufacturing, the jobs at a given work center waiting to be processed. As queues increase, so do average queue time and work-in-process inventory.

random   Having no predictable pattern. For example, sales data may vary randomly about some forecasted value with no specific pattern and no attendant ability to obtain a more accurate sales estimate than the forecast value.

random numbers   A sequence of integers or group of numbers (often in the form of a table) which show absolutely no relationship to each other anywhere in the sequence. At any point, all integers have an equal chance of occurring, and they occur in an unpredictable fashion.

random variation   A fluctuation in data which is due to uncertain or random occurrences.

range   The statistical term referring to the spread in a series of observations. For example, the anticipated demand for a particular product might vary from a low of 10 to a high of 500 per week. The range would, therefore, be $500 - 10$ or 490.

rated capacity   Capacity calculated from data such as utilization and efficiency, hours planned to be worked, etc. Syn: theoretical capacity. Ant: demonstrated capacity.

raw material   Purchased items or extracted materials which are converted via the manufacturing process into components and/or products.

receiving   This function includes the physical receipt of material; the inspection of the shipment for conformance with the purchase order (quantity and damage); identification and delivery to destination; and preparing receiving reports.

reconciling inventory   Comparing the physical inventory figures with the perpetual inventory record and making any necessary corrections.

record accuracy   The conformity of recorded values in a bookkeeping system to the actual values. For example, the on-hand balance of an item maintained in a computer record relative to the actual on-hand balance of the items in the stockroom.

regeneration MRP   An MRP processing approach where the master production schedule is totally reexploded down through all bills of material, to maintain valid priorities. New requirements and planned orders are completely "regenerated" at that time. Ant: net change MRP, requirements alteration.

released order   See: open order.

reorder point   See: order point.

reorder quantity   (1) In a fixed order system of inventory control, the fixed quantity which should be ordered each time the available stock (on-hand plus on-order) falls below the order point. (2) In a variable reorder quantity system, the amount ordered from time period to time period will vary. Syn: replenishment order quantity. See: economic order quantity, lot size.

repetitive manufacturing   Production of discrete units, planned and executed to a schedule, usually at relatively high speeds and volumes. Material tends to move in a continuous flow during production, but different items may be produced sequentially within that flow.

replenishment lead time   The total period of time that elapses from the moment it is determined that a product is to be reordered until the product is back on the shelf available for use.

replenishment period   The time between successive replenishment orders, i.e., replenishment interval. See: replenishment lead time.

requirements explosion   The process of calculating the demand for the components of a parent item by multiplying the parent item requirements by the component usage quantity specified in the bill of material. See: dependent demand, gross requirements, material requirements planning.

resource   Anything required for production of product whose lack of availability would cause failure to meet the plan.

resource profile   See: product load profile.

return on investment   A financial measure of the relative return from an investment, usually expressed as a percentage or earnings produced by an asset to the amount invested in the asset.

review period   The time between successive evaluations of inventory status to determine whether or not to reorder. See: lead time.

rough cut capacity planning   The process of converting the production plan and/or the master production schedule into capacity needs for key resources: manpower, machinery, warehouse space, vendors' capabilities and, in some cases, money. Product load profiles are often used to accomplish this. Syn: resource requirements planning. See: capacity requirements planning.

routing   A set of information detailing the method of manufacture of a particular item. It includes the operations to be performed, their sequence, the various work centers to be involved, and the standards for setup and run. In some companies, the routing also includes information on tooling, operator skill levels, inspection operations, testing requirements, etc.

running time   The time during which a machine is actually producing product. For example, the running time for a machine tool would include time cutting metal and the time moving into position to cut metal, but running time would not include setup, maintenance, waiting for the operator. Ant: idle time.

run time   The planned standard time to produce one or multiple units of an item in an operation. The actual time taken to produce one piece may vary from the standard but the latter is used for loading purposes and is adjusted to actual by dividing by the appropriate work center efficiency factor.

safety capacity   The planning or reserving of excess manpower and/or equipment above known requirements, to support unexpected demand.

safety lead time   An element of time added to normal lead time for the purpose of completing an order in advance of its real need date. When used, the MRP system, in offsetting for lead time, will plan both order release and order completion for earlier dates than it would otherwise. See: safety stock.

safety stock   (1) In general, a quantity of stock planned to be in inventory to protect against fluctuations in demand and/or supply. (2) In the context of master production scheduling, safety stock can refer to additional inventory and/or capacity planned as protection against forecast errors and/or short term changes in the backlog. Sometimes referred to as "overplanning" or a "market hedge." Syn: buffer stock. See: hedge.

sales and operations planning (formerly called production planning)   The function of setting the overall level of manufacturing output (production plan) and other activities to best satisfy the current planned levels of sales (sales plan and/or forecasts), while meeting general business objectives of profitability, productivity, competitive customer lead times, etc., as expressed in the overall business plan. One of its primary purposes is to establish production rates that will achieve management's objective of maintaining, raising, or lowering inventories or backlogs, while usually attempting to keep the work force relatively stable. It must extend through a planning horizon sufficient to plan the labor, equipment, facilities, material, and finances required to accomplish the production plan. As this plan affects many company functions, it is normally prepared with information from marketing, manufacturing, engineering, finance, materials, etc.

schedule control   Control of a plant floor by schedules rather than job orders. Schedules are derived by taking requirements over a period of time and dividing by the number of workdays allowed in which to run the parts or assemblies. Production completed is compared with the schedule to provide control. Most frequently used in repetitive and process manufacturing. See: order control.

scheduled receipt   Within MRP, open production orders and open purchase orders are considered as "scheduled receipts." On their due date, they will be added to the projected available balance during the netting process for the time period in question. Scheduled receipt dates and/or quantities are not normally altered automatically by the MRP system. Further, scheduled receipts are not exploded into requirements for components as MRP logic assumes that all components required for the manufacture of the item in question have been either allocated or issued to the shop floor. See: planned order, firm planned order.

scheduler   A general term which can refer to material planner, dispatcher, or a combined function.

scheduling   The act of creating a schedule, such as a master production schedule, shop schedule, maintenance schedule, vendor schedule, etc.

scheduling rules   Basic rules that can be used consistently in a scheduling system. Scheduling rules usually specify the amount of calendar time to allow for a move and for queue, how load will be calculated, etc.

scrap   Material outside of specifications and of such characteristics that rework is impractical.

scrap factor   A percentage factor in the product structure used to increase gross requirements to account for anticipated loss within the manufacture of a particular product. See: shrinkage factor.

scrap rate   See: shrinkage factor.

seasonal inventory   Inventory built up in anticipation of a peak seasonal demand in order to smooth production. See: anticipation inventories.

seasonality   A repetitive pattern from year to year with some periods considerably higher than others.

second order smoothing   A method of exponential smoothing for trend situations that employs two previously computed averages, the singly and doubly smoothed values, to extrapolate into the future. Syn: double smoothing.

sequencing   Determining the order in which a manufacturing facility is to process a number of different jobs in order to achieve certain objectives. See: dispatching.

service parts   Parts used for the repair and/or maintenance of an assembled product. Typically they are ordered and shipped at a date later than the shipment of the product itself.

service parts demand   The need for a component to be sold by itself, as opposed to being used in production to make a higher level product. Syn: repair parts demand, spare parts.

service time   The time to serve a customer, e.g., the time required to fill a sales order, the time required to fill a request at a tool crib, etc.

setup   The process of changing dies or other parts of a machine in order to produce a new part or product. Syn: changeover.

setup cost   The costs associated with a setup. Syn: changeover cost.

setup time   The time required for a specific machine, line, or work center to convert from the production of one specific item to another. See: external setup time, internal setup time, major setup, minor setup.

shelf life   The amount of time an item may be held in inventory before it becomes unusable.

shipping   Provides facilities for the outgoing shipment of parts, products, and components. It includes packaging, marking, weighing, and loading for shipment.

shop calendar   A special type of calendar used to facilitate scheduling. It is usually expressed in consecutively numbered working days, and excludes weekends, holidays, plant shutdowns, etc.

shop floor control   A system for utilizing data from the shop floor to maintain and communicate status information on shop orders (manufacturing orders) and work centers. The major subfunctions of shop floor control are: (1) assigning priority of each shop order; (2) maintaining work-in-process quantity information; (3) conveying shop order status information to the office; (4) providing actual output data for capacity control purposes; (5) providing quantity by location by shop order for work-in-process inventory and accounting purposes; and (6) providing measurement of efficiency, utilization, and productivity of manpower and machines. Syn: production activity control. See: closed-loop MRP.

shortest process time rule (SPT)   A dispatching rule which directs the sequencing of jobs in ascending order by processing time. Following this rule, the most jobs per time period will be processed. As a result, the average lateness of jobs is minimized, but some jobs will be very late. See: due date rule, slack time.

short-term planning   The function of adjusting limits or levels of capacity within relatively short periods of time, such as parts of a day, daily, or weekly.

shrinkage   Reductions of actual quantities of items in stock, in process, in transit. The loss may be caused by scrap, theft, deterioration, evaporation, etc.

shrinkage factor   A percentage factor in the item master record which compensates for expected loss during the manufacturing cycle either by increasing the gross requirements or by reducing the expected completion quantity of planned and open orders. The shrinkage factor differs from the scrap factor in that the former affects all uses of the part and its components. The scrap factor relates to only one usage. See: scrap factor.

simulation   (1) The technique of utilizing representative or artificial data to reproduce in a model various conditions that are likely to occur in the actual performance of a system. Frequently used to test the behavior of a system under different operating policies. (2) Within MRP II, utilizing the operational data to perform "what-if" evaluations of alternative plans, to answer the question "can we do it?" If yes, the simulation can then be run in financial mode to help answer the question "do we really want to?"

single-level backflush   A form of backflush which reduces inventory on only the next-level-down parts used in an assembly or subassembly. See: backflush, superflush.

single-level bill of material   A display of those components that are directly used in a parent item. It shows only the relationships one level down.

single minutes exchange of die (SMED)   The concept of setup times of less than 10 minutes, developed by Shigeo Shingo in 1970 at Toyota.

single period inventory models   Inventory models used to define economical or profit maximizing lot size quantities when an item is ordered or produced only once, e.g., calendars, tax guides, greeting cards, newspapers, or periodicals, while facing uncertain, i.e., probabilistic, demands.

SKU   Abbreviation for stockkeeping unit.

slack time   (1) The difference in calendar time between the scheduled due date for a job and the estimated completion date. If a job is to be completed ahead of schedule, it is said to have slack time; if it is likely to be completed behind schedule, it is said to have negative slack time. Slack time can be used to calculate job priorities using formulas such as the critical ratio. (2) In the critical path method, total slack is the amount of time a job may be delayed in starting without necessarily delaying the project completion time. Free slack is the amount of time a job may be delayed in starting without delaying the start of any other job in the project. See: critical ratio.

SPC   Abbreviation for statistical process control.

staging   Pulling of the material for an order from inventory before the material is required. This action is often taken to identify shortages, but can lead to increased problems in availability and inventory accuracy.

standard batch quantity (SBQ)   The quantity of a parent that is used as the basis for specifying the material requirements for production. The "quantity per" will be expressed as the quantity to make the SBQ, not to make only one of the parent. Often used by manufacturers who use some components in very small quantities, and/or process-related manufacturers.

standard costs   The target costs of an operation, process, or product including labor, material, and overhead charges.

standard deviation   A measure of dispersion of data or of a variable. The standard deviation is computed by finding the difference between the average and actual observations, squaring each difference, summing the squared difference, finding the average squared difference (called the variance) and taking the square root of the variance.

standard error   Applied to statistics such as the mean, to provide a distribution within which samples of the statistics are expected to fall. See: standard deviation.

standard hours   See: standard time.

standard time   The length of time that should be required to (a) set up a given machine or operation; and (b) run one part/assembly/batch/end product through that operation. This time is used in determining machine requirements and labor requirements. Also, frequently used as a basis for incentive payrolls and cost accounting.

start date   The date that an order or schedule should be released into the plant based upon some form of scheduling rules. The start date should be early enough to allow time to complete the work, but not so early to overload the shop. See: scheduling rules.

static inventory models   See: single period inventory models.

statistical inventory control   The use of statistical methods to model the demands and lead times experienced by an inventory item or group of items. Demand during lead time and between reviews can be modeled and reorder points, safety stocks, and maximum inventory levels can be defined to attempt to achieve desired customer service levels, inventory investments, manufacturing/distribution efficiency, and targeted returns on investments.

statistical process control (SPC)   A quality control methodology which focuses on continuous monitoring during the production process itself rather than post-production inspection of the items produced. The intent is to not produce any defective items, by stopping the process before it drifts out of control.

statistical safety stock calculations   The mathematical determination of safety stock quantities considering forecast errors, lot size, desired customer service levels, and the ratio of lead time to the length of the forecast period. Safety stock is frequently the product of the appropriate safety factor and the standard deviation or mean absolute deviation of the distribution of demand forecast errors.

stock   (1) Items in inventory. (2) Stored products or service parts ready for sale as distinguished from stores which are usually components or raw materials.

stockkeeping unit (SKU)   An item at a particular geographic location. For example, one product stocked at six different distribution centers would represent six SKUs, plus perhaps another for the plant at which it was manufactured.

stockless production   See: Just-in-Time.

stockout   The lack of materials or components which are needed. See: backorder.

stockout costs   The lost sale and/or backorder cost incurred as a result of a stockout. See: stockout.

storage costs   A subset of inventory carrying costs, including the cost of warehouse utilities, material handling personnel, equipment maintenance, building maintenance, and security personnel. See: carrying cost.

subassembly   An assembly which is used at a higher level to make up another assembly. Syn: intermediate. See: component.

suboptimization   A problem solution that is best from a narrow point of view but not from a higher or overall company point of view. For example, a department manager who would not work his department overtime in order to minimize his department's costs may be doing so at the expense of overall company profitability.

summarized bill of material   A form of multi-level bill of material, which lists all the parts and their quantities required in a given product structure. Unlike the indented bill of material it does not list the levels of manufacture and lists a component only once for the total quantity used.

super bill (of material) A type of planning bill, located at the top level in the structure, which ties together various modular bills (and possibly a common parts bill) to define an entire product or product family. The "quantity per" relationship of super bill to modules represents the forecasted percentage of demand of each module. The master scheduled quantities of the super bill explode to create requirements for the modules which also are master scheduled. See: planning bill, modular bill, common parts bill.

superflush A technique to relieve of all components down to the lowest level using the complete bill of material, based on the count of finished units produced and/or transferred to finished goods inventory. See: backflush, single-level backflush.

synchronized production A term sometimes used to mean repetitive Just-in-Time production.

target inventory level The equivalent of the "maximum" in a min-max system. The target inventory is equal to the order point plus the order quantity. It is often called an "order up to" inventory level and is used in a periodic review system. See: min-max system.

teardown time The time taken to remove a setup from a machine or facility. Teardown is an element of manufacturing lead time, but often allowed for in setup or run time rather than separately.

throughput The total volume of production through a facility (machine, work center, department, plant, or network of plants).

time bucket A number of days of data summarized into a columnar display. A weekly time bucket would contain all of the relevant data for an entire week. Weekly time buckets are considered to be the largest possible (at least in the near and medium term) to permit effective MRP. See: bucketless system.

time fence A policy or guideline established to note where various restrictions or changes in operating procedures take place. For example, changes to the master production schedule can be accomplished easily beyond the cumulative lead time whereas changes inside the cumulative lead time becomes increasingly more difficult to a point where changes should be resisted. Time fences can be used to define these points.

time-phased order point (TPOP) MRP (or DRP) for independent demand items, where gross requirements come from a forecast, not via explosion. This technique can be used to plan distribution center inventories as well as planning for service (repair) parts, since MRP logic can readily handle items with dependent demand, independent demand, or a combination of both. See: distribution requirements planning.

time phasing The technique of expressing future demand, supply, and inventories by time period. Time phasing is one of the key elements of material requirements planning.

time series A set of data that is distributed over time, such as demand data in monthly time period occurrences.

time series analysis   Analysis of any variable classified by time, in which the values of the variable are functions of the time periods.

time standard   The predetermined times allowed for the performance of a specific job. The standard will often consist of two parts, that for machine set-up and that for actual running. The standard can be developed through observation of the actual work (time study), summation of standard micro-motion times (synthetic time standards), or approximation (historical job time).

total quality control   An approach encompassing all phases of a manufacturing organization, from design engineering to delivery, that attempts to insure that no defective parts are produced. The basic elements include: process control, easy-to-see quality, insistence on compliance, line stop, correcting one's own errors, 100 percent check, and project-by-project improvement.

TPOP   Abbreviation for time-phased order point.

TQC   Abbreviation for total quality control.

tracking signal   The ratio of the cumulative algebraic sum of the deviations between the forecasts and the actual values to the mean absolute deviation. Used to signal when the validity of the forecasting model might be in doubt.

transit time   A standard allowance that is assumed on any given order for the physical movement of items from one operation to the next.

transportation inventory   Inventory that is in transit between locations. See: pipeline stock.

turnover   (1) See: inventory turnover. (2) In the United Kingdom and certain other countries, it refers to annual sales volume.

two-bin system   A type of fixed order system in which inventory is carried in two bins. A replenishment quantity is ordered when the first bin is empty. When the material is received, the second bin is refilled and the excess is put into the working bin. This term is also used loosely to describe any fixed order system even when physical "bins" do not exist. See: fixed order quantity system.

U-lines   Production lines shaped like the letter "U." The shape allows workers to easily perform several different tasks without much walk time. The number of work stations in a U-line are usually determined by line balancing. U-lines promote communication. See: cellular manufacturing, group technology.

utilization   A measure of how intensively a resource is being used. It is the ratio of the direct time charged for production activities (setup and/or run) to the clock time scheduled for those production activites for a given period of time.

$$\text{utilization} = \text{direct time charged}/\text{clock time scheduled}$$

For example, to calculate labor utilization, the direct labor hours charged is divided by the total clock hours scheduled for a given period of time. Similarly, to calculate machine utilization, the total time charged to creating output (setup and run time) is divided by the total clock hours scheduled to be available for a given period of time.

value analysis   The systematic use of techniques which serve to identify a required function, establish a value for that function, and finally to provide that function at the lowest overall cost. This approach focuses on the functions of an item rather than the methods of producing the present product design.

variable cost   An operating cost that varies directly with production volume; for example, materials consumed, direct labor, sales commissions. Ant: fixed cost.

variable yield   The condition wherein the output of a process is not consistently repeatable either in quantity, quality or combinations of these.

variance   (1) The difference between the expected (budgeted or planned) and the actual. (2) In statistics, the variance is a measure of dispersion of data.

vendor   A company or individual that supplies goods or services.

vendor lead time   The time that normally elapses between the time an order is received by the supplier and his shipment of the material.

vendor measurement   The act of measuring the vendor's performance to the contract. Measurements usually cover delivery, quality, and price.

vendor scheduling   A purchasing approach which provides vendors with schedules rather than individual hard-copy purchase orders. Normally a vendor scheduling system will include a business agreement (contract) for each vendor, a weekly (or more frequent) schedule for each vendor extending for some time into the future, and individuals called vendor schedulers. Also required is a formal priority planning system that works very well, because it is essential in this arrangement to routinely provide the vendor with valid due dates. See: Just-in-Time, paperless purchasing.

visual review system   A simple inventory control system where the inventory reordering is based on actually looking at the amount of inventory on hand. Usually used for low-value items like nuts and bolts. See: two-bin system.

wait time   The time a job remains at a work center after an operation is completed until it is moved to the next operation. It is often expressed as a part of move time.

warehouse demand   The need for an item in order to replenish a branch warehouse. Syn: branch warehouse demand.

waste   Hazardous waste whose disposal is controlled. A byproduct of a process or task with unique characteristics requiring special management control. Waste production can usually be planned and somewhat controlled. Scrap is typically not planned and may result from the same production run as waste.

weighted average   An averaging technique where the data to be averaged are not uniformly weighted and are given values according to their importance. The weights must always sum to 1.00 or 100%.

what-if analysis   The process of evaluating alternate strategies. Answering the consequences of changes to forecasts, manufacturing plans, inventory levels, etc. Syn: simulation.

where-used   A listing of every parent item which calls for a given component, and the respective quantity required, from a bill of material file.

WIP   See: work in process.

withdrawals   (1) Removal of material from stores. (2) A transaction issuing material to a specific location, run, or schedule.

work center   A specific production facility, consisting of one or more people and/or machines, which can be considered as one unit for purposes of capacity requirements planning and detailed scheduling. See: cost center.

work in process (WIP)   Product in various stages of completion throughout the plant including raw material that has been released for initial processing, up to completely processed material awaiting final inspection and acceptance as finished product. Many accounting systems also include the value of semi-finished stock and components in this category. Syn: in-process inventory.

work in progress   See: work in process.

work order   See: manufacturing order. Frequently the term work order is used to designate orders to the machine shop for tool manufacture or maintenance.

work station   The assigned location where a worker performs his job; it could be a machine or a work bench. See: work center.

yield   The ratio of usable output from a process to its input.

zero inventories   A philosophy of manufacturing based on planned elimination of all waste and consistent improvement of productivity. It encompasses the successful execution of all manufacturing activities required to produce a final product, from design engineering to delivery and including all stages of conversion from raw material onward. The primary elements of zero inventories are to have only the required inventory when needed; to improve quality to zero defects; to reduce lead times by reducing setup times, queue lengths, and lot sizes; and to incrementally revise the operations themselves to accomplish these things at minimum cost. In the broad sense it applies to all forms of manufacturing, job shop and process as well as repetitive. See: Just-in-Time, stockless production.

AUTHOR INDEX

SUBJECT INDEX